Attack Warning Red

Founder and organiser of the Observer Corps from 1924 to 1928, Major General E. B. Ashmore CB, CMG, MVO. His work laid the foundations for the RAF's reporting network which was to ensure victory in the Battle of Britain

ATTACK WARNING RED

The Royal Observer Corps
and the Defence of Britain
1925 to 1992

Derek Wood

CARMICHAEL AND SWEET. ENGLAND

To all who have served in the Corps
and particularly those, between 1939
and 1945, who spent endless hours
working in operations rooms, or who
stood in the wind, sun, rain and
frost to ensure Britain's survival

"Be wakeful – be vigilant
Danger may be
At an hour when all seemeth
securest to thee"
                            Southey

First published in 1976 by
Macdonald and Jane's Publishers Limited

ISBN 0356 08411 6

Printed in India by
Lancer International, New Delhi

Revised edition 1992
Carmichael and Sweet Limited
48 Penny Street
Portsmouth PO1 2NL
England

ISBN 0 9517283 1 8

Contents

Foreword

Describing the early history of the Royal Observer Corps, Derek Wood makes the point in this book that the corps did not fit neatly into any Service or Ministry. In a sense that was true: from the outset the corps fostered a strong volunteer spirit, coupled with a healthy egalitarianism, which led in turn to resistance among its members to the concept of a paid Service. This total commitment to the volunteer ethic set the Royal Observer Corps apart from the formal organisation of the peacetime Services. Yet, once it came under the wing of the Air Ministry in 1929, the community of interest was soon recognised and there sprang up a close and harmonious relationship with the Royal Air Force which continues today.

Under a series of wise leaders, the Royal Observer Corps expanded during the 1930s along with the Royal Air Force. It was all done on a shoestring, and it is revealing now to learn that the 16-group structure decided on in 1935 was to cost no more than £10,000 per year. Never before – and I suspect never again – could a nation obtain a vital arm of its defence so cheaply. But it was when Lord Dowding took over Fighter Command that the Royal Observer Corps really achieved its highest purpose. Fully aware of the limitations of the primitive radars available to him he had a clear understanding of the corps' worth as the complement to them and of the vital role it would play in the struggle that lay ahead. Where others were dazzled by the promise of the new technology he stoutly defended the requirement for visual and audio tracking of enemy aircraft. When Winston Churchill dismissed the techniques of the Royal Observer Corps as "stone age" Dowding sprang to its defence, and, of course, he was right.

Derek Wood recounts fully and entertainingly in this book the story of the Royal Observer Corps in the Second World War – and what a magnificent story it is. During the Battle of Britain and afterwards the Royal Observer Corps provided our only intelligence on aircraft operating below 500 feet and, because its members were well trained and as keen as mustard, they achieved an effectiveness in this role which was little short of miraculous. But the activities of the corps were not confined to low-level raid reporting: the operation of the "alarm within the alert", notification of bale-outs and crashes, and a wealth of other intelligence flowed from the Observer Corps posts. As the war ground on the Royal Observer Corps expanded in every direction – helping home "lame ducks", assisting in air sea rescue and taking an heroic part in the D-Day fleet with its members dressed in hybrid uniforms as temporary Naval Petty Officers. The list of its activities is endless. It was all made possible by the ideal of selfless, freely given, volunteer service, and "Attack Warning Red" provides us with a timely reminder of the worth and strength of that ideal.

After the war came the anti-climax of the stand-down from 1945 to 1947, but as Fighter Command expanded at the time of the Korean War, the Royal Observer Corps once again came to its assistance. Valiant efforts were made to regain the lost ground, but although it remained effective throughout the 1950s in identifying and plotting low level raids, the advent of high flying, high speed jet aircraft that could neither be seen nor heard was to prove an insuperable problem. Thus, it was that the role of the corps changed in the early 1960s to that of monitoring nuclear fall-out. As the field force of the United Kingdom Monitoring and Warning Organisation, the Royal Observer Corps continues to play a vital role in the defence of this country and still maintains the close contact with the Royal Air Force which has become so much a part of its history.

To all those who have ever served in the Royal Observer Corps, or who have ever been associated with it, this book will be a joy to read. I count it a great honour to have been asked to contribute this foreword, and I take this opportunity on behalf of the Royal Air Force to salute the Royal Observer Corps and all its members, past and present.

> Air Chief Marshal Sir Andrew Humphrey, KCB, OBE, DFC, AFC,
> Chief of the Air Staff

From the early days of its inauguration in 1925, when volunteers were enrolled as Special Constables; throughout the Second World War during which the corps was the "eyes and ears" of the civil air raid warning system, to the present day when the Royal Observer Corps provides the field force of the United Kingdom Warning and Monitoring Organisation, there have been close and continuous links between the Home Office and the Royal Observer Corps.

Derek Wood has rightly devoted a large part of his book to the period of the Second World War – which was to prove the great testing time for the Observer Corps – and to the Royal Observer Corps' immensely valuable service to Fighter Command in tracking incursions of hostile aircraft overland. However, as a very junior official in the Air Raid Warnings Division of the Ministry of Home Security during part of that time, I can testify from personal knowledge of the no less valuable contribution made by the Royal Observer Corps to the air raid warning system which resulted not only in the saving of many lives, but also in reducing the loss of production time so vital for sustaining the war effort.

When, in the 1950s, following the development of thermo-nuclear weapons with their threat of radioactive fallout, the need arose for a warning system against this new hazard, it was natural that the Home Office should turn once again to the Royal Observer Corps. To those who were aware of the splendid work performed by the Royal Observer Corps in the past, it came as no surprise that they should accept this new and strange task with their customary efficiency. I welcome this opportunity to pay tribute to the many thousands of volunteers of the Royal Observer Corps who have given and continue to give so much of their time in the service of their country.

> Sir Arthur Peterson, KCB, MVO,
> Permanent Under-Secretary of State, the Home Office

Preface

In 1975 the Royal Observer Corps celebrated its 50th anniversary. It is doubtful that any other organisation has accomplished so much over so many years and yet received so little publicity. The people of Britain are largely unaware of the part that the ROC has played in the nation's defence and of its continuing vital task in this nuclear age.

It is estimated that more than 150,000 men and women have served in the corps since 1925 – some for a year or two, many for a decade or more and others for 25 to 35 years. One chief observer in Kent has been in the ROC since 1926 and will undoubtedly complete 50 years. Several observers have even "lost" a few years and remained members well into their seventies, while one is known to have been serving after his eightieth birthday.

The ROC is an object lesson for the politicians. An observer may have a highly paid job while his chief observer can be a bricklayer. The wife in some cases is an officer and her husband an NCO. Company directors serve with trades union officials and managers with shop-floor workers and typists. Class and politics are submerged in a unique voluntary body with a common aim for the good of the nation.

To unravel the complex story of the ROC has taken years of research, and has been made more difficult by the lack of records and the wholesale destruction of those that did exist. Great numbers of files and log books have been burned or have long since rotted away. No central personnel records were maintained until the 1970s, with the result that tens of thousands of people have passed through the Corps leaving no official trace behind.

To complete this history has entailed a massive detective effort, trying to put together the elements of a jigsaw, with pieces scattered up and down the country in old boxes, attics and store rooms. Under these circumstances there must inevitably be some omissions, but it is hoped that they are few.

Derek Wood
Cuckfield, 1976

Acknowledgements

In the history of so diverse an organisation as the Royal Observer Corps the net is inevitably cast very wide and a great number of people become involved. The help which I have received from so many different sources has been most gratifying and has greatly assisted in a long and difficult task.

First I must thank my good friend Stanley Jackson, who has been my right hand through years of research and correlation. A retired observer lieutenant, he served from 1937 onwards as both volunteer and full-time officer. He has laboured over hundreds of files and his advice has been invaluable. His not inconsiderable frame is well known to many serving members and his native Yorkshire wit has ensured that humour has crept into even the worst situations where nothing would add up.

When the question of illustrations was considered I turned to Derek Ballington, now commandant of No 2 Group. He has successfully wrestled with a mass of sketches, old documents and figures to produce top-grade maps and diagrams. The rest of the diagrams, to the same high standard, are the work of Mr C. Minney, also a member of the Corps. Mr Pyemount of Image in Industry made innumerable copy photographs.

Three ROC commandants have held office during the preparation period: Air Commodore D. F. Rixson, Air Commodore E. B. Sismore and Air Commodore R. K. Orrock. My thanks are due to them for their kindness and assistance. I am also indebted to two other former commandants, Air Chief Marshal the Earl of Brandon and Air Commodore J. H. Greswell.

The Ministry of Defence, Air Historical Branch, and the Home Office have both aided the project considerably, the AHB with Mr Louis Jackets (former head of the branch), Group Captain E. Haslam, the present head, and Mr E. Turner.

Past and present members of the corps have given me every assistance. The former deputy commandant, Observer Captain W. Rusby, kept meticulous post-war records and made them freely available, while Observer Commander R. Glover did likewise. The other full-time officers who have been particularly helpful are Observer Commanders R. D. T. Onions, A. Lardner, D. Brooks and L. Coffey, Observer Lt Commanders J. Hoare and J. Murphy and Observer Lieutenants E. Sankey and R. Furneaux.

In the groups themselves several special correspondents excelled in digging out archives and information, including Observer Commanders D. N. James and C. F. Hill; Observer Lieutenants M. F. Hakon, P. E. Trowbridge, T. Cheyne and D. F. Tasker; Observer Officers A. J. Court, N. Parker, R. H. Hartwell, R. Harmer and M. F. Rose; and Messrs G. J. Hancock and H. McGratton.

Former corps officers and members have contributed greatly: T. W. Dobson, D. Finn, G. L. Turner, Ivo Peters, F. R. Hazell, A. P. Hamilton, J. I. Eager, the late Eric Wilton, A. V. Corden, Major Graham Donald, H. R. Whitty, K. H. Gazeltine, Group Captain I. T. Courtney, Sir George Williamson, B. Robinson, John Blake and Mrs B. Hindson.

Among others my particular thanks are due to Robert Wright, the author, Gordon Simmons – a chief observer who undertook the copying of hundreds of sheets of orders and log books – Mrs Betty Ashmore, G. Graham, R. G. Stansfield, Alfred Price, E. A. "Chris" Wren and K. J. Ralph.

To all those others who contributed a note here and a photograph there, or who filled a vital information gap, I offer my thanks.

I am particularly grateful to the ladies who have had to type the manuscript and all the numerous amendments, being my wife (who has also had to put up with eight years of chaos), Mrs Susan Scadding, Mrs Gillian Lindsay-Stuart and Mrs Pamela Munks.

Prologue 1
May 10, 1941

The night blitz on Britain had reached its climax. Across France and the Low Countries final preparations were being made for the despatch of more than 500 Luftwaffe bombers to London. On this full-moon night a maximum effort had been called for before the crews and aircraft were to be moved eastwards for the forthcoming offensive against Russia.

While 700 tons of bombs were checked in their racks and the crews waited for zero hour, an entirely different scene was being played out on the Messerschmitt company's test airfield at Augsburg. A brand-new Messerschmitt 110 twin-engined fighter was taxiing out for take-off. The fuel tanks were full and the visiting pilot had filed his log as a cross-country flight. Although not a works test-pilot or a serving Luftwaffe officer, his rank and flying skill ensured that he could take up combat aircraft as and when he wished.

It was to be a very long cross-country; the 110 was tracked for more than 380 miles before it disappeared out to sea beyond Amsterdam.

In Britain, a beleaguered and somewhat battered fortress, all was being made ready to receive a heavy night attack. Night-fighter crews and gun batteries were ready, the giant Chain Home radar masts searched unceasingly for the first sign of incoming aircraft and the civilian population readied their thermos flasks and blankets for a long stay in the shelters.

One other organisation was also preparing for the onslaught. From the north of Scotland right down to the tip of Cornwall the Royal Observer Corps was waiting. Some 1,500 observer posts, with their plotting instruments, were linked to 40 centres or operations rooms. The observers had as yet no uniforms, just brassards and a steel helmet. With this complex network a continuous day and night watch was kept on the skies overhead. Predominantly made up of volunteers from every walk of life, the Corps had been formed in the 1920s and had developed into a key part of the air-defence system. It was without doubt the most skilled organisation of its kind in the world and a month earlier it had been honoured with the title "Royal" in recognition of its services in the Battle of Britain.

To the ROC groups in the south, the night of May 10–11 1941 was to be long and painful as the operations-room tables became cluttered with tracks and the bombs rained down on the capital. In the north everyone was on the alert but no special raid was anticipated.

At 10.10 p.m. the lone Me110 pilot was approaching the Northumberland coast at a height of 12,000ft, and off Holy Island he jettisoned his underwing fuel tanks. Radar began the track which was given the designation "Raid 42". Thirteen minutes later the aircraft was over land and was immediately reported with sound bearing and angle by A.2 observer post, Embleton. A.2 was in No 30 Group ROC with its operations room in Durham post office.

The aircraft was rapidly losing height but travelling at high speed and at 10.25 p.m. Mr G. W. Green, head observer of A.3 post at Chatton, correctly recognised the silhouette of a Me110 at 50ft in the moonlight – a remarkable achievement in view of the fact that the type was outside its usual range and operational area. Durham transmitted the news to the headquarters of No 13 Group, Fighter Command, where the controller considered it to be a ridiculous report and thought that the aircraft might be a Dornier 17.

In the meanwhile radar had confused the situation by incorrectly reporting Raid 42 over the sea north-east of the point of entry, suggesting that it had turned away. The real aircraft's track however, continued on its westward course across the Durham ROC table. The RAF assumed that the raid had split and accordingly allotted the 110 the designation 42J.

Just after 10.30 p.m. the 110 passed out of Durham Group and into the territory of No 31 Group with its operations room at Galashiels. Two posts – F.2, Jedburgh, and G.1, Ashkirk – glimpsed the aircraft and reported it as an Me110. It was continuously tracked until lost in an unobserved area in the Forest of Ettrick. The quarry re-emerged at 10.45 in No 34 Group ROC with its centre in New Temperance House, Pitt Street, Glasgow. Watching the map table in Pitt Street was an assistant observer group officer, Major Graham Donald.

Major Donald was typical of so many First World War officers who had gravitated to the Royal Observer Corps. He had served in the Royal Naval Air Service and later the RAF, retiring in 1919. He looked after several "clusters" of observer posts and usually called on them between 8 p.m. and 4 a.m. On this night he was visiting the centre to see the controller and find out what was coming into the group from the east. While he was there word was received of the "Dornier 17" coming into Durham. The track laid down in No 31 Group was duly noted, as was the gap thereafter.

A sound plot was obtained at 10.45, but it became confused with a Boulton Paul Defiant despatched from Prestwick to try to intercept the intruder. Despite the RAF decision that the enemy aircraft was a Dornier 17, Glasgow gave it an "X" or unidentified plot and it was labelled as Raid W.1 when a track was re-established on sound alone.

The plotters at Glasgow made some calculations on the aircraft speed based on the rate at which it had been passing through the groups. They estimated that the target was doing more than 300 m.p.h., which was impossible for a Dornier 17. In addition they noted that the Defiant – going flat out – was falling far behind. Donald asked the ROC controller to pass a message to the RAF indicating that W.1 could not be a Dornier 17 and must be an Me110, as reported by Durham and Galashiels. He reminded the RAF controller at Kenton that on March 14, 1941, in between the two big Clydebank raids, a reconnaissance 110 had photographed blazing oil tanks in the area in broad daylight and had been recognised by the fighters that tried to intercept it.

He had vivid earlier memories of being on one of his posts when an aircraft appeared out of the blue and was identified as being hostile on sound alone. The RAF refused to accept it and ordered the aircraft to be given an "X" rating. The post's final report ran "Your 'X' aircraft has just dropped four bombs on Renfrew. May we now be permitted to describe it as hostile?"

Donald's suggestion that the aircraft was an Me110 was greeted in the RAF operations room with "hoots of derision"* and the ROC was sharply told to retain the Dornier 17 label on

---

Where No Angels Dwell, by Air Vice-Marshal Sandy Johnstone.

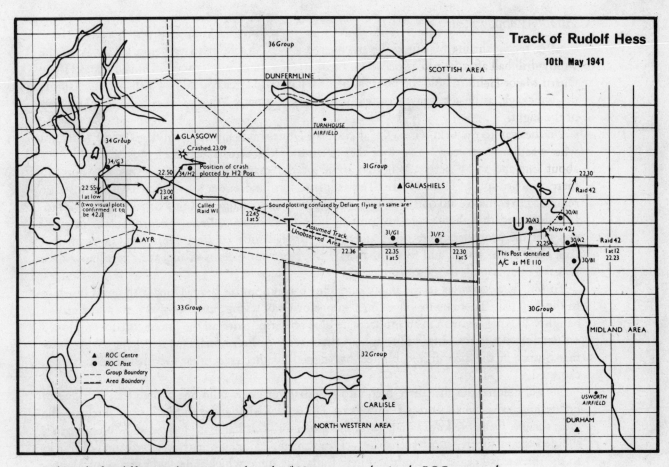

The track of Rudolf Hess in his Me110 on the night of May 10, 1944, showing the ROC groups and posts principally involved

the track. Donald therefore decided to reverse normal night sound plotting procedure and told all the posts in the path of the raid to try for a visual sighting to confirm that it was indeed a 110. One post came on the line to say that it had a visual and that by the look of the wings and tailplane it was an Me110. This was followed by a report from G.3 post, West Kilbride, that the 110 had just shot through the local village at about 25ft and that from their vantage point on the hill the observers had clearly seen every moon-lit detail, right down to the black crosses on the wings. Even then the RAF refused to accept that the aircraft was not a Dornier.

The 110 went out to sea and then turned back, the pilot having checked his position. He pursued a north-easterly zig-zag course, apparently searching for something on the ground. Suddenly H.2 post, on the edge of the Eaglesham Moors, called up excitedly: "One man has just baled out and looks like landing safely". Then: "Plane has come down out of control and crashed in flames." They gave the exact grid reference for the crash location and the time, 11.09.

The 34 Group centre immediately called out the Home Guard and the local police to look for the pilot and possibly one extra man. Major Donald left to conduct his own search, remarking to the controller that the RAF could be informed that "If they cannot catch an Me110 with a Defiant, I am now going to pick up the bits with a Vauxhall!"

After racing through Glasgow he discovered a very docile prisoner being led away to the Busby drill hall after he had knocked on the door of a shepherd's cottage. Donald asked Home Guard Major Helm to hold the pilot in the drill hall until after he had had a chance to examine the wreckage, as he felt that there was something distinctly "queer" about the whole set-up of the flight.

On the way to the field where the aircraft lay Donald was joined by Flying Officer Malcolm who was home on leave. Together they examined the wreckage which was scattered over about one-and-a-half acres. Although some of the magnesium structure was still burning there was no sign of a petrol fire. The tailplane, fins and enough of the wings and fuselage remained to convince anyone with even rudimentary knowledge that this was indeed an Me110. Donald noted that there were no guns or bomb racks, no cameras, no drop tanks in place and that the propellers were not feathered for a dead-stick landing. He rolled the main fuel tank clear of the flames and found that only three or four gallons of fuel were left. How then was the pilot hoping to return to base?

To find some answers to the many questions forming in his brain Donald retraced his steps to the drill hall. There he found a Chief Inspector Gray trying, unsuccessfully, to interrogate a haughty-looking German in an immaculate blue uniform "with all the finesse usually employed on less fortunate motorists." Through an interpreter of Polish origin, Gray kept asking how many were in the aircraft and bluffed by suggesting that two other Germans had just been captured.

Donald pointed out that three men into a two-seater just would not go and that that line of questioning was unlikely to get anywhere. He suggested that he should try to discover the pilot's name. "Oh, we know that," said the Inspector, "his name is Hoffmann." "Nein, nein", shouted the prisoner, "nicht Hoffmann – Hauptmann." Donald gently referred the policeman to the three small eagles on the brand new Luftwaffe tunic which indicated captain, or Hauptmann, rank. He then turned to the prisoner, who seemed to gain some confidence from the sight of a man in blue RAF-type uniform bearing a row of medals including the Distinguished Flying Cross. The Hauptmann rose and bowed with difficulty, his ankle having been injured in the parachute landing.

In answer to Donald's question the officer said that he did not intend to go back to Germany. The whole thing was nearly spoiled by the interpreter suggesting that he was a deserter. Donald spoke some German and also carried a German pocket dictionary. Using these, he managed to elicit the fact that the Hauptmann was some sort of emissary with an urgent secret message to deliver. When Donald relayed this to the assembled company, the Inspector retorted: "We have heard all that balderdash already. He says he has a private message for the Duke of Hamilton and must see him at once, and the damn' liar even has the duke's house marked on his map. What kind of goats does he take us for?"

There was indeed a ring round the duke's residence, Dungavel House. The only snag was that the duke was an RAF wing commander serving at Turnhouse, one of the fighter sectors served directly by 34 Observer Group.

The Hauptmann thawed and began to talk, even giving his name as Alfred Horn, and he laboriously autographed a recognition silhouette card of, appropriately enough, an Me110. Major Donald was certain that he knew the officer's face. He enquired if the Hauptmann knew Munich and was answered in the affirmative. Reference to Löwenbräu beer, however, produced a distinctly sour look, "like a maiden aunt."

There were only two known top German teetotallers, Hitler and Hess, and this was certainly not Hitler.

In a flash Donald realised that he was looking at none other than the deputy Führer of the Third Reich, Rudolf Hess. With his knowledge of languages Donald worked out the derivation of the name. Alfred was simply an old Anglo-Saxon rendering of Alf, or Olf, the Red. In German this would be Rot Olph or, latterly, Rudolf. Donald looked straight at the prisoner and said: "I shall see that your message is conveyed to the duke. I shall also tell him, on my authority, that your true name is Rudolf Hess."

Wondering what on earth could have brought Hess to Britain in the middle of the war, Donald drove back to the ROC centre bearing a large section of Me110 wing complete with black cross. He reported, direct on a teller line, to the RAF duty controller at Turnhouse the basic facts on the aircraft, its pilot and his mission.

He pointed out that he had recognised "Alfred Horn" as Rudolf Hess and recommended that the duke (who was in bed) should see him at the earliest possible moment. Donald stressed that he was in dead earnest and would confirm it all in his written report. He left his telephone number in case the duke wanted to call him.

Bearing in mind that Hitler's blitzkreig efforts had been timed to take place at weekends, Donald decided, on his own initiative, to warn his posts. In the early hours he travelled from one lonely site to another, reporting the night's events and ordering that the two rifles at each post be kept cocked and ready. Moreover, he instructed the observers to challenge anyone approaching the posts and, if they failed to react, to "shoot the legs off them and after that shoot to kill." As many of the men were hill game-keepers and first-class shots, it was fortunate that no strangers were abroad that night.

At 4 a.m. Donald telephoned the centre to ask whether the duke had called back. He had not. Tired out, Donald went to bed.

When he awoke next morning Donald realised that he was out on a limb. His immediate chief in the Royal Observer Corps, Lieutenant Colonel John Kennedy, was over in the wilds of Arran engaged in the siting of three new posts and with him was the next most senior officer, Air Commodore R. Gordon. Neither was due back until Monday. By another stroke of bad luck, the Scottish Area Commandant, ROC, Air Commodore R. Peel Ross, had just been admitted to hospital with a seriously injured knee.

En-route once again to the centre, Donald encountered Inspector Gray who informed him that Army intelligence were convinced that the prisoner was Alfred Horn and remarked that he wouldn't like to be in the ROC officer's shoes after his performance of the previous night. At 34 Group Donald again telephoned Turnhouse and contacted an old friend, Squadron Leader J. Fullerton. He was told that the Duke of Hamilton had not gone straight to see Hess but had believed what the Army had told him about Alfred Horn and had returned to his bed. Donald insisted that the duke must go and see the pilot. The pressure at last began to achieve results on Sunday morning when the Duke of Hamilton and Brandon left for Maryhill Barracks where the prisoner was being held. Despite the fact that Hess revealed his identity and confirmed Donald's report, the duke still found it difficult to believe.

The duke was a personal friend of Winston Churchill, the Prime Minister, and he decided to telephone him at Ditchley. The duke stated that he had interviewed a German pilot who claimed to be Hess. Even at this stage it was clear that he was not convinced. Churchill ordered him to fly south. Using a Hurricane and then a Magister he arrived at Kidlington and was driven to Ditchley. After listening to a first-hand account, Churchill decided to send a German expert from the Foreign Office, Sir Ivone Kirkpatrick.

Thus it was not until Monday that Hess was formally identified. More than 36 hours had passed since the lone ROC officer had discovered the real identity of the mystery pilot and no-one had believed him.

It was the Germans themselves who announced to an astonished world that Rudolf Hess was suffering from severe mental illness and was missing on a flight over the North Sea. Hitler and his associates presumed that he had crashed, as it was unthinkable that the British would not make an immediate announcement if they had captured him. The BBC followed up with a translation of the German communiqué and a belated admission that Hess was safe in a Glasgow hospital. No sooner was the announcement made than the Press was let loose and everyone, even down to the shepherd, claimed to have identified Hess.

The sequel was interesting. George Green, head observer of 30/A.3 post, Chatton, was awarded a British Empire Medal for being the first to recognise the Hess 110 and the sceptical Inspector also got an award – although for what is not clear.

For Assistant Observer Group Officer Graham Donald there was only a mention in the AOC-in-C Fighter Command's despatch on the subject and a veiled admonishment from the intelligence authorities passed on by the Commandant ROC. Nearly 35 years after the event Major Donald's original handwritten private letter to Warrington Morris dated May 14, 1941, concerning the Hess affair and the latter's reply finally came to light in a long-forgotten file. They confirm the episode in all its aspects and are reprinted in the Appendices.

From start to finish the whole Hess affair was 100 per cent Royal Observer Corps, and despite all opposition the Corps persevered at every stage. Thereafter the RAF in the north took very seriously the information that the corps gave, and acted upon it.

Prologue 2
June 13, 1944

The great invasion of Europe was seven days old and allied troops were fighting to expand the Normandy bridgehead.

In Britain radar scanned the night skies, and in the operations rooms WAAF plotters mechanically moved the plaques to indicate the flights of friendly bombers and night fighters.

At 3 a.m. the massive German guns on Cap Gris Nez opened fire, 20 shells falling in the Folkestone area and later nine more exploding inland. The fact was duly noted in a variety of military log books but the only unusual point was the distance inland that the shells dropped, some nearly reaching Maidstone.

In the underground bunker at Bentley Priory, nerve centre of the air defence of Great Britain, an early-morning lethargy had set in. It was 04.09 and the crew were thinking of the joys of a warm bed and a well earned sleep.

Suddenly one of the WAAF tellers sat up as if given an electric shock. She hesitated for a second, as though not believing what she heard in her headphones. Then she called "Diver, Diver" and the whole operations room was galvanised into a frenzy of activity. A dozen hands reached for telephones, the main table plotters suddenly forgot their fatigue and the controller watched in amazement as an extraordinary track progressed at great speed across the table towards London. Nine minutes later the track ceased abruptly and a report was flashed of a heavy explosion near Gravesend. Before there had been time to take stock of the situation, another Diver track had appeared, turned westward, and exploded just north of Cuckfield in Sussex. In quick succession third and fourth tracks were noted; one stopped at Bethnal Green and the other close to Sevenoaks in Kent.

The first robot assault from the air had begun and already six people were dead and nine seriously injured. The V1 flying bombs, with nearly one ton of high-blast-effect explosive apiece, had been launched from camouflaged sites in the Pas de Calais and had claimed their first victims.

The coastal radar stations continued to look seawards but saw nothing. The attack had completely eluded them by flying too low and the operators had been unable to distinguish bombs from the normal traffic and clutter on their cathode ray tubes. How then was it that all the scrambler telephones were now ringing in Whitehall and Winston Churchill's war room was a scene of uproar? The answer lay not with some high-ranking staff officer but with two middle-aged men – a builder and a greengrocer – from the small Kent village of Dymchurch on Romney Marsh. Mr A. M. Wraight and Mr E. E. Woodland were perched up on a Martello tower that had been built to repel Napoleon's invasion. They both wore blue RAF-type battledress with a breast badge which read "Royal Observer Corps."

Nearly two months earlier they had been handed ROC secret operations instruction No 51 entitled "Detection and Reporting of Hostile Pilotless Aircraft." It began by saying that the enemy might launch attacks with pilotless aircraft and it was anticipated that radar stations would be able to detect such aircraft. One prophetic sentence read: "It must be realised, however, that an attack by pilotless aircraft may first be detected by ROC posts." The instruction went on to detail how the threat was to be reported and gave some very vague characteristics, including a speed of 330 m.p.h. and an operational height of between 5,000ft and 10,000ft. The only real clue lay in the statement that after a climb the aircraft would continue in level flight "in both vertical and horizontal plane."

On June 13, Wraight and Woodland were manning the Dymchurch observer post known as Mike Two. They were experienced observers, as the four red service chevrons on their sleeves attested. They had plotted and reported the Battle of Britain, the night-blitz aircraft, the hit-and-run raids and finally the huge armadas of allied aircraft which plied to and fro by day and by night.

The watch had been relatively quiet until, at 04.08, they saw coming across the Channel an extraordinary apparition. Viewed through a pair of high-power US Navy binoculars it looked like a long rocket shape, coloured red from the glare of the flames and with sparks pouring from the rear end. It came straight on with the speed of a fighter and was only 1,000ft above the water. It made a noise like "a Model-T Ford going up a hill." When the strange machine was five miles out from the coast both observers were quite certain what it was; operations instruction No 51 was alive. Having quickly checked the bearing, Woodland raised his telephone mouth-piece and called "Mike Two, Diver – Diver – Diver, one four, north-west, one at one." The plotter at Maidstone Centre was momentarily stunned, but reacted instinctively, bellowing "Diver – Diver" across the operations room.

The tellers on the balcony called "Diver" down every line, including that to the headquarters of No 11 Fighter Group, and in seconds a further call was on its way to Bentley Priory. Also on the Maidstone balcony was the air-raid warning officer and within two minutes he had set the sirens wailing.

Meanwhile Mike 2 had plotted the Diver out north-west at a clock bearing of 53, where it was picked up by Fox 3, Pluckley, and other posts. Over Easy 3 at Lenham sped the V1 and on into the territory of No 19 Group ROC with its operations room at Bromley. Here the Queenie posts picked up the fiery trail before the bomb suddenly dived to earth and blew up at Swanscombe, between Dartford and Gravesend.

The two observers at Dymchurch had not finished on that June night. At 04.15 they plotted another Diver and finally at 05.00 they gave another, again going north-west. One bomb had gone off course and this was reported by the posts of No 2 Group ROC, Horsham, until it finally landed near a viaduct on the main London-Brighton railway line north of Cuckfield.

At 05.30 Maidstone ROC Centre and RAF North Weald conveyed their congratulations by telephone to the two lonely observers at Dymchurch. At 07.07 Maidstone sent the following message to all posts: "Diver procedure cancelled. This means the previous Diver raid is cancelled. In the event of others approaching – shout DIVER, like hell."

All the modern electronic inventions of man's genius had failed to detect the first robot bombers, and it had been left to two pairs of eyes and ears to prove yet again the Royal Observer Corps' motto "Forewarned is Forearmed."

Chapter 1
EARLY DAYS

On the night of May 31, 1915, Hauptmann Linnarz in the 536ft-long military airship LZ 38 penetrated to the East End of London. He dropped 3,000lb of bombs which killed seven people, injured 35 and caused an estimated £18,000-worth of damage. There had been seven previous raids on Britain, but these were close to the coast and only ten people had died. Now Linnarz had brought the war right to the capital of the Empire and the shock was to have profound repercussions which would reach forward to the Second World War.

In 1915 air defences were virtually non-existent. London's anti-aircraft armament amounted to 12 guns, the fighter forces totalled ten small scattered detachments and a proper reporting and tracking organisation had yet to be formed. Such information as there was came from the police, Army units, gun positions and even railway stations. Telephone calls were long delayed and some reports were even sent through the mail. The form for reporting "air-craft" had the following introduction:

"If you see airship or aeroplane try and note these points about her. Then, as quickly as possible, call up 'Anti-aircraft, London' on the nearest telephone. Commence your message with the words 'Aircraft Report,' and proceed to give your information in the following order . . ."

There followed a series of extraordinary questions – "Airship or Aeroplane? Where seen (this should include name of nearest large town). At what time? Proceeding in what direction? Who actually saw it? Did he hear its engine? Does anyone corroborate this? What colour was it? Were there any particular distinguishing marks noticed? If Aeroplane, a) Monoplane or b) Biplane? What type? Any letters painted on it? If Airship how many cars underneath it? Any other information.

By the time the luckless observer had managed to find a telephone, get the London number and go through the whole rigmarole the raider – even at 50 m.p.h. – was probably on his way home.

In Kent the special constabulary were supposed later to telephone "Intelligence London and advise Headquarters 2nd Army, telephone 1050 Tunbridge Wells, and the Chief Constable, 412 Maidstone."

The result of all this was total chaos and a complete inability to establish the position or direction of the incoming airship – even when the controlling authority, the Admiralty, had something worthwhile the process of getting word down to the various defence points took too long for an interception or a co-ordinated gun effort.

At the end of 1915 not a single Zeppelin had been shot down and only one damaged – by a gun at Dover. The following year saw some improvement, however, with the War Office taking over and instituting a searchlight belt stretching from Sussex to Northumberland at a distance of 25 miles from the coast. The patrolling squadrons controlled the searchlights in their area and around London itself the detachments were consolidated into three flights, at Sutton's Farm and Hainault Farm, Essex, and Hounslow, Middlesex.

The observation system was re-organised, with some 200 observer posts established well out from vital areas so that adequate warning could be given. Manning of the posts was at first undertaken by troops, but these were mostly superseded by police.* To improve communications seven warning "controls" were created, each with an AA defence commander and short lines to the trunk telephone network. The air-raid warnings were issued from the controls to districts. These arrangements, together with a crude form of sound locator, were successful in combatting the Zeppelin.

A new menace, however, appeared to supplant the Zeppelin, namely the big biplane bombers, first the Gotha and later the Staaken Giant. On June 13, 1917, twenty Gothas bombed London in daylight and suffered no casualties – an extraordinary feat which produced a public outcry in Britain. The Government reaction, following investigations by the famous South African Lieutenant General (later Field Marshal) Jan Smuts, was to put all sections of ground and air defence of London under the command of one officer. To fulfil the task they chose Major General E. B. Ashmore, then commanding the artillery of the 29th Division north of Ypres.

"Splash" Ashmore, as he was nicknamed (after the shell-hit term), possessed great talents and was undoubtedly the right man for the job. A gunner from the "Shop" at Woolwich, Ashmore was himself a pilot, having received aviation certificate No 281 in September 1912 on a Bristol Boxkite at Brooklands. Some idea of Ashmore's character and determination can be gained from a passage in the late Air Chief Marshal Sir Philip Joubert de la Ferte's book *The Third Service:*

> "He [Ashmore] had learned to fly at Brooklands in the summer of 1912 while working at the War Office. He led a strenuous existence, since he had to be at the aerodrome by 4 a.m. if he was to get instruction and be back in London by 9 a.m., breakfasted and shaved and ready for the day's toil at his desk. He annoyed his brother pupils very much by pushing his way to the head of the queue and, when in the air on the only serviceable machine, by staying up much longer than his allotted ten minutes. In the circumstances, however, he had to be excused as none of the others were working under the same strain."

Apart from expertise in artillery, Ashmore had extensive knowledge of air warfare as he had commanded the Royal Flying Corps wing attached to the 1st Army in France in the autumn of 1915. His awareness of the need for a proper air-defence organisation was prompted by an incident in France when King George V was inspecting No 2 Squadron RFC at Hesdigneul aerodrome. A loud cheer for the sovereign from the assembled men caused the king's horse to rear and fall on him. Ashmore and the squadron commander, Major Beck, carried the king off and he was subsequently taken to a chateau near Aire. AA guns were mounted and scout aircraft patrolled. No aircraft was, however, to fly over the chateau. Despite all this an old unmarked Henri Farman appeared from nowhere and flew right over the house. In his book *Air Defence*, Ashmore referred to the strong impression made on him by the incident:

---

*Major General Ashmore described many of the troops involved as "of poor intelligence and worse discipline."

"It shows that aeroplane patrols are impotent in defence unless they are helped by an elaborate and far-reaching system of observation and control on the ground. It was from this idea that I eventually developed the Observer Corps."

The War Office officially established Ashmore's new command on July 31, 1917, as the London Air Defence Area (LADA). He immediately set about dealing with aeroplane day raids and placed a gun belt 20 miles to the east of London with fighter patrol lanes inside it. Large white arrows were provided at searchlight units, pointing in the direction of the enemy. About 120 fighters were available for the defence of London, plus RNAS machines which were under orders to co-operate. All this was achieved in the space of ten days and in time to meet a Gotha daylight raid on August 12, which was turned back. After a mauling on August 22 the Germans decided that they would have to restrict their activities to altitudes above 10,000ft or under cover of darkness.

Ashmore, with his new ideas, met opposition from the dyed-in-the-wool senior officers on the home establishment, but fortunately Field Marshal Lord French gave him the backing necessary to push through reforms.

The cover of a souvenir booklet produced at the end of the First World War to commemorate the work of the Metropolitan Observation Service, the forerunner of the Royal Observer Corps

Attack Warning Red

For warnings Ashmore had a colour code – "Readiness" for warning troops, police, etc; "Green" for air raid threatened; "Red" for air raid imminent; "White" for enemy clear of the district; "Yellow" for cancelling readiness measures; and "Turn in" for troops, etc. Warnings to the civil population were issued by the Home Office. It is remarkable that 58 years later the nuclear warnings for attack imminent and no further attack or radio-active fallout are "Red" and "White" respectively.

Following a night raid on London on September 4, Ashmore proposed a "balloon apron barrage" within the fighter patrol lines and stretching in an arc from north to south. The balloons were linked and carried weighted wires hanging downwards, hence the word apron. There was, however, extreme difficulty in getting the fighters, including modern Sopwith Camels, anywhere near the bombers at night. Ashmore in his book recalled that in October and December raids:

> "In 131 flights, 58 of them in efficient fighting machines, our pilots had only caught sight of an enemy machine on eight occasions and the eight views produced three combats, only one of which was successful."

What was needed was faster and more accurate information from the ground. As Ashmore put it:

> "Using the *Air Bandit* system of priority telephoning, the observer cordons and other reporting stations could report to the Horse Guards* in three minutes at best. More often the message took three or four times as long to appear before me. The information when it did arrive was often scrappy and not too accurate. Negative information was totally unreliable; I could not be sure, when I had no message from a particular district, that no hostile machine was there."

There was a pressing need for improvement, particularly as the Germans brought into use in December 1917 their big Staaken R.IV four-engined aircraft which carried three times the load of the Gotha, had a top speed of 77.5 m.p.h., an endurance of 6hr–7hr and were fitted with radio and six or seven machine guns. Ashmore therefore set about a complete re-organisation of the observer network, the control system and the communication set-up to go with them.

The Metropolitan Observation Service – the real forerunner of the Royal Observer Corps – had been the key source of information for some time, but it only covered the county of London. Ashmore extended the network outwards to include a variety of other observation posts and defence units and he standardised the method of reporting.

At observer posts a basic instrument was provided, consisting of a flat wheel with the circumference marked in bearings and a radial arm, pivoting about the centre, on which was mounted a sighting rod. The instrument was designed by the Royal Navy Hydrographer, Rear Admiral Parry, and when sighted on an aircraft it gave a bearing and an angle to the target. By comparing readings from two or more posts it was possible to fix the position of the aircraft over the ground. It was basically similar in concept to the ROC instrument of the Second World War, but without a height bar or pointer.

The information from the observer posts was fed to one of 26 sub-controls which worked out positions and then phoned them through to central control in the Horse Guards. Plaques

---

*The nerve centre of LADA.

on maps were used at all controls and the results transmitted in standardised form. Originally all information had been in written form, which was inefficient and time-wasting. It was the GSO.2, Major P. Fooks, who first suggested that there should be an operations table with a map, around which the plotters should sit, using symbols to represent the messages, thus eliminating all writing. Gridded maps were used so that references were the same throughout the system. At each sub-control sat a LADA officer who was in direct communications with LADA HQ.

The plot messages were in code★ and the map table symbols were extremely simple; for instance, a plain circular counter represented a hostile aircraft while a rectangular tab from a key ring represented a formation. On one side was an arrow and the other side was plain. The arrow was only displayed if the direction of flight was known. To avoid the maps being cluttered with useless information, clocks at controls were divided into four quarter-hour periods, the first five minutes coloured green, the next red and the third yellow. The map table symbols were similarly coloured and those of only two five-minute periods were allowed to remain there at any one time.

At LADA central control there were ten plotters around the table receiving information from the "tellers" at sub-controls and placing the counters on the map. Ashmore himself had a seat

---

★In the LADA code, for instance, "Dahlia" meant "seen" and "Daffodil" meant "sounds".

Layout of the London air defences, 1918, showing the inner and outer gunfire areas and the fighter airfields

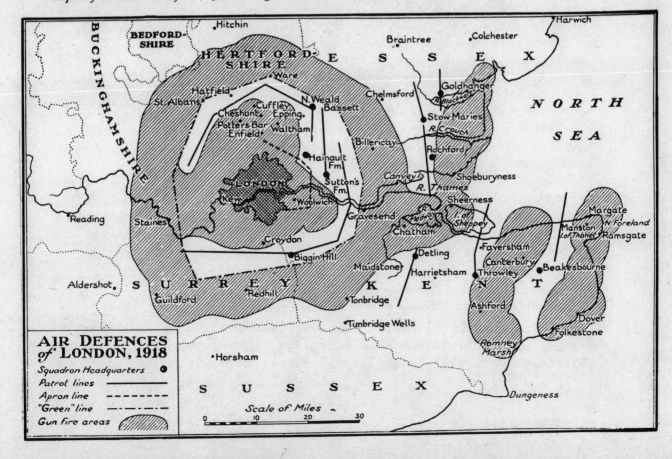

on a dais from where he could see all tracks on the table and dispose his forces accordingly. A personal telephone switch system enabled him to talk direct to any of the sub-controls. To complete the team, recorders maintained miniature maps of the tracks shown on the table, using green, red and yellow pencils. Ashmore estimated that the time taken for a ground sighting to be translated through the system to a symbol on his map-table was of the order of half a minute.

A typical sequence of events during a raid was as follows: watchers on the Essex coast heard an aircraft and reported to a sub-control the horizontal bearing and vertical angle (e.g. "Plane Sounds 50–30"). The sub-control plotted this information, using an assumed height, and thereafter the duty officer would telephone the LADA duty officer in London. The latter would guess whether this was a real raid or perhaps only a motor boat and decide, having regard to the weather and previous reports from other sources, including notification of friendly aircraft flights, whether to sit tight or take air-raid action. In a short time the raid would be either on or off. If it was on, the LADA duty officer ordered "Readiness," the signals superintendent pressed a switch which rang bells everywhere, the PBX operator rang all sub-controls and said the one word "Readiness," while the other signals men warned all the authorities, the staff and signals officers.

The first message likely to reach LADA was that coastal AA guns were firing a barrage at sound, which would be an unseen target. Thus Burnham-on-Crouch would report "Burnham barrage 564 Don 4." This was heard by operator No 3 at LADA and by Rochford and Stow-Maries, where fighter squadrons were based. The LADA operator repeated the message and placed the barrage symbol on the map square 564 D4, choosing the correct colour as shown by the clock. Immediately LADA operator No 5 called his three stations, Chelmsford (next gun line), Hainault Farm and Sutton's Farm (two aircraft patrols), with the message "Larder/all/ Barrage 564 Don 4." Other operators would do likewise and thus, almost simultaneously, all the defences knew where the hostile aircraft was, or was reckoned to be.

In due course other messages arrived, such as the searchlights associated with the two aircraft patrols giving Rochford and Stow information on which bearings were plotted and passed to LADA and elsewhere. If, by sheer luck, two lights held the aircraft while it crossed the baseline between them and control then a definite height was reported, such as "Stow height twelve in five hundred." If a LADA operator passed a message it would be acknowledged by Chelmsford, Rochford and Stow by their saying, in correct order, "Ack, Beer and Cee." If Stow, for instance, missed the message then it would say "Stow" instead of "Cee".

Colonel M. W. Emley recorded, in a confidential lecture in the 1930s, that "The use of this system led to an unexpected and pathetic complaint from an RAF officer that his letter should be changed so that he might be spared the pain of having to say "Beer, beer, beer" for hours on end without getting any."

One further observation by the Colonel is worthy of note in any day and age:

"The GOC himself could not interrupt a message as the operator had control, an acceptance of a deprivation to which I could not persuade some lesser mortals to agree. Interception keys in the fingers of an impatient CO can and do wreck things completely at times."

LADA central control had certain key tactical telephone lines outwards – to Buckingham Palace, the House of Commons, Scotland Yard, the Fire Brigade, the Admiralty, etc – and was also in touch with Calais and Dunkirk. The public warning system was vastly improved because

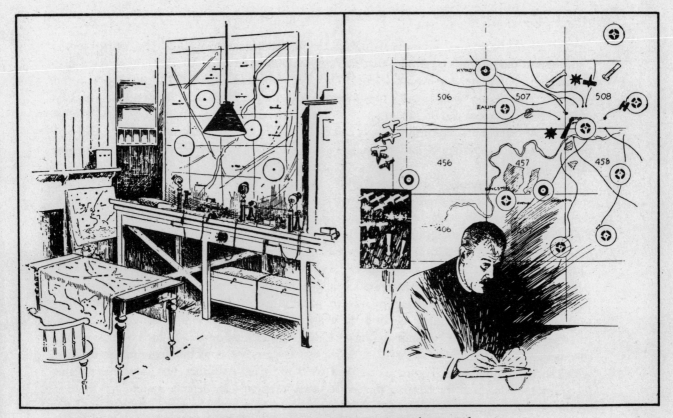

Left An artist's impression of the world's first air-situation operations room at London Air Defence Area Headquarters in the Horseguards, 1918. The rudimentary map table is in the foreground, while the vertical plotting chart—on which observation reports were received—is behind the telephones

Right The vertical chart in the LADA operations room showing the London area, together with aircraft and airfield symbols

of the accuracy and speed of information available from LADA.

Ashmore had his whole system in full working order by the late summer of 1918, but the last German aircraft raid on London had taken place on the night of May 19. On that occasion 13 bombers, including two Staaken R.IVs, reached London. Out of a total force of 33 raiders that arrived over England, three were shot down by guns and three by fighters.

LADA watched, waited and practised until, in November 1918, came the Armistice.

Since 1914 German airships, aircraft and seaplanes had carried out 103 bombing raids on Britain. They killed 1,413 people and injured 3,407 (670 killed and 1,960 injured in London, where they caused damage estimated to be worth just over £2 million). With a relatively small force they had succeeded in disrupting civilian life, holding back industrial output and keeping large numbers of troops and airmen away from the western front.

In *Civil Defence*, one of the official histories of the Second World War, T. H. O'Brien points out that "the two heavy raids on London of June and July 1917, for example, together caused 832 casualties (216 fatal), which amounted to 121 casualties for each ton of bombs dropped, and these casualty figures were to have much significance for the planning authorities of the future."

On November 22 Ashmore submitted proposals for a peacetime air-defence organisation. These included retaining the unified command structure and as much as possible of the gun, balloon, searchlight and observer layout. On the fighter side he suggested that the 6th Brigade airfields should be retained for night flying squadrons in order not to waste all the control room, communications and other facilities that had been established there. Above all he stressed that "ultimate responsibility for the air defences must rest either with the Air Ministry or with the War Office. It would be bad policy to divide the responsibility between the two. Air Ministry control would present certain advantages. A large proportion of the public will always think that the Air Ministry is responsible . . . It is, I consider, an absolute necessity that the whole of the defences of any particular locality, as for example the London Air Defence Area, should be under one commander."

Ashmore was absolutely right in his thinking and it is interesting to note that all his planning and his recommendations were adopted for the air-defence system eventually built up to fight the Second World War. His decentralised controls, with standard information, became the Fighter Groups' sectors and gun and Observer Corps operations rooms; LADA Central Control emerged as the Fighter Command filter and operations room complex; and his forward observation sites became the posts of the Observer Corps and the radar stations. Even the map-table, the raised dais, the colour-change clock and the plotting counters were standard equipment for the RAF in 1939–45. In the command structure the Air Ministry did indeed take over, the geographical area commanders became the Fighter Group AOCs and a supreme authority emerged as the Air Officer Commanding-in-Chief Fighter Command. In his book Ashmore comments: "I was five years too early." In fact it was 18 years before all his ideas came to fruition with the establishment of Fighter Command itself in 1936. Ashmore was never given the recognition he deserved for creating the world's first integrated air defence system and there is no doubt that without his talents the RAF would have had little on which to base its later planning and the Battle of Britain might have had a very different outcome. In 1918–19, however, all Ashmore could do was fight to retain some semblance of an organisation which was fast slipping away in a sea of apathy and false economy.

A conference at the War Office in February 1919 was presided over by Winston Churchill in his dual capacity as Secretary of State for War and Air. It was decided that "It was essential to keep alive the intricate and specialised art of air defence." This was so much hot air. Of the 286 AA guns and 387 searchlights available at the armistice, none remained by 1920, while the 200 or so fighters operationally available each day in 1918 for home defence had dwindled to two active squadrons. Of the observer/control network not a vestige was left.

SUMMARY OF GERMAN AIR ATTACKS ON BRITAIN 1914–18	*Airships*	*Aircraft*	*Totals*
Number which crossed English coast	202	452	654
Bombs dropped (tons)	205	75	280
*Casualties:			
killed	556	857	1,413
injured	1,358	2,050	3,408
Defending aircraft sorties against airships and aircraft	625	1,880	2,505
German airships/aircraft destroyed			
By AA	2	13	15
By fighters	8	9	17
*Numerous injuries were caused by AA splinters			

Ashmore's tenure of office as GOC LADA terminated in December 1920 and he took up the post of Commander Air Defence Brigade RA at Aldershot.

In 1922 the overall responsibility for air defence was transferred from the War Office to the Air Ministry. The Army was to continue to provide guns and searchlights in consultation with the RAF. Operational command was vested in an Air Officer.

A joint sub-committee was set up under Air Commodore J. M. Steel and Colonel W. H. Bartholomew to study air defence based on nine fighter squadrons proposed by the Government out of a total of 25. The Steel-Bartholomew plan, produced in February 1923, envisaged for London an outer observer post belt, an outer artillery zone and an aircraft fighting zone with eight sectors, each with one squadron of aircraft. The aircraft zone reached from Salisbury Plain in the west to Chatham in the east and Duxford in the north. Right in the centre was the inner artillery zone.

The plan was, however, overtaken by events as the Cabinet approved, on June 20, 1923, an air expansion scheme for 52 instead of 25 squadrons of fighters and bombers. This allowed for ten fighter sectors and 17 fighter squadrons. In order to implement the 52-squadron plan another committee was set up in 1924 under Major General C. F. Romer specifically to study command, warning and communications. An observation system was essential if the 52-squadron plan was to work at all and various memoranda were submitted, including – in May 1924 – a scheme for an observation system with posts giving information to observer centres and thence to HQ Fighting Area. Certain centres were to be linked with nearby fighter sectors.

In January 1924 the Committee of Imperial Defence appointed an Air Raid Precautions sub-committee which was chaired by the Permanent Under-Secretary of State for the Home Department. The ARP Committee was to perform most important functions and be closely linked with the growth of the observation system. As Ashmore reported to the ARP committee with reference to observers in the 1914–18 war:

"The observation system provided the information necessary to make the civil warnings effective and may therefore be considered a general, and not exclusively military, concern and responsibility. If this principle is accepted it may be possible to organise again the system of police observation posts that were so effective at the end of the late war."

The Romer Committee also accepted the principle that:

"The civil population will be so vitally affected by air attacks that the responsibility of observation and warning cannot be considered exclusively military."

On this basis any observer system would have to serve both the civil and military interests, and such has been the case for the past 50 years.

One member of the Romer Committee was none other than Major General Ashmore himself, and it was obvious that he was best suited to advise on the setting up of the observation system. Ashmore had, in April 1924, been appointed GOC Territorial Army Defence Formations and Inspector General of Anti-Aircraft. Rather than wait for the full Romer Report, which was scheduled for 1925, he decided to stage some plotting experiments straight away.

Ashmore wanted to find out:

a) The best distance apart to put the posts;
b) The number of posts that could conveniently work to one observation centre;

c)   The best method of passing the "Readiness" signal to the posts and centres;
d)   The best form of reporting; and
c)   The best locating apparatus, if any, required at the post.

He proposed to the ARP committee that there was a good opportunity for a preliminary experiment in August and September 1924, in the area between the Romney Marshes and Tonbridge in Kent, in combination with another experiment in coast watching. The committee agreed "to recommend that the police organisation should be used for providing personnel for observation duties by enrolling special constables for this purpose," and that "civilian personnel should be utilised for the tests in question, details of which should be arranged between the War Office, the General Post Office and the Home Office."

Ashmore wrote to the Chief Constable of Kent, Major H. E. Chapman, asking for his co-operation in setting up a small group of posts and a temporary operations room. The experiment was given the title "Air defence observation in the Weald of Kent, 1924." The head special constable of each of the following locations was asked to direct and provide "specials" for posts which were clustered together in threes for communications purposes:

B.1 Sutton Vallence	C.1 Goudhurst	D.1 Bethersden
B.2 Marden	C.2 Cranbrook	D.2 Ham Street
B.3 Biddenden	C.3 Hawkhurst	D.3 Tenterden

The observation centre or control was set up in a room in the post office of the small town of Cranbrook with the help of the Postmaster. General Ashmore with his signals officer, Colonel Day, toured the area talking to the special constables, telling them how to report and instructing in methods of observation and reporting. Each post was provided with a rudimentary wooden instrument on a map table mounted on a flimsy tripod. A cumbersome head and breast set was to be used for communications, via a telephone box connected to a telegraph pole. The War Office agreed to pay for the observer instrument provided that its cost was kept to the minimum. It resembled a pantograph stood on end with the pivot through the centre of the map table. Two pins on the long arm of the pantograph provided a means of sighting the aircraft.

To plot an aircraft the observer sighted along the upper arm of the pantograph while a second observer moved an upright rod, graduated in thousands of feet, across the map until the height coincided with the bottom arm of the pantograph. The square on which the height rod rested was the one reported to centre as the position of the aircraft. For these first experiments the height of the aircraft was not estimated but passed to the observer from the centre.

The basis of post plotting was always to be the same: a right-angled triangle assembled from the baseline, the sighting adjusted by estimated height and a vertical line between the two. The direction of the baseline came automatically from the bearing on which the aircraft was sighted. The whole idea was simple but effective, and it stood the test of time. Post instruments were orientated by having an aiming line on the map which was sighted on a nearby prominent object or building. The only other piece of equipment issued to posts was an electric torch for looking at the map at night.

Ashmore laid down that "Readiness" was to be called an hour before the time of the exercise when the post office switched lines through to the posts. The No 1 observer at the post took the table, height bar and torch to the site, while No 2 observer connected up and checked the telephone. His instructions for reporting were as follows:

"When the aeroplane is seen or heard, No 1 aims the sight bar on it and says 'On.' No 2 then brings the height bar against the lower bar of the sighting arrangement and reads off the map square. He then reports to the observation centre in the following form: 'Plane seen (or heard) FG2.' If possible he adds the direction of flight; for example: 'Course North.' If there are more aeroplanes than one, he begins his message: 'Two (or more) Planes' or 'Formation.' If more than one post on the same line wants to report at one time, the observation centre will tell all but one to wait: for example, the operator will say 'A.1 and A.3 wait, A.2 report'."

The standardised maps at post and centre were marked with a grid of squares of three miles side, each with a two-letter designation, e.g. HW, NB, etc. These squares were subdivided into four equal portions numbered 1, 2, 3 and 4. Reporting was on the numbered subdivision of a particular three-mile square.

At the Cranbrook post office the centre was set up with a map of the area, on which posts were marked, laid out on a table. Three special constables acted as plotters, each connected to a cluster of three posts and one acted as the recorder showing the aircraft plots with lines on a miniature map. The control officer was Ashmore himself. The coloured counters and the colour-code clock were exactly as in the days of LADA six years before.

All was prepared and day tests were scheduled for August 12, 15 and 19 and for September 9. Night tests were to be carried out on September 2 and 5. Day flights were allocated to a 120-m.p.h. Sopwith Snipe biplane fighter of No 32 Squadron flown by Flying Officer D. M. Fleming. On the late afternoon of August 12 Fleming flew from Kenley to Hawkinge. Watches were synchronised and he took off to fly at 5,000ft along the line of the downs to enter the reporting area from the north.

At Cranbrook Mr Houghton, the post office district engineer, had plugged through the lines and Ashmore waited with his team. At about 6 p.m. Sutton Vallence reported an aircraft seen in square HS and the exercise had begun. Post after post picked up the Snipe as it toured the area, the plotters putting their counters on the table and the recorder pencilling the track on his map. By just after 7 p.m. it was all over, the posts were stood down and Fleming was on his way back to base, to make up his log book and despatch a copy to General Ashmore at the War Office. The three further daylight tests were successfully completed but only one night sortie was made, on September 5, as the weather was too bad for flying on the night of September 2.

The trials proved most encouraging. As Ashmore put it in his letter to the head special constables in September:

"The results have been excellent and I have obtained accurate and immediate records of the flights; records that agree exactly with the pilots' log. The work you have done will be of the greatest value in the future organisation of the air defences."

With the minimum of expenditure and at very short notice Ashmore had proved his point, namely that volunteers working to his system of reporting and tracking could provide the necessary air intelligence over land. In effect, Cranbrook and its temporary posts represented, in miniature, the type of organisation which would occupy a county and be duplicated to cover most of the British Isles.

The mother of all modern air-defence control and reporting systems had been proved with

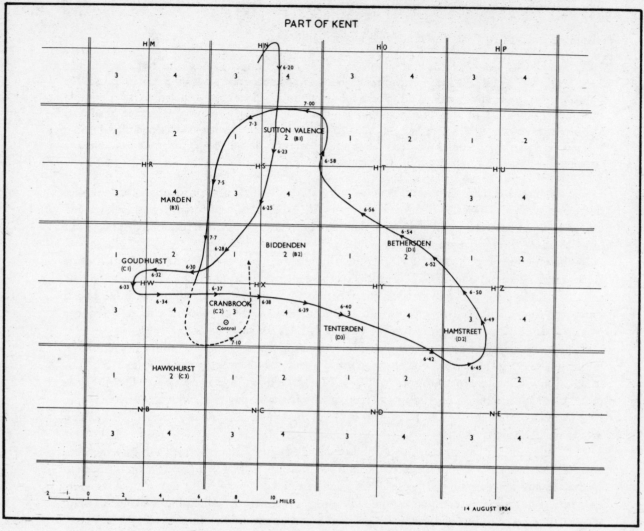

The track of the original plotting and tracking experiment on August 12, 1924. Maj Gen Ashmore set up shop in the post office at Cranbrook while hastily assembled special constables plotted a Sopwith Snipe of No 32 Sqn from nine observer posts. The dotted line shows the progress of the Snipe after the official shut-down time for the exercise. This was the real beginning of the Royal Observer Corps

unpaid volunteers, a makeshift country network and the expenditure of £200 – £300, of which the princely sum of £82 had been charged by the GPO for line connections and time.

Throughout most of its career the Royal Observer Corps has had at least two masters and has carried out a multiplicity of functions. It is perhaps fitting, therefore, that at its birth some difficulty should have been found as to what to file it under. Here was a new formation recruited as special constables under the Home Office, organised and run by an Army major-general and designed to supply information to the Royal Air Force. A classic British compromise!

The problem was solved by opening a file in the Home Office headed "Air raid observation scheme – Correspondence: Chief Constables and General Ashmore as to arrangements." Lacking any classification for such warlike material, the authorities placed it under the heading of "Miscellaneous Criminal." A somewhat inauspicious beginning for a corps still fulfilling vital civil and military functions half a century later.

Chapter 2
THE CORPS ESTABLISHED

General Ashmore had successfully proved his case for an observation system with the 1924 experiments and he was anxious to expand the scheme to a larger area. Accordingly he set about planning exercises to cover two counties, Kent and Sussex, with temporary controls, or operations rooms, in both.

He wrote to the two chief constables asking for special constables to be made available or enrolled, sufficient to man 44 posts in two "Groups". Group operations rooms or centres were to be set up at Maidstone and Horsham. Working on a basic grid and with a spacing of between five and eight miles, Ashmore chose a series of locations and requested GPO telephone lines to be laid on. Both operations centres were in post offices, that at Maidstone being in outbuildings and that at Horsham in the attic. Two "Superintendents" were selected, Mr J. H. Day at Maidstone and Mr H. T. Knott at Horsham.

Volunteers found by the police were sworn in as special constables under conditions of great secrecy and were warned not to tell anyone – not even their relatives. One volunteer, Mr J. I. Eager at Horsham, pointed out that he was a solicitor and therefore could serve for observing duties only and not for ordinary constabulary duties. This was accepted and it became part of later conditions of service.

Posts were proposed at the following places*:

NO I GROUP MAIDSTONE

A.1	*Minster*		F.1	*Ham Street*
A.2	Ash		F.2	Bethersden
A.3	Chislet		F.3	Little Chart
B.1	*Whitstable*		G.1	*Cranbrook*
B.2	Canterbury		G.2	Headcorn
B.3	*Wye*		G.3	Tenterden
C.1	Eythorne		H.1	Catsfield
C.2	*Barham*		H.2	Robertsbridge
C.3	Lyminge		H.3	Beckley

---

*Several posts were removed to other places in the 1920s, some disappeared altogether. Of the original 43 posts, 14 are still operational today, and these are printed above in italics. The 1924–1925 post still on its original site is Ham Street, while the only other posts not resited after 1927 and still operational are Cuckfield and Fernhurst. One post in Surrey, Dunsfold, was to have been set up, as were those at Steyning and Pulborough in Sussex. Apparently these were left in abeyance for a year or so.

D.1	*Eastchurch*		J.1	Horsmunden
D.2	Queensborough		J.2	Ticehurst
D.3	*Sittingbourne*		J.3	*Frant*
E.1	Faversham			
E.2	Sheldwich Lees			
E.3	Lenham			

NO 2 GROUP HORSHAM

K.1	Polegate		N.1	*Cuckfield*
K.2	Warbleton		N.2	Mannings Heath
K.3	Mayfield		N.3	Billingshurst
K.4	*Chiddingly*		O.1	Arundel
L.1	Framfield		O.2	Midhurst
L.2	*Crowborough*		O.3	*Fernhurst*
L.3	Newick			
M.1	*Lewes*			
M.2	Keymer			
M.3	Henfield			

Ashmore travelled the length and breadth of the two counties interviewing "head specials" in the towns and villages involved, supervising the supply of plotting and telephone equipment and arranging the connection of telephone lines. Wherever possible, to cut costs, posts were placed close to a telephone exchange. This often meant that the observers had a short line connection to the exchange, but little view of the sky.

All was ready in time for the exercises which were staged on June 22 and 24, 1925. Three RAF squadrons were used for the test and multiple tracks were established by day and by night. The ARP committee reported on July 8 the success of the exercises and this was followed by recommendations that the observer network be extended to Hampshire and Essex in order to complete the coverage on the main routes from the Continent to London. Representatives from the counties in question had observed the trials at Maidstone and Horsham.

The Committee of Imperial Defence approved the scheme on October 29 thus setting the seal on the existence of the Observer Corps which was already in being. Despite the fact that the Observer Corps could trace its service from the Metropolitan Observation Service of the First World War and had operated again in 1924, the official month of inauguration of the corps proper was to be October 1925.

The terms and conditions for service were laid down as follows:

1. The Observer Corps shall consist of volunteers, enrolled as special constables, who undertake to carry out observation work in the air defence of Great Britain as part of their constabulary duties.
2. Enrolment may be for observation work only, and without acceptance of the general responsibilities of the special constabulary.
3. Upon ceasing to be special constables, members cease to belong to the Observer Corps; but members who so desire may, at the discretion of the Chief of Police, be retained for observation work only after the normal retiring age of the special constabulary to which they belong.
4. The duties are local, and members incur no obligation to carry out observation duties beyond

the district of the local special constabulary.

5. Members undertake not to resign from the Corps after they have been called out for observation duty in connection with a war emergency until either they are released from duty or a week has elapsed after an outbreak of war.

6. Members will act under the direction of the Chief of Police, and such special constabulary officers as he may appoint, as regards attendance for duty at posts and centres and all matters of administration, but for matters of technical training and in operations they will act under the observer group assistants and higher officers of the Observer Corps, and the authorities responsible for air defence.

7. Service in the Observer Corps will rank as approved special constabulary service, and duties performed in connection with the training or work of the corps will rank as police duties for the purposes of the award of the Special Constabulary Long Service Medal.

Three hundred certificates were printed in August 1925 for qualified members of the corps and issued in November under the signature of Major General Ashmore as Inspector of Anti-Aircraft.

Ashmore was already preparing the ground in Hampshire and Essex – plus half Suffolk, with centres at Winchester and Colchester respectively. At Winchester, Ashmore wrote to a retired Brigadier, Noel W. H. Du Boulay, as a result of an approach by the Chief Constable of Hampshire. Du Boulay became the controller at Winchester and he was one of a great number of retired senior officers who took over key Observer Corps tasks in the period 1926–1939.

On the morning of June 1, 1926, Ashmore appeared at the Blue Triangle Club, Parchment Street, Winchester, to brief the Brigadier and some of the special constables recruited for the centre of No 3 Group. He did the same thing at Colchester, interviewing Colonel Herring and a small group of personnel at the penthouse to the GPO Exchange, before forming No 18 Group★.

In a document written in 1927, General Ashmore described his methods as follows:

"The Home Office writes to chief constables, giving the outline of the system. I draw up the tactically ideal lay-out; this is modified after consulting the GPO to make it fit with the existing telephone lay-out. I also consult the chief constables who are able to say whether the necessary men can be procured in any given place. We keep the zones as far as possible to county police boundaries, but the telephone system does not always allow this.

Having thus settled the locality of each post, I go round with a GPO representative and the local police authorities, and we choose the exact spot for the post. The GPO can then erect the extension lines from the local post office to a pole at the observer post itself. The police authorities enrol the special constables, who must live close at hand.

I then make another tour with my chief signal officer, meet all the special constables, distribute the apparatus and instructions, explain the work and orient the map. The CSO explains the telephone which is the ordinary army type connected to the GPO system at the special pole."

The system of recruiting tended to be the same throughout. The chief constable talked to retired officers and businessmen and landowners who, in turn, "persuaded" anyone over whom they had influence.

★The fourth group to be formed was given the number 18 as Ashmore had already done a provisional layout for a large part of England with the intermediate numbers filling the gaps. Unfortunately this expansion did not take place while he was in command.

By the end of 1926, with the network established in four counties, the Observer Corps was there to stay. The methods of plotting were crude but the basis was in fact to be common to all forms of air intelligence, incuding radar, over the next 30 years.

Any aircraft in flight forms a right-angled triangle to a ground observer, the upper side being the direct line from the observer to the aircraft, the base line being the bearing to the observer of the aircraft and the vertical line being that from the aircraft to the point on the earth's surface over which it is flying. From the outset the ground observer could establish, with his instrument, the bearing and the angle from the horizontal of the approaching machine. What he then had to find – in order to derive the correct overland position – was the third side of the triangle. With the early wooden instrument – known to everyone as the "Heath Robinson" – the vertical was established by the height rod, with an estimated figure, being placed up against the lower arm, thus marking a square on the map. For night work the procedure was simply to report a "plane heard NW." If it was overhead, so much the better, but this seldom occurred and sound plots were left to the centre plotter to work out from the cross-cut of direction lines given by two or more posts.

The centre operations rooms operated along the lines of the 1924 experiment, with nine plotters around the map table handling three posts each and using the basic counters to mark the plots. The controller supervised the centre while a recorder maintained a note of the tracks on a small map and a teller looking down on the plotting table reported the tracks to defence headquarters. The headquarters in question was "Fighting Area" at RAF Uxbridge in Middlesex.

In 1925 Air Defence of Great Britain (ADGB) had been set up with Air Marshal Sir John Salmond as Air Officer Commanding-in-Chief. ADGB incorporated Fighting Area and the Wessex Bombing Area, renamed RAF Bombing Formations. Fighting Area, as laid down in the 52-squadron scheme, was divided into the ten fighter sectors, Advanced Fighting Squadrons and the General Officer Commanding Ground Troops. The last mentioned had under him the Inner and Outer London Artillery Zones, searchlight operations and the Observer Corps. There were to be no Observer Corps units in the artillery zones, as these were considered an Army prerogative, and ports and coastal areas were the jealous preserve of the Admiralty. These inconsistencies were to cause problems for many years and were only ultimately resolved when, at a time of crisis, the Observer Corps took over responsibility for all areas of the mainland.

The 52-squadron scheme looked all right on paper but in reality it was only a skeleton which took an unconscionable time to fill out with flesh. The gun/searchlight defences remained impotent with only two pitifully weak AA Brigades authorised.* Modern fighters were lacking. Only three new squadrons were formed in the period 1925–1928 and none in 1928–1929. It was not until the first half of 1932 that the full 17 squadrons were actually in being.

During the whole of the period 1927–1933 not a single new Observer Corps group was formed and the existing four had to soldier on with a strictly limited budget, being virtually unknown to the public and only kept together by the certainty that their work was for the national good. The spirit of the early observers was of the sort which was to carry the Corps through many trials and tribulations in later years.

---

*192 guns were to be allocated under the 52-squadron scheme, laid out in eight brigades, but even by 1931 only 27 per cent of the guns and 22 per cent of searchlights could be manned.

After the tests of 1925 the Observer Corps settled down to a routine. Six basic exercises were held each year during June and July and between the hours of 6 and 7 p.m. These were divided between "communications" and "calibration." The former were intended purely to prove that the telephone lines worked, while the latter involved passing dummy or sometimes live plots to centre. RAF personnel visited the posts and checked the plots against a known flightpath.

During one exercise on June 22, 1927, a VIP team comprised of Major General Ashmore, Wing Commander Holt and Mr C. de C. Parry, HM Inspector of Constabulary, visited Maidstone Centre. In his report Parry described the room in the main street with its operations table, the three areas covered by 12 plotters linked to the posts, the bomber and fighter counters and the colour-change system. Subsequently Parry and Holt visited the Lenham post, where four special constables were on duty. Judging from his report, Parry was suitably impressed.

The air manoeuvres of 1927 gave an opportunity for the network to be tested under more realistic conditions and for the first time since 1918 they represented genuine air exercises, not aircraft providing co-operation with ground troops. The manoeuvres were held on July 25, and the RAF was divided into two groups – "Eastland" representing the attackers, and the fighter squadrons forming the "Defence Forces."

Four single-engined day-bomber squadrons were employed: 11 Squadron with Hawker Horsleys from Netheravon, 12 Squadron with Fairey Foxes from Andover, and Nos 39 and 207 Squadrons with DH.9As from Spittlegate and Eastchurch respectively. For night operations there were three squadrons of Virginia VIIs – Nos 7 at Bircham Newton, 9 at Manston and 58 at Worthy Down. No 99 Squadron at Bircham Newton was flying Hyderabads. The heaviest bomber was the Vickers Virginia, at 17,600lb. It spanned 86ft and could achieve 108 m.p.h., although it normally cruised at around 90 m.p.h. Of the single-engined day bombers the fastest was the elegant Fairey Fox, which reached 156 m.p.h. The DH.9A was a well proven relic from the First World War.

The Intercepter force consisted of the following units:

Squadron	Base	Equipment
1	Tangmere	AW Siskin
41	Northolt	AW Siskin
56	Biggin Hill	AW Siskin
111	Duxford	AW Siskin
3	Upavon	Hawker Woodcock
17	Upavon	Hawker Woodcock
23	Kenley	Gloster Gamecock
32	Kenley	Gloster Gamecock
43	Tangmere	Gloster Gamecock
19	Duxford	Gloster Grebe
25	Hawkinge	Gloster Grebe
29	Duxford	Gloster Grebe

Fastest of the fighters was the Armstrong Whitworth Siskin IIIA at 156 m.p.h. This type first entered service with 41 Squadron in March 1927.

The speed difference between the fighters and bombers was very small, and in the case of the Siskin IIIA and the Fox there was none. The defenders had to be in the right place at the right time if an interception was to be possible. For the Observer Corps there was some confusion between the single-engined day bombers and the fighters, but little problem with the giant lumbering multi-engined machines. As the brief to the corps was to accept two engines for a bomber and one engine for a fighter, the need for recognition of types was manifest early on.

No official statement had been made on the establishment or organisation of the corps but *Flight* reported in its preview of the manoeuvres:

"Watchers on the coast (special constables will be employed as far as possible) will endeavour to spot them [the enemy] and ascertain their numbers and altitude."

At the conclusion of the exercises a senior RAF officer told the press:

"The observers on the coast are all volunteers, special constables. Their work has been extremely good and cannot be praised too highly. It has made remarkable progress in the last twelve months."

Brooke-Popham as Commander-in-Chief sent a congratulatory telegram to chief constables referring to Observer Corps efforts as being "invaluable to the commander of the defending forces." This was hardly surprising, as when the corps was not operating the bombing force had to resort to giving its position to Fighting Area by wireless to allow the defenders any chance at all.

Following the exercises, the officer commanding the defence squadrons wrote: "propose to concentrate next year mainly on the problem of finding the enemy."

As a result of the experience gained, Ashmore decided that more observer personnel would be needed in the event of war. He therefore sanctioned the duplication of centre crews to provide reliefs and the raising of post strengths to at least eight members to make the basis of a duty roster. Beyond this, much resiting of posts was found to be necessary in order that they should have some reasonable view of the skies around them.

By the summer of 1928 the number of posts had been increased and the corps was ready for even larger air manoeuvres, this time carried out in mid-August. There were still no lines for switching to posts and centres during the day, so the exercises had to be carried out from 6 p.m. to 9 a.m.

The "Eastland" bomber force again made its appearance, but this time reinforced by the Auxiliary Air Force at No 1 Air Defence Group with 503, 600, 601 and 605 Squadrons. The auxiliaries had begun to form in 1925, and this was their first participation in the annual manoeuvres. "Eastland" proper was made up of 7, 9, 11, 12, 39, 58, 99, 100 and 207 Squadrons. The only new aircraft in the attacking role were the Fairey 111Fs of 207 Squadron from Eastchurch, which had replaced DH.9As in January 1928. One squadron, No 101, did not take part as it was re-equipping with the fast and highly manoeuvrable Boulton Paul Sidestrand with two Bristol Jupiter engines. The defending force, "Westland," mustered exactly the same 12 squadrons as in the year before, the only difference being that four more of them had converted to Siskins.

It was decided by the authorities that the Observer Corps should at last be presented to the public, and facilities were made available for visits to both posts and centres. The actual sites were not to be disclosed but officialdom revealed that there were 100 posts reporting to four centres. Photographs of posts at work were allowed but none of centres.

Flight's special correspondent, Major F. A. de V. Robertson, spoke of his visit as follows:

"On Wednesday I sped across one of the home counties to visit an observation centre. The room in which it was located was not underground, but probably the centre will go to earth long before there is any chance of our disagreeing with any continental power.★ The Chief Constable was there supervising the activities of his specials. . . . I had heard Sir Robert Brooke-Popham remark a couple of days earlier that it was probably because they were unpaid that the special constables were so good and keen."

The efforts of the Corps were, in fact, so good that they were handsomely acknowledged in the official communiqué. Despite the adulation, there were shortcomings shown up by the exercises. Plots were slow in transmission from centres to Fighting Area and the night plotting proved difficult with the Heath Robinson instrument and the procedures then in force. In addition, the RAF felt that the Observer Corps ought to be extended to cover the outer artillery zone as the reporting gap there made for considerable problems.

The 1928 manoeuvres were to be Ashmore's swan song. He had built the four groups into a vital part of the air-defence system and the pattern he had laid down could be extended right across the country. His very success meant that the Air Staff began to consider that the observer system should be part of the RAF and, as ADGB was the air defence authority, it was proposed that control of the Observer Corps should be transferred from the War Office to the Air Ministry. This was a momentous step which was to mould the thinking and allegiance of the Corps for the rest of its existence.

"Splash" Ashmore retired in 1929 but in May 1940, at the age of 67, he donned uniform again as Commander of the 6th West Sussex Battalion of the Local Defence Volunteers, later the Home Guard. During the Second World War he had only to walk out into Maltravers Street, Arundel, to see one of the essential memorials to his work – an observer post, set high on the Keep of Arundel Castle, maintaining day and night vigil.

★No observer centre was put underground during the whole of the period 1925-1955, when aircraft reporting was the prime task of the organisation.

Chapter 3
AIR-MINISTRY TAKE-OVER

The Romer Committee of 1924 had suggested an observer network covering 18 groups, but only four had been formed. Clearly at some point there would have to be a big expansion, and it was felt that the Air Ministry should be the authority to handle it rather than the War Office. On October 16, 1928, the Home Defence subcommittee recommended to the Committee of Imperial Defence that control of the Observer Corps be passed to the RAF. The committee approved the report at its 238th meeting, held on November 18, 1928, and it was decided that the transfer should take place on January 1, 1929.

ADGB held discussions on the transfer on November 26 and it was agreed that the best method of administering the four observer groups was to affiliate them to the aircraft sector headquarters with which they normally communicated, as follows: No 1 Group Maidstone to Biggin Hill, No 2 Group Horsham to Kenley, No 3 Group Winchester to Tangmere, and No 18 Group Colchester to North Weald. No 3 Group would normally have been allocated to Sector G, but this had headquarters at Northolt – a good distance from the group centre at Winchester. Tangmere was therefore provisionally selected instead.

A further conference was held at the Air Ministry on November 29; Air Vice-Marshal Sir Ivo Vesey was in the chair and the meeting was attended by Army and RAF officers including the AOC-in-C, ADGB, Air Vice-Marshal F. R. Scarlett. It was stated that the War Office was prepared to hand over the Observer Corps as a going concern "without any stores-accounting transaction." No financial adjustment between the War Office and the Air Ministry would be necessary, the transfer including equipment at centres and posts. Any form saturated administrative official in the Ministry of Defence today would wish to be back in the happy era of 1928.

Under the heading "Appointment of a Commandant" the report of the meeting read as follows:

"i) The GOC Air Defence Formations stated that hitherto the War Office had been able to utilise as commandant an officer of one of the RA Brigades of the Outer Artillery Zone who had time to spare for the additional duties owing to the deferred development of the artillery zone. There was, therefore, no precedent for the appointment of a whole-time paid commandant but, if the corps developed as was expected, such an appointment would be necessary.

ii) It was stated that the duties of commandant would include periodical visits to no less than 103 centres* now in existence and that this number might increase by 50 or 60 in the not-too-distant future.

---

*By centres the report meant sites, i.e. Observer Corps centres and posts.

iii) It was agreed that it would not be possible to find an RAF officer with time to spare to undertake the duties of commandant on a part-time basis and the appointment as from January 1 of a whole-time officer would be required.

iv) The chairman stated that he would take up the question of the appointment of a suitable officer and of the emoluments for the post.

It was pointed out that Treasury approval would be necessary for the appointment.

The AOC-in-C expressed the hope that there would not be a longer gap than was necessary between the date of taking over the corps on January 1, 1929, and the actual appointment.

v) The question of the provision of a car and driver for the commandant was deferred for later consideration as a matter of detail.

vi) It was stated that the commandant would require no staff, either paid or unpaid, and that no additional stores staff would be required at sector headquarters."

Under the heading "Other Matters," it was agreed that "The Home Office should be officially informed of the transfer of custody of the Corps to the Air Ministry and that the name of the commandant should be communicated to them as soon as the appointment had been made."

The Air Council wrote to the Under-Secretary of State at the Home Office on December 18, 1928, to acquaint him with the decisions taken. At the same time Air Ministry department S.6 wrote to Mr A. L. Dixon at the Home Office saying: "We shall also have to make entries regarding the Corps in the War Book, i.e. when the Cabinet decide that we are to prepare for air defence we should propose in our general order to the AOC-in-C to tell him to call up the Observer Corps." It added: "Would you wish to be consulted about calling out the Observer Corps?"

The change-over on January 1, 1929, was smooth and had no immediate effect on the working of the Corps. Training became entirely the province of the Air Ministry, but chief constables remained responsible for recruiting and controlling personnel. Points of mutual interest between the Home Office and the Air Ministry were discussed at a meeting of the Committee on Duties of Police in War held at the Home Office on January 24, 1929. It was remarkable how the well worn British committee system managed to sort out problems and initiate changes even where several authorities were involved.

The only thing still outstanding was the choice of the new commandant. This question was resolved with the appointment, on March 8, 1929, of Air Commodore G. A. D. Masterman. This was a good choice, as he had the ability to get on with the extraordinary cross-section of civilians in the Observer Corps, with the police and with the Air Ministry. Masterman set up his office at Hillingdon House, Uxbridge, as had Major General Ashmore, but he was without the benefit of any staff to assist him.

One of his first tasks was to deal with the subject of call-out in the event of hostilities, which was worrying the RAF. Air Vice-Marshal Ellington had written to the Secretary of State complaining that he had "very little, if any, control over individuals of the Observer Corps." He pointed out that before any action could be taken on a call-out telegram, all observers would have to be sworn in under the Chief Constables Act, 1914, and that observers should sign an agreement, similar to that for Territorial Army units, to be called up by the Air Officer Commanding-in-Chief.

Unlike the TA, the Observer Corps received no pay or allowances, which made officialdom even more edgy. Ellington suggested that on call-out for war each observer should be paid a

TA-type gratuity of £5 and daily pay during the "transitory period of apprehended attack and during war." The Observer Corps was such an odd organisation that it did not fit into any of the neat Service compartments. The whole question of status and pay was not to be finally resolved until the outbreak of the Second World War.

Apart from the annual manoeuvres, the Corps kept up its normal activities throughout 1929. There was no sign of any expansion of the network until October, and even then it involved internal reinforcements within the existing groups. At the Joint Chief Constables District Conference, Nos 5 and 6 Districts, held at the Home Office on October 22, 1929, Masterman stated that the Board of Trade had agreed to a scheme for certain Coastguard stations and naval war signal stations★ to be brought into use as coastal observer posts "but regular personnel would not be available for observer duty after the first 24 hours of war."
The stations were as follows:†

Coastguard:	S. Suffolk	– Orford
	Essex	– Walton-on-the-Naze
	Kent	– Reculver, Kingsgate, Deal and Dymchurch
	S. Sussex	– Rye Harbour, Fairlight, Bexhill and Newhaven
	W. Sussex	– Worthing and Selsey
Naval war stations:	Kent	– Dungeness
	Sussex	– Eastbourne (Beachy Head)

The commandant also announced that a lapel badge for the Corps had been designed and was on issue – but only if paid for. He informed the meeting that he was seeking authority to issue badges free to qualified observers. This then was the origin of the Corps crest with its Armada-period warrior holding aloft a blazing torch with the words "Forewarned is Forearmed" beneath. Just who designed the badge no-one knows, but his artistry lives on to this day.

Life in the Observer Corps of the late 1920s and early 1930s was not the rat race of the 1970s. One stalwart on a post housed the telephone box and the instrument in a shed or broom cupboard and six times per year the personnel sallied forth for exercises. If aircraft were involved, an RAF officer would pay a visit to see fair play. He carried with him a rough plot of the proposed times, course and the height to be flown. In quite a few cases the post observers managed to distract the attention of the invigilator and read his brief, with the result that their anticipation and plotting appeared to be quite exceptional. At centres the crews foregathered, laid out the map and the counters and plugged in the telephones in the hope that there would be someone at the other end of the line.

The years 1929 and 1930 were ones of consolidation, filling gaps on the map, improving the standard of post plotting and recruiting more personnel for the centres. Canvas wind-breaks were indented for, RAF despatch riders were used for taking spare kit to posts and celluloid covers were provided for post maps in order to keep the rain off. Badges were only allowed to be worn by personnel after they had been awarded their certificates of efficiency.

★Originally agreed at a conference held on October 15, 1929, under the chairmanship of Air Commodore (later Air Chief Marshal Sir) F. W. Bowhill.

†It is interesting to note that all these sites became regular Observer Corps posts which were used throughout the Second World War, and six of them are still operational.

While the RAF lavished high praise on the corps for its work, there were some who had other ideas. At a Joint Chief Constables District Conference held on December 3, 1930, the Chief Constable of Colchester said that he doubted whether the Observer Corps was much use and it would become even less so as development of aircraft proceeded. His attitude was reflected in the poor state of organisation at Colchester Centre where, until there were some changes three years later, the controller "left everything to his assistant controller."

From 1928 to 1930 the Press were welcomed at centres and posts for the annual exercises, but in 1931 the Air Ministry began to draw a veil of secrecy over the affairs of the corps, for reasons completely unknown. Held between July 20 and 23, 1931, the air exercises were wholly unrealistic as, lacking seaward detection, the defenders required incoming bombers to fly up

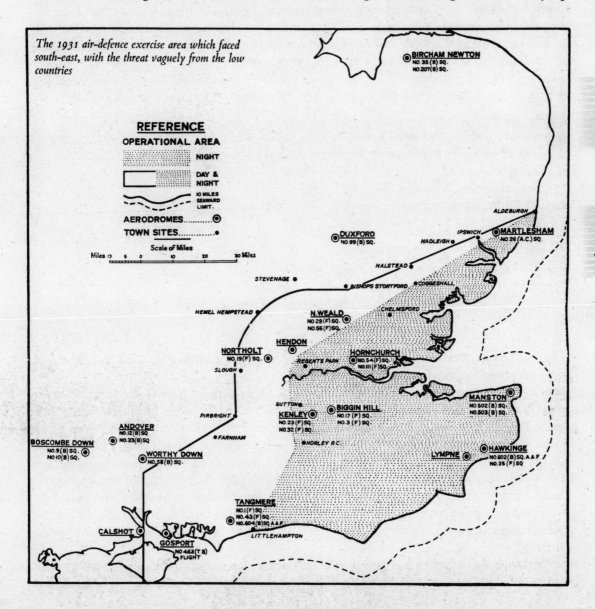

The 1931 air-defence exercise area which faced south-east, with the threat vaguely from the low countries

REFERENCE
OPERATIONAL AREA
NIGHT
DAY & NIGHT
10 MILES SEAWARD LIMIT.
AERODROMES............ ⊙
TOWN SITES............. •

Scale of Miles
Miles 10 5   0   10   20   30 Miles

BIRCHAM NEWTON
NO.35 (B) SQ.
NO.207(B) SQ.

ALDEBURGH

DUXFORD
NO.99 (B) SQ.

IPSWICH
MARTLESHAM
NO.26 (A.C.) SQ.

HADLEIGH

HALSTEAD

STEVENAGE

BISHOPS STORTFORD   COGGESHALL

HEMEL HEMPSTEAD

N.WEALD
NO.29 (F) SQ.
NO.56 (F) SQ.

CHELMSFORD

HENDON

NORTHOLT
NO.19(F) SQ.

REGENTS PARK

HORNCHURCH
NO.54 (F) SQ.
NO.111 (F) SQ.

SLOUGH

SUTTON

MANSTON
NO.502 (B) SQ.
NO.503 (B) SQ.

PIRBRIGHT

KENLEY
NO.23 (F) SQ.
NO.32 (F) SQ.

BIGGIN HILL
NO.17 (F) SQ.
NO.3 (F) SQ.

ANDOVER
NO.12(B) SQ.
NO.33 (B) SQ

FARNHAM

BOSCOMBE DOWN
NO.9 (B) SQ.
NO.10(B) SQ.

SHORLEY R.C.

WORTHY DOWN
NO.58 (B) SQ.

LYMPNE

HAWKINGE
NO.602(B) SQ.A.A.F
NO.25 (F) SQ

TANGMERE
NO.1 (F) SQ.
NO.43 (F) SQ.
NO.604 (B) SQ.A.A.F

CALSHOT

GOSPORT
NO.462 (T B)
FLIGHT

LITTLEHAMPTON

special corridors where the fighters could wait for them. Despite this, there was one clear pointer for the future, namely the bombers which made very successful attacks at low level on Hornchurch, Northolt and North Weald, announcing their arrival with a shower of ping-pong balls. Of the aircraft taking part, one – the Hawker Fury – marked a considerable step forward. It was streamlined, elegant and it was the first RAF fighter in service to fly at more than 200 m.p.h. Only one squadron, No 43 based at Tangmere, had re-equipped with Furies at the time.

One major gap in the London defences was the lack of air-intelligence information on raiders approaching London from the north-west – presumably having broken through the defences to the south and west. To fill this gap the AOC-in-C Air Defence of Great Britain, Air Marshal Ellington, requested Air Ministry approval in November 1930 "To expand the air-intelligence system to the area north-west of London lying between the arms formed by the aircraft zone, i.e. to proceed with the formation of No 17 Observer Group, covering the Hertfordshire area, with an observer centre at Watford." In March, after consultations with Air Commodore Masterman, Ellington put in cost estimates for a group with 18 posts and a centre in the post office at Watford. In the light of current values and inflation it is incredible to realise that the total cost for setting up a whole group in 1930 was put at £633. This figure was broken down as follows:

Observer Centre	£
Approximate cost of GPO equipment including all necessary switchboards, telephones, wiring, etc.	200
Furniture, viz chairs, cupboard for storage of instruments, etc.	21
18 observer posts	
18 complete observer post equipments @ £23.11.0 each	424
Installation charges	18
	£633

Annual communications facilities were expected to cost £106.16s plus £78 for the use of public telephone facilities for the annual exercise.

No 17 Group was to be the guinea pig for the RAF in learning how to set up an observer group, including recruiting and training. The experience was to prove invaluable when new groups began to multiply a few years later. Air Ministry permission for the setting up of 17 Group was officially given on May 15, 1931. So much paper work was involved, however, that the group was only ready to operate in July 1933, just in time for the annual air exercises of that year. Staged from July 17 to 20, the exercises again used the technique of restricted entry for the bombers; one corridor, 70 miles wide, being from Horsham to Swindon and the other, 40 miles wide, from Cambridge to Waltham Abbey. Northland, the defenders, fought Southland, the aggressors, and altogether 318 aircraft (12 fighter and 16 bomber squadrons) were employed.

In 1932 the Air Ministry had completely clamped down on any newspaper visits to RAF stations, let alone the Observer Corps, and this ban was again in force in 1933. The result was some very acid comments by journalists.

In *Popular Flying*, Major C. C. Turner wrote:

"Any attempt to veil such exercises in mystery can only have the effect of attaching to them a kind of importance and a sinister meaning that ought not to belong to them. There is nothing disgraceful in the holding of such exercises; nor is the possession of an air force a matter that can be hidden, or a thing to be ashamed of in the present state of the world.

"In the field of conjecture as to the reason nothing was left unless it be deference to those people who would ban toy soldiers, and (I have heard it seriously argued!) abolish spear-like park railings and replace them by something less suggestive of a lethal weapon. Logically that would be followed by the cutting down of all spruce trees, larches, and many other conifers, to say nothing of church spires; and all factory chimneys (for do they not suggest anti-aircraft artillery?) should be razed to the ground."

Turner went on to point out that the Observer Corps, as usual, "did excellent service." He referred to the fact that the Press had been able to see the corps at work up to 1930 and suggested that people refer back to reports of earlier years to get the details that were now being withheld. Some 40 years on, the whole thing sounds painfully familiar as regards the public attitude to defence as a whole.

Masterman's detailed report on the exercise showed that groups often had periods of no activity which clearly were boring. He cited, however, two particular occasions when the corps was extremely busy, viz:

"18/19 July   During daylight, nine raiding squadrons came in, more than half attacked – 16 combats took place.

19/20 July   Wing raid of 35 Hart aircraft flying west through No 1 Group well tracked – raid of 11 Hart aircraft of No 33 Squadron came in at Dungeness at 15,000."

Although the veil of secrecy had descended on the Observer Corps and access to the exercises was restricted, the first two corps official awards brought the organisation back into the public eye. Mr J. H. Day, Centre Controller Maidstone, and Mr H. T. Knott, Controller Horsham, both received the MBE in 1933.

In that year the RAF changed its whole map system and introduced the "Modified British Grid," which was to last until 1949. With this system, for the first time, there could be no duplication of a position reference anywhere in the British Isles (except Ireland). The grid from 1925 to 1933 had been based on that used for the 1924 experiment*, but with the three-mile-side squares HW, NB, etc, each subdivided into 100 squares numbered from 00 in the top left-hand corner to 99 in the bottom right-hand corner.

The new grid started off with the largest area, 500km squares, with capital letters such as "V." Each 500km square was then broken down into 25 squares of 100km with letters A-Z (omitting I). From there the grid was further broken down into 10km squares numbered from 00, the second numeral increasing to 9 northward and the first numeral increasing to 9 eastward. The references from the point of origin in the south-east corner being known respectively as northings and eastings. From the 10km squares, the next subdivision was into either 2km or 1km squares. For aircraft reproting 2km was considered sufficient, which meant elimina-

---

*See Map page 20.

ting the even numbers. For instance 10km square 96 would be divided into 25 smaller four-figure plotting squares, of which 9363 would be an example. Thus a complete reference to a particular spot in Britain on a 2km basis would be W – the 500km square – followed by G – the 100km square in that area – followed by 96 – the internal 10km square – and 9363 – the 2km square in 96.

The 1933 exercises used the new grid and this meant changing all the centre and post charts. For the posts a 20in-diameter chart was supplied, with the original 16in plotting area marked in with a green circle. Posts approved of the change-over but the centres complained that it took them time to adjust to a report of position "9363" instead of, say, "HY58."

At No 2 Group, Horsham, the centre table was provided with experimental intercommunicating switches, enabling adjacent post areas to communicate with each other at the plotter's option, in order to facilitate the correction of aircraft heights between two posts. The question of height assessment of aircraft was one of the most important where the corps was concerned. Only by continuous practice could observers become expert at height estimating and even then the results could, and did, vary enormously. Wrong judgment of the height of the aircraft as it flew over meant that the position indicated on the map could be wildly wrong. The only way to correct the heights was for posts to have simultaneous observation of same aircraft, whereupon one would place a ruler along its line of site on the map to the position given by the other post. The height rod was then brought up to the cross-cut and a reading taken, which became the "corrected height." The whole performance was made a great deal easier if the aircraft was directly overhead at one of the posts, and it was of course essential that they could hear each other's report over the telephone. At centre one man was employed solely as a "height checker" to verify the heights being given by posts and wherever possible ask them for a corrected height.

On the posts one problem was the rudimentary nature of the instrument. It was not built for speedy plotting, nor was it robust enough to stand up to all-weather operation. From the time that the RAF took over the Observer Corps work had been going on with the design of an all-metal instrument with an integral height bar. At the same period one enterprising head special, Engineer Captain R. H. C. Ball of Sway Post, Hampshire, built new devices of his own. He first perfected a corrected height calculator and then set about making a completely new post instrument which became known as the "Experimental (Ball) Instrument." It was extensively tested at the Milford Post in No 2 Group and, although all details have been lost, it is believed that the design had considerable influence on the evolution of the official Observer Corps instrument, which emerged as the Mark IIA to distinguish it from the Heath Robinson.

Of all-metal construction, the IIA incorporated periphery wheels for moving round a metal table*, a built-in height bar, ring-and-bead sight, spirit level and provision for a torch for night work. With slight modifications, such as extended height bar and rack instead of worm gearing, the Mk IIB was to be standard throughout the corps until the mid 1950s. The only wartime addition to it was the Mickelthwait integral height corrector, which is described in a later chapter.

The Mk IIA instruments were first introduced experimentally, on one selected post in each group, for the 1933 air exercises. Air Commodore Masterman, who had previously relied on "borrowing" the services of personnel at RAF Uxbridge, at last got some assistance in 1933 in

---

*On the Heath Robinson the wooden map table was apt to break up.

the shape of an assistant commandant who was to be paid the princely sum of £200 per annum.

Agreement for the post was reached on February 1, 1933, and in March Group Captain I. T. Courtney was appointed. Group Captain Courtney was to give exemplary service to the corps right through to 1943 and at the time of writing he is aged 81, living in Bournemouth. One of his tasks, in September 1933, was to provide for the commandant a list of comments on equipment and personnel. He was satisfied with all centres except Colchester but, on the subject of posts, pointed out that efficiency depended on the capacity and leadership of the head special and the vocation of the personnel. His summary of immediate needs read as follows:

"a) An efficient controller at Colchester Centre.
 b) A modified height bar.
 c) The provision of efficient field glasses."*

Many more subjects were raised at the Observer Corps Annual Conference held on September 20, 1933. Resiting of a number of posts in all five groups had become necessary as a result of plotting experience. It was also becoming obvious that the lack of posts in defended areas like Portsmouth and the gap between the boundaries of the Horsham and Winchester groups was a grave disadvantage for the air defences. To provide more practice for the corps, particularly at night, the use of civilian flying-club aircraft was considered. Other vital points discussed included the difficulties of sound plotting, the possible duplication of centres for wartime stand-by and the reprinting of the instruction manuals. The last mentioned were the observers' bibles, being small orange-coloured booklets entitled respectively "Handbook for Plotters at an Observer Centre" and "Instructions for Observer Posts," both of which ran to the great length of 11 pages.

All this, however, was to pale into insignificance as a result of the decisions taken in the following year, 1934. From being a cosy close-knit organisation with two headquarters' officers, the corps was to be catapulted into a six-year expansion programme. Posts and centres were to spring up the length and breadth of Britain with new officers and thousands of new observers.

---

*The height bar was for the Heath Robinson instruments, while the field glasses on issue had poor-quality lenses and no eyepiece adjustment.

Chapter 4
EXPANSION

On July 19, 1934, the British Government announced that metropolitan air strength was to be increased to 28 fighter and 43 bomber squadrons, plus flying-boat, reconnaissance and army co-operation units. At the same time planning started on new airfields and a direction-finding radio network, and specifications were issued for, amongst others, eight-gun monoplane fighters. The possibility of France as a potential enemy had long since disappeared and it was a rapidly re-arming Germany that presented the greatest threat. The years of futile disarmament conferences were reaching an end; Adolf Hitler and his Third Reich were reality.

For the first time some common sense began to appear in British air-defence planning. Hitherto all efforts had been directed at providing a screen around the capital city. With the emergence of faster long-range bombers based on Germany, it was at last realised that most of Britain represented a major target. The industrial cities of the Midlands and the North, the big harbours, the main railway junctions and the civil population itself were just as important as London. Once this had been accepted it was inevitable that the Observer Corps had to expand, and in leaps and bounds.

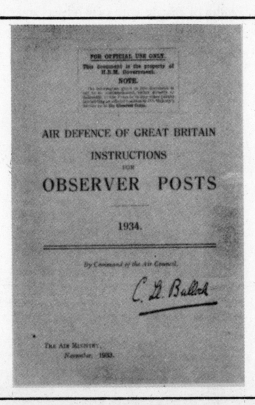

The Observer's bible until well into the Second World War, the little red covered booklet Instructions for Oberver Posts, *which was revised and re-issued from year to year. A publication of similar size was produced for Observer Centres*

FOR OFFICIAL USE ONLY.

AIR DEFENCE OF GREAT BRITAIN

INSTRUCTIONS
FOR
OBSERVER POSTS

1934.

By Command of the Air Council.

C. L. Bullock

The Steel-Bartholomew and Romer reports had attempted to deal with possible attacks from France using slow, short-range aircraft. The defences had therefore been postulated as running ultimately from the Wash to the Bristol Channel. This policy was now to be abandoned. To work out the details of what was required, the Home Defence Committee appointed a sub-committee on air-defence re-orientation under the chairmanship of Air Chief Marshal Sir Robert Brooke-Popham, the ADGB Commander. The Re-orientation Committee considered the entire field of air defence, but one of its conclusions was particularly important:

"That a highly organised intelligence system is essential for the rapid collection and distribution of information regarding the movements of friendly and hostile aircraft throughout the whole area of possible operation."

To implement this the committee recommended that the Observer Corps organisation should be expanded to cover the whole of that part of England enclosed by the east coast up to Middlesbrough, a line drawn thence to Preston, and from there roughly parallel but to the east of the boundary of Wales as far as the south coast. Yet another sub-committee, under Air Commodore O. T. Boyd, was convened to "Investigate the re-organisation and expansion of the Observer Corps consequent upon the re-alignment of the air-defence system." Among those on the committee were Air Commodore Masterman – the Corps Commandant – and Mr J. C. MacIver of the Home Office.

The Boyd Committee reported on January 17, 1935, to the Re-organisation Committee, which gave its seal of approval on February 15, 1935. The report was then passed to the Home Defence Committee, which gave its blessing. In essence the plan was to expand the corps in four stages in parallel with the provision of fighter squadrons, the whole layout to be completed by 1939. It was quite uncanny how the Services were convinced, on the basis of the German re-armament programme, that war would come in that year. They were to be proved absolutely right.

The Boyd Committee re-examined the Romer Report of 1924, which called for 18 observer groups covering the area southward of the line between the Humber and the Bristol Channel. Only five of these groups had in fact been formed, while a sixth, No 16 Group, Norwich, was in process of formation. The requirement, by 1934, was for an even larger organisation than Romer envisaged, covering an area extending south and east of the line Middlesbrough – Preston – Mersey – Crewe – Worcester – Cheltenham – NE of Salisbury – Poole. The committee recommended 16 instead of 18 groups, numbered 1-18 (omitting 13 and 14), and that, starting from No 1 Group in Kent, they should work round England in a roughly clockwise direction. Siting of centres was left to the GPO and the Air Ministry, but Middlesbrough and Hull were specifically vetoed on the grounds that they were "likely enemy objectives." The members of the committee little knew that nearly every city or town chosen as a site for an Observer Corps centre would eventually receive the attentions of the Luftwaffe to a greater or lesser degree. There was to be no form of immunity.

The four stages of development were as follows:

1st stage, March 1, 1935 — Form Groups 12 (Bedford), 4 (Oxford) and 15 (Cambridge); Link Groups 3 (Winchester), 4 (Oxford) and 17 (Watford)

2nd stage, March 1, 1936 — Form Groups 10 (York) and 11 (Lincoln)

| 3rd stage, March 1, 1937 | Form Groups 7 (Manchester), 8 (Leeds) and 9 (York) |
| 4th stage, March 1, 1938 | Form Groups 5 (Coventry) and 6 (Derby) |

All sixteen groups were to be in operation by March 1, 1939, and in order to achieve this it was quite clear that there must be an increase in full- and part-time officials and a division of responsibilities. Accordingly it was proposed that the Observer Corps be divided into Southern Observer Area and Northern Observer Area, with a commandant and deputy commandant in each case. The two areas were to deal with the two commands of Fighting Area and have their communications arranged accordingly. A few clerical, draughtsman and stores staff were also at long last approved. Obviously the senior officers could not cope personally with the hundreds of observer posts that would be involved and the committee considered it essential to appoint an "Observer Group Assistant" responsible for the administration and training of posts in each group. These were to be recruited as part-time officials for six months duty per annum (March 1 to September 1).

The commandant of the Observer Corps, Masterman, wanted a group commandant for clusters of three groups with an OGA for each, but he was out-voted by the other committee members who felt that too many paid official posts would thereby be created. The idea of group commandants, for individual rather than triple groups, did not mature until 1942, at the height of the Second World War.

The rates of pay per annum proposed were: Commandant Observer Corps £600, Northern and Southern Area Commandants £450 each, the two Deputy Area Commandants £300 each and Observer Group Assistants £100. Annual cost of the Observer Corps in 1935 was £2,175 and it was envisaged that when expansion was completed to the 16-group layout the cost would be £10,000 per annum. The bill for the whole expansion was expected to total £15,000.

One final item in the Boyd Committee report is worthy of note:

"The sub-committee is of the opinion that, should the necessity arise, there will not be any difficulty in obtaining an adequate number of volunteers to form an observer organisation with an oversea contingent. The sub-committee does not consider it would be politic for any steps to be taken in regard to this matter at the present time, as if it should become known the possibility of employing the civilian Observer Corps personnel overseas was under consideration, a false impression might be conveyed that an offensive policy was to be pursued, and this might adversely affect recruiting. The sub-committee is of the opinion that in the event of an Observer Corps contingent being required for duty overseas, all personnel required would have to be re-recruited into service in a special category."

When these prophetic words were written, Air Commodore Boyd could hardly have envisaged the vast D-Day invasion fleet of 1944 or the hundreds of Observer Corps personnel aboard the ships, wearing RAF battledress with "Seaborne" shoulder flashes and holding the rank of naval petty officers.

In accepting the Boyd Report Sir Robert Brooke-Popham commented that before the end of the five-year period, finishing in 1939, it would probably be necessary to consider the question of further expansion of the Observer Corps "in the light of anticipated aircraft development and in the light of improvement in the methods of detection developed by research." Sir Robert knew what he was talking about as on February 26, 1935, Mr (later Sir) Robert Watson Watt and Mr A. F. Wilkins of the Radio Research Station at Slough had demonstrated conclusively that radio-wave detection of aircraft was possible. When the Boyd report was approved in April by ADGB the "Radio Direction Finding" (Radar) team was already forming, preparatory to moving to Orfordness on the Suffolk coast.

Since the mid-1920s the Army had been trying to perfect a means of long-range detection whereby adequate warning could be given to the overland intelligence network, in the shape of the Observer Corps. The only hope appeared to lie in sound detectors, and the Army evolved a series of sound mirrors ranging from a 15ft-diameter unit up to a giant 26ft-high, 200ft-wide rectangular concrete monolith. Two of the 200ft mirrors, in concrete, were built on the marshes in Kent★. Extensive tests were carried out in all weathers but the best range that could be achieved was, for a single twin-engined aircraft, 21 miles or roughly three times the range of the human ear. Unfortunately, getting an accurate bearing was difficult, assessing numbers impossible and the risk of confusion with spurious noise sources almost certain. Sound mirrors also gave virtually no assessment of height. The coastal sound locators were used in the air exercises of 1934 and were intended to provide advanced warning for the Observer Corps. The experiment was a flop and work on large concrete locators was stopped in 1935 with the advent of radar. The general sound-locator programme, however, continued along with some very advanced ideas on automated reporting.

Early in 1936 an offshoot of the Air Defence Communications Committee, the Technical Committee for Air Defence Communications – commonly known as the Anson Committee after the chairman, Mr B. O. Anson of the GPO – was set up. Several very well known names were to appear at the meetings of the committee between 1936 and 1939, including Air Vice-Marshal Joubert de la Ferté (AOC, Fighting Area), Mr Robert Watson Watt of the National Physical Laboratory and Air Marshal Dowding. Throughout, one of the members of the Technical Committee was Warrington-Morris, Commandant, Observer Corps. A retired air commodore in charge of a civilian organisation, he was privy to the top secrets of air-defence planning and was able to shape the Observer Corps to fit with the most modern techniques.

Apart from considering the operations room, telephone and teleprinter networks and the reporting network as a whole, the committee was for some time pre-occupied with the "Fixed Azimuth" system. This was an Army-evolved concept which required elevation and baseline to be correlated from two reporting posts – the resultant ground position of a raid being automatically computed at a central operations room and shown on an illuminated display. The primary aids for this system were to be sound locators at AA gun/searchlight sites and Observer Corps posts. It was considered that this would be the only way of getting accurate plots at night.

The method of communication was very advanced even for the present day, the elevation number and baseline code being dialled on an ordinary telephone instrument with a three-digit code. Using a base line between adjacent observer posts, coded calls were to be computed in the form of a grid-square position and height. To make the system work, a computer (sic) was essential and work was put in hand for an electrical calculator using uniselectors made by Siemens. The computer, originally intended for the Army Fixed Azimuth operations room at 56

★At Greatstone, near Lydd, there still stand one 200ft-length and two 25ft-diameter concrete locators, while on the side of the hill at Palmarsh, between Lympne and Hythe, there are 30ft- and 20ft-diameter locators. These are permanent memorials to the efforts of the Army Acoustic Section to give early warning to Britain.

Regency Street, London, SW1, eventually became the key element in radar plotting. Nick-named the "Fruit Machine," it was the world's first-ever air-defence computer which, at Chain Home Stations, automatically worked out the enemy's position and height from bearing and angle. A special demonstration of the fixed-azimuth system was given to the Air Defence Communications Committee by the first Anti-Aircraft Divisional Signals TA at Manston in August 1936. The subject was reviewed by the Committee on September 18, 1936, when Warrington-Morris reported that the fixed azimuth system "was not considered suitable as the present system so far as the Observer Corps was concerned. The observer would have to wait until the azimuth was crossed before a report could be sent, and simultaneous observations by two posts are necessary before a report can be received at the centre." He added that the scheme would mean great difficulty in training, require more posts and individual telephone lines, entail recruiting more personnel at centres and would, overall, incur considerable expense.

The Technical Development Committee subsequently wrote to the main committee asking for clarification on the Air Ministry attitude to sound locators for the Observer Corps. Squadron Leader I. M. Rodney replied on October 8:

"I am directed to inform you, for the information of the chairman of the Development Committee for Air Defence Communications, that the sound locator has not been accepted as standard by the Air Ministry for use by the Observer Corps.

"The instrument at present in use by the Observer Corps consists of a tripod on which is placed a small map table with a squared map. A vertical height bar and sighting arm are used in order to determine the height of the aircraft seen and to indicate the position of the aircraft on the squared map. The base of the instrument is sighted on to some prominent landmark in the vicinity.

"I am to add that the Air Ministry is not at present considering any change in the above system."

This was the death-knell for sound locators in the Observer Corps, and fortunately so. The Army system was brilliant but very complex and expensive. In the upshot the existing observer instrument and layout were more adaptable to expansion and changing conditions, and were cheaper by far. The sound-locator effort was finally to be restricted to small sets for anti-aircraft gun sites. There was nothing wrong with the Army's efforts; it was doing its best to fill a massive gap with inadequate means.

From 1935 onwards the radar system and the Observer Corps expanded hand-in-hand to make a coherent long- and short-range intelligence organisation which served the country exceptionally well in time of need.

The commandant of the corps was privy to some of the secrets in the early years of radar, but the rank and file knew little until after 1938. Even then they understood only that there was a source of information on raiding aircraft which extended well beyond the island shores and a "Sea Plotter" at centres provided the link. The main points of the Observer Corps of 1934-1935 were, however, to keep morale going, improve efficiency and prepare for the building of the new organisation. An officer's inspection report on Wye post in April 1934 summed up the situation:

"Had difficulty in convincing them (the post crew) that Observer Corps is a seriously considered organisation – I hope I have succeeded."

In January 1934 Air Vice Marshal Joubert de la Ferté had taken over Fighting Area from

Bowhill at Uxbridge, and was in charge of 13 squadrons based at seven stations. Joubert described the battle headquarters in these words:

"It was installed in a wooden shack that had once been a chapel. It had no protection against blast or fire, it was cramped, ill ventilated and ill equipped."★

This was the operations room to which the sectors and the Observer Corps reported, and yet there were no permanent telephone lines laid on and, apart from the annual exercises, most of the tests were done with dummy plots relayed from a nearby building. During the 1934 air exercises, held in July, the GPO plugged through a number of lines – all of which failed at one particular point, thus rendering the defences impotent. Permanent lines were thereafter installed at the great cost of £2,000 per year and a new operations room was built with a sound-proof gallery for the Air Officer Commanding.

When an Observer Corps Conference was held at the Air Ministry on November 16, 1934, there was an atmosphere of expectation. Squadron Leader Aitken, Signals ADGB, stressed that permanent accommodation must be made available for centres at post offices or telephone exchanges. At Colchester, for instance, the corps used the linesman's room and the latter had to be turned out whenever the operations room was set up.

To get closer liaison between the RAF and the Observer Corps, a squadron leader from Air Ministry announced that 12 "parent" stations had been selected to be responsible for entertaining members of the posts in their neighbourhood. "All the observers had been asked out for an inspection, usually at weekends, and had been given tea and provided with transport." The Air Ministry had granted one shilling per head up to a total of 500 members for the purpose. For 1935 the visits became a day's training and three shillings per head was paid plus 1½d per mile travelling allowance, where necessary. This was to be the beginning of a remarkable relationship between the RAF and the Observer Corps which was to mature fully in the years 1939-1945.

In the calibration exercise of 1934 a new method of sound plotting was experimented with. Clock bearings were not used; instead, the post reported the number of the square cut by the sound circle on the map. On visual plots, posts were asked to report whether they thought it was a bomber or a fighter. Without any recognition training this was almost impossible. The Commandant asked for reports such as "Aircraft just reported thought to be a bomber, or thought to be a fighter." In his instruction he added: "Class names, such as Hart, Fury, Bulldog, Sidestrand, are not to be used, since they mean nothing to the plotters at the centre."

At centres a dais was being incorporated so that a proper view of the map table could be obtained and special trays were provided to hold the raid counters. On the posts new aids were being issued; these included a very amateurish AP.1480 aircraft silhouette book, a commendatory letter from the Air Council and a pair of blinkers. The last mentioned were used in calibration exercises, where the "blind" observers tried to assess the bearing on a sound plot.

Following trials with the Mk IIA metal observer instrument in the years 1933-34, a number of production sets became available for issue to posts in June and July 1935. A squadron leader from ADGB headquarters travelled round by car handing over Mk IIAs and bringing back the rickety Heath Robinsons. RAF stores depots were also occupied in sending out canvas shelter

---

★ *The Fated Sky*, 1952.

screens which, it was hoped, would keep some of the rain off the luckless observers.

The big expansion programme was well under way in 1935. In September of that year the Corps Commandant undertook his tour of 21 sites in Cambridgeshire, the Isle of Ely, Norfolk, Northampton and Huntingdonshire, to provide for the formation of No 15 Group, Cambridge. The two new Area Commandants – Group Captain V. O. Rees (Northern) and Air Commodore A. D. Warrington-Morris (Southern) – now came into the picture. Rees surveyed and organised No 12 Group, Bedford, in September and No 4 Group, Oxford, in October, while Warrington-Morris saw to the expansion of No 3 Group in September.

In all cases the first move was to find a suitable room for the centre in the town or city involved. The post office or the telephone exchange were most favoured sites or, failing these, an adjacent building. At Cambridge a room exclusively for the Observer Corps was made available. This allowed the table, plotting positions and dais to be permanently *in situ*. Similar arrangements were made in the post offices at Bedford and Oxford.

Older groups were not so fortunate. For instance, 1 Group at Maidstone had to use an outbuilding in the post office yard where the room was normally used as a store; it was small, hot and no dais could be erected. At 2 Group, Horsham, the centre was housed in a small hut usually used as a miniature rifle range and all the apparatus had to be set up specially for each exercise. At 3 Group, Winchester, the centre room was housed in a restaurant and girls' club. Every time an exercise took place the handrail on the stairs had to be dismantled and it took six men to get the plotting table into position. At 16 Group, Norwich, the centre was the cable chamber of the GPO exchange, which was below ground level.

To obtain the necessary centre recruits the chief constable would approach the municipal authorities and large firms. In some cases the head of a firm would become so interested that he would do the recruiting himself among his employees. In 16 Group, Norwich, the Norwich Union Insurance Company filled most of the centre vacancies, while at 9 Group, York, the Terry sweet-manufacturing company filled the ranks of the centre crews and Mr Noel Terry himself (who later refused pay) became the honorary controller. At 10 Group, York, the original recruits came from the Yorkshire Insurance Company, while later gaps were filled by Round Table members and Rover Scouts.

Once the centre was established and the organisation in train, a commandant wrote again to the chief constable or constables of the area asking for a regular policeman to accompany him and a GPO official to the proposed post sites. Wherever possible the designated head special was asked to be present. In rural areas the "landed gentry" provided many recruits from the ranks of gamekeepers, farmers, gardeners and the like. A great many retired officers of all three Services came forward to fill officer and head special vacancies. Local interests were strongly reflected in post membership. An inspection report on the Harrow post stated that "This post consists of masters from Harrow and others of equal intellectual standing" – a magnificent piece of 1930s snobbery.

To each Post was sent a duplicated explanation sheet giving the object of the corps' existence, how the system operated and the methods of manning, training, etc. The *Object* was given as "to report information as to hostile bombing aircraft entering these shores to the authorities responsible for air defence." The code word for putting the observer system into action was "Readiness." The post was informed that "In the event of a national emergency, you will receive the code word from the chief constable of your district."

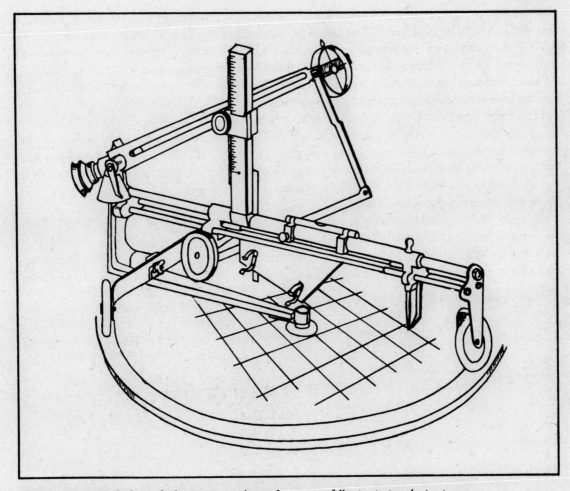

*The post instrument, the basis of Observer Corps plotting for 25 years following its introduction in 1935.
The estimated height of an aircraft was set up on the vertical height bar. The aircraft was then kept in
view through the sighting arm, the movement of which caused the pointer to indicate the correct position
on the gridded map. The second pointer formed part of the later Micklethwait height-correction attachment
for use when two posts were viewing the same aircraft. A telescope was often fitted up the sighting arm
and a torch was fixed in the two clips to show the grid position at night*

By 1935 the pace of German re-armament was quickening perceptibly. It was evident that
modern bombers from Germany, and perhaps the Low Countries, would be able to attack as
far north as Alnwick, Northumberland, westward to cover most of Wales and south-west into
Cornwall. The major part of Britain was therefore vulnerable and the whole approach to air
defence needed re-appraisal. A Re-organisation Committee had been set up in 1934 to examine
the implications of the new threat. The committee reported early in 1935 and recommended a
continuous defence zone stretching from Portsmouth through London up to the Tees. The
concept of an inner fighting zone, an outer artillery zone and a forward observation area was
still maintained. It was out-dated, but until radar was available it was the best that could be
done.

On May 22, 1935, Lord Londonderry, the Air Minister, announced that Scheme C for RAF expansion was to be established. This called for an air force of 122 squadrons, of which 35 were to be fighter-equipped. By February 1936 Scheme C had been superseded by Scheme F for 124 squadrons, all to be ready in 1939. A massive airfield-building programme and a big expansion in air- and ground-crew training was initiated. For air defence, however, fighter squadrons were useless unless they had an observation and warning system. The Home Office, too, realised that, without the Observer Corps, lighting restrictions and air-raid warnings were of little value. A Home Office conference of June 6, 1935, proposed a 1936 exercise – but only within an area covered by the Observer Corps. From that time on the Home Office pressed for nationwide coverage by the Observer Corps or a clear statement that certain areas would be immune from attack, which was impossible. The RAF wanted expansion but was embarrassed at the very logical demands of the Home Office.

Despite all the cross-currents, the expansion of the Observer Corps was going ahead at a very rapid rate. By October 1, 1936, 11 groups were practically complete, three more were to be ready by March 1, 1938, two were to be available by March 1, 1939, and a further two groups were on the list, with an unspecified date for completion. The detailed analysis read as follows:

Groups complete or nearly complete at October 1 1936

GROUP	CENTRE	FIGHTER GROUP	FIGHTER SECTOR
1	Maidstone	Uxbridge	Biggin Hill
			Hornchurch
2	Horsham	Uxbridge	Kenley
			Northolt
			Tangmere
3	Winchester	Uxbridge	Northolt
			Tangmere
4	Oxford	Uxbridge	Northolt
12	Bedford	Uxbridge	Duxford
			Northolt
			Wittering
15	Cambridge	Uxbridge	Duxford
		Nottingham	Wittering
16	Norwich	Uxbridge	Duxford
			Wittering
17	Watford	Uxbridge	Northolt
			Duxford
			North Weald
18	Colchester	Uxbridge	Hornchurch
			North Weald
			Duxford
10	York	Nottingham	Church Fenton
			Digby
			Catterick
11	Lincoln	Nottingham	Digby
			Wittering

Additional groups to be ready by March 1, 1938

7	Manchester	Nottingham	nil
8	Leeds	Catterick	Church Fenton
			Digby
			Catterick
9	York	Catterick	Catterick
		Nottingham	Church Fenton
			Usworth

Additional groups to be ready by March 1, 1939

5	Coventry	Nottingham	Wittering
			Digby
6	Derby	Nottingham	Digby

Additional groups, undated

30	Durham	Catterick	Catterick
			Usworth
31	Edinburgh	Catterick	Catterick
			Usworth

The year 1936 was one of major change, not only for the RAF but also for the Observer Corps. The enlarged RAF was becoming unwieldly and the chain of command unsuitable. The Air Staff therefore decided to break up the Metropolitan Air Forces into autonomous commands: Bomber, Fighter and Training; Air Defence of Great Britain disappeared. Headquarters Fighter Command officially came into being on July 14, 1936, and a remarkable and highly capable officer was appointed as the first Air-Officer Commanding-in-Chief, namely Air Chief Marshal Sir Hugh Caswall Tremenheere Dowding. Known to everyone as "Stuffy," Dowding was just the right man for the job. Organisation and experimentation were his specialities and his task was to create a complete working air-defence system from the ground up.

Dowding began his daunting task with a mixed bag under his command: the embryo of a radar system, No 11 Fighter Group with 11 squadrons, three auxiliary squadrons converting to fighters, a partly formed Anti-Aircraft Division, an Army Co-operation Group and the Observer Corps. For his headquarters he was given the former stately home of Bentley Priory with its large rooms, fine view, dry rot and large colonies of woodworm. Reporting to the AOC-in-C was a new Commandant, Observer Corps. On March 1, 1936, Air Commodore Masterman had retired and his replacement was Air Commodore Warrington-Morris, the former Southern Area Commandant. Group Captain I. T. Courtney was appointed to fill the vacancy at Southern Area.

Masterman had done an exceptional job in his term as Commandant and his work for the corps was to continue for many years in another role, as Western Area Commandant. The new head of the Observer Corps was to see it through its greatest period of expansion and nearly three years of war.

Warrington-Morris entered Dartmouth in the 1890s and his subsequent service covered torpedoes and wireless telegraphy. He transferred to the RAF during the First World War and retired from that Service in 1934.

From July 1936 onwards the Home Office, the Air Ministry and the GPO were in continuous consultation over the extent of Observer Corps coverage. The basis for a warning system had been laid down in January 1936 in a secret Home Office letter to chief constables. For obvious reasons only the area covered by the Observer Corps was affected. "Preliminary" and "action" warnings were proposed for issue to public authorities and certain industries. The country was to be divided into "Warning Districts" based on telephone areas*. Seven to ten minutes' warning of approaching enemy aircraft was anticipated. Through all these developments, both military and civil, the GPO, through the Home Defence Telephone Committee, played a key part. Telephones were absolutely vital for any part of the RAF or the civilian warning systems to succeed. Without publicity or acknowledgement of any sort the telephone planners and engineers laboured to meet an ever increasing demand for defence lines and their maintenance.

The great build-up for the war with Germany went ahead, but the first real results were not apparent until 1937. The air exercise of September 1936 was a biplane affair, with Gloster Gauntlets, Bristol Bulldogs and Hawker Furies and Demons forming the mainstay of the defences and Handley Page Heyfords, Hawker Harts, Boulton Paul Overstrands and Fairey Gordons making up most of the bomber force. The only really new aircraft, a monoplane, was the general reconnaissance Avro Anson. Despite every effort, Bawdsey was the only RDF (radar) station in operation for long-range warning and even this needed recalibration after the first day, September 24. The radar plots could only be used experimentally and were not linked in to the reporting system. Once again the Observer Corps was the only basis on which interceptions could be made.

During the summer exercises of July 29-30, 1936, sound amplifiers were tested in the corps. These were in no way connected with the fixed-azimuth sound locator scheme described earlier in this chapter. The amplifier idea was purely to extend audible range and thereby provide earlier and more efficient warning. The amplifier system consisted of one triple resonated microphone and one double resonated microphone, both of which had been developed as part of the equipment of the Army's 200ft sound mirror. The frequency range for the former was from 90 to 150 cycles, and for the latter from 75 to 95. In this way an octave of low-frequency sound was observed. The resulting electric currents were amplified by a two-valve low-frequency amplifier, and the output was fed into a Ferranti loudspeaker. The amplifier and loudspeaker were incorporated in a special lock-up cabinet sufficiently substantial to be employed for field use. Spares of microphone parts and batteries were supplied with each cabinet. A volume control for sound was provided to enable the listener to deal with disturbing background.

Twelve Amplifier Sound Detecting Units were made up by the Army and delivered to the following observation posts: Walton-on-the-Naze, Faversham, Whitstable, Southminster, Sheerness, Thorpe-le-Soken, Deal, West Mersea, Lenham, Shoeburyness, Canterbury and Kingsgate. The special constables of each group obtained the assistance of a local wireless agent, who took over the unit and supervised its erection on the site before the exercises. The working of the set was carefully explained and a demonstration given of its operation under working conditions, but without aircraft. During the exercise post members were requested to listen to the loudspeaker with a view to obtaining the following information: a) The average time in minutes and seconds that he heard the aircraft in the loudspeaker *before* it was heard by the other members of the post; b) to note whether any high-flying aircraft were heard in the loudspeaker

---

*Like most things from the past connected with the Observer Corps, Warning Districts exist to this day – although now they are for nuclear-attack and fall-out warnings.

VIRGINIA IX & X (2-LION V)

Parachute Training

Span 87'-4"   Length 61'-8"   Height 17'-9"

OSPREY (KESTREL IIMS)

Fleet Fighter Reconnaissance

Span 37'-0"   Length 29'-6½"   Height 10'-5"

Typical official silhouettes of the 1930s. Although designated for parachute training, the Virginia is shown carrying bombs under the centre section, while the Osprey could well be one of several types. Draughtsmanship was not much in evidence

and not heard at all by the other members of the post; and c) whether any difficulty was experienced in working the apparatus.

Difficulty was found in assessing the value of the information obtained because visual observation was not always possible for verification, and aircraft at some distance from the post did not come within the range of the unaided ear. The advantage in time over the unaided ear appeared to be from 1½min to 2min but this was not general as Walton and Kingsgate, too near the sea, generally derived no benefit from the use of the amplifier unit. It was recommended that traffic and other disturbing noises would be very much reduced if the microphones could be placed in pits about 18in to 2ft below ground level, that the sensitivity of the microphone system and amplifier could, with advantage, be increased and that the system could be improved by making the apparatus directional. The whole concept was, however, turned down at a conference held at Bentley Priory on October 5, 1936.

There was one final effort to improve hearing and hence sound plotting on posts. On January 22, 1937, the Air Ministry wrote to Brevet Major P. G. Calvert-Jones, i/c Air Organisation, Fighter Command, enclosing a rough drawing of a suggested sound locator which had been submitted by Captain G. K. Chambers of Sittingbourne, Kent. The instrument consisted of metal tube like a megaphone, 1ft 6in long and containing a baffle unit. It weighed 1lb 8oz and the smaller diameter end was held to the ear by means of a copper handle. The Brevet Major replied to the effect that the Observer Corps was inclined to consider the instrument favourably and a demonstration was held at Bentley Priory on February 23, 1937. One Gauntlet from No 111 Squadron flew as follows: a) at 10,000ft at full throttle; b) at 15,000ft at full throttle, and c) at 15,000ft throttled back. Further trials were held on March 27 and 28 over 12 posts in No 18 Group, Colchester. An army tent was issued to each post for the occasion, presumably so that the member with the ear trumpet might be screened from sight of his target. On June 1, 1937, the Commandant, Observer Corps, in a letter to the C-in-C, advised that the tests had not revealed sufficient positive information to warrant the introduction of such sound amplifiers into the Observer Corps.

Chapter 5
WAR CLOUDS

No 114 Squadron RAF took delivery of its first high-speed twin-engined monoplane bomber, the Bristol Blenheim, at Wyton, Hunts, in March 1936.* At the same time Heinkel 111 medium bombers were arriving in Spain to fight in the civil war and German units at home were beginning to re-equip with the Dornier 17 "Flying Pencil." New fighters were also coming forward in that month – the Me109 in Germany, the Spitfire and Hurricane in Britain. The revolution in the air forces had begun. The new monoplane bombers had speeds far in excess of the old biplanes, together with greatly increased ranges and bomb loads. More and more of Britain was coming within range of the Luftwaffe, with a consequent threat to defence installations, industry and population alike.

To try to make some order out of the chaos of re-armament Sir Thomas Inskip, Minister for the Co-ordination of Defence, requested submission of a report on the "Ideal" air defence of Britain, albeit taking into consideration only the threat of unescorted German bombers. The Home Defence Committee appointed a subcommittee under Sir Hugh Dowding to recommend on the "Ideal" force. On February 9, 1937, the report was submitted, calling for 45 fighter squadrons, 1,200 anti-aircraft guns, 5,000 searchlights, radar, radio control and a big expansion of the Observer Corps.

Fighter sectors were proposed for the Tyne, Newcastle, Forth, Clyde and Bristol areas. Nos 30 and 31 Groups of the Observer Corps, already approved, were to cater for south-east Scotland, but Bristol and the Clyde would require new groups.

The main elements of the "Ideal" plan were rejected until the Munich crisis of 1938, but the Observer Corps part was not only agreed to but augmented. The Home Office had been doing a great deal of research work and was convinced that national coverage by the Observer Corps was essential for all aspects of civil defence. An anti-gas training school had been established at Eastwood Park, Falfield, and this was to be followed in December 1937 by a second school at Easingwold, Yorks – a name that was to become very familiar to observers more than 20 years later.

In addition, the Air Raid Wardens Service was formed on March 4, 1937, and a top-level technical committee under Sir Arnold Wilson was evaluating "Structural Precautions against Air Attacks." The Air Ministry added fuel to that particular fire by deciding that, in the earliest stages of a war, 150 to 600 tons of bombs might be expected daily. It was postulated that with

---

*It was an inauspicious entry into service for the "world's fastest medium bomber," as this first Blenheim ground-looped and was wrecked on arrival.

a special German effort in the first 24hr up to 3,500 tons a day could be delivered. The same analysis gave anticipated casualties for 600 tons of bombs per day as no fewer than 200,000, of whom 66,000 would be killed. These figures were wildly exaggerated, but no-one at the time realised it. The threat appeared such that extreme measures were necessary. The Home Office exerted maximum pressure on the RAF to complete Observer Corps coverage of the country. By 1939 the Air Ministry had reason to be grateful to the Home Office for the extent of the intelligence network that had been built up.

Approved by the Home Office and the Committee of Imperial Defence, observer groups to cover the West Country, Wales and most of Scotland were promulgated in July 1937. The prime requirement was "to meet Home Office needs for rapid and adequate civilian air-raid warning." Three more regular groups were authorised, Nos 34, 35 and 36, to include Stirling, Glasgow and Perth. In addition there was to be extension of the Observer Corps for passive defence, with groups on a less elaborate scale. Fourteen groups were to be formed, Nos 21 to 29, from Devon north to Cumberland. No 32 was to cover Eskdale and the Scottish border and Nos 37 and 38 were to deal with Forfar, Aberdeen and Elgin.

Two groups, 33 for Wigtown and Kirkcudbrightshire and 39 based on Inverness, were left in abeyance for a year. The 14 were labelled as "Observer Groups in the Back Areas" and were issued with simplified forms of centre and post instructions. Posts had no instruments and as late as 1941, many were still using a tacked-down map with a white wooden or cardboard arrow in the middle. Plots were given on where the arrow cut the chart sound circle. Centre procedures were modified and heights on raids were not given. Two special publications were produced: first, in November 1937, a "Handbook for Plotters at an Observer Centre in the Back Areas" and, in 1938, a duplicated folder entitled "Instructions for Observer Centres in the Back Areas."

The effects of the expansion on the Observer Corps itself were profound. New posts were being surveyed daily and centres organised. Distances to be travelled increased and the numbers of people involved were beginning to run into tens of thousands. Recruits had to be found and trained in the face of demands from the regular forces, the territorial and reserve services and civil defence. The miracle was that the job was done and, as was later proved to be, well done.

One other group, of great importance, was also sanctioned in 1937. This was No 19, with its centre at Bromley in Kent, which was intended to straddle London, giving warning to the north, east and south. Completion was required by the end of June 1938. It was to occupy an area previously observed by the Army with searchlight and anti-aircraft units. This division of responsibility and lack of standardisation was at last recognised by the War Office, but the Admiralty remained stubborn to the last and only allowed the Observer Corps into vital harbour zones at the eleventh hour.

Piece by piece the old air-defence map was torn up and, as the fighter sectors expanded to the coast with radar as the first line, so the inner unobserved fighter ring disappeared. The original observer groups closed up so that gaps – such as that which had existed between Winchester and Horsham – were filled with clusters of new posts. As the Fighter Command Battle Order for 1938 stated, the role of the Observer Corps is "to provide information of all enemy aircraft flying over and inside the coastline of Great Britain."

To carry through the mammoth task of organising and maintaining all the new observer groups, additional areas had to be formed. Instead of the original sprawling Northern and Southern Areas, five were proposed and agreed. After consultation with the Commandant Observer Corps, Dowding suggested to the Air Ministry that they should have headquarters as follows:

Southern Area	Bentley Priory, Stanmore
Midland Area	RAF Hucknall
Northern Area	RAF Catterick★
Western Area	Gloucester
Scottish Area	Edinburgh

All these headquarters began forming in 1937 and were operational in 1938. The only subsequent change of site was that for Midland Area, which started at RAF Hucknall and at the beginning of 1938 was transferred to RAF Grantham. Within this area structure Dowding gave the Air Ministry the following amended completion dates for the groups:

1937–38	7 Manchester, 8 Leeds, 19 Bromley, 23 Bristol, 24 Gloucester, 30 Durham, 31 Dunfermline
1938–39	5 Coventry, 6 Derby, 22 Yeovil, 25 Cardiff, 27 Shrewsbury, 29 Lancaster, 34 Glasgow†, 35 Oban
1939–40	21 Exeter, 26 Wrexham, 32 Carlisle, 36 Dundee, 37 No centre ‡
1940–41	38 Aberdeen

By the end of August 1938 Warrington-Morris was able to report that Nos 5, 6, 7, 8, 19, 23, 24, 30 and 31 Groups had been formed, 307 posts had been set up in the new groups and 29 new posts added in Southern Area.

The 21 groups were to be allocated to areas as follows:

Southern Area	Nos 1, 2, 3, 4, 17, 18 and 19
Midland Area	Nos 5, 6, 11, 12, 15 and 16
Northern Area	Nos 7, 8, 9, 10 and 30
Scottish Area	No 31
Western Area	Nos 23 and 24

Because of the rate of expansion and the tremendous burden of work on the small staffs involved, allocation of all groups to their correct area did not take place until October 10, 1938. From early in the same year the whole pace of Observer Corps training had quickened. No fewer than 59 initial and communications exercises were arranged for the period May 24 to July 5, only three being cancelled because of bad weather. For these exercises, which lasted 2hr in the evening, all appropriate fighter group and sector operations rooms were connected to centres. Civil aircraft – of which 219 were used – were engaged for the exercises. Forty

---

★Originally formed in 1935 at Hucknall; moved to Catterick in 1938.

†Initially No 34 Group was to have covered a central Scottish territorial area with an undesignated centre, while Glasgow was to have been 35 Group. In the upshot 34 became Glasgow and 35 was applied to Oban, formed in 1940.

‡No 36 was originally scheduled as Dundee but was actually formed as 36 Dunfermline, while 37 was the number finally allocated to Dundee and 31 became Galashiels.

Attack Warning Red

"concentration aerodromes" were used on a total of 151 occasions, for which 151 RAF officers were seconded to superintend the despatch of civil aircraft on "raids" and to record their times, heights, etc, on return. In addition 12 calibration and 12 service exercises of 3hr each were arranged for the period July 7 to July 26. Eleven were successfully completed, while 13 were affected partially or completely by weather. Tracks for 238 single raids were prepared, using aircraft supplied by Bomber Command. RAF pilots attended at posts during these exercises to record the observations. Track tracings were prepared by the bomber squadrons and were

The official map for the home-defence exercises, 1938. The area of operations had shifted to the eastern counties to meet the expected threat from the Luftwaffe in Germany

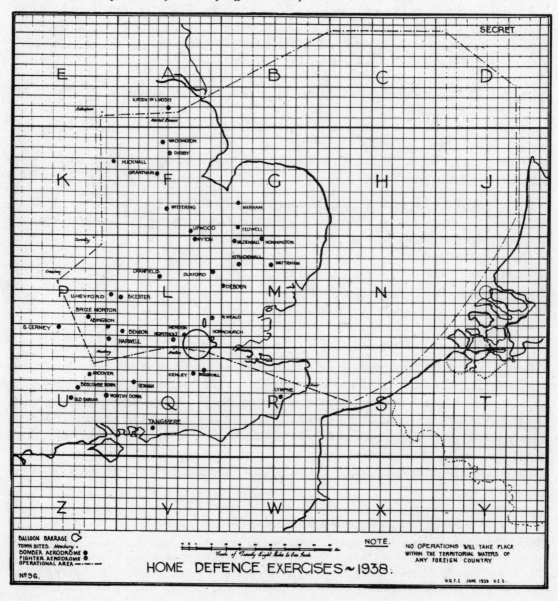

HOME DEFENCE EXERCISES ~ 1938.

then compared with the plot records produced at the centres.

To further cement relations between the Service and the Observer Corps the programme of annual visits to RAF stations by corps personnel was expanded. These served to familiarise the observers with the latest aircraft, and special height-judging competitions provided useful practical training. The highlight of all visits was, however, the flying. Middle-aged gentlemen of all shapes and sizes eagerly took to the air in Tutors, Harts, Hinds, Ansons and Blenheims – in fact anything with wings which had a second seat.

The biggest test of 1938 for the air defences was the annual home-defence exercise scheduled to take place from 9 a.m. on August 5 to 9 a.m. August 7. Five RDF (radar) stations were ready, Great Bromley and Dover having been added since the 1937 exercises. There were deficiencies such as lack of calibration and back-sensing relays to remove the ambiguous picture to the rear of the stations, but the five-station chain was working and sea plots were possible. Raids detected by radar were numbered by the newly created filter room at Bentley Priory, and these numbers were passed on to the appropriate observer groups for overland tracking.

The exercises were entirely aimed at testing the defences against an attack from Germany over eastern England. Nine observer centres (4, 11, 12, 15, 16, 17, 18 and parts of 1 and 19) were affected, together with 265 posts. "Eastland" was the attacking force, with 38 bomber squadrons. For the first time fast monoplane fighters were to be used, in the shape of three squadrons and one flight of Hurricanes. The attackers included twelve Blenheim, nine Battle and four Whitley squadrons.

Because of the critical situation created by Hitler's aggressive intentions towards Czechoslovakia, the RAF was already on war readiness from August 5, when the code word "Diabolo" had been issued.

For the Observer Corps the exercises showed communications problems, poor track continuity and congestion of lines due to reporting of too many friendly aircraft. Lack of post coverage on the ground led to infilling of the gaps and the splitting of Nos 16 Group, Norwich, and 18 Group, Colchester, to form 14 Group, Bury St Edmunds.

Centres were authorised to recruit up to four watches and to provide fortnightly training during the winter, dummy reporting panels being installed so that synthetic reports could be fed to the operations table. Practical post training was more difficult during the winter, but it was suggested that head specials should bring post crews together at least once a month to go through duties and procedures. The process for calling out the corps had been established as far back as 1936, and was as follows:

STAGE 1, *Readiness:*
Full manning of centres and posts with post personnel ready and operating the plotting instrument.
STAGE 2, *Alert:*
Half manning of centres and two observers on each post within sound of the telephone bell. The remaining half of centre crews to be subject to immediate recall if Stage 1 came into operation.
STAGE 3, *Released:*
All personnel released from duty but capable of achieving *Readiness* within 2hr.

When the exercises ended on August 7 the corps little knew that emergency use of the call-out procedures would be made in the following month. The Munich crisis precipitated a full alert and at about 4 p.m. on Monday, September 26, the corps was called out. The majority of telephone lines were through by 6 p.m. 2/N.3 post, Pulborough,★ recorded the events in a notebook:

"*Monday, September 26*
War scare – corps called out. Message received 4.30 to man the post at 6 p.m. Released at 8.30 p.m.
Wednesday, September 28
Orders to have a hut built and stores purchased – bedding etc.
Thursday, September 29
Called out 1 p.m. for continuous duty. Released 10.40 after getting rota working."

Manning was maintained on a rota basis until October 1, 1938, by which time the Prime Minister, Neville Chamberlain, had returned from Germany with his notorious piece of paper. On October 1 the corps was stood down.

The call-out was a god-send for the planners and a host of problems were highlighted. The telephone ring main around London was found to be an essential future element for defence if inter-group telling of tracks was to be maintained. It was also quite clear that for continuous operation the posts could not be left as just telephone connections without protection or means of cooking, resting or simply getting warm. The first step was to provide a wooden hut rather like a garden shed in which a bed could be erected, equipment stored and a stove installed. The hut was to prove a vital asset in war, but because of supply difficulties it took a very long time to equip all posts and many undertook the task themselves.

As the huts went up, posts were told to purchase bedding, cooking and eating utensils, chairs and even Elsan lavatories. Without doubt the most important items in any post's inventory were the kettle and the means of heating it. Some waterproof clothing was also issued to all groups. For centres, tests were being carried out on better methods of identifying raids on the table, including a frame on which could be hung raid number, height and number of aircraft. This was eventually to become standard and, because of its shape, was known universally as the "Gallows Arm." As an interim measure old "F" and "B" counters were re-introduced to denote fighters and bombers respectively. One item on each centre purchase list bore the reference FC/5076/COC dated 28.7.38 and it consisted of six candlesticks with candles.

Additional duty personnel were also ordered for centre watches, these being a table supervisor and a telephonist. The former was to supervise the plotters, straighten tracks and keep the table generally tidy, while the latter was to deal with all messages to and from the fighter group and use public outside lines for messages on bomb incidents, etc, from the police. Already, in 1938, the Observer Corps was considered as the basic organisation for reporting to the RAF details of crashed aircraft and bombs dropped. Salvage centres were in process of formation but, where they did not exist, crash reports were sent direct to designated RAF stations.

Microphone gas masks began to trickle through for use in centres although those for posts were of standard non-microphone military pattern. Many post observers, during anti-gas exercises were heard to ask just how they were supposed to speak into a telephone through a gas mask – no real answer was ever vouchsafed.

It was to be a long time before the Observer Corps was to become a uniformed body and the only forms of identification were badge, tie and brassard. For the National Service Rally of 1938

★This is the standard method of designating a post right through to the present day. 2 — No 2 Group and N.3 = the actual post within the Group.

the corps paraded in civilian clothes. Not to be outdone by the uniformed organisations, Air Commodore Warrington-Morris was at the head of his contingent resplendent in morning coat and top hat!

All sorts of local difficulties arose over post sites, recruiting and communications. Many local inhabitants objected to having an observer post sited near them, as for some extraordinary reason they imagined that it would attract the full fury of the Luftwaffe.

One letter sums up the unreality of the period just prior to the war and the general lack of understanding of the air threat. In reply to a request for siting approval by the Scottish Area Commandant, the Reverend J. Miller of the Manse of Orwell, Milnathort, wrote on October 20, 1938:

"I note you are keen to utilise the field chosen as an observer post, on the Sunday. That being so, I really think you might have chosen some other of the many fields available, and equally suitable, in my parish, than the one adjoining church and manse. I am very anxious to help all I can. Therefore, as you assure me that the occasion for use will be a very rare one, and it is for observation purposes only, I grant the privilege meantime. Please note, however, that I look to your men seeing that, as far as possible, a decorous atmosphere is preserved. Otherwise, I shall withdraw my permission for subsequent years."

The records show that this cleric kept an extremely eagle eye on the post until well into the war when it was resited, much to the relief of the members.

Setting up posts in remote places also produced headaches. When Western Area officers went to look at Abergwesyn, Brecon, for instance, they filed an unusual siting report: "Special case (unique) – no exchange here – only a kiosk – single subscriber went last August – exchange removed to Llantwrtyd Wells." A beautiful spot, Abergwesyn was in a deserted area surrounded by high hills and reports could not be got from anywhere else. The Western Area Commandant wrote to the Director of Telecommunications on October 18, 1938:

"Perhaps on special occasions a single report from Abergwesyn might conceivably be of importance from an intelligence point of view. Hence has come the idea of making this outpost into what I term for want of any better definition 'An on-demand Post' . . . A single watcher can stay by the kiosk. If he is rung up by the centre he replies or, if necessary, he can ring up himself."

So it was that in December 1938 Mr Rees-Hope of Pentwyn Farm was sworn in as head special, along with five observers, and "Watcher Post" 25/L.1 was born. With six feet of extra flex on the public telephone in the kiosk the personnel were able to stand outside and observe; their reports being transmitted by dialling 'O' and asking the operator at Llandrindod Wells for an "Urgent Air Intelligence call to Cardiff 4944." During the 1939 air exercises the post members became soaked to the skin after several hours on duty and authority was given for the provision of a hut with an extension bell. Thus if centre called the post the observer on duty would hare out to the kiosk to pick up the receiver. Eventually, in November 1940, L.1 became a fully fledged post with its own telephone line, and it operated throughout the war and beyond. In 1961 it was provided with a nuclear age underground post but, alas, it fell victim to the financial cuts of 1968 and was closed.

Boredom and lack of aircraft to plot during exercises affected many posts. The head special of Post 8/W.3, Sowerby Bridge, wrote to the Midland Area Commandant in June 1938:

"Also, do please let us at W.3 see or hear a few 'planes sometime, will you? I told Leeds last week that on our post escutcheon we have a crest with the motto 'They also serve who only stand and wait' – Only in fun of course, we'll go on waiting a long time if it will help you."

Group Captain V. O. Rees, the Area Commandant replied:

"I think your motto is excellent. You have no idea how difficult it is to get pilots to stay dead on their course. It is not too easy with bad weather and high winds, and if a machine is blown off its course a couple of miles it gives other posts more work and those on the correct track less work as it misses their post. If the aircraft do not put in an appearance – please wait, 'Watch for you know not when they will come.'"

As 1939 began all the armed services and volunteer organisations were expanding apace. One and a half million ARP workers would be enrolled by the late summer, emergency water tanks and Anderson shelters were sprouting up and the Observer Corps continued to form new groups and reinforce the old ones.

The most important requirement for all was practice. Posts and centres needed many hours of plotting and tracking experience to ensure that vital information got through the system as fast as possible. It was not yet realised that aircraft recognition was to be the vital factor in air intelligence, and to this extent the RAF/Observer Corps training had an element of unreality about it. In fact the Services did not believe that people could recognise different types of aircraft and did virtually nothing by way of finding out if they could, nor in training them for the event. This was a major deficiency, not to be remedied officially until well into the war. Many unnecessary casualties were to be caused as a result.

For the 1939 season the Observer Corps produced a whole list of Service exercises from January onwards, which were to culminate in the Home Defence Exercises from August 8–11. Some exercises were even scheduled for normal working hours to see who could attend. Observers were given practice in all types of weather and with a variety of aircraft at all altitudes. The key problems were found to be loss of communications, lack of track continuity from group to group, and track confusion and duplication due largely to wrong height estimates which altered the speed and position on the centre table.

After Service Exercise No 5 on April 4, 1939, Group Captain Courtney, Southern Area Commandant, reported:

"i) Several raids were not picked up by coastal posts and were sometimes lost inland, and, though it is realised the visibility was very poor, conditions were not unrealistic and both posts and plotters should make every endeavour to get some report of each raid through, the latter by continually informing posts of raids in their vicinity.
ii) The provision of special lines from sector stations to Colchester Centre was tried so as to provide early and continuous information of the movement of fighter aircraft, and proved very helpful; these trials will be continued.
iii) Improvement is necessary in the passing of raid and track identifications from one centre to another as it is essential that such information should be passed in good time so that as soon as a track appears on a centre table its identification is known. It is noticeable that tracks progressively lose their identification as the number of observer groups through which they pass increases.
iv) It is again emphasised that the work of the inter-centre teller is of great importance."

An important air exercise was held on July 8–9, covering the southern and western areas of the corps. A new group – No 14, Bury St Edmunds – took part for the first time and achieved considerable success, even though it had only been completed at the end of June. Overall results were considered to be the best yet and this was largely attributed to the new procedure whereby centres only reported to the RAF those raids given a special number to indicate that they represented "enemy." These numbers were in fact the raid designations given by the Bentley Priory filter room to incoming plots from seaward picked up by radar.

In an attempt to distinguish between "friendly" and "enemy" aircraft without resort to actual recognition of the types involved, the RAF, for the July exercise, used two new methods:

a) Fighters to have undersurfaces coloured half black and half white;
b) Friendly formations to fly in line astern.

The whole procedure helped the observers but was little short of ludicrous for a real war; the enemy had only to adopt the same tactics and the whole reporting network would break down. Nevertheless the July efforts provided a good run-in to the full-scale Home Defence Exercises over the four days August 8–11. These were the largest undertaken in Britain up to that time. Thirteen hundred aircraft, flown from 26 stations, took part, together with the 1st Anti-Aircraft Corps, a Balloon Barrage Group and the Observer Corps. In addition air-raid precautions were tested over a wide area with all authorities and public services involved. The black-out was tried out in London and a large part of eastern England for the first time on the night of August 9–10.

The total area covered by the air exercises was larger than ever before, being south and east of a line Withernsea–Macclesfield–Droitwich–Hungerford–Salisbury–Bournemouth. As usual "Eastland" represented the attacking forces and "Westland" the defenders. The two commanders were respectively Air Chief Marshal Sir Edgar Ludlow-Hewitt, AOC-in-C Bomber Command, and Air Marshal Sir Hugh Dowding, AOC-in-C Fighter Command. For the Observer Corps the exercises gave an opportunity to work under realistic conditions with large numbers of modern aircraft such as Spitfires, Hurricanes, Blenheims, Battles, Hampdens and Wellingtons.

The Corps was permitted to produce tracks only on aircraft detected by radar, as in July, and there was a marriage of radar and observer tracks in an attempt to produce a continuous picture of the air situation. The CH radar chain of 15 stations had gone on the air on Good Friday, 1939, for continuous watch and it was therefore possible to test the system as a whole. In order to analyse the exercise results fully, while still maintaining maximum secrecy, scientists were brought into observer groups to cross-check the link-up of radar and observer tracks. These scientists aptly named themselves "Lost Property Offices" and the resulting analyses were invaluable to Fighter Command in showing up deficiencies in the reporting network.

There were humorous sidelights to the affair. One "Lost Property Office" was run by Mr E. Fennessy from Bawdsey, who later became a group captain and is now Managing Director (Telecommunications) of the Post Office. He recalls that he had some difficulty in liaising with the observer corps men allocated to assist him. The first had a speech impediment and was unintelligible, the second proved to be as deaf as a post and the third to come on duty had had a decidedly liquid lunch in the Mess!

One significant aspect of both the July and August operations was the ease with which small formations of three to six bombers, using cloud, penetrated the defences without being detected.

The CH stations did not see them and, as only radar-initiated tracks were being told by the Observer Corps, they were not showing up on the Fighter Command table. The Observer Corps' priority code-word "Low Raid Urgent" was therefore largely wasted.

Dowding called a conference at Bentley Priory on August 21 to discuss the exercises. Air Vice-Marshal Gossage AOC No 11 Fighter Group, thought that warning was sufficient to allow for interception at the coast, while Air Vice-Marshal Leigh-Mallory, AOC No 12 Group disagreed. Dowding ruled that until radar could guarantee warning 80 miles out to sea, interception of raiders at the coast would not be possible. In his own report on the Exercises, dated August 14, Warrington-Morris opened with the usual congratulatory message from the Air Minister (Kingsley Wood) and then went to say:

"In general, the tracking of 'numbered' raids for the first few hours was not good but it then began to improve and became consistently better during the exercise, and during the last 48 hours was very good indeed.

I do not attribute the early failures to the Observer Corps, but at the commencement of an exercise, we have communication troubles, we have large numbers of formations suddenly appearing on the centre tables and our liaison with the RAF Tellers giving information regarding the tracks of Fighters and the numbering of incoming hostile raids has not reached the state of efficiency which is attained later.

After the initial period it was noticeable that the great majority of incoming numbered raids were well picked up and tracked by the Coastal Observer Groups. This reflects great credit on the sea plotters*. Raids which disappeared from the centre tables further inland were in several cases found to have landed at an aerodrome; this being confirmed by telephone by the observer centre and the bomber station concerned.

I propose to issue the telephone numbers of bomber stations to the observer centres concerned.

Most of the plotting at centres was excellent and indicates the value of the dummy run practices arranged locally by controllers, but there are still a few members who have not got the idea of 'tracking' as distinct from just placing counters on the squares reported by posts.

Too many counters, or double tracking of a raid, tends to confuse the tellers.

The work of the tellers and of the teleprinter operators was excellent, but at one centre I noticed a teller writing down his plot etc. before 'telling' it. This is quite wrong and introduces an unnecessary delay. It may easily add a 2 or 3 mile error to the head of the track and thus mislead the RAF commanders. Every assistance must be given to tellers by keeping clear tracks, and their attention called to new raids appearing on the Table and to changes of course of raids.

The new gallows arms supplied for use with numbered raids were found to be very useful and will be standardised at all centres.

The work of the inter-centre tellers was very good indeed and the special maps supplied to them were of great assistance.

They took all steps possible to hand over raids to adjacent observer centres and it is very largely due to them that numbered raids were continuously tracked over the exercise area.

The posts' crews have a very unpleasant time when the weather behaves as it did during the first two days of the exercise but in spite of this they appear to have been very cheerful and enthusiastic throughout the whole of the exercise. The great majority now realise that in order to enable the centre to track raids at least 3 or 4 reports are necessary on each formation, but they must not speak into their

---

*As mentioned earlier, the name "Sea Plotter" was by way of a cover for the man at the Centre who received from Fighter Command details of raids detected by radar.

microphone simultaneously with a brother post as this only confuses the plotter. In most cases aircraft were picked up very well indeed and the estimates of heights were usually correct. I heard many good reports on low flying raids which were very prevalent due to the low cloud base. Posts' crews should remember the importance of giving at least one more plot after an overhead (visual or sound) as this enables the plotter at the centre to plot accurately the direction in which the raid is proceeding.

As the whole of the information plotted at the centre and transmitted to the Royal Air Force originated at the posts, it is impossible to overrate the value of the information they give. During this exercise, it was not possible to arrange for one type of Bomber to represent enemy and other types to represent friendly aircraft, but in wartime posts' crews should always report if aircraft seen are recognised as British or Foreign."

August was the height of the holiday season and for most of the civilian population questions of air defence and air raids took second place to the need for sunshine and a paddle in the sea. For the Observer Corps the holiday was to end abruptly.

Chapter 6
THE PHONEY WAR

When Neville Chamberlain broadcast on September 3, 1939, and informed the nation that it was at war with Nazi Germany, the least surprised section of the community was the Observer Corps. For eight days and nine nights it had been on continuous watch, and the actual declaration that hostilities had begun was only confirmation of the obvious. Under conditions of great secrecy Dowding had put his whole command on to a wartime basis on August 24. From Warrington-Morris at Bentley Priory the order went out to chief constables to mobilise the observers. Controllers, head specials and every member received a brief message of which the following is typical:

BEDFORD BOROUGH POLICE

Chief Constable's Office
Thursday, August 24, 1939.

URGENT AND IMPORTANT
Please arrange to report for duty at the Bedford Centre each day as from tomorrow as shown below. If you are unable to attend please communicate at once with the controller, Mr Perryman, at the centre.

E. NUGENT CHRISTIE
Chief Constable.

Up and down the country thousands of men suddenly found their normal life permanently disrupted, but they answered the call and for five and a half years thereafter no post or centre was left unmanned.

It is quite unbelievable that the RAF's overland air-intelligence organisation, at the moment of mobilisation, had no real status for its members, no proper terms of service and no pay. In his book *Dowding and the Battle of Britain*, Robert Wright quotes Dowding, after the Munich crisis, as saying: "There was no plan for bringing the Observer Corps to a war footing. They were all volunteers who trained for a few hours in the evenings, after a day's work was done. There was no mobilisation scheme and no authority for paying them." It was a problem which had exercised Dowding from the time he took up his command in 1936. He constantly prodded various departments to obtain a set of terms and conditions for service which would guarantee that the corps could function on a full-time basis.

There had been continuous complaints from personnel in some sections of the country that they really did not think the job was worthwhile and that during exercises they just stood and saw nothing. As late as May 1939 Sir Joseph Hewitt, head special of 10/H.3 post, Cayton,

Yorks, had submitted his own and his colleagues' resignations on the grounds that they had nothing to do.

Early in 1939 an inter-departmental committee under Sir Hugh Dowding had been set up to consider pay and administration of the Observer Corps. In a memorandum dated April 12, 1939, Warrington-Morris pointed out that there were 1) full-time paid headquarters staff with fixed salaries for peace and war, 2) part-time paid headquarters staff who required a pay increase in war, and 3) the main body of volunteer members not receiving pay, but eligible for allowances to compensate for loss of wages in peace and war. The latter was the main worry, as the commandant estimated that with the completion of the 32-group programme (each with one centre and an average of 33 posts) a total number of 27,200 people would be involved – taking an observer centre complement as approximately 175 and a post crew as 21. He suggested special forms showing hours of attendance and rates of pay of 1/3d an hour with 10/– maximum for 8hr in one day. Head specials would earn up to £3 a week and centre controllers £250 a year. No travel, meal or other out-of-pocket expenses were to be paid. To undertake the scheme administrative offices would be needed at the corps and area headquarters.

After the inter-departmental committee had met on May 25, Warrington-Morris wrote a lengthy paper on the possible ranks which Observer Corps officers should hold if they were given commissions in the RAF Volunteer Reserve. He outlined the organisation as covering 60,000 square miles with the 32 agreed centres served by about 1,050 posts. Each group had some 33 posts, but this was in the process of being raised to an average of 36. Each centre was to have six crews plus one reserve, and each post eight crews of two men each plus four men in reserve. All this, he stressed, meant a great amount of officer responsibility. Of his five area commandants, three were retired air commodores and two retired group captains. The deputy area commandants comprised two air commodores, one group captain, two wing commanders, one colonel and a GPO official – all retired.

Warrington-Morris suggested honorary VR commissions as follows:

Deputy Corps Commandant	Group Captain
Area Commandants	Air Commodore
Deputy Area Commandant	Group Captain
Equipment Officer	Wing Commander★
Observer Group Officers and	
Observer Corps Liaison Officer	Wing Commander or Squadron Leader
Assistant Observer Group Officer	Flight Lieutenant

For himself, as Corps Commandant, Warrington-Morris proposed the honorary rank of Air Vice-Marshal.

By August 23, just a day before the call-out, the question of pay and status of observers had still not been settled. The inter-departmental committee had recommended that, as soon as war came, observers should cease to be special constables and should be transferred to the control of the Air Ministry. Dowding had asked for £3.10 a week for observers willing to serve on a full-time basis and the same amount for full-time head specials. The Treasury flatly refused the proposal as it was not, they said, in line with rates of pay for the ARP, Auxiliary Fire Service,

---

★There were at the time only two Equipment Officers for the whole of the country.

etc. While widespread bombing of Britain seemed about to begin, the Treasury was only concerned with the 10/– a week, whether or not Whitehall was flattened in the process.

On August 24 Warrington-Morris wrote in desperation to the Secretary of State for Air saying that Dowding had asked for his proposals to be pressed and adding that "a decision on this point is a matter of the greatest urgency."

Also on August 24, as Observer Corps members were going on duty, Warrington-Morris wrote to Dowding saying that to ensure continuous wartime manning it was proposed to institute two classes of observers:

"CLASS A
Observers who undertake (in writing) to perform 56hr duty each week, for the duration of a war, at such times as are ordered by the controller of their centre or the head special of the post (or by their authorised deputies).
Only qualified members over 35 years of age who are recommended by controllers or observer group officers will be accepted.
They must have good hearing and eyesight.
CLASS B
Observers who undertake (in writing) to perform duty up to a maximum of 24hr each week at their centre or post for a period of three months from the date called out for a war emergency."

Limits were to be set on the number of Class A members and both they and Class B men were to be paid at the same rates. The commandant recapitulated on the functions of head specials, controllers and officers and again made a plea for honorary RAF ranks for officers with no previous service in the armed forces. For retired Service officers he wanted them to be called up in their retired rank and seconded to the Observer Corps. (This latter point would have produced some strange anomalies, with several deputies holding higher rank than their superiors.) The idea of RAF commissions was not, however, taken up and the corps remained essentially civilian in character. If the Observer Corps had been integrated into the RAFVR in this way its history would have been very different and its life probably much shorter.

As it was, after war broke out some corps officers donned their old Service uniforms for lack of anything else to wear. This could have caused acute embarrassment as at least one observer group officer, Sir W. L. O. Twiss of Winchester was a major-general and thus outranked everyone including his area commandant. It was nothing to see an assistant observer group officer dressed as a colonel, trailing behind his observer group officer who was wearing a rather ill fitting captain's uniform. It was also fortunate that head specials wore no uniform as some of them would have been senior to everyone else in the group.

As a panic measure, when the Germans broke through in 1940, it was decided that corps officers should be put into RAF uniforms with ROC flashes and cap badges. A common rank badge was decided upon, consisting of one deep midnight blue sleeve band. As this band was the same depth as that for RAF air rank, Observer Corps officers became known as "air commodores in mourning." It was no surprise, therefore, that many a lowly assistant observer group officer visiting an Army mess was propelled to the top of the table on the mistaken assumption that he must be at least the equivalent of a Brigadier. On one occasion at an hotel near Inverness a very young pilot officer was asked by his doting parents what the two RAF officers were with the black bands on their sleeves. He replied "I don't know, probably something to do with the War Graves Commission."

The lights burned late in Whitehall on August 24 and somehow a typical British compromise was arrived at over pay and conditions for observers. Remuneration was not to exceed £3 a week for either A or B Class observers but the former were only required to undertake 48hr instead of 56hr duty.

An initial notice on the new terms was rushed to centres and posts at noon on August 25, and this was followed on August 31 by a printed broadsheet and a form of declaration to be signed by all observers and returned "within seven days." It was realised that those in charge of posts could no longer be referred to as head specials, as the link with the police had been severed. It was therefore decided to use the term "head observer" to describe the appointment, and so it has remained to this day.

Because of the chaotic situation and the time required to recruit and organise a new accounts department, the police were asked by the Home Office to pay observers at the agreed rates until well into September. In the meantime observers had no contract of service.

The most surprising thing of all, viewed through the materialistic eye of the 1970s, was that a great many observers objected very strongly to being paid – whatever the amount involved. They made their views known in no uncertain manner, as the first draft of a memorandum from section 5, Bedford Observer Centre, shows:

"It is felt that as the Corps was recruited as a voluntary service that the question of pay was not entertained by the members of this section. That if any members are suffering financial loss they should be paid on producing evidence that they are out of pocket. This section is of the opinion that the centre should be fully manned for 24hr and are prepared to fill the vacant places caused by the reduction of personnel without pay provided they can be spared from their several businesses."

While pay and conditions were being wrangled over, the Observer Corps was watching and waiting. The first sirens were sounded at 11.15 a.m. on September 3, 1939, but to no useful purpose. A French aircraft had not filed a flight plan and was therefore considered hostile when picked up by radar. The offender had passed over No 1 Observer Group, Maidstone, and 19 Group, Bromley, but as no-one was supposed to be able to recognise aircraft by type it was only reported as a "plane."

The inability of the whole radar/observer/control network to identify incoming tracks became painfully apparent on September 6, during the "Battle of Barking Creek." At 06.18 a.m. RAF Sector Operations North Weald flashed a message to No 18 Observer Group, Colchester: "Searchlight reports aircraft flying very high over or near West Mersea." Nine minutes later North Weald announced that it had scrambled six fighters to the east, closely followed by two more flights of six. The air-raid sirens were sounded and the Chatham anti-aircraft guns opened fire. Fighter attacked fighter as successive flights intercepted the previous ones on patrol in the Southend area. At 08.55 Mistley police reported a Hurricane down, riddled with bullets, and the corps simultaneously logged another nearby. All fighters had been ordered to land at 08.22 and it was not until the remainder taxied in that Fighter Command realised the Luftwaffe was still at home and the RAF had been fighting itself.

RAF Hucknall asked Colchester for news of a missing Hurricane, L2080, and the centre duly enquired of Ipswich police. The chief constable, mindful of security, refused to give any further information. The farce continued with Hucknall asking for information "re bombs dropped and enemy aircraft brought down." Colchester replied: "None could be given."

After a further equally abortive request for information on enemy aircraft plotted, Hucknall asked for details of the first raid plotted that morning and was told "Raid 5, six at 6000 at 06.50.*" Dowding was furious; radar was in confusion, Anti-Aircraft Command had started the spoof going and the Observer Corps had been unable to sort matters out. Warrington-Morris was told to find out what had happened and he sent an urgent message at 10.10 a.m. to the Controller Colchester, Colonel Herring. At 11.30 the latter replied:

1. Herewith recorder sheets for raid period 06.45 to 09.00.
2. Visibility throughout was poor owing to ground mist, audibility also seems to have been very bad. In several cases where RDF gave position of a raid as immediately over a post, the post concerned could neither see nor hear anything.
3. Posts were unable to state with any certainty whether planes were friendly or hostile."

The whole sorry business was a blessing in disguise, as it marked a turning point for the control and reporting system. Radar reporting was improved, the filter room made more careful raid analyses, positive identification was requested and for the Observer Corps track hand-over and correct recognition became of paramount importance. As officialdom appeared unable or unwilling to organise aircraft-recognition training, the members of the corps themselves undertook the task with remarkable results, as will be shown later.

One immediate outcome of the Barking Creek affair was the issue by Fighter Command, on September 12, of new instructions for telling sea plots:

"*Intention*: The intention is to identify and allot letters or numbers to all tracks of aircraft appearing on the filter-room table. Tracks of incoming bomber, coastal and civil aircraft will be told to command, group and sector operations rooms. The one exception will be tracks of incoming single aircraft in Bomber Lane D (Shoreham – Le Treport).†

Identification: 1) Identified tracks of bomber and Coastal Command aircraft will be lettered as previously. 2) Enemy aircraft will be numbered as previously. 3) Tracks of aircraft that cannot be identified as friendly or enemy will be known as DOUBTFUL RAIDS. These will be lettered "X"‡ followed by a serial number, e.g. X.1, X.2, etc.

Telling: The filter-room teller will tell all incoming tracks that are lettered or numbered. Friendly aircraft will not be told onwards by coastal observer centres. Doubtful raids are, however, to be told onwards from observer centres until they are recognised and reported by posts as friendly or enemy.

Coastal Command Aircraft: Convoy and submarine patrols will be lettered but not told to command table or to lower formations. Moreover these aircraft will not be required to make the D.S. indentification signal.

Training Aircraft on the Coast: Tracks of aircraft in Bomber Lane D or training aircraft in coastal, non-restricted training areas will not be lettered or told by the RDF filter-room.

Date: The new procedure described above will come into force with effect from 12.00 hours, Tuesday, September 12, 1939."

For sight of the actual enemy the Observer Corps had to wait another month, and when the

---

*Clearly one of the flights of fighters sent up from North Weald.

†Various air lanes had been established, along which friendly aircraft were to pass in and out of Britain.

‡This was the beginning of the "X" raid procedure to cover hostile or unidentified aircraft which was continued until long after the war.

Luftwaffe did put in an appearance it was not in East Anglia but far to the north in Scotland. On the morning of October 16 the RAF listening service picked up German radio traffic which indicated a forthcoming raid on Rosyth. This was confirmed when a reconnaissance aircraft appeared over the fleet in the Firth of Forth at 09.27. The raid, by a dozen Junkers 88s flying at 15,000ft, materialised in the afternoon. It was first located by a Chain Home radar which thereafter went off the air owing to a power failure. Reporting therefore fell solely on the Observer Corps. The posts of 31 Group, Galashiels, and 36 Group, Dunfermline, responded well.

Three warships had been hit, however, before 602 and 603 Squadrons intercepted and shot down two Junkers. The posts around Edinburgh had a bird's-eye view as the remaining enemy aircraft skimmed the roofs on their way home. The Luftwaffe re-appeared the following day over the Firth of Forth and disabled the old battleship Iron Duke.

Dowding sent this message to the corps after the raid of the 16th:

"I am very pleased with the way in which the Observer Corps acquitted themselves in this, the first action of the war in which they are able to take part. The visibility conditions were difficult and the bomber formation split up into individual aircraft. In the circumstances I consider that the Observer Corps operated with great efficiency and I should like all concerned to be informed accordingly."

On October 28 No 31 Group had more practice in anger when an He111 was tracked and shot down near 31/J.1 post at Humbie, East Lothian.

East coast posts frequently heard aircraft gunfire as Luftwaffe aircraft engaged in sea reconnaissance and minelaying. On November 23 the liaison officer enquired whether a Heinkel seaplane, shot down on R3199, had been towed in. 19/N.3 post, All Hallows, unofficially reported that the seaplane was towed into Grain at about 22.00 on the 22nd.

By this time two factors were affecting operations of the corps, namely an all-too-familiar attempt to save money and demands by all three Services to undertake new tasks. By the end of October 1939, when it was realised that no vast air armada was to be suddenly unleashed on Britain, cuts in expenditure were demanded by the Treasury. The Commandant, Observer Corps, therefore decided that coastal posts on the east and south coasts to a depth of 30 miles were to remain at "readiness", while those further inland were to be placed on "available" with one member on duty. Inland centres were called upon to have only four plotting positions manned and the paid reserve of personnel to be dispensed with. Centres were supposed to get back to full working in an emergency by having members on 10 min availability every day between 09.00 and 18.00.

The scheme was a bad one and centres would have been completely unable to cope with any sudden raid. The officers and members complained loud and long and bombarded areas and corps headquarters with letters – but all to no avail. The rank and file were particularly incensed as newspapers at the time were carrying completely ill informed letters from the public claiming that the Observer Corps was responsible for the faults of the air raid warning system – whereas all responsibility ultimately rested on the AOC-in-C Fighter Command.

There were many humorous incidents recorded during the twilight period when the corps was getting on to a war footing and at the same time being restricted in its activities. At one o'clock on November 1, 1939, Mr J. Archibald was duty controller at No 38 Group, Aberdeen, when the bell rang and the first real plot appeared on the table. He had been checking that all posts were answering the call and found that only K.2 post, Buckie, was silent. To the amazement of all the officials crowding round, Archibald asked his assistant to ring Mr Valentine, the baker at Buckie. George Williamson, later the group commandant, asked what he wanted the baker for. He replied that Valentine was the head observer at K.2 and it was not reporting. A decade later Archibald admitted, "I had this information by pure chance, having spoken to the baker's sister the previous evening."

While all efforts were directed at economies within the corps, new jobs were being found for it daily. The Royal Navy wanted shipping and maritime incidents to be reported, the RAF required special reports on and flares lit for aircraft returning to base, while the Army considered the corps to be a heaven-sent invasion-reporting network.

To provide a night-time navigation aid for aircraft the RAF asked that a large number of posts be equipped with flares, to be lit at the request of the sector. Pilots were provided with a flare map from which a pattern of light pinpoints could be deduced. A confidential order was issued by Observer Corps headquarters at the beginning of December 1939 outlining the flare

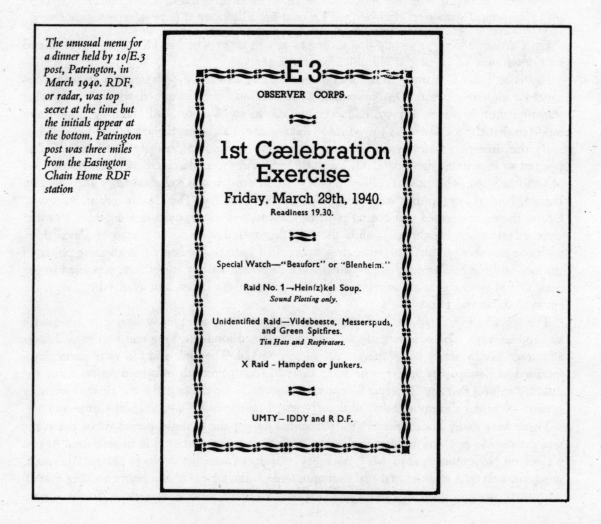

The unusual menu for a dinner held by 10/E.3 post, Patrington, in March 1940. RDF, or radar, was top secret at the time but the initials appear at the bottom. Patrington post was three miles from the Easington Chain Home RDF station

E 3
OBSERVER CORPS.

≈

1st Cælebration Exercise
Friday, March 29th, 1940.
Readiness 19.30.

≈

Special Watch—"Beaufort" or "Blenheim."

Raid No. 1—Hein(z)kel Soup.
Sound Plotting only.

Unidentified Raid—Vildebeeste, Messerspuds, and Green Spitfires.
Tin Hats and Respirators.

X Raid - Hampden or Junkers.

≈

UMTY—IDDY and R D.F.

system and giving lists of posts concerned. RAF sector commanders were to supply the equipment, "together with the name of the local paraffin supplier." Known as "money flares," the equipment consisted of a metal bucket with a lid, with a flare inside which was kept partially immersed in paraffin at all times. On receipt of orders from centre to illuminate, the post observer hooked the flare out of its bucket and placed it on a metal tray "not less than 50 yards from the post site and preferably to the north and east of it so that the prevailing wind will blow smoke away from the post site." A match and a quick jump backwards completed the operation. To extinguish the flare the luckless observer had to hook it up again, throw it back in the bucket of paraffin and bang the lid on.

During March and April 1940 a small number of posts were equipped with four flares which formed the "outer patrol line." These were only lit upon receipt of special instructions. Some money flares were replaced in the summer of 1940 with petrol-burning Coleman lamps, but these were withdrawn in the late summer of that year. With heavy night raids multitudes of flares only attracted the attention of the enemy and confused the defences. The whole procedure was messy, time-consuming and dangerous. Despite the fact that sector commanders were supposed to inform the police that the flares had been authorised, there were to be heated arguments and near fights as home guards, wardens, police and civilians tried to put out the flares while observers attempted to keep them going.

The worst incident with flares took place on July 15, 1940, at 18/J.1 post, Woolverstone, Suffolk. At 12.30 a.m. a naval chief petty officer with nine other petty officers and ratings were returning in taxis to Shotley Barracks after a night out in Ipswich. At Woolverstone they say the money flare being lit and jumped to the conclusion it was the work of fifth-columnists. The post was surrounded and the naval party was challenged by the head observer, Mr J. B. Snell, who was tending the flare. Mr Snell's reward for doing his duty was to be shot in the thigh and a finger by a trigger-happy chief petty officer.

Various less official methods of getting aircraft home to base were also indulged in by the Observer Corps. The St Andrews post, Fife (36/B.1), was particularly well equipped as the members were all men of means, including a retired air commodore and the local chemist who was head observer. The post established excellent relations with RAF Leuchars and the CO there provided them with an RT set in order to help "talk down" lost aircraft to the station. When the CO was posted his replacement took a dim view of Service equipment being loaned out and the set had to be returned. In the ensuing rumpus Air Commodore Peel Ross, Scottish Area Commandant, foolishly tried to sack the head observer. In typical Observer Corps fashion the whole post threatened to resign and the matter was hastily dropped.

The Observer Corps became deeply involved in the subject of a possible German invasion of Britain and the cudgels were taken up by the AOC-in-C Fighter Command, Sir Hugh Dowding. The resulting correspondence was a classic of its kind. It not only showed the interest in and knowledge of the Observer Corps that Dowding had, but also provided a rare insight into his extremely sharp sense of humour and his ability to reduce mountains to molehills.

The C-in-C Eastern Command, Home Forces, started the ball rolling on November 3, 1939 in a letter to Dowding. With reference to invasion and airborne attack he felt that the searchlight units and the observer posts would provide a most effective means of collecting the necessary information and he proposed to attach an officer, with communications, "to the more convenient regimental or group headquarters." GHQ Home Forces, at Kneller Hall, Twickenham, followed this up with a letter to Fighter Command on November 9:

"Sir,

I have the honour to refer to a conversation between Air Officer Commanding-in-Chief, Fighter Command and Wing Commander J. V. Steel, Liaison Officer, General Headquarters, Home Command on November 8, 1939, and to request that communication facilities may be established in an emergency with the Observer Corps Centres in the attached list.

12 Division

No 1 Maidstone　　　　　　　　　Mr J. H. Day
No 2 Horsham　　　　　　　　　　Mr H. T. Knott

Sector Operations Room
Biggin Hill

18 Division

No 14 Bury St. Edmunds　　　　　Capt F. T. Bright
No 16 Norwich　　　　　　　　　Mr C. F. Hill

Sector Operations Room
Wittering

54 Division

No 18 Colchester　　　　　　　　Lt Col H. W. Herring

Sector Operations Rooms
North Weald
Hornchurch

1 Armoured Division

No 12 Bedford　　　　　　　　　Mr B. G. L. Perryman
No 15 Cambridge　　　　　　　　Mr F. W. Bellamy
No 17 Watford　　　　　　　　　Mr C. R. Bolton

Sector Operations Rooms
Debden
Duxford

London Area

No 19 Bromley　　　　　　　　　Mr H. Forbes-White"

Sir Hugh Dowding replied on November 10 to GOC-in-C Home Forces:

"Sir,

I have the honour to acknowledge receipt of your letter dated November 9, 1939, on the subject of communicating facilities.

At the moment a state of extreme confusion appears to exist because at least four different military authorities are in communication with myself or formations under my Command and their proposals are unco-ordinated.

I have asked Air Ministry to permit me to deal direct on this matter, keeping them in touch with our proposals.

If this permission is granted, I shall be very pleased to call upon you at any mutually convenient time.

In the meantime, might I suggest that you instruct Army commands to defer action until they receive some fresh instructions from yourself."

Sir Hugh then wrote to General Sir Walter M. St.G. Kirke, HQ Home Forces on November 12, 1939:

"Dear Kirke,
Various military authorities have been approaching me and my subordinate formations with regard to co-operation in the event of invasion or raids by parachute troops.

The Germans have been extraordinarily successful in keeping us in a constant state of panic by means of every kind of possible and impossible threat, and the curious thing is that we fall for it every time.

The invasion scare is, of course, the wildest of the lot.

We kept back tens of thousands of men who were needed in France in the last War to deal with this bogey. Invasion was unlikely enough then, but now, with the development of Air Power, the probability of its being even attempted appears to me to be infinitesimal.

If, however, we are ordered to provide against this contingency, we must do as we are told.

I have been given to understand that my communications can be of value to you in this connection to 'give an alarm.'

I do not understand what is meant by this. Presumably our first news would come from Agents; and then if the expedition ever started, we should have continuous news of it from sea and air reconnaissance and long before it reached the shore you would have your soldiers waiting there.

I think there has been some vague idea that my Observer Corps might be the first people to see the invasion and so might give the alarm. This is of course not the case. The first news that the Observer Corps would get of the invasion would be in the morning papers.

Nevertheless, as I told Steel, if there is any need for an alarm to be given by means of my Operational lines, I am quite prepared to co-operate if you will provide a list of people to whom you wish the alarm transmitted. Steel has met this requirement by sending me a list of my own Observer Centres.

The main point is that the Observer Corps communication cannot be used for the command of a force which is engaged in repelling an invasion. It is a specialised 'one-way system' and it immediately gets clogged if any attempt is made to use it in the reverse direction.

So much for the invasion:

Now about raids by parachute troops or men landed from Troop Carriers.

I personally regard this danger also as remote, but much less remote than invasion.

I presume that your plans for dealing with it consist of holding a number of highly mobile formations scattered about the country.

The people who are most likely to see parachute troops dropping from an aeroplane are the Observer Corps, who would in any case have been tracking the aeroplane across country from the point where it crossed the coast. On the other hand, I believe that German parachute troops drop from a very low height and, as the Observer Posts are roughly 10 miles apart, they might easily descend in a place which is not visible from my Observer Posts.

Such a parachute descent might be seen by one of the Searchlight Detachments who, in areas where they exist, are more closely spread than the Observer Posts.

The responsibility for reporting any parachute attack is clearly mine, and again, if you will let me have a list of the addresses of those Centre Headquarters, I will undertake the duty of letting them know when a parachute descent has taken place if it has been observed by any Searchlight Detachment or Observer Corps Post."

General Kirke to Sir Hugh, November 15, 1939:

"As a result of our conversation on the possibility of military formations obtaining some warning of parachute descent from the Observer Corps and other organisations under your control, I enclose a list of Military Headquarters to which information should be passed and the Areas in which they are interested, described by Areas covered by the Observer Corps.

I would be glad if you would return the list to me with any alterations or comments you may wish to make, as I would like to include it as an appendix to my defence plan, a copy of which will be forwarded to you through Air Ministry.

It will be made quite clear in the plan that all warnings can only be given once at the commencement of the invasion."

Appendix
In the event of enemy parachutists being seen on land in any of the following observer group areas, Headquarters Fighter Command undertakes to inform the Command Headquarters concerned, i.e.

Observer Group Areas

38, 37, 36, 31, 34	Headquarters, Scottish Command Edinburgh
30, 9, 10, 11	Headquarters, Northern Command York
16, 14, 18, 17, 15, 19, 1, 2	Headquarters, Eastern Command Hounslow"

Sir Hugh Dowding wrote again to Kirke on November 16:

"Thank you for your letter dated November 15, 1939, and enclosures. There are two or three points which I wish to clear up before I start work on arranging for communications.

In the first place, there is a misunderstanding in paragraph 3 of your letter. It was only in the case of giving warning of an invasion that I said I could only give a single message: but we subsequently agreed that no message was necessary for an invasion, that is to say, a landing of troops from ships.

So far as parachute attacks may be undertaken I am prepared to pass a message every time this happens, no matter how often: but I am afraid that I cannot undertake to pass it to a number of recipients. In each case I would undertake to pass it to the nearest Military Authority on your list, and any further communication up or down the Military line would be your responsibility.

I have got a good idea how I can fulfil the requirements indicated in your letter (with the above limitation), but I wonder if it is really all that you will want.

There is no reason why a parachute raid on some important objective should necessarily be made in the Eastern Counties, and I was wondering what your plans were if a parachute attack were made on some objective such as the Gloster aerodrome and factory about 4 miles from Gloucester.

If you are content with the situation I shall be perfectly satisfied and arrange to communicate with the nearest Military Station on your list wherever the landing might take place; but I should not like to finish my work and then find that all had to be altered because of extensive amendments to your list of requirements.

I should propose to send the signal in accordance with the Military Grid, e.g.
"Parachutes dropping VP 3337"
Will this be alright?"

The GOC replied after the manner of one accepting, with gratitude, such communication crumbs as the rich man had allowed to fall from his table, adding:

"I do not propose to take any special measures for dealing with parachute attacks on objectives not situated in the Eastern Counties, as I regard the possibility of such attacks as extremely remote."

Subsequently practice reporting exercises were held within the Corps, with parachute attack messages being passed, prefaced by the words "Dummy, dummy, dummy."

The whole question of invasion communications was to become a key factor after May 1940, but Dowding never budged over his two convictions: firstly, that no invasion could take place unless the RAF had been destroyed; and secondly, that the prime function of the Observer Corps was to be the RAF's overland air-intelligence network for reporting aircraft. Other functions would, of necessity, be purely secondary.

Chapter 7
THE REAL WAR

As the fateful year 1940 dawned Dowding, at Bentley Priory, was working against time to perfect the world's first integrated air-defence system. No other country, least of all Germany, had a control-and-reporting organisation which was anything but a hangover from the techniques of the First World War. The Luftwaffe was not to devise a proper system until after the invasion of Russia in 1941. In Fighter Command there existed all the elements for the conduct of air defence against the manned bomber: radar and human observation, decentralised operations rooms with standard forms of table presentation, good communications, and full radio control of fighters with direction-finding (DF) for position fixing. In addition anti-aircraft guns, searchlights and balloons were all included in the system.

To understand the workings and complexity of the vast machine that had been created it is necessary to explain the layout and the methods by which air defence was conducted. At the heart was Fighter Command Headquarters, Bentley Priory, with its operations and filter rooms housed (as from March 9, 1940) in an underground bunker adjacent to the mansion. This complex was the repository for all the key information coming in from a variety of intelligence sources and it was also the distributor of certain information to the system.

Dowding had three fighter groups, 11 (Uxbridge), 12 (Watnall) and 13 (Newcastle), reinforced in July 1940 by a fourth, No 10 (Box, Wiltshire). Each group had its own operations room and the group commanders were allowed maximum autonomy to conduct the battle as they saw fit. Commanders were, however, expected to reinforce adjacent groups which were being hard pressed. Fighter groups were sub-divided into fighter sectors (seven for 11 Group, six for 12 Group and two for 10 Group). The sector operations rooms received orders from group, ordered fighters into the air and directly controlled them. The operations rooms were situated on or near the sector airfields such as Biggin Hill in C Sector, No 11 Group, and Duxford in G Sector, No 12 Group.

The intelligence network for the system consisted of agents, "Ultra," monitoring stations, the CH and CHL radars and the Observer Corps plus certain inputs from anti-aircraft batteries, searchlight detachments and coastguards. One of the best kept secrets of the Second World War, Ultra was the British-designed decoder which was capable of reading the messages put out by the German Enigma coding machine. The German high command assumed that Enigma codes could not be broken and they were unaware that not only had Britain obtained an Enigma machine before the outbreak of war but had successfully designed its counterpart, Ultra. In 1940 Ultra was in its infancy but Dowding gleaned from it some of the orders issued by Hitler and the instructions given by Goering to the Luftwaffe.

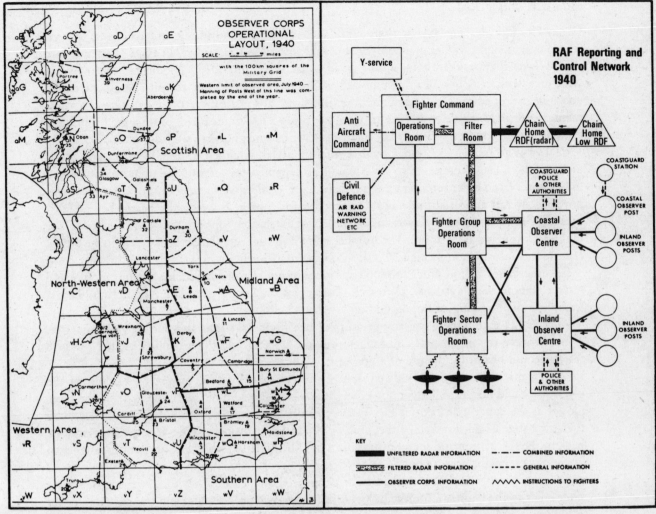

With the monitoring service (better known as the Y-service) as the key cross-check, Dowding had a remarkable picture of the enemy's intentions which allowed him to dispose his limited resources to best advantage. An Air Ministry organisation, the Y-service received virtually no publicity but was of vital importance throughout the war. Using a series of listening stations up and down the country, and employing highly skilled personnel, it was possible to collect, interpret and distribute information from enemy wireless-telegraph, radio-telephone and radar transmissions. Codes were broken, orders of battle discovered from call-signs, position of formations established by direction-finders and, even more important, long warning of an impending attack was often given from the build-up in wireless traffic. The Y-service monitored German air-to-air and air-to-ground messages and even reported on Luftwaffe sightings and its own relayed intelligence assessments. For instance, a Focke Wulf 200 Condor which flew a daily meteorological sortie from Bordeaux was allowed to continue its penetration of British airspace for a long time. The Y-service cracked the code being used and was able to find out the German assessments of the weather over the islands and the likely target for the day. Y information was correlated at a central station and transmitted to the duty Y-service officer at the Fighter Command operations room.

On the radar side in 1940, there were two basic types of installation, Chain Home (CH) and

Chain Home Low. The CH stations, with their massive transmitting and receiving towers, were familiar sights to Germans and British alike although the former, in 1940, were not sure exactly how they worked. CH, with a fixed aerial array, provided "floodlight" cover over a wide area with cathode-ray tube responses on aircraft possible from 40 miles at 3,000ft up to 200 miles at 35,000ft. Height-finding was, however, always a difficulty even with the rudimentary "Fruit Machine" converter then in use. Only a top-grade operator on a well calibrated station, with a good response on the tube, could obtain heights accurate to within 1,000ft.

CHL was a "beam-type" radar, with a rotating aerial, intended to give low cover to complement the CHs. A range of 30 miles could be obtained for aircraft flying at 1,000ft, and a maximum of 180 miles for aircraft at 25,000ft. CHL could give virtually no reading on wave-hopping aircraft at 50ft altitude and it suffered from gaps in between the beams being transmitted. CHL plots were relayed to the nearest CH station for onward transmission to the Fighter Command filter room. For instance the CHL high on the cliffs at Fairlight in Sussex reported its information to the CH station on the marshes at Rye.

For emergency use, in order to plug gaps in the system caused by enemy action, mobile and reserve stations were available. One such station was used in the woods at Angmering, Sussex, following the bombing of Poling CH on August 18, 1940.

At each CH station there was an operator on the cathode-ray tube and one on the converter. The first gave the initial plot and range from the trace, while the second provided the grid reference and height by the use of a goniometer. A typical plot would read:

"Track three – range 45" followed almost immediately by the converter's reading of the grid square and height as "Sugar 3964, height 20,000." These plots were received by the filter plotter at the crescent-shaped table at Bentley Priory and assessed by the duty controller, who then allocated a raid number or the prefix "X" for unidentified. This was then transmitted back to the CH station and subsequent plots would be given as, say: "Hostile 6, now range 20 – Sugar 3131 – height now 15,000."

Once the hostile and X-plots had been designated and cleaned up they were passed by a filter teller to the Fighter Command operations room where Dowding and the duty controller could see at a glance the air situation with a minimum of clutter. Filtered radar plots were also told on from Bentley Priory to the group operations rooms which, in turn, passed them to sector operations rooms and coastal observer centres.

At an observer centre the central map table was manned by plotters, each one dealing with a cluster of three posts. At certain times one plotter could be switched to cover up to six posts at a time. A table supervisor helped prepare the raid plaques, supervised continuity and numbering or lettering of tracks and informed posts of aircraft approaching the coast. On the raised dais overlooking the table were the duty controller, assistant duty controller, duty controller's assistant, sector liaison, tellers (chief, sector and inter-centre), and the recorder. The duty controller was in charge of the centre and could be replaced by his assistant if required. The controller's assistant passed messages on the liaison lines, dealt with crashed aircraft, parachute landings, etc, and kept a log of all messages passed and received.

Sector liaison received information on the telephone from sector operations about movement of friendly fighters. The chief teller told plots to fighter groups by telephone and/or to the teleprinter operator at the centre. Sector tellers told to sectors the same plots the chief teller was passing to group, while the inter-centre tellers passed and received information on tracks entering or leaving the area of the observer group. The recorder kept a continuous record of the tracks appearing on the table.

One further member of coastal centre crews was the sea plotter, who received the filtered radar plots from the fighter group via an Observer Corps representative at the group, known as the observer corps liaison officer (OCLO). This officer also dealt with all RAF group/Observer Corps centre queries and passed down any necessary instructions. Sea plots on the liaison line had absolute priority.

To sort out lost raids there was, at each fighter group, a raid intelligence officer (RIO) who either passed information direct to the Observer Corps or via the OCLO.

Where aircraft were first reported by radar they carried a Fighter Command raid designation throughout. If, however, an enemy or suspected enemy aircraft appeared in a coastal or inland group without having been first found by radar then it was immediately told to the RAF with a letter to denote the centre of origin and a number from one to nine. Once the aircraft had been agreed by the fighter group as hostile the Observer Corps letter and number was removed and an RAF designation given. The designations used in 1940 were as follows:

a) *Allotted by filter rooms*

Category	Designation
HOSTILE	a number
UNIDENTIFIED	"x" plus a number
FRIENDLY FIGHTER	"F" plus a number
FRIENDLY BOMBERS	"R" plus one or two letters
FRIENDLY CIVIL	a single letter
FRIENDLY COASTAL	a single letter
FRIENDLY PHOTO RECCE	"F"
FRIENDLY TEST RUN	"T"
FRIENDLY ARMY CO-OP	"AC" plus a number
FRIENDLY FLEET AIR ARM	"N" plus a number
FRIENDLY TRAINING	"L" plus a number

b) *Allotted by fighter groups*

Category	Designation
HOSTILE	a number
UNIDENTIFIED	"x" plus a number

c) *Allotted by centres*

Category	Designation
HOSTILE	Centre letter plus a number
If recognised as a BOMBER	"ZB" inserted after the word "Visual" or "Heard"
If recognised as a FIGHTER	"ZF" inserted after the word "Visual" or "Heard"
UNRECOGNISED	Centre letter plus a number
FRIENDLY	Centre letter plus a letter
FRIENDLY FIGHTERS	"F" plus, if necessary, the initial letter of sector aerodrome and/or a suffix (split) letter
SPLITS	The designation plus a "split" letter

At an observer centre the map table (scale 1in—1 mile) showed the 10km and 2km grid

THE MICKLETHWAIT HEIGHT CORRECTION ATTACHMENT
STORES REF. No. 6E/339

THE THREADS OF THIS SCREW SHOULD
BE PAINTED WITH SHELLAC BEFORE
BEING SCREWED INTO POSITION.

Plan I
WITHOUT FIXTURE

Plan II
WITH FIXTURE

INSTRUCTIONS.

Part I.

HOW TO FIT TO OBSERVER INSTRUMENT

1 Withdraw four screws "A" (Plan I) and remove the two Brackets "K".

2 Withdraw the four screws "B" (Plan I) and remove the two clips for torch.

3 Screw the height corrector on to the instrument by means of the four screws "A" (Plan 2).

4 Refix the two torch clips by means of the four screws "B" (Plan 2).

5 Release thumb-screw "E" (Plan 2); slip the bracket "D" behind it; then tighten up thumb-screw "E".

6 Fix upright arm of height corrector to top of sighting arm by means of screw "C" (Plan 2).

Part II.

HOW TO USE THE HEIGHT CORRECTOR.

1 Before starting to plot an aircraft it is necessary to see that the pointers "H" and "L" are aligned.

2 When the Post overhears another Post on the same circuit plotting the same aircraft, Number Two of the Post Crew joins up, by means of a straight edge, the positions on the Post Chart of the other Post and the plot given by that Post.

3 Number Two of the Post Crew moves Pointer "H" (Plan 2) to the straight edge.

4 The corrected height is then shown on the scale "P" (Plan 2) at the point at which it is intersected by the upper edge of the moving arm "G" (Plan 2).

5 Until the aircraft is out of sight, plotting can be continued without further adjustment by utilising pointer "H" instead of pointer "L".

6 Pointers "H" and "L" must be aligned before starting to plot another aircraft.

NOTE.—When the instrument is dismantled and placed in the transit case, thumb-screw "E" must be replaced by thumb-screw "J" in order to keep bracket "D" in position.

R.B.P. & Co. Ltd. 2438K

Instructions for fitting the Micklethwait height-correction attachment to the standard Observer Corps post instrument. The diagram was issued in August 1940 by the manufacturer, R. B. Pullin and Co. The attachment was designed by a member of the Corps after whom it was named

squares, the position of the posts and the five-mile "sound circles" around them. For visual reports arrow-shaped counters were employed, while for sound plots a counter resembling a sound trumpet was used. All counters were available in the colours of the colour-code clock to indicate when the plot had been placed on the table and to enable stale information to be cleared away. With sound plots a cross-cut of two bearings gave the aircraft position. Initially no heights were given, but later sound angles from posts were called for which gave an approximate height. On ordinary plots numbered square counters were used, red denoting the number of aircraft involved and blue the height. White-lettered plaques indicated the type of plot, e.g. T=trainer.

It was mandatory that all enemy raid and X-plots be told immediately to the RAF, while any other tracks – such as those of friendly fighters required by RAF Sectors – were on request. For hostile and X-plots the gallows arm★ was used.

★This miniature "clothes horse" carried raid details in the same sequence (i.e. designation, number and height) and stood out above the table top so that it was easy for the tellers on the dais to locate. On the posts the height was estimated and wound on to the height bar. Thereafter the aircraft was located on the sighting arm and the square on which the pointer rested was the position over land. To get corrected heights two posts had to be viewing the same aircraft. One post would put a ruler between the two plots and adjust the height bar so that pointer was back on the aircraft position. The resulting height was then read off. It was a complicated procedure which was time-consuming.

To complete this general picture an enemy aircraft will be followed through from its first detection until it has been passed back as an overland plot by the Observer Corps.

First a CH station has picked up a raider over the Channel at 10,000ft in 100km square R for Robert. The CH operator reports to the Stanmore filter room: "Track 2, range 30 – Robert 8624 – height 10,000 – five plus." At Stanmore the filter officer checks the track and allocates it the raid number 5. This information is relayed via the OCLO at No 11 Fighter Group to No 1 Observer Group, Maidstone. The posts in the likely path of the raid are warned by the plotter to be on the look-out. Shortly afterwards, raid 5 materialises over the coast in the shape of eight Junkers 88s. It is seen by C.3 post, Dover, and the plotting cycle begins. C.3 reports: "C.3 calling, eight planes seen 7592, flying north, height 10,000ft."

At Maidstone centre the supervisor prepares a gallows arm and places it next to the arrow marking the first plot. The tags on the gallows arm read "5-8-10," denoting raid number, strength and height. Looking down from the dais, the tellers note the plot and pass the following message to RAF groups and sectors and to adjacent Observer Corps groups: "Visual – Raid 5 – North-west – R for Robert 7592 – 7592 – 8 at 10." The teller then continues to relay plots until the raid is shot down, passes to another group or goes home.

Sound plots were purely modifications of the basic principle. All forms of plot could be passed either by the voice teller or by means of a teleprinter connected to the RAF defence teleprinter network.

In addition the corps was required to pass information on lights flashed from aircraft, airborne landings, seaborne landings, aircraft in distress, aircraft crashes, aircrew rescued at sea, enemy surface craft at sea, submarines, mine dropping, shipping in distress, explosions, shipping at sea, drifting balloons and suspicious persons or events. This was a formidable list and it turned the Observer Corps into a first-line intelligence organisation through which watch could be kept on literally everything that went on.

Most events were reported to the OCLO at group but in certain cases, such as friendly aircraft crashed, other customers had to be informed. The procedure in these events was to ring the appropriate authority and quaintly preface the call with the words "I want to make an urgent aircraft call."

Having explained the overall system in operation in 1940, we must return to the corps situation as a whole as it was at the beginning of that year.

By January the main enemy was not the Luftwaffe but the weather, combined with boredom. Snow fell, the winds blew, then the ice and fog settled in for good measure. In the centres the cramped closed conditions built up a solid smoke-laden fug so that warmth was no problem. On most of the posts, however, conditions were appalling. It was the first of five winters to be endured in the open. Numerous sites had to be evacuated, but wherever possible contact was maintained with centre by moving to where telephones were still operating. Some personnel were marooned for a week while others stayed until the post was almost snowed up. As cars

---

Early in 1940 a member of the Corps named Micklethwait invented a modification to the instrument whereby an additional pointer with its own horizontal height slide was fitted on the underside. By moving the secondary pointer out to the cross cut, the height automatically appeared on the slide. Known universally as the "Micklethwait Height Corrector", this device was put into production by R. B. Pullen and Co. who built the basic instrument. It was to become standard throughout the Corps until the mid-1950s. Even today to a long-serving observer the name Micklethwait can only mean one thing and he could probably go through the motions of operating it in his sleep.

were useless some observers walked up to 11 miles to perform their duties, while one enterprising man arrived complete with tractor and snowplough and literally cut his way through to the post.

By January 10 some 850 fleece-lined coats had been distributed and balaclava helmets, mittens and the like had been sent by the RAF Comforts Organisation. Despite everything the corps stayed operational, plotting continued and exercises with the RAF were carried on.

There was very little enemy activity except for minelaying and occasional reconnaissance flights over Scotland. One phenomenon surprised both the Observer Corps and the RAF, namely the "white smoke" given off by aircraft above about 30,000ft. Vapour or contrails were to become commonplace by late summer.

Some idea of the improvement in the standard of corps plotting and aircraft recognition is shown by a Hertfordshire post which correctly identified a Spitfire making a contrail at 27,000-ft. Using two posts, the 17 Group centre produced an accurate corrected height on the aircraft.

Plotting lost aircraft was becoming commonplace, one example occurring on the evening of January 26, 1940. A coastal centre was advised that five Ansons were returning from patrol. The weather was very bad, with many coastal posts reporting a blizzard and visibility nil. Three of the Ansons successfully landed at their home station, but two were missing. The first was picked up by a coastal post and was plotted almost to its home station, where it became lost and turned seaward. The other Anson was also picked up going towards the sea, and was again correctly identified by sound alone. Details of the plots were fed to the airfield and it was suggested that one post should light a flare. The result was that one Anson successfully reached home while another came down undamaged on an emergency landing ground two miles from the last post plot.

To while away the long hours observers took to sketching and writing poetry and even songs. A book of poems was eventually published and the "Song of the Observer Corps" was made available as sheet music. Air Commodore Warrington-Morris, the Commandant, was not averse to such amusements and he included many of the verses in his very humorous and chatty circulars to the corps issued fortnightly. Typical of the offerings was one based on the well known ditty "A tall stalwart Lancer lay dying." The Observer Corps version ran:

> "Wrap me up in my fleecy-lined jacket
> And say a good fellow lies low,
> And six stalwart spotters shall carry me
> With footsteps both mournful and slow.
>
> Oh bury me deep 'neath the shelter,
> (Don't resite the hut on my grave),
> And cover me over with sandbags,
> Just think of the money I'll save.
>
> And oft' on a fine summer evening
> When the old moon's on the wane,
> And an enemy raid's in the offing
> I'll come up and help spot the 'plane."

One problem which was to affect the corps throughout the war was the continual disappearance of younger members who reached call-up age or who volunteered for the Services.

Wherever possible the corps tried to retain key men over 30 – but Service demands eventually meant radical changes, as will later be seen.

All those who did go into the Services were asked to write "Observer Corps" under the heading "special qualifications" on the registration form and they were provided with a certificate of service. These men were eagerly snapped up by the RAF and they found themselves at group and sector operations rooms, radar sites and at flying-control sections on airfields.

At Winchester centre for instance, 12 members volunteered for direct entry into the RAF. Four, Messrs C. Bubb, G. Hasted, L. Butt and D. Finch Beavis, were accepted and, together with 14 ex-Observer Corps members from Norwich, Colchester and Watford formed a key part of the Stanmore filter room plotting watch in 1940–41. Of those four observers from Winchester, Hasted was invalided out and continued in the corps until the war's end, Bubb served in the RAF throughout the war, Finch Beavis served in the Middle East and eventually became an air gunner, while Butt, despite wearing glasses, eventually became a successful fighter pilot with a particular knack for shooting down flying bombs; sadly, he was killed.

Many who wore RAF blue in the Second World War had first had their interest in aircraft aroused by volunteer service in the Observer Corps. One such is Group Captain Peter Vaughan-Fowler. Aged 17, he left school at the end of 1939 and had a year to fill before joining the RAF. His father was an Observer Corps officer in Midland Area and he arranged for his son to be enrolled at 5/K.2 post, Buckminster, Leicestershire.

Observer Vaughan-Fowler used his eyes and ears to good effect through 1940 and the early part of 1941. He recalls having to walk three or four miles to the Post through knee-deep snow in the severe winter of 1940–41 and of plotting a flight of swans which were tracked from the north right down to southern England on a day when no aircraft could fly.

The group captain's father departed, in mid 1940, to start an Observer Corps in India. His mother went to join him in 1941 but the ship was torpedoed. Spotted by a Catalina and subsequently rescued, she arrived in London on the boat train just in time to see her ex-observer son off on another train to begin pilot training with the RAF.

Enemy activity over Britain through the early months of 1940 continued to be very slight apart from reconnaissance and minelaying, but one incident was a foretaste of things to come. Early on February 3, 1940, a convoy off north-east England was attacked by Heinkel 111s of KG26 operating from Schleswig. First detected by the CH station at Danby Beacon, the intruders were intercepted by a flight of Hurricanes from No 43 Squadron based at Acklington. The York 9 Observer Group log book takes up the tale:

"08.55   From N/C* X14 V8812 SW – 2 at 3
08.59   Told N/C – heavy engine noise – sound plots in V.51
           From N/C – raid E – V7544 – SE – 1 – no height
           From N/C – X15 – V7915 – W – 2 – no height
09.04   Reported to N/C and Catterick – machine-gun fire heard – direction V.51
09.14   Told N/C post reports X14 doing power dives
09.15   Told N/C post thinks last report refers to fighters not X14 – continue telling
09.18   Told N/C – explosion reported V5713 – thought to be enemy aircraft – heavy explosion
09.28   Told N/C – Y3 fighters appear to have engaged enemy planes in V4535 – V – 4537

*N/C refers to No 13 Group RAF HQ at Newcastle.

09.29   Told N/C 3 fighters engaged 1 Heinkel bomber in V3535 – V3531
09.32   Told N/C post reports Heinkel brought down V3529."

Thus it was that the corps watched and reported the first German aircraft to be destroyed over England since the First World War. The Heinkel had been shot down in the snow near Sneaton Castle by Flight Lieutenant (later Group Captain) Peter Townsend.

As the weather improved so the amount of Service flying increased. Operational training units sprang up in back areas, bomber and fighter exercises increased and secret prototypes of bombers and fighters such as the Avro Manchester, Short Stirling, Hawker Typhoon and Hawker Tornado began to appear more frequently in the skies. Familiar visitors for coastal posts in the south and east were Cierva Autogyros and light aircraft such as the Miles Mentor which flew round and round providing calibration targets for the radar stations.

On April 9 the war came a step nearer with the invasion of Norway and Denmark. Apart from the cunning and stealth with which the attack was carried out there were two elements of vital importance to Britain. Lack of proper intelligence and coastal warning by the Norwegians had allowed the Germans to occupy most of the country with little opposition, and Luftwaffe bombers were now ranged across the North Sea and theoretically capable of penetrating in strength from the north-east. RAF operational sorties immediately increased, with bombers and reconnaissance aircraft hunting for German shipping, while observer posts in Scotland noticed the transit of some very oddly coloured (salmon pink) reconnaissance Spitfires flying out towards Norway.

The Norwegian campaign, however, was just a curtain raiser, for on May 10, German columns poured across the Belgian, Dutch and French frontiers. Winston Churchill became Prime Minister and the coalition Government was formed.

It was fitting that as German paratroops were descending on the forts in Holland the Observer Corps was filing dummy airborne-attack reports to the GOC Northern Command. In England it was just another exercise, but on the Continent it was very real.

At 07.25 on May 10 Colchester observer group noted the following message from Uxbridge: "Flights and squadrons of our aircraft will be frequently taking to the air and we are not to be alarmed." By 20.40 the situation looked slightly different, with a message from 18/D.1 post stating: "Coastguards say that the admiral at Harwich says the Germans may attempt to land troops by parachute or small boats on the Essex coast tonight or tomorrow." Fortunately the Germans were occupied elsewhere. The last salutary note that night was a general call for all observers to ensure that they brought their gas masks with them on duty. "Aberdon" was the code-word used for a gas attack.

As the British Expeditionary Force was pushed back towards Dunkirk and the RAF in France suffered heavy losses, the reality of the situation at last impinged on the island's general conscious-ness. The first of the refugees began to arrive on May 15, in the shape of raid C.7 which was a Dutch aircraft, plotted into the aerodrome at Orford near Bawdsey.

On May 18, as things became grimmer, Warrington-Morris issued the following statement: "The Commandant of the Observer Corps wishes to inform you that he is taking steps to have certain selected posts armed with rifles." By May 22, while the newly formed Local Defence Volunteers were wondering whether to fight with a club or a sword-stick, key groups of the Observer Corps were being issued with rifles, bayonets and adequate ammunition. For groups nearest the firing line the issue was two rifles to a post, a variable number for centres and where-ever possible revolvers for the officers. This action was followed, on May 24, by an urgent message that "All members on duty at posts are to wear their brassards and badges."

The first to be armed after the Continental invasion, the Observer Corps was to remain the only civilian organisation – apart from the police – to carry firearms. The brassard and badge were supposed to protect observers under the Geneva Convention, but if invasion had come they would have provided little help and undoubtedly members of the corps would have been shot out of hand. Fortunately the acid test never came and the post rifles were used for practice, shooting at any German aircraft which hove into view and killing a remarkable number of pheasants, partridges and hares which went into the family stockpots.

1940 **CHANNELS OF COMMUNICATION FOR**
INVASION AND AIRBORNE ATTACK

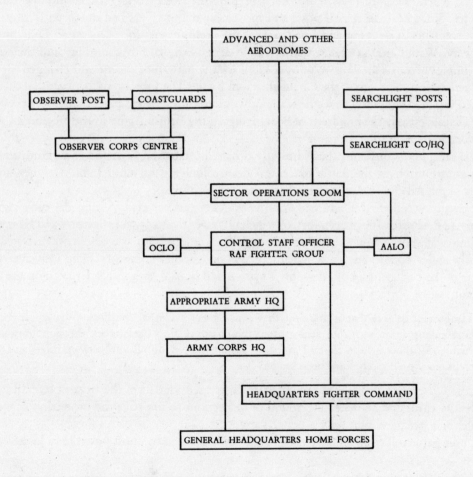

Chapter 8
THE BATTLE OF BRITAIN

"German fighters can now reach this country and post crews will be expected to report types of German aircraft when seen." This terse comment by Warrington-Morris appeared in his circular No 20 of May 29, 1940. It was the day following the surrender of King Leopold of the Belgians, when the hard-pressed divisions of the BEF were reeling back into the Dunkirk perimeter. Since May 20 coastal posts and those near major rivers had noted with interest the mass movements of shipping and small craft as the preliminaries for "Operation Dynamo" got under way. With Goering's boast that he could destroy the BEF by bombing and the concentrated employment of the Luftwaffe over Dunkirk the pattern of the air war changed. Spitfires and Hurricanes poured across the Channel to join battle. The Observer Corps plotted them out and then watched anxiously to see how many would return. For the posts on the Kent coast and in the Thames estuary the hundreds of boats bringing the British Army home presented a never-to-be-forgotten sight.

In the early hours of June 4 the Admiralty declared Operation Dynamo to be complete. The RAF's contribution to the battle in central France lingered on until June 18, when the last fighters of the Advanced Air Striking Force headed for home.

The enemy was now well and truly on the doorstep, and in 41 days since the campaign had opened 944 RAF aircraft had been lost, of which no fewer than 453 were Spitfires and Hurricanes. Dowding was short of pilots and aircraft and his whole system was about to be tested continuously under conditions for which there was no parallel in history. The Observer Corps was one of the cornerstones of Dowding's system and he said later in his despatch on the Battle of Britain:

"It is important to note that at this time they [the Observer Corps] constituted the whole means of tracking enemy raids once they had crossed the coastline . . . Their work throughout was quite invaluable. Without it the air-raid warning systems could not have been operated and inland interceptions would rarely have been made."

For the Observer Corps the situation meant increased vigilance, the issue of overalls, berets and identity cards and an unceasing round of inspections to improve the protection of existing post sites and seek new sites with a better view.★

The blue pattern RAF overalls were greeted with derision by most posts; they looked awful

---

★The sandbags on most posts had by this time started to fall apart and orders were given for a "cement wash" to be poured over them to try to stop the rot.

and they did not fit. As the Wallington, Surrey, post pointed out: "The overalls are cut as if they were to be worn by maternity cases." Most members continued to wear civilian clothes with brassard, badge and tin hat – where available. Many of the tin hats had "Police" written on them, whereupon the enterprising members scratched out all but the letters "OC." The beret was a godsend, as it kept the rain off and cushioned the scraping of the metal telephone head set on many a bald head. The dark-blue beret with badge, has been part of Observer Corps rig-out ever since, although probably no organisation has ever found more shapes in which to wear it.

The identity cards were vital at a time when Local Defence Volunteers were only too happy to shoot anyone who could not prove that he lived next door. Known as "DR.12s," these identity cards carried a photograph of the bearer.

LDV commanders were not averse to poaching on anyone's territory. They even complained about recruiting for the Observer Corps. An edict went forth from Bentley Priory in May that: "Observers have been trained for the purpose of tracking aircraft and should not join other organisations which would have a call upon their spare time."

One of the more hilarious incidents in this connection was concerned with the Earl of Breadalbane. He was most agreeable to a post being sited on his property, at Killin, Perthshire, but strongly resented personnel being recruited through the local police. The poor OGO of No 36 Group wrote to the Scottish Area Commandant on July 24, 1940, stating: "It should be noted here that a state of active warfare exists between the Earl of Breadalbane and the sergeant of Perth constabulary situated at Killin."

The laird had command of the LDV over a large area and left barely a stone unturned in an endeavour to establish his rights. He eventually wrote to Sir Archibald Sinclair, Secretary of State for Air, on August 28, 1940, saying: "I understand, though I am not experienced in these matters, that it is customary courtesy if one is asking a question in Parliament to send beforehand a draft to the minister of the department concerned. I accordingly do so now and shall be very glad to send further details before putting down the question if desired:

"To ask His Majesty's Government by what method and on what qualification members of the Air Observer Corps are selected; whether they are aware that members of the Home Guard have been approached without the knowledge of their own Home Guard commanders by a senior officer of the Royal Air Force and induced to abandon the Home Guard for a paid post in the Air Observer Corps; and whether they approve of a procedure which has unfairly prejudiced the more loyal members of the Home Guard and appears a most unsatisfactory method of recruitment. Further, whether His Majesty's Government will investigate any such which is brought to their notice."

A long two-way flow of correspondence ensued as a result of which the earl was persuaded that there was no case to answer. Democracy at its best clearly remained alive and kicking despite the enemy on the Channel coast.*

Extraordinary things could and almost invariably did happen in 1940, and the Observer Corps was no exception. In a very different vein Lord Esher of Watlington Park, Oxfordshire, wrote to the Air Ministry on June 18, 1940: "I don't want to worry Sir Archibald personally about

---

*The Killin post survived it all and is operational now as 28/F.1.

such a small matter, but I should be most grateful if you would get into touch with whoever runs the Observation Corps by passing this letter on to him." The letter read:

"I have organised an observation post here on the top of the Chilterns, having a wide range of view 750ft above the Oxfordshire plain and within a few miles of Benson aerodrome. We have built a small hut, had the telephone connected, and it is manned by 14 men. These men do other work, and give one night a week, so there are always two on duty from 3 to 6 a.m. Some of them, however, are worried because they have no official status and I think it would be a good thing if we could be allowed to join the Observation Corps. I should be glad to know if it is possible and if so how it is done."

Group Captain Courtney wrote to Warrington-Morris on August 7, 1940:

"I have taken the grid reference as 159131 on one-inch sheet No 105, which marks the post four miles from Nettlebed, eight from Thame and seven-and-a-half from Stradhampton and, by a most extraordinary coincidence, covers an existing blank area in No 4 Group. I have spoken to GPO and there is no objection to the post being designated R.4 and joining with Princes Risborough, Stradhampton and Thame – which I consider would be the best lay-out.

In view of the above circumstances it seems very convenient to incorporate this existing post if you require this blank area covered, which I think is desirable as with the number of training aircraft operating in No 4 Group we do get a number of unknowns – especially at night."

Thus it was that a ready-made private-venture post was incorporated into the corps and with the full collaboration of the Home Guard,* whose commanding officer released six men for observer duties. Watlington today is still operational in the nuclear role as ROC post 3/H.3.

Only one file of Observer Corps inspection reports has survived from 1940, but they make amusing reading at a distance of 35 years. They were written by Group Captain Courtney, Southern Area Commandant. The following are some extracts:

30/4/40 *Post 4/N.1, Sunninghill*
Very misty but appeared very shut in and possibility of moving to Ascot race-course seems barred because there are some 3,000 men accommodated there. Bad noise; interference from two dynamos (?) at waterworks and engine at gasworks not far distant . . . Still short of gas masks and anti-clothing.

6/5/40 *Post 4/O.1, Whitney*
Met head observer; seems sound and goodfellow . . . Suggested field to north of road the other side of cottages better, but apparently this put them within one field of Whitney aerodrome which is opening . . . Only has 11 members so far; The two I saw rather resembled the halt, the maimed and the blind. I think some middle-aged blood would help.

9/6/40 *Post 19/T.1, Eastchurch*
Spoke to coastguard at Warden Point; line has been joined up but minor trouble with ringing at coastguard end . . . Good sandbagged site; concrete floor, but sandbags breaking up despite good cement coating.

23/7/40 *Post 17/B.2, Welwyn*
Good and keen lot; windbreak could be higher with advantage. I think the Bren-gun post to the SE should be provided with a guard rail so that they will never shoot up the post.

*The Local Defence Volunteers were renamed the Home Guard at Winston Churchill's insistence in July 1940.

Commandants of the Observer Corps/Royal Observer Corps 1929-1975

Air Commodore E. A. D. Masterman CB, CMG, CBE, AFC, 1929-1936

Air Commodore G. H. Ambler OBE, AFC, 1942-1943

Air Commodore A. D. Warrington–Morris CMG, OBE, 1936-1942

Air Commodore Finlay Crerar CBE, 1943-1945

Air Commodore The Earl of Bandon CB, DSO, 1945-1949

Air Commodore R. B. Jordan CB, DFC, ADC, 1949-1951

Air Commodore G. H. Vasse CBE, 1951-1954

Air Commodore J. H. T. Simpson DSO, AFC, 1954-1959

Air Commodore J. M. Warfield CBE, 1959–1961

Air Commodore C. M. Wight-Boycott CBE, DSO, 1961–1964

Air Commodore J. H. Greswell CBE, DSO, DFC, 1964–1968

Air Commodore D. F. Rixson OBE, DFC, AFC, 1968–1970

Air Commodore E. B. Sismore DSO, DFC, AFC, 1970-1973   Air Commodore R. K. Orrock DFC, ADC, 1973-1975

Air Commodore M. H. Miller CBE, AFC, 1975 to date

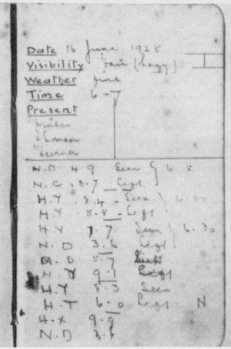

Top right *A Sopwith Snipe of 32 Squadron. It was an aircraft of this type which was plotted by special constables around Cranbrook, Kent in the first Observer Corps experiment on the evening of August 12, 1924*

Bottom left *The basic equipment of an observer post in the 1920s and early 1930s. Mr. A. E. Baker, Head Special of 2/M.3 post Henfield, Sussex seen with the "Heath Robinson" wooden*

post instrument, telephone battery box and the old-fashioned (and very uncomfortable) army type head-and-breast set

Bottom left *A page from the logbook of 1/G.3 "Aircraft Observation Post" during the first full scale exercises in 1925. Two centres, Maidstone and Horsham, were operating in that year. The two left-hand columns indicate squares of the map grid then in use*

Top left *Trying out the new all-metal plotting instrument in 1934. With only a few modifications this piece of machinery was to remain standard through to the 1950s*

Top right *Like something from the space age, three vast concrete sound locators still stand at Greatstone near Lydd, Kent. The rectangular one on the left is 200 ft in length and the circular ones are 25 ft in diameter. These devices were supposed to provide Britain's long-range warning of air attack but for a variety of reasons they proved unsuitable*

Bottom *Typical of the Hawker biplanes which the Observer Corps plotted in the air exercises of the late 1930s is this Hector Army co-operation aircraft based at Odiham. The six-pointed star on the fin indicated a general reconnaissance and Army co-op machine*

Top *An Observer Corps centre of the 1939/40 period; this was the nerve centre of 38 Group Aberdeen in the Autumn of 1939. Standing on the left is the controller, Mr (later Sir) G. A. Williamson who became Scottish Area Commandant in the 1950s*

Bottom *The "rabbit hutch" structure erected in some Groups in the so-called "Back Areas". This is 38/D.2 post Bucksburn late in 1939. These posts had no plotting instrument, only the map table and a white wooden arrow in the middle*

Open to the weather. 2/O.2 post Pulborough, Sussex, deep in the snow of the appalling winter of 1939 and basking in the sunshine during the Battle of Britain in the summer of 1940

The personnel of a typical post of the 1940 period, 15/J.3 Benwick, Cambs in July of that year. Everyone was wearing his Observer Corps badge including the parson in the second row

23/7/40   *Post 17/B.3, Hertford*
Have used old motor tyres filled with sand to make windbreak, in sets of triangles, so that it would be quite bullet-proof.

13/8/40   *Post 19/Q.4, Cobham*
Good site, good view, HO very keen and produced some time ago an ingenious night plotting instrument, quite useful. Showed me a Parker Hale 4mm adapter for use in Service rifle.

24/8/40   *Post 2/M.3, Henfield*
Have already been shot at. Possible alternative concrete tower just west of hut on the asparagus bed.

By June 1940 the RAF was becoming very worried that with so many men under arms British aircrew could well survive a crash or bale-out and still be killed in error on the ground. Accordingly the following signal was sent to all flying stations on June 12:

"Following procedure has been devised to reduce to minimum risk of personnel who force-land or descend by parachute from being mistaken for enemy. When persons approach to apprehend they should stand stiff, holding both hands above head and fingers extended, and announce their identity loudly but make no movement until identity established. If ordered to produce proof or card of identity they should say where it can be found on them but not lower hands to produce without permission, in case their action might be mistaken for reaching for a weapon. If injured and unable to stand personnel should lie flat and stay very still."

The warning was timely but it did not prevent a number of pilots being skewered with a pitchfork or shot in the back-side with 12-bore or ball ammunition. The Observer Corps was fortunately not guilty in these cases, as the members had a good idea of the identity of the air-craft involved.

Invasion was by then not a hypothetical exercise but a distinct possibility. For seaborne attack the coastguards were ordered to report enemy surface vessels to the coastal observer post to which they were connected. From there the information was to be passed by centres to fighter sectors and thence to the military authorities. For airborne landings the corps was to report through the same channels with, if necessary, the Home Guard informing the nearest observer post of anything seen. The corps commandant suggested invasion alarms, by local arrangement, such as the firing of two rifle shots in quick succession. As will be seen from the accompanying diagram, the Observer Corps formed one of the key parts of the invasion-warning system. Dowding's demand that the Corps should not waste its time passing information from centre to local defence forces was adhered to. Corps communications, he stressed, were unidirectional and for the purpose of passing information inwards from posts to centres and onwards. Ultimately the corps became a prime source for invasion information to be passed upwards through the Service network.

Observer posts were supplied with standard Board of Trade distress red-star rocket flares which would be fired when it was known that parachute troops were landing and communication with centre had broken down. Any other post still in communication was to report the firing to centre. This was the beginning of a corps association with small rockets and pyrotechnics which extends to the present day, when warning of approaching radio-active fall-out is given by maroons.

A further visual aid for the corps in 1939–40 was the white canvas "T" which was to be laid on the ground to direct friendly fighters to hostile aircraft when normal communications had broken down or been destroyed. It was a singularly unsuccessful device.

Since the Second World War many efforts have been made to write off Operation Sealion as a threatening exercise which was never intended to be carried out. Close examination to German records, however, shows clearly that Hitler intended to invade Britain by sea and by air if the Luftwaffe could achieve air superiority over south-east England. Dowding learned from agents in France, in July, of the Führer's decision to undertake the Sealion invasion to subdue Britain. At the same time Intelligence revealed German air-transport moves and airborne training exercises which showed that an all-out air drop would precede or accompany the sea-borne attack. The Fighter Command secret intelligence summary for the period noted: "There are indications that a sea and airborne expedition is in an advanced state of preparation". This was long before the invasion barges began to assemble in the Channel ports.

Initially, under the wide-front landing concept, Fliegerdivision 7, based in the Pas de Calais, was to take and hold key areas to the north of Dover and on the downs. When the narrow-front invasion plan (Newhaven to Folkestone) was finally adopted, Fliegerdivision 7 was allotted the main task of seizing and holding the Royal Military Canal which enclosed the Walland and Romney marshes. The marshes would have provided an ideal bridgehead for the 16th Army sailing in from Calais, Rotterdam, Antwerp, Ostend and Dunkirk.

If Sealion had taken place Nos 1 and 2 Groups of the Observer Corps would have been in the front line from the outset, but the posts right in the path of both initial landing forces would have been Dungeness, Rye Harbour, Brookland, Ham Street, Dymchurch and Folkestone. Almost certainly the first warning of airborne landings would have come from one of these posts.

The final German invasion plan for September 1940. Nos 1 and 2 Observer Groups would have borne the brunt of the attack

"SEALION" INITIAL ASSAULT PLAN AND MAIN OBJECTIVES, SEPT. 1940

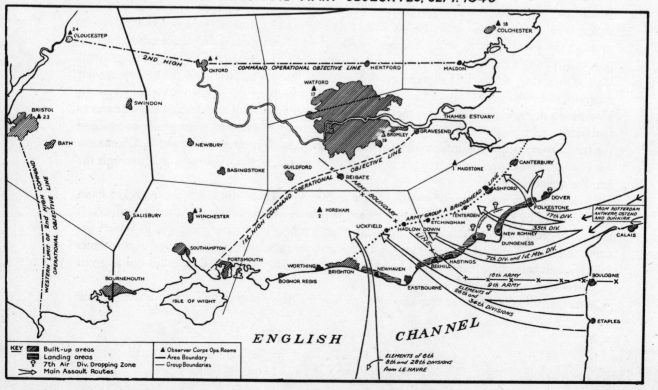

HURRICANE I (MERLIN)
Single-Seat Fighter

Span 40'-0"   Length 31'-5"   Height 11'-3"

12

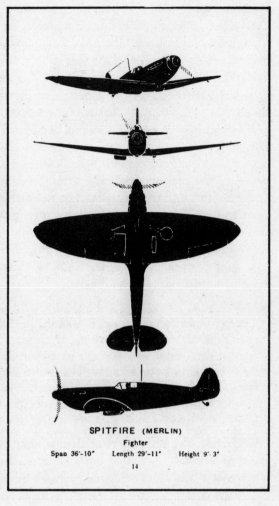

SPITFIRE (MERLIN)
Fighter

Span 36'-10"   Length 29'-11"   Height 9'-3"

14

1940 official silhouettes of the Hurricane 1 and Spitfire 1

Just how much effort was put in on German training for the airborne side of the invasion can be gathered from the log book of Mr Gerhard Puritz, who has worked for many years at the BBC.

After being trained on the Dornier 17M as a reconnaissance pilot he was posted to 1/KG ZbV1 (ZbV: Zur Bezonderen Verwendung=Special Operations Group) operating Ju52s at Märkish Friedland in Pomerania. Training was specifically aimed at towing DFS 230 ten-seat gliders. He started towing practice on August 22 and began night towing with three flights on the night of August 27. Towing with fully loaded Ju52s followed, in Kette (three) and Staffel (six) formation. Air-to-air firing with the dorsal machine gun and window guns on the Ju52 was included in the programme because of the known unpleasantness of Fighter Command.

At the end of August 1940 1/KG ZbV1 despatched an advanced party to France, while back at base the whole Gruppe of 36 aircraft began practising landing in large numbers. On September 18 the unit transferred to Salzwedel, west of Berlin, and thereafter concentrated on rapid movement and quick-loading exercises, roads being considered the prime landing points in Britain. Following the Luftwaffe's inability to defeat the RAF in the Battle of Britain, training slackened off and on November 27 the whole unit was transferred to East Prussia in preparation for the invasion of Russia scheduled for 1941.

If transport Gruppen had arrived over the marshes in September 1940 there would have been little hope for the six observer posts, but they would undoubtedly have been able to despatch the vital warning message that airborne troops had landed.

By August 1940 a scheme called Beetle had been devised for the transmission of wireless-telegraph and radio-telephone information on air and sea landings. As soon as reliable information had been received from the Observer Corps and searchlight detachments it was to be passed to five key military headquarters★ over a special point-to-point wireless network known as the Beetle W/T Organisation. For redistribution of the information to lower Army formations and RAF stations, medium-power long-wave broadcasting stations were installed at the five headquarters. The information that they broadcast was received on ordinary portable radios issued to all RAF stations and various military and naval formations.

In an instruction issued by the SASO Fighter Command on August 18 the basic handling of invasion information was outlined:

"Information received from the Observer Corps or searchlight detachments will reach this head-quarters giving the precise position on the British grid. Preparatory to broadcasting the information on the 'Beetle' W/T Organisation, if instructed by the duty air commodore, the controller will convert the British grid position to a plain-language position, giving the distance and compass direction from a landmark or well known town, e.g., grid position 'WR 2030' would be converted into '2½ miles north-east of Bexhill, Sussex.' The information and the converted position will, if its broadcast is authorised as mentioned in para (b) above, then be passed by telephone by the controller to the duty signals officer who will broadcast the message on the 'Beetle' W/T Organisation."

The firing of a red rocket or flare sending out red stars denoted enemy action on land. A green rocket or flare sending out green stars denoted approach of enemy surface craft, while a white rocket fired from a ship meant attack by an enemy submarine.

Centres in danger areas were in the main guarded by police during the daytime and by the Home Guard at night. Barbed wire and sandbags sprang up around the centres but the posts had largely to fend for themselves. The general rule was "every centre and every post must be continuously manned as long as humanly possible."

Fighter Command issued the following instructions to observer posts on June 11, 1940:

"In the event of invasion by sea or parachute infantry, posts are to remain at their stations as long as possible, giving information of the enemy movements. When they are no longer able to remain at their posts, by approach of the enemy, they are to evacuate them in the following manner:
1. Cut telephone lines.
2. Take their instruments with them.
3. If circumstances do not permit of their taking away their instruments they are to destroy them."

Presumably observers were physically to tear the instrument apart, but just what the German

---

★The five HQs were Scottish Command, Northern Command, XII Corps (Eastern Command), Western Command and HQ Western Area, Plymouth.

army would have been able to do with a genuine intact Mark II observer instrument remains a mystery.

Throughout June German aircraft made widespread incursions over England, particularly along the east and north-east coasts. Most raids were at night and the heaviest attack came on June 18, when more than 100 enemy aircraft were reported and bombs fell in many places. The most serious casualties of the night were at Cambridge, where nine people were killed. The Luftwaffe was exploring the country and testing the defences. It was a month of offensive training and the trying out of such devices as the Knickebein radio blind-bombing system. In addition by keeping up the pressure the Germans hoped to cut British war production and lower civilian morale. In the first case they partially succeeded and in the second they failed.

By the end of June not only had the corps done a lot of plotting under operational conditions but posts had had near misses from bombs, some had been machine-gunned and there had been useful experience of the GPO making rapid repairs to several telephone lines.

1940 official silhouettes of two German types, the Fw 200 Condor and the Messerschmitt Bf109.
Unfortunately the 109 shown was an early version and not the Bf109E which flew against the RAF in
the Battle of Britain

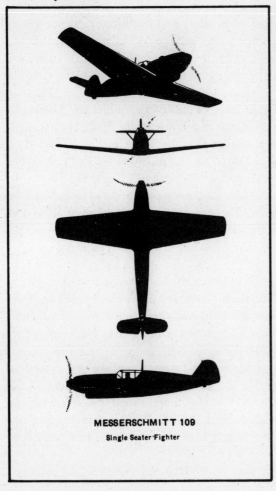

MESSERSCHMITT 109

Single Seater Fighter

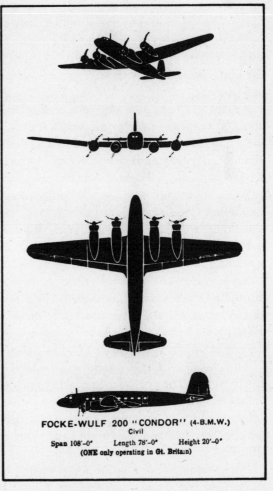

FOCKE-WULF 200 "CONDOR" (4-B.M.W.)
Civil

Span 108'-0"   Length 78'-0"   Height 20'-0"
(ONE only operating in Gt. Britain)

July 1940 marked the opening phase of the Battle of Britain, with the Luftwaffe committing some 135 bombers and dive-bombers and 200 fighters to clearing the Straits of Dover of British shipping. Dowding could muster 52 squadrons of Spitfires, Hurricanes, Defiants and Blenheim I fighters, of which 26 were in No 11 Fighter Group under Air Vice-Marshal (later Air Chief Marshal Sir Keith) Park. Gradually the attacks spread to shipping off the south-west, south-east and east coasts while small numbers of night bombers raided a variety of targets and laid mines from Dover to the Tyne. The inland observer groups had most activity at night while the coastal groups were kept busy 24hr a day and as far west as Cornwall.

In February 1940 Dowding had recommended "a westward extension of the area covered by the Observer Corps." Accordingly on August 26, No 20 Observer Group, Truro, was formed with a small number of posts. This was of considerable assistance to No 10 Fighter Group at Box, Wiltshire, which had been formed on July 13. The second and most crucial phase of the battle opened on August 8, and three days later there was a heavy attack on a land target – Portland – by day. This was followed on August 12 by raids on Portsmouth, five radar stations and coastal airfields. The assault on Fighter Command itself had begun. Despite repeated attacks the CH radars held out and only Ventnor, on the Isle-of-Wight, was out of action for any length of time. Where radars, such as Poling, were badly damaged mobile stations were erected as gap-fillers. The situation concerning fighter airfields, and particularly sector stations, was not good, however, and many were severely damaged. Combined low- and high-level attacks on airfields such as Biggin Hill and Kenley proved very difficult to combat, but for some unknown reason the Luftwaffe did not persevere with low-level strikes except in the case of such coastal airfields as Manston.

August 15, 1940, was one of the most significant days of the battle, when the Luftwaffe attacked simultaneously in the south and the north-east – expecting in the latter area to find little opposition. The German pilots met fierce opposition at every point and were forced to abandon daylight raids from Norway, which could only be accompanied by the vulnerable Me110 twin-engined fighter. Seventy-five German aircraft were destroyed during the day.

As the month wore on the third phase (August 24 to September 6) was entered and the strain on Fighter Command reached almost breaking point. There was an acute shortage of pilots and those there were suffered from severe fatigue. Continuous bombing of airfields made operations very difficult and some stations were reduced to a shambles, but despite everything they kept operating and only Manston was completely evacuated.

September 7 saw a complete change in German tactics which was to swing the pendulum firmly in Britain's favour. Enraged by RAF bombing of Berlin (in retaliation for bombs dropped in error on London), Hitler ordered reprisals against the British capital. If civilian morale could be shattered there might still be hope for Operation Sealion, for which a large but motley collection of vessels was by then packed into the Channel ports.

The change of target caught 11 Fighter Group napping and heavy damage was caused in east London. The resulting fires acted as beacons for the long stream of night raiders which followed. On the night of September 7 the code-word Cromwell was issued and was wrongly interpreted by many units as a warning that invasion had started. Bridges were blown up, vehicles wrecked and the Home Guard and the Army had loaded weapons pointing in every direction.

Night raiding now became a key feature of the war which changed the lives and habits of

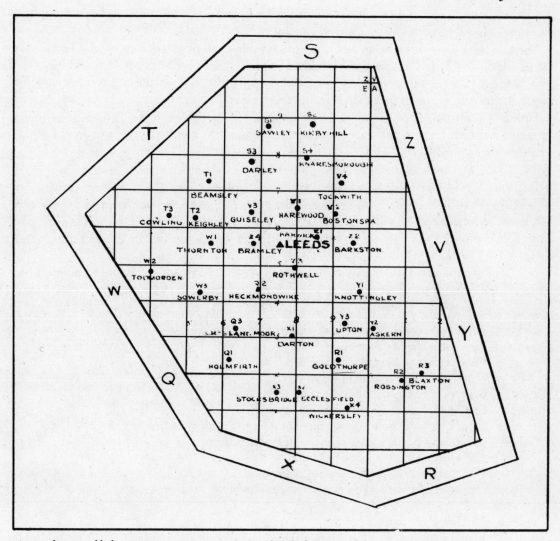

A typical centre table layout in 1940 at No 8 Group, Leeds. The letters round the periphery indicate plotters' positions and the cluster to which they were connected by telephone

millions. Meanwhile the day Battle of Britain was being played out. The crescendo was reached on September 15 when a vast airborne armada set out for London but was broken up and repulsed with the loss of 60 aircraft. Heavy daylight raiding continued until the end of September although the writing was on the wall; the Luftwaffe could not defeat Fighter Command and therefore invasion was impossible.

Because of its severe losses in both pilots and aircraft the Luftwaffe changed its tactics yet again in October, using mixed high-altitude formations of fighter-bombers and fighters plus scattered sorties by medium- and dive-bombers. This was virtually an admission of defeat, and by the end of October the strategic daylight battle petered out. German daylight raids would continue, but they were of nuisance value only and had no bearing on the defeat or otherwise of the British Isles.* The night raids, however, grew in intensity and presented quite another threat, which will be dealt with in the next chapter.

The Observer Corps' part in the first strategic air war of all time had been vital. Throughout the four months July to October the system had been stretched to the utmost. Day and night the plots poured in from the posts; they were sifted and put down on the centre table and the essential information passed to the RAF groups and sectors.

Fighter Command, after a year of working with the corps, found that it had unwittingly obtained a source for any and every sort of information. Where had such-and-such Heinkel crashed? Had the pilot of a Hurricane baled out and was he safe? Had bombs been dropped and what was the location? Were flares being dropped and if so what colour? Was a certain convoy being raided? Had the Corps seen a missing barrage balloon? The questions were endless, but almost always an answer was forthcoming. If the posts did not know they went and found out, while the centres checked with the police and civil defence authorities. In some cases post observers captured the crews of German bombers at gun-point and in others they assisted crashed RAF airmen.

Some idea of the variety of the work done by the corps and strains put upon it can be gained from the following entries selected from September 1940 log of No 18 Group centre, Colchester:

4 *September*

09.25	A.1 post reported 20 bombs dropped in M4527 and 4727.
09.30	Parachutist coming down over M2923.
09.30	Plane crashed in M2523 – unidentified.
	M.2 report plane crashed in sea M5117.
10.02	G.3 report 22 explosions in direction of M4503.
10.07	One Spitfire made forced landing in M0951.
16.50	From Colchester police, answering our query re crashed enemy aircraft:
	One enemy bomber crashed in sea off Foulness Island
	One Hurricane crashed at Mill Beach
	One Spitfire or Hurricane crashed at Purleigh
	One Hurricane crashed on railway line at Rochford.

7 *September*

18.26	To Uxbridge – Raid report:
	Bombs between M0709 and L9911 (HE)
	Bombs between M1727 and M1127 @ 17.44
	Bombs between M5127 and M1753
	Bombs between M4921 and M1755
	Hurricane landed in M7719 @ 17.16
	Hurricane landed in M4115 @ 17.24
	Spitfire crashed in M6513 @ 18.12
	Spitfire crashed in M1917
	Hostile crashed SW M1113 – parachutist
	Hostile crashed M5723 @ 18.12
	Junkers 88 crashed S M1113 – two parachutists

---

*Official figures give 1,733 as German losses during the period of the battle, but it is now known that this is an under estimate owing to certain special Luftwaffe units not submitting full returns and others being disbanded or amalgamated and not showing complete casualty lists. Real losses are believed to be nearer 1,800.

Messerschmitt M6139
Enemy bomber M2713 (Heinkel)

25 September

08.00   *Position at 08.00hr*
Hornchurch and North Weald lines still out
Watford inter-centre line still out
Uxbridge liaison line out
Northolt tellers line out
Lines OK
Watford liaison
Uxbridge teller
Watnall teller
Bromley and Bury inter-centre lines
Hornchurch, North Weald, Debden, Coltishall and Duxford inter-sector lines
All table lines.

20.07   Mr Reynolds, K.2 post, badly injured, his wife killed and child badly injured in raid during the afternoon 25/9/40.

10 September

09.43   Brewster Buffalo aircraft are now flying in small numbers in non-operational duties from naval air stations.

13 September

15.05   Clacton coastguards report Raid X9 to be a Dornier and it dropped screaming bombs 100 yards from their look-out post.

14 September

02.05   To Uxbridge – Raid 17 M1127 or 1327 Dornier, crashed 02.05.

08.42   To Uxbridge – Re message at 02.05, police report plane crashed at Downball School, Sheering – two occupants alive and taken into custody – one dead – plane burned out.

16.19   A Spitfire crashed in M3107 – the pilot did not jump out as he was too low – Debden informed.

23.45   Raid 33 dropped "Molotov Breadbasket" M3111.

15 September

12.13   Multiphone line dead – we cannot ring Uxbridge on liaison line – asked Watford to get in touch with Uxbridge.

23.15   Watford informs us that Bromley cable has been blown up.

17 September

08.20   From Uxbridge – is our emergency lighting set in order? We replied: no, our emergency lighting set is not coupled up and cannot be used – we had to use candles this morning when the current failed.

08.55   To Uxbridge – three unexploded bombs dropped by parachute, A.2 post at Cold Norton, M3117, during night – reported by milkman to farmer to post.

27 September

23.09   To Colchester police – post G.1 report a train travelling from Kelvedon to Colchester has no cover over engine cabin. The light good signal for aircraft.

The belated and short-lived appearance of the Reggia Aeronautica in the air war over Britain came just after the real finish of the battle. The surprising Italian presence was duly noted in the Colchester centre logbook on November 11, 1940★:

> "14.02   Informed Uxbridge – Raid 42R in M7969 appears to be down – column of smoke and Hurricane circling – apparently a Dornier.
>
> 14.09   Informed Uxbridge that post H.2 thinks the first plane down in M96 was an Italian biplane; the second was a Junkers 88. Later reported that the supposed Italian plane fell on land. Uxbridge asked us to see that the wreckage of this plane was guarded. Suffolk police say they have six crashes reported to them – all hostile – are investigating.
>
> 14.28   To Uxbridge – plane brought down in M9167 proved to be Italian. Pilot still alive, also the other plane brought down (a bomber) was Italian. Two men baled out, their parachutes failed to open.
>
> 14.50   Uxbridge asked us to ascertain whether the pilot of the Italian plane crashed M9167 was Italian or German.
>
> 14.52   Informed Uxbridge, pilot was definitely Italian.
>
> 15.37   Passed following additional report from H 2 post to Uxbridge – The Italian fighter was a Fiat 42 – the pilot says there were 42 Fiat fighters escorting German bombers but would not state number of bombers. Uxbridge observed that our post should not have been able to get this."

To anyone who was not there at the time it is almost impossible to describe the atmosphere of that summer of 1940, and it is equally difficult to convey the real picture of the Observer Corps under operational conditions. Two attempts have been made and they are worthy of inclusion here.

The first is an extract from the diary of a newly recruited centre observer, describing his initial visit to the operations room of No 17 Group, Watford, in 1940†:

"... But advancing gingerly a few steps into the room I saw what appeared to me to be a roomful of lunatics playing a game of devil's ludo. About a dozen men were around an irregularly shaped table, some seated, some standing, others leaning across the table to push coloured counters from one point to another.

All were talking – some into their telephones, some to the men next to them and some, it seemed, with one side of their mouths into their phones while with the other side maintaining an argument with their neighbours.

All the time they were busy with their game, pushing coloured counters hither and thither on the squared board, putting new ones on, moving little lettered blocks, keeping the pattern forever changing. On three sides of the table, a few feet away, was a raised platform on which sat other men variously occupied, either talking into telephones or scribbling busily into books or on little pads of paper. One thing they had in common with the men at the table: they were all talking, and from time to time one of the scribblers (or both) would tear a sheet from his little pad and wave it aloft, shouting hoarsely. This in turn drew my attention to two other persons who so far had escaped my notice. Maybe it was their rapid, continuous and unpredictable movements which had caused me to miss them. Indeed they were never still, though at times one or the other would hover

---

★The Italians' first sorties over Britain were on October 25 and 29. In the raid of November 11 casualties were three CR.42 fighters and three Fiat BR.20 bombers. H.2 post was at Grundisburgh in East Suffolk.

†From *Observer's Tale, the Story of Group 17 of the ROC*, published privately in 1950.

momentarily over one of the ludo men and address a few words to him, only to dart away an instant later to snatch the piece of paper waved by the scribbler – for all the world like a sea-gull taking a bit of fish from a child on the Thames embankment. Or he would run to one of the many black-boards placed round the walls, scrawl thereon some weird symbols and then dash to a corner of the room where there was a shelf bearing countless little gadgets of wood and metal and scores of coloured counters hanging on pins. Having secured one of these he would then hurl himself towards one of the ludo players, place the slip and the gadget before him, and then with an upward glance at the clock bellow the strange call 'BLUE ORF'. At the same time he would, with a great scythe-like movement of the arm, sweep a great pile of counters and wooden blocks from the board – which only a moment before, it seemed, had been placed there with infinite care and precision by one of the ludo-players. Not that this appeared to cause any resentment to anybody; indeed the players seemed quite pleased to have their endeavours thus brought to nought and straightway started on a new game.

This madhouse appalled me. The lack of ventilation, the terrible intensity of the occupants and the fact that not one person had taken the slightest notice of me drove me nervous and shaken to retreat to the saner atmosphere of the ante-room, where I strove desperately for a few minutes to summon enough courage to go back to that weird pandemonium. . . ."

The second extract concerns the posts and was written by a member from No 30 Observer Group, Durham, who travelled south at the height of the battle*.

"About a fortnight ago I had occasion to go down to two towns in Kent on business connected with my firm, and while in that district I visited some of the observer posts.

I finished my business in the first town at lunch-time and made my way out towards the coast; at a little village I was introduced to the head observer of B3 post.† We wandered into the 'Royal Oak' and were about half-way through a sherry when we heard the unmistakable sound of aircraft, so decided to make immediately for the post. We had only got about half a mile along the lane when we became conscious that things were happening quickly, so decided to get out and have a look. There were two 'plane formations, each of about 15, all of them apparently Messerschmitt 109s flying at about 20,000ft. As we looked a squadron of Spitfires engaged one formation and fighting commenced; in two or three minutes one Messerschmitt came hurtling down and at about 3,000ft or 4,000ft the pilot baled out. We watched the parachute falling, and we were both sure we could see the pilot attached. The parachute dropped comparatively near. We immediately crossed two or three fields, and on arrival found the military already on the spot – but, mysteriously enough, not a sign of the pilot anywhere. The parachute was of 'Jerry' manufacture, but no trace of the individual concerned could be found.

We proceeded to the post, and after a quiet half-hour the fun recommenced. Three formations of enemy 'planes came in, none of them flying less than about 18,000ft, they seemed to be composed of about one-third Dorniers and two-thirds fighters, mostly 109s. I was immensely struck with the efficient and calm way with which the developing situation was handled by the two observers on duty. For a space of 10–15min they hardly glanced at the chart and only used the instrument and height bar. At the commencement one man, with binoculars glued to his eyes, made it his job to follow closely the first two raiding formations, which were very soon attacked by our fighters. With hardly an unnecessary word he gave the essential information; the man with the head 'phones followed the third raid and still seemed to have ears and eyes left for other parts of the sky.

*These notes originally appeared in the Christmas 1940 edition of "The Watcher," the journal of No 30 Group.
†1/B.3 post, Wye, about five miles north-east of Ashford, Kent.

This is a typical example of the type of conversation:–

'B3 here.... That first formation on 1234 are turning west – second formation on 5678 are being engaged by our fighters – my colleague says nine Hurricanes. Another raid of about 12, half of them two-engined bombers, are over 2345.... B3 here.... That first formation now on 3456 are flying west – the 12 on 2345 have moved to 4567 and are being attacked by a squadron of Spitfires. There seem to be about three or four dogfights going on over 4321 – my partner says an enemy fighter in the second formation is coming down in flames. In the third formation there is some very heavy scrapping now going on in 8765 ... B3 here ... I can hear another raid coming in· from the north-east; I can't look for a moment, but it sounds like about 12 Messerschmitt fighters ... B3 here ... Raid one, on 5432 going west – raid two on 5678 scattered dogfights going on – raid three on 6543 seems to be splitting up – the fourth raid from the north-east we can now see, they are on 7654 and there seem to be about 15 Messerschmitts at over 25,000ft.... I can hear something behind me which sounds like five or six Ansons flying low – do you want them? ... All right ... B3 here ... Raid one is now –' and so on, and so on.

The Avros were correctly identified on sound and I think, if I remember rightly, proved to be about eight in number. Frankly I could not help wondering how long it would take me to learn to deal with a like situation in such a manner; my wondering was cut short by a tearing sound which increased in intensity with each split second. I spun round, scanning the sky, but for a minute or two could not see where the racket was coming from. The noise became a terrific roar, and I don't mind admitting I had the wind up completely and was absolutely certain that half the German Air Force were about to fall on the post. The next moment I saw a Messerschmitt 109, with its engine full on, nosediving straight for the ground at a simply stupendous rate; actually it fell within about a quarter of a mile of the post, and the airscrew, engine and about half the fuselage buried itself in the soil with bits of the plane strewn all round the field.

About an hour later I saw another 109 come down, this time somewhat less than a mile from the post; this plane was, however, in a much better state of preservation.

I then set off to go back, and while on this short journey of about eight miles I was conscious of some very heavy fighting going on. I got out of the car just in time to see a Dornier come down in flames some little distance away and then, unfortunately, I witnessed the crashing of a Spitfire. The pilot, however, baled out when about 800ft from the ground and escaped with a broken leg. I picked up my permit for the defence area at the police office and then spent a portion of the evening at a coastal observer post and about half the night back at B3 post.

A day or two later I managed to get permission to go through the military enclosure at a well known headland, and I took up a position on the edge of the cliff at almost the highest point. From this wonderful viewpoint I witnessed about four major engagements in the air at some 20,000ft up, and also had the thrill of seeing four of the barrage balloons shot down in quick succession. I was so busy watching the progress of two which were blazing and gradually falling over the sea that I quite overlooked the fact that the third balloon was about to fall almost on the spot where I was standing.

Later in the same day I had the very thrilling experience of watching a fight over the water between two Dornier flying boats* and three Hurricanes. We actually saw the Dorniers leave the water under the shelter of the French cliffs, and after an unsuccessful attempt to drop bombs on a torpedo boat which was zigzagging about in mid-channel they were engaged by three Hurricanes. One of the Dorniers escaped, but the other seemed to me to be attacked and hit by two Hurricanes simultaneously. The Dornier literally fell to pieces in the air, and I don't think that there was a trace of any survivors.

---

*Dornier 18s of 3/406.

From what I saw at the three posts I should judge that the efficiency of the observer crews has reached a very high standard. Of course, some of the men I spoke to have been eight, nine and ten years on the job, but they cannot have been having this type of experience for more than a few months.

I certainly felt, as I was leaving the area, a 'sadder and wiser man,' – wiser as I felt I had learned something from these stalwart crews, and sadder in the consciousness that my standard of efficiency in the work was so much below that of many I had been privileged to see."

During the Battle of Britain the corps developed many unofficial links with the RAF. One of these involved the centre at No 7 Group, Manchester, and a corps officer, H. Ramsden Whitty. He knew the RAF well and even had had the local post plotting checked and calibrated with the help of Ansons from Cranage, Cheshire. When the air war started in earnest a private arrangement was made between No 7 Operational Training Unit at Hawarden, Flintshire, and the Manchester centre. Although this was not a fighting unit, Wing Commander (later Air Vice-Marshal) Hallings-Pott formed an armed battle flight with Spitfires. Whenever any "trade" appeared on the 7 Group table or anything looked likely to go in the vague direction of Hawarden, the Observer Corps phoned the airfield and gave full information which continued to be relayed to the pilots in the air. On August 14 this highly illegal system worked perfectly: Hallings-Pott and two other pilots succeeded in shooting down a Heinkel 111, from 111/KG.27, near Chester. In his report the wing commander said he had heard explosions in the district; he did not divulge the real origin of his information.

One other threat manifested itself during the Battle of Britain and it was to remain until the Allied invasion forces of 1944 over-ran the Pas de Calais. On August 22, 1940, the citizens of Dover had their evening rudely awakened by a series of heavy explosions. There were no enemy aircraft in the vicinity and the cause was found to be four-gun German salvos from long-range heavy guns on the other side of the Channel. In fact the first sighting shots had been fired on August 12, and the shelling was to continue until mid-1944 at targets along the coast and well into Kent. For the Observer Corps it became essential to have better protection against shell splinters for posts such as those at Dover and Deal. Special shelters were built, although they could not have withstood a near miss. The general scarcity of money and materials is evidenced by the Southern Area Command's plea to HQ, ROC, in November 1940 for additional cash for protecting 1/C.3 post, Dover, which amounted to the princely sum of £8.15.0.

Apart from reporting aircraft the posts were required, in October 1941, to report certain shell bursts. This was instigated by MI.10 via A1.2G, Air Ministry, to discover whether or not the Germans were using "proximity fuzes" in their ammunition.

Chapter 9
THE BLITZ

As the only source of overland air intelligence in the Battle of Britain, the Observer Corps became involved in a number of disagreements about where information should be routed and how it should be utilised.

Unwittingly the corps was to provide the catalyst for the final round of the No 11 versus No 12 Fighter Group row, which led to the departure of Dowding and Park when they had just won one of the greatest conflicts in the nation's history. The whole affair was sordid and involved intrigue and jealousies at the highest level – hardly credible in the midst of a war for survival.

Air Vice-Marshal Park at 11 Group was the spearhead of air defence, and he demanded early interception and the breaking up of enemy formations by single squadrons or pairs. He **was not** prepared to waste valuable time trying to form massive "balbos" or wings of fighters while the Luftwaffe butchered any target at leisure.

No 12 Group under Air Vice-Marshal Leigh-Mallory, being one remove from the real front line, had adopted a policy of massing forces to bring the maximum strength to bear, regardless of the damage caused in the meanwhile. The concept was formed on ideas propounded by Squadron Leader (later Group Captain) Bader, the legless CO of 242 Squadron based at Duxford.

What neither Leigh-Mallory nor Bader knew was that Dowding based his strategy on the top-secret German planning information available from Ultra, the Y-service and foreign agents. Orders to German air-fleet commanders were to attract the largest possible number of British fighters into the air at one time and destroy them. In the opening stages of the Battle of Britain Luftwaffe pilot reserves were such that they could afford heavy losses in the course of a knock-out blow. By committing fighters in squadron strength on a forward-intercept basis and breaking up enemy formations as early as possible, Dowding succeeded in husbanding his resources while wearing the Luftwaffe down over three long months.

The only way that Dowding could do this was by keeping his two watching networks – radar and the Observer Corps – at the highest pitch of efficiency throughout the battle. He had to know the complete air picture continuously and nothing, in his view, could be allowed to interfere with his "eyes and ears." This explains his pre-occupation with the Observer Corps and the lengths to which he went to protect its facilities from mishandling and overloading.

During August and September Park had become extremely annoyed at having his airfields attacked when 12 Group fighters had been called forward to them. Apparently the 12 Group squadrons had gone elsewhere looking for a fight. Park was also highly suspicious of the big claims being made by 12 Group when they were in action. After one day of high activity he refused to believe the claims of Leigh-Mallory's units and called for a detailed analysis from the Observer Corps of all enemy aircraft seen to crash. The corps, with the assistance of the police and civil defence, just could not match the actual raiders shot down with the claims – and by a large margin. Relations between Park and Leigh-Mallory were not improved by the incident, but it was only later that the AOC-in-C, Dowding, realised just how serious was the enmity between his two group commanders.

So far as the corps was concerned matters came to a head early in November 1940 when Mr Harold Balfour (later Lord Balfour of Inchrie), Under-Secretary of State for Air, submitted a report to the Secretary of State, the Deputy Chief of Air Staff and others, following an unofficial visit to Duxford on November 2. Balfour said that the conflict of operational views between 12 and 11 Group was felt acutely by the units at Duxford which made up the "Balbo" wing formation. He went on:

"The basis of their feeling is that they are at the disposal of 11 Group but are never called upon to function, according to their practised tactics of wing formation, until too late. They have not had a contest with the enemy since the end of September.

"Dealing with the detailed method which is alleged to be followed – this broadly is that they are denied available information because of apparently needless regulations.

"No 12 Group draws its RDF information from Fighter Command, but apparently their officer in Fighter Command control room is not allowed to transmit information concerning RDF plots south of the Thames estuary. This is 12 Group territory. Consequently aircraft can be known to be assembling over – say – Calais and 11 Group have knowledge but 12 Group have not. If the 12 Group representatives could have the full information available to 11 Group this would allow the wing to be on the spot in time to catch the enemy instead of always being late – often somewhere over Maidstone.

"Duxford obtains its Observer Corps information from one of two sources – either the Bromley centre or Colchester, which are linked together by a tie-line. Hitherto the station commander at Duxford has obtained the Bromley information by some private arrangement with Colchester. Today, on the wing being told to go into action, he asked Colchester for information. Colchester stated that Bromley now had orders that on no account were they to give Colchester such information for passing on.

"The station asks that one of two things should happen: either there should be a direct line to Bromley, or Colchester should be allowed to give every bit of information Bromley has (I know that the first alternative is difficult because of land-line loads).

"Squadron Leader Bader and his unit look forward to the time when the enemy may decide to renew their mass daylight raids. Given the wing formation, with the maximum advance information of enemy movements and reasonable time to get to a tactical height and position, he says that he is absolutely certain of taking enormous toll."

Air Vice-Marshal Sholto Douglas (later Marshal of the RAF Lord Douglas of Kirtleside), Deputy Chief of the Air Staff, was a keen supporter of Leigh-Mallory and the "Balbo" theory and he waded in with a letter to Dowding calling for better information support for 12 Group. The Senior Air Staff Officer Fighter Command, Air Vice-Marshal Evill, sent a minute to Dowding on November 6:

"You ask me to make some comments on the enclosures 10A and B.★

It seems to me that there are four points raised in various ways throughout these papers, as follows:

a)   That No 12 Group is not allowed all available RDF information.

b)   That Duxford Sector has been denied Observer Corps information on the Bromley area.

c)   That the Duxford Wing is not called upon by No 11 Group until too late.

d)   That in consequence valuable opportunities for destroying the enemy are being lost.

As regards a), orders were issued in this headquarters on October 11 emphasising the importance of passing the first RDF plots to groups without waiting for tracks to form. And a further order was issued on October 21 to say that No 12 Group was to be given the same information regarding the Dunkirk–Boulogne area as No 11 Group (Air Staff Instructions Nos 5 and 8 respectively).

As regards b), it is true that a practice has grown up whereby Bromley used its inter-centre teller line to Colchester to pass to that centre plots of enemy tracks in the Bromley area for the benefit of Duxford. This practice was stopped recently at the request of the Southern Area Commandant, Observer Corps, who complained that the passing of these plots at busy periods interfered with the essential function of the line which is handing over of tracks between one observer area and another. The proper method is for operational information to pass between sectors, but in this case Bromley only serves as far as North Weald, which is not adjacent to Duxford, so that some special arrangement would be necessary either to double the line between Bromley and Colchester or preferably to put Duxford onto the Bromley teleprinter."

Armed with these facts Dowding replied to Sholto Douglas on November 6:

"Dear Douglas, With reference to your letter dated November 3 on the subject of the 12 Group Wing. I agree that this operation is causing so much friction and ill feeling that I must withdraw the control of combined operations between the two Nos 11 and 12 Groups from the group commanders themselves and issue the orders through my own operations room.

At the same time, the story which Balfour has collected by his direct methods is wrong in its conclusions and in the facts on which these conclusions are based ... The Duxford Sector has certainly been stopped from using an unauthorised system which has caused confusion and inefficiency in the work of the Observer Corps. They have been using the inter-centre telling line to pass distant tracks between Bromley and Duxford, whereas it is required to pass adjacent tracks between Bromley and Colchester. 11 Group had nothing to do with putting a stop to this practice. It was done at the request of the Southern Area Observer Corps Commandant.†"

★Sholto Douglas was referring to progress with radar.

† Group Captain Courtney.

Unbeknown to Dowding events were moving to an inevitable conclusion with the air staff intent on removing both himself and Park. On November 25 Dowding turned over Fighter Command to the newly promoted Air Marshal, Sholto Douglas, while his friend Leigh-Mallory was given 11 Group. In the upshot it did not really matter whether Duxford obtained advanced warning from the Observer Corps or not. Leigh-Mallory took his "Balbo" to 11 Group, where it was found to be of little use in defence and highly expensive in offence. It was not until later in the war that proper wing tactics were worked out and successfully employed.

The departure of Dowding was a sad day for the Observer Corps. From 1936 onwards he had nursed and pushed the organisation, he understood exactly what the corps could and could not do and he was adamant in his refusal to allow anyone to interfere with its basic functions. That the thousands of shirt-sleeved observer volunteers were able to contribute so vitally to the air victory of 1940 was in large measure due to Dowding's respect for and understanding of their abilities and limitations. After seeing radar working, Winston Churchill referred to the corps as "Stone Age"; Dowding knew otherwise.

For months before stepping down from command Dowding had been wrestling with the all-important problem of air defence in darkness. While the Luftwaffe suffered severe losses by day, by night it could roam over Britain with virtual impunity. The night blitz had begun in earnest on September 7, when more than 240 bombers followed up the daylight raids on the East End. Thereafter cities and towns up and down the country suffered to a greater or lesser degree. Places as far apart as Southampton, Cardiff, Birmingham and Liverpool all took their punishment.

For eight months the battle raged until, in May 1941, the Luftflotten began to move eastwards for the assault on Russia. For the Observer Corps the blitz meant the spread of the air war across the whole country. No Group was immune from enemy aircraft and around the main targets the recorders' tracks nightly resembled a series of intricate overlapping spiders' webs.

By some miracle the Observer Corps casualties while on duty in the blitz were remarkably few. Shrapnel and incendiary bombs came down like rain, but there is no record of any observer quitting his post. An extraordinary form of concentration seemed to grip all those on duty. Perched high on an East End building an observer would pause in his reporting only long enough to kick a burning incendiary into the street below. At the centres they seemed totally oblivious of the holocaust outside, calmly plotting, telephoning and recording, while the glass in the windows shivered to a thousand fragments behind the black out screens. For post personnel it was agonising to watch the bombs coming down and fires burning in the area of their own homes, knowing there was nothing they could do until their hours of duty had finished. At centres the incident reports filtered through but no-one left his chair. It was often only in the cold light of the dawn that a worn-out plotter or post observer would wend his way through hosepipes, glass and debris to find his home reduced to a heap of rubble.

Some observers did die, but in general their names went unrecorded. Every so often in a post log it was noted that so-and-so had not reported for duty; normally punctilious, he lay beneath the ruins of a house. To the wardens and rescue teams tearing at the wreckage, his body was that of yet another civilian and his membership of the corps was of little consequence.

To the post observers the London and provincial bombings presented a vista never to be forgotten. They watched spellbound as all around Dante's inferno seemed to become reality. At one post the heat of the incendiaries melted the tar on the roof, while at K.1 post at the top of London University a high explosive bomb went right through the tower roof and wrecked the balcony below. Up to three days before the incident the balcony had been used as sleeping quarters.

One post, 17/J.1 Chigwell, was the unluckiest of all. At 10.30 p.m. on the night of April 19, 1941, observer Bivand knocked urgently on the door of his head observer, Mr H. Spurr. He explained that the public house opposite the post had been demolished and the post itself was badly damaged.

The two men groped their way through debris extending for a quarter of a mile and entered the telephone exchange on which the post was situated. Here let head observer Spurr's official report take up the tale:

"We went into every room, calling out to see if anyone had been left behind, and then made our way with great difficulty to the roof. The roof was strewn with masonry and we found the instrument, windbreak, etc, apparently intact, but the hut, wireless, etc, very badly knocked about. We found observers Bowley and Barton had been removed to Claybury Hospital; the former had a badly damaged face and eyes affected (these have recovered since).

I have heard that he has a fracture of the skull and also has had a lump of shrapnel removed from his thigh. He also had his false teeth smashed in his mouth and subsequently lost. His condition has improved since. Barton was apparently struck with a large lump of timber and has a bruised spine, but may leave hospital in a few days.

He was on the roof at the time and I have heard that Bowley had gone down to the door to answer the bell thinking it was his relief arriving. On opening the door he said, 'Good God it has not gone off' and slamming the door, was evidently blown along the passage with the blast and found lying there badly hurt with his bicycle on top of him. It transpired afterwards that it was a member of the Home Guard who rang the bell to enquire of the position of a bomb that had fallen just previously. The following members were killed:—G. Mackie, A. Nash, J. Pavitt and A. Cockle (an ex-member)★.

Nash has left a wife and two small boys. The other wives perished with them. On April 20 at 0600 hrs I returned to the Post and with the assistance of several members, removed all our property to the tank room below. The Post was out of action until 0600 hrs April 22 on account of line trouble. We have had trouble with the phones since but are now functioning satisfactorily. The steel surround is almost intact."

For the 19 Group, Bromley centre, the night raids went on with monotonous regularity. If it was not London, then enemy bombers were crossing the group on their way to the Midlands.

For instance, in the London attack of December 29, about 240 hostile raids were plotted on the table in $3\frac{3}{4}$ hr. As recorded in *Centre Crew*†:

★These men were killed having a quiet off-duty drink in the pub with their wives when the bomb exploded. Observer Bowley was too badly injured to return to the Corps, but Observer Barton served for the rest of the war.

†Privately published by the late Eric Wilton for the members of Bromley 'B' Crew.

"At the height of the raid the confusion of sound was so great that it became almost impossible to separate the tracks. Furthermore, owing to cable breakages communications between posts and centre were severely dislocated. By 8.30 p.m. 33 lines were out of action. Nevertheless 160 hostile tracks were duly and correctly told to Uxbridge and sectors."

The night of April 16/17, 1941, was however to remain imprinted on the minds of the Bromley crew on duty. Some 450 bombers raided London and the suburbs, dropping nearly 450 tons of high-explosive and 150 tons of incendiary bombs.

The Bromley centre was housed on the ground floor of a large building, Church House, in a prominent position on high ground. At 9.35 p.m. on April 16 a heavy bomb hit the parish church adjacent to the centre, wrecking it completely. Simultaneously a mass of incendiary bombs fell on Church House and nearby properties.

'F' Crew, under acting Duty Controller Mr D. W. Bowen, immediately put its fire squad into action and with the help of the Home Guard 16 incendiaries were extinguished or thrown out.

Soon afterwards the air conditioning plant began to blow smoke and it was found that one incendiary had lodged in the gutter and the fire was taking a hold. The old building was highly combustible and fire engines were unable to get through because of debris.

Within 20 minutes the whole roof was ablaze and it was clear that the structure would collapse. Bowen ordered his crew to leave in small groups each carrying as much equipment as possible. They ran through the gardens to the emergency centre 300 yards away in the old telephone exchange. There they set up shop and prepared to take over.

To avoid a break in reporting the remaining members continued plotting at Church House even though blinded by smoke and with lumps of the ceiling crashing down on the table.

Finally Bowen ordered complete evacuation and, as he walked through the front door, the roof and the upper floors collapsed in a blazing ruin. Despite the chaos and the bombs still falling 'F' Crew got 19 Group back on the air.

As Eric Wilton reported:

"Thanks to the devotion of the Duty Crew and the courage of their Controller, the lapse of time during which the raid went unplotted was only a matter of minutes. The back of the old telephone exchange, in which the Crew were now housed, was on fire. So was the Vicarage next door. A small party of volunteers tackled both these outbreaks, and shortly had them under control. By a quarter to eleven, when G-Crew took over, plotting and telling were proceeding smoothly on such lines as had not been destroyed by the fury of the flames and high explosive."

Several other centres were severely shaken by bombing, but none more than that of No 5 Group, Coventry. Between August and November 1940 Coventry centre had had a succession of near-misses and one direct hit which destroyed the rest room alongside. On the night of November 14/15 more than 500 tons of bombs were dropped following an initial wave of incendiary attacks which illuminated the area.

The 5 Group centre was in the middle of the city on the ground floor of the post office. Directly above the operations room was all the equipment of the main automatic telephone exchange. Miraculously, the post office was about the only building in the central area which did

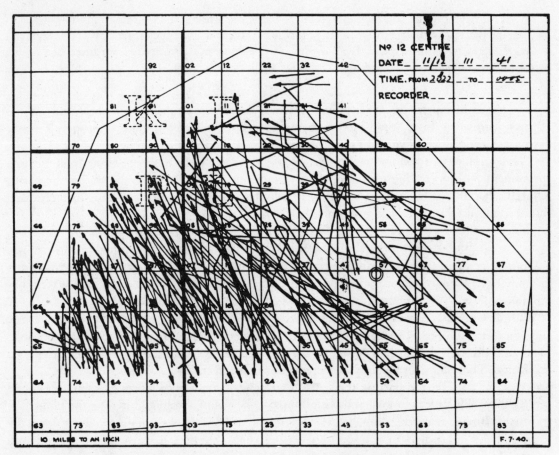

The recorder's sheet at Bedford Observer Centre for a 3hr 43min night period during one of the Coventry blitzes. All the tracks shown are hostile. The confusion created by large-scale night raids can be seen; this was only resolved by the creation of mass raid areas on the table

not receive a direct hit. The fires, however, were so close that fumes poured in through the air filters and the whole building rocked with successive explosions. Telephone lines began to go out one after another and then the lights failed. Candles were lit until the emergency power plant could be got going. Somehow relief men got through the raid and into the centre, but the original duty crew stuck to their posts right through the night. Subsequently the duty controller, Mr Alan Craig, was awarded the British Empire Medal.

Throughout the Battle of Britain and the night blitz there continued to be problems with the public warning system. In some cases sirens were sounded too late, while more often warnings were sounded over large areas where there was no direct attack imminent.

In the summer of 1940 Churchill complained that too much of the Government's time was being wasted in the air-raid shelters. As previously mentioned, the air-raid warning system was controlled from HQ Fighter Command, Stanmore. On the approach of an evening raid the air-raid warning officers on duty in the operations room there – using protractors marked out for different speeds of approach – would issue warnings to the telephone exchanges of the districts which looked as if they might be subjected to attack in about twenty minutes time.

When the sirens were sounded offices were cleared and most people went to the shelters. London was involved in many more alarms than anywhere else and this meant that work was seriously disrupted, often many times each day.

Churchill demanded a system that would produce a second warning when the attack was actually seen to be developing on London, as sometimes the raiders would change direction and no attack would in fact emerge after the sirens had sounded. A new plan known as the Government Subsidiary Air Raid Scheme was therefore evolved. Observer volunteers were called for from groups in Southern Area; initially "A" but later "B" men were employed. They came from posts in Nos 2, 3, 17, 18 and 19 groups. On September 6, 1940, the first party was installed in a makeshift post on the Air Ministry roof, Whitehall, with the aim of giving warning of the immediate approach of hostile aircraft. After a fortnight the observers were moved to permanent posts, one of which was above St James's Park Underground Station. The two posts were known as R.S.1 and R.S.11 and they were to perform invaluable work throughout the war. Several senior Service officers were concerned with the running of the scheme but one in particular, Admiral Legge, deserves mention.

When fully evolved the system worked as follows: a plotting map covering an area of over 15,500 sq miles was used to show enemy movements from the Isle of Wight to Dover in the south and south-east, to Southwold on the east coast, to Mildenhall in the north and to Northampton and Basingstoke in the north-west and west. Two- and four-figure map references and range and bearing plots were obtained from observer centres via two control points. Thus long-range warning was available and the observers knew in which direction to look. When it was certain that London was the target a red button was pressed which sounded alarm bells in the corridors of the House of Commons and in the main Government departments. Ultimately the R.S. posts were responsible for more than 400 buildings including Buckingham Palace over an area of 12 sq miles.

At the same time that the Government subsidiary scheme was being called for in London the question of special warnings to industry was being urgently studied. Millions of man-hours were being wasted because workers were expected to take shelter when the siren sounded even though, in many cases, no raid developed. Some factories, having no faith in public warnings, decided to have roof spotters or "Jim Crows" of their own and this practice was eventually to become nationwide. Official blessing for these spotters was given as early as August 1940. Every effort was made by the Ministry of Home Security to persuade workers to treat the public siren warning as an "alert" so as to allow the minimum dislocation to industrial production. Sanction for an alarm system was given by the War Cabinet on October 14, 1940.

Lord Beaverbrook, Minister of Aircraft Production, called an urgent meeting in the same month at which a variety of senior officials attended, including Observer Corps area commandants or their deputies. The meeting decided that the inner "alarm" message was to be relayed from observer centres and Beaverbrook produced a list of 20 key factories which had to be connected immediately. There ensued a long wrangle on pay, sick leave, hours of work, etc, which exasperated the Minister. After about an hour and a half of fruitless discussion Beaverbrook thumped the table and informed the assembled company that he wanted the inner alarm operating in the 20 factories at once – he did not mean tomorrow. He placed the list on the table and walked out.

On the following day the Scottish Area Commandant, Air Commodore Peel Ross, the

Attack Warning Red

Deputy Area Commandant, Colonel Patterson, and the Controller 38 Group, Aberdeen, Mr (later Sir) George Williamson, were talking over lunch about the new alarm system. The telephone rang; it was an urgent message from No 34 Group centre, Glasgow, saying that post office engineers had just installed an alarm bell to the Rolls-Royce factory at Hillington and what were they to do about it? A circular on the alarm system was sent out by Warrington-Morris in October and followed up in November by detailed instructions from the area headquarters. Alarm controllers and assistant controllers were appointed to Observer Corps group centres and the duties laid down were:

"That as far as possible, an 'alarm' message will be sent to selected factories and other organisations in time for 2min notice to be given to the employees of the approach of enemy aircraft; and that when the attack is over or the enemy aircraft have proceeded to such a distance that their return appears to be improbable a 'release' message will be sent. This is subject to the alarm controller being satisfied that no other enemy aircraft are within about 30 miles and proceeding in the general direction of the factory, etc, which has received the 'alarm' message."

The observer group which pioneered the "alarm" within the "alert" system was No 5 at Coventry. On October 18, 1940, Mr Garlick, the No 5 Group duty controller, received an important visitor – Lord Dudley, the Civil Defence Commissioner for Region 9, which comprised Warwickshire, Staffordshire, Shropshire, Herefordshire and Worcestershire. Lord Dudley had come straight from a Whitehall meeting concerning lost man-hours through air-raid alerts. He carried with him a list of key industrial sites in the Coventry area which required special warning and he wanted someone in No 5 Group to take on the task of organising the "alarm" system. Garlick proposed that a young observer in his mid-twenties, Mr C. J. Forsyth, should undertake the task. Forsyth initially demurred as he was awaiting call-up for the Royal Navy, but his objections were put aside and he was deferred for a period in order to undertake the "alarm" task. Forsyth was appointed regional alarm officer and was fully briefed at the Civil Defence war room of Region 9 at Civic House, Birmingham.

For the next 13 months he worked unceasingly, visiting factories and devising and perfecting a system of bell alarm messages and the training for them. Four observer groups had boundaries adjoining Birmingham (Coventry, Derby, Shrewsbury and Gloucester) and therefore a separate alarm centre was created for these at Civic House early in 1941. Teller lines were linked from group headquarters to the alarm centre, which greatly reduced the time lag in reporting and displaying raids. The local alarms to factories were initiated by centre alarm officers who, in effect, were the forerunners of the Home Office warning officers in the warning and monitoring organisation of the present day, where the Royal Observer Corps is still the field force.

A great deal of effort was necessary to make the "alarm" scheme work and it involved not only briefing the factories but training, organisation and the installation of special GPO circuits. Some factories received bell warnings only, while others also had a speech circuit available which carried a running commentary from the centre to the factory. In his progress report of January 6, 1941, Forsythe commented that:

"Although many schemes are nearing completion throughout the region, Coventry is the only one in operation at this date. Fourteen firms have been receiving alarm and release signals from October 18, 1940, and transmission has been on four separate telephones each connected to three or four factories and all having one common ring on each circuit."

Messrs Pattison and Hobourn Ltd later wrote in:

"Our factory has been running 24hr daily in two shifts, namely from 7.30 in the morning until 6.30 at night with a second shift commencing 7.00 at night and ending at 7.00 in the morning. The system was installed on January 22, 1941, and the number of hours lost through going to air-raid shelters since that date has been nil.

The fact that the alarm has been given to us by the Observer Corps has given the greatest confidence, not only to our 'spotters' but to the whole of our work people, who have the greatest faith in the system."

Forsythe wrote his last report for the month ended October 31, 1941, and by then he was able to state that the total number of schemes in the region was 31 and the total number of factories connected was 801. Despite requests that he continue being deferred, Mr Forsythe said his fare-wells in November 1941 and left to join the Royal Navy, in which Service he spent the rest of the war. He had made a major contribution to the war effort and to the part played in it by the Observer Corps.

Between July 1940 to the end of May 1941 great efforts were made to improve methods of reporting in the dark and in bad weather. Night-fighter radar (AI) in Blenheims in the Battle of Britain was rudimentary and no close control of night fighters existed, although some experiments were carried out with controllers installed at CH radar stations. All too few night raiders were shot down by fighters from September to December 1940.

It was only the advent of GCI (Ground Controlled Interception) radar which changed the picture and ultimately the whole pattern of night defence. With this equipment and its circular screen, or plan-position indicator, it was at last possible to guide intercepters to within AI range of the target. The first GCI was installed for trials at Durrington, Sussex, in October 1940, a further five were in position by Christmas 1940 and 12 were operating by the end of May 1941. The combination of GCI and the new AI Mk 4-equipped Beaufighter at last began to take a toll of the enemy, a total of 166 bombers being shot down by night fighters from March to May.

In the Observer Corps it was decided that a more accurate method of sound plotting would assist throughout the system. Instead of reporting just the square on the five-mile sound circle posts were instructed, late in 1940, to refer to the bearing of the sound and give an estimated height. Thus a post plot would read "plane heard three-thirty at ten thousand." There is no doubt that the new method gave more accurate results, but the plotting was still dependent on the hearing of the observer in question and the effects of the weather. That some success was achieved can be gathered from a circular to group officers and centre controllers in Southern Area issued on March 17, 1941, by Group Captain Courtney:

"I give below extract of a letter received from an RAF sector commander as it gives a guide as to the success of the sound-circle height system which both centres named have been using consistently for some time past.

'On the night of March 12, 1941, at 23.52, a Hurricane from this station intercepted an enemy bomber and was able to fire a two-second burst into it, owing to the excellent interpretation of height, i.e. 10,000ft, given by the Oxford Observer Corps. The aircraft was going south-east over Q.36 square.

Earlier the same evening an enemy aircraft was seen but lost again by another pilot, also at correct height, given by the same centre.

Last night, 13.3.41, while attempting interceptions the Watford centre were giving good heights also, as compared with those given by other means, and these heights – in one case in particular – changed frequently. We were, however, unlucky in the interception.

It has been found that when heights are used when the direction of the sound is at right angles to the track of the aircraft that plotters very soon learn to judge the proportionate distance by eye; and reference to, or the help of, the table supervisor (who in times of 'blitz' is extremely busy) is not necessary.

From experience gained with a number of observer groups in Southern Area who use the sound-circle height system it seems to be the simplest in operation and to have given the best results of the systems tried as this latest comment (given above) shows. I suggest therefore that it be adopted.' "

One other innovation was tried in an attempt to speed up the process of interception, namely the 'running commentary,' and in various forms it was to last until the end of the war. On January 8, 1941, the Observer Corps Commandant issued an instruction to all areas in which he outlined a procedure for post information on a raider to be relayed continuously to a defending fighter. The instruction laid down that at observer centres where there were liaison lines to RAF fighter sectors the duty controller, on seeing that friendly fighters were within ten miles of a raid, should say 'I have an urgent intercept commentary'. Referring to the raid as "bandit", he would then proceed to give relative positions, courses and heights of the fighter and the bandit (and alterations of course and height of the latter), plus area weather information and any anti-aircraft bursts near the enemy. An example of such a transmission would be:

"Fighters two miles south-west of raid 17, which is flying east. Fighter is 2,000ft above bandit – bandit has turned north-east climbing to 10,000ft – continuous cloud above bandit for which he is climbing – AA shells bursting one mile north of bandit."

The system was equally useful in cloudy weather in daylight as it was at night. A typical example of an actual commentary was contained in the Aberdeen centre logbook for the night of April 8/9, 1941:

"Last night we had a great success with the running commentary, and the fighter made contact in poorish moonlight and some cloud when the visibility was not more than a mile and a half and then only for silhouettes. The bandit was not definitely seen to fall into the sea but, as the pilot was exhausting his ammunition, a large portion of the plane flew off past the fighter pilot's windshield and the bandit took a lurch seawards. It was not possible to keep an accurate note of the messages sent by running commentary but two of them were as follows: 'bandit on same track going east', 'both planes same direction, same height, bandit just behind'. This was the last message given as the fighter swung round in a short circle and immediately made contact."

Another typical running commentary was one carried out in Midland Area in which only 29 minutes elapsed between a hostile plot appearing on the table and the enemy aircraft crashing, as shown on the accompanying map.

At 12 Group, Bedford, observer centre a Dornier track appeared on square L.59 at 12.01 going west; 3 minutes later the track of three Hurricanes appeared in square F.30 going south. At 12.08 the Dornier was on L.38 and the Hurricanes about seven miles away. The assistant controller realised the possibility of an interception and got on the liaison line via Duxford to Wittering and gave a running commentary on events to the sector station. At 12.10 the Dornier was on L.07 and the Hurricanes on L.06 about two miles apart, the fighters being ahead of the

3 Hurricanes
/12.04

| 90 | 00 | 10 | 20 | 30 | 40 | 50 | 60 |

K F
P L

KETTERING

| 99 | 09 | 19 | 29 | 39 | 49 | 59 | 69 |

One Dornier
12.01

12.08

HUNTINGDON ●

WELLINGBOROUGH

| 98 | 08 | 18 | 28 | 38 | 48 | 58 | 68 |

12.08
12.20
12.25

NORTHAMPTON

St NEOTS ●
Dornier shot down
12.30

| 97 | 07 | 17 | 27 | 37 | 47 | 57 | 67 |

L
OLNEY
12.25

12.10
12.10

TOWCESTER

BEDFORD ROC CENTRE

12.20

| 96 | 06 | 16 | 26 | 36 | 46 | 56 | 66 |

12.15
BANBURY
12.15
BIGGLESWADE ●

| 95 | 05 | 15 | 25 | 35 | 45 | 55 | 65 |

A typical wartime commentary by the ROC which led to the destruction of an enemy aircraft. By direct broadcasting from the Bedford ROC Centre three Hurricanes were vectored on to the track of a Dornier, and by being given various holding points, directions and heights they were able to shoot it down east of St Neots. The positions/times of both friendly and hostile tracks are shown

bomber. During the next 5 minutes both circled in L.06. At 12.15 the Dornier was in L.06 and the Hurricanes in P.96 about six miles ahead to the west. The Dornier turned east and then north-east, the Hurricanes did likewise and shot ahead. At 12.20 the Dornier was in L.26 and the Hurricanes in L.48, some 12 miles away. This was reported to Wittering and under instructions the Hurricanes circled in L.48 to permit the Dornier to catch up. At 12.25 the Dornier was in L.47 and the Hurricanes in L.58, distance now being reduced to about eight miles. The Hurricanes again circled in L.68 as they lay in wait for the unsuspecting Dornier which continued on its course. They spotted the bomber, dived to engage, and shot it down in flames at 12.30.

Chapter 10
WHAT IS IT ?

The Observer Corps had more than proved its worth in the defence of the nation and Whitehall decided that the time had come to review its status in the light of 16 months of war. Accordingly, in January 1941, the Committee on the Observer Corps was set up, being chaired by Harold Balfour, Under-Secretary of State for Air. One committee member was the Corps Commandant, Warrington-Morris, and evidence was heard from Air Commodore R. Peel Ross and Group Captain I. T. Courtney, Scottish and Southern Area Commandants respectively. As was fitting, the Joint Parliamentary Secretary to the Ministry of Home Security attended all the five meetings of the committee.

Of particular significance was the fact that the AOC-in-C Fighter Command, Air Marshal Sholto Douglas, was present for part of the first meeting. He said that in his opinion the corps had for several years played an important part in the air-defence organisation of the country, that it fulfilled such a rôle at the present time (1941) and that it would continue to do so in the foreseeable future, notwithstanding certain technical developments in the field of air defence which were within the committee's knowledge.★

As a result of what Sholto Douglas had to say the committee based its recommendations on the assumption that the Observer Corps, 'has come to stay."

The committee examined two key aspects of the Observer Corps, the first being status and the second a review of grievances which corps members had put forward in no uncertain fashion. Suggestions had been made that the corps should be converted into a Service organisation either as "part and parcel" of the Royal Air Force or as a military body on the Home Guard model. As recorded earlier, rifles had been issued to the corps after Dunkirk, when invasion was imminent, and doubts were subsequently expressed as to the legal status of the members bearing arms. The Judge Advocate General was consulted and he opined that members of the corps who bore arms would be entitled to the rights and privileges of armed forces under international law during such times as they fulfilled the following conditions:

a) They were commanded by a person responsible for his subordinates.
b) They wore a fixed distinctive sign, recognisable at a distance.
c) They carried arms openly.
d) They conducted their operations in accordance with the laws and customs of war.

He further gave his opinion that these conditions would be fulfilled in the case of members of

---

★Sholto Douglas was referring to progress with radar.

the corps. The committee pointed out that none of the above was to be confused with members' rights "as inhabitants of the territory not under occupation who, at the approach of the enemy, spontaneously take up arms to resist the invading troops without having had time to organise themselves", i.e. "levée en masse." Chapter 14, para 29, of *The Laws and Usages of War on Land* was cited as the source for this particular gem, which meant that the Observer Corps could have it both ways, either as a disciplined force in the general defence or as an undisciplined one rising spontaneously to the attack.

The committee decided that the corps should not be militarised as it would be "inappropriate and unnecessary and would cause serious administrative dislocation (which could not be faced in wartime) to convert into a disciplined military force a body of men composed predominantly of part-time workers which has always prided itself on its democratic character and the almost complete absence of rank distinctions in uniform and precedence." From that time on, whatever the changes in dress, ranks, etc, the corps has always been a civilian organisation administered by the Royal Air Force.

Nevertheless the committee felt that, in view of its long and valuable service, the corps should have a change of title and, if possible with the consent of the King George VI, it should have the prefix "Royal." The Parliamentary Secretary of the Ministry of Home Security stated that the grant of the prefix "Royal" would not give rise to embarrassing repercussions in the civil defence services, which were not employed by the crown and did not have the long period of service which distinguished the Observer Corps.

It is of interest to note that the committee thought that, although the Observer Corps had not been officially started as a separate body until 1925, the police observers of the First World War should be considered as part of the early stages of the corps and this was put forward as part of the argument for changing the title. As this went on record and was accepted, the Observer Corps actually predated its "mother" Service, the Royal Air Force, by about two years.

The question of the title Royal Air Force Observer Corps had been suggested by Dowding in a letter to the Under-Secretary of State for Air dated December 2, 1939. The reply from the Permanent Under-Secretary was amusing:

"The Director of Organisation thinks it not possible that members should be so described because they neither enlisted nor enrolled in the RAF. He puts forward the following alternative: that they should have the honour of the prefix 'Royal,' with their name changed to 'Royal Air Watchers.' It is a matter of taste but I think the name of 'Royal Air Watcher' horrible, quite apart from the fact that the abbreviation 'RAW' would be unfortunate.

My own view is that the organisation should continue to be known as the Observer Corps, that we should agree to their application to be called the Royal Air Force Observer Corps."

The Director of Organisation himself subsequently wrote to Dowding on February 2, 1940, saying that the title Royal Air Force Observer Corps could not be approved. He suggested the following titles:

"Air Watcher Service"
"Air Reporting Service"
"Air Raid Reporting Service."

With the momentous events of 1940 the subject was shelved until the Observer Corps put it forward again in earnest early in 1941. The Air Ministry approached Buckingham Palace and the following reply was received from Sir Alexander Harding, dated February 15, 1941:

> "I have submitted the matter informally to the King, whose views are as follows:
>
> His Majesty quite appreciates the grievance of this corps and would be prepared to give a title 'Royal' provided that this did not have a reaction amongst other civilian corps such as the coastguards or other civilian defence organisations such as the fire brigade.
>
> Moreover, as it is the responsibility of the Home Secretary to make recommendations to the King for the award of the title Royal to civilian organisations, it would be necessary for the application to be submitted through that channel; and it would be for the Home Secretary to ascertain from other Service departments and inform His Majesty how the grant of this privilege would be likely to affect any civilian corps that are auxiliary to them."

Back at the Air Ministry, Wing Commander Sir Lewis Greig referred the request to the Home Secretary, who replied saying that Harding's advice had been given "under a misapprehension" and that the application should go up through Air Ministry channels. While the rank and file of the Observer Corps were blissfully unaware of the honour being suggested, Sir Archibald Sinclair, the Secretary of State for Air, wrote to the First Sea Lord and the Secretary of State for War asking if they had any objections – they had none. It was not until April 5, 1941, however, that Sinclair received a letter from Buckingham Palace:

> "I am sorry there has been such a long delay since I wrote on March 13 about your submission for the grant of the title 'Royal' to the Observer Corps. As you know, the King thought that if this privilege were to be accorded to anyone then the Merchant Navy should have the priority, and for this reason gave instructions that this matter should be investigated before deciding about the Observer Corps.
>
> These enquiries have taken a little time and His Majesty has only just heard from the First Lord of the considerable difficulties which would arise in the case of the Merchant Navy. The King has therefore decided that the latter must wait, and as there is nothing now to stand in the way of the Observer Corps being granted the title 'Royal' His Majesty signed the submission which I return herewith."

In the House of Commons on April 9, 1941, Sir Adam Maitland in a "prepared" question asked the Secretary of State for Air whether he was aware of the opinion in some quarters that the importance of the work of the Observer Corps has not been sufficiently recognised; and whether he was able to inform the House of the results of his recent enquiries into general matters affecting the Observer Corps, and of any proposals of improvement it was intended should be made.

Sir Archibald Sinclair in reply, stated that:

> "I am happy to inform the House that, in recognition of the valuable services rendered by the Observer Corps over a number of years, His Majesty the King has been graciously pleased to approve that the corps shall henceforward be known by the style and description of 'The Royal Observer Corps.' I have recently had under review various questions relating to the status and conditions of service of the corps, and I have arranged to place in the library, for the convenience of members, a summary of conclusions on the main points of principle and detail, and of the action that has been taken or is in progress."

The word was flashed from headquarters to areas and groups and passed over the telephone lines to the posts along with a message of congratulation from Sinclair. Crews going off duty informed the next duty shift and thousands of pints and tots were downed in celebration.

Warrington-Morris said in his Circular No 43:

"I believe that it is almost unprecedented for the title of 'Royal' to be granted during a war and that an honour of this nature is usually withheld until the end of a war."

In his statement to the House of Commons, Archibald Sinclair referred to conditions of service in the Royal Observer Corps. This has been the second subject discussed by the 1941 Observer Corps Committee. As a result of its recommendations the Secretary of State made known certain decisions. A one-piece uniform was to be made available "which can be slipped over civilian clothes,"* while officers continued to wear RAF uniform with ROC insignia and cap badge. For ordinary members a Royal Observer Corps badge with an eagle and the royal crown was promulgated for wear on the coverall and storm coat left breast. This badge, commonly known as the soup plate, lasted through until the mid 1950s. It was promised that the formidable storm-proof coat, the "Zeekee", would eventually be issued on a personal basis while sou'westers, oilskins and gum boots could only be provided at the post sites.

Controllers and assistant controllers at centres were given officer status, officers on duty were allowed first-class instead of third-class travel and observers were allotted the sum of 1d a mile for their cars if they lived more than two miles from their place of duty. Belatedly, members of the corps were to be exempt from fire-watching duties, a point which had caused extreme annoyance among those who were putting in very long hours of observer duty after their normal work had finished.

Finally, it was agreed that liaison between the corps and RAF units should be strengthened and that "The Royal Observer Corps Club" should be given official recognition and a measure of financial support. The emergence of the club was one of those remarkable achievements of Britain in wartime.

As recorded earlier, aircraft recognition was a totally neglected subject in the British Services in the inter-war years – indeed it was considered to be only a pastime for small boys and those grown-ups who had a train- or car-spotting mentality. An attempt was made from 1935 onwards to produce a standard book of aircraft silhouettes, namely Air Publication 1480. This, however, was a laughable affair with black-and-white drawings of extraordinary inaccuracy and very bad draughtsmanship. When war broke out there was no requirement for observers to differentiate between particular types, which could have proved fatal under operational conditions. There were no recognition tests or standards and no training.

On October 19, 1939, for instance, 12/L.3 post recorded in its logbook:

"The HEINKEL 111K BOMBER
This machine has the undermentioned characteristics, which will help to identify it.
1) There are six stubby exhaust ports protruding from *each* side of *each* engine.
2) A machine gun is carried in a 'box' which protrudes below the wings."

Many personnel in the corps, however, felt that, despite the total lack of official interest, they must solve the recognition problem. They bought technical journals like *The Aeroplane* and

*This so-called uniform or "coverall" was of little use and it was eventually superseded by RAF blue battle-dress with ROC buttons, etc.

Flight, collected cigarette cards and cut out every aircraft picture that appeared in newspapers and magazines. Their enthusiasm was generated by the urge to fulfil the observer task efficiently, regardless of official inertia.

Towards the end of 1939 a handful of observers in the Guildford, Surrey, area decided that they ought to get together to try to solve the problem. They called a meeting at the Corona Cafe, High Street, Guildford, and invited Mr (now Sir) Peter Masefield, technical editor of *The Aeroplane*, to give a lecture on "The Recognition of Aircraft." In the chair was Mr James H. Lowings, and 40 members attended. The whole thing was a resounding success and it was decided to form the "Hearkers' Club" to continue the good work. The chairman offered a pair of Hearkers' cufflinks and a silver spoon as prizes in a first-ever recognition competition based on 34 6in by 6in photographs. On this occasion the average score was seven, but one member actually got 28 right out of 34. The enthusiasts at Guildford published six issues of the *Hearkers' Bulletin* in 1940, and as later recorded:

"It was produced at no expense to anyone except the printer, who had the doubtful privilege of doing post duty with the editor (J. Lowings) . . . Its circulation was limited – not, however, by the paper controller but by the extent of the aforementioned printer's suitable offcuts."

Left The notice of a meeting at Guildford in 1939 which saw the beginning of the Hearkers' Club, branches of which were ultimately to spread the length and breadth of the country. Until 1942 the Hearkers' Club (later the Royal Observer Corps Club) pioneered aircraft-recognition training in Britain Right An early Hearkers' Club certificate for the third grade in aircraft recognition, awarded to F. W. Bennelick of the Crowthorne post in December 1940

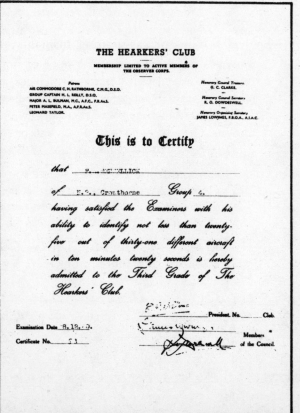

'From monthly meetings the club progressed to weekly get-togethers under the title of the "Hearkers' Club School of Instruction." Its fame spread abroad and more and more observers flocked in to go through elementary, intermediate and advanced stages with their associated recognition tests. Middle-aged men with no previous aviation knowledge began to argue with authority about dihedral, low and high wings and radial versus in-line engines.

The venue – the works of the same long-suffering printer – became overcrowded and the club managed to obtain free accommodation at Guildford Technical College. Masefield gave the club a full page write-up in *The Aeroplane*, saying that the Hearkers had all the answers on "What is it?" The result was overwhelming, with letters pouring in from all over the world. A second Hearkers' Club was formed at Shirley, Surrey, and this was followed by club No 3, Hendon; No 4, Liverpool; No 5, Evesham; No 6, Crowthorne; No 7, Southend; and No 8, Angus.

The climax of the year 1940 came with an examination for all-comers held on November 30. Masefield conducted the test, which was a great success. Mr D. Jenkins, a member from one of the centres, gained 100 per cent in the third- and second-grade tests and 124 out of 125 in the first grade. He was obviously the first master of the recognition art.

The original Guildford enthusiasts, short of money and time, found themselves inundated with new branches. They turned to the commandant of the corps for help. A deputation, headed by Lowings, went to see the commandant and the deputy commandant, Air Commodore H. Le M. Brock. As a result the Hearkers' Club became official in January 1941 and was renamed the Observer Corps Club (from April 1941 the Royal Observer Corps Club). The Treasury made a grant of £352 for administration and the purchase of slides while the honorary organising secretary, Lowings, and later his deputy were made part-time assistant observer group officers. The commandant became president general, the deputy commandant was the chairman and the vice-presidents were the six area commandants. The Air Ministry allowed a petrol grant for all observers to attend one branch meeting per month.

Another private venture event of significance took place on January 2, 1941, when the first edition of *The Aeroplane Spotter* was published by Temple Press. Edited by Peter Masefield, the *Spotter* was an eight-pager printed on newsprint. Apart from a mass of recognition and general aviation material, the *Spotter* carried reports of the Hearkers Club/Observer Corps Club branch meetings. *The Aeroplane Spotter* was to continue until 1948 and it undoubtedly made a major contribution to the war effort.

The Aeroplane Spotter commented on the Observer Corps Club in its issue of February 6, 1941: "Thus had private initiative led the way and demonstrated how the sadly neglected study of aircraft recognition should have been organised from the start. The standard laid down as a minimum required for any efficient observer and embodied in the third-grade test of the club is likely to become the acknowledged basis for all spotters throughout the country."

In the same week another organisation was formed, based on the idea of the Observer Corps Club. To be known as the National Association of Spotters' Clubs, it was to bring together all those outside the Observer Corps who were anxious to study the vexed subject of recognition. They included industrial raid spotters, Air Training Corps units, schools and many other interested groups. Corps members assisted in its formation and many also joined the spotters' clubs.

The Royal Observer Corps Club, meanwhile, was going from strength to strength in 1941,

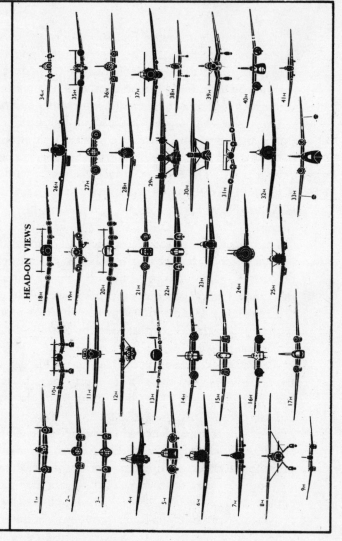

2ND SHEET

THE
ROYAL OBSERVER CORPS CLUB

Silhouettes of British, American, German and Italian
Aircraft listed for the Second Grade Test
of the Royal Observer Corps Club

(*as amended and approved by the General Council of
the Royal Observer Corps Club, May 1941*)

This folder in conjunction with the one recently issued
for the Third Grade, contains every silhouette
required for the Royal Observer Corps
Club Second Grade Test

The General Council of the Royal Observer Corps
Club acknowledge their indebtedness to the Air
Ministry and the Editor of "The Aeroplane" for
permission to use these silhouettes

This folder is printed and published on behalf of the Royal Observer Corps
Club by T & T. Ltd., Leeds, and must not be reproduced

HEAD-ON VIEWS

*Pages from the silhouette folder for the second-grade test of the Royal Observer Corps Club in 1941.
Club methods of recognition training and testing were adopted by all three Services*

organising new branches, conducting graded recognition tests and producing silhouette leaflets
and cards for them. At its peak in late 1942 the ROCC had no fewer than 191 branches from
Lands End to John O'Groats. It had issued about 250,000 silhouette test folders and its members
were lecturing to the three Services, the ATC, the Home Guard and hundreds of spotters'
clubs.

In September 1941 the ROCC began a most ambitious project, the launching of its own maga-
zine, the *Journal of the Royal Observer Corps Club*. A top-grade production, on high-quality art
paper, the *Journal* was a sell-out and production could hardly keep pace with demand. Produced
by amateurs, the publication was again in great demand by organisations outside the corps
and copies found their way to many parts of the world. Where good photographs were lacking
Mr W. G. Woodason and others made highly accurate models and these were photographed
by Mr K. H. Gaseltine of Messrs Ilford Ltd, who served on post 17/D.3. The results were so

good that it was often extremely difficult to tell which was a model and which the real thing. Complex recognition tests were published in the *Journal*, and in fact all the methods employed by the ROC were later adopted by the Services. For test folders, cards and the *Journal* only the most accurate silhouettes were chosen, being a mixture of official drawings produced for AP1480 and those supplied by the *The Aeroplane*.

After 1940 a real effort was made to improve the standard of basic aircraft silhouettes for recognition purposes and qualified draughtsmen/artists began to turn out illustrations accurate in shape and with the correct amount of detail. Every post and centre was supplied with copies of the various editions of 1480, for which there was a continuous flow of amendment sheets. The corps was also issued with AP1480X, an extraordinary manual which was designed to show silhouettes of British prototypes, experimental aircraft and special modifications. In fact many unusual aircraft were omitted from AP1480X while others, such as the long-span Typhoon, were included but never left the drawing board. Before the war the Xs were described as "Miles Experimental" or "Martin Baker Experimental," but with the advent of war this system was changed to numbers from 100 onwards. Thus Experimental 100 was the Fairey Barracuda prototype and 175 was the Twin Hotspur glider. The numbers were quoted in Fighter Command operational messages to the corps and posts were warned to be on the lookout for experimental aircraft number so-and-so to be flying in a certain area with particular markings. Typical examples were:

An early experimental silhouette from AP.1480, showing the Martin-Baker MB.2 prototype. No experimental number was allocated

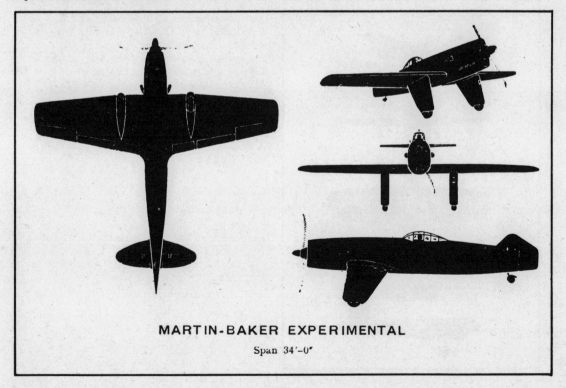

MARTIN-BAKER EXPERIMENTAL

Span 34′-0″

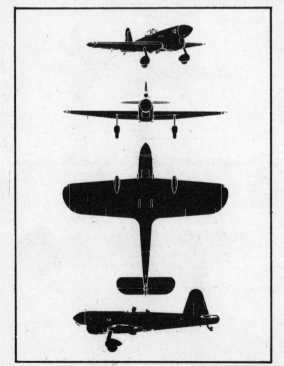

Three silhouettes from Air Publication 1480X. Top left: Experimental 127, the Boulton Paul P.92/2 flying scale model for a four-cannon turret fighter; Top right: Experimental 120, the Martin-Baker MB.3 six-cannon Sabre-powered fighter; Bottom: Experimental 138, the Miles M.20 Merlin-powered wooden fighter prototype

"27.9.41   Experimental aircraft No 112 will be flying with effect from November 10, 1941. Prototype camouflage, colouring and marking. Silhouette contained in AL 25 to AP1480A.

12.11.41   Experimental aircraft No 154 without escort will be flying with effect from November 10, 1941. Prototype markings. Silhouette in AL X3 to 1480."

Experimental No 112 was the Airspeed AS.45 Cambridge – a Mercury-powered advanced trainer – while Experimental No 154 was the Centaurus radial-powered Hawker Tornado, serialled HG641.

Changes of markings and shape were also signalled to centres and posts in the area in which they might be operating, thus:

"8.4.41   From April 15 all operational fighters will have their under surface painted duck-egg blue instead of black and blue. Red, white and blue roundels retained.

7.9.41   Whirlwind aircraft. These aircraft will carry additional markings: a yellow strip on the leading edge from the outer edge of the engine cowling to the wing tip, 5in in width. Two-and-a-half inches wide on either side of the centre line of the wing.

2.11.41   Modified Harrow aircraft with streamlined nose and tail instead of turrets. Centre turrets removed and a row of windows down fuselage side. Now flying in Doncaster area. These aircraft are Army Co-operation Command.

7.11.41   Vickers Wellington Mk VI is now flying. Silhouettes for Mk V, but with Merlin engines. Aircraft bears prototype camouflage, colouring and markings.

8.8.41   Fighter Group headquarters report one Boeing 247D will be flown at some future date from Speke to Boscombe Down. It will be accompanied by one Hudson. The aircraft is the only one of its kind. Painted standard aircraft communication colouring.

19.11.41   Message from Northern Area ROC, RAF station Catterick, Yorkshire. 17.11.41:
In order to enable troops to distinguish between friendly aircraft and aircraft representing the enemy during exercises, a special system of aircraft markings has been introduced.
(a) All aircraft in squadrons working with the 'Enemy' are to have the under surface of the port mainplane painted with 'Siscoline' black distemper, which is to be removed at the conclusion of each exercise.
(b) All aircraft, whether friendly or 'enemy', are to have the aircraft letter painted as large as possible in black in the centre of the under surface of the starboard mainplane.
This marking is to remain until Alert 2 comes into force, when it is to be removed and all aircraft are to revert to standard operational markings."

Many unusual aircraft hove into observers' view during 1941. Manchester, Stirling and Halifax bombers were coming into service in increasing numbers, the Beaufighter was replacing the Blenheim as the standard AI night fighter and cannon-armed Spitfire Vs and Hurricane IICs were taking over from the earlier machine-gun-armed variants. A variety of new American aircraft began to be seen regularly, including the B–17C Fortress 1, the Boston and Havoc, the Tomahawk and even the ill-fated Bell Airacobra. The arrival of Rudolf Hess in May 1941 has been described in the prologue and confirmed that the corps had to be on the look out for, and be able to identify, a great many types in any part of the country.

Other special arrivals in 1941 were more friendly than Hess. On May 5 two Dutchmen took off from Schiphol in a twin-boom Fokker G.1 fighter. Instead of ferrying their charge to Germany they flew to Britain and landed in Suffolk, much to the surprise of the members of the Colchester observer group. The G.1 was subsequently transferred to the Royal Aircraft Establishment, Farnborough, and the Colchester log recorded on May 7:

> "From Uxbridge – F16 one Fokker with C1 one Blenheim escort, ETA Southwold 1630 – ETA Farnborough 1730 via Hatfield and Maidstone. The Fokker aircraft has two engines, is a low-wing monoplane with two tail booms running back from the engines. Fuselage short, running back from trailing edge of wings. Roundels on side, probably yellow."

The second unexpected visitor came in July in the shape of a Belgian SV.4 biplane. The SV.4 involved two Belgian Air Force pilots, Michel Donnet and Léon Divoy, who were determined to continue the fight from Britain. They discovered the SV.4, OO-ATD, covered in dust and without instruments, in a small hangar near a chateau occupied by the Germans. They lashed up basic instruments and purchased black-market petrol originally intended for a Stuka unit. Armed with a Shell company air map they managed, miraculously, to get airborne and at 05.20 on the morning of July 5, 1941, they landed in a field at Thorpe-le-Soken, Essex.

Michel "Mike" Donnet was to have a distinguished career in the RAF, rising to command a Mustang wing in 1944. In the post-war Belgian Air Force he eventually became Lieutenant Général Aviateur Baron Donnet and at the time of writing he is the Belgian representative on the Nato Military Standing Group. Until 1973 Général Donnet was under the impression that his flight to fortress Britain went completely unobserved. The author decided to check such records as existed and discovered that in fact the Royal Observer Corps has seen and reported the aircraft. The Colchester logbooks recorded the incident as follows:

> "B.2 Watch 5.7.41
>
> 05.16   Sound reading M6939. Biplane with a sweep of the wing, not known. 'Raid C.1.'
> 05.29   To Uxbridge. Raid C.1 faded out in 6343.
> 09.45   Message from Mistley ARP control.
>   A plane, evidently C.1 (see message 05.29), is down in Thorpe Sand Pits. A crew of two Belgians are at Thorpe police station, having flown from Brussels. Plane is fairly intact. One mile SSE of Thorpe Church.
> 10.10   We rang Mistley and Thorpe police for news of the Belgian plane and they reported as follows: 'Belgian biplane SV similar to Gipsy Moth. Crew of two, flight sergeant and flying officer of late Belgian Air Force – Plane undamaged – left Brussels at 02.30 hours today – landed at Rose Farm, Thorpe, at 05.30 today – Compass and altimeter only instruments used in the flight – all others had been removed by the Germans. One of the crew speaks English.' "

The SV.4 had passed between Posts 18/D.1, Walton, and 18/D.3, Little Holland, and it landed some two miles south-east of 18/D.2, Tendring. Further messages were sent about this strange happening and on July 6 Debden signalled to ROC Colchester: "Belgian biplane will fly from Thorpe to Martlesham between 18.00 and 19.00hr tonight." The SV.4 was pressed into RAF service as MX457, survived the war and now rests in the Musée de l'Armée et d'Historie Militaire in Brussels.

The Services themselves gradually began to adopt the recognition ideas and techniques of the Royal Observer Corps Club and incorporated them into their own training schedules. The Army was the first to realise the life-and-death importance of knowing "What is it?" and the Anti-Aircraft Command Recognition School was set up by a few enthusiasts at Biggin Hill early in 1940. This became the War Office School of Recognition, first at Withyham, Kent, then in 1942 at Albury, Herts, and later at Deepcut, Hampshire.

The Royal Air Force was slower to react to the problem of recognition, despite many tragic results of faulty identification, and the Aircraft Recognition Wing at No 1 Ground Gunnery School was not started until 1941, at Ronaldsway, Isle of Man. Renamed the Central School of Aircraft Recognition in 1942, it was moved first to Eastbourne and later to Southport and Sutton-on-Hull. One of the best known aviation cartoonists, E. A. (Chris) Wren, became an instructor at CSAR and his "Oddentification" drawings and rhymes were known throughout the Royal Observer Corps and the Services.

To the Royal Navy, however, went the booby prize. For some reason it took their Lordships at the Admiralty longer than anyone else to realise the crying need for proper aircraft recognition training – probably only as long as it took the RAF to recognise ships. Naval gunners happily fired at friend and foe alike, from RAF Boston bombers at Dieppe to their own Swordfish trying to land on a carrier. The Royal Navy was only outshone by the US Navy and US merchant marine where anything with wings had to be hostile; the Royal Observer Corps was later to lend a hand in putting that particular problem to rights.

By May 1941 a final warning drill was worked out for invasion, the possibility of which had again reared its ugly head. In Fighter Command operational instruction No 79/1941, dated May 5, 1941, it was laid down that:

a) The ROC post reported to the ROC operations room:
   (i) The landing of troop carriers,
   (ii) The landing of gliders,
   (iii) The landing of more than six parachutists (six or less, possibly being a friendly crew).
b) The ROC duty controller reported the event to:
   (i) The ROCLO at the associated RAF group and sector,
   (ii) The chief constable of the district concerned,
   (iii) The local Army command headquarters.
c) ROC posts were equipped with pyrotechnic signals:
   (i) A red flare emitting red stars="I have sighted enemy forces on land."
   (ii) A green flare emitting green stars="I have sighted enemy invading forces on the sea."

These orders remained in force until December 1944.

The Observer Corps' contribution to the war effort was not limited to its efforts on duty.

While the Battle of Britain was at its height, in August 1940, Warrington-Morris announced the opening of a fund to buy a Spitfire. Many fighters and bombers were subscribed for by institutions of all kinds and carried a wide variety of names into the air. The going price for a Spitfire, laid down by Lord Beaverbrook's Ministry of Aircraft Production, was £5,000. This was a tall order for those times, considering how poorly paid observers were, but the commandant opened a trust fund with a London bank and waited to see what would happen.

Almost immediately money began to roll in, £20 from one post and £25.15.0 from another. One observer raised £8 by selling verses on different types of aircraft, while another made £11 by charging visitors to look at a bomb crater near his post. By early November £9,350 had been collected and the fund was kept open so that a second aircraft could be purchased. The first contribution of £5,000 was sent to Beaverbrook by Warrington-Morris on November 8, 1940. Beaverbrook replied:

"Will you please convey to members of the Observer Corps this expression of the intense gratitude with which I received from them a gift to provide a Spitfire for the Royal Air Force.

The vigilance which they maintain by day and night is a service essential to the security of our country. It supplements the ceaseless watch kept by the RAF in the skies. It will assuredly have its place in the epic of Britain's defence.

To that debt which the nation already owes them they now add a generosity which must arouse the admiration of us all."

The first Spitfire bearing the words "Observer Corps" and the corps crest, serialled P7666, was delivered to No 41 Squadron at Hornchurch in November 1940 and was flown by Squadron Leader D. O. Finlay, the Olympic hurdler. The Squadron code letters allocated to the aircraft were EB-Z. On his first sortie in this Spitfire on November 25 Finlay shot down an Me109 at 20,000ft over the coast but suffered "a fair amount of damage." A new tail unit and wingtip were fitted and on November 27 Finlay, in EB-Z, scored another Me109 over the sea off Dover. The RAF signalled to the corps:

"Your Spitfire presented to the nation and flown by the officer commanding No 41 Squadron destroyed its second Me109 today. That is two Huns in consecutive engagements. Got any more like this one?"

EB-Z, with other pilots at the controls, flew many patrols in December 1940. While on his third sortie in the aircraft Finlay shared another Me109. In January 1941 Warrington-Morris sent a further cheque to Beaverbrook for £5,000. It was decided to re-christen EB-Z "Observer Corps Spitfire 1" and call the second machine, allocated to 616 Squadron, "Observer Corps Spitfire 2." By February 1941 Spitfire 2 was at Tangmere. The serial is unknown but the unit code was YQ–. In the same month Observer Corps Spitfire 1 was transferred, at Hornchurch, to 54 Squadron and re-lettered KL-Z. Shortly afterwards the pilot, while on patrol over France, was attacked by an Me109 and dived from 20,000ft. He pulled out over the sea but the 109 went straight on into the water.

On April 20, 1941, Spitfire 1 was attacked from behind by 109s and shot down. The pilot baled out and was picked up by the air-sea rescue service. Both aircraft in the meanwhile had been re-christened "Royal."

In late June 1941 Squadron Leader Burton, commanding 616 Squadron, informed the Corps that Spitfire 2 had been on offensive sweeps, had sustained slight damage and had one Me109 to its credit. This was followed early in July by a second Me109. Finally in mid-July during a sweep off France the aircraft was badly shot up, crash-landed in England and was written off. The two Spitfires bearing the Royal Observer Corps crest had accounted for a total of six Me109s and one probable – a brief but glorious history.

While paying for two Spitfires members had also considered the questions of hardship, sickness and even dependent relatives within the corps itself. On June 12, 1941, therefore, a charity known as the Royal Observer Corps Benevolent Fund was registered under the War Charities Act, 1940. Trusts were set up and in 1942 the name was changed to the ROC War Fund. In late 1945 a new declaration of trust was made, the original name was reinstated and administration for the ROC Benevolent Fund was undertaken by the RAF Benevolent Fund, as it still is. The trustees remain the corps commandant and the area commandants.

Chapter 11
RE-ORGANISATION

From the end of May 1941 the German air onslaught on Britain had slackened as the bulk of the Luftwaffe was switched to the east. This did not mean, however, that air activity abruptly ceased. Raiding continued intermittently throughout the year, but with a different pattern. Small numbers of aircraft attacked, often with large bombs, and attempted to concentrate their efforts. On July 8/9 London, Birmingham, Yarmouth, Plymouth, Hull, Tyneside, Newcastle and South Shields were among the cities visited by night; and on September 1/2 a force of fewer than 30 German bombers destroyed 100 houses and caused 121 deaths or serious injuries in Newcastle.

The scale of enemy effort declined from an average of 74 sorties a day in the month of May to 21 sorties a day in July. During the last half of the year the average was down to ten or 12 reconnaissance sorties, one or two being over land and the remainder over shipping, while there were occasional long-range bomber attacks on shipping and local targets.

In the south there was a steady increase in RAF offensive sweeps over France with fighters and light bombers, plus incursions by German fighters and fighter-bombers. To the north the build-up of the RAF was taking place, with continuous training going on.

Where enemy raids were concerned, both inland and at low altitude in coastal areas, it had become evident that closer collaboration was necessary between the RAF and the ROC. Fighter positions were plotted at sector using "Pip-Squeak" automatic direction-finding, while German aircraft were plotted from ROC centre reports. There was inevitably a time lag and the situation was not improved by ROC difficulties with height estimation in poor weather.

One event within the Royal Observer Corps in 1941 was to have lasting significance, namely the admission of women to its ranks. The manpower situation had already become acute and deferment of many men, due to enrol in the Services, could not be delayed. The Manpower Committee continuously reviewed the situation, but it was made clear that ROC members aged 35-40 and in unreserved occupations could not expect deferment beyond October 31, 1941. It was apparent that the Corps would eventually have to rely on: Class A observers (full-time), Class B (part-time), observers in reserved occupations, Class B observers unfit for military service, Class B observers over military age not required for National Service in vital war production industries, and finally women Class A and B.

In July 1941 authority was given for women to be enrolled. There is no note of who was the first women to join, but a trickle of female volunteers began in the late summer and was to become a steady stream for the rest of the war. One of the first to apply in July 1941 was Mrs Mary Breese, the widow of Air Vice-Marshal Breese who had been killed on active service in March of the same year. One of her sons, Flight Lieutenant Breese, had been shot down over Germany and was a POW, while her other son was posted missing while piloting a flying boat over the Atlantic.

One who was to give exemplary service was chief woman observer Flora MacDonald, descendant of the heroine of the same name. She became the controller at the smallest observer group in Britain, No 40, formed in 1941 at Portree on the Isle of Skye. There were only five posts, plus a handful of coastguard watcher posts and a wireless observer unit. The centre was located in the Skye Gathering Hall, Portree. Chief woman observer MacDonald was later awarded the British Empire Medal and she married the 40 Group observer group observer, later group commandant, Observer Lieutenant D. A. Donald.

The influx of women into every section of the war effort went far beyond the mere recruiting of women observers. 1/T.3 post, long used to having daily meditations on a pail in the field, reported in the suggestion book in May 1941:

"Reference: decency, married men, person, care of. These days we have a number of female workers in the adjoining fields and suggest that it would be more decent if a simple screen were erected round the bucket."

The initial shock of women members within the ROC, this hitherto all-male preserve, can hardly be imagined. Dirty stories and bad language had to be curbed, manners improved and some effort made to provide suitable lavatories and washing facilities. The first inroads were into centres, and many posts were highly intrigued to hear for the first time dulcet female tones at the other end of the line. On record is the experience of one post observer who was chatting in the small hours to a woman plotter with a particularly seductive voice. They discussed the films currently showing at the local town and he was clearly about to ask her out when she remarked: "That is a lovely film, I took my little grandson to see it this afternoon."

Entry of women on to posts proved slower and more difficult because of the tough outdoor conditions. In addition they had to contend with small close-knit bands of men who felt that the ROC should remain a strictly all-male world. Through sheer tenacity and ability the ladies won through. They proved that they could undertake any of the tasks required of them equally as well as men and could "rough it" with the best. Without women observers the corps could well have collapsed in the later stages of the war as male recruiting became progressively more difficult. From the end of 1941 to the present day the ROC has been a service for both sexes and no-one can now think of it otherwise. It is, however, to the lasting credit of the corps that it was one of the first uniformed organisations to accept women as complete equals. From the outset they had the same rights and status and could, on merit, be promoted to positions with the same titles as men.

One other group of people also wore ROC armbands and later uniform but, remarkably, they never served in the corps. Scattered over the country were some 1,350 elderly or reserved-occupation men who formed a highly secret and, to this day, almost unknown organisation called the Radio Security Service, or RSS.* It was their job to maintain a radio listening watch for a variety of signals emanating from occupied Europe and even Germany, including those of British secret agents. The coded messages were despatched to a post office box number

---

*One of the first public references to RSS was made in a GPO hand-out issued in Reading in 1968.

in Barnet. The members of RSS operated in nine separate regions, each one in charge of a captain, Royal Corps of Signals. The majority were unpaid and were expected to do 48hr duty a month; in fact some did as many as 200hr.

There was general unease among RSS members because neighbours and others were asking "an increasing number of derogatory and embarrassing questions concerning their apparent non-contribution to the war effort." Also some faced possible call-up but could not reveal the nature of their work. Deep in the recesses of Whitehall the suggestion was made that RSS members might be incorporated into the ROC as a suitable "cover." Accordingly a meeting was convened at the Air Ministry on September 22, 1941; it was attended by, among others, the Deputy Chief of the Air Staff, Air Vice-Marshal N. H. Bottomley; the Deputy Director of Intelligence (S), Group Captain Plant; the head of RSS, Lieutenant Colonel Maltby; and the ROC Commandant, Air Commodore Warrington-Morris. It was agreed that RSS members should be brought on to the nominal rolls of local ROC formations as "special observers." Until new ROC uniforms were available an ROC armlet, beret and badge were to be issued to each RSS member not covered by such a body as, say, the Home Guard.

One beautiful gaffe resulted from this apparently foolproof arrangement. RSS members in Northern Ireland went about saying that they were in the ROC, as instructed, which provoked a lot of curiosity and questioning. This was hardly surprising as no ROC organisation existed in Northern Ireland during the war and the RSS personnel looking for anonymity found themselves sticking out like sore thumbs. The final solution arrived at was for RSS members to tell any nosey-parkers that "we are engaged in secret radio-location work."* This seemed to

---

*Even ROC area commandants were sold the radio-location story and Warrington-Morris remained the only one who knew the facts.

The ROC was able to provide a vital back-up throughout the war for No 80 Wing, the RAF's radio-countermeasures organisation. A typical joint effort occurred on the night of October 21, 1941, when one of the then new Dornier 217s became lost near Pembroke. It was plotted, initially by radar and then by the ROC, as it wandered from west to east across southern England. By reradiating German beacon signals 80 Wing "Meacon" stations were able to convince the German pilot that he was over northern France. When the aircraft finally ran out of fuel it crash-landed at Lydd in Kent; the RAF obtained not only a complete Do217 but also a working model of a new Knickebein bombing-aid receiver. The map shows the Do217's track, the Meacons and their effect and the ROC groups over which the aircraft passed

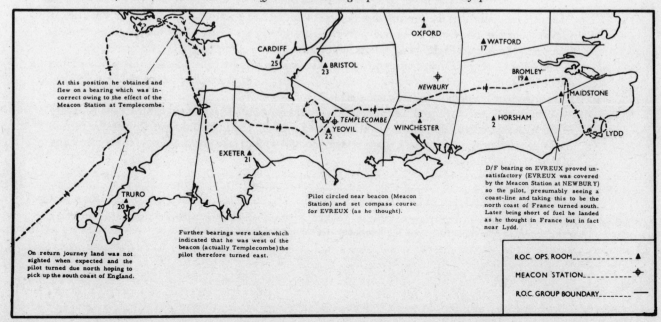

At this position he obtained and flew on a bearing which was incorrect owing to the effect of the Meacon Station at Templecombe.

Pilot circled near beacon (Meacon Station) and set compass course for EVREUX (as he thought).

Further bearings were taken which indicated that he was west of the beacon (actually Templecombe) the pilot therefore turned east.

On return journey land was not sighted when expected and the pilot turned due north hoping to pick up the south coast of England.

D/F bearing on EVREUX proved unsatisfactory (EVREUX was covered by the Meacon Station at NEWBURY) so the pilot, presumably seeing a coast-line and taking this to be the north coast of France turned south. Later being short of fuel he landed as he thought in France but in fact near Lydd.

OXFORD
WATFORD 17
CARDIFF 25
BRISTOL 23
BROMLEY 19
NEWBURY
MAIDSTONE
TEMPLECOMBE
WINCHESTER 3
HORSHAM 2
YEOVIL 22
LYDD
EXETER 21
TRURO 20

R.O.C. OPS. ROOM _____ ▲

MEACON STATION _____ ⊕

R.O.C. GROUP BOUNDARY _____ ▬

work and the real Royal Observer Corps carried on, blissfully ignorant of the existence of its secret shadow.

As 1941 progressed the diminution in air activity and improvements in radar cover inevitably led to calls for reductions in the Royal Observer Corps from a number of Government departments short of manpower. These were combined with growing dissatisfaction in the corps over anomalies within the organisation, and suggestions by the Army that searchlight units might be able to undertake the observer task. New main and emergency centres were urgently needed for the corps, with standardised layout and improved facilities, particularly for women;★ and for some months the air staff had been urging the reorganisation of ROC boundaries in all fighter groups.

Late in 1941 an official review was made of the ROC for no less a purpose than to see whether it could be dispensed with. The conclusion was reached that the corps had to be retained because, as the Director of Fighter Operations, Air Commodore (later Air Chief Marshal Sir) J. Whitworth Jones, put it:

"a) It provides our *only* source of air-raid intelligence about aircraft operating below a height of 500ft.

b) The whole of the 'alarm within the alert' scheme is based on the ROC centre. This scheme has made a major contribution to the acceleration of our war output.

c) Control of permitted lighting in certain of our principal ports depends on the ROC system. This scheme enables the 'three-shift' plan to be worked by stevedores [which] contributes to the Battle of the Atlantic."

Take-over of observation by searchlights was found to be impractical because of layout problems and the inability to maintain 4hr watches. Any strengthening of searchlight posts was impossible owing to ministerial demands for air-defence cuts.

On the subject of new centres, Whitworth Jones reported on January 1, 1942, that pre-war centres were in or too near local telephone exchanges and were unprotected. He pointed out that the centre at Bromley had been knocked out and also that "women cannot be expected to work efficiently under the crude conditions which have been the fate of the ROC in some centres in the past." He described existing buildings and facilities as "dangerous" and as having inadequate accommodation. Whitworth Jones wrote to the Director of Operations:

"There is no doubt that the present arrangements are quite impossible. Both centres at York are at present housed in one wooden hut in a vulnerable position in the centre of the town with no protection against bombing. There are no emergency centres.

The York Observer Corps centres cover our vital east coast ports; all of them liable to low-flying attack, either in the form of bombing or mining (the latter form of attack accompanied by occasional fringe bombing is a nightly feature these weeks).

We should be much obliged therefore if you would now initiate action to construct the necessary Observer Corps centres at York to the standardised pattern. The substitution of women for men in the Observer Corps is, of course, a factor which you will wish to take into account in the construction of these new buildings."

★The first approved design for a centre was that at 17 Group, Watford, which became the prototype for many others, with custom-built operations room and full rest-room and canteen facilities.

Also on January 1, he wrote a letter to the Director of Telecommunications which has seldom been matched in sharpness and humour in official files:

"1)   I have just had put in front of me the most astonishing and abominable lot of filthy files it has ever been my misfortune to gaze upon (and that is saying a lot after 4½ years in this disgusting building)! It deals with all the wranglings, musings and claims by innumerable persons as to what should, and should not, be done in Royal Observer Corps centres.

2)   We find the trouble has been that:
    a)   No clear-cut operational policy for Observer Corps centres has been laid down.
    b)   Fighter Command have been negotiating with various branches of the Air Ministry (largely Director of Tels) with a view to obtaining some service in some particular centre.
    c)   When Fighter Command or the Observer Corps have managed to extract a particular service or convenience for a particular centre for a particular purpose, they have later represented it as *policy* and then used this as a lever to have this service or amenity extended to many other centres.

3)   We have decided to stop the rot.

4)   I have just dictated the guts of a policy paper on this matter. We are going to call a meeting (to which we shall give ourselves the pleasure of inviting you) at which we will:
    a)   approve the policy;
    b)   agree a standard centre for the Royal Observer Corps;
    c)   give every Observer Corps centre the once-over and fix, once and for all, the building reconstruction and new amenities needed.

5)   Having reached this condition of pseudo-stability we may hope that we shall not be worried for (shall we say) a fortnight!"

In March it was being suggested that the ROC should be placed on a full-time basis with members armed and trained for static defence and posts made into a series of strongpoints over the whole country. This idea was abandoned because of the difficulty in getting the requisite number of full-timers, particularly bearing in mind that ROC strength at the time was 34,000, of which only 4,000 were full-time and some 650 were women.

With pressures from within and without it was inevitable that a full-scale reorganisation of the ROC should take place. The corps had been working night and day for more than two years of war with a set-up arranged largely for peacetime operation. There was no standard training syllabus or scheme for instruction for any observer (apart from the volunteers taking the ROC club tests), the command structure between centres and posts was still split and it remained essential to obtain closer co-operation between the RAF and the ROC.

One step in the right direction was the decision, announced in the House of Commons on December 11, 1941, that a two-piece RAF-blue battle-dress was to be issued to all corps members. As *Observers' Tale* recorded, concerning the earlier issue of overalls/boiler suits: "The women in overalls resembled carriage cleaners and the men looked like third-rate plumbers' assistants." The outfits were "laughed out of existence." The blue battle-dress finally arrived in 1942–43 and, with minor variations in badges and buttons, has been with the corps ever since. As this book is written, in 1975, the ROC is still awaiting a modern uniform. The wartime wags who referred to the corps' initials as "Roll on Christmas" and made up the spurious motto "Little and Late" perhaps had a point.

Before continuing with the corps' operations in 1942, however, it is necessary to look closely at the complete reorganisation which took place in that year and in the early part of 1943. The measures taken provided a command structure and training system which is unique and which has stood the test of time.

The first step in providing the essential closer liaison with the Royal Air Force was to change the appointment of Commandant, Royal Observer Corps, from one for a retired officer to that for a serving Air Commodore. To do this meant retiring the indomitable Warrington-Morris, who had successfully steered his extraordinary force through the massive expansion of the late 1930s and the tribulations of war.

His successor, in June 1942, was Air Commodore (later Air Vice-Marshal) G. H. Ambler, who, as an auxiliary, had commanded 609(F) Squadron in 1938–39 and was therefore acquainted with the peculiarities of volunteer formations. After surveying the task thoroughly, Ambler made 18 recommendations summarised as follows:

1) Reorganisation of headquarters ROC.
2) The deputy commandant to be a serving RAF officer.
3) Appointment of an assistant to the deputy commandant.
4) Area headquarters reorganisation.
5) Areas to conform in territory with fighter groups.
6) Area HQs to be housed at fighter group.
7) Group headquarters to be housed at observer centres.★
8) Post personnel to be classified as in reserved occupations on an individual basis.
9) Employment of "mobile" young women at centres.
10) Duty controllers and table supervisors to be classed as in reserved occupations, regardless of age.
11) Training to be compulsory instead of voluntary and to be the liability of HQ ROC as well as the ROC clubs.
12) "B" class, volunteer observers, to be eligible for training pay.
13) A training organisation to be set up.
14) Provision of efficiency badges.
15) Corps reorganisation on a non-military basis but with graded ranks.
16) ROC Employment Order (1941) to be amended to cover "B" as well as "A" members. This would require volunteers to continue in the corps until officially released.
17) Provision of proper conditions-of-service regulations.
18) To counteract the impression prevalent in the ROC that radar development was diminishing the corps' importance.

Most of the points made by Ambler were accepted by the corps as a whole and led to greater efficiency. One, however, No 9, caused a furore which shook the ROC to its foundations, led to a spate of press stories and even to a ministerial statement in the House of Commons.

Employment of "mobile" women, ultimately becoming "immobile women" meant that male observers at centre automatically left when they reached the age of 50. Thus many centre personnel would become redundant and many more would be thrown out as the war progressed and they reached the magic figure of two score and ten. Service at posts was offered by

---

★Under the old system, with centres and posts under separate command, the latter often had a different central address for administration.

way of an olive branch, but of course could not be guaranteed. Being highly individualistic and lacking any rules which precluded public utterances, the corps closed ranks and put pen to paper – to MPs, newspapers and anyone else in authority that they could think of.

Typical of the messages was a telegram dated November 20, 1942, from Cardiff centre to the Prime Minister, the Secretary of State for Air, the Secretary of State for War, the Minister of Labour, the Minister of Home Security, local Members of Parliament individually and also to the editors of *The Times*, *Daily Telegraph*, *Daily Mail*, *Daily Express*, *News Chronicle*, *Daily Herald* and *Western Mail*, Cardiff. It read:

"Members of Cardiff centre, ROC, wholeheartedly protest against dismissal of members over 50 after nearly four years of devoted and efficient service during time of nation's greatest peril. Such action is discouragement of their past efforts. That the reason advanced – that [continued service is a] heavy burden for men of this age – is totally unwarranted is proved by the record of the corps and by His Majesty's recognition of valuable services by conferment of the title Royal Observer Corps. High praise has always been expressed by those responsible for administration of the corps during the period of heavy raids. Order has created consternation and is inconsistent with recruitment of men over 50 for Home Guard and other services. Respectfully request instant consideration as the order issued calls for immediate action."

The row gathered momentum at such a rate that the Parliamentary Under-Secretary of State for Air, Balfour, was forced to make a statement in the House of Commons on November 25, 1942. He said that only 1,400 members were concerned, of whom 25 were over 70 years of age, 280 were between 61 and 70 and the balance between 51 and 60. He unfortunately made reference to the safety of RAF pilots being endangered by the existing ROC set-up and he omitted to mention the many men approaching 50 who would be affected later on.

The whole thing left a very sour taste and was really quite unnecessary. RAF operations rooms had an upper age limit of 35 because, it was said, of the strains involved. Read across to the ROC this was arbitrarily made 50. Apart from the fact that the magic figure 50 suggested that many of those leading the war effort, including the Prime Minister, must be incapable, the decision led to a lowering of morale and a waste of trained manpower.

That some observers at centre were "past it" cannot be doubted, as there were complaints of slow handling of post plots and in some cases of onward telling. The right solution to the problem, nevertheless, would have been to declare all centre personnel over 50 to be on a year-to-year basis. This would have allowed those in authority to weed out the slow runners while keeping men who quite clearly retained the necessary skills and alertness.

Despite the uproar, the establishment remained adamant and the over-50s left. In some cases this took a considerable time, as: "in the event the worst consequences of this gauche and ill considered order were avoided. Duty controllers conspired with the centre controller and devised more or less legitimate stratagems by which a fair percentage of the over-fifties could, after all, be retained. Every possible means was used to delay the resignations of those who had to go."* The remainder of the ROC reorganisation, in general, went smoothly although there were some who felt that the near-military command structure was not to their liking and they, too, left.

Centre Crew by Eric Wilton.

The ROC areas were re-aligned in 1942 to conform more nearly with fighter group territory and area headquarters sites moved closer to the fighter group headquarters. Southern and Western Areas roughly corresponded to Nos 11 and 12 Fighter Groups and were left unchanged, although Western Area HQ moved from Gloucester to Rudloe (No 10 FG). Northern Area took over 36 Group, Dunfermline; 34 Group, Glasgow; and 31 Group, Galashiels, from Scottish Area. North Western Area took over 32 Group, Carlisle; and 29 Group, Lancaster, from Northern Area. Midland Area took over 8 Group, Leeds; and 10 Group, York, from Northern Area. Northern Area HQ moved from Catterick to Newcastle (13 FG, HQ), Midland Area HQ from Grantham to Watnall (12 FG, HQ) and Scottish Area HQ from Edinburgh to Inverness (14 FG, HQ).

Six months after this upheaval, on July 1, 1943, No 13 Fighter Group was abolished and along with it went Northern Area ROC. Its observer groups were redistributed, Nos 36, 34, 31 and 33 (Ayr) going to Scottish Area and 30 (Durham) and 9 (York) going to Midland Area.

At area headquarters the area commandant's post was retained, but the establishment for two deputy area commandants was cut to one, and an adjutant and an operations staff officer were added. The posts of equipment officer and administrative officer at areas were not affected.

Further down the line, at the groups, Air Commodore Ambler made fundamental changes which greatly improved efficiency. Instead of the split command of the controller at centre and the observer group officer with the posts, Ambler made the centres the overall group head-quarters with a group commandant in command, a deputy group commandant (the centre controller), and an increased number of assistant observer group officers. The position of OGO was abolished. At group headquarters an adjutant was also employed and the crew duty con-trollers were upgraded to officer status. Area commandants were given the rank of observer captain (four midnight-blue sleeve rings), group commandants became observer commanders (three rings), centre controllers were appointed as observer lieutenants first class (two thick and one thin ring) while duty controllers and AOGOs became observer officers (one sleeve ring). All these were based on RAF-type ranks except that the sleeve rings were midnight blue and not white. The basic ranks exist today, except for observer lieutenant first class, which in 1974 became observer lieutenant commander.

The whole process had to be gradual in order to avoid manpower gaps, and the timing varied from group to group. To complete the picture, non-commissioned ranks were introduced at posts, being chief observer (equivalent to a sergeant, with three horizontal bars in a laurel wreath on his sleeve) and leading observer (equivalent to a corporal, with two horizontal bars on the sleeve). For a while head observers had no arm badges but carried the title on a label on the breast pocket. Logically, the chief observer was the head observer in charge of the post and the leading observer undertook training duties and acted as deputy. In practice it was often the other way round in wartime, with the leading observer doing the paper work and the chief observer instructing. The ranks were also adopted later at centres – the post controller, for instance, being a chief observer.

Having established a logical chain of command, Ambler could turn to the thorny questions of training and proficiency. At area the operations staff officer was made responsible for training and supervised the AOGOs* who in turn looked after the post instructors. Basic standards of

---

*AOGOs henceforth had to attend compulsory instructors' courses and were age-limited to 50.

post efficiency were laid down, both for plotting and aircraft recognition, and in the latter case there were three standards: basic, intermediate and master, as evolved by the ROC Club in the 1st, 2nd and 3rd grades. For master observers a special proficiency badge was to be instituted in the shape of the plan-view of a Spitfire worn on the arm.

Along with the restructuring came all the paper of the RAF in the shape of forms and yet more forms. Even the chatty circulars of Warrington-Morris gave way to area and group routine orders and operation instructions. From 1942 onwards the ROC was run on (almost) strictly RAF lines, right down to equipment chits for buckets, iron, slop.

For a while the Royal Observer Corps Club lived on, meeting up and down the country, the journal and recognition aids being issued and tests taken. The writing, however, was on the wall. The ROC was being set up on military lines and there was no room for amateur training run by enthusiasts. Both the Air Ministry and the Ministry of Aircraft Production had at last come to realise the paramount importance of aircraft recognition, but they had not been pleased to find that the only real experts in training were a crowd of civilians in the ROC Club. In September 1942 the first edition of a new journal appeared. Called *Aircraft Recognition, The Inter Services Journal*, it was produced by the Aircraft Recognition Material Branch of MAP, which was also responsible for standard silhouette folders, episcope cards, etc, for the Services. Many of the ideas of the ROC *Journal* were copied in the new publication, and it was clear that the two could not exist in competition; nor could the club exist where training had become official and compulsory. In the *Aeroplane Spotter* for December 31, 1942, it was announced:

> "The edict has gone forth that the Royal Observer Corps Club is to be disbanded as from January 3 next. The ROC *Journal* will also cease publication and there will be no more issues of the club's privately circulated recognition material. The work the Club set itself to do will be taken over by the Royal Observer Corps and the recognition material will come from official sources.
> Thus ends one of the most useful voluntary organisations ever set up in this country to assist the war effort."

The requiem was, however, a little premature because – as with all democratic private-venture institutions – the ROC Club refused to lie down. A special general meeting of the club was called at Claridges Hotel, London, on January 3, 1943, and delegates crowded in from all over the country. The headquarters staff expected a vote of thanks and quiet dissolution of the organisation. The delegates thought otherwise; Hitler might be waging war across the Channel but this was a matter of principle!

Air Commodore Ambler gave a lengthy address, explaining the new training scheme and the obvious redundancy for the club that resulted from it. "Mr P. H. Whitfield as chairman of the ROCC appointed by the commandant, and Mr A. P. Hamilton, as the commandant's nominee on the general council, then formally resigned."★

That appeared to be that; but far from it. A full-scale debate then ensued, with strongly raised voices. When the resolution to dissolve the ROC Club was put to the assembly it was roundly defeated; even the commandant could not interfere with the club's constitution or voting rights.

A resolution to change the club's name and to continue it in modified form was carried.

★*Aeroplane Spotter*, January 14, 1943.

Attack Warning Red

Alas, with official support withdrawn the intentions were good but the means inadequate and posts were too busy with compulsory weekly meetings. The ROC Club finally withered away. The foundation of the club as a private institution within an official body, and its tremendous contribution in wartime, have no parallels. It is hardly surprising that it fought to last.

The struggle to keep the ROC *Journal* alive was also a bitter one, but Whitehall had the final weapon – withdrawal of the paper ration. One concession was wrung from authority, namely the right of every observer to receive an individual copy of the *Inter Services Journal*, or its equivalent, for as long as such a journal existed.

In typical corps fashion, however, the ROC *Journal* did not die like a damp squib. The last

"CENTRE" (AS OUR CRAZY ARTIST SEES IT!

The ROC has always had its share of humorists. The best known throughout the war and for many years after was the late H. W. Sessions, who served on the Ryde and Upham posts from 1940 to 1968. His cartoons showed a deep insight into the corps and its members. These are two examples of his work during 1941 and 1942

issue, in December 1942, was double-size at 72 pages, had a defiantly blood-red cover and even included pages of full-colour aircraft photographs. This was the final trumpet of the overworked volunteer editorial committee.

In general 1942 was a year of gloom for Britain: U-boat sinkings mounted, the desert war did not go well and in the Far East it was a continuous tale of disaster and retreat. Austerity on the home front did nothing to improve morale or indicate that the war would not drag on for years. Against this background the Royal Observer Corps had, as related, to undergo a complete reorganisation and cope with the dual problems of more tasks and an acute shortage of man-power. Despite everything the corps continued to do its job with remarkable efficiency and no small amount of humour.

"Head Observer 33/F2, Auchenmalg, to Northern Area Commandant, February 1, 1942:
John McLennon, 'A' Member, walked from the village of Glenluce to Auchenmalg Post, a distance of approximately 6 miles, through drifts from eight to ten feet deep and with a blizzard raging. McLennon suffers from asthma and is very lame. He left home at about midnight and was at Post at 5 a.m."

Report from W. R. English H.Q. 39/D.1, Drumnadrochit:
"1158 Enemy Plane sighted seven miles from the post coming from North East, 3,500ft, making straight for Foyers, passed the post still coming down till over Foyers, then down to 300ft, dropped two or more bombs, went on for a mile and a half in the direction of Whitebridge, turned, came back over his target and believe he dropped more, but owing to smoke and steam could not be sure. He was then making straight for the post, when almost overhead I had a crack at him with my rifle, 8mm, missed with the first but hit him with the second as he slightly changed course and went up into the clouds flying due North 12.3 o'clock. Had we had a machine gun he would never have reached Foyers."

Report from OGO 25 Group, January 24, 1942, re 35/G.4 Siel Island, Argyll:
"On 20/1/42, at about 1430 hrs, Observer D. Dewar had just come on duty at this post, which is on the site of an old British Fort called 'Dunmore'. There is only one path to the top, the sides of the hill being precipitous. The surface was covered with ice and snow.

Observer Dewar, whilst proceeding to collect coal from a hidden cache, slipped on the ice and snow and slid down an incline to the cliff's edge, dropping over 40ft to a ledge and bouncing and dropping about a further 80ft to the bottom.

In his first clear drop he missed a needle point of rock by a foot or so, and the doctor considers that he dislocated his arm, and knocked it in again during his progress down the cliff. After pulling himself together, Observer Dewar walked round the flat at the base of the hill, about a quarter of a mile, to the path leading to the post and went on with his duty. His mate however, insisted on going down for help, and the two observers who had gone off duty returned to help Dewar down the path to his home."

There is no record of the reaction of the other members of the post on finding there was a secret store of fuel known only to the two observers on duty.

While the life on many posts and at many centres was one of routine and often boredom, highlighted by the occasional enemy incursions, the plotting and tracking of all aircraft, particularly RAF aircraft lost or in distress, was of vital importance. Bomber Command's efforts were growing, as were the bomber/fighter sweeps over the Channel.

Chapter 12
"RATS"

During 1942 the whole operational pattern of detection, control and reporting was changing and the Luftwaffe employed its limited resources in the west to the maximum.

Some doubt had been cast on the future role of the Observer Corps in the air-defence network in Fighter Command operational-research section report No 224, dated July 20, 1941. This commented on the difficulties encountered by the ROC in visual and aural reporting at night and in bad weather. An "ideal" layout was put forward, known as the "inland reporting system." In this the main component was to be GCI radar, which might provide not only interception control but also surveillance, with the ROC as a form of manual gap-filler. Forward surveillance would continue to be the longer range CH stations.

A first step was to decentralise filtering to the fighter groups instead of keeping it all at Fighter Command. At the same time ROC centres and GCI stations were to have direct lines to group filters and GCI information was to be available to certain ROC centres. ROC liaison officers were gradually transferred to group filters from group operations rooms, excepting at No 11 Group, the filter room of which continued to be at Fighter Command HQ, Bentley Priory. A new position created at centres was known as the "GCI interrogator," while at the GCI stations themselves the post of "ROC agent" was established. All the final elements for improving the ROC side of the raid reporting organisation were contained in proposals put forward by the C.-in-C. Fighter Command on April 28, 1943. These covered:

1) One uni-directional speech circuit to each ROC group or sector operations room from any observer centre whose boundaries passed within ten miles of the group or sector boundary.
2) One two-way speech circuit from each Observer Corps centre which had 25 per cent of its territory within the group or sector concerned.
3) ROC centres to have long-range plotting boards.
4) ROC operations rooms to have two-way speech circuits with GCI stations; the circuits for use by the ROC in obtaining heights and identification from IFF interrogators, GCI to obtain identifications from ROC.
5) ROC plots to be displayed on inland tables in RAF filter rooms. Uni-directional speech circuits to be provided.
6) Air-raid warnings to be given from ROC centres.★

The ultimate list of ROC centres with GCI communications was laid down as:

★Details of the air-raid warning reorganisation are given in the next chapter.

	ROC CENTRE	GCI
1	Maidstone	Sandwich
2	Horsham	Durrington
3	Winchester	Sopley
4	Oxford	Cricklade and Easthill
5	Coventry	Comberton and Langtoft
6	Derby	Hack Green
7	Manchester	St Annes and Hack Green
8	Leeds	Roecliffe and Staythorpe
9	York	Seaton Snook
10	York	Patrington
11	Lincoln	Orby
12	Bedford	Comberton and Langtoft
14	Bury St Edmunds	Trimley Heath
15	Cambridge	Langtoft
16	Norwich	Neatishead
17	Watford	East Hill
18	Colchester	Trimley Heath
19	Bromley	Wartling
20	Truro	Treleaver
21	Exeter	Exminster
22	Yeovil	Long Load
23	Bristol	Sopley
24	Gloucester	Comberton
25	Cardiff	nil
26	Wrexham	Hack Green
27	Shrewsbury	Hack Green
28/1	Carmarthen	Ripperston
28/2	Caernarvon	Trewan Sands
29	Lancaster	St Annes
30	Durham	Northstead and Seaton Snook
31	Galashiels	Dirleton
32	Carlisle	nil
33	Ayr	Fullarton
34	Glasgow	Fullarton
35	Oban	nil
36	Dunfermline	Dirleton
37	Dundee	nil
38	Aberdeen	nil
39	Inverness	nil

At first it had been thought that inter-centre telling of information between adjacent ROC groups would become unnecessary under the inland reporting system, but radar problems and the methods of attack used by the Luftwaffe in fact made it even more important.

In the new "standard" pattern ROC centres, on which work began in 1942, the controller, the tellers and air-raid warning officials, etc, were seated on a balcony looking down on the map table. To avoid cluttering up the table still further and to give adequate long-range warning of a raid approaching an observer group it was decided to introduce a second map table, the long-range board referred to previously. The long-range board was vertical and required nine observers to man it. It could be clearly seen not only by those on the balcony but also by the plotters on the main table. The map scale on the main table was one inch to one mile, while that of the long-range board was half an inch to the mile; the latter, being vertical, was made of metal and used magnetised counters.

The evolution of the long-range board was typical of ROC improvisation. The Air Ministry had to be convinced that the whole thing was feasible, but delays ensued. In the end the ROC themselves made a mock-up of the LRB which Observer Lieutenant Deeping and the HQ equipment officer, ex-Senior Warrant Officer Austin, took to a friendly engineering firm. The company produced the necessary hardware in metal and an assortment of plaques to use with it. With no RAF sanction, but with the connivance of the commandant, the prototype LRB was set up at No 17 Group, Watford centre and post office engineers rigged lines to it from adjacent centres. A full-scale demonstration was attended by Air Ministry officials and the Senior Air Staff Officer, Fighter Command. The reaction was very favourable, but the inevitable officer from the accounts side of the house asked "who paid?" The commandant was happy to inform him that the manufacturer had made the LRB for nothing.

Work on building new centres and converting old ones went on from late 1942 to late 1943, by which time they were nearly all of the "standard pattern" and complete with long-range boards. Before the ROC had been revamped and the new operations rooms were ready, however, the Germans produced twin threats which caused damage and casualties and kept the observer groups busy in the southern half of Britain. The first consisted of night raids against inland cathedral cities, and the second was low-level fighter-bomber attacks against a variety of coastal targets. The onslaught against religious centres became known as the "Baedeker" raids, while the low-level sorties got the nickname "hit-and-run" or "tip-and-run" raids.

The RAF was also concerned that Luftwaffe aircraft were using yellow under-surface markings to try to hoodwink the defences, as this was the colour employed on British training, communications and experimental aircraft. On September 7, 1942, "supplement No 1 to intelligence summary No 2" was despatched urgently to all centres and posts. This stated that if the enemy used this stratagem the codeword "pressure" would be used, and friendly aircraft would immediately be painted with black stripes on the fuselage underside and a black band around the fuselage. "Pressure" was not cancelled until March 1944.

The Luftwaffe's main areas of activity in 1942 were the Middle East, Italy and, of course, Russia. The high command however, was determined to renew the attack on Britain and Kampfgeschwader 2 was given the task. Since the autumn of 1941 KG 2 had been re-equipping with the new Dornier 217E bomber, which was a marked improvement on the early Do17Z. When the three Gruppen of KG 2 were fully established on Dutch bases with their new charges, the attacks began.

In March and April 1942 sharp raids were made on places as widely separated as Dover, Portland, Grimsby, Middlesbrough and Hucclecote – the site of the Gloster Aircraft factory. On the night of April 23/24 there was a scattered raid on Exmouth, followed the next night by an attack on Exeter. Some 25 bombers killed or seriously injured 135 people. Then followed a succession of raids on Bath (twice), Bristol, Norwich (three times), York, Cowes and again on Exeter. After a three-week lull the attack was renewed, with 80 bombers hitting the city of Canterbury on the night of May 31/June 1. Ipswich was the next to suffer, and then Canterbury again. Finally, near the end of June, another raid on long-suffering Norwich completed the "Baedeker" series. Throughout July raiding went on and a number of towns and cities were hit, some seriously, but the effort was not on the same concentrated scale.

While the ROC was deeply involved in all these raids, with aircraft coming in at low and medium altitude, it was the attacks on Norwich, York and Exeter which affected the corps most. At Norwich, two nights' raids killed more than 220 people and seriously affected the No 16 Observer Group centre. The aircraft used dive attacks, which confused the plotting situation, and on the second night a direct hit on the main telephone cable left only two clusters of posts on the line. Eventually operations were switched to the emergency centre.

When York was raided early on April 29 the single building housing Nos 9 and 10 centres was rocked by high explosives and showered with incendiaries. The teleprinters were put out of action, but plotting continued.

At Exeter on the night of May 3/4 90 aircraft attacked with high explosives, incendiaries and machine guns and 294 people were killed or seriously injured, the main shopping centre was wrecked and 2,000 houses destroyed. The No 21 Observer Group centre at Exeter was set on fire and the emergency centre destroyed. The crew members themselves put out the centre fires.

The Baedeker raids hastened the process of removing vulnerable centres from the middle of towns. At York, separate purpose-built centres were erected on the outskirts of the city, while at Exeter the centre was moved out and the original centre room retained for emergency use.

One very rare type of raid was noted by the corps in September 1942. Just before noon on the 5th of that month a raider was told to Watford centre, which passed it to G.1 post, Cuffley, Herts. G.1 takes up the story:*

"It may be imagined with what surprise we heard centre report casually 'George One – there's a hostile in 54 square.' Hostile on a clear morning like this. Better get the telescope out just in case it comes our way. Suddenly almost above us, much higher than we had expected, we picked up a short wisp of a vortex creeping slowly north. With the naked eye no plane was visible.

Out telescope . . . rest it along instrument height arm . . . up . . . steady . . . got him. He's turning west now. Long pointed equally tapered wings like an elongated Hudson. Twin fins and rudders. That rules out the 177. He's off our table at 30. What a height. We watched the silver shape spewing out its double white vortex, flying steadily westwards.

Centre reports again, 'It's just dropped some dirt on Luton.'

Then we lose sight of it for a while; but suddenly it's coming into us from the north-west. Someone is throwing up some very inaccurate flak by now; a few bursts are seen miles from the target. Two Spitfires climb hard; 10,000ft below.

The London sirens give the warning as the plane swings majestically eastwards, passing almost overhead our post.

What an enormous span. Two small engines set close to the fuselage, long truncheon-shaped nose.

*From *Observers' Tale*. This was a classic case of the difficulty of estimating the altitude of very high-flying aircraft. When G.1 just saw the Ju86 it was probably further south-east in square 63 and only later reached 54, in which Luton was situated. Wrong height assessment led to big errors in ground distance. At that time no other aircraft had been plotted as high as 40,000ft. About a dozen flights over England with the Ju86 were made in 1942.

Look, you can see the black crosses clearly now, even at that height!! . . .
Centre reports: 'it's supposed to be a Ju86P over this country for the first time, flying at 40,000ft.' "

The whole raid resembled a Gotha sortie of the First World War, with the fighters climbing in vain and the anti-aircraft guns firing short. The aircraft involved was, in fact, a Ju86R-1 of 14./KG 6, a unit at Beauvais which existed only for a month.

Another new type which made its appearance at the same time as the Ju86R was the Me210, the "miracle replacement" for the Me110 Zerstörer which had suffered so severely at the hands of the RAF in the Battle of Britain. The 210 first flew in 1939, but a series of accidents and major modifications delayed its entry into service until 1942. In August of that year Versuchsstaffel 210 was deployed in Holland as 16./KG 6 and began operations against Britain.

In *Warplanes of the Third Reich*, William Green states:

"The operational debut of the unit was inauspicious and, despite the relatively high performance of the Me210A-1, two fell to the guns of Hawker Typhoons over Yorkshire on September 6 during one of the first sorties of the type over the British Isles. Two more were lost on operations during the following week, and by September 20 16./KG.6 was reduced to five aircraft of which only three were serviceable."

The incident of September 6 was recorded in the York 9 Observer Group log as:

"12.40 Reported Catterick, two hostile aircraft believed down (Junkers 88s) in V0741 at 11.45 and V4123 at 11.50." After RAF teams had rushed to the locations, Newcastle informed York 9 at 17.17: "The planes shot down this morning were Me210 and not Ju88."

It was not, however, the high-flier or even the medium-altitude bomber which caused the greatest concern in 1942 and 1943. On the contrary, it was the very-low-level intruder, the headache of all air forces.

To understand the nature of the threat and the measures taken against it, it is necessary to look at an overall period of many months. Early in 1942 low-level raids by one or a handful of fighter-bombers began. These were combined in some cases with "pirate" raids where aircraft such as the Do217 dived suddenly from cloud cover on inland targets – particularly factories and airfields. The tip-and-run raiders at wave-top height were extremely difficult to combat. Radar saw nothing, anti-aircraft defences were lacking and by the time fighters were airborne the enemy was already on the way home.

On March 27, 1942, four Messerschmitts bombed Torquay, and within a month Brixham, Bognor Regis, Swanage, Portland, Exmouth, Bexhill, Folkestone, Hastings, Lydd, Dungeness, Poling, Cowes and Newhaven had all been attacked in a similar fashion. A staffel each of Me109s from JG2 and JG26 were responsible for the raids and the aircraft carried either one 550lb or four 110lb bombs. By July 1942 both units had re-equipped with the powerful Focke Wulf 190. This aircraft had first made its presence felt during the February dash up the Channel of the battle cruisers *Scharnhorst* and *Gneisenau*. The Fw 190 was superior in performance to the Spitfire V and was to be a menace until mastered by the Spitfire IX and the Typhoon.

Through the summer the attacks went on, with damage and confusion mounting. Seaside resorts began to resemble shattered ghost towns. The fighter-bombers, or Jabo, appeared out of the blue, fired their cannon, dropped their bombs and were gone before the siren could be sounded or the guns alerted. Bitter complaints began to pour in from coastal towns and MPs

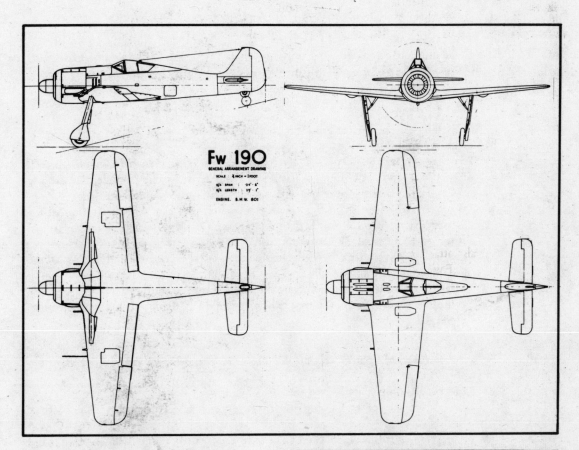

Fw 190

GENERAL ARRANGEMENT DRAWING

SCALE ¼ INCH = 1 FOOT

O/A SPAN   34' 6"
O/A LENGTH 29' 1"

ENGINE. B.M.W. 801

To produce silhouettes for Air Publication 1480 provisional drawings were made from intelligence information and camera-gun shots. The landing of an actual enemy aircraft either damaged or intact led to more accurate silhouettes. Following the arrival of an Fw 190 at Pembrey in flying condition this line drawing was prepared in August 1942 by Air Intelligence Section 2G. From the drawing the accompanying silhouette was prepared and issued in Amendment No 27 to AP.1480B (German) in the same_month

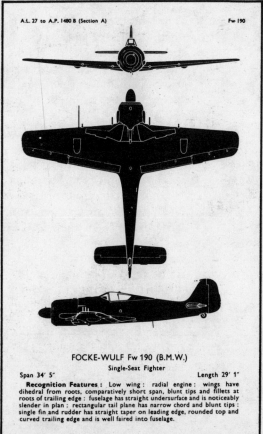

A.L. 27 to A.P. 1480 B (Section A)   Fw 190

FOCKE-WULF Fw 190 (B.M.W.)
Single-Seat Fighter

Span 34' 5"   Length 29' 1"

Recognition Features : Low wing : radial engine : wings have dihedral from roots, comparatively short span, blunt tips and fillets at roots of trailing edge : fuselage has straight undersurface and is noticeably slender in plan : rectangular tail plane has narrow chord and blunt tips : single fin and rudder has straight taper on leading edge, rounded top and curved trailing edge and is well faired into fuselage.

pressed for better warning and more defence. Just how hectic was the life of south-coast posts during the tip-and-run raids of 1942 can be gleaned from entries in the log book of 2/N. 3 post, Worthing, on just two days in August:

"August 12

04.00	21 Wellingtons and four-engined bombers south.
05.44	Air-raid warning.
05.49	Two Fw 190s seen 5917 south at zero. Turned west. Underneath of wings appeared yellow. N.2 reports two Fw 190s attacked Lysander on 3711. Lysander successfully evaded and returned to Shoreham with two holes in wing and one in fuselage.
06.02	Two Fw 190s seen west on 6323 at zero. Guns on pier fired as aircraft approached and passed end of pier. Smith fired four rounds with post rifle. Machine turned out on 5921 and went SE at full throttle. Last plot 6113. (These two machines had also attacked a Lysander off Newhaven.) Under-surfaces of wings and fuselage of the two Fw 190s were painted yellow.
12.08	Message from duty controller congratulating crew on duty at N3, 11.8.42, on recognition of Swordfish in distress. Plane landed safely mainly due to their plotting. Landed at Thorney.

August 19*

04.40	Large numbers of fighters, accompanied by Beauforts, Blenheims and Bostons, out in raid to Dieppe.
05.25	Fighters and bombers started to return.
05.44	Two Fw 190s seen on 5719 going east at 50ft. Zoomed to 2,500ft on 6121.
05.45	Red alert rung.
05.46	Boston coming from east attacked on 6121 by the two Fw 190s, which dived on it and attacked from above and rear on starboard and port sides. Boston immediately burst into flames, crash-landed in sea on 5919 and sank immediately.
	Spitfire north of post flying east to west turned and engaged hostile aircraft. After exchange of cannon fire, Spitfire collided with one Fw 190 while making a vertical diving turn to port. Both machines broke to pieces in the air and crashed in flames. Hurricane had also joined in fight.
	Remaining Fw 190 broke off engagement and went out SE. Hurricane went away west.
06.20	Walrus and two Spitfires searching in 5919. Crash boat reached scene from Little-hampton at 06.30 and was seen to pick up four white objects (bodies).
10.05	24 Fortresses.
10.55	24 Hurricanes, 12 with bombs, 24 Spitfires.
10.56	News from centre; all Fortresses returned to Maidstone area.
11.17	65 Hurricanes, and Spitfires returned.
11.26	Six Bostons (+36 Hurricanes and Spitfires) sweep and 12 Hurricanes (Shoreham).
11.30	Six Bostons, 12 fighters.
11.42	20 return; four Bostons.
12.00	12 Bostons and 48 Spitfires.
12.20	Return from sweep. 11 Bostons, three Blenheims, eight fighters.
12.59	Six Hurribombers east.

---

*This was the day of the abortive allied landings at Dieppe.

13.00	11 Spitfires, six Bostons east 5909.
13.25	Ten Hurribombers, 12 Spits south-east; 16 Spits, six Bostons west.
14.00	24 Spits east.
14.30	12 Spits SE.
14.43	Nine Hurribombers west.
14.45	11 Hurricanes west.
14.53	23 Hurries and Spits west.
14.55	66 fighters SE.
15.00	Three Spits west.
15.32	Air-raid warning.
15.51	20 fighters west.
15.57	Air-raid warning.
16.37	Local alarm.
	Convoy of barges attacked by hostile planes on 6117, at least one barge sunk. Four Fw 190s.
17.32	Alarm Worthing.
18.19	Very heavy explosion.
18.29	Alarm Worthing.
18.40	Ju88 plotted SE on 6319.
19.52	Alarm Worthing. Two Fw 190s east on 5919, 50ft. Pier battery opened fire."

For the ROC as a whole the first step was to check the siting of all posts to assess visibility at 100ft, 500ft and 1,500ft. ROC operations instruction No 7 was issued on August 22, 1942, calling for visibility charts to be prepared. These took several months to prepare and analyse and action on the results was not taken until 1943.

To improve low-level coverage in the reporting chain it was decided to establish some 150 "satellite" posts in a belt 30 miles wide along the south coast and on the east coast as far north as Dundee, as well as on the coast of Lancashire and Cheshire. The satellites were of four kinds: ROC, RAF, searchlight and coastguard. A total of 27 ROC satellite posts were set up, each manned by a single observer; 50 AA Command searchlight sites were linked from the sentry to the nearest ROC post; 22 aerodrome lookouts were connected to ROC posts; and 129 coastguard stations had lines to ROC posts. Many coastguard stations had been part of the ROC reporting network since 1940 and it only remained to provide communications for the remainder. The RAF and the Army manned their own satellites, while ROC personnel manned corps' satellites and also some of those set up at coastguard stations. Each ROC satellite was connected by landline to its parent post and reported as follows: "B.2 satellite, 05 minutes two miles east one at zero, hostile." The plots were passed by the parent post to the centre, where satellites were indicated by a black diamond gummed on to the map table. ROC operation instruction No 9, "Formation of Satellite Posts," was issued on September 22, 1942. In the following month a further effort was made to combat the tip-and-run and low-level pirate raiders with the inauguration of the rocket warning system.

It was decided that 69 ROC posts in coastal areas between the Wash and Land's End should be equipped with Schermuly type A electric projectors firing snowflake illuminating rockets. These consisted of a tube projector fixed to the ground, a breech for cartridges and the rocket, with tail fins, which carried a parachute flare. The code word for the rocket firing system was "Totter," and the first operation instruction for it (No 13) was issued on October 20, 1942. The

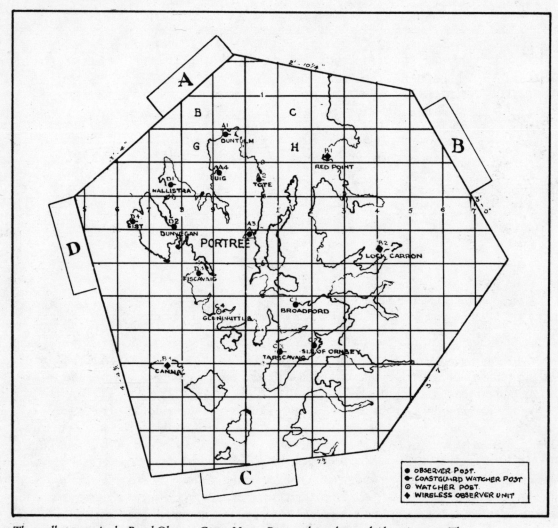

The smallest group in the Royal Observer Corps, No 40, Portree, shown here as laid out in 1942. There were five posts, six coastguard watcher posts, three wireless observer units and one ROC watcher post. There were only four plotting positions round the table

intention was to give immediate warning to AA gun crews and patrolling fighters of hostile aircraft seen at any height below 1,000ft over land or sea. No firing of Totter was allowed during darkness. The schedule of equipment for each post consisted of eight rockets, one projector, nine cartridges with plug attached, one battery holder with lead and socket attached and two batteries. Issues were made immediately to ROC Groups 1, 2, 3, 20, 21, and 22, and later the scheme was extended to Nos 14, 16, 18 and 19 Groups.

To overcome the problem of the sirens being sounded *after* the raiders had passed, 31 posts on the south coast were empowered to issue air-raid warnings direct to siren control points. Such warnings were issued by the post observer when he had seen and positively recognised an enemy aircraft. Some centres were also linked to the warning-telephone network and issued the "red" warning themselves.

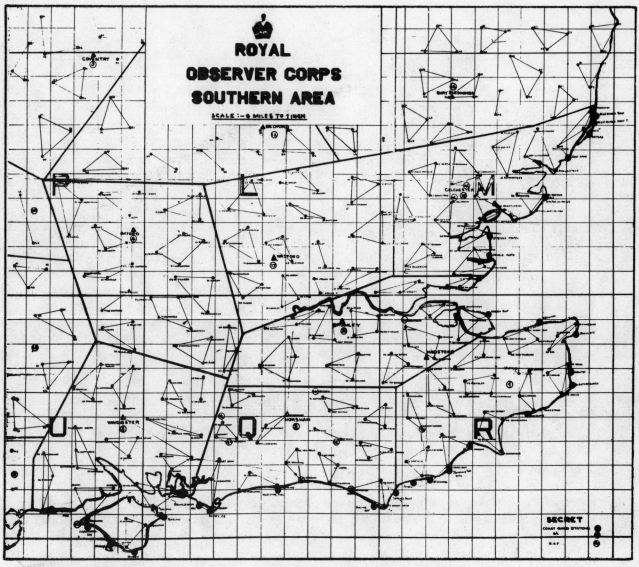

A map of Southern Area ROC prepared in March 1943. The close pattern of post clusters in this vulnerable area is evident. Around the coast are marked coastguard station satellites and satellite posts connected into the main network. These latter were vital at the period for dealing with tip-and-run raids. Also marked are posts connected to searchlight stations

One final improvement to the low-level reporting system was made in 1943 by the introduction of "Rats" procedure. The priority message "low raid urgent" had been in use for a long time, but it was not found to be sufficiently rapid in getting plots through the system. Accordingly, on February 24, 1943, headquarters ROC issued instruction No 17 calling for the use of the priority code-word "Rats" to be used immediately a post sighted and recognised a hostile aircraft flying at any height below 1,000ft. A post would report the word Rats followed by the 100km grid letter and 10km grid number of the post itself, regardless of the actual position of the raid. Thus a report would read "Rats Roger 12." As soon as the centre plotter heard Rats from a post he called out to the tellers, who passed the message on all their lines. Later, in 1944, the procedure was modified so that five or more low-level hostiles were reported as Many Rats.

The ROC groups using Rats procedure were 1, Maidstone; 2, Horsham; 3, Winchester; 14, Bury St Edmunds; 16, Norwich; 18, Colchester; 19, Bromley; 20, Truro; 21, Exeter; and 22, Yeovil. Some of the remaining groups in the country operated Rats for a time, but later reverted to the earlier code – Low Raid Urgent.

The combination of faster reporting, rocket flares, increased coastal gun defences and newer aircraft types such as the Typhoon and Spitfire IX eventually made low-level coastal intrusion too costly for the Luftwaffe, which had to husband its limited resources in northern Europe. Nevertheless the activities of a small force of fighter-bombers achieved dislocation and damage out of all proportion to the numbers employed. It was undoubtedly a most successful enterprise for the German Air Force.

Although low-flying raids gradually decreased in intensity during 1943, *Civil Defence*, by T. H. O'Brien★, records:

"The incidents caused by tip-and-run attack declined progressively from 80 in January of this year to 52 in March, 39 in June and somewhat fewer in the autumn months. In December there were only seven. On a geographical computation throughout the year, Sussex suffered most severely, closely followed by Kent, Devon, Hampshire, the Isle of Wight; Dorset and Cornwall were the other counties most concerned. Any list of towns on which loss of life and damage was inflicted must include Dover, Ashford, Bournemouth, Eastbourne, Hastings, Brighton, Plymouth, Hull, Grimsby and Great Yarmouth."

While the coastal towns were suffering in 1942–43 the ROC became concerned with another dangerous type of intruder. Night after night from the spring of 1942 onwards RAF Bomber Command was launching heavy attacks against German targets. ROC tables became saturated with plots, both outgoing and incoming, and to the activities of the RAF were added those of the US 8th Army Air Force which steadily built up its strength of B-17 Flying Fortresses and B-24 Liberators.

To cope with large numbers of aircraft a system had been inaugurated, in 1941, whereby areas with corners were formed on the operations table. These were classed as area raids, battle zones† and mass raids, while aircraft in close succession were called crocodile raids. Large-scale enemy raids were later classified in the form of "saturation phases." The area-raid principle for both friendly and hostile aircraft was used for the rest of the war and, although not as accurate as individual plotting, avoided the total confusion on the table which had often been the case in the first few months of the blitz.

One thing that area raids did not in general reveal, however, was the existence of a German intruder in the returning bomber stream. With airfield lights on and a steady stream of Stirlings, Halifaxes and Lancasters lining up for a variety of bases, it was a happy hunting ground for Dornier 217s and Ju88s which would suddenly open fire in the circuit or spray the base with bullets and drop bombs.

In 1942 some Bomber Command stations were linked directly to ROC posts and centres in order to speed up intruder warning and to assist with lost RAF bombers. What was wanted,

---

★HMSO series: History of the Second World War.

†Battle zones were, from July 7, 1941, enemy formations breaking up with a "small zone" of ten miles or less in diameter and "large zone" exceeding ten miles in diameter.

*The Hawker Typhoon which was used against the Fw 190 and Me 109 tip-and-run raiders of 1942-43.
The Typhoon was often confused with the 190 in plan view and as a result black and white stripes
were painted under the wings of the former*

however, was some process of elimination so that positive identification could be given of hostile aircraft on intruder missions. In its report No 328 the operational-research section of Fighter Command proposed that Army gun-laying (GL) radar sets should be provided for use in conjunction with ROC centres. The reason given for this suggestion was that once aircraft were over the coast coming inland, apart from recognition by GCI stations of those aircraft carrying IFF Mk 11G there was no positive identification except recognition by sight. The use of GL sets as an identification aid for interrogation and not tracking would enable the ROC to eliminate plots that would otherwise be tracked as unidentified or hostile.

At a conference held at Headquarters Fighter Command three days later it was agreed to recommend to the AOC-in-C that AA Command should be asked to provide GL sets and maintenance personnel. Various difficulties were encountered in providing the special telephone circuits, and it was eventually decided that the ten GL sets to be used should be sited at existing posts and that they should be in operation during darkness. During this time the post concerned would close down, the telephone line from the post being used by the crew of the GL set. In operations order No 46 it was stated that the ten GL sets would be deployed to cover the coast-line of ROC centres at York 10, Lincoln, Colchester (two sets each), Norwich (three sets) and Bury St Edmunds (one set).

The posts equipped with GL radar were 10/L.4, Keyingham; and 10/G.2, Driffield (York 10); 11/K.3, Louth; and 11/G.1, Old Leake (Lincoln); 18/C.3, Lexden; and 18/H.3, Orford (Colchester); 16/V.2, Brundall; 16/N.2, Docking; and 16/Q.3, Melton Constable (Norwich); and 14/E.1, Halesworth (Bury St Edmunds).

At each ROC centre concerned a member known as the interrogator was to read unidenti-fied plots appearing on the ROC table to the GL set in whose area the aircraft was flying. The GL operator would then check whether or not the aircraft was showing IFF. The information passed through the ROC tellers was to be shown in operations rooms by the display, alongside the raid block, of the IFF square as used by filterers in group filter rooms.

This procedure came into effect on November 15, 1942. In a revision of the procedure order at the end of the year the GL interrogator in the ROC centre was instructed to select plots for interrogation in the following order of preference: (1) hostile, (2) unidentified, (3) friendly sea tracks, (4) friendly land tracks. In response to the interrogator's enquiries the GL operator would state that the plot was either "not seen", "unidentified," "friendly" or "SOS". A distinction was also made between the action to be taken by the duty controller at the centre with reference to radar and ROC tracks whose designation was shown, by GL interrogation, to be inaccurate. Tracks which showed broad IFF were to be labelled SOS.

Some idea on the amount of work that the corps did with GL radar can be gained from a report dated February 23, 1943, which showed that more than 8,500 aircraft had been challenged by this means. The results were: number of occasions on which GL sets were responsible for changing "X" to "Friendly" track, 21; number of occasions on which GL sets were responsible for preventing double tracking, 14; number of occasions on which GL sets picked up tracks of aircraft showing SOS, ten.

It was recommended in the report that public wire circuits should be used to provide connections between GL equipment and ROC centres, thus obviating the delay in the passing of plots from the other posts on the cluster. Great difficulty had been experienced by other posts on the same cluster as a GL post in getting their plots through when the GL interrogator was working and this had, on occasion, delayed plots of hostile aircraft. The request for special circuits between the GL sets and the Royal Observer Corps centres was approved by Air Ministry on March 30, 1943.

The GL set used by the ROC comprised three basic units: generator, transmitter and receiver. Each was mounted on its own chassis and was therefore capable of being independently moved. The generator was run by a petrol engine and its current was used to power the transmitter as well as to provide lighting and heating for the transmitting and receiving cabins. The transmitter was enclosed in a cabin which was surmounted by the two transmitting aerials. The main aerial projected a pulse within a predetermined arc, while the secondary aerial was capable of direction on any bearing within the arc. The receiver was housed in a similar though slightly larger cabin which carried an aerial fixed in permanent relation to the cabin roof. The cabin itself was mounted on a pivot which allowed it to be rotated throughout 360°. The rotation of the cabin, and therefore the direction of scan of its aerial, was controlled manually from within the cabin by means of a double crank similar to that provided for propelling small boats at the seaside. The GL unit was under the control of the post head observer, with a small team of three or four RAF personnel for operation and maintenance of the technical equipment. An operational crew comprised three observers and one airman, two observers operating the receiver and reporting to centre and the third manning the transmitting cabin.

Transmission from the main aerial was automatic, while that from the secondary aerial was controlled by the transmitting operator as directed by the receiving operator over the interconnecting telephone link. Reception of mirrored reflections of transmissions within the arc of the transmitter's operational range was automatic and was recognised by blips created on the display on a scan tube. Blips took the form of an inverted "V" of bright light breaking a horizontal line of light on the tube.

Under operational conditions No 1 operator would sit in front of the display with No 2 operator, who would be wearing the head and breast set connecting him to the interrogator in the centre, sitting beside him. No 3 operator sat in the transmitting cabin in front of a panel with the controlling knob for the secondary aerial. When a blip appeared on the tube No 1 would note its bearing and call up No 3 to ask him to operate the secondary aerial on that bearing. When the secondary circuit had been completed on the given bearing the blip would increase in height by three or four times. No 1 observer would then read off the bearing and range of the blip to No 2, who would report "Unidentified" on that bearing and at that range to centre. When IFF was being used by the aircraft it created a second blip on the scan tube of the GL receiver, the blip being a short vertical line to the immediate right of the inverted V; this established its identity as "Friendly."

To further complicate ROC procedures a new British/United States phonetic alphabet was introduced in January 1943, it was covered by ROC signals instruction No 5, dated December 17, 1942. Ack and Beer, etc, which had existed since the First World War, disappeared and in their place came Able, Baker, Charlie, Dog, which were to last until the Nato alphabet of Alpha, Bravo, etc, of the 1950s.

Probably one of the most remarkable operations instructions ever issued to the ROC concerned not aircraft but carrier pigeons. The July 1943 operations instruction No 33 asked for reports of carrier pigeons flying outwards from Britain which might have been despatched by enemy agents. The south- and east-coast posts and satellites were involved, being required to report the grid reference, direction of flight, number of pigeons and height above sea level. The sequence was "George Two, carrier pigeon, 3999, south-east, one at one hundred feet, weather fine, wind south, strong." The instruction had a footnote:

"Doubtful identification should not deter an observer from making a report, but in this case the word 'Doubtful' should precede the word 'carrier pigeon'." Group commandants are to prepare reports in triplicate and despatch them to headquarters on the "first and fifteenth days of each month."

One other requirement, although issued at the behest of the RAF, was hated by most pilots and not thought much of by the Corps members. Through ROC headquarters the Air Ministry had issued, in November 1943, operation instruction No 42: "Reporting of Dangerous Low Flying." This required posts outside designated low-flying areas to report low-fliers, together with exact time and identification letters (squadron code). Many a young pilot officer who landed, after beating up his girl-friend's house or a passing railway train, found himself on the carpet all the minute details of his flight having been supplied by the ROC.

Chapter 13
SAFETY
AND SEABORNE

"Hello Neemo, Hello Neemo, this is Darky, this is Darky, over."

A commonplace wartime ground-to-air message, but to the pilot of Lancaster R for Roger lost in the night with his bomber damaged and low on fuel it was little short of salvation. Somewhere down in the inky blackness was a human being with a radio who could guide the crippled aircraft to an airfield where there would be warmth and safety. The voice might have come from the flying-control section of an RAF station or, in this case, from a lonely post of the ROC, watching and plotting.

The pilot, his recognition lights switched on, thankfully gave his call-sign and waited for the disembodied voice to give guidance. The post observer reported the position of the aircraft to his centre, where the message was passed swiftly to the nearest Fighter Command operations room. Back came the flying-control liaison officer's directions. The observer again called the wandering aircraft: "Hello Koska, R for Roger, Hello Koska, R for Roger, steer 310° ten miles for Fairwood Common, steer 310° ten miles for Fairwood Common."

Hardly believing his luck, the pilot turned on to the new course. Searchlight beams appeared, pointing along the bearing 310°, and then suddenly the twin rows of airfield lights came into view. The ROC had helped yet another lame duck to find its way home and the post went back to plotting other passers in the night.

The pilot little knew that his progress had been reported by post after post and that when he had neared high ground red flares had been made ready to warn him.

It was all part of a massive organisation for assisting friendly aircraft which, by 1944, was tuned to a fine pitch. It had not always been so; the build-up had taken two-and-a-half years and the ROC had been one of the key factors throughout. In the early stages of the war little attention had been given to the problem of getting lost aircraft back to an airfield and it was assumed that radio would solve everything. Radios, however, could be shot up, go wrong or be affected by electrical storms. As recorded in Chapter 6, an attempt was made to provide a flare network for navigation, using the Observer Corps, but this was doomed to failure in a blacked-out country with enemy raiders about.

Through 1940 and the early part of 1941 the corps put through tens of thousands of plots on aircraft which appeared to be lost. The controllers rang the ROCLOs at fighter groups, who in turn tried to find out where the machine had come from and if they could get it down safely. Because there was no co-ordinating authority and the fighter-group operations rooms were laid out for the specific purpose of air defence, many aircraft roamed the country until they ran out of fuel or crashed into high ground. After one raid on Brest in 1941 no fewer than 34 Bomber

Command aircraft failed to find an airfield and crashed.

F. T. K. Bullmore, a squadron leader at flying control, Boscombe Down, played a major role in extracting some organisation from the chaos, initially by using ROC information on a private-venture basis. He propagated his ideas at 12 Fighter Group, Watnall, and was later posted to the Air Ministry to co-ordinate ROC, Fighter Command, Bomber Command and searchlight channels using flying-control liaison officers at each fighter group.

In his book *The Dark Haven* Bullmore is high in his praise of the ROC as a whole and of the part it played in saving lives. He describes one of many visits to the corps as follows:

"One particular post I remember was on the edge of the cliffs of Dunnett Head*, which is the extreme northern tip of Caithness, near John O'Groats. On the occasion of my visit it was a wonderful sunny evening in July. The observers on duty were two old boys, one of whom was a gamekeeper in private life and his comrade the local publican. I spent a long time chatting to them and telling them of the important part they had played in saving an Anson that had been lost and was running short of petrol. They in their turn related some of their winter experiences.

On one occasion they had been isolated in their post for four days and nights because of a blizzard and deep snowdrifts. With no fuel, food or light, these old boys had stuck to their guns although, they admitted, they became a "wee bit depressed" when the gales carried away their telephone line—their only link with civilisation. Although nearly 65 years of age, one of these stalwarts succeeded in climbing up the pole and mending the line which again connected them with the Inverness centre."

In 1941 the standard procedure for an aircraft in distress to obtain searchlight homing – or just to be noticed – was to circle for at least two minutes, fire the combination of coloured lights of the period and send a succession of dots on the navigation lights. The last-mentioned was later amended to the switching on of navigation and downward recognition lights. Any searchlight detachment seeing these signals, or on orders from control, would expose the beam horizontally for 30sec in the direction of the "standard" or "selected" airfield. In order to catch the pilot's eye the beam was then elevated to 45° and depressed again three times quickly and finally left horizontal for a further 30sec. The whole sequence was repeated until the aircraft flew in the right direction, when the beam was to be kept as a horizontal pointer for 2min or until the sound of the aircraft died away. "Canopies" of searchlights were also put up over certain airfields and signal rockets were fired. Because Army searchlights were largely concentrated in defensive belts there were large gaps in the coverage.

Bullmore was mainly instrumental in the RAF obtaining 1,200 surplus searchlights from AA Command which were supplied to RAF airfields to improve the canopy pattern, to RAF camps and sites to provide searchlight homing, and 107 were installed at ROC posts as gap-fillers. On posts operating searchlights it was found necessary to have two additional observers on duty at night to handle the equipment; this meant an additional manning problem. Canopy lights were at first unofficially known as "ROC Lights", but this was frowned upon by the Whitehall section which allocated code names and they were called "Sandra" instead.

From 1941 onwards the RAF began to install TR9D high-frequency short-range radio sets at RAF airfields to help aircraft in distress. The TR9D was a simple transmitter/receiver working on 6,440kHz and with a useful range of about ten miles. In the aircraft it was operated by the

---

*Post 39/J.3, Thurso, now 30/C.1, Barrock.

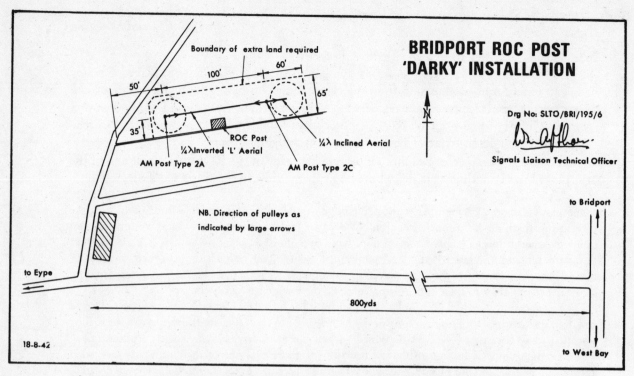

The Air Ministry drawing of a typical "Darky" radio installation at the Bridport, Dorset, post in 1942. Darky posts were responsible for the successful homing of many lost or damaged aircraft

pilot, while on the ground it was fitted with a loudspeaker and was operated by WAAFs. The whole scheme was given the code-name "Darky."

In the autumn of 1942 it was decided by the Director-General of Aircraft Safety to extend the Darky layout to include 45 ROC posts* in areas where RAF coverage was poor. The sites were surveyed, an aerial erected and the TR9 set installed. Darky posts were each allotted to a parent RAF station, which provided technical maintenance and training in R/T procedure. The posts maintained a listening watch from sunset to sunrise, and in daylight on receipt of instructions from centre or when a friendly aircraft was obviously in distress.

ROC operation instruction No 11, dated October 10, 1942, was issued to cover Darky procedure. When a distress message was received a post would reply giving its position in relation to a selected landmark, thus: "Hello Koska, P for Peter; this is the Observer Corps; my position is 120° ten miles from Spalding." Each item was repeated twice. If there was an immediate requirement for the aircraft to land, or if so instructed by the FCLO via centre, the post would give a course to steer.

For an unknown aircraft call-sign the post would use the word "Neemo," while at a later date for civil aircraft using Darky the call-sign "Oakchest" was employed instead of the normal "Koska." Darky posts proved invaluable as part of the overall distress chain and dealt with thousands of messages.

As the safety organisation improved the network had complete co-ordination among the

---

*As RAF stations closed late in 1944 more ROC posts were equipped with Darky, the final figure exceeding 50,

ROC; Fighter Command operations rooms; Bomber, Coastal and Training Commands; and Anti-Aircraft Command. FCLOs performed the vital link and control functions, and by 1944 they were able to call on Darky, searchlight canopies, directional searchlights, airfield pyrotechnics, escort aircraft and "Granite" flares.

Granite was the code name given to an all-ROC operation designed to prevent aircraft flying into high ground in poor visibility. Late in 1943, with the vast increase in air movements at low altitude, particularly of transport aircraft such as the Dakota, it was clear that some form of high-ground warning was essential. Accordingly ROC operation instruction No 34 was issued from Bentley Priory, entitled: "Use of Red Flares by ROC Posts to prevent aircraft from flying into high ground (Code Word 'Granite')." This laid down that Granite posts were to inform centre when the cloud base was down to or below the 1,000ft contour. Four red flares in a rectangle 30ft by 30ft were to be readied in daylight and a simple flare at night, on receipt of the message "stand by for Granite." When the code-word Granite was given the flare or flares were to be lit. Posts were permitted to carry out Granite procedure on their own initiative if there was any danger of an aircraft flying into high ground. At the outset the areas mainly affected were north and north-west Wales, the eastern side of the Welsh hills, east and west sides of the Pennines, the Lake District, south-west Scotland, the Isle of Arran, hills west and north of Montrose and the Ockill hills.

Posts in the following groups were equipped with Granite flares: Derby (16), Manchester (six), Leeds (20), York (17), Wrexham (19), Shrewsbury (18), Caernarvon (13), Lancaster (15),

Diagram showing the working of the organisation for homing lost and damaged aircraft using the Royal Observer Corps. The scheme was perfected from 1942 onwards

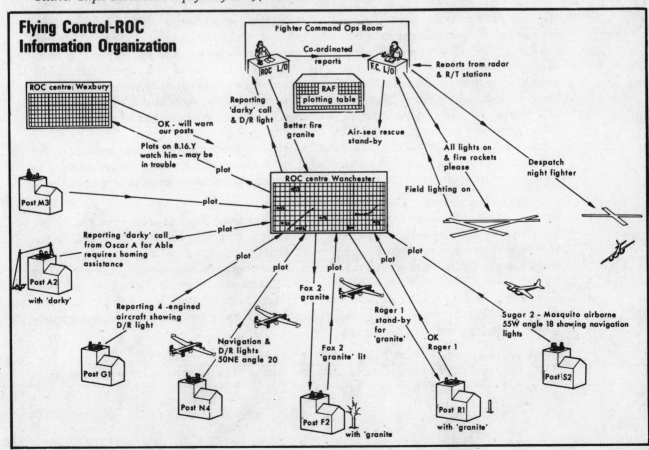

Durham (11), Carlisle (21), Ayr (20), Glasgow (four), Dunfermline (13) and Dundee (13). This made an initial total of 206 posts and these were followed by Exeter with 16 and a whole variety of post sites throughout the country. By April 26, 1945, 340 ROC posts were operating Granite. As an example of its effectiveness, in the area south-west of Newcastle and south of Carlisle there were 13 high-ground accidents from January 1 to December 1, 1943. From June 1 to December 31, 1944, with Granite in operation, high-ground accidents were reduced to three. During the same periods in North Wales the respective figures were 18 and nine.

In addition to the normal Granite sites the RAF called in December 1944 for 15 posts to be equipped with "Augmented Granite." This involved the installation of special HF radio equipment working on 6,440kHz which was called the "Mountain Warning Beacon Transmitter" and gave an audible warning to the pilot.

The overall part played in the Second World War by the ROC in saving lost or damaged aircraft cannot be overstated. A figure of 7,000 aircraft saved was given in 1945, but this is certainly an under-estimate. In the five fighter groups from January 1 to October 21, 1944, the number of incidents in which ROC information directly assisted distressed aircraft to a safe landing totalled 338. For the same period more than 1,800 cases of the use of ROC information were logged by the flying-control liaison section at 12 Fighter Group alone. In No 10 Fighter Group one single case of assistance concerning the ROC involved no fewer than 85 US Army Air Force Dakotas. There were innumerable cases where ROC members rescued aircrew following crashes, directed ambulances and rescue vehicles to crash sites and sent air-sea rescue and other vessels to aircrew down in the sea. Four typical reports of ROC participation in bringing aircraft down safely were:

"June 11, 1944, Halifax of 4 Group at Topcliffe
Reported circling flashing navigation lights by ROC six miles south-east of Oban at 02.15. Oban requested to expose searchlight on to Port Ellen and try to make contact on Darky. At 02.30 aircraft was showing IFF. Oban made R/T contact and passed aircraft course and height to fly to Port Ellen. Made good course for Port Ellen but at 03.00 began to circle off Mull of Kintyre. Machrihanish were asked to light airfield and call on Darky. Aircraft turned north at 03.17 without any contact being made by Machrihanish. Port Ellen, who were also calling, were unable to make contact. R T contact was finally established from Port Ellen 'Occult' site and instructions for reaching Port Ellen were passed to aircraft, which landed safely at 03.37.

Pilot's report stated he was completely lost, experiencing severe icing conditions and was on last fuel tank. Mortars which had to be fired from Port Ellen were of the greatest assistance owing to heavy mist which was covering the airfield. Pilot expressed appreciation for the assistance rendered.

July 7, 1944, Fortress based at USAF Bovingdon
At 21.03 Weston Zoyland reported receiving Darky call from 'Lasca D' asking for Bovingdon, but could not make two-way contact. The weather was very bad with low cloud and storms. Henstridge were asked to obtain a bearing on the HF D/F (6,440kHz) and they reported that they could hear the aircraft on their Darky, asking to land. Exeter instructed to swing their HF D/F to 6,440kHz and call the aircraft. At 21.09, Yeovil ROC to call the aircraft on Darky from their posts L.1 and H.1. At 21.18 Weston Zoyland reported hearing 'Lasca D' saying he is now OK and at the same time ROCLO reported post H.1 had contacted aircraft and given position which was acknowledged. Aircraft proceeded to Bovingdon.

August 12, 1944, Oxford from 21 Flying Training Command at Wheaton Aston
ROC and Army reported this aircraft circling and flashing SOS (E.870). 93 Group asked to watch

track and be prepared to land at Worksop. At 04.00 ROC asked to light Granite flares on high ground to west as aircraft reduced height to 500ft. At 00.52 received report from NW filter room FCLO that Oxford, flown solo by pupil pilot, may be in this area with R/T u/s. Asked controller Church Fenton to send Mosquito to lead Oxford to Worksop. AALO asked to lay on S/L homing to Worksop with three S/Ls south of Sheffield. No other searchlights available. Aircraft continued to orbit. Mosquito fired lights but could not safely reduce height. Aircraft then made course for Worksop, who were instructed to fire mortar. Aircraft landed safely. Pilot was lost in cloud, saw Granite and flew on reciprocal, saw searchlights and Mosquito, picked up Worksop mortar and airfield lighting and got homing instructions on TR9. Pilot and parent station very grateful for assistance.

August 22, 1944, Lancaster of 5 Group, Dunholme Lodge
SOS fix on Lancaster received while aircraft was crossing French coast. Owing to large number of aircraft returning at the time it was not possible to pick out definite track, but a series of good MF D/F fixes enabled FCLO to warn ROC when and where aircraft should cross coast. ROC plotted aircraft immediately it crossed coast at Bexhill and searchlight homing was laid on at Manston, where aircraft made a successful landing on two engines. Pilot reported that two engines had been put out of action in combat."

While the corps was busy saving the lives of aircrew it was also deeply engaged in warning both civilians and the military on the ground. Apart from the local warnings issued to industrial sites and to localities involved in the tip-and-run raids the ROC, by 1943, was at last in a position through alarm controllers, to take over the issue of national air-raid warnings.

The installation of the long-range board at centres gave a clear indication of raids approaching all groups, and this was the key to the devolution of the warning system to the ROC. Alarm controllers were appointed to groups as and when modernisation had been accomplished; many of these were men who resigned from the corps to undertake the exacting duties under the aegis of the Ministry of Home Security. The Cabinet approved the whole scheme in June 1943, and the first "Standard" centre, at Truro, was ready at the end of that month, two days before Air Commodore Ambler left the ROC and was posted to Fighter Command as Deputy Senior Air Staff Officer.

The process of revising centres and transferring air-raid warning control went hand-in-hand, starting with Truro, then passing along the south coast, back across England from Colchester to Wales and thence in a zig-zag pattern right up to Inverness. The final warning transfer from Stanmore and fighter groups to the ROC was completed on April 22, 1944. From that time the national warning messages (Red, Purple and White) were issued throughout the land from ROC groups. England, Scotland and Wales were divided into 157 warning districts, each of which was known by the name of a main telephone exchange and a group of three code letters. These exchanges were called district distributing centres (DDCs) and were responsible for taking the warning messages from the ROC centre warning officer and distributing them. Three types of warning message were used:

Air-raid message "Purple" Issued during blackout hours as an instruction on which exempted light was extinguished. This was a confidential message without the public sirens being sounded.
Air-raid warning "Red" Issued as an instruction for the sounding of the rising and falling "alert" on public sirens, and the mobilisation of the civil-defence services. All exempted lighting was to be extinguished whether or not a "Purple" message had been given. "Red" was intended to give the public about 5min warning of an impending attack.

Attack Warning Red

Air-raid message "White" Issued to cancel both "Red" warnings and "Purple" messages. On receipt of the "White" message public sirens, if they had already sounded the "alert", would then sound the steady note for "raiders passed."

Because of time lags in the reporting system as a whole, the range at which a "Purple" message was issued was calculated from a point 20 miles from the boundary of a warning district (the distance a bomber might see lighting in that district). This allowed $4\frac{1}{2}$ min before a raid reached the warning district boundary. The basic speed of an aeroplane on which these calculations were made was 210 m.p.h., but as speeds increased the ranges were cut.

Warning officers had to show a considerable amount of skill in their assessment of each raid and mentally calculate the speeds involved. Their basic tool was the vertical long-range plotting board. On it they could see all aircraft approaching the group area and decide which warning districts might be affected. The warning officer had to make up his own mind about raids where the group filter room had not labelled them as "X". This often occurred on plots originating with the ROC as "Doubtful" or "Hostile" without radar confirmation. In case any centre was put out of action arrangements were made for an adjoining ROC group to take over while the warning officer transferred to the emergency centre.

Plotting counters used on ROC centre main tables from 1942 onwards

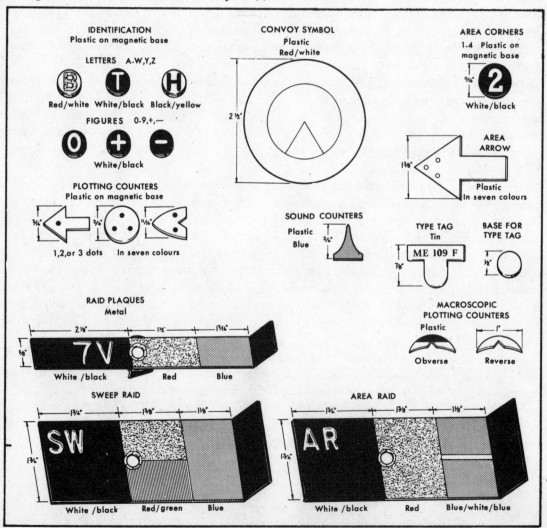

A special policy was adopted in relation to single hostile aircraft, unless there was reason to believe an attack was imminent. Normally the public were not disturbed, but a limited number of warning districts on a special "sensitive list" were informed. The exceptions to the rule were heavy bombers such as the He177 and obvious tip-and-run raiders. A single fighter-bomber or a reconnaissance aircraft was not formally considered sufficient reason for a red warning. This inevitably led to some attacks where the siren was not sounded, despite the fact that the ROC knew exactly where and what the aircraft was. Obviously the public would have been most unhappy to have learned of the single-aircraft rule, but on the basis of slight damage being better than wholesale disruption it was probably sensible. The existence of the "sensitive list" and the policy regarding single aircraft was classified as most secret and was never divulged during the war.

The Corps at the close of 1943 was, in both organisation and technique, at a very high standard of efficiency. Despite a deal of grumbling and a few resignations* the proficiency test system inaugurated by Air Commodore Ambler proved very successful. The post basic test was obligatory and it consisted of (a) a practical and oral test on the post site, (b) a written and oral test on operation instructions and current orders, and (c) recognition and descriptions of 50 aircraft. Eighty marks out of 100 had to be gained for a pass. In mid-1943 the voluntary intermediate test was introduced for posts. This was purely recognition and 85 aircraft had to be recognised out of 100.

Finally on December 12, 1943, the first "master" test, also voluntary, was held throughout the corps. Without doubt this was the most difficult recognition test devised anywhere during the war. Out of 200 different views projected through an episcope, the successful observer had to get 180 correct, including mark numbers where applicable. It was little wonder that Midland Area routine orders stated:

" In view of the exceptionally high standard of recognition ability required to pass it can be said that successful candidates can be regarded as amongst the finest recognition experts in the world."

Several hundred observers just failed to achieve the magic 90 per cent, but 71 did. Two of those who passed and were able to sew the coveted woven Spitfire on their sleeves were observer D. N. James, now Commandant of No 3 Group, Oxford, and observer A. J. Court, now a group officer in 12 Group, Bristol.

Exercises were continuously laid on to test the air defences, notably "Bullseye" and "Eric." Bullseye exercises had started in August 1942 and were covered by ROC operation instruction No 5. They were carried out at night to train Bomber Command crews, searchlights, night fighters, sector operations rooms and the ROC. Command Bullseyes were organised by Fighter Command headquarters and covered several fighter groups, while local Bullseyes were set up by single fighter groups. In addition "coloured" Bullseyes were flown along the red, blue and green set courses from Abingdon, Bassingbourne and Wellesbourne Mountford. The starting line for a Bullseye was marked by intersecting searchlight beams.

In the case of "Eric" exercises, these were started during a comparatively slack period in

---

*The Southern Area Commandant wrote to the Group Commandant, 19 Group, in November 1943 with reference to post 19/T.3, Sittingbourne: "The number of members refusing to take the basic test has been reduced to three. It is confirmed that no exceptions will be made and long service in the corps does not exempt members from taking the test and giving evidence of their efficiency."

January 1943 to test the defences against day and night raiders. Single- and two-seat fighters were used, plus any other aircraft available, and German-type tactics were employed. Such exercises were helpful in streamlining and modifying the control and reporting system but the ROC was, simultaneously, more than fully involved with the vast armada now based on the United Kingdom. During the day Fortresses and Liberators, with Mustang and Thunder-bolt escorts, weaved trails in the sky. Spitfires and Typhoons flew out across the channel along with Mosquitos, Bostons, Mitchells, Marauders and Venturas. In the west and north Welling-

Layout and lines of communication of an ROC centre from 1943. Coastal centres differed only in having a sea plotter on the long-range board to receive coastal radar tracks

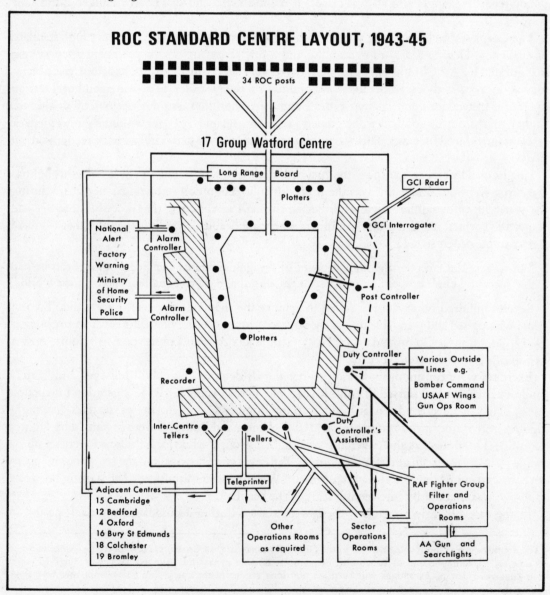

ROC STANDARD CENTRE LAYOUT, 1943-45

tons, Liberators and Halifaxes went to and fro on long-range Coastal Command patrols, while Mosquitoes and Beaufighters scoured the Bay of Biscay and the coasts of Norway and Holland.

Over large parts of the country training flights were continuous, criss-crossed by delivery flights from factory to maintenance unit and MU to operational base. Added to these were experimental, prototype and production test aircraft, calibration and communications machines, gliders and tugs and, in north-west Scotland, the continuous incoming flow of aircraft being ferried from America. By night, from Yorkshire to the south coast, the sky was filled with waves of Lancasters, Halifaxes and Stirlings proceeding to and from the Continent, intermixed with Mosquito pathfinders, intruders and prowling night fighters. Britain at this period was well nicknamed the "unsinkable aircraft carrier," and it was not abnormal for ROC post plots passed over the telephone network in 24hr to total over half a million.

The Fighter Command hierarchy had changed. Sholto Douglas had left Fighter Command for the Middle East at the end of 1942. He had been succeeded by Air Marshal Leigh-Mallory, who in turn had given way to Air Marshal Sir Roderic M. Hill. With the creation of the 2nd Tactical Air Force and a big hand-over of squadrons for the forthcoming invasion of Europe, Hill's Command was renamed Air Defence of Great Britain. This had a whiff of the bracing wires and wooden huts of 1930 about it; fortunately the title was to revert to Fighter Command in October 1944.

Ambler was succeeded as ROC Commandant in June 1943 by Air Commodore Finlay Crerar, who at one time had commanded No 612 Auxiliary Squadron. Finlay Crerar was to guide the corps through one of its most active periods and on into the post-war era.

One of his first tasks was to try to fill the personnel gaps at centres and posts. At October 19, 1943, the corps strength was Class A, 5,883 men and 1,382 women; and Class B, 24,041 men and 1,313 women - making a total of 32,619. To man the long-range boards 665 observers were required, 263 over-50 age-group observers had to be replaced and 103 extra members were needed to afford reliefs at centres.

"Boys" of 16 and 17 had been enrolled, particularly on posts, and many were ATC cadets who proved most useful. A careful eye had to be kept on this and, as Midland Area reported, one boy being paid 9d an hour for duty was found to be aged 14 and not 17 as he had stated. Enrolment was finally limited to 17-year-olds only.

To fill the gaps at centres it was proposed in July 1943 that 700 WAAFs, made redundant by Fighter Command, should become available to the ROC. This seemed a godsend and eventually a total of 244 WAAFs saw service at 13 ROC groups. The number of WAAFs actually posted to the ROC, however, bore no resemblance to either the original promise or the requirement. As late as December 1, 1944, Finlay Crerar wrote to Mr Smith, the head of S.5 at the Air Ministry:

"I am extremely annoyed that you should have vetoed the loan of WAAFs to me by Fighter Command up to the total of 460, which the Secretary of State authorised a year ago. Briefly I need as of today 417 members, or another 200 WAAFs, to complete my requirements at centres alone. Thirty per cent of my crews are undermanned."

On January 1, 1944, Luftwaffe front-line strength in the west totalled 1,410 aircraft. The long-range bomber force consisted of Fliegerkorps IX, in France and the low countries, commanded by General-Major Peltz. Types available for operations in January consisted of Ju88, Ju188 and Do217 bombers and Me410 and FW190 fighter-bombers, plus 56 Heinkel 177s of KG 40 and KG 100. This last-mentioned aircraft was supposed to be Germany's reply to the Lancaster and Halifax, but it had suffered continuous teething troubles.

Peltz had been instructed by Hitler to conduct retaliatory raids against London under the code name Operation Steinbock - which became known in Britain as the "little blitz" or "baby blitz." Steinbock opened on January 21, 1944, with 447 sorties against the metropolis, but the result was extremely disappointing from the German point of view. Out of 268 tons of bombs dropped only 32 tons fell on London, despite attempts at operating pathfinder techniques and the widespread use of "window" silver-paper strips for radar jamming.

Raids on London continued at intervals, the last being on April 18. Hull and Bristol were bombed in March, but from April 20 to May 29 the attack switched firmly to ports in anticipation of the invasion. There were two further raids on Bristol, one on Hull, six on Portsmouth and sorties against Weymouth, Torquay and Falmouth. In all, from January 21 to May 29, just over 2,800 tons of bombs were dropped. Accuracy improved somewhat as crews became more experienced, and the whole series of raids was noticeable for the combination of heavy high-explosive bombs (2,500kg weapons carried by the He177) and masses of incendiary bombs

Two cartoon illustrations from the Ministry of Home Security "Air Raid Warning Instructions," issued in August 1943. This followed transfer of all warning functions to warning officers at ROC centres

"TOTAL BREAKDOWN OF AN OBSERVER CENTRE"

"HE WILL NORMALLY ISSUE A 'RED' WARNING"

dropped from containers. Many of the incendiaries were of the anti-personnel variety.

For the Luftwaffe the little blitz provided much-needed propaganda material, but it also succeeded in wrecking the German bomber arm which might have been used against the Normandy beach-heads. Some 135 bombers were shot down by the RAF and AA Command, while many more crashed on landing or take-off or were hit by British intruder raids on France and the low countries. By April 1 Fliegerkorps IX had barely 200 aircraft on strength compared with 473 on January 20. Thereafter the total of bombers available in the west continued to decline steadily until by June only a handful was available. The air-defence system worked well throughout, with very close co-operation among the ROC, fighter groups and GCIs. The long-range boards proved invaluable, both in track handover and in getting the public warning out in time.

For two members of the corps, the little blitz was a tragedy. The Group Commandant of No 3 Group reported to the Southern Area Commandant concerning a member of the Hambledon Post:

"A shell from one of our AA guns went through the roof of the house occupied by Observer P.C. Guymer and his wife, and exploded in their bedroom. Observer Guymer was killed and she was badly injured . . . Mrs Guymer is also an Observer and a first class one in all respects."

At 3 M.3, Southsea, Hants, another husband and wife team were affected. At 00.45 a.m. on May 23, 1944, a bomb fell within 15 yards of the Royal Beach Hotel on the roof of which M.3 was located. Bricks and stones put the instrument out of action, smashed the wind-screen and littered the site with debris and glass. The Observer and his wife dived for the cubby hole and later emerged unscathed.

As the enemy manned-bomber effort died away in May, the ROC prepared for two very different kinds of major effort, the invasion of Normandy and the V1 robot-weapon attack.

With the spring of 1944 it was clear to the population of Britain that the long-awaited invasion of Europe was just round the corner. The south of England was alive with troops of a multitude of nations, while every country lane seemed to have its complement of guns, tanks or lorries under camouflage netting. Every harbour was choked with ships, landing craft and assault boats.

For the Royal Observer Corps this massing on land and sea was only of passing interest, as all attention was concentrated on reporting, plotting and telling the mass of Allied aircraft which daily filled the sky.

Behind the scenes, however, moves were afoot to give the ROC a vital part to play in "Operation Overlord," the invasion of northern France. On March 11, 1944, the Air-Commander-in-Chief, Allied Expeditionary Air Force, Air Chief Marshal Leigh-Mallory, issued a request for some 2,000 experienced ROC personnel to act as aircraft spotters on defensively equipped merchant ships (DEMS). The authorities were rightly concerned that aircraft-recognition standards were almost non-existent on most of these ships. Unless some experts could be made available there was every likelihood of enemy aircraft passing unrecognised and friendly forces being hit by anti-aircraft fire.

A conference held on April 5, 1944, was attended by the Air Ministry, the Admiralty, HQ ROC, SHAEF, ADGB and the AEAF. The Admiralty wanted the spotters but had limited accommodation available. It was finally agreed that 240 men in pairs could be taken aboard 30

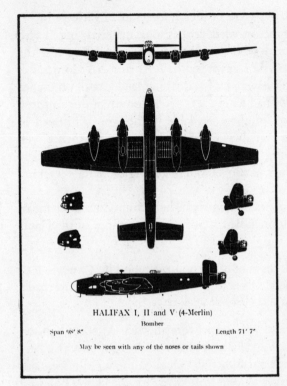

HALIFAX I, II and V (4-Merlin)
Bomber

Span 98′ 8″   Length 71′ 7″

May be seen with any of the noses or tails shown

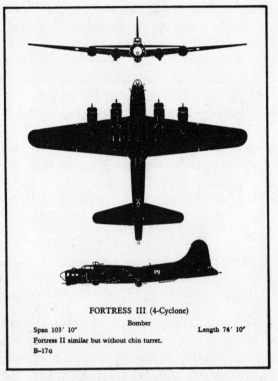

FORTRESS III (4-Cyclone)
Bomber

Span 103′ 10″   Length 74′ 10″

Fortress II similar but without chin turret.
B–17G

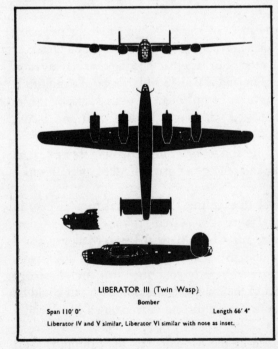

LIBERATOR III (Twin Wasp)
Bomber

Span 110′ 0″   Length 66′ 4″

Liberator IV and V similar, Liberator VI similar with nose as inset.

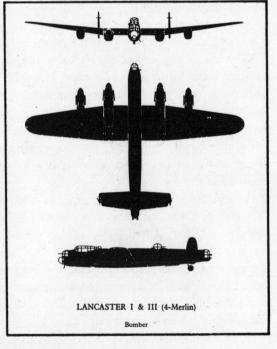

LANCASTER I & III (4-Merlin)
Bomber

The heavy bombers, plotting of which occupied so much of the ROC effort for the last three years of the war

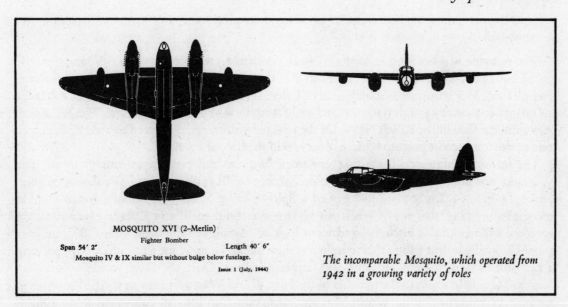

MOSQUITO XVI (2–Merlin)
Fighter Bomber
Span 54′ 2″   Length 40′ 6″
Mosquito IV & IX similar but without bulge below fuselage.

Issue 1 (July, 1944)

The incomparable Mosquito, which operated from 1942 in a growing variety of roles

British LSIs (Landing Ships Infantry) and 90 MT (Motor Transport) ships, while the United States would need 300 men or more. The ROC being a civilian body and largely immobile, it was decided to enlist volunteers into the Royal Navy with the equivalent rank of petty officer for one month with the option of extension to two months if need be. Personnel were to continue to wear ROC uniform with the addition of a navy-blue brassard bearing the letters "RN" and a shoulder badge bearing the word "Seaborne." Members were to be paid a special rate of £1 a day.

Events thereafter moved very rapidly. On April 28, Air Ministry confidential order A.63/L944 entitled "Special Scheme for Royal Observer Corps Participation in Forthcoming Operations," was issued. It outlined details of the whole plan and how observers could apply – through head observers, via group officers and group commandants, to ROC headquarters. At the same time Air Commodore Finlay Crerar sent a personal letter to every post member of the corps:

"I write this message to each of you in every post in the United Kingdom and I want you to read it carefully; I want each of you to consider carefully your own position and make up your mind which path yours must be at this most important crossroads. Much depends on your decision.

Many of you have asked me from time to time whether you could have the chance of taking part in more active operations, and I believe many of you who have for so long been on the defensive will welcome the chance to join in the offensive. I can tell you now of what is not only the most important operational requirement but a handsome and well deserved tribute to the skill and value of the corps to the fighting services.

The supreme command has asked me to provide a considerable number of ROC observers to serve on board ship for recognition duties during forthcoming operations. The highest importance is attached to this request, for inefficient and faulty recognition has contributed largely to enemy successes against our shipping and to losses of aircraft from friendly fire. This request is one which demands the best which the corps can give; it calls for skill in instant recognition, readiness to share the hardships of the fighting services in amphibious operations and personal sacrifice on the part of those members left behind who must carry on . . . No other organisation possesses our skill and experience in aircraft recognition. Our invasion forces need something which we have got. We cannot fail to give it, and give it now."

The response was not long in coming. No fewer than 1,376 observers (701 "A" and 646 "B" men) volunteered, together with 29 officers. Of these, 1,094 reported to the depot at Bournemouth from May 7 onwards. Subsequently 81 were turned down on medical grounds, 209 failed to qualify in the very tough trade test and eight withdrew at their own request. The remaining 796 were enrolled in the Royal Navy. Of the rejected volunteers, 68 agreed to accept posting to one of the south-coast posts to replace observers in the forward zone.

The seaborne volunteers came in every shape and size and every age from 17 to 70. The youngest was almost certainly 17-year-old observer Ian Ramsbotham of Woolaston School, Stoke-on-Trent. Ramsbotham had gained a Spitfire badge in the 1943 master test and could recognise anything that flew. When his service was finished "Petty Officer" Ramsbotham accepted his honourable discharge and went back to school. For the older Class "B" post personnel it usually meant telling their employers they would be away for a month or two, packing a bag and bidding the amazed wife and family goodbye. Only the ROC could take a man who had fought in khaki in the trenches of the First World War, give him an RAF blue uniform for his service in the Second World War and then turn him into an equivalent Petty Officer in the Royal Navy.

The reception depot for the seaborne scheme was set up at the Royal Bath Hotel, Bournemouth, to which a permanent staff of ROC, Royal Navy and RAF officers was attached, under the command of Observer Commander Cooke, seconded from No 11 Group, ROC. The permanent staff consisted of the following:

Observer Commander C. G. Cooke, Commandant
Observer Officer R. E. Reeve, Adjutant

INSTRUCTORS
Observer Lieutenant V. Owers (i/c)
Observer Lieutenant E. H. McLean
Observer Lieutenant A. H. Graham
Observer Officer J. L. Brackenridge
Observer Officer E. H. Heath
Observer Officer W. S. Jackson
Observer Officer A. C. Nisbet
Observer Officer G. T. Scarratt
Observer Officer R. P. Skinner
Observer Officer J. N. Thompson
Observer Officer W. Twiss

ROYAL NAVY
Lieutenant Commander R. Canner (i/c)
Surgeon Lieutenant Glassman
Warrant Gunnery Officer Kelly
Warrant Writer G. A. Moore

ROYAL AIR FORCE
Squadron Leader G. M. F. Warner

ROC liaison officers with defensively equipped merchant ships:
Observer Officers S. G. Tyler, T. E. W. White and J. R. Spence – DEMS Staff Office, Cardiff.
Observer Officers A. Quarmby and D. George – DEMS Staff Office, London.
Observer Officers J. W. D. Evans and S. L. Day – DEMS Staff Office, Southampton.
Observer Officer W. Waring – DEMS Staff Office, Plymouth.

On arrival at the depot, volunteers were subjected to a medical test and a very stiff aircraft-recognition trade test. Those accepted were put through a further intensive course in aircraft recognition and in elementary naval procedures. Initially the recognition test took the form of a film, and one volunteer from the Scottish highlands remarked that it was the first "movie" he had ever seen. To give live practice in picking out hostiles the RAF's flying circus of captured German aircraft laid on fly-pasts. Further naval training was given at HMS *Safeguard*, a land ship in the New Forest. Observers were given the equivalent petty officer rank of Aircraft Identifier and kitted out with RN arm-badges, sou'westers, tin hats, life jackets, sun glasses, rubber boots, etc.

The whole scheme was put together in a remarkably short time and with almost no disagreement among the ministries and Service departments concerned. The effect on the corps as a whole was most marked. Observers from every corner of the land, normally used to the closed environment of a particular post or centre crew, were suddenly flung together for eating, sleeping and working. The barriers of geographical area or of group disappeared and the unity of purpose, thus established, was to be carried on through the annual camps of post-war years. By May 15, 1944, just 16 days after the promulgation of the seaborne scheme, the first observers had been drafted away to their ships. By D-Day on June 6 almost 500 were on board ship; by June 13 this was up to 700. Some returned after one month's service but the great majority remained for two months.

Many had had hair-raising experiences; two were killed by enemy action, 22 survived their ships being sunk, one was injured by shell splinters and one was injured by a flying bomb when his ship was in dock. The members killed were observer J. B. B. Bancroft (MV *Derry Cunihy*) and observer W. J. Salter (SS *Empire Broadsword*).

Messages began to flow in from ships; captains, naval authorities and air commanders – all were unanimous in their praise of the work of the ROC. Special messages of congratulation came in from Admiral Ramsay, Allied Naval Commander-in-Chief, and from Air Chief Marshal Leigh-Mallory, the Air Commander-in-Chief AEAF. The picture became alive with the reports from ships and the observers themselves.

Concerning the SS *John A. Sutter* (aircraft identifiers W. E. Hills and J. F. Rolski), Lieutenant Lyon, commanding US Naval armed guard aboard the ship, wrote to the Commandant, 19 Group:

"Subject named men, formerly members of your command, and now serving as aircraft identifiers on our ship, Merchant Transport 22, attached to my US Naval gun crew, have already proved their weight in gold to us in properly and quickly identifying all aircraft we have encountered in our initial invasion trip.

As an example, on the morning of June 10, with visibility poor, they caused us to hold our fire on two RAF Spitfires which all other ships, except naval units, were firing at for a period of a half hour.

When they reported aboard they told me they could identify anything which they could see. Such has proved to be the case and I find myself, along with my men, relying on them for services far in excess of any other personnel in the crew. It is a pleasure to have them with us, and a great satisfaction to have men so carefully trained to do a job which is so important for the safety of our troops and our cargo."

From the SS *Lysand* it was reported:

"It appears that this vessel has been credited with the Me109 which burst into flames . . . The Master speaks most highly of the behaviour of his DEMS and ROC ratings . . . Aircraft identifier J. Devlin identified the Me109s at the commencement of the attack, while on another occasion aircraft identifier C. S. Reddihough identified a flight of Spitfires and gave a timely warning to the gun crew. The employment of aircraft identifiers in this vessel was therefore fully justified."

Wing Commander P. B. Lucas, Air Staff ADGB, stated:

"The general impression amongst the Spitfire wings covering our land and naval forces over and off the beach-head appears to be that in the majority of cases the fire has come from naval warships and not from merchant ships. Indeed I personally have yet to hear a pilot report that a merchant vessel had opened fire on him."

A Royal Observer Corps DEMS liaison officer wrote:

"I must say I felt very proud of them and the way they were doing their job. They are giving instruction in aircraft recognition to the US gunners and were getting a test ready . . . Naturally, the gunnery officers of DEMS and US armed-guard officers were sometimes sceptical at first, but now they and the ships' Masters are delighted with the venture and the difficulty is going to be to get them to part with the observers who have completed their time.

The officers feel far less worried now that they have expert opinion on identification and as they have learnt from experience that the ROC are correct they rely implicitly on their statements . . . Our men have had complete control over gun crews and not a shot has been fired at our own aircraft in daylight. It should be added that this is in spite of intense fire directed against our own aircraft from the shore and the light landing craft coming to and from the beaches. Two observers reported to me today that they had identified at different times two Me410s, two F w 190s and a third F w 190 immediately on being sighted, which was the direct cause of the first four aircraft being shot down and possibly the fifth . . . I asked one American officer his opinion of our observers and he replied that they had prevented the gun crews from shooting down two of their own Thunderbolts, which speaks for itself . . ."

The ROC efforts during the invasion proved so effective that the AEAF made recommendations for all ships in the invasion fleet to have aircraft identifiers, that the Admiralty should establish a new trade of aircraft identifier and that ROC personnel could be used as instructors. The War Office, at the instigation of 21 Army Group, also wanted help from the ROC and approached the Air Ministry with a view to obtaining the services of some 100 ROC personnel. These were to be stationed near the mulberry-harbour site on the beaches and were to fire signal flares to stop AA fire at friendly aircraft. The War Office letter on the subject was dated August 4, 1944, and it contained one telling paragraph:

"The responsibility is a heavy one and calls for greater expert aircraft recognition than can be provided by the Army, including personnel of Anti-Aircraft Command."

Air Commodore Finlay Crerar went to Normandy to study the Army's problems. Because of the decline in enemy air activity and the Allied advances, it was decided that the provision of 100 observers for the beaches would not be necessary. Instead, Observer Captain V. O. Robinson, North Western Area Commandant, with six other corps officers, visited 65 Army units in France. Robinson's report was submitted on September 25, 1944; it covered the standards of Army aircraft recognition in Normandy and made several recommendations for improvements.

The sequel to the ROC efforts during the invasion came in October 1944 when the Permanent Under-Secretary wrote to Finlay Crerar:

"I am commanded by the Air Council to inform you that they have received from the Lords Commissioners of the Admiralty an expression of their appreciation of the services rendered by seaborne volunteers of the Royal Observer Corps who served in the Royal Navy as aircraft identifiers during the invasion of France.

I am also to inform you that in recognition of their services His Majesty the King has been graciously pleased to approve the wearing of the shoulder badge 'Seaborne' as a permanent part of their uniform by all who took part in this operation and were honourably discharged from the Royal Navy on completion of their contract, or on medical grounds at an earlier date.

The Air Council have learned with satisfaction that as a token of the good work of those members of the Royal Observer Corps who temporarily joined the Royal Navy as aircraft identifiers:

Observer Lieutenant George Alfred Donovan Bourne, Leading Observer Joseph Douglas Witham and Observers Thomas Henry Bodhill, John Hughes, Derek Norman James, Edward Jones, Albert Edward Llewellyn, George McAllan, Anthony William Priestly and John Weston Reynolds

have been mentioned in despatches."

Thirty years later, as this book is being written, there are still serving members of the ROC wearing the Seaborne shoulder flash.

Chapter 14
FLYING BOMBS AND AFTER

While the seaborne observers were adding lustre to the corps' name the south-east corner of England was facing a new form of attack in the shape of the flying bomb. The ROC had a vital role to play in this campaign, and those critics who felt that the days of the "eyes and ears" were numbered were effectively silenced.

Fighting a war on three fronts and faced with day and night bombing of factories and resources Germany had to find a means of hitting back at the British Isles which would not entail the complete destruction of its dwindling bomber arm. As early as 1941 Field Marshal Milch and General Oberst Udet had seen a demonstration of the Schmidt-Argus-Rohr athodyd or impulse-duct engine mounted on a Dornier 217. In essence this was a tube rather like a stove-pipe with slats at the intake end and behind these a series of fuel injectors. When forward speed had been gained the slats opened, admitting air to the tube, fuel was injected and the resulting explosion closed the one-way slats, the exhaust gas expanding out of the rear of the tube. The timed cycle of opening shutters, ignition, closing shutters and combustion gave the engine its peculiar pulsing roar which was to become so familiar in the summer of 1944.

When in 1942 Milch, as Generalluftzeugmeister (director-general of equipment), saw the progress that the German Army was making with Dornberger's brain-child, the A4 or V2 rocket, he decided that the Luftwaffe must have a robot attack weapon of its own. The Field Marshal posted Dipl Ing Lüsser to the firm of Henschel to head a design team aimed at making such a weapon. Mass production of expensive and complex piston engines was out of the question, so the pulse-jet engine came into its own.

In June 1942 the German Air Ministry issued a firm requirement for an expendable, automatically controlled pilotless aircraft to be used in attacks against Britain and particularly London. The design crystallised as a simple torpedo-shaped fuselage with square-cut wings and tailplane and a pulse-jet engine mounted on top over the rear section. A high-blast-effect warhead of 1,870lb was specified and control consisted of a magnetic compass and autopilot with a range-setting/cutout device on the nose. In order to obtain sufficient forward speed for the pulse jet to operate the vehicle was launched up a ramp by means of a steam generator trolley.

The decision to go ahead with the pilotless aircraft was based on a mixture of military and economic necessity and bitter inter-service rivalry. From 1942 onwards it became a race between the Army with the A4 rocket and Luftwaffe with the flying bomb. In December 1942 the first unpowered missile was air-launched from a Focke-Wulf 200 over the Peenemünde Karlshagen research station on the Baltic. In the same month, on Christmas Eve, a powered flying bomb was ramp-launched and flew a distance of 3,000 yards. By July 1943 the machine had flown for a distance of 152 miles and had impacted within half a mile of its target. Full-scale production was ordered and a provisional date of December 1943 was fixed for the opening of the robot attack on Britain.

A tough and enterprising officer, Oberst Max Wachtel, had been in command of the flying-bomb demonstration and experimental detachment at Zempin from June 1943. On August 3 the Luftwaffe sanctioned the formation of Flak Regiment 155(W) to operate the weapon and this absorbed the Zempin experimental detachment. The (W) referred to Wachtel himself and the use of an anti-aircraft title was purely as a cover. The build-up of Flak Regiment 155(W) took place at Bruesterort in east Prussia, which was code-named successively "Windeck" and "Wiesengrund."

The flying bomb was known by a variety of names: Kirschkern (cherry-stone), the original project reference; Feisler 103, the manufacturer's designation; Flakzielgeraet or FZG 76 (AA artillery target apparatus), the cover name used in the Luftwaffe; Höllenhund (hellhound), used by Hitler and the Nazi party; Vergeltungswaffe Eins or V1 (reprisal weapon 1), official German public reference after July 4, 1944; and Maikaefer (Maybug), the standard code name in Regiment 155(W).

Massive preparations were put in hand for the building of 64 main launching sites and 32 reserve sites in a belt from Cherbourg to Calais. By the end of September 1943 no fewer than 40,000 workers from the notorious Todt organisation were working on V1 sites and rail communications. At the end of December 1943 production of V1s was established at 1,200–1,400 a month for January–March 1944 and 3,000 a month by May. From June onwards output was to be raised to 8,000 a month.

In Britain the possibility of rockets or other automatic weapons being used had been considered for a long time, but it was not until early in 1943 that any real notice was taken of German "secret" and "reprisal" weapons. In April Churchill appointed his son-in-law, Duncan Sandys, to investigate such weapons. The main emphasis was on rockets, and little thought was given to a pilotless aircraft. Largely due to the temperament of Lord Cherwell, Churchill's scientific adviser, the investigation and subsequent discussions developed into a verbal brawl.

The original study was code-named "Bodyline" but this was later changed to "Crossbow," which covered all aspects of German secret weapons. The main problem was lack of information on what the weapons actually were and how they would be operated. The picture was further complicated by conflicting British scientific reports and extremely misleading signals from agents on the Continent. Reports of rocket guns, catapults, winged rockets, air mines and aerial torpedoes all served to make critical analysis more difficult.

Because Peenemünde was obviously one of the main research bases for reprisal weapons and it figured largely in agents' messages, a heavy raid by the RAF was made on it between midnight and 01.00 on August 18, 1943. Serious damage was done and the V2 delayed, but no bombs fell on the Luftwaffe establishments engaged on the V1.

In London everyone was groping in the dark and arguing, largely over the reality or otherwise of the V2 rocket. It was only in the Air Ministry Intelligence Directorate that any clear thought was being given to the matter of which weapon was which. This department put forward the idea that there were indeed two weapons, one a rocket and one a flying bomb. On January 3, 1944, the Chief of Air Staff recommended that the Crossbow Committee be disbanded and all studies and intelligence work on German secret weapons be transferred to Air Ministry Intelligence; countermeasures co-ordination henceforth came under Air Commodore Pelly.

The first breakthrough came with the finding by a WAAF Officer, Constance Babbington Smith, at the RAF Central Interpretation Unit, Medmenham, of a reconnaissance photograph of a small aircraft-like object on a ramp at Zempin, the original home of Flak Regiment 155(W). When this was linked with the massive ski-shaped sites mushrooming in France it was certain that the flying bomb was indeed a fact.

It was essential for the defences, both military and civil, to know what sort of threat they were up against. How fast did it go? At what altitude? What was the powerplant? And was it radio-controlled? These questions required urgent answers. All the experts concentrated on the task of finding out but one section in particular, Air Intelligence 2G, produced the answers. In AI 2G was Squadron Leader Golovine, a multi-lingual engineer whose father had been a White Russian general. Golovine had done a great deal of intelligence work in Germany, Jugoslavia and elsewhere before the outbreak of war and he had a particularly enquiring mind. He was very concerned over the powerplant for the flying bomb, about which no-one seemed to have any ideas. He began investigating, to the disgust of Cherwell, who didn't believe in the project. After much fruitless discussion he visited Professor (later Sir William) Hawthorne, a scientific officer at the Royal Aircraft Establishment.

In Golovine's own words:

"I posed the problem: 'What the hell can this be, because we are stuck?' He just looked at me vaguely and said: 'Michael, this is something rather special, I think. It's a constant-volume athodyd'."

After giving an explanation of how an athodyd (pulse jet) worked, Hawthorne and Golovine worked out some basic figures using ordinary petrol as fuel. There was ample to get from France to London; this had to be it, but how could they prove the theory? By a stroke of luck a Major (later General) Jacobsen in Sweden sent a message to London that an odd sort of pilotless aircraft had crashed and some fuel had been collected. Golovine's deputy flew to Stockholm and returned with a bottle of blue fluid. Golovine thereupon rushed round to see his old friend Air Commodore Banks, Director of Engine Research and Development, who had the bottle analysed and found it contained ordinary low-grade petrol. It was indeed a pulse jet fitted to the flying bomb.

Golovine had already prepared a drawing and had assessed the aerodynamics of the V1. He then found problems on whether the structural weights were feasible. After initial rebuffs by the Ministry of Aircraft Production he and Group Captain Silyn Roberts went down to see Sidney Camm, Chief Designer of Hawker. At the end of the second meeting Camm simply said: "Can I have a contract for 10,000 of these airframes?"

Golovine had proved his case, but there remained one last piece of the jigsaw: Was the V1 guided to the target or was it flown on a compass? Wing Commandor Barton, a signals specialist, pointed out that compass settings would have to be done in a non-magnetic building, whereas for radio it would not matter. Golovine thereupon asked for an agent to be parachuted into France with a single brief: to obtain a nail or a screw from the inside wall on one of the ski sites. The man dropped over France, joined the Todt organisation and later returned with a nail. It was made of copper, therefore the flying bomb used an automatic pilot with a compass.

AI 2G then proceeded to assemble an almost complete description of the V1 and its characteristics, including probable flight altitude and speed. This information was fed into Air Defence of Great Britain and from there disseminated to the fighter force, the operations rooms, radar and the ROC (the last-mentioned through operation instruction No 51, issued April 22, 1944).

As a direct result of the deductions of Air Intelligence, the "Diver" procedure had been evolved and the observers at Dymchurch were able to recognise the first V1s when they roared in on the night of June 13, 1944★. It is of interest to note that on June 13 the duty group captain in the command operations room was Group Captain Walker, formerly Deputy Commandant ROC. He telephoned Air Marshal Hill, who passed the message on to Whitehall. Within three minutes of the first V1 crossing the coast Churchill had been told of the fact.

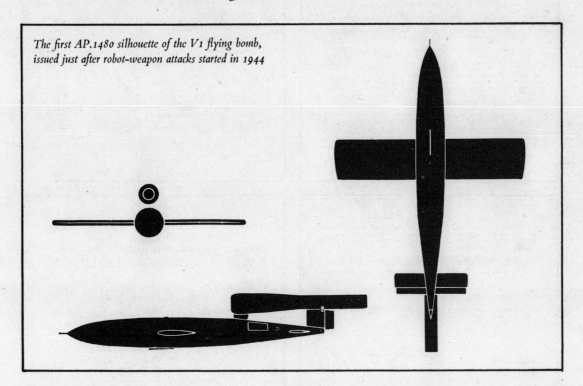

The first AP.1480 silhouette of the V1 flying bomb, issued just after robot-weapon attacks started in 1944

Oberst Wachtel was months late in getting his Flak Regiment operational, and the first firings were at the instigation of Hitler and against the wishes of the Luftwaffe. His ski sites had been smashed by RAF and American bombing, as had the railway marshalling yards which were his supply arteries, while back in Germany there had been production delays because of the attentions of British and American aircraft. Wachtel was forced to delay the first salvoes and build a network of dispersed, simplified and well-camouflaged launching ramps.

It had been the intention to combine V1 mass attacks with a maximum effort by the aircraft of General-Major Peltz's Fliegerkorps IX. Such an all-out assault at the end of 1943 by manned

★ See Prologue, pages 7—8.

S E C R E T

HEADQUARTERS, ROYAL OBSERVER CORPS.
OPERATION INSTRUCTION

OPERATION INSTRUCTION No.....51   DISTRIBUTION:-
DATED ....22.4.44.
CANCELLING ....NIL.   See end of Instruction.
H.Q. REFERENCE...ROC/S.501/OPS.

SUBJECT:-   DETECTION AND REPORTING OF HOSTILE PILOTLESS
AIRCRAFT.

(Code word "DIVER").

INFORMATION.

1. It is possible that the enemy may attack targets in this
country with pilotless aircraft launched from sites in the
Pas de Calais and Cherbourg areas, if, and when he has completed his preparations.

2. It is anticipated that Radar Stations will be able to
detect such aircraft, but may only be able to discriminate
between pilotless and other aircraft by track behaviour,
including the source of origin and line of flight. It must
be realised, however, that an attack by pilotless aircraft
may first be detected by R.O.C. Posts.

3. As pilotless aircraft can operate in conditions which
would preclude operations by normal aircraft, it is to be
expected that the enemy will take advantage of such conditions.
Interceptions of pilotless aircraft may therefore have to be
made in difficult conditions and particular attention to
accurate height determination will be needed. Moreover, it
can be anticipated that these aircraft may fly at speeds up
to 400 miles an hour, and therefore accurate and speedy
reporting is most necessary.

4. Some of the possible characteristics of pilotless aircraft
are detailed in Appendix 'A'. It is stressed that it is unlikely, especially at first, that Post Observers will be able
to distinguish with certainty, pilotless aircraft from others,
particularly by sound. Until, therefore, it is known that
such aircraft have been used, "DIVER" reports are not to be
/originated

-2-   S E C R E T

originated on sound plots unless no reasonable doubt exists
that the sound comes from a pilotless aircraft.

5. According to present information, the only Groups likely to be directly concerned with attacks by pilotless aircraft are the Maidstone, Bromley, Watford, Horsham, Winchester,
Yeovil and Bristol Groups. Such information as is available
about probable targets will be issued later.

6. It is pointed out that these instructions are drawn up
in order that a possible attack by new methods can be
speedily and quickly reported. Amendments will be issued
in the light of experience or when further information becomes available. At the same time all concerned must clearly understand that the need for security regarding these
instructions and their implications is of paramount importance.

INTENTION

7. To lay down a procedure for reporting the presence and
movements of hostile pilotless aircraft.

EXECUTION

Action by Post Observers

Post Observers are:-

8. When "DIVER" procedure is not already in force, to pass to
the Centre the code word "DIVER" preceded by the Post letter
and number immediately they sight a likely hostile pilotless
aircraft.

Example "Able Wun - DIVER".

9. After a short pause to give a plot. This first and all
subsequent plots are to follow normal reporting procedure,
but the code word "DIVER" is to be used in place of the
identification name of aircraft.

Example "Able Wun (Centre replies Able Wun) - "DIVERS" -
8327 - N.W. - Six at Seven?

/10...

-5-   S E C R E T

27 Tracks on the Long Range Board are to be distinguished
by the use of a red circling counter before the Raid
designation on the Tote Board and behind the arrow or shield
on the Long Range Board.

CANCELLATION OF "DIVER" PROCEDURE.

28. Notification of cancellation of "DIVER" procedure will
be received on the sea plotting line by the words
"Cancellation DIVER" repeated three times.

DATE OF EFFECT

29. This Instruction is to come into operation with effect
from 8th May, 1944.

                         J.G.Lim

                   Air Commodore,
                       Commandant,
                   ROYAL OBSERVER CORPS.

DISTRIBUTION.

Headquarters, Southern Area)
             Western Area)   10 copies.

Headquarters, Midland Area)
             N-Western Area) 1 copy each for information.
             Scottish Area)

Group Commandants Nos. 1, 2, 3, 17, 19, 22 and 23 Groups -
                                              8 copies.
             4, 12, 14, 15, 21, 18, 24 and 25
                            Groups - 1 copy.

Head Observers Nos. 1, 2, 3, 17, 19, 22 and 23 Groups -
                                              1 copy.

Ministry of Home Security - 16 copies.
H.Q., A.D.G.B. (OPS.2)   - 2   "
Air Ministry, D. of Ops. (A.D)2 - 6 copies.
O.R.S., A.D.G.B.   - 2 copies.

                                S E C R E T

APPENDIX 'A' to Operation Instruction No. 51 dated 22.4.44.

PILOTLESS AIRCRAFT
Possible Characteristics.

1. Size   - Likely to be about 20 feet in span
                    and length.

2. Silhouette   - Monoplane, with a long fuselage
                    and short nose. The tail plane
                    is probably fairly small.

3. Maximum Speed - Is likely to exceed 400 m.p.h.

4. Average Speed - Speed increases with range from
                    launching point until operational
                    height is reached.

                    Probable speeds are -

                    (i) At 10 miles from launching point
                        250 m.p.h.
                    (ii) At 20 miles from launching point
                        280 m.p.h.
                    (iii) At 30 miles from launching point
                        330 m.p.h.

                    the latter speed being maintained
                    thereafter.

5. Operational Height - Between 5000 and 10,000 feet. 6000
                    feet with a cruising speed of 330
                    m.p.h. is considered probable.

6. Flight Path   - Steady climb to about 6000 feet for
                    25 miles at the speeds given in
                    para.4 above and then level flight
                    in both vertical and horizontal
                    plane.

H.Q. Reference ROC/S.501/OPS.

Pages from the original ROC Operation Instruction No. 51 on "Diver" procedure for dealing with V.1 flying bomb attacks. It was issued on April 22, 1944, nearly two months before the first V.1 crossed the Kent coast and unmanned bombers would have created chaos in south-east England and could well have upset the timetable for the Normandy invasion. As it transpired, Fliegerkorps IX had to carry out the little blitz on its own from January 1944 onwards and suffered such grievous losses that it was no longer a fighting force by the time the V1s were ready.

Wachtel wanted to delay the opening of his offensive, code-named "Rumpelkammer" (lumber room), until he could send over continuous waves of V1s. Berlin's insistence on an immediate start meant that June 13 was a fiasco and the element of surprise was completely lost. The attack was not resumed until the night of the 15th, when 75 flying bombs exploded on land, and a further 65 arrived on the following day. The Fighter Command operational-research branch analysis of the first week of V1 attacks (June 15–22) showed that there were difficulties in identification and a certain amount of disjointed tracking. From the ROC point of view there was, certainly, an amount of double tracking owing to the number of posts from which one flying bomb would be visible.

Landfall was usually made between Dover and Brighton, with the majority of bombs between Dymchurch and Beachy Head. At that time flying bombs were fired from an area extending from Dunkirk to Rouen, the tracks being straight with slight deviation to left or right just before crash. Average airspeed was 340 m.p.h. (between 240 and 400 m.p.h.).

In height there was a remarkable similarity between the height distribution given by radar at 40 miles from coast and that given by the ROC at the balloon barrage. It appeared from each series of estimates that an appreciable proportion of the bombs flew at 3,000ft and above or at 1,000ft and below.

ROC recognition of flying bombs was good, no case being found of a bomb coming in without being identified as such, though it was suspected that the Diver identification was frequently given to the tracks of friendly aircraft. In the matter of hand-over between radar and the ROC in the first week, of the 734 filter room tracks considered to be justified as Diver tracks, 544 were picked up and continued by the corps. The impact of flying bombs on the civil population was serious. After nearly five years of war, blackout and rationing Britain was faced with a weapon lacking human direction or control. It was altogether unnerving, while the actual horizontal blast effects of the weapons themselves greatly exceeded those of ordinary bombs.

Civil-defence planning for rocket and flying-bomb attacks had been going on for many months; they included mass evacuation of London and certain south-coast centres and provision of more shelters. The Chiefs of Staff estimated, in February 1944, that a combined bomber/flying-bomb assault might give an initial weight of up to 625 or even 900 tons of high explosives in 10hr followed by 45–130 tons every 24hr. These figures were substantially scaled down in mid-March but still represented a most serious threat. When the flying bombs did start in earnest rumours began to spread and confidence was at a low ebb. It was not until the morning of July 16 that Herbert Morrison, the Home Secretary, rose to tell the Commons that pilotless-aircraft attacks had begun and the newspapers splashed the story. Just as the Germans had several names for the pilotless aircraft, so did the British: buzz-bomb, P-plane, doodlebug, flying bomb and V1 all found their way into everyday language. On June 19 the Cabinet decreed that the V1 should be officially described as a flying bomb and not as a pilotless aircraft.

Air Marshal Hill had put into operation the Overlord/Diver plan which called for reinforcement of gun defences in London and on the North Downs, relocation of barrage balloons to a line mid-Surrey to mid-Kent and the maintenance of as many fighters as possible on patrol over the coast. Hill was hampered by the limited fighter force available because of the demands of the Normandy invasion. The most successful interceptions of the fast-flying V1s were made by Tempest Vs and Spitfire XIVs, but even these had to be stripped and polished to extract every ounce of performance. The newly introduced Meteor jets were fast enough but only one squadron, No 616, was available – at Manston from August 1944. Despite all efforts, in the fortnight after June 19 half the flying bombs reaching the coast were getting through to London.

As had occurred on the night of June 13, when the first V1s arrived, the pick-up of coastal radars was generally inadequate and was often confused with friendly aircraft over the channel and France. A great responsibility therefore lay on the ROC. The observer groups most affected were Horsham, Maidstone and Bromley, and through these groups the V1s cut a path which became known as doodlebug alley. Many V1s penetrated to the Watford and Colchester Groups, while Winchester had a number aimed mainly at Southampton.

Even if radar was uncertain, the post observer in daylight, night or bad weather could pick out the V1s by sight or sound. It was therefore decided to establish RAF forward air controllers at the Maidstone and Horsham centres, using a twin-channel VHF/RT mobile at each location and special liaison circuits to the Biggin Hill sector. The RAF controllers were therefore able to direct the fighters straight from the ROC table plots. More than 200 V1s were destroyed in this way from the two centres. The success of this method of interception was largely the result of trials carried out earlier at the Lincoln observer centre in conjunction with the RAF Digby sector of No 12 Fighter Group.

It had become essential to improve the low-level radar cover in the main area of V1 flights, and the United States agreed to loan a microwave early-warning (MEW) radar which was earmarked for France. This equipment had been on test at Start Point in the west of England and it was most suitable for early warning and fighter direction. The MEW went into operation at

The Hawker Tempest, which had the speed to catch the V1

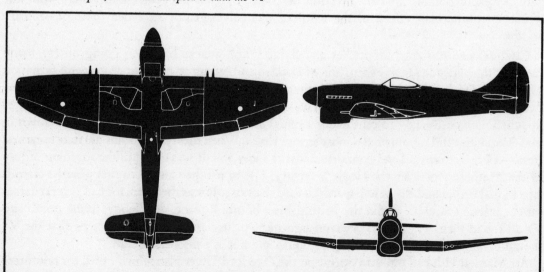

SUMMARY OF INTERCEPTION OPERATIONS AT ORBY G.C.I. STATION.

PERIOD : from 0800 hrs. 19 / 3 / to 1800 hrs 20 / 3 / 44.

1. OPERATIONS commenced at 2110 hrs. 19 / 3 and ended at 2250 hrs. 19 / 3 / 44
owing to cessation of E/A.

2. CREW.

Watch	B			
From ...	1730 hrs. 19 / 3	hrs. /	hrs. /	
To ...	2300 hrs. 19 / 3	hrs. /	hrs. /	

3. CONTROLLER.

A. At Sector	F/O Dean		
B. At Station	S/L Clark, F/O Shimeld, F/O Board, Sgt. Barratt, Cpl. Tricker.		
From ...	1730 hrs. 19 / 3	hrs. /	hrs. /
To ...	0830 hrs. 20 / 3	hrs. /	hrs. /
Interceptions :— (a) Attempted	8 with D.18 6 with D.31		
(b) Handed to Fighter	8 with D.18 6 with D.31		
(c) Combats	1 with D.18		

4. WEATHER REPORT FROM SECTOR.

Sunset 1913 hrs. Sunrise 0708 hrs.

Moonrise 0423 hrs. Moonset 1238 hrs.

Age of moon Last quarter

Time ...	1600-2359 hrs.		hrs.		hrs.		hrs.		hrs.	
Height	Wind		Wind		Wind		Wind		Wind	
	Speed	Dir'n	Speed	Dir'n	Speed	Dir'n	Speed	Dir'n	Speed	Dir'n
Surface	15-25	WNW								
5,000'	35-40	320								
10,000' ..	40-	320-								
15,000'	80	330								
20,000'										
Cloud	3-7/10, 2,500-3,500									
Visibility	Good									
Freezing Level ...	3,000'									

5. ENEMY ACTIVITY.

Time activity commenced 2103 hrs. 19 / 3 approximately.

Time activity ceased 2250 hrs. 19 / 3 / .

By 1944 collaboration between the RAF and the ROC had reached a peak of efficiency. These report sheets from Orby GCI radar station show typical night operations by radar-equipped Mosquitoes in a "Window" electronic countermeasures environment. The resulting destruction of a Heinkel 177 bomber is confirmed visually by the ROC.

6. FIGHTER AIRCRAFT.

Sequence	1.	2.	3.	4.	5.	6.	7.	8.
Squadron	307	307						
Call Sign	Duckpond 18	Duckpond 31						
Type of A/C. ...	Mos.	Mos.						
Letter ...	HK.119 Mk.VIII	HK.522 Mk.VIII						
Pilot ...	F/O Brophocki	F/O Pelka						
A.I. Operator	F/L Ziolkowski	F/O Gasecki						
Time when F/A Taken over from Sector	2037	2034						
Handed back to Sector	2257	2250						
Remarks on Serviceability...	O.K.	O.K.						

7. DETAILS OF ATTEMPTS.

No.	Time	Commencement of Interception.						Hand Over of Chase to Fighter		Result
		Enemy A/C.			Fighter A/C.					
		Pos'n	Ht.	A/S.	Call Sign	Pos'n	Ht.	Time	Pos'n	
1.		About 15 separate attempts were made with Duckpond								
2.		31 (Controller: F/O Shimeld) and Duckpond 18 (Cont.								
3.		F/O Board). All were made on the Western extremity								
4.		of the "Window" area as it was being sown towards the coast. Interceptions were started just over 60 miles								
5.		East of Skegness.								
6.		Fixer Channel was very full, so a/c were brought								
7.		clear after each attempt, and always kept between the "Window" and the coast.								
8.		6 contacts were given by D.31. All were on Friendlies								
9.		or "Window". 8 contacts were obtained by D.18. The								
10.		last in his case was in G.3887 square. This he identified as a HE.177 flying on about 280°. He								
11.		opened fire on the hostile at 16,000 ft. and saw it in flames beneath him. D.18 did not see it crash, but							(combat
12.		R.O.C. saw an a/c crash into the sea in that area at 2148 hrs. (two minutes after 18 gave contact).								
13.										
14.										
15.										

*Attempts to Intercept will finish at one of these stages:
Abandoned (A), Failed (F), Handed to F/A(HO), Detection (AI), Visual (V), Combat (C).

N.B.—" Abandoned " applies only to those attempts which the Controller chooses to discontinue before reaching the stage of " Hand Over," e.g., Attempts against "Friendlies."

8. COMMENT BY CONTROLLER.

A. Enemy activity was/was not on a large scale and consisted of approximately _____ raids which were visible on the "Bowl." "Window" sown very densely.

B. Identification was/was not especially difficult owing to friendly bomber activity :—

C. Advance warning was/was not adequate :—
   (i) Heights :—
   (ii) Courses :—

D. Fighter aircraft were/were not always well placed :—

Attempt No.	Comments on Attempts. The Controller is asked to observe the following points :— (i) The criterion of an attempt is the giving of one vector towards a raid. (ii) The individual attempts should be discussed separately. (iii) The raid number and direction IN or OUT with respect to the target should be given when possible.
	"Window" was observed about 90 miles East of Skegness. Duckpond 31, and Duckpond 18, were taken East, each controlled from an interception cabin. The trend of the incoming hostiles appeared to be N.W. A further two a/c, Lunchon 42 and 48, were also taken out E., ready for handing to the Cabins as contacts were obtained or, alternatively, bringing back inland for Orbit Beacons ahead of the incoming raids. The latter course was adopted, and a further a/c, Lunchon 55, was also taken to an orbit beacon.
	Head on attempts at 18-20,000 ft. were made by Duckpond 31 and 18. As the "Window" was proving very troublesome, endeavour was made to keep both between it and the coast, ready for S/L reinforcement if all G.C.I. attempts proved abortive.
	Duckpond 31 obtained six contacts at ranges from zero to 60 miles from the coast. None of these resulted in combats and one visual obtained was on a friendly a/c.
	Duckpond 18 obtained 8 contacts in approximately the same area. Three of these were on friendlies, and were identified as such by the pilot. The fourth contact was 15/16 miles or so East of Skegness, on an a/c flying a course of about 290°. This was identified as an HE.177 by the pilot, who fired on it at a height of 16,000 ft. and claims to see it going down with flames coming from it. The pilot did not see it crash, but the time of the combat 2146 hrs. appears to coincide with an R.O.C. report of an a/c crashing into the sea in G.38 square at 2148 hrs. This appears to tally perfectly with D.18's claim.
	The area covered by "Window" was 70 miles by 50, but it did not penetrate more than some 10/12 miles inland.

Fairlight, Sussex, on June 29, and was linked to both Maidstone and Horsham ROC centres. From its inception until the time it was handed back at the end of August, this MEW was responsible for directing the "kills" of 142 V1s. As top priority the Telecommunications Establishment, Malvern, built the Type 26 radar, similar to MEW, which was successfully used in conjunction with the Type 24 long-range height-finder.

To further improve the chances of destroying V1s before they got to London, Snowflake/Totter rockets were used by the ROC. Some coastal posts already had these rockets and they were now instructed to fire them during daylight when a flying bomb was sighted within two miles of the post. Thus, as with the tip-and-run raiders, fighter patrols would be warned of the direction of the attack. With the large increase in the balloon barrage to the south-east of London to counter the flying bombs there was a considerable danger of fighters, concentrating on interception, flying into the barrage. It was accordingly decided to equip 32 posts on the south, east and west of the Diver balloon barrage with red Snowflake rockets, to be fired whenever an aircraft within three miles of the post was seen to be approaching the direction of the barrage. These posts were made up of 17 from Bromley, Maidstone and Horsham groups and 15 wireless observer units.

By early July it had become clear that the defensive layout was unsatisfactory and the kill rate too low. General Pile, in concert with Air Marshal Hill, succeeded in putting through a plan for complete redeployment. This involved a gun belt from Beachy Head to Dover, 5,000yd deep and firing 10,000yd out to sea. Fighters operated over the sea and in the area between the guns and the balloon barrage. Minimum height for fighters over the gun belt was 8,000ft, which left a full 2,000ft between them and the height of bursting shells.

The guns started to move south on July 14, 1944. More than 1,000 light and heavy anti-aircraft pieces, 30,000 tons of stores, 23,000 men and women of AA Command and a complete signals network were involved. A great improvement in AA kills of V1s also came about as a result of the supply of American SCR 584 fire-control radars and associated predictors, together with proximity fuzes for the shells.

Experience with radar and the ROC led to better fighter direction and the number of V1s shot down by the intercepters rose appreciably. Pilots had problems in hitting the V1s without themselves being blown up, and a number resorted to the trick of tipping them up with one wing-tip.

For the south-eastern groups of the ROC it was a period of unremitting toil. Not only had the flow of V1s to be dealt with accurately and speedily, but at the same time the day and night bomber fleets, the intruders, the fighters, the transports and the aircraft in distress all had to be plotted and looked after. The long-range boards at centres proved invaluable to ROC controllers and Home Office warning officers. Air-raid sirens were sounded promptly and interference with factory production was kept to a minimum.

The first phase of the V1 attacks lasted from June 13 to September 5, 1944. The Luftwaffe had hoped to maintain a rate of fire of one bomb every 26min from each of 55 launchers, but shortage of supplies and technical defects reduced this to one every 1–1½hr. Despite setbacks and interference, Wachtel's regiment succeeded, in the first phase, in launching more than 9,000 V1s against London and 53 against Southampton. Of these, more than 1,000 crashed after take-off and 3,463 were shot down by the defences. A total of 3,262 avoided the guns, fighters and balloons and crashed on land, of which 2,340 reached the London civil-defence region. The attack only ended because the Allied armies overran the launching areas and forced Flak Regiment 155 (W) to evacuate.

During July a new element had been introduced into the V1 attack, namely air-launching from converted Heinkel 111 bombers. Following experiments late in 1943 He111s were adapted to carry one V1 under either port or starboard wing. Aircraft of KG.3 launched about 400 bombs: 90 at Southampton, 300 at London and some 20 against Gloucester. Some were also launched off the east coast.

When the ground launchers were captured the aircraft of KG.3 were merged with other units and re-opened the offensive, initially from Holland and later from Germany. These V1s were concentrated off the east coast, the first nine appearing on the night of September 5. Altogether about 1,200 V1s were air-fired between September 16, 1944, and January 14, 1945.

On Christmas Eve, 1944, 50 He111s launched V1s aimed at Manchester from between Skegness and Bridlington. Only one reached the city itself. Others came down in several eastern and Midland counties, but the main brunt fell on the area of the Colchester observer group. To meet the threat the defences had been extended, first as far as Chelmsford and later up to Great Yarmouth.

This meant that, as in the south-east, coastal posts found themselves right in the front line and literally in amongst the guns. Typical was the experience of post 18/H.1, Aldeburgh. At 20.24 on the evening of November 5, 1944, a somewhat shaken observer reported to Colchester that Diver 286 had passed within 10ft of the post with the motor still running; it had torn through the adjacent AA battery and crashed into their tents, setting them alight. He added that, as ammunition was heaped near the post and the warhead had not gone off, the position appeared to be far from safe. Permission was given to evacuate the post but the crew decided to stay put. It was subsequently discovered that the V1 had hit one of the guns and the warhead had miraculously split into more than 100 pieces without exploding. The fire had been caused by petrol from the V1s tanks.

In the early hours of January 14, 1945, the last air-launched V1 to reach Britain came down at Hornsey. It appeared that the flying-bomb offensive was over, except for the continued rain of weapons which fell on Belgium. In February 1945, however, intelligence reports on bomb

The "Flight" drawing of the V1 flying bomb, showing the layout of this simple but dangerous weapon which kept a large section of the ROC at full stretch for several months

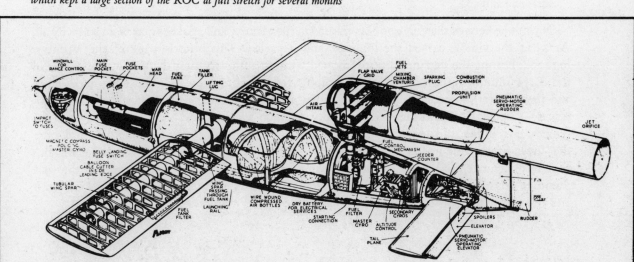

fragments in Belgium suggested that a longer-range V1, which could be fired at Britain from bases in Holland, might be in the offing. The air defences were again redeployed, and on March 3 the final phase of the V1 campaign opened with a ramp-launched missile which landed on Bermondsey.

Flak Regiment 155(W) had been re-formed in Holland, this time under the direction of the SS, and three launching sites had been prepared. Using wooden wings, the revised V1 could achieve a range of 220 miles instead of the original 152. The attack was to be short-lived, as evacuation of Holland was anticipated, and on March 30 the SS ordered the suspension of all V1 operations. In its 26 days the third phase (March 3–29) yielded 275 V1s launched, and of these only 125 were observed by the defences and 91 were shot down. The last bomb to land in Britain fell on Datchworth, near Hatfield, on the morning of March 29.

Air Chief Marshal Sir Roderic Hill, in his official report on *Air operations by ADGB and Fighter Command in connection with the German Flying Bomb and Rocket Offensives 1944–1945* submitted in April 1948, said: "The part played by the Royal Observer Corps – the silent service of the air defences – was an epic in itself."

One incident at the height of the V1 attacks was unique and is unparalleled in any of the regular Services. Members of the royal family made a number of visits to posts and centres between 1939 and 1943, the King himself having toured units in the Colchester group late in 1940. On June 18, 1944, at 22.40, Observer (later Observer Lieutenant) F. R. Hazell and the Reverend D. Southeard were on duty at 17/E.4 post on the Brunswick Tower of Windsor Castle. Visibility was exceptional, with St Paul's and Big Ben clearly to be seen up to 22 miles away. They had been plotting more than a dozen V1s which had crashed within visual radius of the post when a page appeared and informed them that King George VI and Queen Elizabeth would be paying a visit in "one minute." The centre at Watford was alerted by a message that "VVVIPs" were on their way.

The royal party consisted of the King and Queen, Princess Elizabeth and the Queen's nephew, the Honourable Andrew Elphinstone. Detailed explanations were given on how ROC posts worked and the King and Princess Elizabeth showed that they could identify nearly every aircraft in the corps pack of recognition cards. In *Observers' Tale* it is recorded that:

> "The Princess looked up and said: 'Are you going to plot that Wellington?' Number one did some quick work with the binoculars and was able to give number two: 'Wellington, over post – north-east – one at nine'."

During the hour of the visit two V1s crashed in the vicinity and steel helmets were worn by all. At 23.11 the visitors signed the logbook and departed. This historic page of the Windsor logbook, bearing the signatures, was removed without authority after the war by a member of the corps and not returned; only photographic reproductions remain. The King and Queen and the Princess returned the next night when, in addition to Observer Hazell, the chief observer – Captain K. F. Sworder – was on duty. Captain Sworder had been head observer of the Cuffley post in the mid-1930s and in 1937 had been appointed observer group officer. Under the "over-fifties" rule in 1943 Sworder stepped down and became a head observer again, this time to inaugurate the Windsor Castle post and see it through to the closing stages of the war. Sworder was one of the many in the corps over its 50 years who have left officer appointments and re-appeared as non-commissioned officers or ordinary observers.

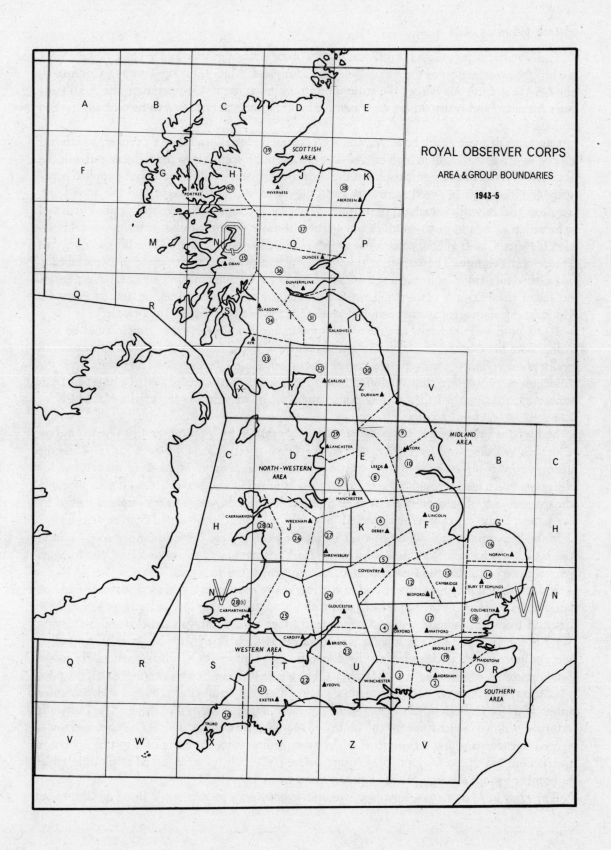

ROYAL OBSERVER CORPS

AREA & GROUP BOUNDARIES

1943-5

Attack Warning Red

The V1 attacks in 1944–45, while calling for maximum vigilance and accuracy, were only part of the overall effort of the corps. Bomber Command, ADGB, Flying Training Command, the US 8th and 9th Air Forces, the communications units, Army Co-operation, the Air Transport Auxiliary and many others were involved and all their aircraft had to be plotted, tracked and assisted.

One form of enemy raid, however, the ROC could do little about: the V2 rocket, which had caused so much argument in high circles in 1943, was not susceptible to the fighters, radar or the ROC. It was not until August 1944 that the authorities, from Swedish and Polish-supplied hardware and information, could accurately assess the nature of the V2. It emerged as a 46 ft-long, 12.7-ton rocket with a warhead of 1,650lb. Propelled by liquid oxygen and alcohol, it could achieve a peak height of 50–60 miles and a range of more than 200 miles. After much deliberation the Vice-Chiefs of Staff considered the V2 menace had passed as the Allies pressed on across France and Belgium. The arrival of the first V2 at Chiswick on the evening of September 8, 1944, therefore came as something of a surprise. Between September 8 and March 27, 1945, no fewer than 1,054 V2s impacted on Britain, with a spread over London and 11 counties. Considerable damage was caused and there were 9,277 dead and injured as a result.

ROC posts were required to give a bearing and angle on rocket trails which could be seen rising from the Continent and also to inform centre of the approximate position of impact. In really good visibility posts reported rocket trails from incredible distances. Sightings from the Midlands were frequent, but the longest-range one was almost certainly on the night of December 29, 1944, when half a dozen posts south-east of Manchester reported a V2 which hit London, 200-odd miles away.

Many posts and centres in the south were severely shaken by V2s and the first one to land on Chiswick was described by 17/D.2, Acton, as "The biggest shaking we ever had." While the action varied from group to group, training continued in earnest. The second master test for the corps was staged throughout the country on Sunday, December 17, 1944. It was probably the toughest aircraft-recognition test of all time, with a film on which aircraft images flashed by for 3–6sec. Some 6,500 observers entered, but only 164 gained the coveted Spitfire arm badge.

In the late summer and winter of 1944 Luftwaffe aircraft were few and far between so far as the ROC was concerned. One occasional visitor, however, was the high-flying Arado 234B jet which reconnoitred the British east coast from September onwards.

Suddenly in March 1945, as the end of the war really seemed in sight, the Luftwaffe had one last desperate fling. On the night of March 3 about 100 aircraft, at low altitude, penetrated the defences from Northumberland to Oxfordshire intent on shooting-up airfields and destroying RAF bombers in the air. The attacks were concentrated on 14 airfields but bombs and bullets were scattered over a wide area, to the discomfiture of many ROC posts, particularly in the Lincoln group. On the night of March 3 Observer J. P. Kelway was driving to 11/L.1 post, Hackthorn, to take over duty. He met a damaged German bomber at zero feet and was killed instantly in the explosion. Altogether some ten RAF bombers were shot down. The Luftwaffe returned with a smaller force on the nights of March 4, 19 and 20. The ROC had operated a special intruder-warning service to RAF bomber groups since the issue of a special operation instruction, No 27, on May 14, 1943. Appropriate ROC centres were linked to plotting tables at bomber groups through private uninterrupted trunk lines (PUTs).

The raids in March 1945, however, were serious enough to warrant a Bomber Command

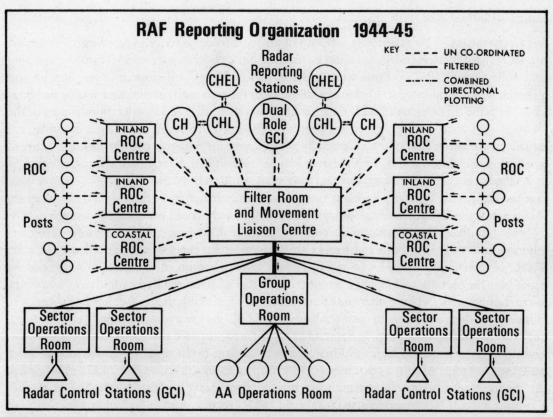

RAF Reporting Organization 1944-45

Radar Reporting Stations

KEY
- – – – UN CO-ORDINATED
- —— FILTERED
- –·–·– COMBINED DIRECTIONAL PLOTTING

CHEL   CHEL
CH   CHL   Dual Role GCI   CHL   CH

INLAND ROC Centre

ROC

INLAND ROC Centre

Posts

COASTAL ROC Centre

Filter Room and Movement Liaison Centre

INLAND ROC Centre

ROC

INLAND ROC Centre

Posts

COASTAL ROC Centre

Sector Operations Room   Sector Operations Room

Group Operations Room

Sector Operations Room   Sector Operations Room

Radar Control Stations (GCI)   AA Operations Room   Radar Control Stations (GCI)

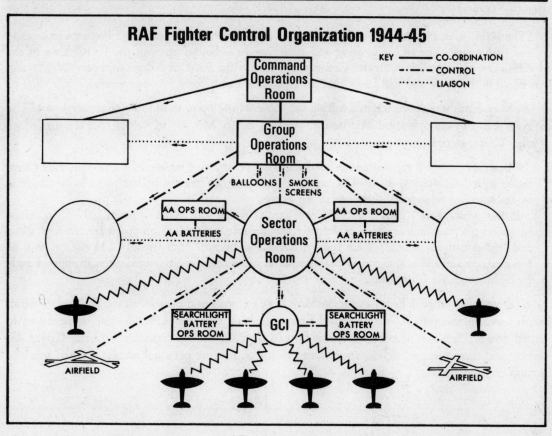

RAF Fighter Control Organization 1944-45

KEY
- —— CO-ORDINATION
- –·–·– CONTROL
- ········ LIAISON

Command Operations Room

Group Operations Room

BALLOONS   SMOKE SCREENS

AA OPS ROOM   Sector Operations Room   AA OPS ROOM

AA BATTERIES   AA BATTERIES

SEARCHLIGHT BATTERY OPS ROOM   GCI   SEARCHLIGHT BATTERY OPS ROOM

AIRFIELD   AIRFIELD

request to the ROC for immediate warning of hostile intruder activity. Accordingly, on March 19, ROC headquarters issued operation instruction No 57 covering the special intruder warning and code-named "Bugs." Posts were ordered to call "Bugs" on suspecting an intruder and give the 100km grid letter and 10km grid number of the post itself, in the same way as had been done with the tip-and-run raiders. As a further precaution all AA gun operations rooms in the "Diver" gun areas were linked to the nearest ROC centre in order to obtain a direct speech broadcast on enemy aircraft tracks. Friendly aircraft were forbidden to pass through the "Diver" gun area at less than 6,000 ft. This measure was promulgated in operation instruction No 58.

As the last enemy manned-aircraft raid took place on March 20, these special procedures were not used in anger. With the Russians sweeping into Germany from the east and the Western Allies across the Rhine, the final collapse of Nazi Germany could not be long delayed.

From July 1944 certain groups well removed from the main danger area were ordered to open plotting lines to RAF groups and sectors only when certain types of tracks needed to be told. ROC groups dealing with Nos 10 and 11 Fighter Groups continued as before. In August of the same year the plotting and telling exercises, which had gone on regularly for almost five years, were discontinued. In November 1944 the regulations concerning the civil-defence services were relaxed, but there could be no such relief for the ROC. As the events of March 1945 showed, they had to stand to their posts. In September 1944 it was proposed that radars on the north coast and the ROC centres at Oban and Portree should be shut. In the upshot this was turned down and it was not until April 1945 that nine ROC groups in the north were released and stood down. At the meeting on April 26 at which this was decided, Air Vice-Marshal Ambler of Fighter Command (ROC Commandant 1942–43) paid the ROC one of its most handsome tributes of the war. He said:

"The ROC is an integral part of the command and without it the command becomes practically non-operational. The whole plotting and radar system is bound up with the ROC. One of the difficulties which will face Fighter Command is that, if the ROC is disbanded, every WAAF and airman in the command will know that the command had become non-operational."

As May came voices were raised asking why the whole corps could not be stood down. The answer came with operation instruction No 59, dated May 5, in which Air Commodore Finlay Crerar stated:

"When the ceasefire is announced the air-defence organisation, of which the Royal Observer Corps forms an important part, *may* still be required to defend the country against possible air incursion by uncontrolled elements of the German Air Forces.

In this event, those Royal Observer Corps groups which still remain operational will continue to maintain a precautionary state of defence until definite orders to stand down are received. Posts and centres concerned will remain fully manned and aircraft, both friendly and enemy, will be reported, tracked and told in the normal manner in order that they may be dealt with appropriately by Fighter and AA Commands."

So it was that when VE-day came on May 8, 1945, posts and centres viewed the celebrations with some misgivings. It was not until four days later that the ROC was at last allowed to stand down. Messages of congratulation flowed in from the Government and the Royal Air Force, and these were passed down the lines along with more personal messages from area and group commandants.

Top *The primitive conditions in some groups is well illustrated by this picture of 21/C.2 post at Chulmleigh, North Devon, in August 1940. Lieutenant Colonel Bowen, Head Observer, is on the left and Observer F. J. Wheaton on the right. The latter was still in the corps in 1976 as Leading Observer of the Chulmleigh post*

Middle *Dornier 17s of KG.3 crossing the Belgian coast en route for southern England at the height of the Battle of Britain. This was typical of the formations plotted every day by the Observer Corps*

Bottom *A Battle of Britain raid as recorded in the logbook of 9 Group, York. Entries show the progress of the abortive Luftflotte 5 attack on the North East from bases in Norway on August 15, 1940. The 12 Spitfires scrambled from Acklington at 12.36 were from 72 Squadron. Raid 10, given initially as six plus at 12.42, had been increased to 20 plus at 12.52 and by 12.59 was being told as 30 plus. In fact it consisted of 63 Heinkel IIIs of I and III/KG.26 and 21 Me110s of ZG.76. Interceptions by 41, 72, 79, 605 and 607 Squadrons, plus concentrated anti-aircraft fire, accounted for eight He IIIs and seven Me 110s. Only one casualty was suffered by the RAF, Pilot Officer K. S. Law of 605 Squadron, whose Hurricane crashed into a hedge. Law was taken to Hartlepool hospital with head lacerations and shock*

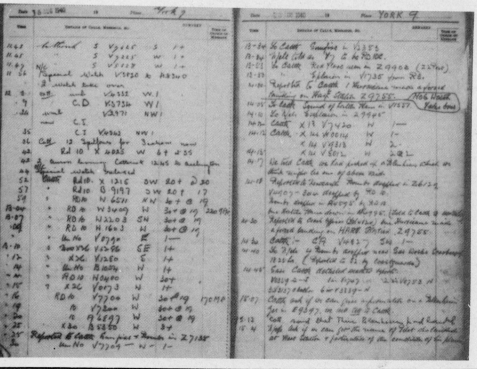

The Observer Corps has always had a mind of its own; the reactions of the Officer Commanding RAF Station Catterick when he received this 1940 Christmas Card from York 9 Observer Group have not been recorded

His Majesty King George VI visiting one of the Colchester group posts during the Battle of Britain. It is believed to be 18/E.3 Braintree which the King visited on October 29, 1940. In this picture it can be seen that the post surround is made out of straw bales and, for the occasion, the two observers on duty appear to have been equipped with some form of standard raincoat

The first of two Spitfires paid for by the Observer Corps in the winter of 1940/41. Both carried the corps crest and name. This aircraft, shown here at Hornchurch, was code-lettered EB–Z and was flown by the CO of 41 Squadron, Squadron Leader D. O. Finlay, who is standing beside it

All that remained of Church House, Bromley, headquarters of 19 Observer Group, on the morning of April 17, 1941. The Centre was completely destroyed by fire bombs the previous night and the duty crew were forced to move into the stand-by Centre in a nearby building

The wartime DR.12 identity card of Major Graham Donald, Assistant Observer Group Officer in 34 Group, Glasgow. Major Donald correctly identified Rudolf Hess after his flight to Britain in 1941

Women observers began to appear in strength in the ROC in 1942 and this group was photographed at 11 Group Lincoln. Raincoats and badges were all that the ladies initially were given but later, like their male colleagues, they went into RAF battledress

Top *The "cubby hole" at an observer post circa 1943. The extraordinary range of items on the shelves bore no resemblance to an RAF stores manifest. The two observers in the picture were at "Available" which meant that they could have a meal, etc., as long as one wore the telephone head-and-breast set.*

Middle left *Late in 1942 the ROC were issued with Snowflake illuminating rocket flares under the code word "Totter". These were fired to show fighters and guns the position of German low-level tip-and-run raiders and later V.1 flying bombs. A chief observer at Beachy Head in Sussex is shown loading a Totter rocket into the firing tube*

Middle right *Among the ususual aircraft plotted by the corps during the war was the Hillson FH.40 Mk. 1 designated officially as Experimental Aircraft No. 205. This was a Hurricane with an additional strut-mounted "slip wing". The intention was to gain range by take-off at higher all-up weights, the slip wing being jettisoned subsequently*

Bottom *All of the experimental aircraft flown in Britain during the war were plotted at one time or another by the ROC, including the first British jet-propelled aeroplane, the Gloster E.28/39 shown here*

Top *A closer look at the enemy. Observers of 17 Group, Watford examine an FW 190 during a Group meeting at Leavesdon Aerodrome in 1944*

Bottom *The scene at an ROC centre after the installation of the Long-Range Board which is shown in the background. On the main table, of 2 Group, Horsham, in 1943, are being plotted Mustangs, Spitfires and a variety of bombers*

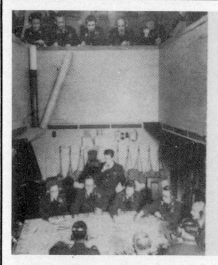

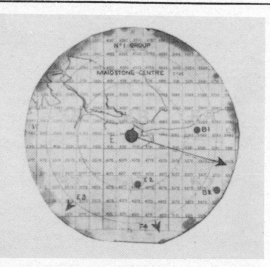

Top left *An ROC centre of the revised and modernised type set up from 1942. This is 19 Group, Bromley operations room in 1943 showing the main map table and the balcony. Seated at the latter are the tellers and recorder on the extreme right*

Top right *The wartime post chart of 1/E.1, Faversham, Kent, showing the modified British grid, five-mile sound circle and an outer circle and the position of neighbouring posts*

Middle *As the war progressed most of the rudimentary posts gave way to more permanent structures with better amenities. Typical of the purpose-built posts is 8/Q.1 at Holmfirth, Yorks. There were rooms downstairs and the observation platform and cubby hole on top. To the right is the early pattern post hut*

Bottom *Throughout the war the Junkers 88 was a frequent visitor to Britain by day and by night. This Ju 88 G-1 with Lichtenstein SN-2 radar landed at Woodbridge, Suffolk in July 1944 and was thereafter flown in RAF prototype markings*

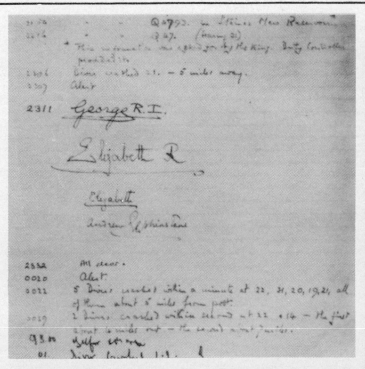

Top left *In the midst of the V.1 attacks King George VI and Queen Elizabeth visited the ROC post on the Brunswick tower of Windsor Castle where Observer Hazell and the Reverend Southeard were on duty and plotting a flock of V.1s coming down within sight of the post. This is a photograph of the page in the logbook of 17/E.4 with the Royal signatures*

Top right *ROC observers served on board ship for the invasion of France under the Seaborne scheme. Seen here is a chief observer at Bournemouth complete with life jacket, "Seaborne" shoulder flash and "RN" arm badge*

Bottom *In addition to ground-launched flying bombs a large number were carried under the wings of Heinkel IIIs of KG.3, which unit air-launched them off the south and east coasts of England*

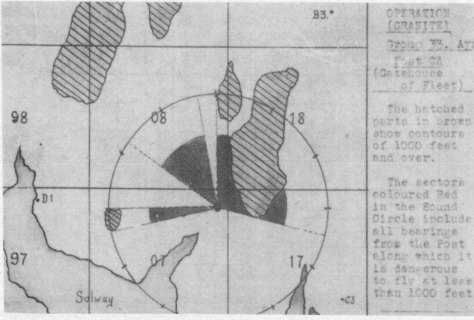

Operation "Granite", which involved the lighting of flares to stop friendly aircraft flying into high ground, was a conspicuous success. Each ROC post had a specially prepared chart showing the high ground in the locality and this one was for 33/C.4 Gatehouse of Fleet, near the Solway Firth

Air Commodore the Earl of Bandon, the ROC's first post-war commandant, instituted the practice of holding an annual camp for the corps at an RAF station, which practice has continued most successfully to this day. Shown here are corps members marching off from the tent lines at the first ROC Camp at RAF Thorney Island in 1948

Fast flying jets began to replace the piston engined types in the late 1940s and the ROC had to adjust to new conditions. Seen here are a US Air Force F-80 Shooting Star and a pair of RAF Meteor 4s taking part in Exercise "Foil" in June 1949

Finally, on May 12, 1945, posts completed their last plots and centre recorders filled in their last sheets. At 17.00 the great network of telephone lines and teleprinters fell silent, and the sinews of the air-defence network ceased to function. In its report on the stand-down of the ROC *The Aeroplane* summed up the achievements of the corps in a few lines:

"The general public knew nothing of the activities of the ROC and little realised that the one organisation which was in closest contact with operations of war was this pseudo-military body. In fact the ROC was probably responsible for more damage to the enemy's war effort than most of our home-based military forces of a similar character, which must be unique in the annals of civilian national service."

GERMAN AIR ATTACKS ON BRITAIN 1939–45*

Estimated weight of weapons dropped		*Metric tons*
Bombs (excluding incendiary and AP)		64,393
Flying-bomb warheads		5,823
V2		1,054
	Estimated total	71,270
Civilian casualties (excluding Home Guard)		
	Killed	60,595
	Seriously injured	86,182
		146,777
	Slightly injured	150,833

*Source *Civil Defence*, by T. H. O'Brien, HMSO

Chapter 15
STAND-DOWN
AND REVIVAL

As the lights went up again in Britain it was difficult for the population to realise that there would be no more sirens, blackout, bombs or gunfire and that perhaps the only use for the air-raid shelter was for growing mushrooms. Members of the ROC could not get used to an armchair by the fire in the evening instead of the usual preparations for the night shift at post or centre. At the sound of any aeroplane they would instinctively look up and search the skies. No statistics were kept about the corps' efforts in wartime, but it is possible to calculate that nearly six million man/woman days of duty were performed by members and literally hundreds of millions of plots were passed through the system.

After stand-down volunteers adjusted to the increase in their leisure time, but for the full-time "A" men it meant finding a new job or registering at the local Labour Exchange. Post head observers, as always, had to clear up and put everything in apple-pie order. They wrestled with streams of forms and letters on pay, uniforms, petrol coupons and where such-and-such a piece of equipment had gone. Only coal stores and latrine buckets could be written off, the former as no one knew how to collect them and the latter because even the RAF could not face their return.

The Commandant, Finlay Crerar, with a nucleus of full-time officers kept headquarters going at Stanmore while at each area and group "caretaker" officers looked after affairs. All personnel had been asked, before the war's end, to indicate whether they would continue in peacetime on a voluntary basis as and when the ROC was re-formed. Some 78 per cent replied in the affirmative, and there the matter was to rest for nearly 18 months.

In the meanwhile, however, three events took place which were to be a source of great pride and pleasure to the whole corps. To mark its gratitude to the ROC for wartime achievements the Air Ministry decided to organise a massive rally and air display at RAF North Weald, Essex. At least one member of each post and centre crew in the country was invited to attend from the evening of Saturday, June 23, 1945, to the morning of Monday, June 25. It was the first time that representatives from every ROC unit had been gathered together in one place. More than 1,800 ROC personnel attended the rally and an exceptional programme was laid on, including a flying display the like of which had not been seen since pre-war Hendon days.

On show in the static park, and flown off at the end, were Mosquito, Lancaster, Fortress, Halifax, Walrus, Liberator, Wellington, Warwick, Beaufighter, Dakota, York, Stirling, Mustang, Spitfire, Tempest, Typhoon, Thunderbolt, Hellcat, Firefly, Corsair, Avenger, Ju88, Fw190, Sunderland and Catalina. Also in the ground was the ROC's old enemy, the V1 flying bomb. The actual flying display included four squadrons of Mosquitoes escorted by six squadrons of Mustangs, supply-dropping by Halifaxes, a Hamilcar landing, a Horsa tow-off by a Dakota, three Czech Spitfire squadrons and aerobatics by a Meteor III and a Tempest. In complete contrast a Sikorsky R-4B helicopter hovered over the crowd. This was the first public demonstration of the Meteor, despite the fact that the corps had been plotting the type since its flight tests started in 1942.

King George VI had approved the design of a Royal Observer Corps ensign, in RAF blue with the Union Jack in one corner and bearing the corps badge. The ensign was dedicated at a service at North Weald on Sunday, June 24, and it was borne to the drumhead by Observer Lieutenant J. D. Pollock, VC, of 33 Group, Ayr.

On Sunday afternoon all the observers paraded for inspection by Lord Beatty, Under-Secretary of State for Air, who had earlier presented the ensign. Beatty said: "I want to express the gratitude of the Royal Air Force for the work which the Royal Observer Corps has done so efficiently during the war." He then presented the Commandant, Finlay Crerar, with a silver cup on which were engraved the words:

"From the Royal Air Force to the Royal Observer Corps in token of a worthy comradeship, 1939-1945."

The whole contingent of 1,800 observers then carried out the first-ever ROC march past, to the accompaniment of the RAF band and with Lord Beatty taking the salute. Drill has never been part of the ROC curriculum, but somehow the corps has always been able to find either enough trained men in its ranks to get a squad smart and efficient or somebody else's warrant officer or RSM to do the job.

The first big occasion for the corps to parade actually occurred just before the North Weald rally. On June 10, 1945, the King, accompanied by the Queen and Princess Elizabeth, addressed a farewell parade in Hyde Park of 2,500 representatives of "the citizen armies of civil defence." Pride of place in the march was given to the Royal Observer Corps. *The Times* reported that in a speech before the royal party arrived Mr Herbert Morrison, wartime Home Secretary, added "a particular word of praise for the Royal Observer Corps, the eyes and ears of all our defences, without whom neither Fighter Command, nor the Ministry of Home Security nor the Anti-Aircraft Command could have done its job."

The third major parade for the corps did not come until after the war in the Far East had finished in August 1945. Preparations were made for an enormous victory parade through London with every element of the armed forces and the civilian services represented, together with formations from all the Allies and the countries of what was then the British Empire. The parade took place on June 8, 1946, the ROC contingent consisting of the Commandant, 12 officers, 60 observers and 12 women observers. At the saluting base in the Mall were the royal family, the Service commanders and the politicians, including Winston Churchill.

Some insight into the occasion and the character and humour of the older observers who took part can be gained from extracts of notes written by the late Observer V. Griffin of 23/G.3 post, Devizes. He was chosen by lot to represent his post and No 23 Group and, on June 6, reported to Kensington Gardens where a great array of men were living under canvas and rehearsing for the parade. The ROC were unfortunately accommodated alongside the pipe band of the Royal Garwhal Rifles, who practised their "agony bags" continuously. Observer Griffin takes up the story:

"It was not for long before we were on the march with the RAF band leading and the whole RAF contingent, including the RAF Regiment and a band of 24 Iraqi Levies – to the shouts of the RAF drill instructors yelling 'swing those arms; watch that dressing; heads up', and everything that goes to make up a drill instructor's dictionary.

I had been all through this many years ago and it seemed second nature to respond to all these commands, but not so with a good many of our boys and it speaks well of them how they got down to it and turned out on the 8th.

Off we went all along the Serpentine, doing everything but march into it, control marshals getting excited and harassed trying to make guardsmen out of airmen and observers. I tell you it looked hopeless and I could see that our drill Flt Sgt and officer thought the same. Their voices were gradually getting more hoarse each time they shouted."

After a nights' sleep, the Observers were on parade once more at 9 a.m., but:

"Our flight sergeant instructor did not turn up on parade, having to report sick. It was said he had been taken to a mental home."

Continuous drill, however, turned the contingent into a smart, well knit unit and promptly on the morning of the 8th they fell in:

"All spick and span with berets adjusted just so and in line of 12 abreast when the parade marshal shouts out 'Be ready to march off in twenty seconds.' Dead on 10 a.m. we marched off the parade ground for the last time, headed by the RAF band, to the assembly at Hyde Park. Arriving at the assembly ground, we took up our position. Here we were joined by our lady observers who had been in training at Bushy Park with the WAAF contingent. They too looked fit and said they were looking forward to the thrill of the march but were pleased to join us.

Now began the eight miles march through London, which was much of a muchness, one mighty roar of human voices with now and again the strains of the RAF band which was leading us and the problem of keeping step and in that straight line of 12 abreast.

The remarks one heard were very interesting. Someone in the crowd would say 'Royal Observers' and a great cheer would go up. On the whole I should say by the searching glances given us that we were a mystery unit. One remark, as a person spotted 'Seaborne' on one of our shoulders, was very interesting. 'Seaborne' the voice said, 'Never heard of them.' As arranged, the parade was to have 20 minutes halt. This caught us in Oxford Street. The break brought its humour. The onlookers from windows two to seven storeys, began pelting us with sweets, cigarettes, cakes and apples; a tin hat would have been an asset.

Coming to the Cenotaph, the command was 'Eyes Inwards' as we paid tribute to those comrades of the 1914-18 war. This was one of my thrills and one that touched me very deeply, for it brought back old memories of my comrades of the Great War whom I had seen killed all around me while I was spared – at Loos, Festubert, Neuve Chapelle, Ypres, the Somme and Mametze Wood; not one at a time but in hundreds and they had no known grave.

As we entered the Mall the clouds came lower and lower and we were greeted by the roar of aircraft overhead. Could an observer keep his eyes down? They were Sunderlands followed by screeching fighters.

Well, the great moment was at hand, actually a matter of seconds. One could feel the tenseness in the ranks as we waited for our chief, Air Commodore Finlay Crerar, to give the command 'Royal Observers Corps, Eyes Left' and then give his salute.

All I hope is that he was proud of us when he said it. Personally, I see no reason why he shouldn't be, for had we not been given the 'Royal,' this speaking for itself? Personally, for my own post G.3,

Devizes, and G.1 and G.2, with whom we worked together in unison, not forgetting those at Bristol Centre, particularly those of the first two years, I know we had put our all into the job. 'Royal Observer Corps, Eyes Front,' his hand cut smartly away and swinging again and it was all over.

The Albert Memorial was a welcome sight as this meant the turning from the highway into camp was near. This we reached well soaked, but not downhearted, for hadn't we stood tied up like dogs on the end of 9 ft of telephone cable for six years exposed to every type of English weather? The last rite was the issue of a chit with the commandant's compliments, granting the owner one pint of free beer in the NAAFI. I was not the last one in the canteen."

The ROC also provided a 61-strong contingent for the Battle of Britain memorial service in Westminster Abbey on September 16, 1945. Since that time the corps has regularly participated in the annual Battle of Britain commemoration, the armistice-day service at the Cenotaph and the festival of remembrance at the Albert Hall.

Another cause for satisfaction to the ROC was known to only a handful of officers. The RAF had decided, a month after the war's end, to test the German raid-reporting and control system under operational conditions. A comparison was needed with the Fighter Command C and R system, which differed fundamentally in concept from its German counterpart, including the observer organisations involved.

The German aircraft-reporting service (Flugmeldedienst or Flumdienst) was first organised on a national basis in 1932. In 1939 it was taken over by the Luftwaffe and the volunteer members were called up for full-time military service. The layout comprised observer posts (Flugwachen or Fluwas) at 10–15km intervals, reporting to central observer posts (Flugwachkommandos or Flukos). Posts consisted of a hut with windows all round and the eight observers lived on the site (including a cook and one non-commissioned officer. Three observers formed a duty crew. The method of reporting was very crude by comparison with the ROC, consisting of number, direction of flight in clock code and height, the last-mentioned being described as low, medium or high. No plotting instrument was provided and aircraft-recognition ability was almost nil. To these deficiencies was added the lowering of standards, both mental and physical, for observers as the war went on. Thus the Flugmeldedienst, while performing to the best of its limited ability, only succeeded in providing a very confused air picture with wide track and height variations and little identification of what the aircraft involved actually were.

In order to try out the whole German set-up, the RAF re-activated a complete section of the German C and R network, including operations rooms, radar stations (with six types of radar), Y-service stations and observer posts. The area chosen overlapped Denmark and Germany, and German prisoners of war were brought back to operate the stations, which included 21 observer posts and one observer centre, at Kolding.

The exercise, code-named "Post Mortem," from June 25 to July 7, covered 14 separate simulated attacks by Bomber Command with up to 200 heavy bombers, Mosquitoes, the whole gamut of RAF jamming devices and large-scale dropping of window. A total of 131 officers and NCOs were employed in observing the exercise, including one ROC officer.

In the subsequent RAF report on the exercise, it was stressed that "the use of unrestricted radio and other countermeasures played a major role in reducing the efficiency of the German air-reporting and control system." This meant that the Luftwaffe had reluctantly been falling back on visual and aural information of a much lower standard than that available to the RAF through the ROC. Of the Flugmeldedienst, the report said:

"The observer system was inferior to its British counterpart. Plotting was inaccurate, time lags were excessive and the Germans preferred to accept information derived from the inland radar stations."

The potential effect of electronic countermeasures was to play a big part in the decision to re-establish the ROC as an integral part of the peacetime air-defence network. On June 14, 1945, the Director of Operations had written to the Secretary of State:

"We now know that as a result of the success obtained by our countermeasures against German radar, the German defence system in the last year of the war had to rely more and more on visual and aural reporting. In any future war, therefore, we must be prepared to deal with similar counter-measures against our own radar; consequently, the retention of a highly efficient ground observer organisation will be necessary."

It was fortunate that this view was taken, as certain senior RAF officers wanted to change the whole basis of the ROC and incorporate it into the RAF as part of the Volunteer Reserve. This would have led to the complete disappearance of the corps in its existing form and its appeal as a uniformed civilian organisation.

As early as August 3, 1944, Sir Roderic Hill, commanding Air Defence of Great Britain, had written to the Under-Secretary of State for Air calling for a unified and revised raid-reporting organisation for the post-war period. He was satisfied that no radar development then envisaged could supplant the essential elements provided by human ear and eye which covered reliable identification, low cover inland, continuous cover in mountainous country, a multiplicity of other duties and immunity from jamming and interference. Hill added:

"In any event, I consider it to be of vital importance that in a modern raid-reporting system the *ground observers should provide information supplementary to radar information* in such a manner that both types of information are co-ordinated at the earliest stage, and that the radar *and ground-observation units should at all levels be in the one organisation under the one command.*

It is evident that the ROC in its present form could not fit into such an organisation. Posts should report to a suitable form of central radar station so that the present type of 'centre' would not be required. All personnel concerned in the organisation must work as a team in the same uniform, each branch (radar and ground observer) having a good knowledge of the whole system, the personnel in each being eligible to interchange on passing the necessary tests.

I envisage that after the war such an organisation would be operated by a nucleus of RAF personnel, the main body of personnel, however, being supplied by the RAFVR or AAF. *I therefore strongly recommend that as soon as possible after the conclusion of the war in Europe the ROC in its present form should be disbanded, but that ex-ROC personnel should be encouraged to join the RAFVR or AAF for duties in the revised reporting organisation.*"

In his conclusion Hill stated:

"Though I regard the disbanding of the ROC in its present form as essential in the interests of operational efficiency, I cannot emphasise too strongly that it is only the system which needs altering. Nothing said in this letter must be taken as in any way deprecating the high esteem in which the ROC is regarded by this headquarters, the inestimable service which it has rendered in this war, or the excellent record for enthusiasm and efficiency which the corps has built up and maintained. Nevertheless, it is my considered opinion that in view of the fully operational role which it is called upon to play it has suffered serious disadvantages in the past through being a civilian organisation, and to an appreciable extent, therefore, its usefulness to the system has been curtailed.

Besides being an operational requirement, I feel that the disbanding of the corps and the transfer of a number of its personnel into the RAF would surmount a number of difficulties which have presented themselves in the past."

This was strong medicine indeed, and Hill's comments were to be amplified in a key memorandum on "Raid Reporting and Control Aspects of the United Kingdom Air Defence Organisation," produced by Fighter Command in November 1945. Started by Hill and eventually issued by Air Marshal Sir James Robb, the next AOC-in-C Fighter Command, the memorandum was a masterly study written largely by Group Captain J. Cherry, Wing Commander D. H. Grice and Squadron Leader A. C. Case. It covered every aspect of the C and R organisation and one of its key recommendations was that the radar and observer systems should be merged into one RAF system in two phases. The memorandum also suggested that air defence should be based on certain radar facilities which, at the end of the 1950s, finally materialised as master radar stations.

All the suggestions made concerning the ROC would undoubtedly have been brilliant under ideal circumstances and with unlimited money available; in post-war Britain neither condition applied. In addition, both Hill and the writers of the memorandum lacked practical observing experience and therefore laid great stress on the need to have observers who were mobile. This, of course, was the exact opposite of what was actually efficient in practice. The war had shown clearly that the best form of eye and ear observer was one who knew his locality intimately and could detect any variation in surroundings, noise and weather. This knowledge required long years of practice and moving observers about from place to place would have destroyed it.

That there would be a peacetime observer organisation was not in doubt as, on July 7, 1945, the Chiefs of Staffs Committee had submitted a report on the "air defence of Great Britain during the ten years following the defeat of Germany." This report specifically recommended that:

"The raid-reporting and control organisation should contain means for detection and recognition by ground observers.

In the composition of the forces for the air defence of Great Britain there should be included the Royal Observer Corps (or similar ground observer organisation)."

Because of the doubts raised by the Fighter Command memorandum, the actual reconstruction of the ROC was delayed by many months, which was ultimately to affect the corps' operational efficiency and its strength. It was not until March 1946 that the Secretary of State for Air was able to submit to the Cabinet a defence committee paper which stated:

"Since there is at present no alternative available, it is essential to the needs of air defence to proceed with the organisation of a post-war Royal Observer Corps. I accordingly request approval in principle to the formation of a post-war Royal Observer Corps, before entering into discussions with the Treasury about the financial aspects of a post-war organisation."

The ROC, meanwhile, had been existing on a care-and-maintenance basis which, including grants to members, pay of whole-time officers and clerks and uniforms, was costing £232,000. An additional £100,000 was inserted into the accounts as an estimated cost to the public of communications, although the lines were mostly not being used and the GPO did not charge the Air Ministry.

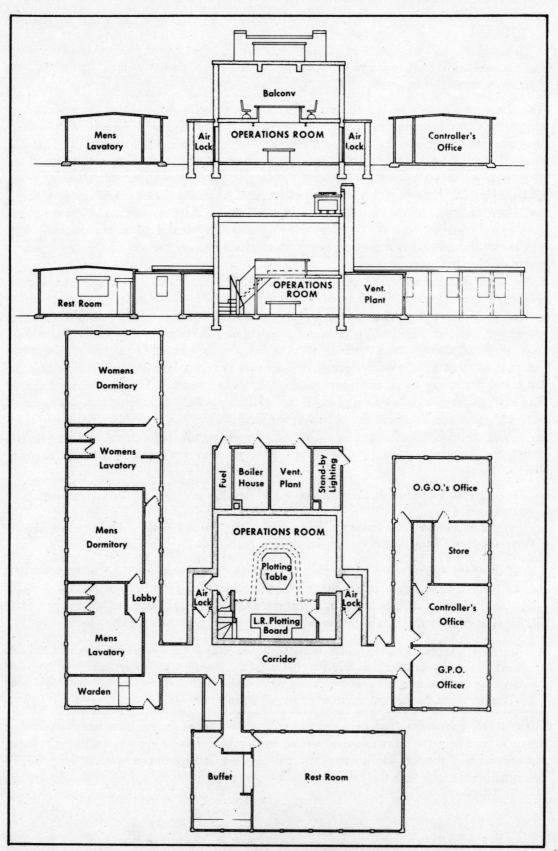

Layout of a typical custom-built ROC centre of the type put into commission from late 1942. These centres continued in use until the advent of nuclear fall-out protected centres in the 1960s

In November 1945 Air Commodore (later Air Chief Marshal) The Earl of Bandon succeeded Air Commodore Finlay Crerar as commandant. Lord Bandon, known affectionately in the RAF as "Paddy" or "the Abandoned Earl", was an officer of great personality and humour and he was to provide the tonic so necessary for a corps which was virtually in limbo. His tasks were twofold: to maintain morale under very difficult circumstances and to lay the foundations for the post-war revival. He was to face many months without any officially announced policy for re-organisation and with a nucleus of only 230 men and women actually employed in the corps. No centres were operationally in use and there were only a few cluster meetings for posts to attend. Some posts kept up their own meetings regardless, but there was no official training syllabus.

Corps members attended air displays whenever they were held, and in 1946 they assisted at air races and with the world's air-speed record. In September 2/S.3, Worthing, and 2/N.2, Middleton, posts supplied observers to give warning of the approach of RAF High-Speed Flight Meteors along the south-coast course. They had the excitement of watching Group Captain E. M. Donaldson achieve a new record of 616 m.p.h.

At the first post-war Society of British Aircraft Constructors display and exhibition at Radlett, Herts, a sprinkling of fortunate ticket holders could be seen in ROC uniform.

One pleasant surprise for long-serving wartime members came at the beginning of 1946 with the distribution of well earned Defence Medal ribbons. Special certificates of service were issued to those who had served for more than six months but had not completed the requisite time for the Defence Medal.

Another hopeful sign was the re-appearance of the monthly *Inter Services Aircraft Recognition Journal* which had been such a useful training tool from September 1942 until it was suspended in September 1945. The first of the new issues was dated July 1946 and every other month from August onwards a four-page supplement, entitled *The Royal Observer Corps Gazette*, was included.

As the months went by it became clear that a lot fewer than 78 per cent of the members would ultimately be available to serve with the revived ROC*. Some older observers found other interests, while many moved to different parts of the country and did not renew their contacts with the corps. ATC cadets and 16- to 17-year-olds, who had given a good account of themselves in the closing stages of the war, were conscripted into the Services and young women from the centres found full-time occupations in marriage.

As early as December 3, 1945, an examining committee on the post-war organisation of the ROC had held its first meeting. The re-formed corps was to be based largely on proposals put forward by the Air Ministry's S.5 Division. The examining committee held five meetings, the last on January 31, 1946, and no fewer than 33 people from a variety of departments were involved. The corps' representatives were the commandant, Observer Commander C. G. Cooke, Observer Commander I. D. R. Sims and Observer Lieutenant H. Austin. Basically the layout was to be the same as in wartime, with five areas and 40 groups, although No 40, Portree, was in fact to remain closed. In the main the posts were to be left according to the stand-down layout. Full-time officers could not be guaranteed more than three years' employment, which seemed to indicate a short life for the organisation.

---

* 78 per cent would have represented an available force of 489 officers and 24,578 men and women observers.

Various changes were made to bring the corps into line with peacetime needs. At headquarters ROC the deputy commandant post was established as that for a full-time observer captain, and the operations staff officer was to be an observer commander and not an RAF wing commander as previously. The post of corps commandant could be filled by either an air commodore, RAF, or an observer commodore. In the event of the latter occurring the operations staff officer's task was to revert to a wing commander, RAF.

At the areas the commandants were to be part-time and their deputies full-time, and this system was paralleled in the groups. This was a fundamental departure from the wartime system, when all area and group commandants were employees of the Air Ministry. Considerable discussion went on over the proposed change to part-time senior commanders involving both administration and operations. The decision was finally taken on the basis that, as the ROC was a part-time voluntary organisation, the "legal representation and protection of the spare-time element dictated the command structure." As far as the full-time officers were concerned, it was pointed out that if the spare-time element ceased to exist then the full-time would automatically cease to be civil service commissioned ROC officers, although retaining their identity as civil servants. The system of command by volunteers at areas and groups, with full-time deputies in both cases, has stood the test of time.

The proposed complement of observers for centres was laid down as the number of positions multiplied by $3\frac{1}{2}$ and again by $1\frac{1}{3}$ to provide for three crews and adequate reserves. An upper limit of 16 was set for personnel at each post. The establishment for the corps was laid down as 57 whole-time officers, 415 spare-time officers and 27,901 spare-time observers. Total annual cost for post-war corps was estimated at £423,590.

Subject to the overriding authority of the Air Council, the administration of the ROC rested with the Air Ministry, while operational policy direction and responsibility for training was vested in the AOC-in-C Fighter Command. A new royal warrant was prepared for the establishment of the corps.

On November 15, 1946, the commandant was able to send out a letter to all wartime observers who had stated an interest in joining the peacetime ROC. He enclosed a pamphlet giving details of service, etc, and an enrolment form. Terms of service were for observers to enrol for not less than three years and put in at least 36hr training per year. Annual grants were laid down as £1 5s for observers and £2 10s for chief observers. In the event of a national emergency, observers had to be prepared to devote at least 12hr weekly to ROC duty.

On the evening of November 16 Mr Herbert Morrison, Lord President of the Council, called in a BBC broadcast for volunteers for the ROC. He said that as Minister of Home Security during the war he was able to see at close quarters the quiet and courageous efficiency with which the corps carried out its many and varied duties. Its assistance was invaluable to the Royal Air Force. It was these same men and women, he went on, who were wanted in re-forming the corps. Headquarters followed up, on December 19, with training memorandum No 1, which stated: "As from January 1, 1947, the corps will commence active training."

At long last the corps was to take its place again as an integral part of Britain's air defences. The time lapse, however, had not made things easy. Apart from the disappearance of a large number of those people originally expected to sign on as volunteers, the physical state of the corps was poor. Posts situated on top of buildings had, in many cases, been pulled down and in coastal areas the buildings themselves had been derequisitioned and returned to their civilian owners. Other post structures had become dilapidated or had been attacked by vandals. Of some no trace remained.

As early as August 17, 1945, the group commandant No 4 Group reported to area that on VJ night the post look-out and rest hut at 4/O.2, Boar's Hill, had been completely burned out during the celebrations. At 1/D.2 Post, Dover, situated in a military camp the local soldiery had smashed the post itself and wrecked the hut. The adjutant of No 1 Group described it as being in "a really disgusting condition."

Certain groups had their centres intact, apart from an accumulation of dust, but at others the centre had been completely dismantled or was in process of finding a new home. This made training extremely difficult. Communications also presented a vexing problem, with telephone lines removed or, in the case of some posts, left terminated in the old-fashioned earwig-filled box on a telegraph pole.

The pre-war practice of a complete observer group visiting an RAF station once a year was revived. One of the groups which quickly took advantage of this was No 14, Bury St Edmunds. On a Sunday in July 1947 nearly 300 members descended on the RAF Bomber Command airfield at Stradishall, Suffolk. Flights were provided for them in a York, two Lancasters, Dominies, Ansons, Oxfords and even a Miles Messenger.

As soon as it became clear that there would only be about 9,000 volunteers from among the old wartime hands, recruiting for the ROC was opened to the public. In February the first men and women began to come forward to sample the joys of observing. They consisted of ex-servicemen with no reserve commitment, 16- and 17-year-olds not immediately due for national service, and a fair sprinkling of women, including ex-Wrens, ATS and WAAFs. They were full of enthusiasm, but needed time to be trained.

Only nine months after the corps had resumed training there was an emergency call-out. Early in September 1947 intelligence information reached Whitehall that Jewish terrorists of the Stern gang were going to attempt to drop explosives on London from a light aircraft. The emasculated radar network was hard-put to look for and recognise a light aircraft. The only answer was to put the ROC on the job. On the afternoon of Friday, September 5, Air Commodore Bandon telephoned Observer Captain St Clair Smallwood, Southern Area Commandant, and requested that Nos 1 and 2 Observer Groups be put on to an operational footing straight away under the code name "Operation Zion."

Southern Area informed the respective group commandants and the word was passed to centre personnel at Maidstone and Horsham and to post chief observers. Despite the "rust" in the system, 267 officers and observers were on duty within 4hr and both groups were operational with lines plugged through to the No 11 Fighter Group filter room. Where posts had no telephones they continued plotting and kept a log of all passing aircraft. The RAF maintained standing patrols of fighters and posts were open until 1 o'clock in the morning, when the "all clear" was given as a result of the terrorists being caught by the Paris police.

The emergency call-out provided useful experience for the first post-war exercise, which was staged in Southern Area on September 21, 1947, appropriately enough Battle-of-Britain Sunday. Six of the seven groups in the area, with 220 posts, went into action. For many posts it meant a return to the atmosphere of the 1920s: a field or the sea-shore with a telegraph pole, a length of cable, the battery box and the instrument. Needless to say it rained, but gradually the weather cleared and posts and centres began the familiar routine of plotting, tracking and telling.

Attack Warning Red

This was the first occasion on which the ROC was called on to deal with jets in any numbers, the regular squadrons providing Meteor IVs and Vampire Is. There were also the old faithfuls, like the Spitfire and the Mosquito operated by the auxiliaries, Tiger Moths from Reserve Command, a sprinkling of civil aircraft and one joker, a lumbering Ju52 which appeared over No 1 Group, Maidstone. Among the tracks from London to the south coast was one for an airliner carrying the Foreign Secretary, Ernest Bevin, to Paris.

Chapter 16
BACK IN BUSINESS

During the stand-down period of the ROC between May 1945 and January 1947 many schemes were proposed for speeding up the flow of information from post to centre and onwards to the RAF. Radio was tested in place of telephone landlines and one very advanced idea involved automatic displays lit on the operations room table by the post observer pushing a button – the only speech necessary being a statement of type and height. None of these plans, however was to come to fruition and the resuscitated corps was thrown back on wartime experience and procedures.

The numbers available were too low to get the whole country network on its feet, while communications were little short of appalling. In Scotland, the west and north-west England there were, for instance, whole groups without a centre, few proper post sites and no telephones. Live training was, therefore, impossible and morale suffered.

For the 1,420 posts and 39 centres on the nominal role in 1948 the telephone was the vital artery. In wartime most ROC links had been permanently connected by private wires which did not go through the normal public telephone system. Because the post-war ROC required to use its communications only for exercises and in the event of an emergency, permanent lines could not be afforded. The post office therefore provided emergency circuits, normally carrying everyday traffic but switched to the ROC as required. Interlinked cluster emergency circuits together with centre multi-line switchboards and teller and sea broadcasts represented a massive undertaking for even an organisation such as the post office, which was wrestling with post-war demands for more domestic telephones and overall modernisation. It was to take several years to put communications into reasonable order and the necessity for having emergency circuits instead of permanent lines has provided headaches for corps and the post office ever since.

The enforced "rest" from 1945 to 1947 would have been the ideal time to re-assess the threat of faster jet aircraft, to thin out and resite posts and set up permanent centres in new locations. No money was available, however, and the Chiefs of Staff, together with Attlee's Government, had agreed that no war threat would exist for ten years. Thus the Royal Observer Corps resumed its reporting role on the basic lines of 1944–45 but within an emasculated air-defence network containing a limited number of fighter squadrons and a fraction of the radar sites required.

The antagonism of the Soviet Union and the massive power available to that country were initially ignored. Russian intentions were only fully realised in June 1948 when all motor traffic and rail transport into the western zones of Berlin were stopped. The "Iron Curtain" had finally come down and on June 26 and 28 respectively the Americans and the British began the famous Berlin airlift which was to last until October 1949.

On July 16, 1948, it was announced that two United States Air Force Groups, with a total strength of 60 B-29 Superfortresses, had been assigned to Britain for temporary duty. The Third Air Division, USAF, was set up and American military aircraft were back in Britain to stay.

Behind the scenes the Government and the RAF were urgently considering a major programme of air-defence expansion. The system had become so run down that it was to take years to put it back on its feet. The Ministry of Supply approached Marconi and requested a complete study of Britain's radar defences. This was followed in 1949 by contracts to overhaul the whole network, many of the stations having been either closed in 1945 or sealed. When the stations were opened up again the equipment was found to be in a very poor state and in need of re-engineering to meet modern requirements. All the vast aerial arrays on the majority of CH stations had to be rebuilt completely and this could not be completed until 1951. The existing GCI sites also required a great deal of work. Because of these manifold deficiencies the ROC was viewed by the Air Staff as being absolutely vital to provide the overland picture for Fighter Command. Even though it was beset with recruiting, communications and building problems the corps was to hold the ring for over three years while the neglect of radar from 1945–1948 was made good.

The key role they were playing was scarcely realised by many post observers on exercises. All too often their ill-fitting uniforms were soaked through, post structure and hut were non-existent and the rickety wooden tripod legs of the instrument often fell to pieces, depositing the heavy metal map table on a luckless observer's feet. Telephones had a habit of emitting loud screams and crackling noises or they cut out altogether. Where lines had not been laid on the observers solemnly wrote the plots down and put them in the mail the next day.

During a tour of posts in one 1948 exercise the AOC-in-C Fighter Command and the corps commandant were "astonished" to find observers operating under exposed conditions with no buildings and inadequate clothing. After the "strongest representations" to the Air Ministry, authority was obtained for the issue of Sidcot flying suits, airmen's greatcoats and ground sheets (for use as capes) on the scale of four per post. This was regarded as an interim measure but with little hope of proper replacements being available for a long time. Some idea of the poor state of supply at this period can be gained from the records up to September 30, 1949, which showed that the ROC had indented for 5,226 Sidcot suits (received 1,463), 4,975 greatcoats (received 3,118) and 4,812 ground sheets (received 3,619). Centres with permanent accommodation were undoubtedly well off, but a shortage of recruits meant one plotter spending hours coupled to six posts at a time. At groups without a centre training could only be theoretical and the announcement of air exercises was usually greeted with ironic laughter.

Over many years the ROC had been considered as a possible organisation for re-equipment with radar to provide an electronic overland picture. On November 2, 1948, the Air Ministry officially informed headquarters ROC that authority had been officially given for the issue of radar to the corps. All groups in Southern Area were invited to put in volunteers to operate and maintain the equipment. Throughout the winter observers were interviewed and finally a team was selected from No 17 Group, Watford, consisting of Chief Observer T. W. Caesar, Observers J. R. Potter and J. G. Wright and Woman Observer J. Deverell.

The real problem, however, lay not in finding suitable ROC personnel but in getting hold of a radar set. The RAF in 1948–49 was no better off as regards an overland low-level radar than it had been in 1940. It was finally agreed to issue an AMES Type 6 Mk VIII set to the corps and the complete equipment was inspected at RAF Henlow in March 1949. Chief Observer Caesar was attached to Henlow for a week's course on the set. As the Type 6 was hardly light-weight and certainly not mobile enough it was rejected.

In May 1949 it was learned that an American lightweight mobile set, AN/TPS2, was still in Britain, and it was received at Stanmore in June. From then until August 11 training meetings were held weekly and on several week-ends. The equipment was brought up to full operational standard and by mid-July was ready for air test and calibration. The air test showed that the equipment failed on low-flying aircraft at distances greater than 25 miles.

The first active trial took place under operational conditions on August 14, 1949, during a Midland Area exercise. The equipment was set up at Ampthill, just south of Bedford and was operated by ROC members. This was the first direct ROC use of radar since the days of GL sets during the war. The Ampthill experiment was considered to be a success and plans were made for its use in the 1949 major exercise, Bulldog. On August 19, however, there was an abrupt reversal of policy. The AOC-in-C Fighter Command informed HQ ROC that it had been decided that the handling of radar equipment was not the task of the ROC and that he wished that nothing should divert the efforts of the corps from the all-important function of visual identification and plotting. Significantly, the AOC-in-C added that no equipment had yet been designed which would give adequate early warning of low-flying aircraft inland.

It took more than two years from VE day for Britian to realise the strides that the Soviet Union was making in military aircraft. There was a tendency to dismiss the Russians as being somewhat primitive and certainly unlikely to challenge the West in terms of long-range bombers and high-speed fighters. This fitted in well with the "no war for ten years" theorists. Two particular days in 1947 provided shocks which were to open the eyes of the Air Staff and begin the process of revitalising air defence. On May 1 the annual Mayday celebrations in Moscow included about 100 jet aircraft: some prototypes, some pre-production and a high proportion of production machines. In the last-mentioned category were the Yak-15 single-jet and MiG-9 twin-jet fighters. Even greater surprise came at the Aviation Day parade at Tushino on August 3, 1947, when amazed foreign observers saw three Soviet-built versions of the Boeing B-29 bomber flash by at low altitude. Designer Tupolev and his team had succeeded in copying the B-29 down to the last nut and bolt. The Soviet Air Force was on the way to posses-sing a force of pressurised high-altitude bombers with a range of more than 3,000 miles. This changed the whole strategic situation.

With advanced Soviet aircraft appearing, together with a spate of new types from Britain and America, it was essential that recognition training be overhauled. The silhouette manual, Air Publication 1480, was re-issued in mid-1948, this time double the page size of the pre-war and wartime editions. The wheels began to turn in the Ministry of Supply to produce episcope cards, folders and recognition posters. Flash trainers were badly needed for projecting aircraft views briefly on screens, but "technical difficulties" with shutter operation delayed their intro-duction. The episcope cards were excellent but the ROC had nothing to show them on. The recommendation that every post should have an episcope for training was made in 1947. By the end of 1949 it had produced "nothing but a considerable amount of correspondence." The Ministry of Supply found great difficulty in finding any firms that would tender at a suitable price. There was also a dismal lack of recognition films both for the RAF and the ROC. The Inter-Services Committee, which dealt with the subject, had a target of one film a month but only succeeded in finishing seven films in two years.

Courses at the RAF Central School of Aircraft Recognition at Kirton-in-Lindsey continued until April 1949, when the school was closed. The personnel were transferred to Fighter Command at Stanmore, where the school was eventually re-established and did most valuable work.

The ROC continued with its basic and intermediate tests, despite the difficulties. All those who had passed the intermediate test were eligible for the master test, which took place for the first time after the war on April 10, 1949 (centres), and April 24, 1949 (posts). Operations rooms were introduced to the joys of a written paper on centre work only, while posts continued with aircraft recognition. A total of 314 members of posts and 102 from the operations rooms gained the coveted "Spitfire" badge. A handful succeeded in entering and passing both tests.

Remarkable as it may appear, throughout the whole of its life up to the stand-down in 1945 the ROC rank and file had never had a consolidated instruction manual. The posts and centres had existed on their little red pamphlets plus a mass of operations instructions and amendments which were only available in limited quantities to officers and NCOs.

During 1948 two officers at HQ ROC were given the task of producing the first "Royal Observer Corps Training Manual" in which it was intended to set out "clearly and concisely" the main functions of the ROC and its personnel at centres and posts. The manual took a long time to prepare, as the procedures involved had to be tried and tested to see that they all worked in practice. The authors well knew that every member of the corps would spend time trying to find any errors and even more time writing to authority about them. At last in August 1949 Air Publication 3215 was promulgated by command of the Air Council and the long and laborious process of distribution to members began. In the course of time AP 3215 was to be modified, amended, re-issued and re-amended as the corps changed its tasks and techniques, but it lives on today as the standard training manual.

During the immediate period following the re-activation of the corps Lord Bandon was anxious to institute an annual camp on Territorial Army lines. He wanted to bring together observers from many parts of the country and give them both tuition and evening relaxation, thus breaking down the boundaries of area, group and county.

His first approaches to the Air Ministry met with a rebuff and he therefore began negotiating with Billy Butlin, the holiday-camp owner, with a view to taking over one of his sites for a period. When news of this dastardly venture into the world of sordid commerce reached the Air Ministry there was a sudden change of heart and RAF Thorney Island was offered to the corps for four weekly camps in September 1948, the personnel living under canvas. The whole performance was a great success, with lectures, parades, VIP visits, experience flights, rifle practice and height- and speed-judging competitions combined with first-grade entertainment. Annual camp was henceforth to be a permanent feature of ROC life.

Live exercises were essential to bring together the threads and give realistic practice to all elements of the control and reporting network, not least the ROC. On May 9, 1948, Midland Area, covering 40,000 sq miles, carried out an exercise involving 120 Service aircraft. Air Commodore Lord Bandon took the AOC-in-C Fighter Command, Air Marshal Sir William Elliot, down to Bedford centre to view the proceedings. Scottish Area followed up on June 20, when five out of the eight Scottish groups staged the first exercise in the area since stand-down. Aircraft were drawn from auxiliary, university air and communications squadrons. The groups involved were 31, Edinburgh; 33, Ayr; 34, Glasgow; 37, Dundee; and 38, Aberdeen. Six hundred Observers turned out and 111 posts were manned. At that time the ROC strength for the whole of Scotland was only 1,600 members, compared with 7,000 in wartime.

Because of the lack of communications North Western Area was unable to hold a full operational exercise until October 1949. Various smaller local exercises were held up and down the country, including "synthetic" exercises. These sometimes consisted of an observer standing out in the open in pea-soup fog and, at the appointed hour, solemnly tearing open an envelope and reading to centre the plot on a non-existent Me410 going north at 200ft.

On some exercises members were unable even to gain access to their posts. For instance, the group commandant, No 19 Group, reported to the Southern Area commandant on December 3, 1948, concerning 19/Y.4 post, New Cross: "When members reported for duty on Sunday, November 28, 1948, it was found that the post had been taken over by the school (Aske Hatchem Grammar School, Dulwich) meteorological society. The padlocks on the post cubby hole had been removed and replaced with new locks and there was a notice on the cubbyhole, signed by one of the masters of the school, 'KEEP OUT.' The chart table is now surmounted by a weather gauge."

All this work was vitally necessary in order to provide a run-up to the real test for the newly revitalised air defences of Britain. With the Soviet Union flexing its muscles it was essential that the effectiveness of the limited fighter-defence facilities available be assessed by large-scale wartime-atmosphere air exercises.

By 1948 the need for re-assessment had become urgent, as Fighter Command had not fought a large-scale defensive air war against manned aircraft since 1940–41. Accordingly an RAF training exercise, code-named "Dagger," was turned into the first large-scale post-war trial, with as near operational conditions as facilities and manning allowed. For this exercise the whole gamut of attack was run, including low-, medium- and high-level raids simulating the first three days of a sudden outbreak of war. The ROC could only participate on Saturday and Sunday, September 4 and 5; the opening day, September 3, and the two ensuing days, the 6th and 7th, were left entirely to the radar network. ROC Midland and Southern Area were involved, supported by Scottish, North Western and Western Areas. There was no operation in Midlands Area from dawn to 09.00 on the Sunday and Oxford centre was unmanned throughout, the new centre building not being occupied until February 1949. Altogether 678 posts and 17 operations rooms participated, with a total of 6,260 personnel involved.

A wide variety of aircraft took part, including Wellingtons, Hornets, Meteors, Mosquitoes, Buckmasters, Lancasters and USAF B-29s in the attacking role and Meteors, Vampires, Hornets, Spitfires and Mosquito night fighters forming the defence. Just as in pre-war days, the Bomber Command attackers were known as Southland and the defenders as Northland.

The lessons learned from the exercise were salutary and the whole system creaked and groaned under the strain of operating continuously over a long period. The radar network generally was found to be technically and operationally below wartime standard, transmission of plots through the system was found to be inordinately lengthy and only two out of 19 low-level raids were detected by the Chain Home Extra Low (CHEL) stations. Apart from the shortage of useable radar equipment the main fault lay in telling of plots and in the filter rooms –

where excessive delays occurred throughout the exercise.

Dagger was a considerable success for the ROC, most especially where low-flying raids were concerned, the RAF describing ROC tracking as "outstandingly good." On September 5 there were eight raids at 500ft or less and, because of splits, these raids formed 12 tracks which gave rise to some 1,500 track miles overland. All were detected by the ROC and tracking was continuous over 92 per cent of the overland tracks thus formed.

As a further test for low-level intruder attack, Midland Area ROC took part in an exercise code named "Hedgehop" on October 24, 1948. The groups involved were No 10, York; No 11, Lincoln; No 14, Bury St Edmunds; No 15, Cambridge; and No 16, Norwich. Because of shortages at the RAF filter room at Watnall, No 6 Group, Derby, provided plotters. Aircraft employed were Meteors, Hornets, Mosquitoes and Spitfires from No 12 Fighter Group.

For 1949 the main test of the air defences was called "Exercise Foil," being divided into three phases between June 25 and July 3. No fewer than 500 aircraft took part, including B-29s, Lincolns, Mosquitoes, Lancasters, Vampires, Meteors, Spitfires and, for the first time, American F-80 Shooting Stars. Many aircraft operated from BAFO in Germany and a Dutch Meteor squadron was detached to Britain for the event. As in Dagger, raiders came in at all altitudes and to add realism Vampires flew as simulated jet bombers at low level and at 30,000ft.

The ROC operated in daylight hours over two week-ends, mobilising all groups in Southern Area, seven in Midland Area, three in Western Area and a skeleton in two groups in North Western Area, the last-mentioned being affected by the lack of post telephone circuits. Where groups were seriously under-manned, observers from more fortunate locations travelled long distances in order to fill the gaps. As an example, no fewer than 60 observers from Scotland travelled south to man Lincoln observer centre.

Wren's impression of ROC participation in exercise Foil in 1949. The drawing first appeared in "The Aeroplane" for July 8, 1949

Hardly had the results of Foil been digested than the corps was called out for a further week-end to participate in exercise Bulldog on September 24–25, 1949. In this exercise, particular attention was paid to low-level, high-speed jet intruders which proved to be a considerable headache and called for very rapid action at both posts and centres. The code-word "Rats" was experimentally re-introduced for the exercise, which meant waves of nostalgia for those observers who had served in wartime.

Air Commodore R. B. Jordan succeeded Air Commodore the Earl of Bandon as Commandant ROC on February 1, 1949. The RAF was placing great reliance on the corps and the big stumbling block was lack of personnel. This, therefore, was the theme of Jordan's first message published in the June 1949 issue of the *Royal Observer Corps Gazette*. He stressed that the "corps is only about half the size it should be" and called for a big improvement in recruiting, particularly of women observers for duty at centres. He added: "Without adequate numbers of women to man our centres, our observers at their posts are useless, because their information cannot be collected and passed upward to the RAF operations rooms of Fighter Command."

At the same time that Jordan was wrestling with recruiting, a new broom was sweeping at Bentley Priory. The colourful and well known air marshal, Sir Basil Embry, had been appointed AOC-in-C Fighter Command in succession to Sir William Elliot in April 1949. Embry took a long, hard look at his control and reporting organisation and decided that the ROC should be much more closely integrated with the RAF. On January 16, 1950, the Air Council approved the transfer of complete operational and administrative control of the ROC to HQ Fighter Command. Only personnel problems were left in the hands of the Air Ministry. Embry decided to control the corps in the same way as a fighter group and gave HQ ROC the status of a group headquarters, which in turn gave the commandant group commander status and the right to fly his pennant.★

On February 20, 1950, Embry informed Nos 11 and 12 Fighter Groups and the Commandant ROC of the transfer of control in the following letter:

"It has been decided to place the Royal Observer Corps under the operational and administrative control of headquarters Fighter Command. This decision has been made for the same reasons that led to the transfer of the Royal Auxiliary Air Force squadrons from Reserve Command. The Royal Observer Corps from now on will come under my control and I propose that its headquarters will remain as at present constituted, and will be treated in much the same way as a group in Fighter Command. As such it will be responsible for the efficient individual training, organisation, administration and recruitment of the corps so that it can fulfil its role in the air-defence system.

The integration of the ROC areas and centres with the other elements of the air-defence system within a sector is the responsibility of the respective sector commanders. Whereas the ROC is responsible for the preliminary training of the individual, the sector commander is to train ROC units as an operational part of the air-defence team. This will mean the closest liaison between the ROC and the rest of the operational elements of the sector in order that each can appreciate the other's job, and how it fits into the overall air-defence system.

Sector commanders will realise that the ROC is a voluntary civilian body; its members are not subject to Air Force law despite the fact that they wear uniform. They are, of course, extremely

---

★In the present nuclear reporting role the ROC as a whole has lost the RAF group status, but the commandant retains the position of an RAF group commander.

proud of their corps and of its achievements during the last war.

I therefore wish sector commanders by visits, etc, not only to gain complete understanding of the function and problems of the ROC but to take a firm grip in getting the ROC units up to necessary standard of operational efficiency."

ROC groups were allocated RAF sectors as follows:

ROC GROUP

RAF Metropolitan Sector	No 1	Maidstone
	17	Watford
	18	Colchester
	19	Beckenham
	2	Horsham
RAF Southern Sector	3	Winchester
	4	Oxford
	22	Yeovil
	23	Bristol
	24	Gloucester
	25	Cardiff
	21	Exeter
	20	Truro
	28/1	Carmarthen
RAF Scottish Sector	31	Edinburgh
	34	Glasgow
	35	Oban
	37	Dundee
	38	Aberdeen
	39	Inverness
	36	Dunfermline
RAF Western Sector	7	Manchester
	26	Wrexham
	27	Shrewsbury
	28/2	Caernarvon
	29	Lancaster
	32	Carlisle
	33	Ayr
RAF Northern Sector	8	Leeds
	9 & 10	York
	30	Durham

RAF Eastern Sector	5	Coventry
	6	Derby
	11	Lincoln
	12	Bedford
	14	Bury St Edmunds
	15	Cambridge
	16	Norwich

The whole pattern of air defence was about to undergo a massive change. In September 1949 President Truman announced that he had evidence that an atomic explosion had occurred in the Soviet Union. At the same time intelligence organisations in the West began to receive alarming news that the Russians were forging ahead in the sphere of advanced military aircraft. Prototypes of high-speed jet fighters and bombers had been seen and it was clear that the Soviet Air Force had been grossly underestimated. The biggest shock came late in 1949 when intelligence evidence showed that Russia had successfully developed a swept-wing high-subsonic fighter designed around the Rolls-Royce Nene engine which Sir Stafford Cripps had supplied to Russia as a good-will gesture. By December 1949 the Air Defence Intelligence (Technical) section of the Air Ministry, with the help of the United States, was able to prepare accurate and detailed drawings of the "Type 14", which was to emerge as the redoutable MiG-15 fighter. From this a silhouette was prepared and issued a year later to the ROC and to the Services.

On June 25, 1950, North Korean forces crossed the 38th parallel and invaded South Korea. Initially only known Russian piston-engined types of aircraft were used, but on November 1, 1950, American Mustangs over the Yalu river were attacked by six MiG-15s. Obviously the type was in large-scale use and the performance achieved had to be read right across the Soviet Air Force, including bomber developments. It was against this background of surprise at Soviet technical advances that Fighter Command began to improve its standards.

Mobile radar convoys were first produced to supplement the modernised CH, CHL, CHEL and GCI chain and this move was followed by a plan for the complete rebuilding of the radar chain and the sector operations centres with underground facilities proof against nuclear attack. Known as "Rotor", the programme had a special progress committee chaired by Air Commodore (later Air Marshal Sir) W. P. G. Pretty. The Committee began work in earnest in December 1950. This plan was, of course, unknown to the ROC, other than the commandant, and all efforts in 1950 were devoted to meeting the potential Soviet threat with the resources available.

On April 4, 1949, the North Atlantic Treaty had been signed in Washington by Belgium, Britain, Canada, Denmark, France, Holland, Iceland, Italy, Norway, Portugal and the United States. Under Article 5 of the treaty the signatories agreed that "an armed attack against any one or more of them in Europe or North America shall be considered an attack against them all." This looked excellent on paper, but the general state of West European defence was lamentable. Radar networks differed in concept and equipment – or were non-existent – while aircraft were few and in many cases obsolescent. There was no central control, and warning and track-handover facilities did not exist. It was against this background that the annual exercise "Emperor" was staged, in three phases, between October 7 and October 15, 1950. This was the largest exercise held since 1945, and as the ROC exercise instruction stated:

"The Royal Observer Corps is to participate during certain phases of the exercise, when the whole of the groups throughout England and Wales will become operational simultaneously for the first time since the Second World War."

The American, Belgian, Danish, Dutch and Norwegian air forces arrived to participate, and in all 1,000 aircraft took part. The RAF, lacking any modern home-built bomber, had acquired the first of its Boeing B-29s (named Washington), while the US 3rd Air Division fielded not only B-29s but the new B-50D with underwing fuel tanks and also the Republic F-84 Thunderjet. To complicate matters Vampires with external fuel tanks were hostile and those without were friendly.

For the ROC the whole thing had a smell of wartime about it. In Exercise Bulldog in 1949 and in Exercise Stardust in April 1950 the all-too-familiar code-word "Rats" had been provisionally used instead of "Low Raid Urgent." For Emperor "Rats" was officially adopted and "Low Raid Urgent" disappeared, never to return. For the low-level Rats raids a new technique of VHF/RT broadcast direct from Rats controllers at ROC operations rooms to airborne fighters was carried out in Nos 1, 14, 16, 18 and 19 Groups of Southern Area. This was similar in most respects to the direct radio/fighter control from Nos 1 and 2 Groups used during the V1 attacks. For Exercise Emperor the broadcast was known as "Terrier Procedure," the Terrier being the fighter intercepting the hostile aircraft.

The wartime operations instruction No 53 on Rats had been re-issued in modified form in September 1950. It called for post plots on Rats both visual and sound, in the latter case only if the observers were satisfied the type fell into the right category. Rats were defined as "hostile or unidentified aircraft flying at heights of 1,000ft or less over sea or land, as estimated from the level of the post." The centre duty controller was instructed to give Rats plots absolute priority at all stages and ensure maximum speed in telling to the RAF plotter. Many lessons were learned from Emperor and the Rats/Terrier procedure was adopted as standard, although the fighter-control element was later moved from the ROC centres to the RAF sector operations centres.

Like Rats, many of the old Second World War operations procedures had been dusted down, revised and re-issued. Thus it was that post observers had to relearn No 52, States of Preparedness; No 49, Heights reported from ROC Posts; No 18, Reporting and Plotting by Sound; No 25, Action to aid the Safety of Friendly Aircraft; and No 43, Reporting from ROC Posts. At centres there were No 40, Mass Procedure; No 48, Main telling Procedure for individual tracks; and No 46, The handover of tracks by Inter-Group Telling, Long-Range Board Plotting, and by liaison. Even the air-raid warning system, with its air-raid warning officers on the ROC centre dais, was back in business. For this, operations instruction No 35, Air Raid Warnings, first issued in August 1943, was reprinted. Once again the ROC was also in the weather business. Apart from the routine weather logs kept at each post and available for query by centre, specially designated posts in all groups passed detailed "Rocmet" weather reports through the system at set intervals.

There had been one other innovation for Emperor, namely the geographic reference system. The modified British grid had been used by the whole of the C and R system throughout the Second World War as the basic means of referring to any spot as represented on a map. It only covered England, Scotland and Wales, however, and was not capable of extension to Continental Europe. The emergence of Nato made it imperative that there should be a common map-reference system for international use. Geographic reference, or Georef for short, was decided upon and was officially adopted throughout the Fighter Command C and R organisation on September 25, 1950, just in time for Emperor. For the whole of the ROC it meant forgetting everything so patiently memorised on British grid and trying to keep in mind that they were looking at 2min rectangular areas and not 2km squares.

During the year the ROC was not only absorbed with the rapidly changing operational pattern but also with domestic developments of considerable significance. The year 1950 was the 25th anniversary of the corps' formal existence and this was celebrated by all groups during the week of April 16–22. One major event was the staging of an exercise on April 16 covering Kent, Surrey and Sussex, including the whole of the area observed during the first Nos 1 and 2 Group exercise in 1925. For this the RAF provided Meteors, Vampires, Spitfires, Mosquitoes and Lincolns. At the Cranbrook post in Kent the head observer, G. Couchman, one of the original members, welcomed Mr A. Baker who had been the head special there in 1925.

To mark the silver jubilee of the ROC King George VI consented to become the corps Air Commodore-in-Chief. The request to the Monarch had been put forward in February, but Palace officials felt some other title should be used. The records showed that Air Commodore Ambler was, in 1942, thought to be the only serving RAF officer who would command the corps and that it would later revert to an ROC officer, hence the promulgation of the title observer commodore. In fact serving RAF officers had been commandants from Ambler onwards and to this day it is a regular RAF posting. On the recommendation of the Air Council the King assumed the title Air Commodore-in-Chief on April 11, 1950.

One further royal assent was to give great satisfaction to members in this year and this was issuing of a royal warrant for the establishment of the Royal Observer Corps Medal. It had been hoped that the medal would be awarded after eight years' service, as in the case of Special Constabulary Medal, but the regulations finally laid down a period of 12 years. The ROC Medal bearing the sovereign's effigy on one side and the Elizabethan coast watcher on the other was officially instituted on January 31, 1950. The ribbon is light blue, dark blue and silver-grey stripes and is worn "after the Special Constabulary Medal and before the Union of South Africa Commemorative Medal." One half only of full-time salaried or paid service by ROC personnel in peacetime can be reckoned and it therefore takes a full-time officer 24 years to get his medal unless he has served as a volunteer, which period is counted in full. When the ROC Medal was instituted no consideration was given to the normal "clasp" which would denote multiples of the 12 years. It was not many years, therefore, before some very strange ad-hoc devices began to appear on the left breast of some observers who felt that their 24 years should be recognised outwardly. The problem was solved by the institution of a clasp to the medal and a rose emblem on the ribbon.

Finally, 1950 saw the disappearance of the large civil-defence-type breast badge which observers had worn on their battledress since 1942. On August 3, 1950, the Air Council adopted the proposal that the breast badge be replaced by ROC shoulder flashes, similar to those worn by the RAF Regiment. Under the flash the number of the group in which the member served was also to be incorporated. Altruism was not really the key to this decision. Flashes were cheaper; the Air Ministry reckoned that they could write off the £1,600-worth of breast badges in stock and recover the outlay on flashes in seven years.

Chapter 17
POST-WAR PEAK

To meet the threat posed by the massive expansion of the Soviet Air Force the RAF embarked on "Rotorplan" in 1951. This involved the transfer of sector operations centre and GCI radar personnel to underground bunkers safe from conventional bombs and most of the effects of kiloton nuclear weapons, apart from a direct hit.

Originally it had been intended that the Chain Home radar stations, with their tall lattice masts, should be retained for long-range warning. An entirely new British high-power radar, the Type 80, became available, however, and it offered such advanced performance that it was decided to phase out the CH stations. The programme was vast and expensive involving, apart from the underground buildings and the radars, a complete new communications network and 1,620 display consoles of all types. The Type 80 sets were installed at most of the new sites, but some older equipment remained in use as gap-fillers. The Type 80 gave a range of 200 miles on high-flying aircraft and its inauguration changed the whole air picture.

The Rotor system was built over the period 1951 to 1954, with the bulk of the stations being commissioned by the end of 1953. For the ROC the Rotorplan ultimately meant a complete upheaval, but in the years 1951–53 there were constant alterations in internal layout, communications circuits and operational procedures.

For 1951, ROC areas conducted their own exercises, those in Western Area, for instance, being known by the name Wessex and those in Southern Area as Southex. Some groups also laid on exercises, but these were limited in scope and usually relied on passing civil and military traffic for practice. Rapidly increasing speeds of jet aircraft and the need to cut down transmission time for plots through the system led to the need for reports to be made on the basis of a larger area than the standard two-minute areas. Various groups experimented with quartering and lettering the ten-minute areas on the post charts, which in effect meant reporting by five-minute instead of ten-minute areas.

Taking this idea one stage further, No 2 Group was permitted, during exercises Southex V and Southex VII in 1951, to use a procedure whereby the five-mile circle was divided into quarters, A, B, Y and X, which was very similar to a method employed in certain groups in 1939–40. When fast, low-flying jets appeared the observer used his finger to mark where the aircraft was estimated to be on the chart and reported "Mike wun – Meteor – Able – Southeast – wun at two." The centre plotter would then place the correct coloured visual counter on the main table in the centre of the segment of the post sound circle indicated by the letter given. The system proved successful and, in modified form, was used throughout the corps, the term "finger plotting" becoming standard parlance. Further experiments with finger plotting were

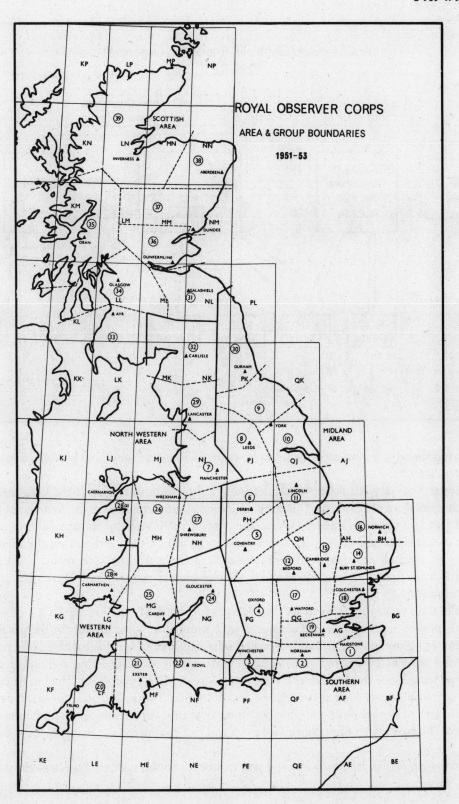

ROYAL OBSERVER CORPS

AREA & GROUP BOUNDARIES

1951-53

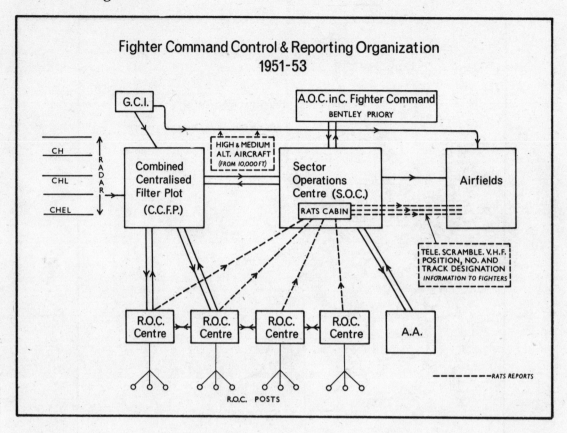

made during the 1951 annual air exercise, code-named "Pinnacle" and held between September 28 and October 3.

The Royal Auxiliary Air Force was undergoing a three-month call-up at the time and 11 of these squadrons were available for full-time operation. Innovations were the first use of radar-equipped jet night fighters (Meteor NF.11s and Vampire NF.10s) and the appearance in small numbers of Canberra and RB-45 jet bombers. The arrival of the Canberra on the scene was ultimately to upset all pre-conceived ideas about air defence. Fighter Command was bent on refining its tactics against the high-flyer and the hedge-hopper and the Rats/Terrier scheme was in full operation.

The following year, 1952, was to see big changes for the RAF and for the ROC. The RAF reached its post-war peak in aircraft strength, with more than 6,300 aircraft in the inventory. There were 45 fighter, 25 bomber and 12 coastal squadrons available, albeit with a large proportion of what must be considered obsolescent aircraft. While the USAF was fighting in Korea with swept-wing F-86s and the Chinese were using Soviet MiG-15s, the RAF had to be content with straight-wing types such as the Meteor and Vampire. The ROC was still beset with the problem of lack of proper posts and the poor siting of many. Air Commodore Jordan had been pressing for the production of prefabricated posts and had conducted a country-wide survey of sites.

In March 1951 Jordan left the corps and was promoted to the rank of Air Vice-Marshal. He was succeeded by Air Commodore G. H. Vasse, a tall man of robust proportions; he was universally known as "Tiny." Vasse inherited the post problem, on which little or no progress seemed to be made in Whitehall. In April 1951 approval was given for no fewer than 411 ROC posts to be resited and 93 new ones to be constructed. Fighter Command was responsible for siting and, through the superintending engineers of official works areas, the new positions had to be assessed, approved and all the formalities of acquisition gone through. Many landowners were loth to part with even a small plot and lengthy negotiations usually ensued.

Post structures themselves presented even more problems, and it was largely through Air Vice-Marshal Jordan's pressure within the RAF itself that the prefabricated post scheme eventually became a reality. In 1952 Messrs Orlit Ltd, Colnebrook Bypass, Bucks, produced definitive drawings of two types of post: Type A, which was at ground level; and Type B, which was raised on four 6ft legs.

The basic design was the same, with precast concrete or wooden sections fitted together to form a rectangle 10ft long by 6ft 8in wide. On the front left a door was provided which opened into a 3ft 6in-wide cubby hole, where the telephone box was installed; from this a 4ft-high doorway (intended for dwarfs) gave access to the walled observation platform with a central pedestal for the observer instrument. Sections of corrugated iron fitted on to wooden cross members to form the cover for the platform. The whole assembly was crude and uncomfortable, but had the merits of being capable of mass production. After all, anything was better than nothing and the "Orlit post," as it came to be known, was a considerable improvement on having the instrument erected in the middle of a ploughed field. The process of getting Orlits installed was not, however, completed until 1954–55 (by mid-1954, 338 Orlits had been erected). That

The "Orlit" prefabricated post for aircraft observation, introduced into the ROC between 1952 and 1955. More than 400 were completed, some at ground level and others on stilts as shown. Some Orlits can still be seen at old post sites in various parts of the country

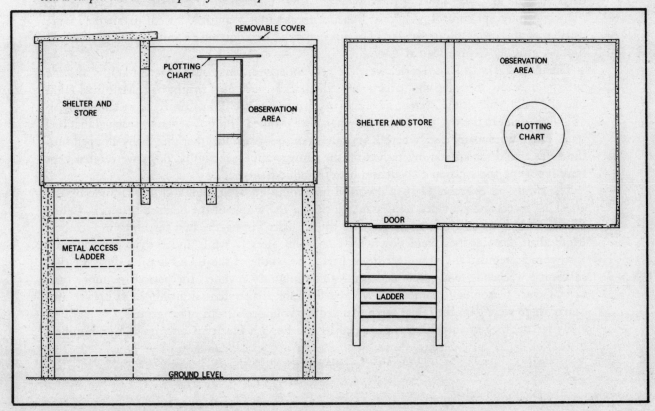

the structures were durable cannot be doubted, as a few still exist today as reminders of the period when the ROC was still the "eyes and ears of the RAF."

To assist with the permanent Fighter Command headache, Rats, the ROC reverted to a procedure which had proved effective during the tip-and-run and V1 raids, namely the use of flares. A large number of posts were provided with Very pistols or "Signals Dischargers (Pistols) 1½in No 4 Mk 1," together with suitable signal cartridges. These were to be fired when Rats appeared and were to alert fighters on patrol. Very pistols were only supplied to country posts, as the dangers in built-up areas were manifest. Despite exceptional precautions, however, there were a number of cases where Very cartridges set fire to hay-ricks, cornfields and even public lavatories on playing fields. As an example at Beyton post in Suffolk on October 12 a Very pistol was fired to denote a low flying raid and the observer on duty reported:

"The flare was fired and landed reasonably near to two stacks owned by Messrs. R. Black & Sons, Brook Farm, Beyton. For a few minutes my attention was occupied by other duties. When next I checked in the direction of the stacks (approximately a minute after firing the flare) a small flame was noticed on the ground near to the stacks. Two other observers on the post immediately ran to the stacks to try to smother the flames before reaching the stacks. On their arrival, the flames had reached the stacks and were rapidly spreading up the sides. To me, still at the post, it was then apparent the fire was beyond the control of the observers and I immediately issued instructions by telephone for the fire service to be summoned."

The RAF could only operate the Rats/Terrier procedure when the ROC was operating, and this usually meant at weekends. Meteors, Vampires and later Venoms were employed in daylight only in pairs, the two aircraft being officially referred to as "Playmates." The pairs were plugged into telescramble (station RT) and were scrambled from the operational-readiness platform. One pilot flew at 800ft while the other was at 300ft, the high man looking for ROC flares and the low man looking for the target. After take-off both aircraft were switched to the sector intercept control broadcast, but had no close GCI control. Speeds maintained were usually of the order of 400–430kt. The normal type of controller's call would be "Bandit sighted, crossing Cromer 240 at 1,000."

The real snags with Rats/Terrier were the very short endurance of the Meteor at low altitude and the difficulty in seeing the flares against the background on a bright day. Main fuel tanks plus the belly tank on the Meteor gave only 35min endurance. Pilots aimed to reach base with 60 gallons a side in the wings, and the high man always called "Bingo" when he reached that fuel state. There were many cases where Rat chasers ran so low on fuel that they belly-flopped into the fields round the airfield or crashed on the runway approach. ROC posts were often kept busy reporting the location of bent and battered aircraft.

The annual air exercises of 1952 involved maximum effort at high and low altitude by the attacking forces and provided unpleasant shocks for the whole of the defence network. Called "Exercise Ardent," the operations covered three phases during the first fortnight in October. More than 6,000 sorties were flown by 1,000-plus aircraft while more than 200,000 men and women, regular and volunteer, took part. The whole of the ROC was on duty for two successive weekends, with posts and centres continuously manned for periods of more than 24hr. Centre personnel in some cases worked for 12hr at a stretch with only short breaks, and where there were gaps the tables were manned by volunteers from other groups.

By far the biggest surprise was provided by the English Electric Canberra B.2 jet bomber, of which four squadrons were operating from Binbrook, Lincolnshire. Ordered to drop from their normal height of 45,000ft down to 35,000ft, the Canberras still proved exceptionally difficult to intercept, F-86 Sabres achieving the feat twice and the Meteors and Venoms only once. Radar could see the Canberras at 35,000ft, but photographic reconnaissance Mk 4s at 45,000ft were sometimes not noticed. For the ROC the combination of speed and height provided severe headaches. Estimates of altitude varied considerably, courses zig-zagged and some posts were told acidly by the plotter than the aircraft they were reporting was over the next county.

Washingtons, B-29s and B-50s made up the main heavy-bomber force, being backed up by the aged Lincoln. Although at its top post-war strength Fighter Command could muster only straight-winged Meteors, Vampires and Venoms. The only modern swept-wing intercepters available were those of No 1 Royal Canadian Air Force Wing at North Luffenham. The RAF had numbers of aircraft but not quality.

Coincident with the medium- to high-level raids there was a steady stream of Rats attacking airfields and even getting through to Bentley Priory itself. F-84 Thunderjets were especially successful at low level and often caught the defences napping, despite the ROC tellers screaming "Rats" down the sector and station telephone lines.

One particular raid led to an extension of ROC territory. One hundred-plus bombers at night rendezvoused over the north-west Atlantic, sneaked over Cape Wrath and then down through central Scotland. The bombers finally split formation, attacking Edinburgh and Glasgow and they were not intercepted until well into England. Quite clearly more posts were needed in northern and north-western Scotland to ensure that the gap could be closed. On the night in question the long-range boards had remained empty. All that had been received at groups had been a few unco-ordinated reports such as "Heard – wun fife – distant – south – two plus at no height – piston – out."*

The first of many new Scottish posts was formed at Port Patrick in December 1952 and this was followed in 1953–54 by Aultbea, Girvan, Tomatin, Braid Hills, Traquair, Kirkmichael, Kinbrace and Strontian. Later further posts were set up on Skye and the Outer Hebrides to give adequate warning to the west.

In 1952 King George VI died and the corps was without its Air Commodore-in-Chief. The King had taken a great personal interest in the corps, on which he had conferred the title "Royal," and his passing was keenly felt. The Princess who had watched the V1s from the post on Windsor Castle in 1944 now became Queen. In the *London Gazette* of June 1, 1953, it was announced that Her Majesty Queen Elizabeth II had been pleased to assume the appointment of Air Commodore-in-Chief of the Royal Observer Corps; the royal link continued, to the great satisfaction of all members.

As the corps passed into 1953 it began a process of change which was to continue for nearly a decade. Fighter Command was gradually putting its vitals underground and changing its sector layout to match the advanced radars being deployed. New techniques were being introduced to meet the threat at both high and low altitudes, and the Churchill Government felt that if the Russians were going to strike in the West it could well be in 1953. As each sector transferred to its new location all the telephone circuits had to be changed, and the emergency

---

*The reporting procedure for sound plots had been modified since the war, and the practice of giving 2/2+ or 5/5+ and the words piston or jet was introduced in June 1952.

circuits from the Rats keyboard at sector to ROC groups often took time to install and test. A typical change-over of the period was the transfer of RAF Metropolitan Sector from Trimley Heath to Kelvedon Hatch on March 9, 1953. Both operations rooms continued running their general situation maps simultaneously until the controller at Kelvedon Hatch considered that his communications and VHF broadcast were fully operational.

The ROC was absorbed in trying to find a way to keep accurate tracks on the high fliers and speed up reporting and track handover. The change in RAF sector layout gave the opportunity for the ROC to redraw its map country-wide, with areas re-aligned to coincide with the new RAF sectors. The concept received the full support of Sir Basil Embry and of his successor as AOC-in-C Fighter Command, Air Marshal Sir Dermot Boyle, who took office in the spring of 1953.

A tremendous amount of planning work was necessary before the scheme for ROC reorganisation was ready. The final plan involved the coverage of England, Scotland and Wales by six instead of five areas: *Metropolitan* (HQ, Uxbridge) absorbed the old Southern Area; *Southern Area* (HQ, Rudloe, near Bath) absorbed the old Western Area; *Eastern Area* (HQ, Norwich) took over part of the old Midland Area; *Western Area* (HQ, Preston) absorbed the old North-Western Area; *Northern Area* (HQ, York) took over part of the old Midland Area; and *Scottish Area* (HQ, Edinburgh). The names North-Western and Midland Areas disappeared.

The groups themselves were turned upside down, with nine of the old group headquarters ceasing to function and territories and posts being redistributed across the new group borders as necessary. The final list of 30 Groups was:*

No 1 Group	Beckenham	(16)	No 16 Group	Shrewsbury	(15)
No 2 Group	Horsham	(17)	No 17 Group	Caernarvon	(11)
No 3 Group	Oxford	(14)	No 18 Group	Leeds	(17)
No 4 Group	Colchester	(15)	No 19 Group	Manchester	(12)
No 5 Group	Watford	(15)	No 20 Group	York	(17)
No 6 Group	Norwich	(17)	No 21 Group	Lancaster	(11)
No 7 Group	Bedford	(17)	No 22 Group	Carlisle	(7)
No 8 Group	Coventry	(17)	No 23 Group	Durham	(17)
No 9 Group	Yeovil	(11)	No 24 Group	Edinburgh	(13)
No 10 Group	Exeter	(14)	No 25 Group	Ayr	(12)
No 11 Group	Truro	(11)	No 26 Group	Glasgow	(14)
No 12 Group	Bristol	(15)	No 27 Group	Oban	(8)
No 13 Group	Carmarthen	(16)	No 28 Group	Dundee	(13)
No 14 Group	Winchester	(17)	No 29 Group	Aberdeen	(10)
No 15 Group	Derby	(17)	No 30 Group	Inverness	(10)

The groups disbanded and redistributed were: 14, Bury St Edmunds; 15, Cambridge; 25, Cardiff; 36, Dunfermline; 24, Gloucester; 11, Lincoln; 1, Maidstone; 26, Wrexham; and 10, York. Some of these names re-appeared again in group and boundary changes in the 1960s in

*Figures in brackets denote the number of post-clusters (including overlap clusters) and therefore the number of plotters' positions for each group.

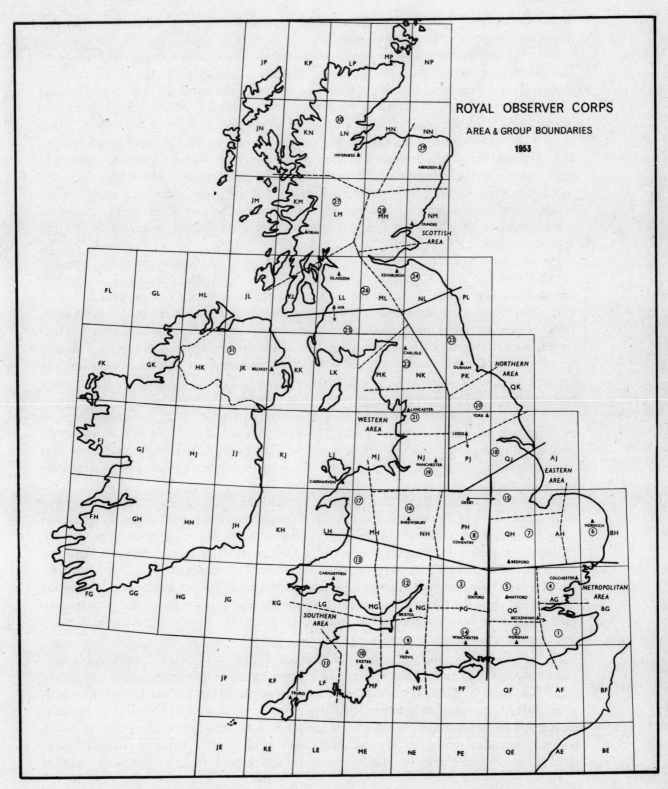

the nuclear reporting role. The only group which has kept its original centre name and number throughout 50 years is No 2 Group, Horsham.

The redundant operations rooms were retained for use as training centres. In addition to the changes in geographical plan, certain new facilities were provided at the 30 reconstituted groups. Posts were reclustered to provide the best picture/communications layout and a number of posts on group boundaries were grouped into "overlap clusters" whereby they could report to two or more adjoining group centres. To speed up inter-centre plotting and telling, "guide circuits" were introduced. These involved a "guide operator" with up to 9ft of telephone cord and a head-and-breast telephone set which provided liaison from the table, group to group. The guide operator moved around the table, passing information as required. The only problem was tucking away the surplus telephone cord and the only real solution to this was a complicated system of weights and pulleys, which was not recommended. Because of the complexities of the communications lines involved, financial approval was given for the construction of GPO apparatus rooms at ROC groups.

The whole re-organisation of the corps was scheduled to be effective from November 1, 1953. On that date the GPO cancelled all existing circuit arrangements, except at Truro, Exeter, Carmarthen, Caernarvon, Oban, Dundee, Aberdeen and Inverness. Over the greater part of the United Kingdom, therefore, from November 1 there was a state of "nil cover" as far as the ROC was concerned. From this there was a gradual build-up to full operational cover as GPO circuits were reconnected. The situation was critical and the air-defence commander wished to be advised every week on the state the ROC had reached. Each group commandant was required to submit reports on GPO circuit connections every Friday night until the network was completed, including details of posts resited and wired.

While the re-organisation was under way a further extension of ROC coverage was being programmed. Sir Basil Embry had visited Northern Ireland and met a number of influential people. He subsequently received letters asking why the Royal Observer Corps did not exist in the province. As he was concerned over the west-about threat, Embry approached the commandant.

Observer Commander Rusby and Observer Lieutenant Lardner were sent for a fortnight to carry out a survey of Northern Ireland. Rusby subsequently recommended that an operations room be established at Belfast, together with about 60 posts. The scheme was approved and Observer Lieutenant D. Johnson was posted to Belfast as deputy group commandant and Observer Officer A. C. Thomas as group training officer. The headquarters building chosen for the new No 31 Group was an old wartime anti-aircraft control room at Houston Park in the Orangefield area. Recruiting was opened for four operations-room crews and personnel to man 58 observer posts scattered across Antrim, Londonderry, Tyrone, Fermanagh, Armagh and Down.

The first man to be officially enrolled in Northern Ireland, on April 1, 1954, was No 8001 Observer Albert M'Curdy, who was later to become a duty controller. Altogether 28 people enlisted on April 1, of whom ten were women. A large number of the recruits who flowed in were ex-RAF, including two former chaplains. The Royal Navy also provided an ex-naval captain and an ex-lieutenant commander. Brigadier R. J. C. Broadhurst, a retired army officer with a distinguished record, was approached by the RAF to take on the job of group commandant. He was to remain in the post for two years. By September 1, 1954, 100 people had enrolled and by December 1 there were 200 – a remarkable achievement in the opening up of an entirely new territory as far as the ROC was concerned. Despite every trial and tribulation in recent years, No 31 Group continues and it does credit to those who helped form it 21 years ago.

The main air exercise for 1953 had been "Momentum," staged in August and covering three phases, two of which were at weekends. More than 6,000 sorties were flown by aircraft of Fighter, Bomber, Coastal and Flying Training Commands, together with the Royal Auxiliary Air Force, the RCAF and the USAF. In addition the Royal Navy put up strikes by Sea Furies, Attackers and Wyverns. High-speed Rats attacks were flown by Vampires, Venoms, Sabres and F-84s. American B-45s put in high-altitude attacks, but the most difficult targets of all were the Canberras which for the first time were operating without height and speed restrictions. A dozen Canberra squadrons were involved and at 45,000ft they roamed the country with virtual impunity. While Rats plotting and telling by the ROC was good, great difficulty was found in maintaining accurate tracks on the Canberras, particularly at night with no contrails visible.

The year 1954 can be considered as the high-water mark of the Royal Observer Corps in its role as the visual and aural aircraft-detection agency for the RAF. Instead of 39 groups in a ragged formation across the country, there were now 30 mainland groups with neat boundaries coinciding with the fighter sector layout. Posts had been reclustered and the overlap clusters smoothed the inter-group handover. No 31 Group was just beginning.

In March 1954, Air Commodore J. H. T. Simpson succeeded Air Commodore Vasse as corps commandant and Observer Captain W. Rusby succeeded Observer Captain Cooke as deputy commandant. The ROC annual camp for the year was staged at RAF Waterbeach.

Throughout its years of existence the ROC had not been subject to Queen's Regulations, and requirements had been laid down on an ad hoc basis. To the official mind this was untidy and inappropriate for a uniformed body playing a key part in our defence. Accordingly, in March 1954, "Regulations for the Royal Observer Corps" were issued by the Air Council as Air Publication 3306. These covered general conditions of service, conduct, uniform, training, pay and allowances, administration, etc. In revised form, and now issued by the Defence Council, AP3306 is still in force.

The standards of training had improved considerably and enthusiasm was high, with 9,484 members entering for the annual master test and 1,321 winning Spitfire badges. So many observers had obtained Spitfires on several occasions that it was decided to institute a red Spitfire badge to denote the passing of five master tests. As members continued to pile up passes each year it was later agreed that ten master passes should be marked by a red star under the Spitfire, 15 by two red stars and 20 by three red stars. There had been a marked increase in the quality and quantity of aircraft-recognition training aids, and the corps continued to win major awards in the field. The Silver Hurricane Trophy for the top team in the all-England aircraft-recognition contest for 1954 was won by 5/C.4, St Albans, and they completed a hat-trick as the corps had won in 1952 and 1953. To assist in recognising Soviet aircraft without recourse to such names as Mikoyan and Polikarpov, Nato introduced code-names and titles like Badger, Fresco and Coach worked their way into the ROC vocabulary.

At centres, training was being greatly facilitated by the "Beckenham synthetic trainer," first tested in the Beckenham group operations room in 1950. A simple but effective device, the Beckenham trainer consisted of a vertical aluminium screen on which was affixed a chart of the whole plotting table or a few post clusters as required. Miniature models of aircraft, bearing indications of type, strength and height, were moved over the face of the chart by the use of magnets at the back. Up to 12 observers with head and breast sets could transmit reports to plotters in the operations room. The tracks could then be displayed in the normal manner and practice given in telling them. Both post and centre observers could gain realistic experience cheaply and regardless of the weather and external telephone connections. The groups made up the trainers themselves, to a standard specification, and Fighter Command authorised the payment for materials involved which, in 1950, was estimated at the princely sum of £3 15s.

For the air exercises of 1954 the re-organisation of the corps was virtually complete, as was the revised RAF sector layout. Code-named "Dividend," the exercise took place between July 16 and July 25. The area involved was east of a line drawn through Lyme Regis – North Wales – Isle of Man – north-east Irish coast, and it excluded territory north of the Caledonian Canal. The control and reporting network used for the ROC was:

RAF SECTOR	CENTRALISED COMBINED FILTER PLOT	ROC GROUP	
Metropolitan (Kelvedon)	Hill House	No 1	Beckenham
		2	Horsham
		4	Colchester
		5	Watford
Southern (Box)	Box	3	Oxford
		9	Yeovil
		12	Bristol
		14	Winchester
Eastern (Bawburgh)	Watnall	6	Norwich
		7	Bedford
		15	Derby/Lincoln
Northern (Shipton)	Watnall	18	Leeds
		20	York
		23	Durham
Western (Longley Lane, Preston)	Whittingham Lane	8	Coventry
		16	Shrewsbury
		19	Manchester
		21	Lancaster
		22	Carlisle
		25	Ayr
Caledonian (Barnton Quarry)	Barnton Quarry	24	Edinburgh
		25	Ayr
		26	Glasgow
		27	Oban
		28	Dundee
		29	Aberdeen

Six groups were outside the exercise area and therefore did not take part. For the "Terrier" organisation operational in Phase 2, January 24–25, 17 ROC groups were designated. In Metropolitan, Eastern, Northern and Caledonian Sectors, Terrier control was exercised from the SOC, while in Southern Sector control was given to the ROC operations rooms under the direction of the SOC. RAF controllers, known as "ROC controllers," were put in four ROC group operations rooms.

The control facilities at the SOCs appeared on the VHF panel in the "Rats cabin" on keys indicating the ROC centre to which the lines were connected. Where necessary, observer groups (other than in Southern Sector) could be given control by throwing the centre VHF keyboard switch from "SOC" to "local." When a fighter was handed over from, say, Eastern to Southern Sector, the ROC exercise controller at Eastern SOC would inform the Bedford ROC duty controller of the Terrier fighter identity, e.g. "Fighter Allocation on 34N is Placid Red." Bedford repeated the information to Oxford, where the "ROC controller" took over. In Southern Sector ROC groups, VHF radio tellers broadcast Rats plots with sequences such as "14 William Canberra – Peter Fox 5557 – South West – Peter Fox 5557 – South West."

In Dividend, widespread use was made of Very pistols at ROC posts, but only on certain types designated as hostile, flying below 5,000ft and within one mile of the post.

During the exercise aircraft classified as hostile were: *British:* Avenger, Canberra, Firefly, Lincoln, Meteor, Sea Fury, Sea Hawk, Vampire, Varsity, Venom and Wyvern; *American:* B-26 Invader, B-45 Tornado, B-47 Stratojet, C-47 Dakota, F-80 Shooting Star, F-84 Thunderjet, F-86 Sabre and KC-97 Stratocruiser. Friendly fighters were F-86 Sabre, Meteor, Vampire and Venom. To complicate matters Sabres, Meteors and Vampires operated in both hostile and friendly fighter roles, the means of identification being single, tight pair or box formation, at high altitude and carrying drop tanks. In addition, in Phase 2, Meteors and Vampires without drop tanks and in sections of three operated as Rats.

A special night anti-intruder organisation was set up in Metropolitan and Eastern Sectors to defend the night-fighter stations of West Malling and West Raynham, using a modified Rats procedure. Finally, the Home Office warning organisation was in full operation and air-raid warning offices functioned at ROC groups and passed the warnings to the warning districts.

During Dividend the ROC was stretched to its maximum since the Second World War. Apart from the changed layout, there were many new procedures and a very heavy workload for the centres. At posts the weather was generally poor, with rain squalls at low altitude. Rats flitted in and out of cloud, while vapour trails often provided only a glimpse. The wind and rain made night plotting extremely difficult.

When the dust had settled ROC headquarters, along with Fighter Command, analysed the results of Dividend. Clearly the increase in jet aircraft speeds at high and low altitudes called for radical changes in plotting and tracking methods. Too many aircraft were being lost, double-tracked or not handed over in time for an interception to be made. To many posts it was painfully obvious: a formation of Thunderjets would appear out of cloud at 100ft and be across the neighbouring airfield while the observer was still bellowing Rats down the telephone. The centre plotter was under similar pressure. Attempts had been made to produce a new ROC instrument capable of rapid operation and prototypes had been shown at ROC annual camp. Speeds were, however, too great and it was clear that the days of an observer instrument were numbered.

The ROC was short of vital personnel and in the summer many were away on holiday or, in country districts, out harvesting. Operations-room training showed a definite need for improvement with more practical work, while it was stressed by headquarters that the plotter was the vital link. Something had to be done to improve the manpower situation, simplify procedures throughout and training. The ROC intensified its recruiting efforts, particularly among "H" reservists of the armed forces, and tried to stop the continuous wastage that always occurs with a voluntary organisation in peacetime. Half of all training was put on a practical rather than a theoretical basis, the master-test syllabus was altered and more synthetic exercises were scheduled.

To simplify the task it was decided to abolish the giving of sound angles from the instrument on heard plots, change the communications keyboards at centres and initiate a series of trials of new plotting, tracking and telling procedures. Northern Area tried a system of reporting by bearing, direction and distance; this was followed up by Metropolitan Area doing the same thing with post instruments removed, and an overall test in Southern and Scottish areas. The whole effort was a build-up towards the annual exercise "Beware," held in September 1955. Western Area was excluded as it was not taking part in Beware. Bearing, direction and distance were adopted in September for use on all tracks with optional variations in detailed procedure. Instead of sound angles, estimated heights were given both by day and by night. Instruments were removed and Georef references were not used. For Beware, Fighter Command at last had a modern swept-wing intercepter available in the shape of the Hawker Hunter, while Bomber Command had one squadron of Valiant four-jet bombers in addition to the twin-engined Canberras.

The new procedures in the ROC showed that progress was being made. As a result, a new operations instruction, No 54, was issued to all posts on November 1, 1955. The post chart was denuded of all save the outer "minute" ring, a reference circle at five miles radius, other posts within ten miles, the coastline, the aiming line and an arrow to denote posts beyond ten miles. No instrument was used and all reports were to be made regardless of whether the aircraft had been identified. All reports were to give an estimated height. For aircraft more than five miles from the post the estimated distance in miles was given, while on sound plots the word "distant" was used. Typical examples of the new form of reporting were:

Rats M3 – 15 – West – 1 at 2 – Meteor.

A.1 – Navigation Lights – 25 – South – 1 at 12 – Piston.

F.2 – Heard – 42 – Distant – South – 1 at 20 – Jet.

A.1 – Now Dividing – 15 – South – 4 at 20 – Meteors – and 20 – South West – 3 at 20 – Meteors.

For fast-flying friendly jet aircraft the code word "Jab" was introduced as a counterpart to "Rats." Plotting on aircraft circling, landing, taking off and in distress was continued in modified form, as was mass plotting for large formations. Simultaneously, a new instruction was prepared for centres and main table plaques and symbols were redesigned. Despite all this effort there were fears at ROC HQ, Stanmore, that the corps was gradually losing its vital place in the control and reporting organisation.

The RAF anticipated a future Soviet threat as being from bombers of Mach 0.95 or even Mach 2.0 performance coming in at heights of from 45,000ft to 60,000ft. New supersonic fighters were on the drawing boards which would be able to intercept bombers on purely radar direction, either on the other side of the Channel or out in the North Sea. Experiments at the Boulmer radar had led to a decision to concentrate location, command and control at a small number of master radar stations equipped with new Type 80 sets. Some older GCI stations were retained, but even these eventually succumbed to the axe.

The process was a gradual one, but in the ultimate the sector operations centres (with their Rats cabins and general situation tables) and the filter centres would disappear. All the 1953 re-organisation was seen to be of little avail, as the complex ROC communications network laboriously built up by the GPO would not be connected to the RAF's nerve centres. Amid the gloom, however, a completely different requirement for the ROC's services was being formulated in another Government Department. This was to put the corps firmly back into the home-defence field and project it forward into the 1970s.

Chapter 18
THE BOMB

When atomic bombs were dropped from B-29s on Hiroshima and Nagasaki in August 1945 more than 97,000 people were killed and some 91,400 were injured. A great many more died later from the effects of nuclear radiation. The world was horrified at the destructive effect of this "doomsday" weapon, but it was the actual blast and fireball on which attention was focussed and not the possible long-term effects from residual radio-active fall-out.

From the kiloton "nominal" atomic bomb (equivalent to 20,000 tons of TNT) of Hiroshima, the great powers evolved the most appalling weapon of all, the megaton thermonuclear hydrogen bomb yielding upwards of the equivalent of one million tons of TNT. In November 1952 the United States exploded a hydrogen bomb on the ground in the Pacific. This achievement was, however, eclipsed by the Soviet announcement, in the summer of 1953, that they had successfully tested a hydrogen bomb dropped from an aircraft, the explosion taking place at high altitude. America's first airborne hydrogen bomb was not demonstrated until May 1956.

In the meantime one United States hydrogen bomb test at Bikini Atoll on March 1, 1954, was to prove of lasting significance and demonstrated a further threat to the continued existence of mankind. The Bikini bomb, of 15 megatons, was a "dirty" device in which the fusion element was contained in a casing of fissile material. The result was that the now familiar giant mushroom cloud carried vast quantities of radio-active particles to a height of more than 20 miles, where the wind spread them over an area of 7,000 square miles. The American authorities had done little in the way of long-range meteorological forecasting in the upper atmosphere for the tests. They were, therefore, taken by surprise at the extent to which gamma radiation appeared as the particles descended. Japanese fishermen far from the explosion site were affected, and islands 200 miles downwind of the detonation site reached dangerous levels of radiation.

The possible dangers of fall-out had become apparent to the US authorities during earlier tests and the information was passed to the Nato allies, including the United Kingdom. The Home Office, as the Ministry controlling civil defence, began to assess the threat as it would affect Britain – a vulnerable island with highly concentrated population and industrial centres.

On February 22–24, 1954, the first radio-active fall-out study was held at the Civil Defence Staff College, Sunningdale. The attack postulated was a ten-megaton bomb, exploded at ground level in the north-west corner of Birmingham. Assuming constant winds, the fall-out plume spread eastwards, reaching Great Yarmouth 9hr after the burst.

The study showed that evacuation in the path of the fall-out plume was impracticable and dangerous. In order for people to receive any measure of protection from their homes they must stay put until radio-activity had decayed to a tolerable level. Of necessity this meant there had to be some sort of warning system based on the large-scale continuous monitoring of fall-out levels. The system had to be operated by an organisation covering the whole country from fixed sites and with installed communications. All the syndicates in the study favoured the use of Royal Observer Corps posts to monitor and report fall-out, with observer groups passing the reports to Fighter Command and thence to Whitehall. The actual plotting of the fall-out pattern was foreseen as taking place in the civil-defence room at each fighter sector. Thereafter progress was rapid. Early in March the Director-General of Civil Defence, General Sir Sidney Kirkman, wrote to the Chief of the Air Staff, Marshal of the RAF Sir William Dickson, asking for the assistance of the ROC in reporting fall-out. The CAS agreed that the whole matter should be looked into and suggested that the Deputy Chief of the Air Staff, Air Marshal Pike, arrange meetings between the Home Office, the Air Ministry and representatives of Fighter Command.

In its initial approach the Home Office enumerated the reasons why the ROC was the most suitable body for fall-out reporting: spacing of ROC posts gave the right reporting density; posts had private lines independent of manual exchanges; corps members were accustomed to handling instruments; Home Office staff were already installed at both ROC groups and RAF sectors, and at the latter full meteorological information was available. It was also suggested that the ROC might fulfill a supplementary function by using special equipment to identify the power of the bomb and the height of the burst. In order to carry out the task the Home Office indicated that the corps would have to be issued with radiac instruments, undergo special training, be given protected accommodation and have further protection for its communications. The man in the Home Office principally concerned with the setting up of the monitoring organisation was R. F. H. Firth, Assistant Secretary J.3 Division.

All parties involved attended a conference on April 4, 1955, with Air Commodore K. B. B. Cross in the chair. It was agreed that the ROC could undertake monitoring as a secondary role without prejudice to the primary aircraft-reporting role. To obtain final sanction the permission of the Air Council had to be sought. Air Council approval in principle was given on May 5, 1955, and the Treasury became involved because expenditure was necessary and a general election was about to take place.

The Home Office wanted ROC centres moved to less vulnerable areas and given fall-out protection along with the posts. They also thought that comprehensive radio back-up for reporting would be needed. The RAF was luke-warm about these proposals, as all Fighter Command's efforts were concentrated on improving the radar network and providing super-sonic fighters for off-shore interception. It was becoming clear that if the Home Office was to have its ROC network suitably equipped and protected then it would have to take on both the expenditure and the physical work involved. An initial ad hoc outlay of £3,500 was approved by the Treasury for training ROC instructors and building brick hutches at ROC groups to contain radio-active sources.

The basis of the fall-out warning system was to be the air-raid warning organisation, dismantled in 1945 and restarted in 1949. Warning officers had been recruited by both the Home Office and the Scottish Home Department and some 6,000 sirens had been installed, of which 5,000 were remotely controlled. All gave the warbling and steady notes of the wartime "alert" and "raiders passed" respectively.

The first inkling that the corps at large received of a possible new role came on March 1 during the 1955 defence debate. The Home Secretary announced that the Government recognised the need to set up an organisation to monitor radio-activity after a thermonuclear-weapon attack and to give warnings of fall-out. He revealed that negotiations were in progress with the Air Ministry over using the ROC as the national nuclear warning and monitoring organisation. In strict confidence senior officials of the existing air-raid warning teams, ROC area and group commandants, deputy group commandants and group training officers were informed that the corps would undertake the fall-out task.

By the beginning of June the corps had officially been given the job of reporting fall-out. On June 15, 1955, the Secretary of State for the Home Department, in reply to a written question by Mr Ian Harvey, MP, announced in the Commons:

"I am glad to be able to inform the House that arrangements are being made for the Royal Observer Corps, in conjunction with the air-raid warning organisation, to undertake this important new function in addition to their existing duties."

On June 16 Air Commodore Simpson wrote to areas and groups outlining what was intended and this was, in turn, passed on to all observers. The ROC was to tread a new path, one that would ultimately represent its primary and not its secondary role. The Home Office decision to ask the corps to undertake fall-out, and later bomb-burst, monitoring represented a high compliment to all the skills in reporting, displaying and telling of information that had been amassed through the years. It is no exaggeration to say that had the Home Office chosen to set up an organisation of its own it would have taken five years longer and cost a great deal more.

Arrangements were made for two courses to be held at the Home Office Defence School at Easingwold, Yorkshire, from June 13-18 and June 20-25, 1955. Half the full-time officer cadre of the corps attended each course.

The courses were introduced by the ROC Commandant, Air Commodore Simpson. He was followed by Mr Firth, who talked about the features of radio-activity, the effects of nuclear weapons, protection, and the purpose of the warning organisation being created. He explained that meteorological information would be a guide to the likely movement but a ground reporting organisation was needed to report where the fall-out was beginning to come down. He described how the Navy would want to know which ports were still available; rail authorities would want to know where trains could run and the RAF would require to know which airfields could be used.

It was hoped that deliveries of instruments and radio-active sources would become available in October 1955 and that by the end of the winter the corps would be functioning in the new role. It was envisaged that reports would be made from ROC group operations rooms to the sector operations centres, "where scientists will try to forecast areas likely to be receiving fall-out." These ideas were regarded as experimental and the courses were warned that "many changes in procedures may have to be made before they are right." It was also the firm intention that the new role was secondary to aircraft recognition and there would be no clash of roles. Observers would be required to take cover in the event of fall-out affecting their post.

The course proceeded with an appreciation of the threat and its effects, radiation, fall-out, protective measures and the instruments to be used, including measuring the dose for a person, the radiac survey meter, radiac calculator and the contamination meter. Most of the officers found themselves overwhelmed by the terminology, jargon and description associated with the new role.

Training in the corps started in the autumn and at each of that year's ROC training camps the indefatigable Mr Firth spoke about the new role and ranged over most of the items covered in the full-time officer courses held in June.

"Fall-Out Training Instruction No 1" was issued by HQ ROC on September 19, 1955. It outlined a programme whereby the full-time officers who had been to Easingwold were to instruct the part-time officers. These in turn would lecture at centre crew meetings and at post "cluster" meetings, where the basic facts would be passed on and such radiac instruments. as were available would be demonstrated. Priority was given to post personnel training, as without the post observer's ability to use the instruments and report correctly the whole concept was useless. From January 1, 1956 all observers who had satisfied an instructor that they were qualified to use the individual dosimeter and the radiac survey meter had these facts noted on their personal cards maintained at group headquarters.

Civil Defence were already using radiac survey meters and it was thought that the ROC might employ the same instrument, perhaps with modifications for remote reading. The basic warning of impending attack was to be given over the unidirectional carrier line broadcast system which formed part of the GPO telephone network.

"Good Fortune," a field-trial exercise on nuclear fall-out, was held in September 1955 using RAF western sector and the observer groups reporting to it. A synthetic pattern was fed into each centre and upwards to sector, where an analysis was made by one scientist with clerical assistance. Readings were only taken every half hour and the resulting picture therefore suffered from delays and inaccuracies. As a result of the field test it was decided to have post readings of a dose-rate meter every five minutes.

At the Air Raid Warning Training School in London the type and frequency of readings were determined, and trials there included the use of experienced, trained RAF tellers. It was calculated that two tellers in an ROC operations room would work at six sequences a minute and could clear a group of 60 posts in five minutes. A Home Office meeting, attended by the ROC Commandant and the Deputy Commandant, led to the corps being asked to devise suitable procedures to meet the requirements. The resulting trials were held at HQ No 5 Group, Watford.

From December 1955 to January 1956 operations-room crews tried out various methods, similar in some respects to the plotting techniques used in the aircraft mass-raid procedure. Readings were displayed on a plaque over each post on the main table. This was quite simple to do, but there was difficulty in getting observers to appreciate that they were doing something different and to treat it with the requisite care. On January 20, 1956, a very smooth performance was achieved in a trial run at Watford and the Home Office officials present were much impressed – they were assured of the corps' ability to do the new job competently.

The Home Office hoped to be able to install "shadograph" bearing indicators and blast-pressure-type bomb-power indicators at posts, to allow bomb-burst positions, heights and powers to be calculated. Two types of display were allowed for at sectors, the first showing forecasts and actual reports of the progress of the fall-out front as it moved across the country and the second showing completed fall-out dose rates at all posts at a standard time of 7hr after a burst.

The first major Home Office fall-out exercise, "Cloverleaf," was carried out on April 7 and 8, 1956, with the following groups taking part:

Nos 6, 7 and 15 reporting to Eastern Sector (Bawburgh);
Nos 18, 20 and 23 reporting to Northern Sector (Shipton);
Nos 8, 16, 19, 21 and 22 reporting to Western Sector (Whittingham Lane CFP).

Only operations-room personnel participated and posts were not involved. Warning officers acted as the liaison between centres and sectors. Special main-table plaques were issued, cut down to 3in size, and on these were mounted magnetised plotting counters to indicate the intensity of fall-out. The dummy post reports were relayed to the plotters from the Beckenham Trainer in the centre training room. The methods employed were described by authority as working "unbelievably well."

The lessons learned were applied during the 1956 RAF autumn air exercise in September, during which both aircraft plotting and fall-out reporting were undertaken one after the other. Nos 1, 2, 4, 5, 3 and 14 Groups were trained for the fall-out task with special reporting procedures, under the exercise code-name "Outward Bound." Posts were sent sheets listing the reports to be made, starting with a first fall-out report and the time and followed by five-minute readings. "Fall-out Training Instruction No 2" was issued to cover the new procedures.

The centre main table was divided into two sections and the tellers passed the indicated fall-out readings from north to south. If a post lost communication an old-fashioned convoy symbol was used to show that it was out of action. On the main table the dose-rate was displayed by magnetic numerals on a plaque, coloured red on one side and blue on the other. Each five minutes on the clock in the operations room was coloured red or blue and the side of the plaque appropriate to the colour on the clock was used. By this means any stale dose-rates would be noticed and told to the SOC before any more up-to-date readings.

The main results of the exercise were to show that fall-out reporting could be undertaken efficiently, but that the aircraft reporting commitment was in decline. With the concentration on master radars, the corps was losing its direct lines to the centralised filter plots at sectors. From this point on the ROC role for Fighter Command was low-level only over a steadily diminishing area.

To make the nuclear warning system work, the Home Office had to provide underground posts and protected accommodation for centres, together with all the necessary instruments and equipment. As early as May 1956 the Home Office had laid down a programme for the siting of underground posts which would consist of concrete bunkers buried in the ground and capable of sustaining a four-man crew for a week. The minimum area required for the shelter was a circle 50ft in diameter on flat ground without obstruction, and many overground post sites, particularly those on buildings, did not lend themselves to digging holes in the ground.

The prototype experimental underground post was built at 2/N.1, Farnham and the first trials were carried out there on September 29–30, 1956. The post consisted of a reinforced-concrete structure protected on top by a 7½in-thick concrete slab and 3in of earth. A vertical 15ft shaft gave access to two rooms at the bottom, one used as the repository for a chemical closet and the other, 15ft × 7ft 6in, laid out as a monitoring room. Canvas chairs, a table, store cupboard and a pair of two-tier metal-frame bunks were provided. Two-section steel doors were provided at the top of the entrance shaft which carried louvred ventilators, as did a small air shaft at the opposite end of the structure. Lighting was provided by a battery-powered 12V bulb. Apart from hatch conversion to a single trap door, the addition of more ventilators and improvements in equipment, the standard ROC post remains the same today.

At Farnham, four post members manned the underground shelter for the first phase, while in the second phase the crew consisted of two Home Office Scientific Advisory Branch staff and two ROC members. During phase two the post was completely sealed and communications maintained via the other two members in the overground post. Rations, bedding and general barrack equipment were provided by the RAF. The ROC team on this historic occasion consisted of Leading Observer H. T. Barrett and Observers F. Kent, A. Dimes and G. M. Elphick. Barrett and Elphick remained in the underground post for 30hr, while Kent and Dimes manned the above-ground post in phase two. The final paragraph of the ensuing report stated:

"The general consensus of opinion is that it would be quite feasible to spend a much longer period in the shelter and the favourable reaction of the personnel engaged in the trial proved encouraging."

The underground post and protected headquarters programmes were massive undertakings, involving 1,563 posts and 31 centres. There were two types of centres, semi-sunk and surface; each had to have its operations room with dais, standby generator plant, sleeping accommodation, kitchens, air conditioning, air filters, communications, water and food storage, etc. When sealed the centre had to be capable of operating for a week under fall-out conditions. Custom-built group headquarters cost an average of £45,000 (semi-sunk) and £41,000 (surface) – figures which today appear laughably low. Certain Army and RAF protected operations rooms proved suitable for conversion. No 12 Group, Bristol, and No 31 Group, Northern Ireland, took over AA gun operations rooms, while No 30 Group, Inverness, and No 21 Group, Preston, occupied disused RAF sector operations centres.

The design of the Underground posts was based on that at Farnham, where trials of equipment and methods of operation continued for some time. Some posts were conversions of basements in buildings, like Martello Towers or, in the case of Windsor Castle, a much modified coal cellar. In the main, however, the custom-built underground structure, as erected at Farnham, was accepted as standard.

Every post site in Britain had to be surveyed to see if it was suitable for the fall-out role. Posts on buildings with no open space adjacent were ruled out and had to be resited, sometimes at a considerable distance. In many cases new post sites were not suited to the aircraft-reporting role, but fall-out had priority. The Air Ministry Works Department Lands Officers, the works representatives and the ROC worked together to complete the siting arrangements.

The Home Office wanted 100 posts built in the first year and about 250 a year thereafter. Inevitably with budget restrictions, all the paper work and the actual building to be done, often in inaccessible spots, the programme began to stretch out. By mid-1958, 94 underground posts had been taken over and 110 were in course of construction. All over the country, holes in the ground appeared, in which concrete walls began to sprout. Some posts in dry earth were easy to build, while those on clay had a permanently water-filled hole which required constant pumping. The most difficult of all were those on hard rock, such as granite, where the space had to be hewn out. The basic cost of building a post was £1,250, but local conditions caused variations between £1,000 and £2,000. Today building an average post would cost £8,000, or the same as for a small house.

While the Home Office was rapidly organising the protection and re-equipment of the corps for fall-out duties, more posts were being formed in Scotland to plug the west and north-west-about holes in the ROC's aircraft-reporting network. These posts were eventually to prove vital in completing the national nuclear reporting set-up.

In May 1955 a vacancy had occurred for a full-time group officer in the ROC with locality undisclosed. Seventeen applicants came forward for the board, little knowing what was in store. One of them was Donald Campbell, who had served as a spare-time observer. At Bentley Priory, Air Commodore Simpson asked him what his reaction would be if he were posted to the wilds of Skye and the west coast of Scotland. To the Commandant's amazement, Campbell replied: "I would be delighted." Simpson did not believe his ears until Campbell explained that he knew the area well and was a west highlander. He remarked later that "the light dust cloud hazing the drive was caused by 16 ex-candidates departing at horrified speed." As usual, the ROC had found the right man for the right job. Nominally attached to group headquarters at Inverness, he was given a free hand to establish his own headquarters on the Isle of Skye.

The posts had been sited and constructed and Campbell, like a dentist, had only to extract the teeth in the form of recruits in the most sparsely inhabited part of Britain. The residents were very suspicious of anything resembling a uniform. Despite this Campbell, with a mixture of tact and native cunning, managed to set up a chain of posts whose loyalty and endurance stand high in the annals of the ROC. Despite objections from group headquarters, Campbell lived in a single-berth sleeping van. He averaged a complete tyre change every 10,000 miles and three broken springs a year; bad roads, snow, floods and local hospitality were the normal occupational hazards. Like so many observers before them, the west highlanders reacted favourably to a polite request but were adamant in the face of dictation.

Their spirit of service can only be described as remarkable. For the annual master test it was not the questions or the pictures that worried people so much as the weather. "With a raging blizzard over the whole west coast and the venue at Portree, the Uig crew (17 miles and 40min under normal conditions) turned up late for the test, soaked and exhausted. Their open jeep had failed at the last drift two miles from the village. The combined Ardvasser (46 miles) and Broadford (30 miles) crews with a farm tractor bulldozing the whole way got home at 7 o'clock the next morning. Lochinver, returning from Invergordon (86 miles), were blocked at 2 a.m. while still 16 miles from home. Its crew 'stole' a snow plough to complete the journey."

Campbell eventually established five posts on Skye, seven on the mainland and, finally, four in the Outer Hebrides. "ROC night" had come to be recognised in an extraordinary variety of places. Campbell completed his work in 1962 and the sub-HQ was closed down. Scotland was a blossoming territory for the ROC, and between March 1952 and June 1962 no fewer than 44 new posts were formed.

Aircraft reporting continued through the exercises of 1956 and 1957, but in the latter year the writing was clearly on the wall. The RAF sector operations centre concept was dying and all control was passing to the master radars. The carefully thought-out ROC plans for the Rotor network were coming to nought. The Defence White Paper of 1957, prepared by Mr Duncan Sandys, stated that further advanced fighter and bomber development would be abandoned and everything would be concentrated on Bomber Command's nuclear deterrent force.

"Tripwire" had come into operation, which meant that the V-force would hit back if there was any sort of strike against the United Kingdom. Low-level reporting still existed, but the reporting lines were drying up and only East Anglia, with the V-bomber stations, could expect to retain the aircraft role. The RAF, in fact, referred to the corps as part of the deterrent. Aircraft plotting and reporting went on, but fewer and fewer RAF aircraft participated and observers had to resort to plotting Viscounts and DC-3s as "Rats."

Quite apart from the ROC reporting network, the Home Office had been engaged in setting up 11 Civil Defence regions, with regional and sub-regional headquarters capable of taking over in the event of the break-down of central Government control following a nuclear attack. Essential food and fuel were stockpiled, while Civil Defence emergency rescue and salvage columns were set up. The Post Office worked out plans for a complete emergency communications network based on microwave techniques and repeater stations.

In general, the public reaction to all this was: "If the bomb comes, everyone is going to die, so why bother?" Nothing could have been further from the truth, but it seemed extremely difficult for the Government to put over a picture of what might really happen and the chances of survival – if there was adequate warning and everyone took cover. Unfortunately, successive Governments, both Labour and Tory, have been excessively coy over telling the people what to do about nuclear bombs and fall-out, and this has led to misunderstanding and confusion.

It was against this background that some members of the ROC resigned. They had been steeped in aircraft reporting and the RAF and they felt that the fall-out role was just a pointer to the corps losing its identity and becoming a remote off-shoot of the Civil Defence Corps. Firth, at the Home Office, was well aware of this undercurrent and he went out of his way, in lectures in 1957, to stress that there would be no "take-over" of the corps.

Returning to the corps' progress in the 1950s, in 1957 the ROC participated in the air-defence exercise "Vigilant," which included a nuclear attack phase called exercise "Treble Chance." Both phases were timed for May 25 and 26; Nos 6, 7, 15, 18, 20 and 23 Groups were involved with aircraft plotting and Nos 1, 2, 4, 5, 6, 7, 15, 3, 9, 10, 11, 12, 13 and 14 with fall-out. A variety of aircraft were employed, including Valiants, Hunters, Skywarriors, Skyraiders, Stratojets, Super Sabres, CF-100s and Mystères. Javelins were also operated as friendly fighters. Eastern Area was required to report Rats to Bawburgh SOC, but fall-out had overall priority.

Fall-out information was displayed on long-range boards at centres and a provisional procedure was tested whereby local warnings could be distributed by warning officers with the ROC in the event of group/sector communications breaking down. Aircraft were reported by all clusters until fall-out was in operation, except in Eastern Sector where aircraft plotting was of operational importance. Centres used new plaques on the main table showing the dose-rate readings of a full cluster. For the posts it was a boring time, watching aircraft passing overhead and only being able to read simulated dose-rate readings from a sheet of paper.

During Treble Chance various other trials were carried out, including linking Air-Defence Operations Centre to Whitehall, issuing fall-out warnings to ships at sea, obtaining fall-out readings at fighter stations and testing the effect of complete breakdown of communications at an RAF sector. Finally, for the first time, attack warnings were initiated direct from the display at a master radar station.

In September 1957 a further exercise was held, "Dutch Treat," in which Holland received information from Eastern Sector of fall-out which might reach it across the North Sea. Caledonian, Eastern, Northern and Western Sectors and three civil-defence regions were involved.

By 1958 the whole question of ROC reporting of aircraft was in the balance. The RAF wanted the visual and aural reporting role to be continued as an insurance, but was far from clear as to how the information was to be used. The biggest blow was the loss of the general situation maps at RAF SOCs. The ROC was limited to telling to the Rats table and already some observer groups had no outlet even to this. The accent was on the V-bomber deterrent force and surface-to-air guided weapons such as Bloodhound. Airfields were being closed, the Royal Auxiliary Air Force Squadrons closed in 1957 and regular fighter units were being steadily reduced.

A low-level intruder flying at 600 m.p.h. – ten miles a minute – took just sixty seconds to cover the diameter of a post sound circle. In the operations room this represented 10in across the table covered in one minute and 25 miles in one two and a half-minute colour change of the counters. Speed of reporting and plotting was essential. The Fighter Command research branch undertook some studies of control and reporting to deal with very-low-level attack against specific targets, e.g. bomber bases. The scheme involved providing as much radar warning as possible, reporting by the ROC direct to master radars (using pre-arranged locations for reference) and standing fighter patrols.

A live exercise using these techniques was held on May 16-18, 1958, in No 4 Group, Colchester, and No 6 Group, Norwich. The CHEL stations which still existed gave radar warning and ROC information was fed directly to Trimingham Master Radar and then broadcast to the fighters. The performance put up by the corps was very encouraging, with 80 per cent of the posts succeeding in tracking the raids, the missing 20 per cent being caused by weather conditions. Tracks were produced continuously up to about the maximum distance of 50 miles and the ROC alone was able to claim credit for half the interceptions achieved.

The trial was continued in the autumn RAF exercise and two further live tests were made in 1959. A fifth test, scheduled for 1960, was cancelled and the idea fizzled out. One unfortunate aspect of the exercises was the necessity to hold them on Saturdays and Sundays. One Sunday afternoon the radar track faded after only a few plots and an extrapolation seemed to show the raid heading for Norwich; the defence was positioned accordingly. Evensong in Norwich Cathedral was rudely shattered by the unmusical noise of two Hunters at 500ft and it provoked bitter reaction from the dean.

While Eastern Sector was trying out the new low-level techniques, in May 1958 Exercise "Four Horsemen" was going on in Northern, Eastern and Western Sectors. Communications were disrupted on a scale likely to occur in war. This realistic exercise was based on assumptions of the number of Soviet aircraft available for operations, how many would get through and how many would carry H-bombs. Meteorological officers at sectors were fed with actual weather charts, and for the first time bomb triangulation was carried out at ROC centres. Triangulation had previously been done at sectors and it consisted of teams working out the ground-zero position (the point over which the bomb exploded), height and power of a nuclear burst from information supplied synthetically, but later to be available from posts. In many ways the procedure was similar to that carried out in the fixing of aircraft sound reports, but with bomb-power added.

Fighter Command was the first RAF operational command to show a real interest in the need for nuclear burst and fall-out information. It was required for the Air Defence Commander in the Air Defence Operations Centre at Bentley Priory in order that effective operations could be planned and conducted during and after a nuclear attack. He had to know which airfields were free from damage or had been damaged by bursts and which were free from the threat of fall-out or, if they were threatened, the estimated time of arrival of fall-out. From this information it was possible to deploy fighters to safe airfields so that they remained available for use in the next air battle. Aircraft already airborne had to be diverted if their base was damaged, under fall-out or threat of fall-out.

During the spring of 1958 ROC officers on a course at Sunningdale were taken to see the ADOC. They viewed a Fighter Command synthetic exercise in progress. Hostile tracks were produced from films made in the FC Exercise Branch, which represented blips on the master radar screens. The fall-out exercise coincided with the air attack pattern. The burst and fall-out information was assumed to have been received from the appropriate SOC, although it was being "told" internally. Airmen, wearing plimsolls, crawling about on a general situation map in what, during the Second World War, had been the intruder room in ADOC, locating the position of nuclear bursts, drawing lines in chalk to define areas of the UK threatened by fall-out and marking areas actually affected by fall-out.

The first major exercise in which nuclear information was passed from the SOCs to the ADOC took place as early as 1956. There followed a long period of tests, during which both procedures and displays were modified. Early in 1958 a working party was set up at Fighter Command, one member of which was the ROC Operations Staff Officer. The work-load at Fighter Command was also such that personnel for fall-out planning and manning were hard to find. As the ROC was part of Fighter Command and provided the basic fall-out information, it was logical for the AOC to turn to the corps to fill the gap.

For the annual air exercise, in October 1958, volunteers were called from No 5 Group, Watford, to man the fall-out reporting section at ADOC. Others were required for ADOC telling duties at the SOCs. Special training was given by the Home Office Air Raid Warning School in London to observers going to ADOC and to the SOCs. Apart from the case of the wartime ROC liaison officers this was to be the first time in its history that the corps had actually worked in the operations room at Fighter Command. The exercise was a dual aircraft/fall-out one, code-named "Sunbeam/Night Bird." A rehearsal was held on October 11 and the real thing took place on October 17–18. Selected observer groups were involved with both low-level aircraft and fall-out and some with fall-out only. As the logbook of 9/C.1 post, Keynsham, Somerset, showed, those on purely fall-out reporting resented their inability to report aircraft. "This was a pity," the record ran, "As Hornet Moth, Chipmunk, Dove, Heron, Comet and Sea Vixen were observed."

Fighter Command put up 25 squadrons and three NATO commanders were involved, in addition to Bomber Command and the 3rd USAF based in Britain. The "enemy" consisted of Canberra, Valiant, Vulcan, Victor, Lincoln, B-66, B-45, F-100, F-84 and B-47 aircraft. Extensive raids, with full jamming support, were flown against the radar network and nuclear weapons were simulated. Whenever it was reported that a bomb had burst, ROC posts and centres in the area switched to fall-out reporting.

At ADOC a vertical perspex screen had replaced the general situation map in the old intruder room. Two observers maintained the display from the back, working on information received over internal circuits from the fall-out reporting section, which was a partitioned-off part of the room. Liaison officers, using landlines, passed the display information to Bomber Command HQ and Royal Navy HQ at Portsmouth. Sixteen observers were needed to run the fall-out reporting section and facilities were fairly crude – the "workmap," for instance, consisting of a paper edition of a Georef chart pinned on a trestle table. Attack warnings in Sunbeam/Nightbird were initiated for the most part from master radar stations instead of from the SOCs.

Attack Warning Red

One major defect that became apparent was the delay in passing fall-out information to the ADOC. Three types of prediction were required:

INITIAL: The plume for the 3hr after the bomb burst, drawn by a scientist and showing hour time lines.

ACTUAL: Areas actually affected and defined by the extent of post reports with time lines showing speed of advance of the fall-out front.

SUBSEQUENT: These were based on the actual behaviour of the fall-out front, due to the prevailing winds, and were therefore more reliable. Time lines indicated time of arrival of fall-out downwind.

Initially there was a tendency for the production of these plumes on the displays in SOC to be delayed, and consequently much of the information had become stale by the time it was told. The defect persisted until a system was introduced wherein "initial prediction template details" were issued from the SOC to the ADOC. These consisted of the scientists' evaluation of the current meteorological forecast and comprised bearings and distances which, when plotted, produced a template. When they were applied to a ground zero of a ground-burst weapon the area threatened by fall-out, together with ETA downwind, could be traced on the display by the plotter.

Chapter 19
FAREWELL TO AIRCRAFT

The years 1959 to 1961 saw the ROC turn inexorably away from the aircraft-reporting role and become more and more immersed in its nuclear function as the field force for the warning and monitoring organisation*. Aircraft exercises became more rare and in most cases they involved a group or groups with posts reporting to the centre but with no outlet from there to the RAF. Anything with wings, military or civil, was plotted but often the skies remained empty apart from the odd Tiger Moth or Viscount. A shortage of Service aircraft flying at week-ends even led to Chipmunks and Ansons being designated as Rats in one Southern Area inter-Group exercise in 1959.

Air Commodore Warfield had succeeded Air Commodore Simpson in May 1959 and on September 7, 1960, the former received a new directive on operational requirements of the ROC from Air Marshal Sir Hector McGregor, AOC-in-C Fighter Command. The long-awaited blow had come. The priorities laid down were:

a) The reporting of nuclear bursts;
b) Low-level aircraft recognition and reporting over a designated area of eastern England;
c) The reporting of radio-active fall-out.

The designated low-level area boundary zig-zagged down from Redcar in Yorkshire through Nos 20, 18, 15, 7 and 5 Observer Groups. Nos 4 and 6 Groups were included complete. The area was designed to cover the V-bomber bases and their approaches and operational practice was to be given in tracking aircraft flying below 5,000ft. The groups involved were the envy of their less fortunate colleagues in the north, west and south.†

Outside the area, groups were required to preserve the skills of aircraft recognition and low-level reporting but without the provision of special facilities for live training – which meant that no RAF aircraft were laid on for the purpose. The corps was also asked to "preserve an understanding" of the procedures for reporting such events as aircraft in distress, mine-laying and airborne landings, etc.

While the aircraft role was being restricted throughout the country, posts and centres were wrestling with bomb-burst and fall-out procedures which continually changed as practice showed ways of speeding up and streamlining the system.

Exercises began with an enemy attack using atom and hydrogen bombs at various places.

---

*With the official nuclear deterrent policy and the unlikelihood of conventional attack, the air-raid warning system had naturally evolved into the warning and monitoring organisation.

†Many posts were resited for the underground task and lost their overground structures.

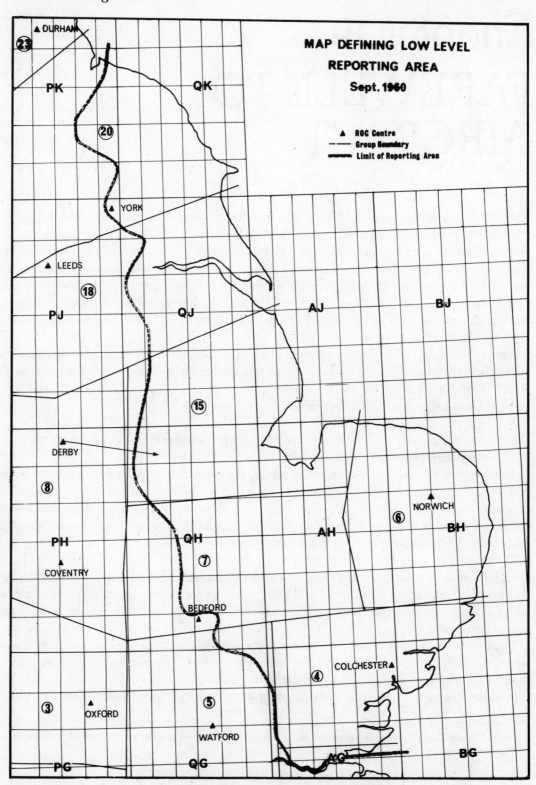

The final phase of operational visual reporting for the ROC, the low-level reporting area in the east, designed to cover the bases of the V-bomber deterrent force

Both air and ground bursts were fed in, the latter causing subsequent fall-out. Taking a certain set of meteorological conditions, the passage of fall-out could be predicted by the experts and a full picture drawn. The whole position was then worked backwards so that up to 200,000 synthetic dose-rate readings could be produced for reading at ROC posts. Each head observer received an envelope with dummy "shadograph" burn-papers and readings for the pressure indicator and the radiac survey meter. At the appointed time posts reported "nuclear burst" together with the bearing and elevation shown on the papers. Thereafter they gave fall-out readings in roentgens per hour. At centre bursts were reported to sector, where they were allocated names from a long list, such as Magic for Metropolitan Sector and Cocoa for Caledonian Sector. In Northern Sector one of the bomb code names was Nuisance.

Thereafter a three-man triangulation team set to work to analyse the bomb or bombs, the members being the tote-operator, a triangulator and an assessor. The burst times at each post were shown on a blackboard, together with bearings, elevations and pressure readings. Bearings from the posts were laid off on a table map, which gave a triangulated fix on ground zero and the various distances from the bomb. A ready reckoner enabled angles of elevation and distances from bursts to be converted into burst heights. Finally, with the aid of graphs the pressure readings and distances could be converted into bomb powers such as half-megaton, five-megaton, etc. On receipt of this information and the latest weather forecast, scientists at sectors could begin to work out a prediction of where the fall-out plume would go and when. First arrival of fall-out at posts and readings thereafter allowed for more accurate predictions of fall-out strength and decay.

What the corps lacked, however, were the instruments on which reports under attack conditions could be made. Four men sitting in a hole with a telephone and nothing else were useless. The only production radiac instrument available to the corps from the outset was the Radiac Survey Meter No 2. This had two serious drawbacks: it was scaled to 300 roentgens/hour only and it had to be carried outside the post to be read. Thus observers would be continuously exposed to large doses of radiation against which the underground post was intended to shield them.

During 1958 a prototype of a new instrument known as the "Fixed Survey Meter," was produced. The indicator unit of this could be mounted on the table in the post and connected by cable to a pipe running up through the concrete roof, at the end of which was fitted an ionisation chamber. The advantages of the FSM were that it could be operated from within the underground post and it read to 500R/hr. Readings in excess of 5,000R/hr were possible by withdrawing the ionisation chamber down the pipe. The FSM was not available in quantity until the autumn of 1960. Thereafter it became the standard fall-out measuring instrument in the corps, with the RSM No 2 being used for back-up.

To measure the peak over-pressure of the blast wave of the bomb at each post, the Atomic Weapons Research Establishment produced the Bomb-Power Indicator, or BPI. Several designs were tested before the device was finally approved, again in the autumn of 1960. Essentially the BPI consisted of an above-ground baffle plate mounted on a steel pipe going down into the post. At the bottom of the pipe an indicator unit with bellows was connected to a pointer on a dial. The air from the blast wave would pass down the pipe to the bellows and show pressures up to 5lb/sq in on the dial.

The last of the basic instruments for the posts was the shadograph, which became known as the Ground Zero Indicator or GZI. This consisted of a 10in-high cylindrical container with four small holes facing the cardinal points of the compass. Inside, photographic paper was fitted into four plastic cassettes, each with a marked graticule. In the event of a nuclear burst the image of the fireball was projected through one or more of the pinholes and burned distinctive marks on the sensitised paper. From these the bearing and elevation of the burst could be read off and it was usually clear whether it was a ground or an air burst. GZIs were mounted on metal base plates alongside the post entrance hatch.

As an additional warning device for nuclear bursts, in case they took place before the ROC could become fully operational, the warning and monitoring organisation looked at a device known as the Bhangmeter. Originally developed by the United States, the Bhangmeter had been used in both the British and American nuclear tests. It was an electronic device with a photocell light receiver mounted above ground and a control panel and recording unit under cover. The Bhangmeter was dependent on the light output in the fraction of a second immediately following bomb detonation. A Polaroid camera was used to produce a print showing the bomb characteristics in a form which closely resembled the cathode-ray tube of a 1940 CH radar station. The equipment suffered from limited angle of coverage, however, it was susceptible to lightning and it had to be modified to measure up to megaton-range yields. The Ministry of Aviation had retained six Bhangmeters; these were taken over by the Home Office and installed at selected SOCs and ROC groups. An alarm was fitted to the sets and they would have automatically taken a photograph if a nuclear flash had appeared within their range of vision.

While the various tools of the trade were being tested, developed and put into production the corps was examining the conditions in an underground post and living equipment needed for up to a week's shut-down while radio-active fall-out decayed to an acceptable level.

Several preliminary environmental trials were carried out at the prototype post at Farnham and on December 1–3, 1959, three Home Office scientists and Observer Lieutenant L. G. Honisett, a group officer, descended the ladder for a 48hr sojourn below ground. The object of the trials was to test the value of bellows for rapid ventilation, the effects of repeated exposure to nine or more hours of foul air followed by short periods of ventilation, the general effects of 48hr enclosure and to collect observations on food, drink and sanitation. The post was rigged with complex measuring instruments and the occupants underwent tests after 9hr with the hatches shut. Despite the monitoring room temperature of 60°F the insidious cold of the concrete floor crept through flesh and bone. Various types of food were eaten, but the only hot drink was provided by self-heating cans of soup and these gave off carbon monoxide. The sole lighting was a 12V bulb fed from a battery and with this it proved impossible to read instruments and work without the aid of torches. When the four men ascended the ladder to the outside world on the morning of December 3 they had completed an experiment which was to provide the basic knowledge from which posts would be equipped and operated under wartime conditions.

The Home Office and the ROC were gradually evolving an organisation which could report the detonation of atomic or thermonuclear weapons over Britain, provide details of the bombs' characteristics and predict the fall-out pattern so that warning could be given to the population and the Services.

In the RAF a great deal more attention was being given to bomb and fall-out problems and to the use of the ROC. Synthetic exercises, known as "windmills," were held regularly during the period 1958–61 at the ADOC at Bentley Priory. They were of 8hr duration and occurred at mid-week, which presented acute problems for corps manning.

Observer Lieutenants R. Glover and J. M. Clark were made responsible for producing the synthetic exercises for the RAF and the former had had the task of recruiting and organising the ROC members at the ADOC. Despite the awkward times involved, No 5 Group, Watford, always succeeded in producing sufficient volunteers. As there were no eating facilities available for observers, all those serving at ADOC were given the temporary unpaid rank of chief observer and allowed to use the Sergeants' Mess. Problems occurred when these members forgot to take the rank badges down when attending their own post meetings. They were met by frosty stares from their genuine chief observers.

Two major exercises were held in 1959, "Cloud Dragon" on April 25–26 and "Dust Devil" on July 25. Metropolitan, Southern, Eastern and Northern Sectors took part in Cloud Dragon and the first attempt was made to practise liaison with several NATO countries – France, Belgium, Holland and Denmark. The Home Office set the exercise and fall-out was simulated as passing across the North Sea and the English Channel. Dust Devil formed part of a large-scale Fighter Command exercise and was designed to enable the command to study, under live conditions, the problems of redeployment under fall-out conditions. Fighter Command gave precise attack details and the Home Office/ROC produced a synthetic picture to suit.

Early in 1960 a speech broadcast was introduced from ADOC to the command and group headquarters of the RAF in the United Kingdom; the Air Traffic Control Centre, Uxbridge; the Air Ministry Operations Centre; and Royal Navy HQ, Fort Southwick. The various organisations required the information being collected at ADOC and it was logical to pass it out from the centre via speech circuits.

The ROC was called upon to train Service personnel to receive and display information at each terminal of the broadcast. Eventually, however, it became clear that with normal postings the same men were not available year after year, and with the ending of conscription RAF manpower for the job became virtually non-existent. The task of providing special-duties teams of personnel to form nuclear reporting cells at the terminals therefore devolved upon the ROC. These teams have been expanded through the years and today provide essential services for the RAF and the Army at a variety of headquarters.

During exercise "Signal Fire" in April 1960 Air Marshal Sir Hector McGregor, AOC-in-C Fighter Command, visited the fall-out reporting section at the ADOC and discussed with ROC officers the problem of obtaining very rapid positive evidence that a nuclear attack on Britain had started. The ROC and the sectors could provide such information. What the AOC wanted was for a message to be flashed to ADOC as soon as posts had bomb-burst indications. In the following month, May, the RAFLOs at sectors were asked to give flash messages during exercise "Dust Bowl." The experiment was not a complete success but it did prove that the requirement could be met, once a suitable procedure had been worked out. When post observers had overpressure readings on the BPI of 0.3lb/sq in or more they were to give a suitable code word followed by the post designation. The centre plotter immediately shouted the code word across the operations room loud enough for the SOC teller to hear. He or she then passed it straight to sector, from where it was relayed to the ADOC. The ROC controller at ADOC had an intercom to the AOC-in-C's "bridge," through which he passed the code word and the Georef letters of the 1° area in which the post originating the call was situated. Simultaneously the message was told to the plotter on the general situation map in front of the "bridge" so that the AOC had it on visual display together with the aircraft track information. The system was first tested in exercise "Observe Wun" on October 9, 1960; it proved very successful and the code word is still in use. The post snap report, shouting of the code word across the operations room and the subsequent relaying of the message bore all the hall-marks of the Diver procedure of 1944.

With the growing emphasis on the nuclear task it was logical for the Home Office to take over operational control of fall-out reporting and to assume a greater financial burden where the ROC was concerned. Discussions were initiated in 1959 which resulted in the Home Office agreeing to pay 80 per cent of the bill for the ROC from 1960 onwards. Two years later this was amended to 90 per cent, the RAF paying the remainder.

By dint of trial and error through a succession of exercises a total system was being evolved for detection, and reporting of nuclear attack and subsequent fall-out. Once evolved, this could alert all the military and civil defence authorities and warning to the population could be given.

The problems still be solved for UKWMO were: means for rapid mobilisation; provision of a standard attack warning communications network; availability of clear and separate audible warnings to the public of nuclear attack and impending fall-out; vulnerability of existing land-line communications and provision of better training aids.

"Emergency call-out" came high on the list of priorities. A series of code words were used to indicate a simple alert at a period of heightened tension, a reinforced alert with manning-up switching of telephone lines and distribution of equipment and stores, and a general alert which meant final readiness for war. As before the war, centres and posts evolved their own measures for emergency call-out.

Warnings were standardised at ROC posts for attack and fall-out with hand sirens for the former and maroons sounding a Morse "D" for the latter. The sirens took time to deliver and there were problems with maroon development by the Royal Armaments Research and Development Establishment. Until maroons were available fall-out warning was to be by "gong or whistle," exactly as the police had given warning of the approach of Zeppelins in the First World War. It was essential that there be different types of warning so that the public would stay under cover once fall-out was imminent. With the completion of the FSM production programme the warnings were classified as red for attack imminent, grey for fall-out expected in about 1hr and black for imminent danger.

The increased threat from long-range nuclear-warhead missiles led, in 1961, to an agreement between the USA and Britain for the building of the Ballistic Missile Early Warning Station (BMEWS) at Fylingdales in Yorkshire. With the speed of a missile attack it was vital to get the fastest possible warning out. ROC posts at the time received their attack warnings from the plotter at centre and this was too time-consuming.

The Home Office produced plans for a nationwide network of "alarm" sets known as the carrier warning system. The carrier receiver itself consisted of a battery-powered low-frequency receiver with a built-in loudspeaker and volume control. They were to be installed at 15,000 points where public warnings were issued – police stations, fire stations, hospitals, public utilities, civil and Service HQs, military units, ROC groups and posts and, in certain circumstances, in private houses. The system worked as follows: as soon as warning of attack was given by BMEWS, NATO or master radar it was flashed by the ADOC to the BBC and to 250 carrier control points, usually at police stations. From there it was broadcast over all carrier receivers to a total of 20,000. In the case of fall-out the carrier control points would pass the warnings to particular warning districts which each covered about 100 square miles. Every carrier receiver was marked with its district number, e.g. Bedford 32.

Increased security for landline communications entailed improved sites for centres and better lines for posts. Only a few clusters in the country were on private wires and the rest were on emergency switching. As the building programme went ahead in 1961–2 changes in groups were announced. The posts of No 19 Group, Manchester, and No 21 Group, Lancaster, were combined and transferred to a new 21 Group headquarters at Longley Lane, Preston. Lancaster and Manchester became secondary training centres. Various boundary changes occurred in Scotland and 26 Group HQ at Bishopriggs was transferred to Glasgow, No 17 Group HQ, Caernarvon, was transferred to Wrexham and in 1963 No 5 Group, Coventry, was transferred to Lawford Heath, Rugby.

For training it was essential to get a practice set for the Fixed Survey Meter. Observers had to learn check procedures and operation and they only saw the instrument when it was brought round from headquarters. An ingenious device was therefore invented which looked exactly like the FSM but was operated by clockwork. Known as the Fixed Survey Meter Trainer, it could be fed with a celluloid pattern which moved the dial needle to register varying amounts of fall-out. This made exercises far more realistic but it meant an added chore for the exercise planners, who had to convert tens of thousands of readings into gradients on the patterns. The FSMT was first tested on a group basis on April 8, 1962, at No 14 Group, Winchester. The whole of Southern Area tried it on May 20. One thousand FSMTs were available by March 1962 and it was standard throughout the corps by September of the same year. The whole contract for the FSMT was worth £65,000.

To provide emergency communications it was decided that all group headquarters and one

Wren's artistic round-up of the opening of the protected centre at No 4 Group, Colchester, in March 1961, which appeared in "The Aeroplane" for March 10

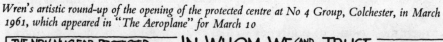

post in every cluster should be equipped with VHF radio. Relay masts were to provide the links and radio posts became known as "master posts." In the chaotic situation following a nuclear attack it was hoped that sufficient landlines would remain between posts for the master post to be able to report two or more fall-out readings to centre. The first trials with radio were carried out in the Winchester Group in the autumn of 1961. Equipping the whole corps with radio has been an exceptionally long job and even now, as this is written, the last groups are still awaiting equipment.

The major fall-out exercise for 1962 was called "Fallex 62" and it was described as "patchy," with the eastern part of the country fully extended but some groups only slightly affected. This was to be a problem with any realistic test where bombs dropped only in certain areas and the remainder were limited to monotonous fall-out readings or "no reading" for hours on end.

Over the period September 28–29 the fall-out exercise "Double Six" was combined with the defence exercise "Matador 2." Eastern, Northern and Western Areas took part. Aircraft reporting was carried out in the eastern low-level area for which a trial had taken place in 4, 6, 7 and 15 ROC Groups at the end of August. Posts were given plenty of experience with Rats procedures and the aircraft used in Matador 2 to simulate low-level attacks were American F-101 Voodoos and RB-66s.

During Fallex 62, logarithmic charts were used for recording fall-out and Dose Rate 7 procedures were inaugurated at centres. These functions were normally carried out at the SOC but it had been decided that the groups should be able to provide customers with all the necessary information in the event of SOC communications being put out of action.

An additional task was given to the corps in 1963 in the shape of deposition measurement. This entailed the master posts using the Radiac Survey Meter to measure the actual rate of fall-out decay by collecting sample trays and measuring them every hour. From this information scientists could work out not only the decay and deposition rates but also the time at which fall-out was complete.

It was essential to test the facilities at centres as well as those at posts, and in April 1963 a manning experiment was carried out in No 1 Group, Maidstone. It was originally to have been tried in February, but heavy snow meant a postponement. The operations room was manned for 48hr by four officers and 29 observers split into three shifts (one third in bed, one third working and all out when the red warning was sounded). At posts one in each cluster was shut down for the 48hr, with air changes at the regulation intervals. All equipment available except the pre-packed blankets was used, and during the whole period 30 nuclear bursts were dealt with. This provided very valuable information on wartime conditions and assisted in the major exercises "Observe Wun" and "Dust Storm" held in May and June 1963 respectively. One further 1963 exercise was "Kingpin/Double Four."

It was during the years 1959 to 1964 that the Campaign for Nuclear Disarmament made itself felt and the Aldermaston marches became part of the calendar. The CND movement was motivated by the highest ideals but it tended to be somewhat hysterical and ignore facts as they existed. It also led to the rise of many left-wing fringe organisations which demonstrated on any and every occasion and put out bulletins which seldom bore any resemblance to the truth. Despite the fact that the ROC existed to protect the population from nuclear attack and its after effects, it was openly assailed by lunatic splinter groups whose knowledge of nuclear warfare was as limited as their use of the English language. The Oxford Centre, for instance, was bedaubed with slogans just before it opened. In Scotland the fanatics demonstrated at any site connected with Civil Defence, including the ROC. One brilliant broadsheet issued by "Solidarity Glasgow" described 27/N.3 Kirkintilloch Post in the following terms:

"Inchterf, on the road to Kilsyth. A quarter-mile from the main entrance the ventilators of an Observer Corps shelter can be seen. According to local rumour there is a huge 'cave', the size of Hampden Park underneath. This is probably where the troops who will be used to keep order and to cart away the bodies of those who have not been atomised by the H-bomb which will explode over Glasgow, will be kept."

The reactions of the members of Post 27/N.3 are not on record, but devoutly would they have wished for a space the size of Hampden Park instead of their little 15ft by 7ft 6in monitoring room.

During the whole period of building and re-equipment the corps continued with its normal cycle of training meetings, joint crew and cluster meetings, visits to airfields, courses at civil-defence schools and, inevitably, the annual intermediate/master test. As the years went by the written papers for the last-mentioned became more complex and the recognition film accounted for a smaller percentage of the marks. By 1965 the film had been replaced by sheets of printed photographs. This saved money in cinema hire and allowed the test to be held at RAF stations, town halls, works canteens, etc.

In May 1961 Air Commodore C. M. Wight-Boycott had become commandant in place of Air Commodore Warfield. Wight-Boycott was well aware of the corps' background, as he had served on night fighters and on Fighter Command operations staff in the Second World War. In 1950, when on the staff of a fighter sector, he had been responsible for liaison with the ROC and arranging RAF co-operation in exercises.

Two of his more pleasant duties after assuming command were to present the 5,000th ROC medal and a rather special "medal" to a railway engine. The engine in question was Battle of Britain class loco No 34050 "Royal Observer Corps" bearing the corps crest. At Waterloo station on July 2, 1961, before a guard of honour of 50 observers, Wight-Boycott unveiled a metal enlargement of the ROC medal fitted on the cab. The proceedings completed, 300 observers boarded the special train and departed for a day trip to Bournemouth. 34050 was the only engine in Britain ever to wear a long service decoration.

The 5,000th ROC medal came on September 7, 1962 at RAF Hereford, when it was presented by the Commandant to No 8161 Observer M. P. Marsh of 12/F.4 post, Newport, Mon.

Wight-Boycott had his first taste of ROC camp at RAF Binbrook in July 1961. The Air Ministry news letter for July 28 of that year aptly describes the type of people that he met:

"At Binbrook one found men and women of all ages, kinds and callings – the 60-year-old tombstone writer and the 16-year-old engineering apprentice; the Life Guardsman of World War I and the housewife with three children and a husband looking after them in Bedford while she went to camp; the husband, wife and daughter from Winchester; the grandfather and his grandson side by side in the Binbrook classroom; the well-to-do businessman and squire and the pensioner; the observer officer and the woman observer who spent the second week of their honeymoon in camp.

They came from the four corners of Britain – from Northern Ireland and from Cornwall, from the Fenlands and the shores of the Bristol Channel, the Yorkshire moors and the moors of Devon. And this year, for the first time, came men from the Shetlands where four observer posts were lately opened. Fourteen of the 36 observers in the Shetlands made the long trip to Lincolnshire. One of them had never been off the islands; had never seen a train. Most observers used the railways to get to Lincolnshire, but, like those from Northern Ireland, the Shetlanders had to make a voyage too. They had to cross 180 miles of the North Sea to Aberdeen for their train. These bronzed, hardy men from Britain's northland said they were finding their first camp extremely interesting and were enjoying the experience."

Wight-Boycott was concerned over the speed with which the corps could be brought to full operational readiness at short notice. He therefore initiated practice alerts for all corps officers two or three times a year without prior warning. Further down the line, centres and posts arranged emergency call-out lists and went on duty as if an emergency had been declared. After one such test, a deputy group commandant wrote to officers and chief observers: "It should be borne in mind that the DGC gets no sadistic pleasure in arranging these 'call-outs' and likes a day off too now and then."

The year 1963 was particularly busy for the eastern groups in the aircraft-reporting role but, alas, it was to be by way of a swansong as the RAF was on the verge of abandoning its "eyes and ears" and concentrating solely on electronic devices.

On July 27 the RAF held a full-scale penetration exercise involving the five observer groups in the low-level belt. Posts used a modified form of Rats procedure with reports such as "Rats Golf Two – zero niner – miles four – north west – two planes;" and "Rats Golf Two – two zero – miles 1 – crossing coast *NOW* – Vulcan." Each post filled in track record sheets on which bearings and range rings in miles were marked. At centres Rats tracks were shown with chinagraph arrows on perspex on what was termed the "low-level defence screen." Behind the perspex was a map of the land and some sea, the whole gridded with Georef. Main tables used only large arrow counters and no colour change. Tracks were told to ROCLOs at Bawdsey, Trimingham and Patrington master radars. Low-level defending Hunters were put up by No 234 Squadron, Leconfield, and Nos 1 and 54 Squadrons from Waterbeach. The Hunters flew in pairs with two drop tanks each on the patrol line system. A further eight fighter squadrons were available to deal with the medium- and high-level raids which were not the concern of the ROC. The first penetration consisted of two raids of eight Valiants at low level, supported by one raid of 30 Victors and Vulcans at medium and high levels. The second penetration, one hour later, was by 20 aircraft at medium and high levels. The Valiants made "pop-up" attacks on the Bloodhound 1 surface-to-air missile bases while high-level aircraft simulated Blue Steel air-surface missile release 80 n.m. offshore. Bomber Command used electronic counter-measures while the defences employed a co-ordinator in a Canberra.

The major national fall-out exercise for 1963 was called "Double Four" and was held in September to coincide with a Fighter Command exercise "Kingpin." A similar exercise known as "Dust Storm" was staged in August 1963.

In May 1964 exercise "Spring Link" was held using the SOCs in Caledonian, Northern, Western and Eastern Sectors and the ROC groups therein. The object was to provide RAF commanders with the operational problems posed by fall-out. This was followed in September by national exercise "Dust Bath."

During 1964 exercises, tests were made in Yeovil Group of "tele-talk" in place of the familiar head and breast telephone. Tele-talk was an 8in-square box containing both microphone and

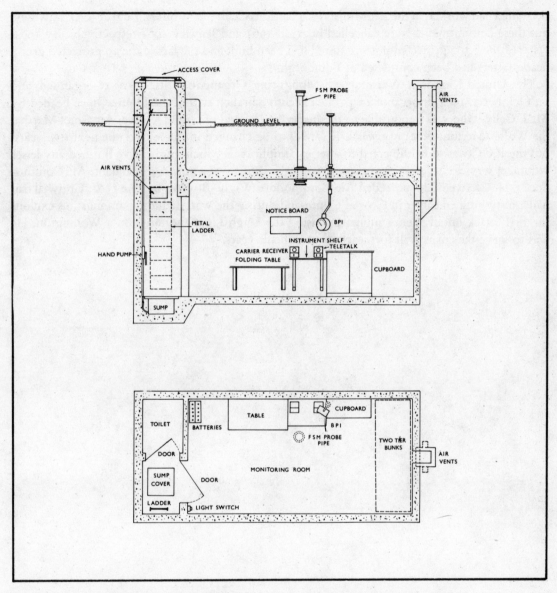

Plan and side-view drawings of a standard Royal Observer Corps underground monitoring post, of which there were 873 operational in the United Kingdom in 1975

amplifier. It was transistorised and key-operated. The signal strength of landline communications was greatly improved and tele-talk eventually became standard to all ROC posts. Cost of installation was £15 a post.

While aircraft reporting was gradually disappearing, the ROC commitment to the RAF in nuclear reporting cells at military establishments was growing. By July 1964 ROC volunteer teams were operating at the 13 major headquarters. In addition there was a RAFLO and one observer for RAF liaison and Bhangmeter operation duties at all six UKWMO sectors. ROC personnel had worked in the Air Ministry Operations Centre in Whitehall and at RAF Bawdsey, but these commitments were cancelled in April 1963 and January 1964 respectively. By 1964, 1,500 of the 1,562 protected posts required had been built and the last of the 29 protected group headquarters had been completed at Edinburgh.

The United Kingdom Warning and Monitoring Organisation itself was re-organised, and on October 1, 1964, it became a separate executive branch within the Home Office headed by Mr J. Gelly, who was responsible to the Inspector General of Civil Defence, Air Chief Marshal Sir Walter Merton. Not only was UKWMO to be changed in shape over the next five years, but the ROC was to be subjected to a series of upheavals which might have finished any lesser volunteer service. Steering the corps through the shoals was a new commandant, Air Commodore J. H. Greswell. He succeeded Air Commodore Wight-Boycott in June 1964. Greswell had had a distinguished career in Coastal Command during the war, including amongst his exploits the first attack on an enemy submarine using the Leigh Light mounted on a Wellington. He was to serve the corps well for nearly four difficult years.

Chapter 20
SURVIVAL

In the summer of 1965 the RAF finally decided that it no longer required the services of the Royal Observer Corps in the low-level reporting role. Thus the low-level belt disappeared and the last 280 or so active overground structures became redundant – although of course the posts had a full part to play in the nuclear task.

Cutaway drawing of a typical ROC underground post—in this case a "Master Post" on a cluster equipped with radio for the relay of reports in the event of telephone breakdown

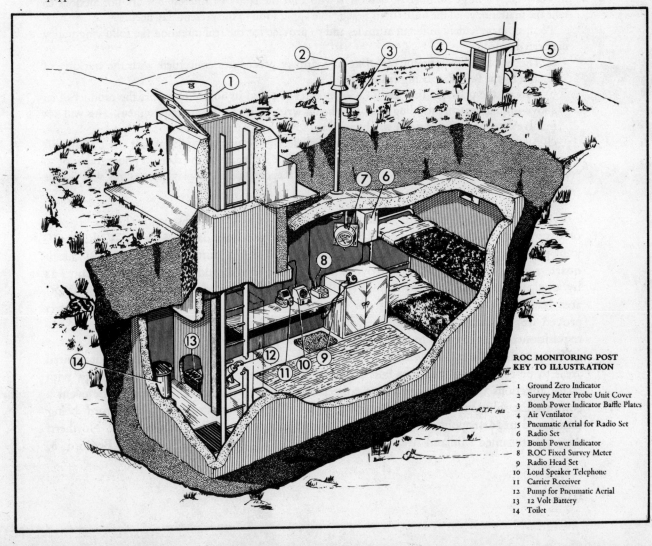

**ROC MONITORING POST
KEY TO ILLUSTRATION**

1 Ground Zero Indicator
2 Survey Meter Probe Unit Cover
3 Bomb Power Indicator Baffle Plates
4 Air Ventilator
5 Pneumatic Aerial for Radio Set
6 Radio Set
7 Bomb Power Indicator
8 ROC Fixed Survey Meter
9 Radio Head Set
10 Loud Speaker Telephone
11 Carrier Receiver
12 Pump for Pneumatic Aerial
13 12 Volt Battery
14 Toilet

Air Commodore Greswell took part in a high-level study which decided the future of the ROC in the light of the RAF's decision. It was finally affirmed that the ROC was to remain a uniformed organisation under the administrative control of the RAF. The corps' role was, however, changed to: (1) reporting nuclear bursts; (2) reporting radio-active fall-out; and (3) low-level aircraft recognition and reporting. This meant in effect that the RAF would like the ROC to maintain its ability to recognise aircraft and provide rudimentary plotting and tracking facilities, if required, but it was not prepared to pay for the privilege by providing any live aircraft exercises or special communications. This was a sad blow to the aircraft enthusiasts in the corps, and the visible signs came later as 900 overground posts deteriorated or were knocked down for lack of maintenance; money and communications were solely vested below ground. For 40 years the corps had been a key element in the air-defence reporting system and now it was to concentrate on different, but equally vital, work. In a memorandum to all area and group commandants, Greswell summarised the situation thus:

"It is well known that 'aircraft' is a subject which the real enthusiast will study at home irrespective of whether he is a member of the ROC or not – or if he is a member, irrespective of whether or not 'aircraft' feature in the ROC training syllabus. At the other end of this spectrum is the observer for whom aircraft hold no particular charm, and for these the subject is just another ROC chore. In between is a large number of observers who find the study of interest but are not anxious to take the matter beyond the limits of its practicable application to the present-day need.

To meet these widely different attitudes and to provide for the real intention the following policy has been decided:

a) The whole of the present reporting and display procedures concerned with the tracking of aircraft by the ROC are being cancelled.

b) Instead, the principle that the ROC continues to retain its ability to report the product of an above-ground watch, including aircraft, is being written into the future requirement. This will not involve detailed procedures but will be confined to the broad intention.

c) Aircraft recognition will continue to be included in the training syllabus and a test of aircraft knowledge will feature in the annual tests. This will be by means of the sheet of photographs of 30 aircraft introduced for the tests last year (1964). Reporting and display procedures will not be included either in the syllabus or in tests."

Even before the RAF's intentions had been made completely clear, discussions had been going on over yet another re-organisation of ROC group and area boundaries. At a UKWMO/ROC joint planning meeting in March 1965 it was proposed that a joint Home Office/ROC headquarters be established at Kestrel Grove, Stanmore. Groups should be reduced from 29 to 28 by amalgamating Exeter, Truro and Yeovil into two groups and adjusting sector and ROC area boundaries with a reduction from six to five of the latter. Co-location of headquarters proved impossible as Kestrel Grove, which HQ ROC was sharing with MATO, was de-requisitioned and the corps found itself still at Bentley Priory.

The commandant agreed with re-allocation of groups to sectors "operationally" but wanted areas to be retained in situations best suited to ROC needs. The idea of master groups with sector functions was mooted, but this concept was only to come about later. In the event a compromise solution was reached, with 14 Group, Winchester, and 3 Group, Oxford, being transferred to Metropolitan Area and 23 Group, Durham, going to Western Area. Northern Area was renamed Midland Area on November 1, 1965, and thereafter Groups 7, Bedford; 8,

Coventry; 15, Lincoln; and 6, Norwich; were transferred to it. On January 1, 1966, Eastern Area was disbanded.

Around this time it was also decided that the basic post team should be three (post strength 12) and for master posts four (post strength 16). With centre crews this meant a requirement for 25,000 personnel overall, whereas the actual strength of the corps was 17,000. As if to reassure members of the need for their services, during a review of Home Defence in the House of Commons in February 1966 it was stated that:

"The warning and monitoring organisation, on which the country is dependent for warning of attack and the monitoring of radio-activity, and in which the Royal Observer Corps plays so valuable a part, will be maintained at a high level of efficiency. Further improvements in the system are planned."

This last comment referred to "data transmission," which will be dealt with later.

While axing of the aircraft-reporting role was in progress and the intensification of the nuclear burst/fall-out reporting task was in progress, other plans were being laid for a very special celebration. The year 1966 marked the 25th anniversary of the corps' assumption of the style and description "Royal." To celebrate this occasion Her Majesty the Queen presented the ROC with a banner at Bentley Priory on June 24. One hundred and three officers and 653 observers from all over the country paraded for the royal review.

The banner was dedicated by the Chaplain-in-Chief Royal Air Force, handed to Her Majesty by the Commandant, and passed to the banner-bearer. In view of the corps' previous connections it was fitting that the banner party should have consisted of the Bearer, Observer Officer J. D. Ballington, a wartime sapper, and the escort Leading Observer G. E. Matthews AFM, ex-RAF, Acting Chief Observer F. W. Sherrard, ex-Royal Marines, and Leading Observer N. Page, ex-Royal Army Service Corps. The Banner Orderly was Observer T. J. Dunne, ex-RAF. In 1945 it had been an ensign, in 1966 a banner, and this only went to show the confusion that could arise over the corps' status as a uniformed civilian organisation. The Queen was presented with a jewelled ROC brooch, which she wore for the remainder of the proceedings, and as she inspected the massed ranks group by group. Later in the afternoon Her Majesty talked informally to a wide variety of corps members assembled on the Bentley Priory sports field. Once again the ROC showed that, although drill was not in its curriculum, it could be as sharp as many regular Service units when on parade.

During 1967 several shortcomings in the corps were remedied, including the questions of ration packs for posts, poor post lighting and bad centre-to-sector communications. Self-heating cans put out noxious fumes, so it was decided to issue posts with balanced packs of canned food and have them heated on Tommy cookers. This is still not the optimum solution and other methods are being sought. On post lighting, the small bulb which was impossible to read by was scheduled for replacement by fluorescent strip lighting, 4w and 6w versions of which had been tested at the Elstree and Edenbridge posts. At the power end it was realised that lighting/radio batteries could not be hauled out of posts during an emergency period for charging at the local garage. Provision was therefore made for the supply of four-stroke petrol/electric charging sets at all posts. With these, posts could continue to maintain batteries at full charge until the last moment of a crisis. Two types were issued and they cost £45 or £52 each. The total bill for supplying PE charging sets was £80,000.

The most significant technical development was, however, in the field of communications with the perfecting of data transmission by means of teleprinters instead of using voice telling over a telephone wire. This was to alter the whole layout and working of sectors and groups. Data transmission had been looked at from 1962 onwards, including proposals for its use by posts. In 1964 a data transmission committee was formed under the chairmanship of Observer Commander A. J. Lardner with assistance from the UKWMO and two Fighter Command works study officers. The site used for experimental work was the secondary training base at Beckenham, the headquarters of No 1 Group having moved back to Maidstone. At the beginning there was nothing to be seen, but at the end of 18 months a complete prototype operations room had been installed, crews had been trained and demonstrations had taken place. The first full-scale exercise took place in July 1965. Early in 1966 the go-ahead was given by the Home Office for data transmission and the expansion of the radio network.

The Beckenham layout was to be applied to all ROC groups, and it meant a complete change from all the accepted layouts back to the 1920s. The main map table and the long-range board disappeared. In their place were GPO machines and, on one side, vertical transparent displays "A" and "B." Instead of the officers sitting up on the balcony, the plotters now occupied that position. These display plotters each had marked rotating black boards on which first fall-out readings and post communication states could be shown. When filled in and turned around, the boards provided all the necessary information for the tellers on the opposite balcony, who could then pass it on to the teleprinter operators. The log-chart tellers relayed post information to the chart plotters. Also on the ground floor was the tape centre.

Crew members had to be completely retrained and instructions rewritten. New names began to appear, such as tape-centre orderly, tape-centre store operator and tape-centre traffic clerk. The first live exercise with data transmission was Metex 1/67, held on August 20, followed by exercise "Test Pilot" on September 10, when the posts took part, and then the main annual exercise "Intex 67." Data transmission was subsequently introduced into all ROC centres, the scheme being completed in 1970.

While the technical side was being perfected, a Home Office/ROC working party was examining yet again the group structure of the corps. In 1953 the ROC was turned inside out to adjust to the RAF's sector boundaries. With the disappearance of the aircraft role it became essential to change the layout to suit nuclear burst and fall-out reporting. The working party's terms of reference involved post/cluster strength in relation to data transmission, relocation of posts and clusters to ensure minimum vulnerability of landline and radio communications, and achievement of financial economies where possible. Initially there was an attempt to make ROC boundaries conform with local-authority areas, but this was soon discarded by the Home Office and the ROC. Arithmetical division of the posts was also abandoned. The working party then decided that safety of communications was the only real criterion on which the layout should be based. The result was an interim report produced by the working party in May 1967 for consideration before a final detailed layout was completed. This included the closing down of Leeds and Watford centres, the relegation of Oban and Truro to sub-group status and the reclustering of all posts. It also proposed the relocation of Bristol (Lansdown) at Hereford and of Coventry (Lawford Heath) at Burton-on-Trent. HQ ROC did not agree and discussions continued over many months.

At the same time, communications specialists had been examining the UKWMO sectors.

It was found that these, as "left-overs" from the time that the Home Office were lodgers with the RAF, were based on long and vulnerable communication links. It was decided, therefore, to house the sectors in "blisters" attached to certain ROC centres. Communication links were thereby shortened and, where the blisters were attached, communications ran only from one room to another.

In later group changes within ROC areas a star arrangement was adhered to wherever possible, with the sector group in the middle. The first site selected for a blister was in Metropolitan Area, at No 2 Group, Horsham. This was followed by adaptations at 15 Group, Lincoln (Midland Sector); 12 Group, Bristol (Southern Sector); 21 Group, Preston (Western Sector); and 28 Group, Dundee (Caledonian Sector). These were far-reaching modifications in the corps' structure and at the same time separate proposals were put up at high level for the integration of the warning and monitoring organisation/ROC rank structure.

Rumours of the possible changes spread on the corps' own bush telegraph and news stories appeared in the *Daily Telegraph* and *Sunday Telegraph* in June suggesting that the ROC was to sever its relations with the RAF. Letters of protest and telephone calls poured in to ROC headquarters. Whitehall immediately denied that there would be a change in the links and associations with the RAF and the commandant issued a special message to all members. Air Chief Marshal Sir Walter Merton, Inspector-General of Civil Defence, wrote to Air

ROC humour continues: Bill Thacker, a serving observer, is probably the most popular cartoonist and his work has appeared in many journals. These two cartoons epitomise the corps' attitude to life, which has altered little over 50 years

"The Corps does not concern itself with any facet of Politics . . . for instance you can see from the Observers' pay that they are not involved in any way with the Redistribution of Wealth"

"Now THAT must be the chap my ROC uniform was made for"

Marshal Sir William Coles, C-in-C Technical Training Command, and asked him to reassure corps members during the course of his inspection of the ROC Camp at Coningsby in July.

In January 1968 the Labour Government, in the midst of an economic crisis, decided on massive cuts in home defence. They assessed the chance of a nuclear war in the next few years to be so small that they could afford to reduce spending by £18 million The Auxiliary Fire Service, the Civil Defence Corps and the TAVR III were disbanded. Home defence was henceforth on a care-and-maintenance basis with vast quantities of specialised equipment like fire engines and rescue trucks being sold off, and 84,000 volunteer personnel dispensed with. Previously the watchword had been "rescue" for any future nuclear war; from then on it was to be "survival." It looked as if the ROC too might be swept away under the blade of the Treasury axe.

On January 18, 1968, the Under-Secretary of State for the Home Department made the following statement in the House of Commons:

"The Royal Observer Corps will be retained as part of the warning and monitoring organisation and the WRVS will be retained because of its very considerable and notable peacetime service. The Government have taken these decisions because they believe that the risk of nuclear war does not, in the present circumstances, justify home-defence expenditure on the scale of recent years.

The warning and monitoring organisation, manned mainly by the Royal Observer Corps, will continue. It has the task of warning the public of an imminent attack with nuclear weapons – sometimes referred to as the 'four-minute warning' – and subsequently to warn them of the presence of radio-active fall-out. The organisation also has an ability to provide more detailed information, particularly on fall-out, to services which can make use of it.

There are powerful reasons why this organisation should not be disbanded. The capital cost of the organisation has already been met – its buildings, equipment and communications are, for the most part, complete. Furthermore, the preservation of the technique is more complex than in most other fields. Therefore we are making an exception to the general principle of winding up the volunteer organisations and keeping the Royal Observer Corps in being, although there will be some re-organisation and reduction to secure economies."

So the corps was to remain in being but the sting was in the tail in the word "economies." The Government required the warning and monitoring organisation to take a cut in expenditure from £2 million to £1.7 million. Translated into ROC terms, this meant only £988,000 being available (£890,000 from the Home Office and £98,000 from the Ministry of Defence). Air Commodore Greswell was faced with two alternatives; a virtually dormant and untrained corps of existing size, lacking proper meetings, training and interest, or one which was severely cut in size and personnel but at the same time fully active and efficient. Air Commodore Greswell, quite naturally, chose the latter course.

The bombshell came on February 19, 1968, in the shape of a circular to all area and group commandants. Six hundred and eighty-six posts were to close; post establishment was limited to ten, including the head observer; Watford and Leeds Groups were to be closed; Truro and Oban Groups were reduced to satellite status; and the appointments of 11 whole-time officers were disestablished. In terms of the overall establishment, the corps was to be reduced from 25,000 to 12,500, but since the strength was actually 17,500 the number of observers made redundant totalled around 5,000. The reduced coverage of posts meant a less detailed fall-out warning picture. At the same time deposition measurement was abandoned.

All over Britain head observers received notes saying that their posts were redundant as from April 1, 1968, and that all personnel must be "disposed of" by June 30. Post crews that had worked together as close-knit teams for many years found themselves on the scrap-heap. Some members resigned in disgust, some transferred to centres where recruits were always wanted, while others crowded on to nearby posts which were to remain operational, only to be asked to resign later in order to achieve the magic number of ten. An amount of "dead wood" was inevitably cleared away in the course of this major act of surgery, but the corps also lost large numbers of dedicated and efficient observers, so many in fact that recruiting drives were necessary before six months had passed.

Final meetings were held at most posts on which closure notices had been served. Typical are the last logbook entries of 9/C.1, Keynsham, Somerset, a very enterprising and efficient post:

> "April 5, 1968.
> 19.15   In the recent re-organisation of the Royal Observer Corps, our post was declared redundant and ceased to be operational as from last Monday, April 1, 1968. As the personnel on post 9/C.1 are to be dispersed as soon as possible, it has been decided to assemble at our post site this evening at the start of what will probably be our last post meeting, to say farewell to 'Charlie Wun.' Both the protected post and the observation post are open.
> 20.00   Both posts closed for the last time.
>
> Ivo Peters."

While the ROC wrestled with the problems of cuts and re-organisation, it witnessed the passing of two very old friends, Fighter Command and Bomber Command, which were merged into the new Strike Command on April 30, 1968. The corps had worked with and served both through five and half long years of war, and it had formed part of Fighter Command since its inception in 1936.

On April 25 a ceremonial parade and fly-past was held at Bentley Priory to mark the disbandment of Fighter Command. It was a sad commentary on events that the ROC banner was paraded alongside the standards of only eight fighter squadrons – a far cry from the 68 squadrons of July 1940.

One of the results of the formation of Strike Command was that the ADOC at Bentley Priory was replaced by the Strike Command Operations Centre (STOC) at High Wycombe. In the event of war the attack warning would be given nationwide by Home Office officials at STOC, using the carrier broadcast system.

On June 28, 1968, Air Commodore Greswell retired and his place as commandant was taken by Air Commodore D. F. Rixson. He faced a very difficult situation, with the corps strength being reduced by nearly one third, coincident with a new sector building programme and the introduction of data transmission. It was essential that the status of the corps be both privately and publicly maintained to ensure that morale was kept up among the remaining observers. Rixson discussed the matter at high level in the Home Office and the Ministry of Defence and the ROC case was successfully put over. Rixson found that he was faced with an acute shortage of personnel in many areas, particularly in sparsely populated areas, and, remarkable as it may seem, a recruiting programme was initiated.

So far as the RAF was concerned, the old links had tended to become remote in the years 1966 to 1968, but from then on they revived. In October 1969 the RAF standing instruction on

"Responsibilities of the Royal Air Force towards the Royal Observer Corps" was amended and re-issued for the first time since 1950. The document outlined the functions and status of the corps and the co-operation required from the RAF, including air-experience flights.

While the ROC had been perfecting its techniques, the Home Departments had fully developed their specialist teams at both groups and sectors. The teams had originally been headed by group senior warning officers and chief sector warning officers respectively. In 1969 these appointments were re-designated as chief warning officers and sector controllers. The sector controller is the principal field representative of the Home Departments in the sectors of the United Kingdom Warning and Monitoring Organisation. Under his direct control at a sector/group control are 21 personnel including senior sector scientists, scientists, a chief warning officer and warning officers. At group controls there are 13 personnel of the Home Departments, including the holder of the recently created post of group controller, and a chief warning officer. Some dual appointments of group controller and ROC group commandant have now been made. Personnel of the Home Departments are responsible for the analysis of meteorological forecast data, the issue of warnings and the interpretation of nuclear burst and fall-out information. As the years have passed the teams recruited by the Home Departments and Royal Observer Corps have become blended into a homogeneous entity with distinctive tasks to achieve the same common objective.

Reverting to the Corps itself, on September 30, 1969, Observer Captain W. Rusby OBE, retired as Deputy Commandant, having held the post for a record 16 years. In a lecture at the time he summarised the vicissitudes that the Corps had been called upon to endure during those years:

"Consider also for a moment the fact that the 16 years from 1953 to 1969 have seen this corps of ours turned upside down and inside out in a manner that nobody of the wartime days would ever have thought possible. We've been organised and re-organised and re-organised – we've been transposed from rugged creatures who gazed at the heavens in the sun and the wind and the rain, to become denizens of a gloomy underworld, where we read instruments and are obsessed by a hazard that cannot even be seen. We've progressed from the tools of Heath Robinson to a welter of modern equipment, we've been completely rebuilt and have even rebuilt our rebuilt ops rooms – and about the only thing we have not changed in this momentous 16 years is the simple dedication to the corps of the part-time volunteer. This, thank God, has remained constant despite the most astonishing upheavals."

For certain groups aircraft reporting of an unusual kind returned in 1970–71. The ROC was asked to provide assistance to the Royal Aircraft Establishment in monitoring sonic booms during the supersonic trials of the Concorde 002 airliner under the RAE code name Trafalgar. The supersonic corridor ran on a straight line from the extreme north of Scotland, over Oban and thence over Truro. Twelve special overpressure monitoring points were established by the RAE, but in addition individual timed reports, covering points within the sonic boom "carpet," were needed. Selected observers from 75 posts in Southern, Western and Scottish Areas were asked to fill in a form giving details of the boom heard, their personal activity at the time and local weather conditions. Oban Centre itself played a part in the Concorde trials and was in direct communication with the RAE.

On fall-out reporting the corps' task was extended in 1970 to cover mobile monitoring. After a nuclear attack posts still operating would, once fall-out had decayed to 'a safe level,

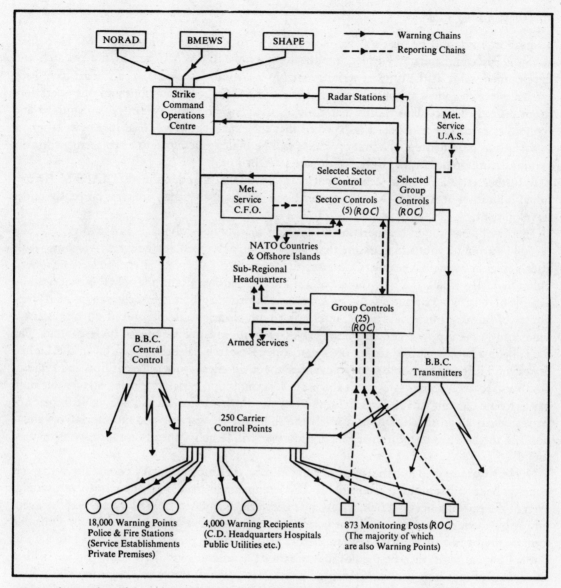

Diagram showing the nuclear warning and reporting chains in Britain as they exist today. Points where the ROC participate are shown, but there are in addition ROC nuclear reporting cells in the Strike Command operations centre and at a number of other Service headquarters

reconnoitre certain areas. Fall-out dose-rates and local conditions would be noted and then reported to centre from the post.

In December 1971 Air Commodore E. B. Sismore took over as commandant on the retirement of Air Commodore Rixson. During his period of command Air Commodore Sismore visited several organisations abroad dealing with nuclear and aircraft reporting. Particularly close links were forged with the Royal Danish Ground Observer Corps, these being assisted by the fact that Sismore had been master navigator during the daring Mosquito raid on the Gestapo headquarters at Copenhagen and Odense in 1945, for which he was subsequently awarded the Order of Dannebrog. Air Commodore R. K. Orrock succeeded Air Commodore

Sismore in 1973, and he, in turn, was succeeded in 1975 by Air Commodore M. H. Miller, as the corps commandant. Further modifications of the UKWMO are in the research and development stage at the time of writing. At No 2 Group, Horsham, experiments have been carried out with a view to combining the sector and ROC group functions into one operations room instead of two. This means that control, manning and display can be streamlined and economies made in personnel. It is expected that the experiments will lead to a new design of sector/group headquarters, the first of which will be built at Hereford as a replacement for the existing Southern Sector/12 Group headquarters at Bristol.

A further technical aid at centres will come with the introduction of DIADEM (Directional Indication of Atomic Detonations by Electromagnetic Means), which is currently under development.

There will continue to be operational problems that require solving in order to get the best possible warning layout and to ensure that, as far as humanly possible, the system remains viable after a nuclear attack has begun. One great unknown is the ultimate effect of electromagnetic pulse, or EMP, which is a by-product of a nuclear explosion at altitude. EMP is theoretically capable of destroying or putting out of action transistorised equipment, such as radios and computers, of burning out aerial feeders, interfering with electrical circuits and of putting massive sudden surges into power and telephone cables, even if the latter are buried underground. The overall effect is of lightning strikes on a vast scale. Research has been going on in the United States and in Britain for some years to evaluate the EMP effect from different sizes and types of bomb and to evolve some safeguards against it. Disconnecting aerials during an attack, shielding of electronic equipment and even the revival of the old-fashioned thermionic valve in place of transistors are all possible solutions. Clearly the ability of the warning and monitoring organisation and the Services to fulfil their functions in war will largely depend on the answers that are found.

Nuclear warfare is so horrific, even to contemplate, that most ordinary people shy away and honestly believe that nothing can be done. The arrangements made in Britain, however, would, even in the case of a heavy attack, ensure that between six and ten million lives could be saved, simply by adequate attack and fall-out warning being given. For instance, in a Sector a possible scenario might be a heavy attack with numerous ground and air bursts ranging up to 3 Megatons. The following might then be the possible situation: 4 million-plus dead and $\frac{1}{4}$ million with a lethal dose of radiation of 600 Roentgens-plus. There would, however, be around 1 million people with radiation sickness, but likely to recover and probably 16 million uninjured survivors. These estimates would only be valid if there was full warning and the population took cover. Without warning many millions more would be dead or dying. Using the BBC, the carrier control points and the carrier receiver-equipped warning points (such as ROC posts) a four-minute warning could be given of attack and imminent danger warnings of fall-out would follow from the work of the posts, groups and sectors.

After the holocaust it might be necessary to run sections of the country temporarily as individual autonomous regions. To this end full preparations have been made for Government on a regional and sub-regional basis whereby civilian and service experts covering all aspects of government and administration would be assembled as soon as the international situation made war appear inevitable. Britain could virtually be reduced to the state of having little kingdoms as in the early middle ages, but within them maximum effort would be made to use

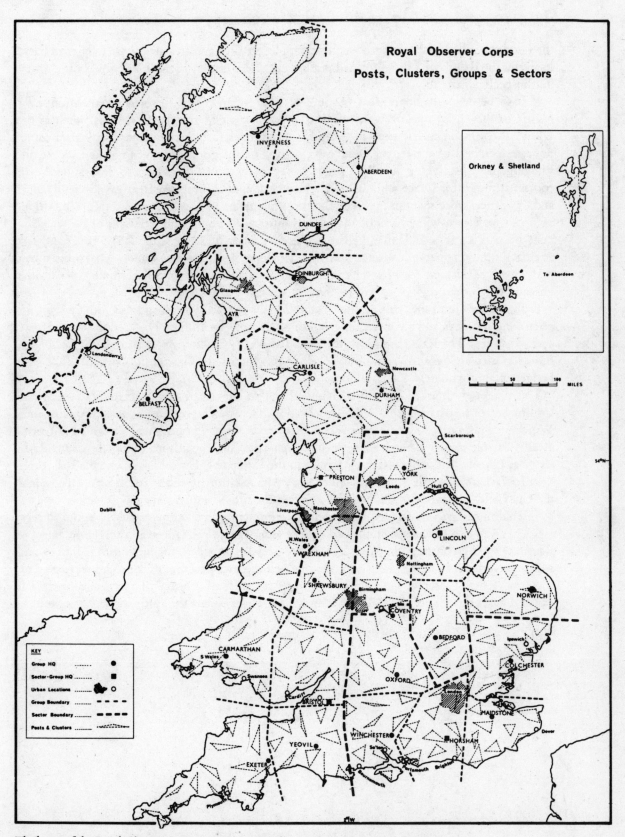

Royal Observer Corps
Posts, Clusters, Groups & Sectors

Orkney & Shetland

To Aberdeen

0   50   100   MILES

KEY
Group HQ .... ●
Sector-Group HQ .... ■
Urban Locations .... ○
Group Boundary .... ― ― ―
Sector Boundary .... ▬ ▬ ▬
Posts & Clusters ....

The layout of the Royal Observer Corps, as it now exists, showing the areas, groups and post clusters the resources still available to succour those people left alive and to start on the long road back. In all this the ROC, with its uniformed personnel and communications links, would have a vital but unspecified part to play.

It is to be devoutly hoped that no-one, be it great power or terrorist organisation, ever resorts to the use of nuclear weapons. It is nevertheless essential that a network such as the UKWMO be maintained in peacetime, ready for the attack that everyone prays will never come. For the members of the Royal Observer Corps it means giving up evenings and weekends, studying, training, taking tests and participating in exercises. It may also mean specialised courses at the Home Office schools and attendance at annual camp. Apart from all the practical and theoretical work that this involves, the corps maintains a knowledge of aircraft recognition.

In view of the growing threat of Soviet conventional air power and the swing of the scientific pendulum, it is just possible that the RAF, one day, might again need the ROC's eyes and ears as a back-up to the nation's science-based air defence system. No-one knows what other threat may develop, but if it requires the employment of the most advanced computer of all – the human being – then the ROC will be there to measure, assess, report and warn.

Probably the most remarkable thing of all is that the corps volunteers put up with discomfort, often long journeys and a considerable call on their time for minimal reward in terms of pay and allowances. The ROC itself costs the nation under £1 million per year, for a force of ten thousand men and women – a minimal price to pay for safety. This is out of a total UKWMO budget of approximately £2.8 million.

The year 1975 marked the fiftieth anniversary of the corps official inauguration by the Committee of Imperial Defence. The celebrations were widespread and varied. For instance, Winchester Group rebuilt a Barnes Wallis dambuster spinning bomb and presented it to the RAF; Carlisle staged a band concert; Norwich took ROC families flying in a Friendship airliner; Lincoln held a thanksgiving service in the Cathedral; Horsham presented a bell tower door to the parish church which was unveiled by Mrs Ashmore, General Ashmore's widow; and the Cuckfield Post unveiled a memorial stone on the fiftieth anniversary day, October 29.

The culmination came on October 31 when a commemorative dinner was held in the officers' mess at RAF High Wycombe in the presence of Her Majesty the Queen and HRH the Duke of Edinburgh. As was fitting, the heads of all three Services attended, together with Ministers and senior Government officials. ROC officers representing every section of the corps were present.

As the Royal Observer Corps moves into its second half century of active life, its role is vastly different to that of 1925. The task may have changed but the spirit remains the same.

Appendix 1

Headquarters and Area Organisation 1925 to 1975

HEADQUARTERS – OBSERVER CORPS (1925 to 1941);
ROYAL OBSERVER CORPS (1941 onwards)

1925   Formed as part of AA/RA Command of the
Army. Headquarters at Hillingdon House, Uxbridge
1929   Transferred from Army to control by Air
Ministry
1938   Headquarters transferred to Headquarters, Fighter
Command, RAF at Bentley Priory, Stanmore
1941   Title "Royal" conferred by His Majesty King
George VI

Command
1925 to 1929   Corps commanded by a staff officer,
AA Command RA
1929 to 1942   Corps commanded by an air officer RAF
(retired)
1942 to date   Corps commanded by a serving Air
Commodore, RAF

Founder
Major General E. B. Ashmore CB, CMG, MVO, RA
  1925 to 1929

Commandants
Air Commodore E. A. D. Masterman CB, CMG, CBE,
  AFC, RAF (retired)   1929 to 1936
Air Commodore A. P. Warrington-Morris CMG, OBE,
  RAF (retired)   1936 to 1942
Air Commodore G. H. Ambler CBE, AFC, RAFVR
  1942 to 1943
Air Commodore F. Finlay Crerar CBE, RAFVR
  1943 to 1945
Air Commodore Rt. Hon. The Earl of Bandon CB,
  DSO, RAF   1945 to 1949
Air Commodore R. B. Jordan CB, DFC, ADC, RAF
  1949 to 1951
Air Commodore G. H. Vasse CBE, RAF   1951 to 1954
Air Commodore J. H. T. Simpson DSO, AFC, RAF
  1954 to 1959

Air Commodore J. M. Warfield CBE, RAF   1959 to
  1961
Air Commodore C. M. White-Boycott CBE, DSO,
  RAF   1961 to 1964
Air Commodore J. H. Greswell CB, CBE, DSO, DFC,
  RAF   1964 to 1968
Air Commodore D. F. Rixson OBE, DFC, AFC,
  MBIM, RAF   1968 to 1970
Air Commodore E. B. Sismore DSO, DFC, AFC,
  MBIM, RAF   1971 to 1973
Air Commodore R. K. Orrock DFC, ADC, MBIM,
  RAF   1973 to 1975
Air Commodore M. H. Miller CBE, AFC, RAF
  1975 to *Serving*

Assistant Commandants
Air Commodore C. E. H. Rathbone CB, DSO, RAF
  (retired)   1939 to 1943
Observer Captain H. St. Clair Smallwood OBE
  1953 to 1961
Observer Captain W. R. Wilkinson OBE, JP   1953 to
  Serving
Observer Captain J. Neil Thompson MBE   1961 to
  Serving

Deputy Commandants
Group Captain I. T. Courtney CBE, RAF (retired)
  1936 to 1938
Air Commodore H. Le M. Brock CB, DSO
  1938 to 1942
Observer Captain V. O. Robertson OBE, MC
  1943 to 1945
Observer Captain C. G. Cooke OBE   1945 to 1953
Observer Captain W. Rusby OBE   1953 to 1970
Observer Captain R. A. F. Falconer OBE, DFM
  1970 to 1972
Observer Captain C. J. Rowlands MBE   1972 to *Serving*

Senior Staff Officers – Operations
Observer Commander H. G. Newman, Operations
  Staff Officer   1943 to 1945

Observer Commander R. R. Poole, Operations Staff
Officer   1947 to 1949
Observer Commander W. Rusby OBE, Operations Staff
Officer   1949 to 1953
Observer Commander F. W. Mitchell MBE, Operations
Staff Officer   1953 to 1969
Observer Commander A. J. Lardner, Senior Operations
Officer   1969 to 1972
Observer Commander D. Brooks, Senior Operations
Officer   1972 to 1975
Observer Commander R. L. Smith, Senior Operations
Officer   1975 to *Serving*

Senior Staff Officers – Administration
Observer Commander Walker, Senior Administration
Officer   1943 to 1945
Mr. A. B. Archer (HEO), Staff Officer Administration
1945 to 1960
Mr. A. Manning (HEO), Staff Officer Administration
1960 to 1971
Observer Commander R. R. Glover, Senior
Administration Officer   1972 to *Serving*

SOUTHERN AREA
Formed 1935 to administer territory south of a line
drawn approximately from Southwold to Oxford

Headquarters locations
RAF Bentley Priory, Stanmore, Middlesex   1935 to 1936
RAF Uxbridge, Middlesex   1936 to 1953
1937 Territories west of a line running approximately
north from Selsey Bill were annexed to form the basis
of a new Western Area
1953 Title "Southern Area" was transferred to the
territories administered from the hitherto "Western
Area", from its HQ at RAF Rudloe Manor, and the new
title "Metropolitan Area" applied to that previously
known as "Southern"

Headquarters location
RAF Rudloe Manor   1953 to date

Commandants
Group Captain I. T. Courtney CBE   1935 to 1942
Observer Captain A. P. Hamilton OBE   1942 to 1945
Observer Captain H. St. Clair Smallwood OBE
1947 to 1953
Observer Captain I. D. R. Sims OBE   1953 to *Serving*

Deputies
Air Commodore C. E. H. Rathbone CB, DSO and
1935 to 1942
Group Captain H. L. Reilly DSO   1935 to 1942
Observer Commander W. R. Wilkinson OBE
1943 to 1944

Observer Commander J. P. Pickford OBE, DL
1944 to 1945
Observer Commander F. W. Mitchell MBE   1947 to
1953
Observer Commander J. Seaden   1953 to 1964
Observer Commander C. J. Rowlands MBE
1964 to 1972
Observer Commander R. D. T. Onions   1972 to *Serving*

WESTERN AREA
Formed 1937 to administer territories west of a line
drawn approximately north from Selsey Bill to
Bridgenorth and west to Aberystwyth

Headquarters location
RAF Rudloe Manor   1937 to 1953

1953 Title "Western Area" transferred to territories
hitherto known as North Western Area and the title
"Southern Area" adopted

Headquarters locations
RAF Barton Hall, Preston, Lancs   1953 to 1966
Longley Lane, Gooshargh, Preston, Lancs   1966 to date

Commandants
Air Commodore E. A. D. Masterman, CB, CMG,
CBE, AFC   1937 to 1943
Observer Captain J. W. Saunders   1943 to 1945
Observer Captain I. D. R. Sims OBE   1947 to 1953
Observer Captain W. R. Wilkinson OBE   1953 to
Serving
Observer Captain F. C. Lockyer OBE   1953 to 1968
Observer Captain K. . Terry   1968 to *Serving*

Deputies
Observer Commander J. H. Evers-Swindell   1943 to
1945
Observer Commander J. H. G. Seaden   1947 to 1953
Observer Commander W. H. Wilson MBE   1953 to
1961
Observer Commander H. Robins MBE   1961 to 1964
Observer Commander H. Falconer OBE   1964 to 1970
Observer Commander R. Smith   1970 to 1975
Observer Commander D. Brooks   1975 to *Serving*

NORTH WESTERN AREA
Formed 1941 to administer territories west of the
Pennines and between Central Wales and the Scottish
Border

Headquarters location
RAF Barton Hall, Preston, Lancs   1941 to 1953

Commandants
Colonel V. O. Robinson OBE, MC, TD 1941 to 1943
Observer Captain V. O. Robinson OBE, MC, TD
 1943 to 1944
Observer Captain W. R. Wilkinson OBE 1944 to 1953

Deputies
Air Commodore A. W. F. Glenny MC, DFC 1941
 to 1942
Observer Commander W. R. Wilkinson OBE 1942 to
 1943
Observer Commander J. S. Pattison 1943 to 1945
Observer Commander W. J. Wilson MBE 1945 to
 1953

1953 Title North Western Area abolished and territory
renamed "Western Area"

NORTHERN AREA
Formed 1935 to administer territories north of a line
drawn approximately from Southwold to Oxford

Headquarters location
RAF Hucknall, Notts 1935 to 1938
1938 on the formation of "Midland Area", Northern
Area territory confined to that bounded on its south by
a line drawn approximately from Cleethorpes to
Huddersfield, on its west by the Pennines and to the
north by the Scottish Border

Headquarters location
RAF Catterick 1938 to 1943
1943 Northern Area closed and the Durham, Leeds and
York Groups transferred to "Midland Area"
1953 Northern Area reformed to administer those parts
of former Midland Area not embraced by the newly
formed "Eastern Area"

Headquarters locations
Shelley House, Acomb, York 1953 to 1963
31 Priory Street, York 1963 to 1966
1966 Northern Area disbanded, its territory transferred
to the reformed Midland Area

Commandants
Group Captain V. O. Rees OBE 1935 to 1938
Air Commodore A. L. Godman CMG, DSO 1938 to
 1943
Observer Captain W. R. Wilkinson OBE 1953 to 1961
Observer Captain E. Tyrrel OBE 1961 to 1966

Deputies
Group Captain P. B. Hunter 1938 to 1943
Observer Commander J. L. Waugh MBE 1953 to 1964

Observer Commander J. M. Clark 1964 to 1966

MIDLAND AREA
Formed 1938 to administer territories of the former
Northern Area to the south of a line approximately
from Cleethorpes to Huddersfield and east of the
Pennines

Headquarters locations
RAF Grantham 1938 to 1940
Mostyn Lodge, Grantham 1940 to 1942
RAF Watnall, Notts 1942 to 1953
1953 Area disbanded and territories divided and dispersed
to the newly formed Eastern Area and the reformed
Northern Area
1966 Midland Area reformed to
administer territories surrendered by the redundant
Eastern and Northern Areas

Headquarters location
RAF Spitalgate, Lincs 1966 to 1976
Fiskerton, Lincs 1976 to *In use*

Commandants
Group Captain V. O. Rees CBE 1938 to 1942
Observer Captain W. G. Hanson OBE 1942 to 1953
Observer Captain E. Tyrrel OBE 1966 to 1970
Observer Captain J. Chilton 1970 to *Serving*

Deputies
Captain J. W. Saunders 1938 to 1942
Observer Commander J. Roseigh MBE 1942 to 1952
Observer Commander J. L. Waugh MBE 1952 to 1953
Observer Commander J. M. Clark 1966 to 1975
Observer Commander L. Coffey 1975 to *Serving*

EASTERN AREA
Formed 1953 to administer territories hitherto forming
the southern parts of Midland Area
1966 Area disbanded and territories returned to the
reformed Midland Area

Headquarters locations
RAF Horsham St. Faith, Norwich 1953 to 1963
RAF Old Catton, Norwich 1963 to 1966

Commandant
Observer Captain S. F. Vincent CB, DSO, DFC, AFC
 1953 to 1966

Deputies
Observer Commander C. G. Cooke OBE 1953 to 1962
Observer Commander R. C. Harrod MBE 1962 to 1966

METROPOLITAN AREA
1953 Title given to territory hitherto known as "Southern Area"

Headquarters locations
RAF Uxbridge, Middlesex   1953 to 1972
Horsham, Sussex   1972 to *In use*

Commandants
Observer Captain H. St. Clair Smallwood OBE   1953 to 1954
Observer Captain B. Parkes MVO   1954 to 1963
Observer Captain J. W. Foster OBE, DFC   1963 to *Serving*

Deputies
Observer Commander D. Miller MBE   1953 to 1963
Observer Commander D. W. Egginton   1963 to 1968
Observer Commander R. R. Glover   1968 to 1972
Observer Commander A. J. Lardner   1972 to *Serving*

SCOTTISH AREA
Formed 1937

Headquarters locations
Alva Street, Edinburgh   1937 to 1939
Walker Street, Edinburgh   1939 to 1943
Stonefield House, Inverness   1943 to 1947
14 Carleton Terrace, Edinburgh   1947 to 1973
Craigiebarns, Dundee   1973 to *In use*

Commandants
Air Commodore Peel-Ross DSO, AFC   1937 to 1944
Observer Captain J. M. Miller MC, TD   1944 to 1947
Observer Captain Sir G. A. Williamson   1950 to 1958
Observer Captain J. R. L. Halley   1958 to 1965
Observer Captain R. MacFarlane   1965 to 1968
Observer Captain A. J. S. Stewart   1968 to *Serving*

Deputies
Air Commodore Gordon   1938 to 1943
Mr. Geoffrey Moore   1939 to 1943
Colonel Patterson   1938 to 1941
Observer Commander J. M. Miller MC, TD   1941 to 1944
Observer Commander W. J. Wilson MBE   1944 to 1945
Observer Commander Q. Dunlop BSc   1947 to 1967
Observer Commander D. W. Egginton   1967 to 1969
Observer Commander D. Brooks   1969 to 1972
Observer Commander H. W. Williamson   1972 to *Serving*

NO	ORIGINAL DATE OF ISSUE	TITLE	REMARKS
1	9.7.42	Signals Instruction No 1	
2	1.8.42	Raid Designations	
3	2.8.42	Amendments to Operations and Signals Instructions	
4	8.8.42	Exercise "Grouse"	
5	12.8.42	"Bullseye" Exercises	Bomber Command training exercises
6	13.8.42	Notification of new types of aircraft	
7	22.8.42	Visibility and Hearing at ROC Posts	Country-wide charting of Post sites
8	21.9.42	Plotting and Telling	
9	22.9.42	Formation of Satellite Posts	150 satellites on south and east coasts
10	12.10.42	Assistance to Aircraft in Distress	
11	10.10.42	"Darky"	Supply and operation of radio sets to ROC Posts to aid aircraft in distress. Amended: 7.7.43 and 22.4.44
12	12.10.42	Reporting by ROC of low flying raids	Preliminary orders to deal with tip-and-run raiders. Cancelled: 10.1.43
13	20.10.42	Rocket Warning of Enemy Daylight Raids (Code Word "Totter")	Firing of parachute "Snowflake" flares to warn of tip-and-run raiders. Instruction amended: 1.7.43
14	9.11.42	Employment of third Observer at certain ROC Posts	Third man on coastal Posts to fire Totter rocket
15	11.11.42	Non-directional Sea Plots	Passing of plots from CH radar to ROC Sea Plotter with minimum delay
16	16.11.42	GL Recognition by ROC	Replaced by Ops Instr No 19
17	24.2.43	Reporting by ROC of Low Raids	Rats procedure. Amended: 27.5.43 and 7.5.44
18	14.12.42	Reporting by sound from ROC Posts	Introduction of standard procedure using clock code in minutes and sound angles. Amended: 28.4.43
19	21.12.42	GL Sets at ROC Posts	
20	29.12.42	Reports of Enemy raids from ROC Posts	Standard method of reporting on enemy activity. Amended: 1.5.43
21	20.1.43	Exercise "Eric"	Air defence exercises
22	27.1.43	Notification of Movements of Friendly Aircraft	To reduce congestion with too many aircraft being told. Amended: 29.2.44
23	3.2.43	Separate Telling from Filter Rooms of Ancillary Information	Experiment to limit telling messages
24	22.3.43	Angle Heights	Post reports using angles
25	4.4.43	Aircraft in Distress	Basic procedures for aircraft indicating SOS. Amended: 17.9.44
26	21.4.43	Procedure Relating to New Raid Designations	Revisions to raid designation system introduced in 1942. Appendix A on snap designations added 13.5.43. Revised 11.12.44

No	Date	Subject	Notes
27	14.5.43	Intruder Warnings to Bomber Groups	Priority tracking of enemy aircraft to plotting tables at Bomber Groups
28	15.5.43	Special Satellite Posts	Extra satellite posts in 5 ROC Groups to gap-fill against low raiders
29	17.5.43	ROC Action in regard to friendly aircraft in distress and crashed	Reporting to and liaison with Flying Control Liaison Officers
30	15.6.43	Unidentified Tracks	Differentiating between hostile and friendly tracks. Amended 6.7.43
31	25.9.43	Telling of ancillary information	
32	5.7.43	Record Sheets	Records for RAF use
33	14.7.43	Reporting of Carrier Pigeons in Flight	Intention to find pigeons used by enemy agents. Revised: 21.7.44. Cancelled: 18.12.44
34	25.3.44	Use of Red Flares by ROC Posts to prevent Aircraft from Flying into High Ground (Code Word "Granite")	Burning of red flares by ROC Posts in vicinity of high ground. Amended: 20.1.45
35	5.8.43	Air Raid Warnings	Warning states and use of Long Range Board
36	18.8.43	Inter Centre Telling – Long Range Board	Procedures for LRBs to reduce congestion and improve speed. Amended: 28.9.43
37	28.8.43	Alarm Bells at Centres	Alarms inside Centres for alert when Hostile or Unidentified shown on table
38	1.9.43	Synchronisation of Centre Clocks	Cancelling signals Instruction No 1
39	25.9.43	Colour Change and Timing of Plots on Centre Tables	Reversion to 3-colour plotting and 2½ minute colour change Amended 11.9.44 and 7.12.44
40	15.10.43	Area Reporting by Mass and Zone Telling and Plotting	
41	4.11.43	National Air Raid Warnings. Telephone and Electrical Circuits: Testing of	
42	10.11.43	Reporting of Dangerous Low Flying	Came into operation 1.1.1944
43	27.11.43	Reporting from ROC Posts	Standard methods laid down
44	18.1.44	Reporting of Marker Flares Dropped by Enemy Aircraft	
45	24.2.44	Inter Centre Telling	Long Range Board and main table Procedures. Amended: 6.11.44
46	2.1.44	Long Range Board Plotting	Amended: 6.11.44
47	4.2.44	Main Table Plotting Procedure	Amended: 6.11.44 and 7.12.44
48	29.2.44	Main Telling Procedure	
49	20.3.44	Heights reported by ROC Posts	
50	20.3.44	Testing of Unidirectional Circuits	
51	22.4.44	Detection and Reporting of Hostile Pilotless Aircraft. (Code Word "Diver")	First instruction re: V.1. Amended: 10.7.44 and 26.1.45
52	17.5.44	States of Preparedness	Minimum standards at Posts and Centres
53	3.6.44	Priority Call "Low Raid Urgent"	Hostile aircraft at less than 1,000ft
54	5.6.44	Liaison with GCI Stations	
55	14.6.44	Reporting of Shipping (Code Word "Stick")	ROC reporting limited to ship reports ordered by Centre and those in distress
56	28.12.44	"Augmented Granite"	Use of mountain warning beacon transmitters at selected Posts
57	19.3.45	Intruder warning to Bomber Groups (Code Word "Bugs")	
58	29.3.45	Counter Measures against enemy intruder aircraft	Gun Operations Rooms linked to ROC Centres
59	5.5.45	Stand-Down of the Royal Observer Corps	

Appendix 3

Aircraft Recognition List for RAF and Fleet Air Arm, Late 1941

Anson
Albacore
Airspeed T.4/39 (Exp. 112)
Airspeed S. 23/37. (Exp. 117)
Audax
Battle
Battle (Trainer)
Beaufighter I
Blenheim I and IV
Beaufort
Botha
Buffalo
Boston
Barracuda I (Exp. 100)
Boulton & Paul ½ scale model of F.1/37 (Exp. 127)
Beaufighter II (Exp. 129)
Blenheim V (High Altitude) (Exp. 131)
Blenheim V (Direct Support) (Exp. 132)
Catalina
Dominie (DH. 89)
Dragon (DH. 84)
Dragonfly (DH. 90)
Defiant
Envoy III
Express Air Liner (DH. 86B)
Electra (Lockheed 10A)
Falcon
Fulmar
Flamingo (DH. 95)
Folland 43/37 (Exp. 103) Sabre Engine
Folland 43/37 (Exp. 123) Hercules Engine
Fokker Four Engined. F22 & F26
Gladiator
General Aircraft S.23/37 (Exp. 107)
Gloster F. 9/37 (Exp. 108) Taurus Engine
General Aircraft T.47 (Exp. 109)
General Aircraft Glider 10/40 (Exp. 113)
Gloster F.9/37 (Exp. 114) 2 Peregrine Engines
General Aircraft Glider 10/40 (Revised Edition) Exp. 125
Gauntlet
Harvard

Hector
Henley III
Hurricane I and II
Hereford
Halifax
Hampden
Hudson
Havoc I
Hornet Moth (DH. 87B)
Hind
Hillson Bi-Mono (Exp. 133)
Harrow
Hart
Lysander Mark II and III
Leopard Moth DH. 85
Lerwick
London
Lysander Special (Exp. 110)
Lancaster (Exp. 124)
Liberator
Mentor
Magister
Moth-Minor (DH)
Moth (DH.60)
Manchester
Martlet
Mohawk
Maryland
Master
Master II (Exp. 105)
Mosquito (Exp. 111)
Martin Baker F.18/39 (Exp. 120)
Master III (Exp. 122)
Miles Monarch
Overstrand
Oxford I, II and III
Percival Proctor
Percival Q.6
Piper Cub
Puss Moth
Phillips and Powis (Exp. 118)

Attack Warning Red

Queen Bee
Rapide (DH. 89A)
Roc
Stinson (Reliant)
Swallow
Spitfire I, II and V
Spartan Cruiser
Short Scion
Stirling
Stranraer
Sunderland
Shark
Seal
Skua
Swordfish
Seafox
Spitfire III (Exp. 101)
Sea Otter (Exp. 106)

Saunders Roe R.5./39 (Exp. 126)
Tomahawk I
Taylorcraft
Tiger Moth
Tutor
Tornado I (Exp. 102)
Typhoon I (Exp. 121)
Vega Gull
Vickers B.1/35 (Exp. 104)
Wallace II
Wellington I (C)
Whitley I, II, III & V
Walrus
Whirlwind
Whitney-Straight
Warwick II (Exp. 128)
Wellington V (Exp. 130)

Appendix 4

Distribution of National Air Raid Warning Districts Among ROC Centres 1943 to 1945

ROC CENTRE	WARNING DISTRICTS
Aberdeen	Aberdeen
No 38 Group	Elgin
	Fraserburgh
Ayr	Ayr
No 33 Group	Brodick
	Campbeltown
	Kilmarnock
	Stranraer
Bedford	Banbury
No 12 Group	Market Harborough
	Northampton
Bristol	Bath
No 23 Group	Bristol
	Dursley
	Swindon
	Salisbury
Bromley	London Central
No 19 Group	London Croydon
	London East
	London South
Bury St Edmunds	Bury St Edmunds
No 14 Group	
Cambridge	Cambridge
No 15 Group	Huntingdon
	Newmarket
	Peterborough
	Spalding
Cardiff	Aberystwyth
No 25 Group	Cardiff
	Carmarthen
	Llandrindod Wells
	Merthyr Tydfil
	Milford Haven
	Newport
	Swansea
Carmarthen	Not used for NARWs
No 28/1 Group	
Caernarvon	Not used for NARWs
No 28/2 Group	
Carlisle	Carlisle

ROC CENTRE	WARNING DISTRICTS
No 32 Group	Dumfries
	Keswick
	Penrith
Colchester	Chelmsford
No 18 Group	Colchester
	Ipswich
Coventry	Birmingham
No 5 Group	Coventry
	Leamington
	Leicester
Derby	Burton-on-Trent
No 6 Group	Derby
	Macclesfield
	Stoke-on-Trent
	Montrose
Dundee	Dundee
No 37 Group	
Dunfermline	Dunfermline
No 36 Group	Perth
Durham	Bishop Auckland
No 30 Group	Hexham
	Morpeth
	Newcastle
Exeter	Barnstaple
No 21 Group	Exeter
	Okehampton
	Plymouth
	Torquay
Galashiels	Berwick
No 31 Group	Edinburgh
	Galashiels
Glasgow	Glasgow
No 34 Group	Greenock
	Lanark
	Lochgilphead
	Oban
Gloucester	Cheltenham
No 24 Group	Evesham
	Gloucester
	Hereford
	Worcester

Attack Warning Red

Horsham No 2 Group	Brighton Guildford Horsham Worthing	*Portree* No 40 Group *Shrewsbury* No 27 Group	Not used for NARWs Shrewsbury Stafford
Inverness No 39 Group	Fort William Inverness Kyle Wick	*Truro* No 20 Group	Wellington Wolverhampton Bodmin Falmouth Scillonia
Lancaster No 29 Group	Barrow Blackburn Douglas, I.O.M. Kendal Lancaster Preston	*Watford* No 17 Group	Truro Bedford London, Bishops Stortford London, St. Albans London West Luton
Leeds No 8 Group	Bradford Keighley Leeds Sheffield Wakefield	*Winchester* No 3 Group	Aldershot Andover Portsmouth Winchester
Lincoln No 11 Group	Lincoln Louth Melton Mowbray Newark Nottingham Skegness	*Wrexham* No 26 Group	Bangor Caernarvon Chester Colwyn Bay Machynlleth Newtown Oswestry
Maidstone No 1 Group	Canterbury Folkestone Hastings Maidstone Tunbridge Wells	*Yeovil* No 22 Group	Wrexham Bournemouth Bridgwater Minehead Shepton Mallet
Manchester No 7 Group	Crewe Liverpool Manchester Rochdale Wigan	*York* No 9 Group	Taunton Weymouth Yeovil Darlington Harrogate
Norwich No 16 Group	Great Yarmouth Kings Lynn Norwich		Middlesbrough Scarborough
Oban No 35 Group	Not used for NARWs	*York* No 10 Group	Bridlington Doncaster
Oxford No 4 Group	Aylesbury Oxford Reading		Hull Scunthorpe York

Appendix 5

Correspondence on Hess flight between Major Graham Donald and Air Commodore Warrington Morris

Letter dated May 14, 1941

"Dear Air Commodore Warrington Morris,

Probably you will have read my report upon the tracking, reporting and identifying both the German plane and the pilot between 23.00 hrs. and 24.00 hrs. on Saturday night, the 10th inst., by *34 Observer Group* of the Royal Observer Corps.

As this flight of Rudolf Hess to Scotland may well prove to be a turning point in the War, I feel that the honour of being the first Group to identify the plane correctly as a Me 110, and the pilot as Rudolf Hess, should be clearly acknowledged as being to the credit of 34 Group.

I want you to regard this letter as being entirely personal and confidential to yourself, as it is merely intended to amplify the brief report which I made on Sunday the 11th, immediately after the event.

The point which I could not tactfully embody in an official report was that after I definitely identified "Captain Alfred Horn", my remarks to the assembled police and Home Guard were simply greeted with hoots of derision. I solemnly assured them that our prisoner had escaped from Germany, that his remarks indicated there was a "split" in the Nazi party, that he personally knew the Duke of Hamilton, and that he was definitely Rudolf Hess, the deputy Fuhrer of the German Reich. The amusement was terrific. George Robey never aroused more!

I finally asked the police, HG etc. to take very special care of our very special prisoner, and said that I would endeavour to pass his message to the Duke of Hamilton immediately.

I immediately went back to our Glasgow Centre. There, I am glad to say, our Duty Controller, Mr W. Paisley, and the crew, all gave credence to my report. I then telephoned Turnhouse Aerodrome, where the Duke of Hamilton is a Wing Commander. I spoke to the Duty Controller, told him the plane *was* a Me 110 (stripped), that the pilot came over meaning to surrender, that he had a message for the Duke, that he knew the Duke. I also told him that, if the name "Alfred Horn" meant nothing to the Duke, he could say on my authority that the pilot's real name was Rudolf Hess. I am afraid that the Duty Controller began to find the story funny also! I did my best to convince him I was in dead earnest and that the Duke should be notified at the earliest possible moment. Whether this was done or not, I cannot tell.

I knew only too well that if Hess was to be induced to "come clean" (in film language) and to be really helpful, it was essential to treat him especially well from the start. I fear he was treated as a very ordinary prisoner for the first twenty-four hours or so.

On Sunday, I heard unofficially from the police that the whole story was looked upon as balderdash. My OGO (Lieutenant Colonel Kennedy) and our DAC (Air Commodore Gordon) were both inaccessible over in the Isle of Arran and I was seriously considering telegraphing Mr Churchill about the whole show. On Monday, however, I managed to contact the DAC and the OGO and showed them my written report which has been forwarded to you.

The whole thing is now, of course, history.

I do feel, however, that the Air Council, or our grand Prime Minister, should be informed that *one efficient Unit* of Britain's defence at least was aware that a Messerschmitt 110 was over Scotland (all other reports said a Dornier 215), reported to police and Home Guard where it crashed, and also reported that the pilot was Rudolf Hess. That one efficient unit, I am proud to say, *34 Observer Group of the Royal Observer Corps.*

An Observer's primary duty is to be observant, and to be good at "identification". The Rudolf Hess show seems to come under the head "identification" I think!!

Please believe I am not anxious for my own name to come into this. The work was *team* work between Posts, Centre and AOGO and a pat on the back for 34 Group would buck up the esprit de corps greatly.

I hope I have not done anything unduly unorthodox in writing you personally like this. I merely wish to amplify my official report a bit. In any case, please regard this rather diffuse "amplification" as being confidential to yourself.

I would not like to cause any offence, if my writing direct to you should not be correct procedure.

One other point. There was one young Officer present in the HG Headquarters who actually backed up my recognition of Hess as being reasonable. His name is

    Pilot Officer F. I. Malcolm, RAF
    Army Co Op Squadron
    Western Zoyland
    Somerset.

If consulted, he will undoubtedly bear out my account of the events.

I think it would be very gratifying to the ROC as a whole to be so closely connected with such a historic event.

    Yours faithfully,
    Graham Donald
    Major
    AOGO 34 Obs Group."

Warrington Morris replied on May 18, 1941, :

"RUDOLF HESS. Flight on May 10, 1941 Raid 42.J.

Thank you for your very interesting letter regarding the above. I congratulate you on being able to suggest to some of the Posts that the aircraft might be a Me 110 due to its high speed, and your subsequent 'recognition' of the pilot. It is of course quite understandable that, at first, such recognition should be received with incredulity and that it required a great deal of perseverance on your part to persuade anyone to accept it as a possibility and to report the matter to higher authority.

I now have sufficient information to be able to write an official report. The aircraft was first recognised as a Me 110 when seen by a Post in Northumberland, and again by two Posts in No 31 Group, but both the Fighter Group and Sector insisted that it must be a DO 215.

I have nothing to indicate that any Post in No 34 Group gave a definite recognition and it was only when you suggested that the E/A might be a Me 110 that one of the H Posts thought this likely.

There is only one point which Air Intelligence have spoken to me about, i.e. it appears from your report that after Hess had informed you that he had landed deliberately, you dug up enough German to get a bit more out of him.

As you are probably aware there is a special organisation of officers to interrogate prisoners as soon as possible after capture and they are anxious that no one else should do so before their arrival as it tends to make the prisoner more careful in what he says.

I do not consider that it applies in this case, as Hess came here deliberately and presumably with the intention of talking, and I consider that you showed great initiative in your action at the Centre and subsequently. You must indeed be pleased at having been a "Principal" in such an epoch making event.

    Yours sincerely,

    A. P. Warrington Morris"

Appendix 6
ROC Camp Venues

1948	Thorney Island	1955	Stradishall	1962	Horsham St Faith	1969	Watton
1949	Thorney Island	1956	Wattisham	1963	West Raynham	1970	Watton
1950	Waterbeach	1957	Tangmere	1964	Newton	1971	West Raynham
1951	Waterbeach	1958	West Malling	1965	Weeton	1972	Brawdy
1952	Waterbeach	1959	West Malling	1966	—	1973	Lindholme
1953	Waterbeach	1960	Binbrook	1967	Coningsby	1974	Lindholme
1954	Waterbeach	1961	Binbrook	1968	Honington	1975	Colerne

Appendix 7
Royal Observer Corps Ranks 1975

Observer Commodore
Commandant ROC*

Observer Captain
Deputy Commandant
Assistant Commandant ROC
Area Commandant

Observer Commander
Senior Administration Officer HQ ROC
Senior Operations Officer HQ ROC
Deputy Area Commander
Group Commandant

Observer Lieutenant Commander
Operations 1 HQ ROC

Operations 2 HQ ROC
Personnel Services Officer HQ ROC
Supply Officer HQ ROC
Area Staff Officer
Deputy Group Commandant

Observer Lieutenant
Operations 1A HQ ROC
Administration Officer HQ ROC
Group Staff Officer

Observer Lieutenant
(*Honorary Rank on promotion from
Observer Officer*)
Duty Officer
Group Officer
NRC Officer
ROC Sector Officer

Observer Officer
Duty Officer

Group Officer
NRC Officer
ROC Sector Officer

Chief Observer
Assistant Duty Officer
Assistant Sector Officer
Communications Supervisor
Tape Centre Supervisor
Triangulation Supervisor
Head Observer (Post or NRC)

Leading Observer
Post Controller
Instructor (Post or NRC)

Observer
Basic Rank for Post, Operations Roon
and NRC Personnel

*Normally Commandant ROC is serving RAF officer of Air Commodore rank

Appendix 8
ROC Group Headquarters in Town and Cities

ABERDEEN
Formed in 1939 as No 38 Group
Redesignated No 29 Group 1953
Locations
Old Infirmary Building, Woolmanhill, Aberdeen
   1939 to 1961
Quarry Road, Northfield, Aberdeen   1961 to *In use*
Protected Accommodation opened May 15, 1961
Emergency Centre, Rosemount Church Hall
Controller
G. A. Williamson
Observer Group Officer
Colonel J. Simpson
Group Commandants
Observer Commander R. S. Pattison   1943 to 1945
Observer Commander Sir G. A. Williamson   1947 to
   1950
Observer Commander J. Farquharson   1950 to 1955
Observer Commander J. Archibald   1955 to 1962
Observer Commander J. MacDonald MBE, MA
   1963 to 1968
Observer Commander A. MacKenzie   1968 to *Serving*
Stand-Down Caretaker
Observer Lieutenant R. Leith

ABERDEEN
Formed 1940 as No 33 Group
Redesignated No 25 Group, 1953
Locations
Nile Court, Ayr   1940 to 1943
Masonic Hall, Ayr   1943 to 1945
Nile Court, Ayr   1947 to 1951
Bellrock Avenue, Prestwick   1951 to 1962
Monkswell House, 17 Waterloo Road, Prestwick
   1962 to *In use*
Protected Accommodation opened 1962
Emergency Centre, Academy Hall, Ayr
Controller
Alex McHarg
Observer Group Officer
Sir James Reid Kay

Group Commandants
Observer Commander J. Kennedy   1943 to 1945
Observer Commander R. Broom   1947 to 1956
Observer Commander J. Whitesides   1956 to 1974
Observer Commander J. F. Graham   1974 to *Serving*
Stand-Down Caretaker
Observer Lieutenant H. McCall
Notes
Group non-operational from 1947 to 1951. Centre
personnel continued synthetic training at Nile Court
and travelled to Edinburgh for exercise participation
throughout the period. Full Group status resumed with
the move to Bellrock Avenue, Prestwick.

BEDFORD
Formed 1935 as No 12 Group
Redesignated No 7 Group 1953
Locations
GPO Telephone Exchange, Bedford   1935 to 1943
Days Lane, Biddenham, Bedford   1943 to *In use*
Protected Accommodation opened 1962
Emergency Centre, Montrose Hall, Harper Street,
   Bedford
Controller
B. G. L. Perryman
Observer Group Officer
Major A. M. Dawes
Group Commandants
Observer Commander L. C. H. Fuller MBE   1943 to
   1945
Observer Commander H. A. N. Tebbs MBE   1947 to
   1965
Observer Commander J. Chilton   1965 to 1968
Observer Commander W. J. Gooden FRSH   1968 to
   Serving
Stand-Down Caretaker
Observer Lieutenant J. Grimmer MBE

BELFAST
Formed 1953 as No 31 Group

Locations

Houston Park, Orangefield, Castlereagh, Belfast   1953
  to 1963

Knox Road, Lisburn, Co. Antrim, (Protected
  Accommodation   1963 to *In use*

Group Commandants

Observer Commander R. J. C. Broadhurst   1953 to 1956

Observer Commander A. O. B. Trail OBE, DL, JP
  1956 to 1962

Observer Commander G. C. Hutchinson   1962 to 1965

Observer Commander J. J. Barnes MBE   1965 to
  Serving

BRISTOL

Formed 1937 as No 23 Group

Redesignated No 12 Group 1953

Locations

Little King Street, Bristol (rear of Library)   1937 to 1943

Worcester Terrace, Bristol   1943 to 1945

Kings Square Avenue, Bristol   1947 to 1958

Lansdown, Bath   1958 to *In use*

Protected Accommodation opened August 22, 1959

Emergency Centre, Kings Square Avenue, Bristol

Group Commandants

Observer Commander F. C. Lockyer   1943 to 1945

Observer Commander C. H. Davey MBE   1953 to 1970

Observer Commander R. G. Pitt   1970 to *Serving*

Stand-Down Caretaker

Observer Lieutenant H. F. Tarring

BROMLEY/BECKENHAM

Formed 1938 as No 19 Group (embracing territory
south and east of London, previously observed by TA
Searchlight Units)

Redesignated No 1 Group, 1953

Locations

Church House, Bromley   1938 to 1945

Dura Den, Park Place, Beckenham   1945 to 1960

Controller

Major B. Binyon OBE

Observer Group Officer

Colonel A. Fitzgerald OBE

Group Commandants

Observer Commander B. Binyon OBE   1943 to 1947

Observer Commander J. N. Thompson MBE   1948 to
  1956

Observer Commander T. Birch   1956 to 1958

Observer Commander J. N. Thompson MBE   1958 to
  1960

Stand-Down Caretaker

Observer Lieutenant E. W. Carvosso

Notes

In reorganisation of 1953 Group absorbed territory
formerly attached to Maidstone and was redesignated

No 1 Group. Maidstone HQ was retained as a
Secondary Training Centre. In 1959 the situation was
reversed and the headquarters of the Group returned to
Maidstone. The premises at Dura Den, Beckenham were
retained as a Secondary Training Centre until 1968.

BURY ST EDMUNDS

Formed 1939 as No 14 Group (embracing Posts formerly
attached to Cambridge, Colchester and Norwich Groups)

Location

The Guildhall, Bury St Edmunds

Controller

Captain F. T. Bright MBE, DFC

Group Commandants

Observer Commander F. T. Bright MBE, DFC   1943 to
  1950

Observer Commander C. D. Bright MBE   1950 to 1953

Stand-Down Caretaker

Observer Lieutenant F. Mitchell MBE

Note In re-organisation of 1953 Group disbanded. Posts
transferred to Bedford, Colchester and Norwich Groups.
Guildhall premises retained as a Secondary Training
Centre, attached to No 6 Group Norwich. Training
Centre closed in 1968.

CAERNARVON

Formed 1940 as No 28/2 Group

Redesignated No 17 Group under reorganisation of 1953

Closed 1962 on transfer of control to Wrexham.

Premises retained as Training Centre until September
  1966

Locations

Telephone Exchange, Caernarvon 1940 to 1942

Caernarvon Castle   1942 to 1945

Northgate Street, Caernarvon   1947 to 1966

Emergency Centre, Telephone Exchange, Caernarvon

Controller

C. C. Valence Esq

Observer Group Officer

Captain J. W. Saunders

Headquarters, 31 Bangor Street, Caernarvon

Group Commandants

Observer Commander E. H. Davies   1943 to 1944

Observer Commander W. R. Snell MBE   1944 to 1945

Observer Commander W. H. E. Matthews   1947 to
  1962

Stand-Down Caretaker

Observer Lieutenant A. F. Green

CAMBRIDGE

Formed 1935 as No 15 Group

Locations

GPO Cambridge   1935 to 1943

Meadowfields, Newmarket Road, Cambridge   1943 to 1953

Emergency Centre, University Arms Hotel, Regent Street, Cambridge
Controller
Observer Group Officer
Major E. F. Grant-Dalton
Group Commandants
Observer Commander T. E. Grayson   1943 to 1945
Observer Commander H. G. Newman   1947 to 1953
Note
In re-organisation of 1953, Group was disbanded. Posts transferred to Bedford and Lincoln Groups.
Headquarters premises retained as Secondary Training Centre attached to No 7 Group, Bedford, until 1965.

CARDIFF
Formed 1938 as No 25 Group
Locations
GPO, Westgate Street, Cardiff   1938 to 1940
Insole Court, Llandaff, Cardiff   1940 to 1943
Ely Rise, Llandaff, Cardiff   1943 to 1946
RAF Caerau, Ely, Cardiff   1946 to 1953
Controller
G. L. Hannah
Observer Group Officer
G. P. Thomas
Group Commandants
Observer Commander G. L. Hannah   1943 to 1948
Observer Commander L. E. W. Williams   1948 to 1953
Stand-Down Caretaker
Observer Lieutenant C. D. Noel
Note
In re-organisation of 1953, Group disbanded. Posts attached to No 12 Group Bristol, or to No 13 Group, Carmarthen. HQ premises at RAF Caerau retained as Secondary Training Centre, attached to No 12 Group Bristol, until 1968.

CARLISLE
Formed December 1939 as No 32 Group
Redesignated No 22 Group under re-organisation of 1953
Closed March 1954 – Territories dispersed to Ayr, Durham and Lancaster Groups
Reformed January 1962 as No 22 Group following closure of Lancaster Group HQ and the transfer of title, 21 Group HQ to Preston
Locations
Huntingdons Funeral Company's underground stables, West Walls, Carlisle   1939 to 1941
10 Norfolk Road, Carlisle   1941 to 1954
No 14 MU RAF Carlisle   1962 to *In use*
Protected Accommodation opened 1962
Controller
Colonel F. R. W. Graham

Observer Group Officer
Brigadier Pringle – Headquarters, Bank Street, Carlisle
Group Commandants
Observer Commander F. R. W. Graham   1943 to 1944
Observer Commander C. J. Rowlands MBE   1944 to 1945
Observer Commander Potter   1947
Observer Commander R. Ritson   1947 to 1953
Observer Commander R. J. F. A. Lawder   1953 to 1954
Observer Commander K. Maynard   1962 to *Serving*
Stand-Down Caretaker
Observer Lieutenant C. J. Rowlands MBE

CARMARTHEN
Formed 1940 as No 28/1 Group
Redesignated No 13 Group October 1953
Locations
Lyric Cinema Basement, King Street, Carmarthen   1940 to 1949
Parade Road, Picton Terrace, Carmarthen   1949 to *In use*
Protected Accommodation December 1961
Controller
Captain Davies
Observer Group Officer
Lieutenant Colonel Hammersley DSO
Group Commandants
Observer Commander J. P. Pickford OBE, DepLL   1943 to 1945
Observer Commander J. Thompson   1945 to *Stand-Down*
Observer Commander J. P. Pickford OBE, DepLL   1947 to 1969
Observer Commander L. Watkins OBE   1969 to 1974
Stand-Down Caretaker
Observer Lieutenant W. S. Jackson
Note
Group absorbed western part of No 25 Group, Cardiff, on latter's closure under 1953 re-organisation.

COLCHESTER
Formed 1926 as No 18 Group
Redesignated No 4 Group, 1953
Locations
Top Floor of Post Office, High St, Colchester   1926 to 1927
Corn Exchange, High St, Colchester   1927 to 1931
GPO Exchange (penthouse), Colchester   1931 to 1943
Errington Lodge, Lexden Rd, Colchester   1943 to *In use*
Protected Accommodation opened March 4, 1961
Emergency Centre, Colchester Library, Culver St, Colchester. If bombed out, lines rerouted to Cambridge
Controllers
Lieutenant Colonel –. Nicholls   1926 to 1928

Lieutenant Colonel H. W. Herring MC   1928 to 1943
Observer Group Officer
Major J. Sandeford
Group Commandants
Observer Commander D. Miller MBE   1943 to 1945
Observer Commander J. R. Nixon MBE   1945 to 1961
Observer Commander E. G. J. W. Kent MBE   1961 to
    Serving
Stand-Down Caretaker
Observer Lieutenant J. R. Nixon MBE

COVENTRY/RUGBY
Formed 1938 as No 5 Group
Redesignated No 8 Group, 1953
Locations
GPO, Hertford Street, Coventry   1938 to 1941
Broadwater, Earlsdon Avenue, Coventry   1941 to 1963
Lawford Heath, Rugby   1963 to *In use*
Protected Accommodation opened November 2, 1963
Controller H. Garlick
Observer Group Officer
Commander Graveney RN (Ret)   1938 to 1939
C. A. Lakin   1940 to 1943
Group Commandants
Observer Commander C. A. Lakin MBE   1943 to 1959
Observer Commander S. Wooley MBE   1960 to 1968
Observer Commander J. W. Chilton   1968 to 1970
Observer Commander B. Morris   1970 to *Serving*
Stand-Down Caretaker
Observer Lieutenant R. S. Palmer

DERBY
Formed 1937 as No 6 Group
Redesignated No 15 Group 1953
Locations
GPO Telephone Exchange, Derby   1937 to 1942
Highfields, The Broadway, Derby   1942 to 1961
Emergency Centre, Congregational Church Hall,
    Victoria Street, Derby
Observer Group Officer
W. B. M. Fielden MC
Group Commandants
Observer Commander W. B. M. Fielden MC   1943 to
    1945
Observer Commander H. G. Newman   1945 to 1950
Observer Commander F. Rodgers MBE   1950 to 1961
Stand-Down Caretaker
Observer Lieutenant F. Farnsworth
Notes
In 1953 re-organisation Group absorbed practically whole
territory that had hitherto formed No 11 Group,
Lincoln. Lincoln Group was disbanded but HQ premises,
at RAF Waddington, retained as a Secondary Training
Centre attached to Derby. In 1961, Protected

Accommodation for the Group opened at Fiskerton near
Lincoln. Group HQ transferred to Fiskerton and
premises at The Broadway, Derby, retained as a
Secondary Training Centre until 1968.

DUNDEE
Formed 1939 as No 37 Group
Redesignated No 28 Group, 1953
Locations
St Cuthberts Hall, Dundee   1939 to 1942
Craigiebarns, Dundee   1942 to *In use*
Emergency Centre – East Hall, St Andrews Church,
    King St, Dundee
Protected Accommodation opened April 29, 1961
Controller
R. R. Overstone
Observer Group Officer
N. J. H. Goodchild
Group Commandants
Observer Commander N. J. H. Goodchild   1943 to
    1947
Observer Commander J. R. L. Halley   1947 to 1958
Observer Commander A. J. S. Stewart DFC, MA
    1959 to 1969
Observer Commander A. D. Douglas   1969 to *Serving*
Stand-Down Caretaker
Observer Lieutenant N. J. H. Goodchild
Note
Group absorbed the territory of former No 36 Group,
Dunfermline in re-organisation of 1953.

DUNFERMLINE
Formed 1938 as No 36 Group
Locations
Ministry of Labour Building, Dunfermline   1938 to
    1943
Victoria Works, Pilmuir Street, Dunfermline   1943 to
    1945
RAF Petreavie Castle   1947 to 1953
Emergency Centre, Squash Racquet Court, Abbey
Park House, Dunfermline
Group Commandants
Observer Commander R. C. Blackwood MC   1943 to
    1945
Observer Commander D. George   1947 to 1953
Stand-Down Caretaker
Observer Lieutenant D. George
Notes
Group disbanded in re-organisation of 1953. Majority of
Posts then attached to Dundee to form No 28 Group.
Pitreavie Castle retained as Secondary Training Centre
until 1968.

DURHAM

Formed 1937 as No 30 Group
Redesignated No 23 Group, 1953
Locations
GPO, Providence Row, Durham   1937 to 1951
The Sands, Durham   1951 to *In use*
Emergency Centre, Durham Castle
Protected Accommodation opened June 1961
Controller
E. G. Jones, MBE, MA
Observer Group Officer
Lieutenant Colonel F. H. Charlton, DSO
Group Commandants
Observer Commander F. H. Charlton DSO   1943 to 1945
Observer Commander R. V. Dickenson   1947 to 1948
Observer Commander R. L. Hay   1948 to 1953
Observer Commander T. W. Dobson MBE   1953 to 1973
Observer Commander K. Whitfield   1973 to *Serving*
Stand-Down Caretaker
Observer Lieutenant E. G. Jones MBE MA
Notes
Emergency Centre used operationally for a few months during 1943, while structural alterations to permit the mounting of a Long Range Board were undertaken at the Providence Row premises. In 1953 re-organisation Group absorbed some of the Posts from former Galashiels Group.

EDINBURGH

Formed 1947 with the transfer of No 31 Group
  Headquarters from former location at Galashiels
Redesignated No 24 Group, 1953
Locations
14 Carleton Terrace, Edinburgh   1947 to 1962
RAF Turnhouse, Edinburgh   1962 to *In use*
Protected Accommodation opened October 1964
Group Commandants
Observer Commander R. C. Blackwood MC   1947 to 1949
Observer Commander I. R. Smith   1949 to 1954
Observer Commander G. B. Scott   1954 to 1965
Observer Commander J. W. R. White   1965 to 1973
Observer Commander W. M. Holmes MBE   1973 to *Serving*
Stand-Down Caretaker
Observer Lieutenant T. L. W. Stallibrass

EXETER

Formed 1940 as No 21 Group
Redesignated No 10 Group, 1953
Locations
"Speranza" (over GPO), High Street, Exeter   1940 to 1942

"Barnfield", Southernhay East, Exeter   1942 to 1945
GCI Station, RAF Exminster   1947 (*few months*)
Ex-RAF Sector Ops. Room, Poltimore Park, Exeter
  1947 to 1961
Protected Accommodation, Poltimore Park, Exeter
  1961 to *In use*
Emergency Centre, The Quay, Exeter (1942/43 only)
Observer Group Officer
J. Griffiths-Morgan, Barrister at Law
Group Commandants
Observer Commander L. P. R. L. Cooke   1943 to 1945
Observer Commander W. R. Snell MBE   1947 to 1954
Observer Commander R. H. G. Neville OBE, MC
  1954 to 1957
Observer Commander F. C. Sturgiss OBE   1958 to 1971
Observer Commander K. G. Tyers BSc   1971 to *Serving*
Stand-Down Caretaker
Observer Lieutenant W. R. Snell MBE
Notes
During enemy raid on Exeter, May 3/4, 1942, former Centre at Speranza destroyed. Emergency Centre used operationally for nine months in 1942/43 while structural alterations to facilitate the installation of a Long Range Board in progress at Barnfield. Appointment of Group Commandant remained vacant from April 1957 to April 1958. The DGC Observer Lieutenant D. W. Egginton administered Group during this period.

GALASHIELS

Formed 1938 as No 31 Group
Closed, 1946 on transfer of Group Headquarters to
  Edinburgh
Location
Corn Exchange, Walker Street, Galashiels   1938 to 1945
Emergency Centre, Town Hall, Galashiels
Controller
T. Lees Esq
Observer Group Officer
Major R. C. Blackwood MC
Group Commandant
Observer Commander J. R. Dickenson   1943 to 1945
Stand-Down Caretaker
Observer Lieutenant T. L. W. Stallibrass

GLASGOW

Formed 1939 as No 34 Group
Redesignated No 26 Group, 1953
Closed 1962.
Locations
New Temperance House, Pitt Street, Glasgow   1939 to
  1949
RAF Bishopbriggs, Glasgow   1949 to 1962
Emergency Centre – 89 Wellington Street, Glasgow

Controller
Major R. B. Wharrie MC
Observer Group Officer
Sir Windham E. F. Carmichael-Anstruther Bart DSO, DL, JP
Group Commandants
Observer Commander Sir Windham E. F. Carmichael-Anstruther Bart DSO, DL, JP   1943 to 1944
Observer Commander J. Hartley   1944 to 1950
Observer Commander E. J. B. Irving   1950 to 1962
Stand-Down Caretakers
Observer Lieutenant R. C. Harrod   1945 to 1946
Observer Lieutenant Ian Murray   1946 to 1947
Note
Group disbanded 1962. Some of its territory absorbed by No 25 Group, Ayr, remainder by No 27 Group, Oban.

GLOUCESTER
Formed 1937 as No 24 Group
Closed 1953
Locations
GPO Exchange, George Street, Gloucester   1937 to 1942
Northgate Mansions, Gloucester   1942 to 1953
Emergency Centre, Shire Hall (Basement), Gloucester
Controller
P. Hough Esq
Observer Group Officer
Flight Lieutenant B. E. Barwell
Group Commandant
Observer Commander C. H. Davey MBE   1943 to 1953
Stand-Down Caretaker
Observer Lieutenant P. Hough
Note
Group disbanded in re-organisation of 1953. Major part absorbed into Bristol Group.

HORSHAM
Formed 1925 as No 2 Group
Locations
Attic of GPO, The Carfax, Horsham   1925 to 1929
"The Lindens", 11 North Street, Horsham (Centre at TA Rifle Range)   1929 to 1938
TA Drill Hall, Denne Road, Horsham   1938 to *In use*
Protected Accommodation opened April 1962
Controller
H. T. Knott MBE
Observer Group Officer
Lieutenant Colonel W. G. Moore OBE
Group Commandants
Observer Commander W. G. Moore OBE   1943 to 1945
Observer Commander M. H. W. Smithers   1945 to 1955
Observer Commander J. N. Thompson MBE   1955 to 1959

Observer Commander T. W. Birch   1959 to 1964
Observer Commander W. S. Gardiner CB, OBE, DFC, AFC   1964 to 1969
Observer Captain W. Rusby OBE   1969 to 1974
Observer Commander J. D. Ballington   1974 to *Serving*
Stand-Down Caretaker
Observer Lieutenant R. J. Phelps
Notes
Emergency Centre set up in The Masonic Hall, Denne Road, Horsham, in late 1942 and used operationally whilst premises capable of accommodating a Long Range Board prepared at The Drill Hall.

INVERNESS
Formed 1939 as No 39 Group
Redesignated No 30 Group in 1953
Locations
Caledonian Hotel (Annex), Inverness   1939 to 1945
"Raigmore". Inverness   1947 to *In use*
Protected Accommodation opened December 13, 1961
Observer Group Officer
J. O. A. Fraser-MacKenzie Esq
Group Commandants
Observer Commander J. O. A. Fraser-MacKenzie MBE   1943 to 1945
Observer Commander E. E. Fresson OBE   1954 to 1956
Observer Commander C. E. Cagienard   1956 to 1970
Observer Commander D. S. Bell DFC, AFC   1970 to *Serving*
Stand-Down Caretaker
Observer Lieutenant J. W. Barnett

LANCASTER
Formed June 1939 as No 29 Group
Redesignated No 21 Group, 1953
Locations
Lancaster Castle   1939 to 1942
Bank Chambers, Church Street, Lancaster   1942 to 1945
Lancaster Castle   1947 to 1956
Willow Lane, Lancaster   1956 to 1961
Emergency Centre, Timms Cafe, Church Street, Lancaster
Controller
H. Cross Esq
Observer Group Officer
Lieutenant Colonel L. I. Cowper OBE, DL
Group Commandants
Observer Commander L. I. Cowper OBE, DL   1943 to 1948
Observer Commander W. Wolfendale MC   1948 to 1949
Observer Commander E. B. Riley   1949 to 1961
Stand-Down Caretaker
Observer Lieutenant I. R. Smith

Note

The Group disbanded December 31, 1961. Territory combined with northern part of former Manchester Group to form No 21 Group, Preston. Premises at Willow Lane, Lancaster, retained as a Secondary Training Centre until 1967.

LEEDS

Formed 1938 as No 8 Group
Redesignated No 18 Group, 1953
Closed October 1968
Locations
Vicar Lane, Leeds   1938 to 1939
GPO Leeds   1939 to 1942
Grove House, Grosvenor Road, Leeds   1942 to 1964
Harrogate Road, Yeadon   1964 to 1968
Protected Accommodation, April 11, 1964
Observer Group Officer
Captain H. Jowett MBE
Group Commandants
Observer Commander H. Jowett MBE   1943 to 1945
Observer Commander J. Freeman   1947 to 1954
Observer Commander Kitching   1954 to 1956
Observer Commander A. Pegler   1956 to 1961
Observer Commander K. Terry   1961 to 1963
Observer Commander W. Beaumont   1963 to 1968
Stand-Down Caretaker
Observer Lieutenant J. L. Waugh MBE
Notes
Group absorbed large part of territory of former No 10 Group, York, and restyled No 18 Group. When Group disbanded, 1968, greater part transferred back to No 20 Group, York.

LINCOLN

Formed 1935 as No 11 Group
Redesignated No 15 Group, 1953
Locations
GPO Exchange (Upper Floor), Lincoln   1935 to 1938
St Peters-at-Arches, Lincoln   1938 to 1942
St Martins Hall, Lincoln   1943 to 1947
RAF Waddington, Lincoln   1947 to 1960
Fiskerton, Lincoln   1960 to *In use*
Protected Accommodation opened, December 10, 1960
Controller
Captain C. H. Drummond
Observer Group Officer
Captain H. Denham-Smith
Group Commandants
Observer Commander C. G. Cooke OBE   1943 to 1944
Observer Commander R. R. Poole   1944 to 1945
Observer Commander E. Fitch   1947 to 1948
Observer Commander G. A. Vetch MBE, TD   1948 to 1953

Observer Commander F. Rodgers MBE   1961 to 1966
Observer Commander R. H. Johnson   1966 to *Serving*
Stand-Down Caretaker
Observer Lieutenant R. R. Poole
Notes
In re-organisation of 1953 Group territory merged with that of former No 6 Group, Derby, to form No 15 Group, Derby. Premises at Waddington retained as Secondary Training Centre. Group Headquarters returned to Fiskerton in 1960.

MAIDSTONE

Formed 1925 as No 1 Group
Locations
GPO (Outbuildings), Maidstone   1925 to 1929
Corn Exchange Buildings, Maidstone   1929 to 1942
"Fairlawns", (Basement), London Road, Maidstone   1942 to *In use*
Protected Accommodation opened June 25, 1960
Emergency Centre, Telephone Exchange
Controller
J. H. Day MBE
Observer Group Officer
Colonel Bamford
Group Commandants
Observer Commander Cunliffe-Fraser   1943 to 1944
Observer Commander C. G. Cooke OBE   1944 to 1945
Observer Commander D. M. Edwards   1947 to 1953
Observer Commander J. W. Foster OBE, DFC   1961 to 1965
Observer Commander E. T. Green   1965 to *Serving*
Stand-Down Caretaker
Observer Lieutenant E. C. Smallwood
Notes
In 1953 re-organisation Group territory merged with that of former No 19 Group with its HQ at Beckenham. Fairlawns retained as a Secondary Training Centre. Group HQ returned to Maidstone in 1961 leaving Beckenham in secondary role.

MANCHESTER

Formed 1937 as No 7 Group
Redesignated No 19 Group, 1953
Locations
GPO, Spring Gardens, Manchester   1937 to 1942
"Danebury", Slade Lane, Levenshulme, Manchester   1942 to 1961
Controller
Major G. W. Naismith
Observer Group Officers
Lieutenant Colonel E. G. Tuite-Dalton MC   1937 to 1940
Captain A. R. C. Huntingdon   1940 to 1942

Group Commandants
Observer Commander A. R. C. Huntingdon 1943 to
    1945
Observer Commander J. B. Russell 1947 to 1961
Stand-Down Caretaker
Observer Lieutenant E. B. Michaelis
Notes
Group disbanded December 31, 1961. Territory merged
with much of former No 21 Group, Lancaster, to form
the new No 21 Group, Preston. Premises at Levenshulme
retained as Secondary Training Centre until 1970.

NORWICH
Formed 1934 as No 16 Group
Redesignated No 6 Group, 1953
Locations
GPO, Dove Street, Norwich (Basement) 1934 to 1940
GPO (New Premises), St Andrews, Norwich 1940 to
    1942
"Fairfield", Lime Tree Road, Norwich 1942 to 1947
RAF Old Catton (later renamed Chartwell Road)
    Norwich 1947 to *In use*
Protected Accommodation opened September 27, 1961
Controller
C. F. Hill
Observer Group Officers
Colonel Kerrison 1934 to 1937
Colonel Jacob 1937 to 1939
C. G. Cooke 1939 to 1942
Group Commandants
Observer Commander C. F. Hill MBE 1943 to 1945
Observer Commander E. C. Reeve 1945 to 1952
Observer Commander C. F. Hill MBE 1952 to 1970
Observer Commander H. J. Teague 1970 to *Serving*
Stand-Down Caretaker
Observer Lieutenant T. Flack
Notes
From 1942 onwards St Andrews premises retained as
Emergency Accommodation and used operationally in
late 1942 after Main Cable to "Fairfield" had been
damaged by enemy action. They were again used in
1943 while structural alterations to accommodate a
Long Range Board were carried out at "Fairfield".

OBAN
Formed 1940 as No 35 Group
Redesignated No 27 Group, 1953
Closed 1973. Territory absorbed by No 30 Group,
Inverness. Accommodation retained as comms. centre
Locations
Telephone Exchange, Drimvargie Terrace, Oban 1940
    to 1945
Albany Street (Nissen Huts), Oban 1947 to 1962
North Connel, Argyll (ex-RAF Station) 1962 to 1973

Protected Accommodation opened May 26, 1962
Controller
C. A. MacAllister
Observer Group Officer
Major J. C. Struthers DSC
Group Commandants
Observer Commander J. C. Struthers DSC 1943 to
    1944
Observer Commander D. A. J. Boyle 1944 to 1945
Observer Commander W. A. Nimmo 1947 to 1959
Observer Commander V. W. Huntington 1959 to 197
Stand-Down Caretaker
Observer Lieutenant Wilson

OXFORD
Formed 1935 as No 4 Group
Redesignated No 3 Group, 1953
Protected Accommodation opened May 15, 1965
Locations
GPO Oxford 1935 to 1941
New Bodleian Library, Oxford 1941 to 1945
Drill Hall, North Way, Oxford 1947 to 1949
Woodstock Road, Wolvercote, Oxford 1949 to 1965
Cowley Barracks, Oxford 1965 to *In use*
Controllers
H. Bennet 1935 to 1939
R. J. Hickmott 1939 to 1943
Observer Group Officers
Brigadier L. P. Collins CB, CSI, DSO, OBE 1935 to
    1942
Captain F. Gardiner MBE, MC, JP 1942 to 1943
Group Commandants
Observer Commander F. Gardiner MBE, MC, JP
    1943 to 1953
Observer Commander R. L. Crofton MBE, AFC, BSc
    1953 to 1959
Observer Commander D. N. James 1959 to *Serving*
Stand-Down Caretaker
Observer Lieutenant T. Dixon

PORTREE, Isle of Skye
Formed 1941 as No 40 Group
Closed 1945
Location
Skye Gathering Hall, Portree
Controller
Chief Woman Observer Flora MacDonald BEM
OGO and later Group Commandant
Observer Lieutenant D. A. Donald
Notes
The Group consisted of five Posts and a small Centre.
Posts now form part of the Inverness Group.

PRESTON

Formed January 1, 1962, as No. 21 Group, covering
territories formerly controlled by the redundant
Lancaster and Manchester Groups
Location
Longley Lane, Goosnargh, Preston (Premises converted
from former Fighter Control Operations Block)
Secondary Training Centres at the retained former
Headquarters at Willow Lane, Lancaster and
Levenshulme, Manchester, closed 1967 and 1970
respectively
Group Commandants
Observer Commander J. B. Russell   1962 to 1963
Observer Commander A. Dalton MBE   1963 to 1972
Observer Commander J. G. Brown   1972 to *Serving*

SHREWSBURY

Formed 1938 as No 27 Group
Redesignated No 16 Group, 1953
Locations
Shire Hall, (Cellars), Shrewsbury   1938 to 1943
London Road, Shrewsbury   1943 to 1962
Holywell Street, Shrewsbury   1962 to *In use*
Protected Accommodation opened January 13, 1962
Controller
C. S. Aspbury
Observer Group Officer
Major L. E. Bury CBE
Group Commandants
Observer Commander H. L. Gornal   1943 to 1955
Observer Commander H. P. Barber MBE   1955 to
  Serving
Stand-Down Caretaker
Observer Lieutenant G. C. Tyler OBE

TRURO

Formed 1940 as No 20 Group
Redesignated No 11 Group, 1953
Locations
GPO Exchange, Truro   1940 to 1942
Masonic Hall, Union Place, Truro   1942 to 1949
Fairmantle Street School, Truro   1949 to 1962
Albert Place, Daniel Street, Truro   1962 to 1973
Protected Accommodation opened May 4, 1963
Emergency Centre, Cricket Pavilion, Truro School,
St. Clements Hill, Truro
Observer Group Officer
Mr. Beasley
Group Commandants
Observer Commander N. H. Bushby MC   1943 to 1945
Observer Commander J. A. Boret CBE, MC, AFC
  1948 to 1962
Observer Commander W. V. Green   1962 to 1973

Stand-Down Caretaker
Observer Lieutenant S. Roseveare
Note
Group disbanded in 1973, its Posts being absorbed by
No 10 Group, Exeter.

WATFORD

Formed 1931 as No 17 Group
Redesignated No 5 Group, 1953
Locations
GPO Buildings, Market Street, Watford   1931 to 1943
Cassiobury Drive, Watford   1943 to 1968
Protected Accommodation opened November 18, 1961
Controller
C. R. Bolton
Group Commandants
Observer Commander H. R. Whitty   1943 to 1945
Observer Commander B. Parkes MVO   1946 to 1959
Observer Commander G. A. D. Bourne MBE   1959 to 1967
Observer Commander W. J. Gooden   1967 to 1968
Stand-Down Caretakers
Observer Lieutenant S. N. Prewitt   1946
Observer Lieutenant R. C. Harrod   1947
Notes
Group disbanded in re-organisation of 1968. Its Posts
dispersed to the Bedford, Horsham and Oxford Groups.
Premises at Cassiobury Drive retained as a Training
Centre attached to Metropolitan Area Headquarters,
Uxbridge, until 1973 and put up for public sale 1974.

WINCHESTER

Formed June 1926 as No 3 Group
Redesignated No 14 Group, 1953
Locations
Blue Triangle Club, Parchment Street, Winchester
  1926 to 1929
Telephone Exchange, Brook Street, Winchester   1929
  to 1940
Northgate House, 28 Jewry Street, Winchester   1940 to 1943
Abbotts Road, Winchester   1943 to *In use*
Protected Accommodation opened June 3, 1961
Emergency Centre, Northgate House   1943 to 1945
Controllers
Brigadier General N. W. H. Du Boulay CMG   1926 to 1933
Colonel G. N. Salmon CMG, DSO   1933 to 1943
Observer Group Officer
Major General Sir William Twiss KCIE, CB, CBE, MC
  1938 to 1943
Group Commandants
Observer Commander Sir William Twiss KCIE, CB,
  CBE, MC   1943 to 1945
Observer Commander W. Belton MBE   1947 to 1969
Observer Commander J. Bridle   1969 to 1972
Observer Commander S. G. Deedman   1972 to *Serving*

Stand-Down Caretaker
Observer Lieutenant B. L. Day

WREXHAM

Formed 1939 as No 26 Group
Closed in re-organisation of 1953 – territory merged
    with Caernarvon Group
Reopened 1962 as No 17 Group Headquarters
Locations
Telephone Exchange, Wrexham   1939 to 1942
1 Acacia Pavril, Wrexham   1942 to 1945
Tenters Square, Wrexham   1947 to 1953
Borras, Wrexham   1962 to *In use*
Protected Accommodation opened 1962
Controller
O. B. Evans
Observer Group Officer
Major F. Sutton DSO
Group Commandants
Observer Commander F. L. Gore CIE, DSO, OBE
    1943 to 1944
Observer Commander E. W. Fitch   1944 to 1945
Observer Commander D. Garfield-Davies OBE   1947
    to 1953
Observer Commander P. Kirby   1962 to 1964
Observer Commander R. E. Wilcox-Jones   1964 to
    Serving
Stand-Down Caretaker
Observer Lieutenant E. Vaughan-Jones

YEOVIL

Formed 1938 as No 22 Group
Redesignated No 9 Group, 1953
Locations
Princes Street, Yeovil   1938 to 1941
53 Southwoods, Yeovil   1941 to *In use*
Protected Accommodation opened September 30, 1961
Controller
W. R. Snell MBE
Observer Group Officer
Wing Commander D. Stewart MBE, MC, AFC
Group Commandants
Observer Commander D. Stewart MBE, MC, AFC
    1943 to 1953
Observer Commander W. R. Snell MBE   1953 to 1964
Observer Commander F. H. Shutt   1964 to 1972
Observer Commander D. J. Bridle   1972 to *Serving*
Stand-Down Caretaker
Observer Commander Stewart

YORK

Two Groups were formed in 1937, No 9 Group covering
the North Riding of Yorkshire and No 10 Group
covering the East Riding of Yorkshire and the Northern
part of Lincolnshire.

In re-organisation of 1953 northern part of No 10 Group
attached to that of No 9 Group and redesignated No 20
Group, while remaining southern part attached to
Leeds and redesignated No 18 Group, Leeds.
In re-organisation of 1968 No 18 Group disbanded. Its
territory, covering the East and West Ridings of
Yorkshire, transferred to No 20 Group, York, while that
in North Lincolnshire transferred to No 15 Group,
Lincoln. The Northern Posts of the previous 20 Group
transferred to No 23 Group, Durham.
Locations
GPO, Lendall, York (Consisted of a large wooden hut at
    rear of GPO, with a central entrance with a lobby
    common to both Groups affording entrance to each
    Centre located in larger rooms at opposite ends of the
    hut.)   1937 to 1943
Knavesmire, York (Purpose-built prefabricated buildings,
    100 yards apart on Common Land under special
    permission for the duration of the war, of the City of
    York Pasture Masters.)
    for No 10 Group   1943 to 1953
    for No 9/20 Group   1943 to 1961
Shelley House, Acomb, York   1961 to *In use*
Protected Accommodation opened December 16, 1961
Emergency Centres
No 9 Group, Yorkshire Museum, St Mary's Abbey, York
No 10 Group, The DeGrey Rooms, Blake Street, York
Controllers
No 9 Group (Honorary) Noel Terry
No 10 Group H. Goulton-Leonard
Observer Group Officers
No 9 Group Major Parrot
No 10 Group Captain J. Roseigh MBE
Group Commandants
No 9 Group
Observer Commander J. Elmhirst   1943 to 1950
Observer Commander W. L. Prest   1950 to 1953
No 10 Group
Observer Commander C. J. Ingleby DSO, DL   1943 to 1945
Observer Commander F. F. Hepworth   1947 to 1949
Observer Commander J. S. Cahill   1949 to 1953
No 20 Group
Observer Commander E. S. Turner   1953 to 1962
Observer Commander C. Burton   1962 to *Serving*
Stand-Down Caretakers
No 9 Group
Observer Lieutenant W. L. Prest
No 10 Group
Observer Lieutenant W. Rusby
Notes
No 9 Group HQ was removed following its closure in
1953. No 10 Group HQ was accepted by The Pasture
Masters in lieu of reparation in 1961 and converted into
a sports pavilion and changing rooms.

Top left *For years after the war many posts had nothing but a telephone connection in a field, just as their predecessors in the 1920s. This is a West Country post in the early 1950s, with no protection against the elements and only the basic items – instrument, telephone and binoculars. The Jeep was the property of a visiting officer*

Top right *On January 31, 1950 the Royal Observer Corps Medal was officially instituted, to be awarded on the completion of 12 years satisfactory voluntary service, or 24 years full-time*

employment. Later, clasps were awarded for each additional 12 years, together with rosettes for the ribbon

Bottom *At Headquarters Fighter Command at Bentley Priory on May 17, 1953, the AOC, Air Marshal Sir Dermot Boyle, presented the first 19 ROC medals. He is seen here presenting a medal to Observer Officer A. Clarke of 16 Group, Norwich. Behind Sir Dermot are the corps commandant, Air Commodore Vasse, and the deputy commandant, Observer Captain Cooke*

Some posts organised their own aircraft co-operation for plotting and height judging practice. Post 9/C.1, Keynsham enlists the aid of Captain Applegate in an Auster 6 in May 1954

The late 1950s, and the table at 1 Group cluttered with tracks, including six Vulcans, Valiants, Hunters, Meteors, a Thunderjet and a Sea Fury plus civil types like the Viscount and the Convair-Liner

Top left *"Rats", two low-flying Javelin fighters over 2/N.1, Farnham in Surrey*

Top right *The interior of the first underground protected post for the nuclear role as it appeared during experiments in 1959/60. The strange apparatus in the middle of the room was an oversize pair of bellows intended to give a rapid change of air in the monitoring room under operational conditions*

Bottom *From 1955 onwards the familiar post instrument disappeared and plotting was done using bearing and estimated height only. "Finger plotting" was the only way in which the corps could cope with the increasing speeds of jet aircraft.*

An underground post in the course of construction. The first picture shows the concrete walls being erected in a large hole in the ground; in the second picture the concrete roof is being prepared; in the third picture the post structure, with entrance hatch, ventilators, blast pipe and probe pipe, is virtually complete and awaiting only a generous covering of earth (7/F.1 Riseley, Beds.)

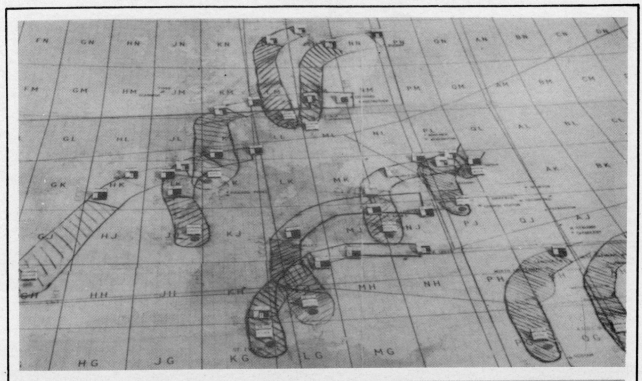

Top *A general situation map at the Air Defence Operations Centre during exercise Dutch Treat in September 1957. The fall-out plumes from a number of nuclear explosions have been marked on the map and over the ground zero of each burst is its code name*

Bottom *The old and the new. By the early 1960s the programme of underground post building had been completed. Many posts had moved to entirely new locations but some had their underground accommodation built alongside the old structure. This picture shows the Cuckfield, Sussex, post with its Orlit aircraft observation post still standing and in the foreground the underground post with instruments installed*

A protected ROC centre, custom-built for the nuclear role and capable of operating for a week under fall-out conditions. This particular building is of the "semi-sunk" variety with the main floor underground

When the new protected centres were built the map table and Long-Range Board were installed and fall-out plotting continued with counters and plaques as in the aircraft role. Later, when data transmission was introduced, the plotters moved to the balcony and the old type maps disappeared. In this photograph personnel from 1 Group are operating with the earlier system

Top left *An ROC underground post at Elstree showing a crew of three under operational conditions. The equipment on the table consists of an individual dosimeter, the charging unit for the dosimeter, the carrier receiver the teletalk unit for communication with Centre and the fixed survey meter*

Top right *The Queen presents the Corps Banner to the Banner Bearer, Observer officer J. D. Ballington, on the occasion of the Royal Review of the ROC in June 1966 to mark the 25th anniversary of the grant of the title "Royal"*

Bottom *The Queen reviews observers from every part of the Country. Behind the Queen, Air Commodore Greswell and, on the right, Observer Captain Rusby*

All the ROC Area and Group Commandants gathered together for the first time on the occasion of the Royal Review in June 1966

The vertical displays A and B used at centres to show the position of nuclear bursts and fall-out. Women observers mark the displays while a Home Office official makes an assessment at Oxford Group Centre

There are five sector controls in the United Kingdom, all attached to an ROC Group Headquarters. At this sector control national displays and the international liaison section are shown with Home Office and ROC personnel at work

Appendix 9
Royal Observer Corps Posts 1924 to 1975

TERMS AND ABBREVIATIONS USED:

C/G	Coast Guard
Darky	HF Radio for communication with aircraft lost or in distress
G.L.	Posts equipped with gun-laying radar for IFF interrogation
Granite	Posts equipped with flares for warning aircraft of the proximity of high ground
Augmented Granite	Normal Granite flares plus HF transmitter producing a high ground warning signal in an approaching aircraft
HSL	Homing searchlight for directing aircraft to nearest airfield
Money Flare	Paraffin flare for homing RAC aircraft at night
Satellite	Sub-Post, sited to observe territory not visible from parent Post; connected by extension to Post telephone circuit
Totter	Rocket flares for directing fighters on to track of enemy aircraft or V1s
U/G	Underground protected Post accommodation for the nuclear role
Watcher Post	A Post without direct telephone links. Reports made from nearby public or private telephone

In order to avoid confusion, old county names have been used. All Post locations are given in the form of six figure national grid references.

ENGLAND

BEDFORDSHIRE

Ampthill
Opened 1937 L.027378, 12/M.2; 5/F.2 1953; U/G Nov 1963; 7/G.3 Oct 1968; *In use*

Bedford
Opened 1937 L.066518, 12/R.3; resite to L.084435, 7/F.2 Nov 1953; U/G; *Closed Oct 1968*

Eaton Socon
Opened 1937 L.163595, 12/R.2; 7/R.2 Nov 1953; U/G; *Closed Oct 1968*

Newport Pagnell
Opened 1937 P.871445, 12/M.3; 7/F.1 1953; U/G; *Closed Oct 1968*

Pavenham
Opened 1937 P.973557; 7/R.3 Nov 1953; U/G March 1964; 7/F.3 Oct 1968; *In use*

Riseley
Opened 1937 L.047626, 12/R.1; 7/R.4 Nov 1953; U/G March 1964; 7/F.1 Oct 1968; *In use*

Sandy
Opened 1937 L.152495, 12/S.1; 4/E.1 Nov 1953; U/G March 1964; 7/G.1 Oct 1968; *In use*

Shefford
Opened Dec 1939 L.153381, 12/S.3; resite to L.158388 July 1960; U/G Aug 1961; *Closed Oct 1968*

Toddington
Opened 1937 L.009263, 17/L.3; 5/Q.1 Nov 1953; U/G; *Closed Oct 1968*

Turvey
Opened 1937 P.957526, 12/M.1; resite to P.973557, 7/R.3 Nov 1953; U/G; *Closed Oct 1968*

BERKSHIRE

Arborfield
Opened Dec 1936 O.758663, 4/T.1; 2/K.2 Nov 1953;
U/G Jan 1961; 14/K.2 Dec 1962; *Closed Oct 1968*

Bradfield
Opened Oct 1935 U.609729, 4/T.2; resite to U.600712,
May 1937, Money Flare, 1940; 14/K.4, Nov 1953;
resite to U.602712, U/G, April 1968; *In use*

Cold Ash
Opened Oct 1935, U.519694, 4/T.3; 4/V.1, May 1937;
4/S.1, April 1939; 14/L.2, Nov 1953; U/G Sept 1959;
Closed Oct 1968

Crowthorne
Opened Dec 1935, U.846645, 3/L.2; 4/N.2 March 1940;
2/R.4 Nov 1953; U/G Aug 1960; *Closed Oct 1968*

East Ilsley
Opened Oct 1935 U.484807, 4/V.2; 3/N.2 Nov 1953;
U/G June 1959; *Closed Oct 1968*

Great Shefford
Opened Oct 1935 U.375739, 4/V.3; 4/V.1 April 1939;
4/L.1 Nov 1953; U/G July 1960; *Closed Oct 1968*

Longworth
Opened Oct 1935 4/X.3; 4/O.3 July 1940; 3/P.4 Nov
1953; resite to U.288996, March 1956; resite to
U.413997, June 1958; U/G Sept 1959; *Closed Oct 1968*

Newbury/Kintbury
Opened June 1940 U.401665, 4/S.3 Kintbury; resite to
U.451651, renamed Newbury, Sept 1948; 4/V.3 March
1950; 14/L.3 Nov 1953; U/G July 1958; 14/B.2 Oct
1968; *In use*

Shurlock Row
Opened Dec 1936 U.826739, 13/E.4; 4/P.2 April 1938;
resite to U.820747 July 1942; 5/L.4 Nov 1953; resite to
U.830847 July 1947; U/G Dec 1961; *Closed April 1968*

Streatley
Opened Oct 1935 U.575801, 4/Y.1; 3/J.3 Nov 1953;
U/G Aug 1959; 14/C.1 Oct 1968; *In use*

Sunninghall/Ascot
Opened Sept 1935 U.934674 (Top of Water Company's
reservoir); 3/L.1; 4/N.1 March 1940; resite to
U.921689 (Ascot Racecourse Grandstand Tower),
1200 hrs, March 23, 1943; 19/M.1 Nov 1945; 5/L.3
Nov 1953; resite to U.923685 May 1961; U/G April
1962; *Closed Oct 1968*

Uffington/Ashbury
Opened Dec 1936 U.306886, 4/X.2 Uffington; resite to
U.271847, 3/N.4 Nov 1953; U/G July 1960; 3/K.2
Oct 1968; *In use*

Wantage
Opened Oct 1935 U.407870, 4/V.1; 4/X.2 April 1936;
3/N.3 Nov 1953; U/G Sept 1959; 3/K.1 Oct 1968; *In
use*

Windsor
Opened Aug 1943 U.972771 (Brunswick Tower,
Windsor Castle), 17/E.4; 5/L.2 Nov 1953; Non-standard
Underground Post created in former coal cellar beneath
the Castle, with concealed BPI Pipe in a lawn fronting
State Apartments. The GZI Mounting on the Brunswick
Tower, as 3/A.3 Sept 1967; 2/A.3 Oct 1968; *In use*

BUCKINGHAMSHIRE

Beaconsfield
Opened Nov 1931 U.943914, 17/E.1; resite to
U.924895 Oct 1940; 5/N.3 Nov 1953; U/G June 1958;
3/L.2 Oct 1968; *In use*

Bletchley/Fenny Stratford
Opened May 1936 P.883336, 12/N.1 Fenny Stratford;
resite to P.877323, renamed Bletchley, March 1950;
5/F.4 Nov 1953; U/G Dec 1960; *Closed Oct 1968*

Brill
Opened Oct 1935 P.639151, 4/H.1; 4/Q.1 April 1936;
4/Z.3 June 1940; 3/H.3 Nov 1953; U/G May 1958;
Closed April 1968

Buckingham
Opened April 1936 P.706330, 12/O.1; 5/G.3 Nov 1953;
U/G April 1968; 3/G.3 Dec 1962; 3/H.1 Oct 1968; *In
use*

Cheddington
Opened Nov 1931 P. 898080, 17/F.1; 17/L.1 April 1938;
resite to P.916170 April 1944; 5/Q.2 Nov 1953; U/G
July 1960; 7/H.1 Oct 1968; *In use*

Great Missenden
Opened Nov 1931 P.901023, 17/F.2; 5/N.1 Nov 1953;
resite to P.924022 Oct 1959; U/G Dec 1961; 3/L.1
Oct 1968; *In use*

Marlow
Opened Nov 1939 U.855869, 17/E.3; 4/P.1 May 1938;
5/L.1 Nov 1953; U/G Jan 1960; *Closed April 1968*

Olney
Opening date not known, U.892457; U/G 5/F.1 March
1964; 7/F.3 Oct 1968; *In use*

Princes Risborough/Radnage
Opened Oct 1935 P.787052, 4/S.2 Radnage; resite to
P.806027, renamed Princes Risborough, March 1937;
5/N.4 Nov 1953; resite to P.801016 Sept 1963; U/G
July 1964; *Closed April 1968*

Slough
Opened 1933; 17/E.2 (Lascelles Road, Slough); re-site to Horlicks factory tower early 1943; *Closed December 1943*

Stone/Weston Turville
Opened Oct 1935 P.788122, 4/R.2 Stone; 4/Z April 2, 1940; 5/G.3 Nov 1953; renamed Weston Turville June 1955; U/G Sept 1959; *Closed April 1968*

Stony Stratford
Opened Aug 1949 P.775413, 12/X.2; 7/G.2 Nov 1953; 3/G.3 Dec 1962; U/G July 1966; *Closed April 1968*

Whitchurch
Opened Feb 1938 P.975209, 12/N.3; 4/Z.1 June 1939; resite to P.793210 Nov 1952; 5/H.1 Nov 1953; U/G Nov 1957; 3/H.2 Oct 1968; *In use*

CAMBRIDGESHIRE

Abbots Ripton
Opened 1937 L.219776, 15/E.2; 7/S.3 Nov 1953; *Closed Oct 1968*

Arrington
Opened 1937 L.321502, 15/L.1; 5/E.2 Nov 1953; U/G April 1961 7/G.2 Oct 1968; *In use*

Benwick
Opened 1937 L.346897, 15/J.3; resite to L.336911, 7/N.4, Nov 1953; resite to L.338888 May 1960; U/G July 1960; *Closed Oct 1968*

Bottisham
Opened Aug 1938 L.537614, 15/C.2; resite to L.562623, 7/P.4, Nov 1953; U/G Jan 1962; 4/A.1 Oct 1968; *In use*

Caxton
Opened 1937 L.299596, 15/D.3; 7/Q.3 Nov 1953; U/G Jan 1961; *Closed Oct 1968*

Cherry Hinton
Opened 1937 L.493546 (Gog-Magog Golf Course), 15/C.4; 4/D.1 Nov 1953; U/G Aug 1961; 4/A.3 Oct 1968; *In use*

Chrishall/Ickleton
Opened Oct 1937 L.448404, 17/H.1 Crishall; 15/L.3 Dec 1939; 4/D.4 Nov 1953; resite to L.475415, renamed Ickleton, July 1959; 4/J.1 Oct 1968; *In use*

Harston
Opened 1937 L.493437, 15/L.2; 7/D.3 Nov 1953; *Closed Oct 1968*

Linton
Opened 1936 L.566469, 15/C.3; resite to L.554465 May 1938; 4/D.2 Nov 1953; U/G Nov 1961; 4/D.3 Oct 1968; *In use*

Littleport
Opened 1936 L.558866, 15/K.3; 7/N.2 Nov 1953; resite to L.564853 March 1960; U/G Aug 1960; *Closed Oct 1968*

Manea
Opened 1936 L.474888 15/J.2; 7/N.3 Nov 1953; U/G March 1961; *Closed Oct 1968*

March
Opened 1936 L.402953, 15/J.1; 7/N.1 Nov 1953; U/G July 1961; 6/H.1 July 1968; *In use*

Parson Grove
Opened 1936 F.379098, 15/A.2; 7/M.1 Nov 1953; U/G March 1960; 6/D.1 Oct 1968; *In use*

Soham/Fordham
Opened 1936 L.596743, 15/B.3 Soham; 7/P.2, renamed Fordham, Nov 1953; resite to L.618810 Jan 1955; resite to L.601773 Jan 1960; U/G April 1961; 6/H.2 Oct 1968; *In use*

Stretham
Opened 1936 L.512749, 15/B.1; 7/P.1 Nov 1953; U/G Feb 1962; *Closed Oct 1968*

Sutton/Mepal
Opened 1937 L.446789 (Brewery roof), 15/B.2, Sutton; 7/Q.1 Nov 1953; resite to L.441801, RAF Mepal, Dec 1958; U/G Aug 1960; 6/H.3 renamed Sutton, Oct 1968; *In use*

Upwell
Opened 1936 P.504022, 15/A.3; 7/M.2 Nov 1953; U/G Oct 1959; 6/D.3 Oct 1968; *In use*

Whittlesey
Opened Nov 1959 L.287983, 15/G.1; 7/M.3 Nov 1953; U/G June 1958; 7/B.2 Oct 1968; *In use*

Willingham/Histon
Opened 1936 L.428646, 15/C.1, Histon; 7/Q.2 Nov 1953; resite to L.412651, renamed Willingham, Jan 1961; U/G Oct 1961; 7/E.2 Oct 1968; *In use*

CHESHIRE

Aldford
Opened 1937 J.418588, 7/G.2; 16/N.1 Nov 1953; resite to J.417586 Jan 1960; U/G Dec 1960; 17/D.2 Aug 1961; *In use*

Altrincham
Opened 1937 J.738879, 7/E.1; Granite 1943; 19/K.4 Nov 1953; 16/F.4 April 1961; resite to J.715889 May 1964; U/G Oct 1965; 16/A.1 Oct 1968; *In use*

Audlem
Opened 1938 J.661448, 27/B.2; 16/P.2 Nov 1953; U/G Oct 1965; 16/B.3 Oct 1968; *In use*

Attack Warning Red

Bromborough/Neston
Opened March 1937 J.344808, 7/H.2 Bromborough; 19/F.3 Nov 1953; resite to J.316796 Oct 1961; U/G 21/M.3 June 1963; 17/D.1 Oct 1968; renamed Neston, Nov 1972; *In use*

Caldy/Hoylake
Opened 1938 J.216891, 7/H.1 Hoylake; 19/F.2 Nov 1953; resite to J.221869 March 1955; resite to J.241878, renamed Caldy, Nov 1956; U/G Jan 1961; 21/M.2 Jan 1962; *Closed Oct 1968*

Faddiley
Opened 1938 J.587532, 27/B.1; 16/N.2 Nov 1953; U/G Aug 1959; *Closed Oct 1968*

Helsby
Opened 1937 J.493754, 7/F.3; 19/J.2 Nov 1953; 16/H.2 April 1961; U/G Oct 1962; 16/A.3 Oct 1968; *In use*

Knutsford
Opened 1937 J.748794, 7/D.3; Granite 1943; 19/K.3 Nov 1953; U/G Nov 1959; 16/F.3 Oct 1965; 16/B.3 Oct 1968; *In use*

Macclesfield
Opened 1938 J.900718, 7/D.2; Granite 1943; resite to J.925725, 19/L.2, Nov 1953; U/G Oct 1965; *Closed Oct 1968*

Malpas
Opened 1938 J.487482, 27/A.1; Granite 1943; 16/N.3 Nov 1953; resite to J.495480, U/G, July 1962; 16/C.1 Oct 1968; *In use*

Middlewich
Opened 1937 J.708663, 7/F.1; Granite 1943; 19/K.2 Nov 1953; 16/F.2 Dec 1957; U/G Oct 1965; 16/D.1 Oct 1968; *In use*

Northwich
Opened 1937 J.665746, 7/E.2; Granite 1943; 7/F.4 Oct 1945; resite to J.673723 Nov 1950; 19/J.4 Nov 1953; U/G, 16/R.4, Oct 1965; *Closed Oct 1968*

Poynton
Opened 1937 J.901027, 7/D.1; Granite 1943; resite to J.902832 May 1939; 19/L.4 Nov 1953; resite to J.932827 Jan 1961; 16/L.4 June 1961; U/G March 1962; 16/B.1 Oct 1968; *In use*

Preston-on-Hill
Opened 1941 J.571819, 7/E.2; 19/J.1 Nov 1953; U/G June 1965; 16/R.1 July 1965; *Closed Oct 1968*

Sandbach
Opened 1938 J.765621, 27/C.1; Granite 1943; 16/P.1 Nov 1953; U/G Sept 1963; *Closed Oct 1968*

Saughall
Opened 1937 J.365703, 7/C.1; resite to J.368693 Jan 1938; 19/H.4 Nov 1953; U/G Feb 1959; 17/D.3 Oct 1968; *In use*

Tarporley
Opened 1937 J.538638, 7/F.2; 19/J.3 Nov 1953; U/G July 1965; 16/R.3 Feb 1967; 16/A.2 Oct 1968; *In use*

Willaston/Crewe
Opened 1938 J.674534, 27/B.3 Willaston; 16/P.4 Nov 1953; resite to J.722521, renamed Crewe, Nov 1962; U/G Jan 1964; *Closed Oct 1968*

CORNWALL

Bodmin
Opened 1940 X.068664, 20/H.4; HSL 1941; Totter 1943; 11/K.3 Nov 1953; U/G June 1961; 11/B.3 Oct 1968; 10/M.3 April 1973; *In use*

Callington
Opened 1940 X.366692, 21/J.1; Totter 1943; 20/K.1 Feb 1944; 11/C.3 Nov 1953; U/G March 1960; 10/E.3 Oct 1968; *In use*

Coads Green
Opened 1940 X.302765, 20/S.3; Satellite created on X.289746, March 1942; Totter 1943; 20/K.3 Feb 1944; 11/C.2 Nov 1953; U/G March 1960; *Closed Oct 1968*

Constantine
Opened Feb 1942 W.755292, 20/T.4, tic-line to C/G Station; Totter 1942; 11/G.1 Nov 1953; resite to W.719296 July 1955; U/G July 1959; *Closed Oct 1968*

Downderry
Opened July 1940 X.314549, 21/J.2; Tie-line to Looe C/G Station 1941; 20/S.3 March 1944; 11/D.3 Nov 1953; U/G June 1961; 10/H.3 Oct 1968; *In use*

Helston
Opened Oct 1940 W.702252, 20/T.3; HSL 1941; tie-lines to Coverack and Porthleven C/G Stations, 1941; Totter 1942; 11/G.2 Nov 1953; U/G April 1958; 11/C.2 Oct 1968; 10/N.2 April 1973; *In use*

Kilkhampton
Opened Oct 1940 S.260120, 20/N.1; Satellite, Bude C/G Station 1941; 11/A.2 Nov 1953; resite to S.257134 Sept 1959; U/G Oct 1961; 10/C.1 Oct 1968; *In use*

Launceston
Opened July 1940 X.334842, 21/K.2; 20/K.2 Feb 1944; 11/C.1 Nov 1953; U/G June 1961 10/E.2 Oct 1968; *In use*

Liskeard
Opened Oct 1940 X.257648, 20/S.2; Totter 1943;

11/D.1 Nov 1953; U/G June 1961; 10/H.3 Oct 1968; *In use*

The Lizard
Opened Dec 1941 W.713121, 20/Q.3; Tótter, also tie-lines to Porthanstock and Lizard C/G Stations, 1942; 11/G.4 Nov 1953; U/G July 1958; 11/C.3 Oct 1968; 10/N.3 April 1973; *In use*

Madron
Opened April 1940 W.436331, 20/M.3; HSL 1941; tie-line to Penzer Point C/G Station and Totter, on resite to W.438334, 1942; 11/H.3 Nov 1953; U/G Nov 1961; 11/C.1 Oct 1968; 10/N.1 April 1973; *In use*

Marazion
Opened Nov 1941 W.645212, 20/T.1; Totter and tie-line to Halsferran Cliff C/G Station 1942; resite to W.538303, 11/G.3, Nov 1953; U/G Aug 1958; *Closed Oct 1968*

Mevagissey
Opened June 1940 X.019434, 20/R.1; Totter 1942; 11/E.2 Nov 1953; resite to X.006423 Feb 1958; U/G 1960; 11/D.1 Oct 1968; 10/P.1 April 1973; *In use*

Millbrook
Opened July 1940 X.435515, 20/J.4; 11/D.4 Nov 1953; U/G Dec 1960; 10/H.2 Oct 1968; *In use*

Mitchell
Opened Aug 1942 W.841537, 20/P.4; 11/J.4 Nov 1953; U/G Feb 1963; 10/A.2 Oct 1968; 10/L.2 April 1973; *In use*

Nanpean
Opened Oct 1940 W.974541, 20/H.3; HSL 1941; Totter 1942; 11/E.1 Nov 1953; U/G July 1959 *Closed Oct 1968*

Newquay
Opened July 1940 W.832604, 20/P.3; 11/J.1 Nov 1953; resite to W.851637 Aug 1960; U/G Aug 1961; *Closed Oct 1968*

Otterham
Opened Oct 1940 X.148885, 20/N.3; HSL 1941; 11/B.3 Nov 1953; U/G July 1962; 10/E.1 Oct 1968; *In use*

Par
Opened Nov 1940 X.103543, 20/R.2; HSL 1941; Totter 1942; tie-line to Fowey C/G Station 1942; resite to X.104556 March 1951; 11/E.4 Nov 1953; U/G Aug 1961; 11/B.2 Oct 1968; 10/M.2 April 1973; *In use*

Penryn/St. Ithians
Opened Nov 1940 W.759354, 20/P.2 St. Ithians; Totter 1942; *Closed 1945*. Reopened June 1953, renamed Penryn, 20/F.2; 11/F.2 Nov 1953; U/G April 1958; 11/D.3 Oct 1968; 10/P.3 April 1973; *In use*

Polperro
Opened July 1940 X.202508, 20/S.1; Totter 1942; tie-line to Nore C/G Station and Looe 1942; and Darky 1942; 11/E.3 Nov 1953; resite to X.211549 Sept 1959; U/G June 1960; *Closed Oct 1968*

Praze
Opened Oct 1940 W.665351, 20/Q.1; Satellite, Portreath C/G Station 1941; Totter 1942; resite to W.673366, 20/F.3, Nov 1953; U/G Aug 1961; *Closed Oct 1968*

St. Agnes
Opened June 1941 W.727486, 20/P.1; Totter 1943; 11/J.2 Nov 1953; U/G Aug 1961; 11/A.3 Oct 1968; 10/L.3 April 1973; *In use*

St. Anthony
Opened Jan 1941 W.859326, 20/T.3; Totter 1943; tie-line to C/G Station; 11/F.4 Nov 1953; U/G May 1960; *Closed Oct 1968*

St. Breward
Opened Oct 1940 X.098775, 20/O.2; 11/L.3 Nov 1953; U/G Sept 1960; 11/B.1 Oct 1968; 10/M.1 April 1973; *In use*

St. Columb Major
Opened Feb 1941 W.923622, 20/O.4, HSL 1941; Totter 1943; 11/K.2 Nov 1953; U/G April 1964; 11/A.1 Oct 1968; 10/L.1 April 1973; *In use*

St. Ives
Opened July 1940 W.517386, 20/M.1; Satellites at St Just & Penzer Point C/G Stations, HSL, 1941; Totter 1942; 11/H.1 Nov 1953; resite to W.522380 Sept 1961; U/G July 1962; *Closed Oct 1968*

Saltash
Opened July 1940 X.424589; 20/J.3; 11/D.2 Nov 1953; resite to X.298586 Sept 1957; U/G June 1959; *Closed Oct 1968*

Sennen
Opened July 1940 W.359255, 20/M.2; HSL 1941; tie-line to Tol-Pedd-Penwith, Treen. C/G Station 1941; Totter and Darky 1942; 11/H.2 Nov 1953; U/G June 1963; *Closed Oct 1968*

St Mary's, Scilly Isles
Satellite at C/G Station with direct line to Centre

Tintagel
Opened July 1940 X.050885, 20/O.1; 20/N.4 Oct 1942; 11/L.4 Nov 1953; U/G July 1960; *Closed Oct 1968*

Trebetherick
Opened Oct 1942 W.945801, 20/O.3; 11/L.2 Nov 1953; U/G Aug 1960; *Closed Oct 1968*

Truro
Opened Oct 1940 W.815459, as Satellite; Full Post status, 20/T.1, 1943; 11/J.3 Nov 1953; resite to W.837463 March 1954; resite to W.823437 March 1955; U/G Aug 1961; *Closed Oct 1968*

Veryan
Opened Jan 1940 W.913388, 20/T.2; Satellite at Pentargus Point, Darky, 1942; 11/F.1 Nov 1953; resite to W.920375 Sept 1962; U/G July 1963; 11/D.2 Oct 1968; 10/P.2 April 173; *In use*

Wadebridge/Padstow
Opened Oct 1940 W.912762, 20/O.1 Padstow; resite to W.922741 Nov 1942; 11/K.1 Nov 1953; renamed Wadebridge June 1956; resite to W.949718 June 1960; U/G Aug 1961; *Closed Oct 1968*

Week St. Mary
Opened April 1941 X.234984, 20/N.2; 11/B.2 Nov 1953; U/G June 1960; *Closed Oct 1968*

CUMBERLAND

Allonby
Opened Oct. 1939 Y.098432, 32/F.1; Granite 1943; Augmented Granite 1944; 22/L.2 Nov 1953; resite to Y.084430 Aug 1959; U/G May 1960; 22/H.1 Oct 1968; *In use*

Alston
Opened Oct 1939 Y.724462, 32/D.1; 22/P.2 Nov 1953; U/G May 1961; 23/F.3 Oct 1968; *In use*

Armathwaite
Opened Oct 1939 Y.504486, 32/C.3; Granite 1943; 22/P.3 Nov 1953; resite to Y.509453 Aug 1954; U/G Oct 1965; *Closed Oct 1968*

Bassenthwaite
Opened 1948 Y.229328, 32/E.4; 22/N.4 Nov 1953; U/G May 1961; 22/J.1 Oct 1968; *In use*

Bootle
Opened Nov 1938 D.104889, 29/O.1; Granite 1943; 21/D.2 Nov 1953; resite to D.103893 Aug 1958; U/G Oct 1965; 22/G.2 1965; *Closed Oct 1968*

Brampton
Opened Oct 1939 Y.532604, 32/C.2; Granite 1943; 22/P.4 Nov 1953; U/G Jan 1959; 22/G.3 Oct 1968; *In use*

Caldbeck
Opened Oct 1939 Y.316413, 32/E.1; Granite 1943; 22/N.1 Nov 1953; resite to Y.337391 March 1955; U/G April 1962; 22/F.4 Oct 1968; *In use*

Cockermouth
Opened Oct 1939 Y.115320, 32/F.2; Granite 1943; 22/M.1 Nov 1953; resite to Y.124330 Dec 1954; U/G May 1960; *Closed Oct 1968*

Culgaith
Opened Oct 1939 Y.598305, 32/D.3; resite to Y.615294 March 1940; 22/O.4 Nov 1953; U/G May 1960; 22/K.1 Oct 1968; *In use*

Dalston
Opened Oct 1939 Y.367477, 32/G.2; 32/E.4 May 1942; Granite 1943; Augmented Granite 1944; 22/L.3 Nov 1953; resite to Y.380484 Feb 1961; U/G April 1962; 22/F.3 Oct 1968; *In use*

Eskdale
Opened Nov 1938 D.143998, 29/N.3; Granite 1943; 21/D.4 Nov 1953; 22/G.4 July 1961; resite to D.135001 Feb 1962; U/G Oct 1965; 21/A.1 Oct 1968; *In use*

Greystoke
Opened Oct 1939 Y.443309, 32/E.2; Granite 1943; 22/N.3 Nov 1953; U/G Nov 1960; *Closed Oct 1968*

Keswick/Threlkeld
Opened Oct 1939 Y.287229, 32/E.2 Keswick; resite to Y.307244, renamed Threlkeld, Aug 1951; 22/N.2 Nov 1953; U/G May 1961; 22/J.3 Oct 1968; *In use*

Kirkbride
Opened Oct 1939 Y.228584, 32/G.1; 22/K.3 Nov 1953; resite to Y.228582 Feb 1961; U/G May 1962; 22/F.1 Oct 1968; *Closed 1973*

Millom
Opened June 1941 D.179783, 29/O.4; resite to D.175792 May 1950; 21/E.2 Nov 1953; U/G April 1964; *Closed Oct 1968*

Penrith
Opened July 1951 Y.504293, 32/D.4; 22/O.1 Nov 1953; U/G May 1960; 22/J.2 Oct 1968; *In use*

Roadhead
Opened Oct 1939 Y.519748, 32/A.2; Granite 1943; 22/J.2 Nov 1953; U/G May 1961; 22/G.1 Oct 1968; *In use*

Rockliffe/Kingstown/Carlisle
Opened Oct 1939 Y.396597, 32/J.2, Rockliffe; Granite 1943; resite to Y.393587, renamed Carlisle, (roof of Castle which also housed the Centre) Nov 1953; resite to Y.383593, renamed Kingstown, Jan 1961; 22/F.2, renamed Carlisle, Oct 1968; *In use*

Seascale
Opened Nov 1938 Y.043001, 29/N.2; resite to Y.035017 Dec 1939; Granite 1943; 29/N.2 Dec 1950; 21/D.1 Nov 1953; U/G Jan 1959; 22/G.1 Oct 1965; *Closed Oct 1968*

Silloth
Opened Oct 1939 Y.108532, 32/G.4; 32/G.2 Jan 1942; 22/L.1 Nov 1953; U/G May 1960; *Closed Oct 1968*

Whitehaven
Opened Nov 1938 Y.986189, 29/N.1; Granite 1943; 22/M.3 Nov 1953; U/G April 1961; 22/H.2 Oct 1968; *In use*

Wigton
Opened Oct 1939 Y.252493, 32/G.3; Granite 1943; 22/L.4 Nov 1953; U/G April 1962; *Closed Oct 1968;* Reopened, 22/F.1 1973; *In use*

Workington
Opened Oct 1939 Y.009295, 32/F.3; Granite 1943; 22/M.2 Nov 1953; U/G Nov 1962; 22/H.3 Oct 1968; *In use*

DERBYSHIRE

Ashover
Opened Jan 1938 K.356637, 6/L.1; Granite 1943; 18/E.3 Nov 1953; U/G Nov 1959; 8/B.3 Oct 1968; *In use*

Baslow
Opened Jan 1938 K.241723, 6/O.3; Granite 1942; 18/E.2 Nov 1953; U/G Dec 1963; *Closed Oct 1968*

Brassington
Opened Nov 1943 K.225555, 6/L.4; Granite; 8/H.2 Nov 1953; U/G Oct 1964; 8/D.1 Oct 1968; *In use*

Buxton
Opened Jan 1938 K.065753, 6/N.1; resite to K.075747 July 1941; Granite 1942; resite to K.088757 April 1948; 18/E.4 Nov 1953; U/G Sept 1959; 8/A.4 Oct 1968; *In use*

Chinley
Opened Oct 1937 K.033814, 7/C.3; resite to K.052812 Sept 1949; 19/M.2 Nov 1953; resite to K.035811 April 1955; U/G Nov 1960; 16/M.2 Aug 1962; *Closed Oct 1968*

Castle Gresley/Church Gresley/Overseal
Opened Dec 1937 K.292167, 6/S.2 Overseal; 8/N.1 Nov 1953; resite to K.279179, renamed Castle Gresley, July 1958; U/G June 1959; renamed Church Gresley April 1964; 8/F.2 Oct 1968; *In use*

Etwall
Opened Dec 1937 K.284322, 6/S.1; resite to K.271324 June 1938; resite to K.283322 April 1943; 8/A.2 Nov 1953; U/G Feb 1961; 8/D.3 Oct 1968; *Closed 1975*

Glossop
Opened Oct 1937 K.006947, 7/C.1; 19/M.1 Nov 1953; 16/M.1 April 1961; U/G June 1965; 21/M.2 Oct 1968; *In use*

Hartington
Opened Jan 1938 K.130602, 6/N.2; Granite 1942; resite to K.129599 Aug 1942; 8/H.1 Nov 1953; U/G Jan 1958; 8/C.1 Oct 1968; *In use*

Hope
Opened Oct 1937 K.171832, 7/C.2; 18/E.1 Nov 1953; resite to K.140796 Oct 1962; U/G Dec 1962; *Closed Oct 1968*

Hulland
Opened Jan 1938 K.250485, 6/L.3; Granite 1942; 8/A.1 Nov 1953; resite to K.278465 April 1959; U/G Nov 1959; *Closed Oct 1968*

LONG EATON/CLIFTON
Opened Dec 1937 K.477338, 6/T.2 Long Eaton; Granite 1942; 8/K.3 Nov 1953; resite to K.540336 Nov 1963; U/G Oct 1964; 8/E.3, renamed Clifton. Oct 1968; *In use*

Melbourne
Opened Dec 1937 K.380253, 6/T.3; 8/M.1 Nov 1953; resite to K.365248 March 1960; U/G Feb 1961; *Closed Oct 1968;* Reopened, 8/D.3, 1975

Pleasley Hill
Opened Dec 1937 K.507646, 6/K.3; resite to K.509644 Nov 1939; Granite 1942; 8/D.1 Nov 1953; U/G Sept 1961; *Closed Oct 1968*

Ripley
Opened Jan 1938 K.410507, 6/L.2; Granite 1942; Augmented Granite 1944; 8/J.4 Nov 1953; resite to K.386505 May 1964; U/G Oct 1964; 8/D.2 Oct 1968 *In use*

Spondon
Opened Dec 1937 K.413368, 6/T.1, Granite 1942; 8/K.4 Nov 1953; resite to K.408380 May 1962; U/G Nov 1963; *Closed Oct 1968*

Staveley
Opened Dec 1937 K.445752, 6/O.2; Granite 1942; resite to K.435760 1942; Augmented Granite 1944; 18/N.3 Nov 1953; U/G Jan 1964, 18/F.4 April 1966; *Closed Oct 1968*

Whitwell
Opened Dec 1937 K.529771, 6/P.3; Granite 1942; 18/T.4 Nov 1953; U/G May 1959; 18/L.4 April 1966; 8/B.1 Oct 1968; *In use*

Attack Warning Red

DEVONSHIRE

Ashburton/South Brent
Opened July 1940 X.754683, 21/H.3 South Brent; Granite and Totter, 1943; 21/H.2 June 1944; renamed Ashburton June 1951; 10/T.2 Nov 1953; U/G Aug 1963; 10/G.3 Oct 1968; *In use*

Axminster
Opened Sept 1938 22/S.2; Totter and Satellite, T.311974, 1943; 9/K.4 Nov 1953; U/G June 1962; *Closed Oct 1968*

Bampton
Opened Sept 1938 S.960234, 22/X.1; resite to S.973187, 10/Y.3 Nov 1953; U/G Oct 1961; 9/E.3 Oct 1968; *In use*

Barnstaple
Opened July 1940 S.580312, 21/B.3; tie-line to Northoe C/G Station 1941; resite to S.584296 Oct 1952; Granite 1943; 10/M.1 Nov 1953; U/G July 1959; *Closed Oct 1968*

Bere Alston/Yelverton
Opened July 1940 X.525692, 22/L.1 Yelverton; resite to X.530695 Oct 1940; Satellite, Stoke Point 1941; Totter and Granite, 1943; 21/K.1 July 1944; resite to X.456653, renamed Bere Alston, 10/P.3, Nov 1953; U/G Aug 1961; 10/J.3 Oct 1968; *In use*

Brixham
Opened July 1940 X.954566, 21/G.3; Totter 1942; 21/J.3 June 1953; 10/S.4 Nov 1953; U/G Nov 1960; 10/K.2 Oct 1968; *In use*

Christow/Chudleigh
Opened July 1940 X.867800, 21/F.2 Chudleigh; Totter and Granite 1943; 21/M.4 Jan 1945; resite to X.831831, 21/G.1, Feb 1953; 10/V.3 Nov 1953; renamed Christow July 1955; U/G Sept 1960; 10/F.2 Oct 1968; *In use*

Chulmleigh/Winkleigh
Opened July 1940 S.685146, 21/C.2 Chudleigh; resite to S.692152 June 1941; Granite 1943; 10/M.3 Nov 1953; resite to S.681168 April 1954; resite to S.619094, renamed Winkleigh Oct 1960; U/G Nov 1962; 10/C.2 Oct 1968; *In use*

Croyde
Opened July 1940 S.434385, 21/B.1; 10/L.3 Nov 1953; U/G Dec 1961; 10/A.3 Oct 1968; *In use*

Collompton/Kentisbeare
Opened Sept 1938 T.016076, 21/D.2 Collompton; Granite 1943; 10/X.4 Nov 1953; resite to T.053070, renamed Kentisbeare Nov 1954; U/G June 1962; 9/E.2 Oct 1968; *In use*

Drewsteignton
Opened July 1940 X.712908, 21/F.3; Satellite, Budleigh

Salterton C/G Station 1941; Totter 1942; 10/0.4 Nov 1953; U/G Aug 1960; 10/F.1 Oct 1968; *In use*

Exeter/Pinhoe
Opened July 1940 X.924953, 21/E.1 Exeter; 21/D.1 June 1941; Granite and Totter 1943; resite to X.975953, renamed Pinhoe May 1953; 10/W.2 Nov 1953; resite to X.996933 Sept 1961; U/G May 1962; 10/G.1 1968; *In use*

Exminster
Opened April 1941 X.931880, 21/E.1; Satellite, Ladram Bay C/G Station 1941; Granite 1943; 21/F.2 Jan 1945; 10/V.1 Nov 1953; resite to X.944869 Nov 1955; resite to X.910843 Sept 1963; U/G Feb 1964; *Closed Oct 1968*

Exmouth
Opened July 1940 Y.019800, 21/E.2; Totter 1942; Satellite Y.029799 1942; resite to Y.046813 Jan 1952; 10/W.3 Nov 1953; U/G Sept 1960; *Closed Oct 1968*

Feniton/Ottery St Mary
Opened Aug 1940 Y.059952, 22/T.3 Ottery St Mary; 21/E.4 Feb 1954; resite to Y.102968 Nov 1941; Totter 1943; 10/W.1 Nov 1953; renamd Feniton Sept 1954; resite to Y.104004 Oct 1956; U/G June 1959; *Closed Oct 1968*

Five Barrows
Resite to S.733368, 10/Z.2 April 1954; U/G Post Sept 1959; *Closed 1968*

Gara Bridge/Loddiswell
Open 1953 X.727477, 10/R.3 Loddiswell; resite to X.762532 May 1957; renamed Gara Bridge Nov 1958; U/G 1960; *Closed Oct 1968*

Hatherleigh
Opened Aug 1940 S.552047, 21/A.2 (roof of folly resembling castle); Granite 1943; 10/N.2 Nov 1953; resite to S.545047 Aug 1959; U/G Nov 1961; *Closed Oct 1968*

Hartridge/Farway Common
Opened Aug 1943 T.182067, 22/T.3 Hartridge; Totter 1943; 9/K.2 Nov 1953; resite to T.169981 Oct 1955; resite to T.172986, renamed Farway Common Jan 1958; U/G July 1959; *Closed Oct 1968*

High Bickington/Beard Moor
Resite to S.602203, 21/?, Jan 1952; 10/M.2 Nov 1953; U/G April 1961; *Closed Oct 1968*

Holbeton/Bigbury-on-Sea
Opened July 1940 X.664448, 21/H.2 Bigbury-on-Sea; Satellite X.723555 (East end of approach to RAF Bolt Head) Nov 1942; Totter 1942; 21/M.1 Sept 1951; resite to X.653447, renamed Holbeton April 1952; 10/Q.4 Nov 1953; resite to X.602488 May 1962; U/G Aug 1963; *Closed Oct 1968*

Holsworthy
Opened June 1940 S.352040, 21/K.1; 20/L.3 March 1944;
11/B.1 Nov 1953; U/G June 1960; 10/C.3 Oct 1968;
In use

Hornscross
Opened June 1940 S.376232, 21/B.2; 20/L.2 April 1944;
resite to S.375236, 11/A.1 Nov 1953; U/G June 1960;
Closed Oct 1968

Ilfracombe/Combe Martin
Opened 1940 S.508474, 21/B.4 Combe Martin; Granite
1943 10/L.1 Nov 1953; resite to S.543482, renamed
Ilfracombe, May 1955; resite to S.628446, renamed
Combe Martin, May 1960; U/G May 1964; *Closed
Oct 1968*

Ivybridge/Modbury
Opened July 1940 X.646574, 21/H.1 Ivybridge; Totter
1942; Granite 1943; 10/R.1 Nov 1953; resite to X.677547,
renamed Modbury May 1957; U/G Sept 1959; 10/E.1
Oct 1968; *In use*

Lydford
Opened July 1940 X.510856, 21/K.3; Granite 1943;
21/A.3 June 1944; 10/0.2 Nov 1953; resite to X.528857
Dec 1955; U/G Dec 160; 10/F.3 Oct 1968; *In use*

Lynton
Opened July 1940 S.713498, 21/C.1; Granite 1943; 21/B.2
Oct 1944; 10/Z.1 Nov 1953; resite to S.726482 Sept
1959; U/G April 1961; 10/B.1 Oct 1968; *In use*

Manaton/Lustleigh
Resite from Lustleigh to X.764782, 21/New Post,
Manaton, Sept 1951; 10/V.2 Nov 1953; *Closed Oct 1968*

Marlborough/Salcombe
Resite from 21/M.2, Start Point, at request of BBC, to
site of war-time satellite, X.733386, as 21/H.3, 1950;
resite to X.709407, 10/R.2, Salcombe Nov 1953;
renamed Marlborough June 1955; U/G Aug 1959;
Closed Oct 1968

Moretonhampstead
Opened Aug 1940 X.741846, 21/F.4; Granite & Darky,
1942; 10/0.3 Nov 1953; U/G June 1959; *Closed Oct 1968*

Newton Abbot/Ashburton
Opened July 1940 X.754683, 21/F.1 Ashburton;
Granite and Satellite, Teignmouth, 1943; 21/M.1 Nov
1945; 21/H.3 Jan 1951; renamed Newton Abbot 1951;
10/T.1 Nov 1953; resite to X.844691, Sept 1961; U/G
Aug 1962; *Closed Oct 1968*

North Tawton/Bow
Opened Aug 1940, S.667028, 21/A.3 North Tawton;
Granite 1943; 10/N.3 Nov 1953; resite to S.675023 May
1955; resite to S.734028, renamed Bow, Oct 1959; U/G

Sept 1963; *Closed Oct 1968*

Noss Mayo
Opened May 1953 X.540466, 21/Q.3; 10/Q.3 Nov 1953;
Closed 1957

Okehampton
Opened Aug 1940 X.608955, 21/A.1; Granite 1943; resite
to X.539939, 10/C.1, Nov 1953; U/G Nov 1962; *Closed
Oct 1968*

Paignton/Totnes
Opened July 1940 X.796597, 21/J.1 Totnes; Satellite
X.826625 Nov 1942; Granite 1943; resite to X.855595,
10/S.1, Nov 1953; resite to X.846608, renamed Paignton
June 1962; U/G Aug 1963; *Closed Oct 1968*

Plympton
Opened July 1940 X.560510, 21/L.3; Satellite X.536577
June 1942; Totter and Granite 1943; 21/K.1 Dec 1944;
21/L.1 Sept 1950; 10/Q.1 Nov 1953; U/G April 1958;
Closed Oct 1968

Sharperton
Opened Oct 1940 X.590731, 21/L.2; Totter 1943; 21/K.2
Aug 1944; resite to X.559703 June 1952; 10/J.1 Nov
1953; U/G April 1953; *In use*

Sampford Percival/Tiverton
Opened Aug 1940 T.019143, 22/X.4 Sampford Percival;
10/X.2 Nov 1953; resite to T.930115, renamed Tiverton,
Nov 1954; U/G Aug 1960; *Closed Oct 1968*

Seaton
Opened Sept 1938 Y.240899, 22/S.3; Totter 1943; resite
to Y.234911, 22/G.1 June 1944; 22/T.1 Sept 1949; 9/K.3
Nov 1953; U/G 1960; 9/G.2 Oct 1968; *In use*

Shirwell/Combe Martin
Opened July 1940 S.577745, 21/B.4 Combe Martin;
resite to S.565403, renamed Shirwell, 10/L.4, Nov 1953;
U/G June 1959; 10/A.1 Oct 1968; *In use*

Sidmouth
Opened 1943 Y.110868 21/E.3; 10/W.4 Nov 1953; U/G
July 1962; 9/G.3 Oct 1968; *In use*

South Molton
Opened July 1940 S.704265, 21/B.1; Granite 1943; 21/C.3
Sept 1953; resite to S.728246, 10/M.4, Nov 1953; resite to
S.713246 July 1955; U/G June 1959; 10/B.2 Oct 1968; *In use*

Stockleigh Pomeroy/Bickleigh
Opened July 1940 S.885032, 21/D.3 Bickleigh, Granite
and Totter 1943; renamed Stockleigh Pomeroy Jan 1951;
10/X.3 Nov 1953; U/G June 1959; 10/D.2 Oct 1968; *In use*

Stockenham/Torcross/Start Point
Opened Sept 1940, X.813378, 21/H.4 Stokenham;

Satellite X.829432 and Totter, 1942; 21/O.2 Nov 1944; 21/J.3 July 1946; 21/M.3 Nov.1950; renamed Torcross May 1951; 10/S.4 Nov 1953; resite to X.815379, 10/S.2 Start Point, June 1960; *Closed Oct 1968*

Strete/Stoke Fleming
Opened July 1940 X.869498, 21/G.2 Stoke Fleming; Satellite, Hope's Nose 1941; Totter 1943; 21/J.2 May 1952; resite to X.836470, 10/S.3 Strete, Nov 1953; U/G Aug 1959; 10/K.3 Oct 1968; *In use*

Tavistock
Opened Oct 1940 X.491735, 21/L.4; Granite and Totter 1943; 21/K.1 1944; 10/P.2 Nov 1953; resite to X.475773 Jan 1961; U/G Feb 1962; *Closed Oct 1968*

Teignmouth/Bishopsteighton
Opened July 1940 X.999740, 21/F.3 Bishopsteighton; resite to X.917751 March 1941, 21/M.3 March 1945; 21/G.3, renamed Teignmouth, Jan 1947; 10/V.4 Nov 1953; U/G Oct 1959; *Closed Oct 1968*

Torquay
Opened April 1942 X.913680, 21/G.4; Totter 1943; Satellite X.943636 1943; 10/T.3 Nov 1953; resite to X.926698 Oct 1954; U/G May 1961; 10/G.2 Oct 1968; *In use*

Torrington
Opened July 1940, S.482203, 21/B.1; 20/L.1 Feb 1944; 11/A.3 Nov 1953; resite to S.531239 Dec 1959; U/G Oct 1960; 10/A.2 Oct 1968; *In use*

Wembury/Plymstock
Opened July 1940 X.501486, 21/L.2 Wembury; Totter 1943; 10/Q.2 Nov 1953; resite to X.498518, renamed Plymstock, Dec 1961; U/G July 1964; 10/J.2 Oct 1968; *In use*

Whitestone/Crediton
Opened July 1940 S.827001, 21/D.1 Crediton; Granite and Totter 1943; 21/F.1 Aug 1951; resite to X.865947, renamed Whitestone, 10/N.4, Nov. 1953; U/G June 1959; *Closed Oct 1968*

Witheridge
Opened July 1940 S.806138, 21/D.2; Granite 1943; 21/O.1 Oct 1944; resite to S.767114, 10/N.3, Nov 1953; U/G June 1959; 10/D.3 Oct 1968; *In use*

Woolacombe
Opened May 1954 S.484426, 10/L.2; U/G Feb 1962; *Closed Oct 1968*

DORSETSHIRE

Abbotsbury
Opened Sept 1938 Y.573848, 22/Q.4; Satellite on Sea Wall 1942; Totter 1943; resite to Y.559854 Sept 1951; 9/H.1 Nov 1953; resite to Y.561865 Nov 1956; U/G March 1959; *Closed Oct 1968*

Bere Regis
Opened Sept 1938 Y.858948, 22/Q.2; 22/P.4 April 1942; Totter 1943; 22/E.3 Feb 1944; 9/G.1 Nov 1953; U/G May 1963; 9/K.1 Oct 1968; *In use*

Blandford Forum
Opened Sept 1938 T.884043, 22/0.2; resite to T.874052 April 1942; Totter 1943; 14/C.4 Nov 1953; U/G June 1962; *Closed Oct 1968*

Bridport/Burton Bradstock
Opened Sept 1938 Y.465947, 22/S.1 Bridport; tie-line West Bay C/G Station 1942; resite to Y.460923, 22/Q.3, and Totter, Oct 1942; resite to Y.392935, 9/J.3, Nov 1953; resite to Y.480907 Oct 1964; U/G, renamed Burton Bradstock Dec 1966; 9/H.2 Oct 1968; *In use*

Buckland Newton
Opened Sept 1938 T.679049, 22/R.1; 22/F.4 May 1953; 9/F.4 Nov 1953; U/G Dec 1958; 9/J.1 Oct 1968; *In use*

Canford Cliffs
Opened Sept 1938 Z.055889, 22/P.3; Totter 1942; 14/D.1 Nov 1953; U/G June 1960; *Closed Oct 1968*

Fontwell Magna
Opened Aug 1940 T.865181, 22/N.2; 14/C.1 Nov 1953; resite to T.876164 Aug 1961; return to T.865181, U/G Feb 1962; 9/F.2 Oct 1968; *In use*

Foreland
Satellite opened, Z.658875 (C/G Station), Oct 1943, Totter 3/J.2; *Closed Sept 1944*

Gillingham/East Stour
Opened Sept 1938 T.816364, 22/N.1 Gillingham; resite to T.797267, 9/H.1 Nov 1953; resite to T.772267 (Matthews Brewery roof) Nov 1953; Post abandoned Oct 1958 following Brewery Fire. Resite to T.771238, renamed East Stour, Nov 1960; U/G April 1963; *Closed Oct 1968*

Maiden Newton/Evershot
Opened Sept 1938 Y.610997, 22/H.2 Maiden Newton; 22/Q.1 March 1944; 9/F.3 Nov 1953; resite to Y.610030 Dec 1960; U/G, renamed Evershot, June 1962; *Closed Oct 1968*

Portland Bill
Opened Sept 1938 Y.677789, 22/Q.1; Satellite, Y.651732, Stopes Tower, & Totter, 1942; 22/J.3 July 1945; 9/H.2 Nov 1953; resite to Y.682713 Jan 1960; U/G Aug 1960; 9/J.3 Oct 1968; *In use*

Preston
Opened Jan 1943 Y.700820 (White Horse Hill), 22/J.1;

9/H.3 Nov 1953; resite to Y.708891 Oct 1958; U/G Dec 1961; *Closed Oct 1968*

Sturminster Newton
Opened Sept 1938 T.793146, 22/N.2; 22/O.1 Sept 1942; 22/R.1 Sept 1944; resite to T.789128 Aug 1949; 9/F.1 Nov 1953; U/G June 1959; *Closed Oct 1968*

Verwood
Opened Jan 1943 U.093098, 22/O.4; 22/P.4 Feb 1944; resite to U.089106 14/C.4, Nov 1953; resite to U.093098 Sept 1956; U/G April 1958; *Closed Oct 1968*

Wareham
Opened Sept 1938 Y.938873, 22/P.1; Totter 1942; resite to Y.931864 Aug 1943; 14/D.4 Nov 1953; U/G Aug 1959; *Closed Oct 1968*

West Lulworth
Opened Sept 1938 Y.828797, 22/Q.3; Satellite, Lampton Herring C/G Station 1941; 22/E.3 Sept 1943; 9/C.3 Nov 1953; U/G Mar 1959; 9/K.3 Oct 1968; *In use*

Wimborne Minster/Broadstone/Wichampton
Opened Sept 1938 Y.987952, 22/O.2; Wimborne Minster; resite to Y.984955 Sept 1939; 22/P.3 May 1947; renamed Broadstone May 1951; 14/E.4 Nov 1953; resite to Z.006974 Aug 1959; resite to Z.005056 July 1963; U/G Aug 1963; 14/G3, renamed Wichampton, Oct 1968; *In use*

Worth Matravers
Opened Sept 1938 Y.974778, 22/P.2; tie-line, St Alban's Head C/G Station and Totter, 1942; 22/N.1 July 1944; 14/D.2 Nov 1953; U/G Feb 1962; 9/K.2 Oct 1968; *In use*

Yetminster
Opened April 1939 T.600106, 22/M.4; 22/R.3 April 1942, 9/F.2 Nov 1953; U/G Jan 1961; 9/H.1 Oct 1968; *In use*

DURHAM

Aycliffe
Opened Dec 1936 Z.290219, 30/G.2; resite to Z.292219, Granite, April 1943; 20/J.1 April 1955; 23/S.1 Jan 1962; resite to Z.291211 Aug 1962; U/G Dec 1963; *Closed Oct 1968*

Brusselton/West Auckland
Opened Dec 1936 Z.181267, 30 G.3 West Auckland; Granite 1943; resite to Z.201174 renamed Brusselton 1960; U/G July 1961; *Closed Oct 1968*

Castleside
Opened Jan 1941 Z.086483 30/K.1; Granite 1943; 23/P.3 Nov 1953; U/G June 1962; 23/G.2 Oct 1968; *In use*

Egglescliffe
Opened Dec 1936 Z.424147, 9/Z.1; 9/T.2 Oct 1943; resite to Z.426148 Dec 1943; 20/J.3 Nov 1953; resite to Z.436121, 23/S.3 July 1962; U/G Dec 1964; *Closed Oct 1968*

Easington/Seaham Harbour
Opened Dec 1936 Z.431499, 30/E.3; resite to Z.431496 (St John's Church Tower) June 1942; resite to Z.430468, 23/A.1, Nov 1953; U/G April 1962; 23/H.2 Oct 1968; *In use*

Gainford/Piercebridge
Opened Dec 1936 Z.174180, 30/H.1 Gainford; Granite 1943; resite to Z.234153, 23/C.2 renamed Piercebridge Nov 1953; U/G Aug 1960; *Closed Oct 1968*

Hartlepool
Opened Dec 1936 Z.509346, 9/P.1; resite to Z.514349 April 1938; 9/N.1 Sept 1943; 20/K.1 Nov 1953; resite to Z.485337 Aug 1960; U/G May 1962; 23/K.1 Oct 1968; *In use*

Hastings Hill/Washington
Opened Dec 1936 Z.313564, 30/E.2 Washington; resite to Z.311584 April 1943; resite to Z.352544, renamed Hastings Hill, May 1949; U/G June 1959; 23/H.1 Oct 1968; *In use*

Horden
Opened Dec 1936 Z.434411, 30/F.1; 23/A.2 Nov1953; resite to Z.454390 Sept 1960; U/G April 1962; *Closed Oct 1968*

Pit House
Opened March 1954 Z.201399, 23/B.1; U/G Jan 1969; *Closed Oct 1968*

Sacriston
Opened Dec 1936 Z.247467, 30/J.3; Granite 1942; 23/N.2 Nov 1953; U/G, resite to Z.223480 May 1955; 23/H.3 Oct 1968; *In use*

Sadberge
Opened May 1942 Z.338166, 9/T.4; 20/J.2 Nov 1953; U/G July 1961; 23/K.2. Oct 1968; *In use*

Seaton Carew
Opened April 1940 Z.525285, 9/P.4; 9/N.4 1943; 20/K.2 Nov 1953; U/G Aug 1960; 23/T.2 March 1966; *Closed Oct 1968*

Sedgefield
Open Jan 1940 Z.364302, 30/F.3; 23/A.3 Nov 1953; U/G July 1960; 23/K.3 Oct 1968; *In use*

Sherburn Hill
Opened Dec 1936 Z.338420, 30/F.2; resite to Z.330417 Sept 1938; 23/A.4 Nov 1953; U/G Jan 1959; *Closed Oct 1968*

Attack Warning Red

Springwell
Opened Dec 1940 Z.261566, 30/E.4; 23/N.4 Nov 1953; resite to Z.286589 Aug 1954; U/G May 1959; *Closed Oct 1968*

Stanhope
Opened Dec 1936 Z.001396, 30/J.2; resite to Y.992407 June 1953; 23/C.1 Nov 1953; U/G Nov 1960; 23/J.1 Oct 1968; *In use*

Tantobie
Opened Jan 1941 Z.086483, 30/K.1; Granite 1942; 23/P.3 Nov 1953; U/G June 1962; 23/G.2 Oct 1968; *In use*

Tow Law
Opened Nov 1938 Z.134384, 30/J.1; Granite 1943; 23/B.4 Nov 1953; U/G Oct 1958; 23/J.2 Oct 1968; *In use*

Wearhead
Opened Oct 1939 Y.860402, 32/D.2; 30/J.4 Sept 1940; resite to Y.854388, 32/D.2 April 1942; 23/D.2 Nov 1953; U/G Jan 1961; 23/J.4 Oct 1968; *In use*

Westerton/Spennymoor
Opened Jan 1941 Z.250341, 30/G.1 Spennymoor; resite to Z.239310 renamed Westerton Aug 1953; 23/B.2 Nov 1953; resite to Z.245312 June 1959; U/G Nov 1960; 23/J.3 Oct 1968; *In use*

Whitburn
Opened Dec 1936 Z.401616, 30/E.1; resite to Z.407624 June 1940; 23/N.3 Nov 1953; U/G June 1959; *Closed Oct 1968*

Wolviston
Opened Dec 1936 Z.427193, 9/P.3; resite to Z.463264 Aug 1940; 9/T.1 Sept 1943; 20/K.4 Nov 1953; U/G June 1960; 23/T.4 May 1966; *Closed 1968*

Woodland
Opened July 1959 Z.050244 23/C.4; U/G Nov 1960; 23/L.1 Oct 1968; *In use*

ESSEX

Billericay
Opened Nov 1937 Q.672940; 18/M.2; 18/K.3 March 1938; resite to Q.675934 March 1943; 4/P.4 Nov 1953; resite to Q.670911 Sept 1962; U/G Aug 1963; 4/K.3 Oct 1968; *In use*

Bradwell-on-Sea
Opened Nov 1929 M.006072, 18/A.1; resite to M.013069 April 1940; 4/M.2 Nov 1953; resite to M.011074 Oct 1959; U/G Sept 1960; 4/L.1 Oct 1968; *In use*

Braintree
Opened April 1929 L.767227, 18/B.2; 18/E.3 June 1935; resite to L.757231 Jan 1941; Darky 1942; resite to L.787237 Dec 1947; 4/L.1 Nov 1953; U/G June 1959; *Closed Oct 1968*

Brightlingsea
Opened April 1929 M.089162, 18/D.3; resite to M.095346 (on track between Taybor's Oyster Beds), 18/C.3, April 1938; resite to M.077162 (Batenicus Tower, West Mareg Point) Oct 1939; 4/J.3 Nov 1953; resite to M.064186, U/G Jan 1959; *Closed Oct 1968*

Canvey Island
Opened Oct 1937 Q.815828, 19/O.2; 1/B.1 Nov 1953; resite to Q.773836, 4/R.2, Feb 1961; U/G June 1962; *Closed Oct 1968*

Castle Headingham
Opened Jan 1931 L.765231, 18/E.2; resite to L.789358 June 1935; 4/C.4 Nov 1953; U/G Sept 1961; *Closed Oct 1968*

Chigwell
Opened Oct 1937 Q.442922, 17/M.2; 4/Q.1 Nov 1953; resite to Q.434947 (RAF Chigwell) April 1959; U/G Aug 1961; 4/Q.3 Nov 1965; 4/J.3 Oct 1968; *In use*

Chipping Ongar
Opened Nov 1937 Q.554034, 19/O.1; 17/M.1 March 1938; 4/Q.1 Nov 1953; resite to Q.559057 Jan 1959; U/G July 1959; 4/J.1 Oct 1968; *In use*

Clacton/Holland-on-Sea
Opened April 1938 M.194162, 18/D.3 Holland-on-Sea (Telephone Exchange roof); resite to M.191149 (Clock Tower roof, Alton Hall Hotel) June 1950; 4/J.2 Nov 1953; resite to M.162134 (Martello Tower), renamed Clacton, Feb 1961; Non-standard U/G, lower room of Tower with dual Probe Pipes projecting through opposite walls, Dec 1961; *Closed Oct 1968*

Earls Colne
Opened April 1929 L.850291, 18/E.2; resite to L.857282 April 1934; 18/F.2 May 1938; 4/G.2 Nov 1953; U/G Oct 1960; 4/H.3 Oct 1968; *In use*

Finchingfield
Opened April 1929 L.682316, 18/E.1; resite to L.693319 Aug 1944; 4/G.3 Nov 1953; resite to L.695328 Oct 1960; U/G Nov 1961; 4/G.1 Oct 1968; *In use*

Foulness
Opened Jan 1939 R.004929, 18/M.2; 4/N.2 Nov 1953; resite to Q.004029 Dec 1957; U/G June 1960; Closed Oct 1968; Reopened, 4/L.2, Jan 1971; *In use*

Good Easter
Opened Oct 1937 L.624123, 18/K.4; 18/B.3 March 1938;

18/H.4 April 1939; resite to L.629117, 18/B.3, Oct
1941; 4/L.3 Nov 1953; U/G Oct 1959; *Closed Oct 1968*
Reopened, 4/G.2, 1975

Great Baddow
Opened Nov 1937 L.732033, 18/K.1; resite to L.722045
Oct 1940; 4/P.1 Nov 1953; resite to L.740056 Oct 1960;
U/G Nov 1961; *Closed Oct 1968*

Great Dunmow
Opened April 1929 L.624228, 18/B.1; resite to L.634225
(Windmill), 1944; 4/L.4 Nov 1953; resite to L.645245
March 1957; U/G Jan 1959; *Closed Oct 1968*

Great Horkesley/Langham
Opened May 1937 L.973307, 18/F.1 Great Horkesley;
resite to L.988326 April 1943; 4/F.4 Nov 1953; resite to
M.009305, renamed Langham, Nov 1960; U/G Sept
1961; 4/H.1 Oct 1968; *In use*

Great Wakering
Opened Nov 1929 Q.957887, 18/A.5; resite to Q.955885
May 1935; 19/O.1 Feb 1938; 4/N.3 Nov 1953; U/G
Sept 1961; *Closed Oct 1968*

Harold Wood
Opened Nov 1937 Q.526928, 17/M.3; 4/Q.2 Nov 1953;
U/G Oct 1960; *Closed Oct 1968*

Hatfield Broad Oak
Opened Oct 1937 L.569163, 18/B.2; 17/M.2 March
1938; resite to L.558165 May 1942; 17/H.4 Nov 1945;
resite to L.546161, 4/H.2, Nov 1953; U/G Feb 1960;
Closed Oct 1968

Hatfield Peverel
Opened April 1929 L.791120, 18/B.3; 18/G.3 April
1938; 4/K.4 Nov 1953; resite to L.797125 May 1954;
U/G July 1959; *Closed Oct 1968*

Henham
Opened Oct 1937 L.548282, 17/H.1; 4/H.1 Nov 1953;
U/G Nov 1961; 4/C.3 Oct 1968; *In use*

Kelvedon
Opened April 1929 L.858190, 18/C.1; resite to L.853196
May 1936; 18/G.1 April 1938; resite to L.851191 Feb
1948; 4/K.1 Nov 1953; U/G May 1960; *Closed Oct 1968*

Latchington
Opened Jan 1939 L.883009, 18/A.2; 4/N.1 Nov 1953;
U/G April 1960; *Closed Oct 1968*

Lexden
Opened April 1929 L.968546, 18/C.3; resite to L.971226
May 1942; G/L 1942; 4/F.3 Nov 1953; *Closed Oct 1968*

Little Waltham
Opened Jan 1939 L.711134, 18/B.2; 4/L.2 Nov 1953;
U/G Feb 1959; 4/C.2 Oct 1968; *Closed 1975*

Maldon
Opened April 1929 L.852068, 18/A.3; 18/G.2 Dec 1941;
4/K.3 Nov 1953; resite to L.837071 Dec 1959; U/G May
1960; *Closed Oct 1968*

Manningtree
Opened April 1929 M.103316, 18/D.1; 18/J.2 May 1938;
4/F.2 Nov 1953; U/G Aug 1960; *Closed Oct 1968*

Nazeing
Opened Feb 1938 L.424063, 17/M.3; 17/G.3 Sept 1949;
4/Q.4 Nov 1953; U/G April 1960; *Closed Oct 1968*

New Malden
Opened Oct 1937 Q.213689, 19/X.1 (Telephone Exchange
roof); 5/M.2 April 1955; resite to Q.212697 July 1963;
U/G Oct 1963; *Closed Oct 1968*

Orsett
Opened Oct 1937 Q.545811, 19/P.1; 1/B.4 Nov 1953;
U/G Jan 1959; *Closed Oct 1968*

Rochford
Opened April 1929 Q.877015, 18/A.4; resite to Q.883009
April 1934; 18/M.3 April 1938; resite to Q.879934,
4/N.3 Nov 1953; U/G Jan 1962; *Closed Oct 1968*

Southend/Leigh
Opened Sept 1938, Q.874959, 19/O.4 Southend (Palace
Hotel roof); 1/A.1 Nov 1953; 4/R.1 July 1960; resite to
Q.835873, U/G, renamed Leigh, Jan 1966; 4/L.3 Oct
1968; *In use*

Southminster
Opened April 1929 Q.958998, 18/A.2; 18/M.1 April
1938; resite to Q.964992 Jan 1941; 4/M.3 Nov 1953;
U/G Oct 1959; *Closed Oct 1968*

Tendring
Opened April 1929 M.144247, 18/D.2; Darky 1942;
4/J.4 Nov 1953; U/G Jan 1959; 4/E.3 Oct 1968; *In use*

Tolleshunt D'Arcy
Opened Jan 1939 L.923113, 18/G.2; 18/A.3 March 1942;
4/M.4 Nov 1953; U/G June 1959; *Closed Oct 1968*

Vange
Opened Dec 1937 Q.727881, 19/P.3; resite to Q.718876
June 1950; 4/P.3 Nov 1953; U/G Nov 1958; *Closed Oct 1968*

Walton-on-the-Naze
Opened Nov 1929 M.260266, 18/D.4; resite to M.262237
(Walton Hall roof) July 1940; resite to M.252213 April
1962; U/G Aug 1962; *Closed Oct 1968*

West Mersea
Opened April 1929 M.014124, 18/C.2; resite to M.007129
Nov 1935; 4/M.1 Nov 1953; resite to M.019123 June
1956; U/G July 1960; *Closed Oct 1968*

Wickham Bishop
Opened Oct 1952 L.855127, 4/K.2; U/G June 1959;
4/M.2 Oct 1968; *In use*

Woodham Ferrers
Opened Nov 1937 Q.798988, 18/K.2; 4/P.2 Nov 1953;
U/G Aug 1959; 4/K.1 Oct 1968; *In use*

GLOUCESTERSHIRE

Alderton/Evesham
Opened Nov 1937 P.008327, 24/N.3 Alderton; Granite
1942; resite to P.003324 May 1949; 3/C.4 Nov 1953;
resite to P.019408 Aug 1962; renamed Evesham Dec
1962; U/G May 1963; *Closed April 1968*

Almondsbury/Thornbury
Opened Jan 1938 T.609842 Almondsbury; 23/K.4; resite
to T.596834 Sept 1944; 12/H.1 Nov 1953; resite to
T.647888 Sept 1961; U/G May 1962; renamed
Thornbury Sept 1962; *Closed Oct 1968*

Andoversford
Opened Dec 1937 P.028195, 24/L.2; Granite 1942; resite
to T.596834 Sept 1944; 3/A.1 Nov 1953; resite to
P.032208 May 1956; resite to P.049219 Sept 1961; U/G
Sept 1963; 3/E.3 Oct 1968; *In use*

Blakeney
Opened Dec 1937 O.668061, 24/P.2; 12/K.1 Nov 1953;
U/G Sept 1961; *Closed Oct 1968*

Cleve Hill/Stoke Orchard
Opened Sept 1939 O.987283, 24/L.4 Cleve Hill; 24/N.4
March 1941; Granite 1942; 3/C.3 Nov 1953; resite to
O.983283, renamed Stoke Orchard, June 1962; U/G Oct
1964; *Closed Oct 1968*

Dursley
Opened Jan 1938 T.754984, 23/L.1; resite to T.861989
April 1940; 24/K.4 March 1942; resite to T.733996,
12/K.3, Nov 1953; U/G Sept 1961; 12/J.3 Oct 1968;
In use

Hallen/Avonmouth
Opened May 1938 T.518782, 23/K.3 Avonmouth; resite
to T.520807 May 1953; 12/H.3 Nov 1953; resite to
T.553803, renamed Hallen, Sept 1958; U/G Sept 1960;
12/L.4 Oct 1968; *In use*

Hill
Opened Sept 1941 T.654969, 24/P.4; 12/K.2 Nov 1953;
resite to T.654953, 12/E.2, Aug 1959; resite to T.643953
Aug 1961; U/G Dec 1962; *Closed Oct 1968*

Leighterton
Opened Jan 1938 T.823920, 23/L.3; 12/L.1 Nov 1953;
resite to T.830893, 12/J.1, June 1962; U/G May 1963;
12/J.2 Oct 1968; *In use*

Little Sodbury
Opened 1954 T.759825, 12/J.2; resite to T.768839 Jan
1959; U/G May 1960; 12/L.1 Oct 1968; *In use*

Marshfield
Opened 1938 T.768725, 23/M.3; 12/J.3 Nov 1953; U/G
April 1958; 12/L.2 Oct 1968; *In use*

Minsterworth/Westbury-on-Severn
Opened Dec 1937 O.756168, 24/O.1 Minsterworth;
12/L.4 Nov 1953; resite to O.731145 May 1961; renamed
Westbury-on-Severn Sept 1962; U/G Sept 1963;
Closed Oct 1968

North Cerney
Opened Dec 1937 P.031081, 24/L.1; 3/B.2 Nov 1953;
resite to P.029081 May 1956; U/G Nov 1962; 3/J.1 Oct
1968; *In use*

Northleach
Opened Jan 1941 P.096146, 24/L.4; 3/A.2 Nov 1953;
U/G June 1962; *Closed Oct 1968*

Poulton
Opened Dec 1937 P.112027, 24/L.3; 3/A.3 Nov 1953;
resite to P.101005 May 1956; resite to P.100020 July
1959; U/G Nov 1962; *Closed Oct 1968*

Rodmarton/Kemble
Opened Dec 1937 T.937976, 24/K.3 Rodmarton; 3/B.3
Nov 1953; resite to Y.937985 April 1954; resite to
T.967963 June 1961; renamed Kemble Oct 1961; U/G
March 1962; 3/J.3 Oct 1968; *In use*

St. Briavels
Opened Dec 1937 O.559041, 24/P.3; 12/L.4 Nov 1953;
U/G June 1961; 12/H.1 Oct 1968; *In use*

Stow-on-the Wold
Opened Jan 1938 P.19367, 4/J.3; Granite 1943; 3/L.1
Nov 1953; U/G April 1960; 3/E.1 Oct 1968; *In use*

Stroud/Stonehouse/Middle Lypiatt
Opened Dec 1937 O.698032, 24/K.1 Stonehouse
(Wycliffe College roof); resite to O.829030 June 1949;
12/K.4, renamed Middle Lypiatt, Nov 1953; renamed
Stroud June 1954; resite to O.831086 June 1961; U/G
April 1963; Closed Oct. 1968; Reopened, 12/J.1,
Nov 1970; *In use*

Tirley
Opened Nov 1937 O.802279, 24/O.2; 12/M.3 Nov 1953;
U/G June 1959; *Closed Oct 1968*

GREATER LONDON

Acton
Opened May 1938 Q.215802 (Min of Pensions Building
roof, Bromyard ave), 17/K.2; 17/D.2 May 1939; 5/A.4

Nov 1953; resite to Q.158819 Sept 1960; U/G Oct 1961;
Closed Oct 1968

Brixton
Opened April 1939 Q.313758 (Telephone Exchange roof,
Gresham Road), 19/X.3; 5/A.3 Nov 1953; resite to
Q.211748 (Palewell Common), Jan 1965, U/G May
1966; *Closed Oct 1968*

Crouch End/Highgate/Bowes Park
Opened May 1938 Q.300881, 17/K.2 Crouch End
(Telephone Exchange roof); resite to Q.283877
(Highpoint Flats roof), renamed Highgate, June 1941;
5/B.3 Nov 1953; resite to Q.301904, renamed Bowes
Park, Jan 1964; U/G Feb 1964; 2/B.1 Oct 1968; *In use*

Gower Street
Opened 1939, Roof of GPO Parcels Office, Mount
Pleasant, 17/K.1; resite to London University Roof Nov
1939; 5/A.1 Nov 1953; *Closed 1963*

Harrow/Colindale
Opened March 1932 Q.153878 (Northwick Park Golf
Club), 17/D.3; resite to Q.149888 (roof of, Harrow View,
Automatic Telephone Exchange), June 1942; 5/M.1 Nov
1953; resite to Q.199881, renamed Colindale. Aug 1960;
U/G July 1961; *Closed Oct 1968*

Hounslow
Opened Oct 1937 Q.139579 (Hounslow Telephone
Exchange roof), 19/X.3; 17/D.1 July 1939; 5/M.3 Nov
1953; resite to Q.089749 (London Airport), U/G, July
1966; *Closed Oct 1968*

Newcross/Dulwich
Opened April 1938 Q.355770 (Telephone Exchange roof),
19/Y.4 Newcross; Post destroyed by enemy action during
1940 and temporarily resited on roof of Robinson's
Flour Mills, Deptford. Resite to Q.359761 (roof of Aske
Hatcham Grammar School), Oct 1940; 5/A.2 Nov 1953;
resite to Q.340727, renamed Dulwich, March 1963;
U/G May 1965; 2/B.1 Oct 1968; *In use*

Uxbridge/Northolt
Opened March 1932 Q.054840 (Uxbridge Telephone
Exchange roof), 17/D.2; 17/E.3 April 1938; 5/M.4 Nov
1953; resite to Q.095850 (Northolt RAF Station), U/G,
July 1967; 2/A.2 Oct 1968; *In use*

Winchmore Hill/Enfield
Opened April 1938 Q.322948, 17/G.2 Winchmore Hill
(Laburnham Telephone Exchange roof); 5/B.1 Nov
1953; resite to Q.288997 Dec 1957; U/G, renamed
Enfield, Dec 1960; *Closed Oct 1968*

HAMPSHIRE

Atherfield (IOW)
Satellite, opened Sept 1943 Z.454791 C/G Station, Totter,
3/C.1; *Closed Oct 1944*

Barton
Satellite, opened July 1943 Z.240929, C/G Station, 3/N.1;
Closed Jan 1945

Boscombe/New Milton
Satellite, opened July 1943 Z.711914 (San Remo Hotel
roof), 3/H.4; full Post status and Totter, Aug 1943;
14/E.3 Nov 1953; resite to Z.233931, renamed New
Milton, June 1960; *Closed Oct 1968*

Botley
Opened 1926 U.512133, 3/E.1; resite to U.509147 Dec
1940; Totter 1943; 14/S.1 Nov 1953; resite to U.498117
March 1962; U/G Nov 1962; 14/H.2 Oct 1968; *In use*

Brightstone (IOW)
Satellite, Z.423816 C/G Station, 3/G.4; *Closed 1944*

Brook Bay
Satellite, opened Oct 1943, 3/G.2; *Closed Oct 1944*

Chandlers Ford
Opened 1926 U.434200, 3/E.3; resite to U.423193 April
1939; Totter 1943; 14/Q.3 Nov 1953; resite to U.413197
March 1963; U/G April 1964; *Closed Oct 1968*

Cheriton
Opened 1926 U.580288, 3/C.2; 3/B.2 July 1940; resite to
U.582281, 14/H.4 Nov 1953; U/G Dec 1959; 2/F.1 Oct
1968; *In use*

Christchurch
Opened Sept 1938 Z.149929, 22/O.1; 3/H.1 March 1940:
Totter 1942; resite to Z.152935, 14/E.2, Nov 1953;
resite to Z.143954 Dec 1956; U/G Sept 1959; 14/G.2 Oct
1968; *In use*

Compton
Opened 1926 U.775146, 2/P.3, 3/D.1 April 1939; Totter
1943; resite to U.796149, 14/H.2 Nov 1953; U/G Dec
1962; *Closed Oct 1968*

Copythorne
Opened 1926 U.312154, 3/F.1; resite to U.286161 Oct
1942; Totter 1943; 14/P.1 Nov 1953; resite to U.307138
July 1962; U/G, U.329164, July 1964; *Closed Oct 1968*

Exbury/Stone Point
Opened 1926 U.430002, 3/G.1 Exbury; Money Flare
1940; resite to U.437017, 3/F.3 June 1940; 3/G.4 May
1947; 14/S.3 Nov 1953; resite to U.457986, renamed
Stone Point, June 1955; U/G April 1962; 14/H.3 Oct
1968; *In use*

Attack Warning Red

Fleet/Odiham
Opened Oct 1935 U.810537, 3/L.4 Fleet (Oakley's Store roof); resite to U.800520 Dec 1935; resite to U.773520, 4/M.2, March 1940; 2/J.1 Nov 1953; resite to U.004491, renamed Odiham, July 1961; U/G Sept 1961; *Closed Oct 1968*

Fordingbridge
Opened 1926 U.148141, 3/H.2; 14/P.4 Nov 1953; resite to U.167142 June 1961; U/G Jan 1962; 14/C.1 Oct 1968; *In use*

Freshwater (I.O.W.)
Opened May 1934 Z.337874, 3/J.1, 3/G.3 Jan 1936; Money Flake 1940; resite to Z.353858, Totter, 1943; 14/F.4 Nov 1953; U/G Jan 1959; 14/J.3 Oct 1968; *In use*

Froxfield Green/Langrish
Opened 1926 U.706254, 3/D.1 Langrish; 3/B.1 renamed Froxfield, April 1939; resite to U.727259 Sept 1953; 2/H.1 Nov 1953; U/G April 1959; 2/F.2 Oct 1968; *In use*

Gratley
Opened 1926 U.280420, 3/A.3; resite to U.268409 May 1939; Money Flare 1940; 14/N.2 Nov 1953; U/G June 1961; 14/E.2 Oct 1968; *In use*

Hambledon
Opened 1926 U.646151, 3/D.2.1 resite to U.649146 April 1930; Totter 1943; 14/H.3 Nov 1953; U/G April 1959; 2/F.3 Oct 1968; *In use*

Hardley
Opened Sept 1938 T.996174, 22/N.3; 14/C.2 Nov 1953; U/G Oct 1960; *Closed Oct 1968*

Havant
Opened 1926 U.770068, 3/D.3; resite to U.721073 (Post Office roof) Dec 1937; resite to U.692065 (Belmont Hill) Dec 1938; 2/G.1 Nov 1953; resite to U.685065 Oct 1957; 14/G.1 Dec 1962; U/G Jan 1968; 2/M.3 Oct 1968; *In use*

Hayling Island
Opened Jan 1940 Z.688997, 3/M.1; resite to Z.725986 June 1941; Totter 1943; *Closed Jan 1946.* New Post opened July 1948 Z.746980; 2/G.1 Nov.1953; resite to Z.733006 May 1963; U/G Jan 1964; *Closed Oct 1968*

Headley/Bordon
Opened 1926 U.820364, Parish Green, Headley, resite to Farthing Field Dec 1929, 3/L.1; resite to U.794339 Aug 1961; U/G Sept 1963; 2/N.4 renamed Bordon, Jan 1966; 2/C.2 Oct 1968; *In use*

Hengistbury Head
Satellite, opened July 1943 Z.174906, C/G Station, 3/N.4 *Closed 1944*

Herriard
Opened 1926 U.671444, 3/B.3; Money Flare 1940, 3/C.1, 1940; resite to U.671442 May 1940; 3/K.1 June 1943; 14/J.4 Nov 1953; U/G March 1959; 2/C.3 Oct 1968; *In use*

Hill Head/Lee-on-Solent
Opened Jan 1940 U.551018, 3/M.2 Lee-on-Solent; 3/M.2, renamed Hill Head, March 1940; resite to U.538024 Dec 1940; Totter 1943; 14/S.2 Nov 1953; resite to U.528028 April 1961; U/G Aug 1961; *Closed Oct 1968*

Keyhaven
Satellite, opened July 1943 Z.240929; *Closed May 1945*

Kingsclere
Opened Oct 1935 U.526584, 3/HK.3; 4/S.4 March 1940; 14/R.1 Nov 1953; U/G June 1960; *Closed Oct 1968*

Kings Worthy
Opened 1926 U.490326, 3/C.1; resite to U.492530 June 1929; 3/K.3 July 1943; *Closed May 1946.* New Post, opened Jan 1947 U.494332; 14/R.3 Nov 1953; resite to U.495337 Aug 1955; U/G Oct 1960; 14/F.2 Oct 1968; *In use*

Lockerley Green
Opened 1926 U.292264, 3/F.3; Money Flare 1940; 3/E.4 June 1943; 3/F.3 May 1947; 14/Q.4 Nov 1953; resite to U.313250 Oct 1963; U/G March 1966; 14/H.1 Oct 1968; *In use*

Longparish
Opened 1926 U.430442, 3/A.1; resite to U.437434 June 1940; 3/K.1 Jan 1941; 3/A.4 June 1943; 14/R.4 Nov 1953; U/G June 1961; *Closed Oct 1968*

Luccombe Bay (IOW)
Satellite, opened 1943, Z.585800, 3/C.4; *Closed Jan 1945*

Lyndhurst
Opened 1926 U.300083, 3/H.1; Totter 1942; 3/F.4 1942; 14/P.2 Nov 1953; resite to U.300079 June 1956; resite to U.289089 April 1961; U/G Jan 1962; 14/H.4 Oct 1968; *In use*

Marchwood
Opened 1926 U.387116, 3/F.2; resite to U.387074 May 1940; Totter 1943; 14/S.4 Nov 1953; resite to U.383095 Feb 1962; U/G Oct 1968; *Closed Oct 1968*

Medstead
Opened 1926 U.658369, 3/B.2; 3/C.1 May 1934: 3/K.4 March 1940; 14/J.3 Nov 1953; resite to U.663366 Dec 1953; U/G Dec 1963; *Closed Oct 1968*

Needles (IOW)
Satellite opened June 1943 Z.294849; *Closed Oct 1944*

Newport (IOW)
Opened Oct 1935 Z.496878, 3/J.1; Totter 1943; 14/F.1
Nov 1953; resite to Z.518891 April 1961; U/G July 1962;
14/J.1 Oct 1968; *In use*

Niton (IOW)
Opened May 1934 Z.504767, 3/J.3; resite to Z.508761
Jan 1943; Totter 1943; 3/C.2 Sept 1943; 14/F.3 Nov
1953; U/G May 1962; 14/J.2 Oct 1968; *In use*

Overton
Opened Oct 1935 U.521498, 3/K.2; 14/R.2 Nov 1953;
U/G Oct 1960; 14/F.3 Oct 1968; *In use*

Ringwood
Opened 1926 U.152055, 3/H.3; resite to U.193058,
Totter, 1943; 14/F.3 Nov 1953; resite to U.173022 April
1962; U/G Nov 1962; *Closed Oct 1968*

Sandown (IOW)
Opened May 1934 Z.595838, 3/J.3; Totter 1942; 14/F.2
Nov 1953; resite to Z.617853 Sept 1961; U/G April 1962;
Closed Oct 1968

Seaview (IOW)
Opened Jan 1940 Z.615922, 3/J.4; 14/G.3 Nov 1953; U/G
Feb 1962; *Closed Oct 1968*

Selbourne
Opened Jan 1934 U.746335, 3/B.2; 3/L.3 Dec 1940;
2/J.2 Nov 1953; U/G March 1960; 14/J.2 Dec 1962;
Closed Oct 1968

Southsea
Opened Jan 1940 Z.652981 (Royal Beach Hotel roof),
3/M.2; Totter 1943; *Closed Nov 1946.* New Post opened
Sept 1947, Z.637999 (Commercial Chambers roof);
14/G.4 Nov 1953; resite to Z.633991 Oct 1959; U/G
Aug 1961; *Closed Oct 1968*

Stockbridge
Opened 1926 U.356352, 3/A.2; Money Flare 1940; resite
to U.369359 July 1941; 14/Q.1 Nov 1953; resite to
U.382354 Oct 1954; U/G Feb 1962; *Closed Oct 1968*

Stratfield Turgis
Opened Oct 1935 U.700588, 3/K.1; 4/M.1 March 1940;
2/M.3 Nov 1953; resite to U.702590 Jan 1960; U/G Aug
1960; 14/K.3 Dec 1962; 14/F.1 Oct 1968; *In use*

Sway
Opened 1926 Z.286987, 3/G.2; resite to Z.277999 Nov
1942; Totter, 3/N.2, 1943; resite to Z.293982, 14/E.1,
Nov 1953; U/G Feb 1963; *Closed Oct 1968*

Upham
Opened 1926 U.535204, 3/E.2; resite to U.542211 May
1940; Totter 1943; 14/Q.2 Nov 1953; U/G Feb 1959;
Closed Oct 1968

Woody Point
Satellite, opened 1943 Z.536762, C/G Station, 3/C.3;
Closed Aug 1944

HEREFORDSHIRE

Burghill
Opened Dec 1937 O.484453 24/S.2; 12/E.4 Nov 1953;
U/G Nov 1961; 12/D.1 Oct 1968; *In use*

Fownhope
Opened Dec 1937 O.580343, 24/U.3; 12/N.2 Nov 1953;
resite to O.575337 Aug 1954; resite to O.592340 April
1959; U/G Nov 1961; *Closed Oct 1968*

Harewood End
Opened Dec 1937 O.525270, 24/R.2; 12/N.3 Nov 1953;
resite to O.530275 May 1956; U/G July 1961; 12/E.3 Oct
1968; *In use*

Hucclecote/Barewood
Opened Dec 1937 O.865170, 24/K.2 Hucclecote; Granite
1942; resite to O.881189 Oct 1951; 3/B.1 Nov 1953;
renamed Barewood Feb 1959; U/G June 1959; 12/J.1
Oct 1968; *Closed 1970*

Lea
Opened Dec 1937 O.652223, 24/O.3; 12/L.1 Nov 1953;
resite to O.676826 Aug 1954; resite to O.672220 April
1959; U/G June 1961; 12/E.2 Oct 1968; *In use*

Ledbury/Trumpet
Opened Dec 1937 O.703373, 24/U.2 Ledbury; 12/M.4
Nov 1953; resite to O.695357, renamed Trumpet, Sept
1954; resite to O.880372 April 1961; U/G Oct 1963;
12/E.1 Oct 1968; *In use*

Leominster
Opened Dec 1937, O.492593, 24/T.1; 12/A.2 Nov 1953·
resite to O.513577 Aug 1954; U/G Nov 1961; *In use*

Lyonshall
Opened Dec 1937 O.324653, 24/S.3; Granite 1942;
12/A.3 Nov 1953; U/G Nov 1963; *In use*

Pencombe
Opened Dec 1937 O.600529, 24/T.2; resite to T.617533,
12/N.1 Nov 1953; U/G Nov 1961; 12/B.1 Oct 1968;
In use

Peterchurch
Opened Dec 1937 O.349385, 24/S.1; 12/Q.3 Nov 1953;
resite to O.265392 Aug 1954; resite to O.362394 Dec
1959; U/G Nov 1961; 12/D.3 Oct 1968; *In use*

Pontrilas
Opened Dec 1937 O.400274, 24/R.1; 12/P.1 Nov 1953;
resite to O.387268 Aug 1954; U/G Nov 1961; 12/D.2
Oct 1968; *In use*

Ridgway Cross
Opened Dec 1937 O.722473, 24/U.1; 12/M.1 Nov 1953;
U/G June 1959; *Closed Oct 1968*

Upper Sapley/Shelsley Beauchamp
Opened Dec 1937 O.734630, 24/V.1 Shelsley Beauchamp;
Granite 1942; 12/C.3 Nov 1953; resite to O.744637 July
1955; resite to O.709626 Aug 1962; U/G renamed Upper
Sapley, June 1966; 16/L.3 Oct 1968; *In use*

Whitchurch
Opened Dec 1937 O.542179, 24/P.1; 12/L.2 Nov 1953;
resite to O.542181 Feb 1962; U/G May 1961; *Closed Oct
1968*

Wigmore
Opened Aug 1939 O.410690, 27/H.2; Granite 1943;
12/D.3 Nov 1953; resite to O.410688 Oct 1958; U/G
Nov 1961; *Closed Oct 1968*

HERTFORDSHIRE

Ashwell
Opened Nov 1931 L.272392, 17/A.1; 17/A.4 May 1938;
17/S.2 April 1939; 12/S.2 Dec 1939; 5/E.3 Nov 1953;
resite to L.268385 May 1954; U/G April 1960; 7/J.1 Oct
1968; *In use*

Berkhampstead
Opened Nov 1931 L.001087, 17/F.3; 5/P.3 Nov 1953;
resite to L.988091 March 1958; U/G July 1960; *Closed
Oct 1968*

Brent Pelham
Opened Oct 1937 L.433306, 17/H.2; 4/H.4 Nov 1953;
resite to L.425315 March 1955; U/G Nov 1961; 7/K.1
Oct 1968; *In use*

Cuffley
Opened May 1936 L.288017, 17/G.1; 5/C.3 Nov 1953;
Closed Oct 1968

Elstree
Opened March 1932 Q.181948, 17/C.2; 5/B.4 Nov 1953;
U/G May 1959; 2/A.1 Oct 1968; *In use*

Great Offley
Opened Nov 1931 L.136274, 17/G.3; 17/A.1 April 1938;
5/D.4 Nov 1953; U/G July 1959; 7/J.3 Oct 1968; *In use*

Hertford
Opened Nov 1931 L.339127, 17/B.3; resite to L.314131
June 1934; 5/S.2 Nov 1953; resite to L.324118 March
1956; resite to L.293145 Aug 1960; U/G Jan 1961; 7/K.3
Oct 1968; *In use*

Kimpton
Opened Nov 1931 L.173179, 17/G.2; 17/B.1 May 1938;
5/D.3 Nov 1953; resite to L.181178 Oct 1958; U/G Nov

1958; *Closed Oct 1968*

Kings Langley
Opened Nov 1931 L.068001, 17/C.1; resite to L.067019
Oct 1949; 5/P.2 Nov 1953; U/G Nov 1959; 7/H.3 Oct
1968; *In use*

Letchworth
Opened Nov 1931 L.215328; 17/A.3; 5/D.1 Nov 1953;
resite to L.202325 Jan 1960; U/G Sept 1960; *Closed Oct
1968*

Markyate Street
Opened Nov 1931 L.065166, 17/G.1; resite to L.058155
Nov 1935; 17/L.2 May 1938; 5/P.1 Nov 1953; U/G May
1960; 7/J.2 Oct 1968; *In use*

Much Hadham
Opened Oct 1937 L.436198, 17/H.3; 4/H.3 Nov 1953;
U/G May 1962; 7/K.2 Oct 1968; *In use*

Park Street
Opened Nov 1931 L.149236, 17/C.3; resite to L.141043
Nov 1935; 5/C.4 Nov 1953; resite to L.154042 July
1960; U/G Jan 1961; *Closed Oct 1968*

Rickmansworth/Chorley Wood
Opened Nov 1931 Q.053945, 17/D.1 Rickmansworth;
resite to Q.043948 Nov 1935; 17/F.1 April 1938; 5/N.2,
renamed Chorley Wood, Nov 1953; U/G July 1959;
Closed Oct 1968

Walkern
Opened Nov 1931 L.282263, 17/A.2; resite to L.303261
Aug 1949; 5/D.2 Nov 1953; U/G Nov 1958; *Closed Oct
1968*

Walkington
Opened Nov 1937, Q.286638 19/Y.2 (Fire Station roof);
resite to Q.288622 Nov 1938; 2/Q.3 Nov 1953; U/G
June 1960; 2/B.3 Oct 1968; *In use*

Welwyn/Hatfield
Opened Nov 1931 L.242143, 17/B.2 Hatfield; renamed
Welwyn Nov 1934; 5/C.1 Nov 1953; resite to L.207111
April 1957; U/G Oct 1958; 7/H.2 Oct 1968; *In use*

HUNTINGDONSHIRE

Buckden
Opened Nov 1949 L.178677, 15/D.2; U/G Aug, 1968;
Closed Oct 1968

Castor/Fleeton
Opened July 1950, L.208972, 15/G.2 Fleeton; 7/M.3 Nov
1953; resite to L.135993 Oct 1960; renamed Castor, Nov
1960; U/G Feb 1962; *Closed 1968*

Ramsey
Opened 1938 L.275849, 15/E.3; 7/S.2 Nov 1953; U/G
June 1960; 7/E.1 Oct 1968; *In use*

Sawtry
Opened Nov 1949 L.157841 15/E.1 7/S.1 Nov 1953;
U/G 1958; 7/B.2 Oct 1968; *In use*

St Ives
Opened Nov 1949 L.306723 15/D.1; 7/Q.4 Nov 1953;
resite to L.278688 Dec 1958; U/G May 1959; 7/E.3 Oct
1968; *In use*

Wansford
Opened June 1947 F.079009, 15/F.1; 7/L.2 Nov 1953;
U/G Feb 1962; *Closed Oct 1968*

KENT

All Hallows
Opened Sept 1938 Q.837786 (Slough Fort), 19/N.3;
1/A.1 Nov 1953; 1/B.1 June 1960; U/G Nov 1961;
Closed Oct 1968

Ash
Opened April 1929 R.293585, 1/A.2; resite to R.299578,
Totter, May 1942; 1/M.1 Nov 1953; resite to R.293582
Nov 1959; U/G May 1962; *Closed 1968*

Barham
Opened 1925 R.208499, 1/C.2; resite to R.216509, 1/D.1,
Sept 1939; Totter 1943; 1/M.4 Nov 1953; U/G June
1960; 1/C.3 Oct 1968; *In use*

Bearsted
Opened Nov 1937, Q.794559, 19/Q.2; 1/R.2 Nov 1953;
resite to Q.694560 July 1962; U/G Sept 1902; *Closed
Oct 1968*

Bethersden
Opened 1924, 1/D.1; 1/F.1 1925; resite to Q.929405
1953; U/G Feb 1962; *Closed Oct 1968*

Biddenden
Experimental Post B.3, 1924

Borough Green
Opened May 1939 Q.619573, 19/R.3; 1/D.2 Nov 1953;
U/G March 1960; 1/A.2 Oct 1968; *In us*

Brasted
Opened Jan 1939 Q.469569, 19/S.1; 1/D.3 Nov 1953;
U/G Sept 1962; *Closed Oct 1968*

Brookland
Opened Dec 1939 Q.988255, 1/M.4; 1/N.3 Sept 1947;
1/H.1 Nov 1953; U/G Feb 1962; *Closed Oct 1968*

Canterbury
Opened 1925 R.131155, 1/B.2; 1/P.2 Nov 1953; resite to

R.162583 March 1959; U/G Aug 1961; *Closed Oct 1968*

Chislet/Upstreet
Opened 1925, 1/A.2 Chislet; 1/A.1 1929; 1/B.3 May
1938; resite to R.235635 Dec 1941; Totter 1943; 1/L.4,
renamed Upstreet, March 1944; 1/N.3 Nov 1953; resite
to R.233635, U/G Oct 1961; *Closed Oct 1968*

Cliffe
Opened 1938 Q.732767, 19/N.2; 1/B.3 Nov 1953; U/G
June 1961; *Closed Oct 1968*

Cobham
Opened Nov 1937 Q.819645, 19/Q.1; 1/R.1 Nov 1953;
Closed 1956

Cranbrook
Experimental Centre, room above Post Office, 1924
Experimental Post, C.2, Q.778346, 1924; 1/C.1 1925;
1/G.2 1930; resite to Q.763355 Sept 1942; 1/E.3 Nov
1953; U/G Sept 1968; 1/D.2 Oct 1968; *In use*

Dartford/Greenhithe
Opened Nov 1937 Q.534738, 19/Z.4 Dartford; 1/C.2
Nov 1953; 1/C.1 Dec 1960; resite to Q.608734, renamed
Greenhithe, Sept 1963; U/G Dec 1965; 1/A.1 Oct 1968;
In use

Deal/Kingsdown
Opened 1929 R.372540, 1/C.4 Deal; Totter 1942; 1/M.2
Nov 1953; resite to R.372481 July 1954; renamed
Kingsdown Sept 1954; resite to R.372540 April 1956;
1/M.2, renamed Deal, Dec 1959; resite to R.374494 Dec
1959; U/G, renamed Kingsdown, Dec 1966; 1/C.2 Oct
1968; *In use*

Dover
Opened Jan 1938, 1/C.3; 1/D.2 Sept 1942; Totter 1943;
resite to R.328417 (Dover Castle), 1/L.1 Sept 1943; U/G
May 1962; *Closed Oct 1968*

Dungeness
Opened 1929 R.088167, 1/F.5; resite to R.092178 April
1934; 1/M.1 Dec 1938; Totter 1943; 1/N.1 July 1943;
1/K.3 Nov 1953; resite to R.025198 July 1961; U/G
1965; 1/J.2 Oct 1968; *In use*

Dymchurch
Opened Nov 1929 R.100290 (Martello Tower), 1/F.6;
1/M.2 April 1938; Totter 1943; (First Post to recognise
and report V1 Flying Bombs); 1/K.2 Nov 1953; resite to
R.104316 Sept 1961, 1/J.3, U/G, Aug 1962; *In use*

Eastchurch
Opened 1925 Q.996713, 1/D.1; resite to Q.996716 Oct
1935; 19/T.1 Aug 1940; resite to Q.998716 Nov 1952;
1/Q.1 Nov 1953; resite to Q.993708 Jan 1961; U/G Oct
1961; 1/B.2 Oct 1968; *In use*

Attack Warning Red

Edenbridge
Opened Oct 1937 19/S.2; resite to Q.458466 Jan 1943; 2/S.2 Nov 1953; U/G July 1960; *Closed Oct 1968*

Eltham
Opened March 1938 Q.428746, 19/Z.3; resite to Q.442719 1/C.1 Nov 1953; U/G May 1965; *Closed Oct 1968*

Eythorn
Opened 1925, 1/C.1; resite to R.292492 Nov 1941; Totter 1942; 1/M.3 Nov 1953; U/G Nov 1960; *Closed Oct 1968*

Farningham
Opened Jan 1938, 19/Z.2; resite to Q.540667 Oct 1942; 1/D.4 Nov 1953; 1/C.1 Oct 1960; resite to Q.534669 Oct 1961; U/G May 1963; *Closed 1968*

Folkestone
Opened Dec 1939 R.211353 (Martello Tower), 1/D.3; Totter 1942; 1/L.2 Nov 1953; resite to R.241366 Aug 1959; U/G 1961; 1/J.1 Oct 1968; *In use*

Hamstreet
Experimental Post D.2, R.007332, 1924; 1/F.1 1931; Totter 1942; 1/M.2 Sept 1943; 1/K.4 Nov 1953; U/G Nov 1961; 1/E.3 Oct 1968; *In use*

Hawkhurst
Experimental Post C.3, 1924

Headcorn
Opened 1925 Q.829447, 1/G.2; 1/G.1 1929; Totter 1942; resite to Q.827447 July 1948; 1/J.4 Nov 1953; U/G Nov 1961; *Closed Oct 1968*

Herne Bay
Opened Nov 1929 R.194684, 1/B.4; 1/P.1 Nov 1953; resite to R.170649 Feb 1965; U/G Sept 1965; *Closed Oct 1968;* Reopened, 1/C.4, 1976

Hoo
Opened Nov 1937 Q.781740, 19/Q.1; 19/N.1 Jan 1939; resite to Q.779735 Jan 1942; 1/B.2 Nov 1953; U/G Oct 1960; 1/B.1 Oct 1968; *In use*

Horsmonden
Opened 1925 (roof of "Wisteria"), 1/J.1; Totter 1943; resite to Q.698385 May 1951; 1/E.3 Nov 1953; U/G May 1960; *Closed Oct 1968*

Kingsgate
Opened 1929 R.395709, 1/A.1; 1/A.3 Jan 1939; Totter 1942; 1/K.3 June 1944; 1/N.1 Nov 1953; U/G June 1961; *Closed Oct 1968*

Lenham
Opened 1925, 1/E.3; resite to Q.986516 Aug 1940; 1/Q.1 Nov 1953; 1/Q.3 Dec 1958; resite to Q.902537 Sept 1961; U/G Oct 1962; *Closed Oct 1968*

Linton
Opened March 1942 Q.764510, 1/G.4; 1/E.2 Nov 1953; U/G 1962; 1/D.1 Oct 1968; *In use*

Little Chart
Opened 1925, 1/F.3, *Closed shortly afterwards*

Lyminge
Opened 1925, 1/C.3; resite to R.170408 Nov 1934; 1/M.3 April 1938; Totter 1942; 1/L.3 Nov 1953; U/G Nov 1960; *Closed Oct 1968*

Marden
Experimental Post B.2 1924

Minster
Opened 1925 R.309650, 1/A.1; resite to R.313657 (Laundry Hill), Totter, 1942; 1/N.2 Nov 1953; U/G 1962; 1/C.1 Oct 1968; *In use*

Oare/Faversham
Opened 1925, 1/E.1 Faversham; renamed Oare May 1936; resite to R.001629 July 1947; 1/Q.2 Nov 1953; U/G Oct 1961; *Closed Oct 1968*

Orpington/Farnborough/Knockholt
Opened Nov 1937 Q.445648, 19/Z.1 Orpington; 1/C.3 Nov 1953; resite to Q.472614, renamed Farnborough, Nov 1960; U/G Sept 1962; 1/A.3 renamed Knockholt, Oct 1968; *In use*

Penshurst/Tonbridge
Opened Nov 1937 Q.587448, 19/R.2 Tonbridge; resite to Q.592468 (Tonbridge Castle) July 1940; 1/E.1 Nov 1953; resite to Capitol Cinema roof April 1959; resite to Q.526471 Nov 1961; renamed Penshurst May 1963; U/G March 1965; 1/D.3 Oct 1968; *In use*

Pluckley
Opened 1929 Q.921453, 1/F.3; resite to Q.923459 Dec 1937; 1/J.1 Nov 1953; U/G June 1961; 1/E.1 Oct 1968; *In use*

Queensborough
Opened 1925, 1/D.2; *Closed shortly afterwards*

Rainham
Opened Nov 1939 Q.811653, 19/Q.1; resite to Q.819645, 1/R.1, Nov 1953; U/G June 1961; *Closed Oct 1968*

Sedlescombe
Opened Nov 1939 Q.781185, 1/H.1; 1/J.3 July 1942; Totter 1942; Darky 1942; 1/L.1 April 1946; 1/G.2 Nov 1953; U/G Sept 1961; *Closed Oct 1968*

Sevington/Willesborough
Opened June 1940 Q.043405, 1/M.1 Willesborough; 1/F.1 Jan 1941; 1/K.1 Nov 1953; resite to Q.038406 Nov 1954; renamed Sevington March 1956; U/G June

1961; *Closed Oct 1968*

Sheerness
Opened Jan 1930, 1/D.1; resite to Q.938749, 19/T.2, May 1940; 1/A.2 Nov 1953; 1/B.2 Dec 1960; resite to Q.926718, U/G, Feb 1962; *Closed Oct 1968*

Sheldwich Lees
Opened 1925, 1/E.2; resite to R.014567 May 1943; 1/P.3 Nov 1953; U/G April 1962; *Closed Oct 1968*

Sittingbourne/Rodmersham Green
Opened 1925 Q.907631, 1/D.3 Sittingbourne; 19/T.3 June 1940; resite to Q.917615 Aug 1951; 1/Q.4, renamed Rodmersham Green, Nov 1953; resite to Q.898613 Dec 1961; U/G Oct 1962; 1/B.3 Oct 1968; *In use*

Snodland
Opened Nov 1937 Q.695611, 19/Q.3; 1/R.4 Nov 1953; U/G 1962; *Closed Oct 1968*

Sutton Valence
Experimental Post B.1 1924

Tenterden
Experimental Post D.3 1924; 1/G.3 1925, Q.885332; Totter 1943; 1/J.3 Nov 1953; resite to Q.873347 April 1957; U/G May 1959; *Closed 1968*

Wateringbury
Opened Nov 1937 Q.862522, 19/R.1; 1/H.3 Nov 1953; U/G Dec 1959; *Closed Oct 1968*

Whitstable/Blean
Opened 1925 R.101648, 1/B.1 Whitstable; 1/F.4 Nov 1953; resite to R.096616, renamed Blean, May 1966; U/G Sept 1976; 1/C.4 Oct 1968; *Closed 1976*

Wye
Opened 1925 R.053196, 1/B.3; 1/F.4 May 1939; Totter 1943; resite to R.056460 July 1948; 1/L.4 Nov 1953; U/G Jan 1959; 1/E.2 Oct 1968; *In use*

LANCASHIRE

Atherton
Opened Oct 1937 D.684044, 7/B.3; Granite 1942; resite to D.692044 Feb 1952; 19/B.3 Nov 1953; U/G, 21/P.3, Feb 1959; 21/L.3 Oct 1968; *In use*

Backbarrow
Opened May 1940 D.363839, 29/X.3; Granite 1942; 21/E.1 Nov 1953; resite to D.358842 Dec 1956; U/G June 1965; *Closed Oct 1968*

Bacup
Opened Oct 1937 D.863231, 7/A.2; 19/A.4 Nov 1953; resite to D.865228 Nov 1964; U/G, 21/Q.4, June 1965;

21/M.1 Oct 1968; *In use*

Barrow-in-Furness
Opened May 1940 D.172690, 29/O.2; Granite 1942; 21/E.3 Nov 1953; 21/D.3 Oct 1968; *In use*

Bickerstaffe/Burscough
Opened July 1940 D.445045, 7/K.4 Bickerstaffe 19/E.4 Nov 1953; resite to D.427105, renamed Burscough, Dec 1961; U/G April 1962; 21/N.4 May 1962; 21/K.2 Oct 1968; *In use*

Billinge Beacon/Ashton-in-Makerfield
Opened July 1941 D.525014, 7/E.4 Ashton-in-Makerfield; 7/J.1 Sept 1943; 19/E.3 Nov 1953; U/G, renamed Billinge Beacon, Jan 1960; 21/N.3 Nov 1964; *Closed Oct 1968*

Blackpool/Weeton
Opened Oct 1937 D.306373 (Imperial Hotel roof), 7/L.4 Blackpool; resite to D.309364 (Talbot Rd Car Park roof) May 1947; 21/G.4 Nov 1953; resite to D.377357, renamed Weeton, May 1964; U/G March 1966; *Closed Oct 1968*

Brinscall/Chorley
Opened Oct 1937 D.595197, 7/K.1 Chorley; 7/A.4, Granite, May 1942; 19/C.3, renamed Brinscall, Nov 1953; resite to D.593230 Oct 1954; U/G Nov 1962; 21/L.1 Oct 1968; *In use*

Broughton-in-Furness
Opened Nov 1938 D.207879, 29/0.3; Granite 1942; resite to D.218889 Aug 1943; Augmented Granite 1944; 21/D.3 Nov 1953; U/G Oct 1965; 21/A.2 Oct 1968; *In use*

Caton
Opened Nov 1938 D.521657, 29/P.2; Granite 1942; 29/Q.4 May 1951; 20/F.3 Nov 1953; resite to D.513657 March 1957; resite to D.541649 June 1961; U/G May 1962; *Closed Oct 1968*

Chorlton-cum-Hardy
Opened Sept 1941 J.830931, 7/D.4; 19/L.1 Nov 1953; resite to J.830931 Feb 1960; U/G Sept 1961; *Closed Oct 1968*

Denton/Hyde
Opened Oct 1937 J.938943, 7/C.4 Denton; Granite 1942; 19/M.3 Nov 1953; resite to J.958926, 16/M.3, renamed Hyde, Nov 1961; U/G Dec 1962; *Closed Oct 1968*

Fleetwood
Opened Nov 1938 D.311468, 29/Q.2; resite to D.314477 June 1941; resite to D.325482 Nov 1950; 21/G.1 Nov 1953; U/G June 1965; *In use*

Flookburgh
Opened Nov 1938 D.368756, 29/P.1; 29/X.1 June 1940; resite to D.361760 Oct 1949; 21/E.4 Nov 1953; resite to D.368742 Aug 1958; 21/E.3 Nov 1963; U/G June 1965; 21/D.1 Oct 1968; *In use*

Formby/Woodvale
Opened Oct 1937 D.278056, 7/J.1 Formby; 7/K.1 Nov 1943; 19/E.1 Nov 1953; U/G, 21/N.1, July 1962; Post abandoned because of erosion 1964. Resite to D.304095 May 1965; U/G July 1968; 21/K.1 Oct 1968, renamed Woodvale; *In use*

Forton
Opened Nov 1938 D.496504, 29/Q.3; Granite 1942; 21/H.1 Nov 1953; U/G June 1965; *In use*

Great Eccleston/Catforth
Opened Dec 1937 D.422392, 7/L.1 Great Eccleston; 21/G.3 Nov 1953; resite to D.455368 Aug 1962; U/G May 1963, renamed Catforth; 21/H.3 Oct 1968; *In use*

Hawkshead
Opened Feb 1939 D.351978, 29/T.1; 29/W.1 July 1940; Granite 1942; 21/C.2 Nov 1953; U/G Oct 1965; 22/L.3 Oct 1968; *In use*

Heysham
Opened Nov 1938 D.411607, 29/Q.1; Darky and Granite 1943; 21/F.2 Nov 1953; resite to D.409601 March 1960; U/G Nov 1961; 21/D.2 Oct 1968; *In use*

Longridge
Opened Nov 1938 D.612378, 29/R.2; Granite 1942; resite to D.617382 March 1953; 21/H.1 Nov 1953; resite to D.621389 Nov 1959; U/G Oct 1960; *In use*

Lytham
Opened Oct 1937 D.335274, 7/L.3; 19/D.1 Nov 1953; 21/D.1 Jan 1962; U/G May 1963; 21/G.2 Oct 1968; *In use*

Mellor
Opened Oct 1937 D.659312, 7/A.3; Granite 1942; 19/C.1 Nov 1953; U/G July 1959; *Closed Oct 1968*

Padiham
Opened Oct 1937 D.797349; 7/A.1; 19/B.1 Nov 1953; 21/P.1 June 1962; U/G March 1963; 21/J.3 Oct 1968; *In use*

Parbold
Opened Oct 1937 D.508106 7/K.2; resite to D.516126 Feb 1941; 19/C.2 Nov 1953; resite to D.528125 Dec 1961; U/G Oct 1962; *Closed Oct 1968*

Prestwich
Opened Oct 1937 D.815032, 7/B.2; 19/B.4 Nov 1953; resite to D.831048 Sept 1957; U/G Dec 1958; 21/M.3

Oct 1968; *In use*

Shaw
Opened Oct 1937 D.929098, 7/B.1; Granite 1943; 19/A.3 Nov 1953; resite to D.930105 Feb 1955; resite to D.923103 Sept 1960; U/G July 1965; *Closed Oct 1968*

Southport
Opened Oct 1937 D.272178, 7/K.3; resite to D.317153 Sept 1950; 19/D.2 Nov 1953; resite to D.324167 Sept 1959; U/G July 1960; *Closed Oct 1968*

Speke
Opened Oct 1940 J.438866, 7/J.4; 19/F.4 Nov 1953; resite to J.422831 June 1958; U/G March 1959; 21/M.4 Sept 1962; *Closed Oct 1968*

St. Helens
Opened Oct 1937 J.487945, 7/J.4; 19/E.2 Nov 1953; 21/N.2 April 1962; U/G June 1965; 21/K.3 Oct 1968; *In use*

Turton
Opened Oct 1937 D.734152, 7/B.4; 19/B.2 Nov 1953; resite to D.724143 June 1955; U/G, 21/P.2, June 1965; 21/L.2 Oct 1968; *In use*

Warrington
Opened Oct 1937 J.615893, 7/E.3; 19/K.1 Nov 1953; resite to J.618912 June 1958; U/G May 1959; 16/F.1 Feb. 1963; *Closed Oct 1968*

Waterloo
Opened Oct 1937 (Esplanade Gdns,) 7/J.3; resite to Sandheys Rd, 7/J.1; resite to J.316980 1943; 19/F.1 Nov 1953; resite to Hall Rd, Blundellsands, 1959; U/G 1960; *Closed Oct 1968*

LEICESTERSHIRE

Billesdon
Opened 1948 K.717023, 5/A.1; 7/K.1 Nov 1953; resite to K.716022 Jan 1959; U/G July 1959; *Closed Oct 1968*

Birstall
Opened Dec 1937 K.599097, 5/A.1; 5/H.1 July 1940; resite to K.585084 July 1943; 8/L.4 Nov 1953; resite to K.590107 Nov 1963; U/G Dec 1964; 8/G.3 Oct 1968; *In use*

Buckminster
Opened Nov 1949 K.873224, 5/K.2; 15/G.1 Nov 1953; U/G May 1961; 15/K.2 Oct 1968; *In use*

Cold Overton/Wissendine/Langham
Opened 1947 K.833122, 5/K.1 Langham; resite to K.842137 Dec 1952; 15/G.3, renamed Wissendine, Nov 1953; resite to K.806097 May 1954; renamed Cold Overton April 1956; U/G April 1959; 7/A.1 Oct 1968; *In use*

Colerton
Opened July 1954 K.387164, 8/M.4; U/G April 1959;
Closed Oct 1968

Fleckney
Opened Dec 1937 P.641937, 5/A.2; resite to P.638932
March 1943; 8/L.3 Nov 1953; U/G Oct 1960; 8/J.2 Oct
1968; *In use*

Hathern/Shepshed
Opened Dec 1937 K.437194, 5/H.3 Shepshed; 8/M.2 Nov
1953; resite to K.495218, renamed Hathern, Jan 1954;
U/G Nov 1960; 8/C.1 Oct 1968; *In use*

Lutterworth
Opened Dec 1937 P.535848, 5/B.1; 8/P.2 Nov 1953;
resite to P.520855 Aug 1962; U/G Aug 1963; 3/B.1 Oct
1968; *In use*

Markfield
Opened Dec 1937 K.485097, 5/H.2; resite to K.487103
Jan 1940; 8/M.2 Nov 1953; resite to K.500092 March
1961; U/G Oct 1966; *Closed Oct 1968*

Melton Mowbray
Opened May 1948 K.750206, 5/K.3; 15/G.4 Nov 1953;
resite to K.742214 Sept 1954; U/G May 1959; *Closed
Oct 1968*

Rearsby
Opened Nov 1940 K.663138, 5/H.4; 8/L.2 Nov 1953;
U/G July 1961; 8/G.2 Oct 1968; *In use*

Stoke Golding
Opened Dec 1937 P.398968, 5/G.2; 8/P.4 Nov 1953;
U/G May 1960; 8/J.1 Oct 1968; *In use*

Thurlaston/Croft
Opened Dec 1937 P.489990, 5/A.3 Thurlaston; 5/G.3
May 1939; 8/P.1, renamed Croft, Nov 1953; U/G July
1959; *Closed Oct 1968*

Twycross
Opened Dec 1937 K.329061, 5/G.1; 8/N.2 Nov 1953;
U/G June 1960; *Closed Oct 1968*

Wymeswold
Opened Dec 1937 K.616236, 5/H.1; 5/J.3 May 1939;
8/L.1 Nov 1953; U/G Nov 1961; *Closed Oct 1968*

LINCOLNSHIRE

Alford
Opened 1936 F.458750, 11/H.3; 15/M.3 Nov 1953;
resite to F.410741 June 1960; U/G June 1961; 15/F.2 Oct
1968; *In use*

Bardney
Opened 1937 F.125689, 11/F.1; 15/L.4 Nov 1953; U/G

Aug 1960; 15/H.3 Oct 1968; *In use*

Barton-on-Humber
Opened April 1940 A.031203 (Beacon Hill), 10/L.1;
18/S.1 Nov 1953; U/G May 1959; *Closed Oct 1968*

Baumber
Opened June 1936 F.229734, 11/K.2; 15/L.1 Nov 1953;
U/G June 1961; 15/H.1 Oct 1968; *In use*

Billingborough
Opened May 1939 F.106336, 11/B.2; 15/K.4 Nov 1953;
U/G Oct 1963; 15/L.2 Oct 1968; *In use*

Billinghay
Opened June 1937 F.142552, 11/F.3; 15/K.1 Nov 1953;
resite to F.133562 Aug 1960; U/G Aug 1961, 15/H.2 Oct
1968; *In use*

Binbrook
Opened May 1941 F.227940, 11/K.4; 15/B.2 Nov 1953;
U/G Oct 1959; *Closed Oct 1968*

Bishop Norton
Opened June 1936 K.982922, 11/L.2; 18/C.2 Nov 1953;
U/G May 1959; *Closed Oct 1968*

Boston
Opened Feb 1937 F.311446, 11/E.1; 15/P.4 Nov 1953;
resite to F.330486 March 1962; U/G Feb 1963; 15/M.1
Oct 1968; *In use*

Bottesford
Opened May 1953 K.843396, 5/J.1; 15/F.3 Nov 1953;
U/G Feb 1960; *Closed Oct 1968*

Bourne
Opened Feb 1936 F.095214, 11/C.2; 11/G.2 Nov 1949;
15/H.1 Nov 1953; resite to K.097226, U/G Aug 1961;
15/L.3 Oct 1968; *In use*

Burgh-on-Bain
Opened June 1936 F.208895, 11/K.1; 15/B.3 Nov 1953;
resite to F.214841 Jan 1959; U/G Oct 1959; 15/E.2 Oct
1968. *In use*

Castle Bytham
Opened May 1936 K.989177, 11/C.1; 15/E.4 Nov 1953;
U/G Sept 1961; *Closed Oct 1968*

Chapel St. Leonards
Opened Aug 1938 F.553727, 11/H.2; 15/N.1 Nov 1953;
resite to F.561735 Jan 1959; U/G Oct 1961; *Closed Oct 1968*

Claypole
Opened Nov 1949 K.848487, 11/M.4; 15/F.2 Nov 1953;
U/G Feb 1960; 15/G.2 Oct 1968; *In use*

Coningsby
Opened May 1939 F.228597, 11/N.3; 15/L.3 Nov 1953;

resite to F.257561 June 1954; U/G Nov 1963; 15/J.3 Oct 1968; *In use*

Crowland
Opened Aug 1938 F.234102, 15/G.4; 15/Q.3 Nov 1953; U/G Nov 1962; *Closed Oct 1968*

Donington/Quadring Eaudyke
Opened March 1937 F.237335, 11/E.2 Donington; 15/K.3 Nov 1953; renamed Quadring Eaudyke Jan 1954; U/G Sept 1963; 15/M.3 Oct 1968; *In use*

East Kirby
Opened July 1936 F.326633, 11/G.2; 15/N.4 Nov 1953; *Closed Oct 1968*

Eastoft
Opened July 1936 E.805157, 10/B.1; 18/Q.1 Nov 1953; 20/Q.1 Jan 1963; resite to E.805155 Nov 1963; U/G Feb 1965; 15/A.2 Oct 1968; *In use*

Epworth
Opened July 1936 E.792043, 10/B.2; 18/Q.3 Nov 1953; resite to E.789045 Nov 1960; U/G Jan 1961; *Closed Oct 1968*

Fosdyke
Opened Dec 1936 F.322325, 11/D.2; Darky 1943; 15/P.3 Nov 1953; resite to F.307347 March 1964; U/G Oct 1964; *Closed Oct 1968*

Fulstow
Opened June 1939 F.340971, 11/J.3; 15/A.4 Nov 1953; U/G March 1961; *In use*

Gainsborough
Opened June 1936 K.823891, 11/L.1; 11/L.3 Oct 1939; 11/A.4 Feb 1940; 11/L.4 Sept 1943; 18/C.1 Nov 1953; resite to K.820891 Oct 1961; U/G Dec 1961; 15/C.1 Oct 1962; *Closed Oct 1968*

Grantham
Opened Aug 1939 K.903332, 11/M.3; 15/J.3 Nov 1953; U/G Aug 1958; 15/K.1 Oct 1968; *In use*

Greetwell
Opened April 1939 F.009719, 11/F.2; 15/E.2 Nov 1953; resite to F.003697 June 1962; U/G Oct 1962; *Closed Oct 1968*

Hackthorn
Opened Aug 1936 F.002825, 11/L.1; Granite 1942; resite to F.186453, 15/K.2 Nov 1953; U/G Feb 1963; *Closed Oct 1968*

Holbeach
Opened April 1939 F.378248, 11/D.3; resite to F.3853251 April 1949; 15/Q.1 Nov 1953; resite to F.364263 July 1955; U/G Oct 1964; 15/M.2 Oct 1968; *In use*

Honington
Opened 1937 K.928450, 11/B.2; 11/M.2 Feb 1947; 15/J.4 Nov 1953; U/G April 1965; *Closed Oct 1968*

Humberstone/Cleethorpes
Opened July 1936 A.312045, 10/D.1; resite to A.324069 Nov 1950; 18/A.1 Nov 1953; resite to A.327056 Jan 1962; 15/A.1 June 1963; U/G Sept 1963; *Closed Oct 1968*

Immingham/Roxton
Opened July 1936 A.187146, 10/D.3 Immingham; 18/L.2 Nov 1953; resite to A.183117 Feb 1961; U/G March 1961; 20/V.2, renamed Roxton, Sept 1963; 15/B.2 Oct 1968; *In use*

Ingoldsby
Opened May 1938 F.011297, 11/B.3; 15/J.2 Nov 1953; U/G 1959; *Closed Oct 1968*

Little Steeping/Winceby
Opened May 1936 F.317688, 11/H.2 Winceby; 11/N.2 Aug 1939; 15/N.4 Nov 1953; resite to F.426617, renamed Little Steeping, May 1958; U/G July 1963; 15/J.2 Oct 1968; *In use*

Long Sutton
Opened Nov 1949 F.437246, 15/H.1; 15/R.1. Nov 1953; resite to F.479284 July 1955; resite to F.474293 Dec 1959; U/G July 1962; *Closed Oct 1968*

Louth
Opened Oct 1936 F.321883, 11/J.3; G.L. Post 1943; 11/K.3 May 1949; 15/M.1 Nov 1953; resite to F.337848 Jan 1959; U/G Oct 1969; 15/F.3 Oct 1968; *In use*

Mablethorpe
Opened June 1938 F.499689 11/J.1; 15/M.2 Nov 1953; resite to F.502863 May 1958; U/G June 1961; 15/F.1 Oct 1968; *In use*

Market Deeping
Opened 1938 F.138108, 15/G.3; 15/H.3 Nov 1953; U/G March 1960; 7/B.1 Oct 1968; *In use*

Market Rasen
Opened Dec 1936 F.117885, 11/K.3; 11/C.3 Jan 1947; 15/B.4 Nov 1953; resite to F.090876 Jan 1960; U/G Feb 1962; 15/E.1 Oct 1968; *In use*

Moulton Chapel
Opened Nov 1949 F.324176, 15/A.4; 15/Q.4 Nov 1953; U/G March 1960; *Closed Oct 1968*

Navenby
Opened March 1937 K.990582, 11/M.1; 15/E.3 Nov 1953; resite to K.983547 U/G July 1958; 15/L.1 Oct 1968; *In use*

North Kelsey
Opened Nov 1940 A.053021, 10/C.4; 18/L.3 Nov 1953;
U/G May 1959; 15/D.2 Oct 1968; *In use*

North Summercoates
Opened July 1936 F.428965, 11/J.2; 15/A.3 Nov 1953;
resite to F.447947 Oct 1962; U/G 1964; *Closed Oct 1968*

Old Leake
Opened Nov 1937 F.412499, 11/G.1; G.L. Post 1943;
15/P.1 Nov 1953; resite to F.446486 Nov 1956; U/G
April 1963; *Closed Oct 1968*

Sandholme Bank
Opened Aug 1953 F.379392, 11/New Post; 15/P.2 Nov
1953; U/G Feb 1960; *Closed Oct 1968*

Saxilby
Opened May 1936 K.895759, 11/A.1; 15/C.4 Nov 1953;
U/G April 1960; *Closed Oct 1968*

Scawby
Opened July 1936 E.954052, 10/C.1; 18/L.4 Nov 1953;
U/G May 1961; 20/Q.2 Sept 1962; 15/D.1 Oct 1968;
In use

Scotter
Opened July 1936 E.897008, 10/B.3; 10/C.3 May 1947;
18/Q.2 Nov 1953; U/G May 1961; 20/Q.2 Sept 1962;
15/D.1 Oct 1968; *In use*

Skegness
Opened 1937 F.572652, 11/H.1; 15/N.2 Nov 1953; resite
to F.556656 March 1962; U/G March 1964; 15/J.1 Oct
1968; *In use*

Sleaford
Opened June 1936 F.071463, 11/B.1; resite to F.074489,
15/J.1 Nov 1953; U/G April 1961; *Closed Oct 1968*

Spalding
Opened Aug 1936 F.230227 11/D.1; 15/H.2 Nov 1953;
resite to F.269213 March 1962; U/G Oct 1964; *Closed
Oct 1968*

Swallow
Opened July 1936 A.177025, 10/D.2; 18/B.1 Nov 1953;
U/G May 1959; *Closed Oct 1968*

Tetford
Opened May 1937 F.330764, 11/N.1; 15/M.4 Nov 1953;
U/G Dec 1960; *Closed Oct 1968*

Wainfleet St. Mary
Opened April 1936 F.512585, 11/G.3; Darky 1942;
15/N.3 Nov 1953; resite to F.519569 Oct 1964; U/G Jan
1965; *Closed Oct 1968*

Winterton
Opened July 1936 E.935189, 10/C.2; 18/S.3 Nov 1953;
U/G May 1959; 20/S.3 June 1965; 15/A.1 Oct 1968; *In
use*

Wooton
Opened July 1936 A.077152, 10/C.3; 10/D.4 1942;
18/L.1 Nov 1953; U/G Jan 1961; 15/B.1 Oct 1968; *In use*

NORFOLK

Aldeby
Opened Oct 1938 M.433932, 14/D.1; 6/D.4 Nov 1953;
U/G June 1959; *Closed Oct 1968*

Aylsham/Marsham
Opened 1934 G.204297, 16/R.3 Aylsham; 6/S.2 Nov
1953; resite to G.196226 Aug 1960; U/G, renamed
Marsham, March 1961; 6/C.3 Oct 1968; *In use*

Brancaster
Opened 1934 F.772428, 16/N.1; 15/S.1 Oct 1953; 6/T.2
Nov 1957; U/G Jan 1960; 6/A.1 Oct 1968; *In use*

Brundall
Opened 1934 G.327086, 16/V.2; G.L. Post 1943; 6/R.2
Nov 1953; resite to G.343082 Jan 1959; U/G June 1960;
6/P.2 Oct 1968; *In use*

Caister
Opened Nov 1934 G.506117, 16/T.4; 6/E.1 Nov 1953;
U/G June 1959; *Closed Oct 1968*

Cley-next-the-Sea
Opened Nov 1934 G.048445, 16/P.2; resite to G.062441,
6/H.1, Nov 1953; U/G 1958; *Closed Oct 1968*

Coltishall
Opened Nov 1934 G.277206, 16/V.1; resite to G.262188,
6/R.1, Nov 1953; U/G Dec 1957; *Closed Oct 1968*

Cromer
Opened Nov 1934 G.214425, 16/Q.1; 6/G.1 Nov 1953;
resite to G.189423 April 1954; resite to G.231416 Jan
1956; U/G Nov 1958; *Closed Oct 1968*

Dersingham
Opened Nov 1934 F.694312, 16/O.3; 15/S.4 Nov 1953;
resite to F.695319 Nov 1957, 15/S.2; U/G Jan 1959;
6/T.4 Feb 1968; 2/A.2 Oct 1968; *In use*

Diss
Opened June 1939 M.115810, 14/G.1; 6/P.3 Nov 1953;
U/G June 1960; 6/K.3 Oct 1968; *In use*

Docking
Opened June 1939 F.671371, 16/N.2; G.L. Post 1943;
15/S.3 Nov 1953; U/G Oct 1961; *Closed Oct 1968*

Downham Market
Opened March 1936 F.597027, 15/K.1; 7/A.4 Nov 1953;
U/G Aug 1960, resite to F.601035; 6/D.2 Oct 1968; *In use*

East Dereham
Opened Nov 1934 F.996138, 16/Y.2; resite to F.999095, 6/K.1, Nov 1953; U/G Aug 1959; *Closed Oct 1968*

Fakenham
Opened Nov 1934 F.914280, 16/P.3; resite to F.956293, 6/J.1, Nov 1953; U/G Dec 1958; *Closed Oct 1968*

Freethorpe
Opened Nov 1934 G.414045, 16/T.1; 6/E.3 Nov 1953; U/G Dec 1959; *Closed Oct 1968*

Garboldisham
Opened Sept 1939 L.994814, 14/D.3; resite to M.015816 June 1953; 6/L.2 Nov 1953; U/G Aug 1961; 6/J.2 Oct 1968; *In use*

Gressenhall/Litcham
Opened Nov 1934 F.893182, 16/Y.1 Litcham; resite to F.985188, 6/J.3, renamed Gressenhall, Nov 1953; U/G Sept 1959; 6/B.2 Oct 1968; *In use*

Guist/Elnam
Opened Nov 1934 F.987202, 16/W.3 Elnam; resite to G.005268, 6/S.4, renamed Guist, Nov 1953; U/G Dec 1958; *Closed 1968*

Harleston
Opened Oct 1939 M.257827, 14/C.3; 6/P.2 Nov 1953; U/G March 1958; *Closed Oct 1968*

Hellesdon
Opened Nov 1934 G.201113, 16/W.2; 6/R.3 Nov 1953; U/G Dec 1959; 6/P.1 Oct 1968; *In use*

Hingham
Opened Nov 1934 G.037019, 16/X.3; 6/Q.4 Nov 1953; U/G Dec 1957; *Closed Oct 1968*

Honingham
Opened Nov 1934 G.102113, 16/X.1; 6/Q.1 Nov 1953; resite to G.094102 April 1954; U/G March 1962; 6/F.3 Oct 1968; *In use*

Hockham
Opened Nov 1938 L.972922, 14/B.1; resite to L.954928, 6/K.2, Nov 1953; U/G Aug 1959; *Closed Oct 1968*

Hunstanton
Opened Nov 1934 F.675418, 16/N.3; 15/S.1 Nov 1953; U/G Nov 1957; *Closed Oct 1968*

King's Lynn
Opened March 1936 F.611218, 15/H.2; 15/R.3 Nov 1953; resite to F.549241 Jan 1958; resite to F.603227 Sept 1959; U/G Oct 1960; 6/A.3 Oct 1968; *In use*

Loddon
Opened Oct 1934 M.369982, 16/T.3; Darky 1942; 6/D.1 Nov 1953; U/G Feb 1961; *Closed Oct 1968*

Long Stratton
Opened Oct 1938 M.203919, 14/C.1; 6/P.1 Nov 1953; U/G June 1959; *Closed Oct 1968*

Martham/Repps
Opened 1934 G.476177, 16/S.1 Martham; resite to G.428167, 6/P.3, renamed Repps, Nov 1953; U/G March 1958; *Closed Oct 1968*

Melton Constable
Opened Nov 1934 G.051328, 16/Q.3; G.L. Post 1943; resite to G.041378, 6/H.2, Nov 1953; U/G 1958; 6/B.1 Oct 1968; *In use*

Middleton/South Wooton
Opened Aug 1954 F.669230, 15/R.2 South Wooton; resite to F.672160, renamed Middleton, July 1959; U/G March 1960; *Closed Oct 1968*

Mundesley
Opened Jan 1934 G.319362, 16/H.1; 6/G.2 Nov 1953; resite to G.323357 April 1954; resite to G.301367 June 1960; U/G Aug 1960; 6/C.2 Oct 1968; *In use*

Mundford
Opened June 1939 L.798936, 14/A.1; 6/K.3 Nov 1953; resite to L.807952 Jan 1958; U/G Nov 1961; 6/E.3 Oct 1968; *In use*

Narborough
Opened Nov 1934 F.748108, 16/Z.1; resite to F.741074, 7/A.1 Nov 1953; U/G Jan 1959; 6/E.1 Oct 1968; *In use*

New Buckenham
Opened Oct 1938 M. 093907, 14/B.2; 6/P.3 Nov 1953; U/G June 1960; *Closed Oct 1968*

North Walsham
Opened March 1954 G.241326, 6/G.3; U/G Dec 1957; *Closed Oct 1968*

Reepham
Opened Nov 1934 G.112225, 16/W.1; resite to G.085189, 6/S.3, Nov 1953; U/G Sept 1962; *Closed Oct 1968*

Runham/Flegborough
Opened Nov 1934 G.436151, 16/S.3 Runham; resite to G.460114, 6/E.4, renamed Flegborough, Nov 1953; U/G March 1962; 6/G.4 Oct 1968; *In use*

Saxthorpe
Opened Nov 1953 G.115293, 6/S.1; U/G Dec 1957; *Closed Oct 1968*

St. Germans/Terrington
Opened Nov 1949 F.534155, 15/H.3 Terrington St John; 15/R.4 Nov 1953; resite to F.579127 June 1955; renamed St Germans Feb 1958; U/G Jan 1959; *Closed Oct 1968*

South Creake
Opened Nov 1934 F.851350, 16/O.1; 6/H.3 Nov 1953;
U/G July 1961; 6/B.3 Oct 1968; *In use*

Southery
Opened Sept 1936 L.616947, 15/K.2; 7/A.3 Nov 1953;
U/G Aug 1959; 6/E.4 Oct 1968; *In use*

Stalham
Opened Nov 1934 G.392251, 16/S.1; 6/F.4 Nov 1953;
U/G Sept 1959; 6/G.1 Oct 1968; *In use*

Stoke Ferry
Opened May 1940 F.699007, 16/Z.3; 7/A.2 Nov 1953;
U/G May 1961; *Closed Oct 1968*

Swaffham
Opened Nov 1934 F.815096, 16/Z.2; resite to F.824113,
6/J.3 Nov 1953; U/G Dec 1957; *Closed Oct 1968*

Thetford
Opened Dec 1938 L.866824, 14/A.2; resite to L.841042,
6/L.1 Nov 1953; resite to L.864855 Feb 1961; U/G
Sept 1961; 6/J.1 Oct 1968; *In use*

Walcott
Opened Nov 1934 G.369301, 16/R.2; 6/F.1 Nov 1953;
resite to G.375317 April 1958; U/G Dec 1960; *Closed
Oct 1968*

Watton
Opened Nov 1939 F.912009, 16/Y.3; 6/K.4 Nov 1953;
resite to F.929040 Jan 1959; U/G Aug 1959; 6/E.2 Oct
1968; *In use*

Wells-next-the-Sea
Opened Nov 1934 F.961420, 16/P.1, 6/H.4 Nov 1953;
U/G Dec 1958; *Closed Oct 1968*

West Beckham/Matlaske
Opened Feb 1954 G.136344, 6/Matlaske; renamed
West Beckham Dec 1954; resite to G.140388 Oct 1960;
U/G Jan 1961; 6/C.1 Oct 1968; *In use*

West Raynham/Massingham
Opened Nov 1934 F.801242, 16/O.2 Massingham; resite
to F.858254, 6/J.4, Nov 1953; U/G Aug 1959; *Closed
Oct 1968*

West Walton
Opened Nov 1949 F.472138, 15/A.1; resite to F.464138,
15/Q.2, Nov 1953; resite to F.479142 May 1954; U/G
July 1960; *Closed Oct 1968*

Wymondham
Opened July 1934 G.121008, 16/K.2; 6/Q.3 Nov 1953;
resite to G.126988 Aug 1955; U/G June 1959; 6/K.1 Oct
1968; *In use*

Corby
Opened 1938 P.932906, 12/L.4; 7/L.4 Nov 1953; *Closed
Oct 1968*

Crick
Opened 1938 P.579713, 12/P.3; 8/Q.2 Nov 1953; *Closed
Oct 1968*

Daventry
Opened 1938 P.577608, 12/P.2; 8/Q.3 Nov 1953; *Closed
Oct 1968*

Duddington
Opened Nov 1949 K.991007, 15/F.2; 7/L.1 Nov 1953;
U/G March 1961; 7/A.2 Oct 1968; *In use*

Duston
Opened Oct 1954 P.717615, 12/H.1; resite to P.8713604,
7/H.4, Nov 1953; U/G Feb 1962; 7/C.3 Oct 1968; *In use*

Earls Barton
Opened Dec 1953 P.870648, 7/J.2; U/G March 1960;
7/D.3 Oct 1968; *In use*

Winterton
Opened Nov 1934 G.499197, 16/S.2; 6/F.2 Nov 1953;
U/G Oct 1963; *Closed Oct 1968*

NORTHAMPTONSHIRE

Bennefield
Opened June 1955 P.960899; U/G, 7/L.4, June 1958;
7/D.1 Oct 1968; *In use*

Blakesley
Opened 1938 P.623504, 12/O.3; 8/G.1 Nov 1953;
Closed Oct 1968

Brackley
Opened 1938 P.584374, 12/C.2; 3/G.4 Nov 1953; U/G,
3/D.2, 1968; *In use*

Brixworth
Opened 1938 P.755709, 12/K.2; 7/J.3 Nov 1953; U/G
May 1960; 7/C.2 Oct 1968; *In use*

Chipping Warden
Opened 1939 P.941481, 12/J.1; Granite 1943; resite to
P.505519, 8/F.2 Nov 1960; U/G Jan 1962; 3/F.2 Dec
1962; 3/D1 Oct 1968; *In use*

Clipston
Opened 1938 P.703826, 12/K.1; 7/J.4 Nov 1953; U/G
Nov 1959; 7/C.1 Oct 1968; *In use*

Cogenhoe
Opened 1938 P.822606, 12/H.3; resite to P.817577,
7/H.2, Nov 1953; *Closed Oct 1968*

East Carlton
Opened Nov 1949 P.835887, 12/K.3 ; 7/K.3 Nov 1953;
U/G Feb 1964; *Closed Oct 1968*

East Haddon
Opened 1938 P.672678, 12/P.1; resite to P.671676 Nov
1953; *Closed Oct 1968*

Harlaston
Opened Dec 1937 K.196097, 6/S.3 ; 8/N.4 Nov 1953;
U/G 1961; 8/F.4 Oct 1968; *In use*

Kettering
Opened 1938 P.874804, 12/L.3 ; 7/J.1 Nov 1953; *Closed
Oct 1968*

Oundle
Opened Nov 1949, L.037888, 15/F.4 ; 7/L.3 Nov 1953;
resite to L.033906 May 1961; U/G Dec 1964; *Closed Oct
1968*

Raunds
Opened 1938 P.988746, 12/L.3 ; 7/S.4 Nov 1953; U/G
Dec 1961; 7/D.2 Oct 1968; *In use*

Roade
Opened 1938 P.749518, 12/N.3 ; 7/H.3 Nov 1953; *Closed
Oct 1968*

Sutton Bassett
Opened 1938 P.777907, 5/A.4 ; 7/K.4 Nov 1953; U/G
Nov 1959; 7/A.3 Oct 1968; *In use*

Wellingborough
Opened 1938 P.879677, 12/H.2; resite to P.869649, 7/J.2,
Nov 1953; *Closed Oct 1968*

NORTHUMBERLAND

Amble/Redrow
Opened July 1940 U.254042, 30/B.2 Amble; 23/L.2 Nov
1953; resite to U.271003 July 1959; U/G Feb 1961;
renamed Redrow June 1961; *Closed Oct 1968*

Bamburgh
Opened Jan 1937 U.165350, 30/A.1; 23/K.1 Nov 1953;
U/G Nov 1963; 23/A.2 Oct 1968; *In use*

Beal/Hagerston/Fenham Hill
Opened Dec 1940, 30/N.2 Beal; HSL 1942; resite to
U.067427 Nov 1943; 23/J.2, renamed Hagerston, Nov
1953; resite to U.071412, renamed Fenham Hill, Nov
1955; resite to U.076427 Oct 1961; U/G Jan 1964;
Closed 1968

Bellingham
Opened Oct 1939 Y.847838, 32/B.2; 23/Q.3 Nov 1953;
U/G March 1961; 23/D.2 Oct 1968; *In use*

Blyth
Opened Jan 1936 Z.306796, 30/D.1; resite to Z.299796
June 1940; resite to Z.321812 Feb 1949; resite to Z.299796
June 1953; 23/M.1 Nov 1953; resite to Z.322785 Jan
1958; U/G May 1961; *Closed Oct 1968*

Byrness
Opened Dec 1957 T.774034, 23/R.3; resite to T.782031
May 1961; U/G April 1965; 23/B.1 Oct 1968; *In use*

Chatton
Opened Jan 1937 U.053286, 30/A.3; Granite 1942;
23/K.4 Nov 1953; resite to U.072323 Dec 1955; U/G
Oct 1960; *Closed Oct 1968*

Ellington
Opened Jan 1937 Z.280929, 30/C.1; 23/L.3 Nov 1953;
resite to Z.285925 Feb 1962; U/G Aug 1962; 23/E.1 Oct
1968; *In use*

Embleton
Opened April 1938 U.226224, 30/A.2; helped in tracking
Rudolph Hess 1941; 23/K.2 Nov 1953; U/G Jan 1964;
23/A.3 Oct 1968; *In use*

Gilsland
Opened Oct 1939 Y.641658, 32/C.1; Granite 1943
22/P.1 Nov 1953; resite to Y.839659 Dec 1959; U/G Oct
1961; 22/G.2 Oct 1968; *In use*

Great Whittington
Opened Jan 1937 Z.000706, 30/L.2; Granite 1943; 23/Q.4
Nov 1953; resite to Z.008714 Sept 1960; U/G June 1962;
23/D.3 Oct 1968; *In use*

Harbottle
Opened Jan 1937 T.931048, 30/M.2; Granite 1943;
resite to T.936057, 23/M.2 Nov 1953; 23/R.4 Sept 1954;
U/G Dec 1960; 23/C.4 Oct 1968; *In use*

Hartburn
Opened Jan 1937 Z.096856, 30/L.4; Granite 1943; 23/Q.2
Nov 1953; U/G Aug 1960; 23/E.4 Oct 1968; *In use*

Hart Heugh
Opened May 1955 T.986253, 23/J.4; U/G Feb 1964;
23/A.4 Oct 1968; *In use*

Haydon Bridge
Opened Oct 1939 T.838658, 32/B.3; 23/D.1 Nov 1953;
U/G Jan 1961; 23/F.1 Oct 1968

Kenton
Opened Jan 1940 Z.220676, 30/D.2; 23/M.3 Nov 1953;
resite to Z.215674 July 1959; U/G Feb 1962; *Closed Oct
1968*

Kielder
Opened Oct 1939 Y.627928, 32/B.1; resite to Y.431919

Aug 1952; 23/E.3 Nov 1953; U/G March 1961; 23/Q.5
Feb 1968; 23/D.1 Oct 1968; *In use*

Kirkwelpington
Opened Jan 1937 Z.050819, 30/L.1; 30/L.4 Granite,
1943; resite to Y.996857, 23/Q.1 Nov 1953; *Closed 1956*

Longhorsley
Opened Jan 1937 Z.142943, 30/C.2; 23/L.4 Nov 1953;
resite to Z.147919 July 1954; resite to Z.142944 Jan
1955; U/G Dec 1960; 23/C.3 Oct 1968; *In use*

Longhoughton
Opened Jan 1937 U.224145, 30/B.1; HSL 1943; 23/K.3
Nov 1953; resite to U.260155 Nov 1961; U/G Oct 1962;
Closed Oct 1968

Milfield
Opened June 1939 T.930346, 30/N.4; resite to T.928347
Aug 1941; Granite 1942; 23/J.3 Nov 1953; resite to
T.931346 Dec 1959; U/G Oct 1960; 23/A.1 Oct 1968;
In use

Otterburn
Opened Jan 1937 T.896923, 30/N.1; 30/L.3 Nov 1954;
23/R.3 Nov 1953; resite to Y.909951 Oct 1962; U/G
June 1963; 23/B.2 Oct 1968; *In use*

Ponteland
Opened Jan 1937 Z.165756, 30/L.3; Granite 1943,
23/P.1 Nov 1953; resite to Z.156695 June 1961; U/G
Feb 1962; 23/G.1 Oct 1968; *In use*

Prudhoe
Opened Aug 1940 Z.092623, 30/K.4; Granite 1942;
23/P.4 Nov 1953; U/G June 1962; 23/G.3 Oct 1968; *In use*

Rothbury
Opened Jan 1937 U.063011, 30/M.3; Granite 1942;
23/R.2 Nov 1953; resite to U.065989 June 1960; U/G
Sept 1963; *Closed Oct 1968*

Shilbottle
Opened Jan 1937 U.189075, 30/B.3; 23/L.1 Nov 1953;
resite to U.191081 June 1960; U/G Feb 1961; 23/C.2 Oct
1968; *In use*

Slaley
Opened Dec 1936 Z.973579, 30/K.2; Granite 1942;
23/D.2 Nov 1953; U/G Jan 1961; 23/F.2 Oct 1968; *In use*

Stannington
Opened April 1938 Z.212802, 30/C.3; 23/M.4 Nov 1953;
U/G April 1961; 23/E.3 Oct 1968; *In use*

Tynemouth/Whitley Bay
Opened April 1937 Z.324787, 30/D.4 Whitley Bay;
resite to Z.370698 April 1938; 23/M.2, renamed
Tynemouth, Nov 1953; resite to Z.347691 Nov 1957;
resite to Z.351713, renamed Whitley Bay, Nov 1963;

U/G Oct 1964; 23/E.2 Oct 1968; *In use*

Whitfield
Opened Oct 1939 Y.779576, 32/B.4; 23/D.4 Nov 1953;
U/G Dec 1960; 23/F.4 Oct 1968: *In use*

Whittingham
Opened Jan 1937 U.072112, 30/M.1; Granite 1942;
23/R.1 Nov 1953; resite to U.073114 Sept 1961; U/G
Sept 1962; 23/C.1 Oct 1968; *In use*

NOTTINGHAMSHIRE

Blyth
Opened Dec 1937 K.548969, 6/P.1; resite to K.626863
Nov 1941; Granite 1942; 18/M.3 Nov 1953; resite to
K.635862 Nov 1963; U/G May 1964; 15/C.2 Oct 1968;
In use

Burton Joyce/Lowdham
Opened Dec 1937 K.675468, 6/V.2 Lowdham; 8/K.1
Nov 1953; resite to K.643445, renamed Burton Joyce,
March 1954; U/G June 1961; 8/E.2 Oct 1968; *In use*

Collingham
Opened Nov 1949 K.837628, 11/A.3; 15/E.4 Nov 1953;
U/G Feb 1960; *Closed Oct 1968*

Cotgrave
Opened Jan 1938 K.652345, 6/V.3; 8/K.2 Nov 1953;
U/G June 1961; *Closed Oct 1968*

Dunham-on-Trent
Opened Nov 1936 K.804747, 11/A.2; 15/E.1 Nov 1953;
resite to K.822738 Jan 1961; U/G July 1961; 15/G.1 Oct
1968; *In use*

East Markham
Opened Feb 1943 K.729737, 11/A.4; 15/T.2 Nov 1953;
U/G April 1961; 15/C.2 Oct 1968; *In use*

East Retford
Opened July 1938 K.678070, 6/P.2; resite to K.704816
March 1942; 18/T.1 Nov 1953; U/G Jan 1960; *Closed
Oct 1968*

Edwinstowe/Ollerton
Opened July 1938 K.648676, 6/K.1 Edwinstowe; resite
to K.656673 Nov 1942; Granite 1942; 8/T.1, renamed
Ollerton, Nov 1953; 18/L.3, renamed again, Edwinstowe,
July 1962; U/G Nov 1963; *Closed Oct 1968*

Farnsfield
Opened Dec 1937 K.640577, 6/K.2, resite to K.635586,
Granite Post, 1943; 8/J.2 Nov 1953; U/G Sept 1961;
8/B.2 Oct 1968; *In use*

Harby
Opened March 1948 K.754306, 5/J.2; 15/F.4 Nov 1953;

U/G Feb 1960; 15/K.3 Oct 1968; *In use*

Hucknall
Opened Dec 1937 K.518492, 6/V.4; Granite 1942;
8/J.3 Nov 1953; U/G March 1964; 8/E.1 Oct 1968;
In use

Newark
Opened Jan 1936 K.788523, 6/V.1; 15/F.1 Nov 1953;
resite to K.753572 Oct 1959; U/G Nov 1963; 15/G.3
Oct 1968; *In use*

Walkeringham/Wiseton
Opened July 1941 K.770929, 10/B.4 Walkeringham;
10/B.3 July 1944; 18/M.2 Nov 1953; resite to K.756917,
18/H.2, Nov 1963; U/G May 1964; 15/D.3, renamed
Wiseton, Oct 1968; *In use*

Weston-on-Trent
Opened Dec 1939 J.984279, 6/Q.3; 8/A.4 Nov 1953;
resite to J.981279 Jan 1960; U/G Sept 1960; 16/G.2 Oct
1968; *In use*

OXFORDSHIRE

Boars Hill
Opened Feb 1940 P.526029, 4/O.2; resite to P.486029
Nov 1948; 3/P.3 Nov 1953; U/G June 1960; 3/G.2 Oct
1968; *In use*

Culham/Sutton Courtenay
Opened Oct 1935 U.514949, 4/X.2 Sutton Courtenay;
renamed Culham, June 1949; U/G Aug 1960; *Closed
Oct 1968*

Deddington/Bloxham
Opened Dec 1938 P.464319, 4/Z.4 Deddington; 12/Q.2
March 1939; 3/K.2 Nov 1953; resite to P.451345,
renamed Bloxham, May 1960; 3/F.1 Oct 1968; *In use*

Edgehill
Opened 1939, 12/J.2; Granite 1942; 3/F.4 Nov 1953; resite
to P.373468 June 1961; U/G March 1963; 3/D.3 Oct
1968; *In use*

Enstone
Opened March 1940 P.372239, 4/Q.1; 3/K.3 Nov 1953;
U/G June 1959; 3/F.2 Oct 1968; *In use*

Filkins/Carterton
Opened Dec 1936 P.241053, 4/Y.2 Filkins; 3/L.3 Nov
1953; resite to P.251072 April 1959; renamed
Carterton June 1959; U/G Nov 1961; 3/E.2 Oct 1968;
In use

Hailey/Witney
Opened March 1940 P.347094, 4/O.1 Witney; resite to
P.342099 April 1942; resite to P.349131 April 1949;
renamed Hailey June 1952; resite to P.347129, 3/P.1,

Nov 1953; U/G June 1959; *Closed April 1968; Reopened
3/G.3, June 1971; In use*

Kidlington
Opened Oct 1935 P.498136, 4/Q.3; resite to P.502119
April 1936; resite to P.498132, 3/P.2, Nov 1953; U/G
June 1959; 3/G.3 Oct 1968; *Closed June 1971*

Kidmore End/Shiplake
Opened Feb 1940, U.696300, 4/T.3, Kidmore End;
resite to U.727779, March 1949; resite to U.688000 Sept
1949; resite to U.695801, 5/K.1, Nov 1953; resite to
U.756777, July 1957; resite to U.759778, U/G, Sept 1959;
renamed Shiplake, Nov 1962; 14/C.2 Oct 1968; *In use*

Middleton Stoney
Opened Oct 1935, P.543238, 4/Q.2; 3/H.4 Nov 1953;
U/G June 1959; 3/G.1 Oct 1968; *In use*

Nettlebed/Checkendon
Opened Oct 1935 U.704870, 4/S.3 Nettlebed; 4/P.3
April 1939; 5/J.2 Nov 1953; resite to U.669862, U/G,
renamed Checkendon, March 1961; 3/J.2 1966; *Closed
Oct 1968*

Shipton-under-Wychwood
Opened Dec 1936 P.287193 4/Y.1; Granite 1943; 3/L.2
Nov 1953; U/G June 1959; *Closed April 1968*

Stradhampton
Opened Oct 1935 U.601981, 4/S.1; 4/R.2 1941; 3/J.4
Nov 1953; resite to U.625979 Dec 1956; U/G, 3/J.4, May
1958; *Closed Oct 1968*

Swalcliffe
Opened Dec 1936 P.374378, 4/Z.2; Granite 1943; 12/Q.1
Feb 1945; 3/F.3 Nov 1953; U/G June 1962; *Closed
April 1968*

Thame
Opened Oct 1935; P.721058, 4/R.3; 5/H.4 Nov 1953;
U/G Sept 1959; 3/H.2 Sept 1962; 3/H.3 Oct 1968; *In
use*

Watlington
Opened Feb 1941 U.704935, 4/R.4; resite to U.711936
May 1951; 5/J.1 April 1957; U/G Dec 1959; 3/J.1 Aug
1962; 3/L.3 Oct 1968; *In use*

RUTLANDSHIRE

Empingham
Opened June 1939 K.946095, 11/C.3; 15/G.2 Nov 1953;
U/G May 1961; *Closed Oct 1968*

Uppingham
Opened Nov 1949 P.856992, 5/A.3; 7/K.2 Nov 1953;
U/G May 1960; *Closed Oct 1968*

SHROPSHIRE

Bridgnorth
Opened July 1938 O.715924, 27/G.3; 16/H.3 Nov 1953; resite to O.735932 Nov 1960; U/G May 1961; *Closed Oct 1968*

Church Stretton
Opened June 1938 O.465929, 27/J.1; 16/E.1 Nov 1953; U/G April 1965; 16/H.3 Oct 1968; *In use*

Clun
Opened March 1939 O.302808, 27/J.4; 26/Q.1 Sept 1939; 26/P.3 June 1941; 27/J.4 Dec 1943; resite to O.295810 Aug 1949; 16/B.1 Nov 1953; U/G Oct 1959; 12/B.1 May 1963; *Closed Oct 1968*

Cockshutt
Opened July 1938 J.432288, 27/L.1; Granite 1943; 16/K.1 Nov 1953; U/G April 1965; *Closed Oct 1968*

Craven Arms
Opened June 1938 O.435830, 27/J.3; 16/E.3 Nov 1953; resite to O.420836 Dec 1964; U/G June 1965; *Closed Oct 1968*

Ditton Priors
Opened Sept 1938 O.605891, 27/G.2; Granite 1943; 16/E.2 Nov 1953; resite to O.605893 Nov 1964; U/G May 1965; *Closed Oct 1968*

Dorrington
Opened June 1938 J.474031, 27/K.2; Granite 1943; 16/G.3 Nov 1953; resite to J.743027 Jan 1961; U/G March 1961; *Closed Oct 1968*

Great Bolas
Opened June 1938, J.630210, 27/M.2; 16/J.4, Nov 1953; U/G May 1965; 16/F.3 Oct 1968; *In use*

Hadnall/Bomere Heath
Opened June 1938 J.517198, 27/L.2 Hadnall; Granite 1943; 16/K.2 Nov 1953; resite to J.489201 Oct 1964, U/G, renamed Bomere Heath, April 1965; 16/E.1 Oct 1968; *In use*

Ludlow
Opened Sept 1939 O.518756, 27/H.1; Granite 1943; 16/B.2 Nov 1953; resite to O.504744 Nov 1959; U/G May 1961; 12/B.2 Dec 1962; 16/K.2 Oct 1968; *In use*

Lydbury North
Opened June 1938 O.355861, 27/J.2; 16/E.4 Nov 1953; resite to O.359859 Oct 1964; U/G May 1965; 16/E.1 Oct 1968; *In use*

Market Drayton
Opened Aug 1938 J.678353, 27/M.1; 16/K.1 Nov 1953; resite to J.661345 Nov 1964; U/G April 1965; 16/F.1

Oct 1968; *In use*

Minsterley
Opened June 1938 J.371053, 27/H.3; Granite 1943; 16/G.4 Nov 1953; U/G March 1965; 16/E.2 Oct 1968; *In use*

Much Wenlock
Opened July 1938 J.625013, 27/E.1; Granite 1943; 16/H.4 Nov 1953; resite to J.614986 Nov 1960; U/G May 1961; 16/H.2 Oct 1968; *In use*

Nescliffe
Opened July 1938 J.387187, 27/L.3; Granite 1943; 16/G.1 Nov 1953; U/G May 1965; 16/E.3 Oct 1968; *In use*

Oakengates
Opened July 1938, J.696100, 27/E.3, 16/J.3 Nov 1953; U/G Aug 1961; 16/F.2 Oct 1968; *In use*

Oswestry
Opened Aug 1939 J.296299, 26/O.3; Granite 1943; 16/L.1 Nov 1953; U/G, 17/Q.1 Nov 1961; *Closed Oct 1968*

Press
Opened May 1939 J.560331, 27/M.3; 16/K.4 Nov 1953; U/G April 1965; *Closed Oct 1968*

Sambrook
Opened Feb 1939 J.715243, 27/D.2; 16/J.1 Nov 1953; U/G May 1965; *Closed Oct 1968*

Rushton Spence
Opened Jan 1938 J.941631, 6/N.3; Granite 1943; 19/L.3 Nov 1953; resite to J.941628 Nov 1956; 16/L.3 April 1961; resite to J.939632 Jan 1965; U/G; Oct 1965; 16/B.2 Oct 1968; *In use*

Stottesdon
Opened July 1938 O.683826, 27/G.1; Granite 1943; 16/A.4 Nov 1953; U/G Sept 1965; 16/J.2 Oct 1968; *In use*

Upton Magna
Opened July 1938 J.548122, 27/K.1; 16/G.2 Nov 1953; resite to J.549125 May 1964; U/G April 1965; 16/H.1 Oct 1968; *In use*

Whitchurch
Opened Oct 1938 J.547422, 27/A.3; 16/P.3 Nov 1953; resite to J.555420 Nov 1959; U/G Oct 1960; *Closed Oct 1968*

SOMERSETSHIRE

Bruton
Opened Sept 1938 T.684345, 22/M.2; 9/D.3 Nov 1953;

U/G May 1959; *Closed Oct 1968*

Chard
Opened Aug 1940 T.309089, 22/T.4; resite to T.310091 Dec 1942, Granite and Totter 1943; Post destroyed by fire, August 1, 1950; 9/K.1 Sept 1953; U/G July 1955; 9/G.1 Oct 1968; *In use*

Childen Polden
Opened Aug 1940 T.387382, 22/L.4; Granite 1942; 9/A.3 Nov 1953; U/G Sept 1959; 9/B.3 Oct 1968; *In use*

Clevedon
Opened Jan 1938 T.408720, 22/J.1; 12/H.3 Nov 1953; U/G July 1959; 12/L.3 Oct 1968; *In use*

Clutton
Opened June 1953 T.642600, 23/New Post; 9/C.2 Nov 1953; U/G June 1959; 9/C.1 Oct 1968; *In use*

Crewkerne
Opened Sept 1938 T.441072, 22/Y.3; resite to T.429072 Oct 1938; 22/S.4 Nov 1940; Satellite 1942; Totter 1943; 22/Y.4 July 1944; 9/J.2 Nov 1953; U/G Sept 1961; 9/H.3 Oct 1968; *In use*

Dunster
Opened Sept 1938 S.996466, 22/K.2; resite to S.996458 Sept 1941; Granite 1942; 10/Y.1 Nov 1953; resite to S.988456 Aug 1954; resite to T.005444 Dec 1960; U/G Feb 1962; 9/A.1 Oct 1968; *In use*

Exford/Winsford
Opened Sept 1938 S.913350, 22/K.3 Winsford; resite to S.841378, renamed Exford, Aug 1940; 10/Z.3 Nov 1953; U/G April 1961; 10/D.1 Oct 1968; *In use*

Exton/Dulverton
Opened April 1942 S.934345, 22/K.4 Exton; 10/Y.2 Nov 1953; resite to S.881272 June 1962; renamed Dulverton Feb 1963; U/G May 1963; *Closed 1968*

Frome
Opened Jan 1938 T.765485, 23/F.3; 9/D.1 Nov 1953; U/G May 1962; 9/D.2 Oct 1968; *In use*

Glastonbury
Opened Sept 1938 T.497381, 22/M.1; resite to T.493382 Jan 1944; 9/L.1 Nov 1953; U/G Sept 1959; *Closed Oct 1968*

Hatch Beauchamp
Opened Sept 1938 T.306231, 22/Y.2; resite to T.312218 Feb 1940; Granite 1942; 9/L.3 Nov 1953; U/G Oct 1962; *Closed Oct 1968*

Highbridge/Burnham-on-Sea/Puriton
Opened Sept 1938 T.311568, 22/L.3 Highbridge; resite to T.302481, tie-line to Burnham-on-Sea C/G Station; renamed Burnham-on-Sea March 1942; 9/A.1 Nov 1953; resite to T.292431, renamed Puriton, July 1961; U/G June 1963; *Closed Oct 1968*

Holford
Opened Sept 1938 T.162428, 22/L.1; Darky and Granite, 1942; 9/A.2 Nov 1953; U/G June 1962; *In use*

Keynsham
Opened Jan 1938 T.653679, 23/K.1; resite to T.669659 April 1942; 9/C.1 Nov 1953; U/G Dec 1957; *Closed Oct 1968*

Langport
Opened Sept 1938 T.418285, 22/Y.1; Granite 1942; 9/L.4 Nov 1953; U/G Dec 1958; 9/B.2 Oct 1968; *In use*

Long Ashton
Opened Jan 1938 T.548708, 23/K.2; resite to T.541694 April 1946; 9/B.1 Nov 1953; U/G Dec 1960; *Closed Oct 1968*

Lydeard St. Lawrence
Opened Sept 1938 T.122314, 22/X.2; Satellite, Elworthy Barrows 1942; Granite 1943; 10/Y.4 Nov 1953; resite to T.097334 May 1954; resite to T.122314 Sept 1958; U/G Oct 1961; *Closed Oct 1968*

Marston Magna
Opened Sept 1938 T.593255, 22/M.2; Satellite created T.588278 1941, to facilitate "Cross Plotting", not hitherto possible, between M.1, M.2, M.3, Y.3 and E.3; 9/E.2 Nov 1953; resite to T.590255 April 1962; U/G Nov 1962; 9/F.4 Oct 1968; *In use*

North Petherton/Kingston St. Mary
Opened Sept 1938 T.283332, 22/L.2 North Petherton; Satellite T.233304 and Granite, Oct 1942; 9/L.2 Nov 1953; U/G on former satellite site, renamed Kingston St. Mary, April 1962; *In use*

Porlock/Minehead
Opened Sept 1938 S.886475, 22/K.1 Porlock; tie-line. Hurlston Point C/G Station 1942; Granite and Darky 1943; 10/Z.4 Nov 1953; resite to S.945476 renamed Minehead, Jan 1960; U/G Dec 1961; *Closed Oct 1968*

Portishead
Opened May 1953 T.465776, 23/New Post; 12/H.4 Nov 1953; resite to T.496774 Nov 1956; resite to T.448758 Dec 1962; U/G Sept 1964; *Closed Oct 1968*

Radstock
Opened Jan 1938 T.686549, 23/F.2; 9/C.3 Nov 1953; resite to T.688544 May 1956; U/G May 1959; *Closed Oct 1968*

Shepton Mallet
Opened Jan 1938 T.625432, 23/F.1; resite to T.605428

March 1944; 9/D.2 Nov 1953; U/G May 1959; 9/C.2 Oct 1968. *In use*

Stoke-Under-Ham or Hamhill
Opened Sept 1940 T.478174, 22/Y.3; 9/J.1 Nov 1953; U/G Feb 1959; *Closed Oct 1968*

Temple Combe
Opened Aug 1940 T.703218, 22/M.4; Satellite T.772226 March 1942; tie-line to Searchlight Unit, Henstridge Aerodrome, Nov 1942; 22/R.4 Sept 1952; 9/E.3 Nov 1953; U/G June 1961; 9/F.3 Oct 1968; *In use*

Wellington
Opened Sept 1938 T.154206, 22/X.3; Granite 1942; 10/X.1 Nov 1953; resite to T.152234 July 1955; U/G April 1958; 9/E.1 Oct 1968; *In use*

Westbury-Sub-Mendip
Opened Jan 1938 T.507507, 23/H.1; resite to T.500508, 9/A.4 Nov 1953; U/G April 1961; *Closed Oct 1968*

West Harptree
Opened Jan 1938 T.560565, 23/J.1; resite to T.546561, 9/B.4, Nov 1953; U/G Nov 1961; 9/V.3 Oct 1968; *In use*

Weston-Super-Mare/Bleadon
Opened Jan 1938 T.318615, 23/J.2 Weston-Super-Mare; resite to T.317582 (Windmill) following enemy attack on town (28/29 June), July 1942; 9/B.2 Nov 1953; resite to T.345578, renamed Bleadon, May 1957; U/G April 1959; 9/B.1 Oct 1968; *In use*

Winscombe
Opened Jan 1938 T.426577, 23/J.3; resite to T.540570 Aug 1953; 9/B.3 Nov 1953; U/G July 1960; *Closed Oct 1968*

STAFFORDSHIRE

Armitage
Opened Dec 1937 K.092162, 6/Q.2; resite to K.077156 Nov 1944; 8/B.1 Nov 1953; U/G Nov 1962; 8/F.1 Oct 1968; *In use*

Bobbington
Opened Oct 1938 O.815909, 27/F.3; 16/A.1 Nov 1953; U/G April 1965; *Closed Oct 1968*

Blyth Bridge/Longton
Opened Dec 1937 J.955720, 6/M.3 Blyth Bridge; resite to J.926425, renamed Longton, Oct 1941; 16/Q.2 Nov 1953; resite to J.930402 June 1954; U/G Oct 1965; *Closed Oct 1968*

Brierley Hill
Opened Aug 1938 O.918868, 27/F.2; 16/A.2 Nov 1953; resite to O.918893 Oct 1961; U/G Feb 1965; 16/L.1 Oct

1968; resite to O.916895 Nov 1972; *In use*

Burslem/Endon
Opened 1937 J.877511, 27/C.2; Granite 1943; resite to J.892491, 16/Q.1 Nov 1953; U/G 1962; *Closed Oct 1968*

Cannock/Cheslyn Bay
Opened Dec 1937 J.973115, 6/R.1 Cannock; resite to J.985108 Jan 1938; 8/B.4 Nov 1953; resite to J.969082, renamed Cheslyn Bay, June 1959, U/G May 1960; 16/J.1 Oct 1968; *In use*

Grosall
Opened July 1938 J.831205; 27/D.3; 16/J.2 Nov 1953; resite to J.842211 Jan 1961; U/G Oct 1968; 16/G.3 Oct 1968; *In use*

Glascote/Polesworth
Opened Nov 1953 K.244022, 8/N.3 Glascote; U/G April 1962 renamed Polesworth July 1963; 8/F.3 Oct 1968; *In use*

Hoar Cross
Opened Dec 1937 K.144232, 6/Q.1; resite to K.142231 Nov 1938; 8/A.3 Nov 1953; U/G June 1959; *Closed Oct 1968*

Ipstones
Opened Dec 1937 K.017503, 6/M.1; Granite 1943; 8/H.1 Nov 1953; U/G Nov 1958; 8/C.3 Oct 1968; *In use*

Pattingham
Opened July 1938 O.826986, 27/F.1; resite to O.826985, 16/H.2 Nov 1953; resite to O.817971 Sept 1962; U/G July 1963; 16/J.3 Oct 1968; *In use*

Shenstone
Opened Dec 1937 K.102048, 6/R.2; resite to K.116055 Oct 1941; 8/B.2 Nov 1953; U/G Dec 1960; *Closed Oct 1968*

Silverdale
Opened July 1938 J.815477, 27/C.3; Granite 1943; 16/Q.4 Nov 1953; U/G Oct 1962; 16/D.2 Oct 1968; *In use*

Standon
Opened July 1938 J.816345, 27/D.1; 16/Q.3 Nov 1953; resite to J.818344 Jan 1965; U/G Oct 1965; 16/G.1 Oct 1968; *In use*

Uttoxeter/Rocester
Opened Dec 1937 K.119394, 6/M.2 Rocester; resite to K.097296 May 1942; 8/H.3 Nov 1953; renamed Uttoxeter Aug 1961; U/G April 1962; 8/C.2 Oct 1968; *In use*

Walsall/Willenhall
Opened Dec 1937 O.965987, 6/R.3 Willenhall; 8/B.3 Nov 1953; resite to O.958998, renamed Walsall, Dec

1962; U/G Aug 1963; *Closed Oct 1968*

Wheaton Aston/Boscobel
Opened July 1938 J.858127, 27/E.2 Wheaton Aston;
16/H.1 Nov 1953; resite to J.832090 June 1955; resite to
J.830089 Oct 1965; U/G, renamed Boscobel (Shropshire)
May 1966; *Closed Oct 1968*

SUFFOLK

Aldeborough
Opened 1936 M.460582, 18/H.1; 6/A.2 Nov 1953; 4/A.2
1958; resite to M.476607 Jan 1959; U/G Dec 1959;
Closed Oct 1968

Bacton
Opened Oct 1938 M.062668, 14/H.1; 6/M.3 Nov 1953;
U/G July 1958; 4/B.2 Oct 1968; *In use*

Badingham
Opened Oct 1938 M.322676, 14/F.1; 6/N.3 Nov 1958;
U/G March 1959; *Closed Oct 1968*

Beyton
Opened Oct 1938 L.943626, 14/J.2; 6/M.4 Nov 1953;
U/G April 1958; 4/B.3 Oct 1968; *In use*

Botesdale
Opened Oct 1938 M.054744, 14/G.4; 6/M.1 Nov 1953;
U/G April 1958; *Closed Oct 1968*

Bungay
Opened Nov 1938 M.338894, 14/C.2; 6/N.1 Nov 1953;
resite to M.322865 May 1961; U/G Jan 1962; 6/K.2 Oct
1968; *In use*

Bury St. Edmunds
Opened Oct 1940 L.838642, 14/J.3; resite to L.829647,
7/B.2, Nov 1953; U/G April 1962; 4/B.1 Oct 1968; *In
use*

Clare
Opened April 1929 L.764448 (bank of Norman Bailie,
Clare Castle), 18/G; 14/K.3 May 1938; resite to L.766452
Oct 1941; 4/C.3 Nov 1953; resite to L.773441 Feb 1959;
U/G Dec 1959; 4/D.2 Oct 1968; *In use*

Claydon
Opened Jan 1931 M.154498, 18/J.2; 14/H.2 May 1938;
18/J.1 June 1941; resite to M.135493 Dec 1941; 4/B.3
Nov 1953; U/G Sept 1959; *Closed Oct 1968*

Coombes
Opened 1938 M.043571, 14/H.3; 6/B.1 Nov 1953; U/G
1964; *Closed Oct 1968*

Crowfield
Opened 1938 M.159562, 14/H.2; 6/B.2 Nov 1953; U/G
1965; 4/F.1 Oct 1968; *In use*

Culford
Opened Oct 1938 L.851707, 14/M.2; 6/L.4 Nov 1953;
U/G July 1960; *Closed Oct 1968*

Debenham
Opened Oct 1938 M.169641, 14/G.3; 6/M.2 Nov 1953;
U/G March 1958; *Closed Oct 1968*

Ellough/Barnby
Opened Jan 1954 M.418850, 6/N.2 Ellough; resite to
M.462878 April 1960; U/G June 1960; renamed Barnby
Dec 1960; 6/G.3 Oct 1968; *In use*

Felixstowe
Opened March 1938 M.292347, 18/L.3; resite to
M.294331 (Martello Tower) July 1940; Totter 1941;
4/E.3 Nov 1953; U/G June 1962; M.293331; *Closed
Oct 1968*

Framlingham Earl
Opened May 1939 G.274012, 16/V.3; 6/Q.2 Nov 1953;
resite to G.250024 Jan 1960; U/G June 1960; *Closed
Oct 1968*

Grundisburgh
Opened April 1928, 18/H.2; 18/L.1 May 1938; resite to
M.230514 (Windmill) July 1940; 4/E.1 Nov 1953; U/G
April 1960; *Closed Oct 1968*

Hadleigh
Opened April 1929 M.031422, 18/F.2; resite to
M.033423 Nov 1933; 18/J.3 May 1938; 4/F.1 Nov 1953;
resite to M.036427 Sept 1960; U/G Aug. 1961; 4/E.2
Oct 1968; *In use*

Halesworth
Opened July 1938 M.396776, 14/E.1; G.L. Post 1943;
6/C.4 Nov 1953; resite to M.401788 Feb 1960; U/G
Sept 1960; *Closed Oct 1968*

Hartest
Opened 1938 L.838523, 14/K.1; 7/C.2 Nov 1953; U/G
Jan 1960; *Closed Oct 1968*

Haverhill
Opened June 1930 L.670274, 18/E.3; resite to L.676462
May 1937; 14/L.3 May 1938; 4/C.4 Nov 1953; U/G
Sept 1959; *Closed Oct 1968*

Hopton/Gorleston
Opened 1934 G.530026, 16/T.2 Gorleston; resite to
G.536996, 6/E.3, renamed Hopton (grounds of Home
Office Sector Operations Room), March 1960;
U/G 1961; *Closed Oct 1968*

Kentford
Opened Nov 1938 L.714653, 14/M.3; 7/B.3 Nov 1953;
U/G Aug *1959*; *Closed Oct 1968; Reopened 1975 as* 4/A.2

Lakenheath
Opened Aug 1944 L.727827, 14/A.3; 7/B.1 Nov 1953;
U/G April 1968; 6/J.3 Oct 1968; *In use*

Lavenham
Opened April 1929 L.714492, 18/F.1; 14/A.2 May 1938;
14/K.2 Sept 1939; resite to L.916488 Aug 1942; 4/B.4
Nov 1953; U/G Oct 1959; *Closed Oct 1968*

Lowestoft
Opened Oct 1938 M.546959, 14/D.2; 6/D.2 Nov 1953;
U/G June 1959; 6/G.2 Oct 1968; *In use*

Mildenhall/Islehem
Opened Oct 1949 L.705746, 14/M.1 Mildenhall; 7/B.4
Nov 1953; resite to L.688755 Oct 1954; renamed
Islehem April 1958; U/G Aug 1959; *Closed Oct 1968*

Newmarket/Cheveley
Opened 1939 L.627607, 14/L.1 Newmarket; 7/P.3 Nov
1953; resite to L.962265, renamed Cheveley, Nov 1960;
U/G 1962; 4/A.2 Oct 1968; *Closed Aug 1974*

Orford
Opened Nov 1929 M.425477, 18/H.2 (balcony, Orford
Quay Watch Room); GLPost 1943; resite to M.412493
Nov 1948; 4/A.3 Nov 1953; U/G April 1961; *Closed
Oct 1968*

Pakefield
Opened April 1938 M.535883, 14/D.4; 6/D.3 Nov 1953;
U/G Dec 1957; *Closed Oct 1968*

Saxmundham
Opened 1938 M.394634, 14/F.2; 6/A.1 Nov 1953, U/G
1960; *Closed 1968*

Shottisham/Alderton
Opened May 1929 M.346547 (North Edge of Screwe
Mere), 18/L.2 Shottisham; 18/H.3 June 1941; resite to
M.347408 July 1944; 4/E.2 Nov 1953; renamed Alderton
Jan 1955; U/G Nov 1960; 4/F.2 Oct 1968; *In use*

Southwold
Opened April 1938 M.506749, 14/E.2; 6/C.2 Nov 1953;
resite to M.512774 Sept 1959; U/G June 1961; *Closed
Oct 1968*

Stanton/Honington
Opened Sept 1938 L.959736, 14/J.1 Stanton; 6/L.3 Nov
1953; renamed Honington March 1961; U/G June 1961;
Closed Oct 1968

Stradbroke
Opened Nov 1936 M.234742, 18/S.1; 14/G.2 July 1939;
6/N.4 Nov 1953; resite to M.237743 May 1959; U/G
Aug 1959; 4/C.1 Oct 1968; *In use*

Stratford
Opened May 1938 Q.387842 (Juppa Road Telephone
Exchange roof), 17/K.3, 5/B.2 Nov 1953; resite to
Q.416824 Oct 1960; U/G April 1961; 4/J.2 Oct 1968;
In use

Sudbury
Opened April 1929 L.881416, 18/F.3; 4/G.1 Nov 1953;
resite to L.884424 Sept 1954; resite to L.889437 Feb
1958; U/G March 1960; 4/E.1 Oct 1968; *In use*

Westleton
Opened Oct 1938 M.445692, 14/E.3; 6/C.3 Nov 1953;
U/G March 1958; 4/C.2 Oct 1968; *In use*

Wickhambrook
Opened Oct 1949 L.747542, 14/L.2; resite to L.752540,
7/C.1; Nov 1953; U/G April 1959; 4/D.1 Oct 1968;
In use

Wickham Market
Opened Feb 1938 M.305551, 14/F.3; 4/A.4 Nov 1953;
U/G March 1961; 4/C.3 Oct 1968; *In use*

Woolverstone
Opened April 1929 M.187383, 18/H.1; 18/J.3 May 1938;
18/L.2 Jan 1941; resite to M.195386 (Woolverstone·Hall
roof) March 1943; resite to M.195373, 4/E.4, Nov 1953;
U/G July 1961; 4/F.3 Oct 1968; *In use*

Wrentham
Opened Oct 1938 M.529819, 14/D.3; 6/C.1 Nov 1953;
resite to M.528840 Feb 1959; U/G June 1961; *Closed
Oct 1968*

SURREY

Chiddingfold
Opened June 1929 (Chiddingfold Village Green), 2/R.1;
resite to U.956355 May 1933; Granite 1943; resite to
U.949348, 2/N.2 Feb 1949; U/G Nov 1959; *Closed Oct
1968*

Clandon
Opened Oct 1937 Q.043515, 19/V.3; resite to Q.051507
May 1941; Granite 1943; 2/P.1 Nov 1953; U/G Post
June 1959; 2./D.2 Oct 1968; *In use*

Claygate/Oxshott
Opened Sept 1940 Q.166632, 19/Y.3 Claygate (Ruxley
Towers, NAAFI H/Q); 19/V.4 Nov 1940; 2/Q.1 Nov
1953; resite to Q.145623 Nov 1961; renamed Oxshott
March 1962; U/G May 1962; *Closed Oct 1968*

Cranleigh
Opened 1929, Q.049394, 2/O.1; 2/R.2 May 1939; resite
to Q.064379 Feb 1942; Granite 1943; 2/P.4 Nov 1953;
resite to Q.019359 Oct 1958; U/G Sept 1961; 2/G.1
Oct 1968; *In use*

Attack Warning Red

Farnham
Opened June 1929 Q.838470, 2/R.3; resite to Q.838474 Dec 1937; 3/L.3 May 1939; resite to Q.834495 March 1940; Totter 1943; 2/N.1 Nov 1953; prototype Under Ground Post, used in all initial trials, May 1957; 2/C.1 Oct 1968; *In use*

Godstone/Nutfield/Redhill
Opened Oct 1937 Q.344511, 19/S.3 Godstone; resite to Q.332501 Aug 1942; Granite 1943; 2/S.1, renamed Nutfield, Nov 1953; resite to Q.314501 Aug 1963; resite to Q.295479, renamed Redhill, Oct 1964; U/G Feb 1965; 2/E.2 Oct 1968; *In use*

Headley
Opened Oct 1937 Q.205540 (Common land N/E of Headley Cricket Ground), 19/V.1; Granite 1943; resite to Q.204539 June 1952; 2/Q.4 Nov 1953; U/G April 1966; *Closed Oct 1968*

Hogs Back
Opened March 1943 U.975486, 4/N.2; Granite 1943; 19/M.2 April 1947; 2/R.2 Nov 1953; U/G Aug 1957; *Closed Oct 1968*

Holmwood
Opened Oct 1937 Q.172456, 19/V.2; Granite 1943; 2/P.2 Nov 1953; U/G Jan 1960; 2/E.3 Oct 1968; *In use*

Knaphill/Camberley/Deepcut
Opened Sept 1933 U.956584, 4/L.3 Knaphill; 19/N.3 Jan 1941; 19/M.3 Aug 1954; 2/R.3 Nov 1953; resite to U.911592 Jan 1962; U/G Nov 1963; renamed Deepcut June 1964; 2/D.3, renamed Camberley, Oct 1968; *In use*

Milford
Opened June 1929 U.940651, 2/R.2; resite to U.935640 (Rodbro' Hill) May 1938; 2/R.4 May 1940; 3/L.3 June 1940; resite to U.936649 (Mousehill Down) Sept 1940; 2/R.3 Jan 1941; Granite 1943; 2/N.2 Nov 1953; resite to U.947431 Feb 1960; U/G July 1960; *Closed Oct 1968*

Weybridge
Opened Oct 1937 Q.081661, 19/X.2; 2/R.1 Nov 1953; U/G April 1963; 2/D.1 Oct 1968; *In use*

SUSSEX

Arundel/Littlehampton
Opened 1925 (N Bank, East of Arun Bridge), 2/O.1; Arundel; resite to Q.189065 Aug 1939; resite to Q.019073 (Castle Keep), June 1942; 2/N.1 Nov 1953; 2/E.3 May 1957; resite to U.996033 (Ford Airfield), renamed Littlehampton, Nov 1961; U/G May 1962; 2/J.3 Oct 1968; *In use*

Beachy Head/Pevensey
Opened Nov 1929 V.591957, 2/K.2 Beachy Head; 2/K.3 Sept 1940; Totter 1942; 2/B.2 Nov 1953; resite to Q.655038 (Martello Tower), renamed Pevensey Ma 1955; resite to Q.646027 Sept 1961; U/G Sept 1962; 1/G.2 Oct 1968; *In use*

Bexhill/Cooden
Opened Nov 1929, 1/H.1 Bexhill; 1/J.2 April 1933; resite to Q.709089 (Golf Course), renamed Cooden, Nov 1940; 2/H.2 May 1943; resite to Q.758077 April 1949; 1/C.3 Nov 1953; resite to Q.759076 Dec 1961; U/G Oct 1963; *Closed Oct 1968*

Beckley
Opened 1925, 1/H.3; Closed shortly afterwards

Billingshurst
Opened 1925 Q.100256, 2/N.3; 2/O.2 1929; Granite 1943; resite to Q.098258 Feb 1949; 2/L.1 Nov 1953; U/G June 1958; *Closed Oct 1968*

Bognor/Middleton
Opened 1939 Z.976003, 2/N.2 Middleton; resite to Z.89200 (roof of "Villa Place", Elmer Road) Aug 1940; Totter 1942; resite to A.933989 (Old Church Tower, Market Street, Bognor Regis), renamed Bognor, June 1949; 2/F.2 Nov 1953; resite to Z.984004 July 1961; U/G Aug 1963; *Closed Oct 1968*

Brighton/Rottingdean
Opened Aug 1938 Q.362026, 2/L.2 Rottingdean; Totter 1942; site abandoned Dec 1946. New site, Q.329045 (Radio Building roof), renamed Brighton, Feb 1955; U/G Oct 1962; 2/K.3 Oct 1968; *In use*

Catsfield
Opened 1925, 1/H.1; Closed shortly afterwards

Chiddingly
Opened 1925 Q.545143, 2/K.4; 2/K.3 1929; 2/V.3 May 1939; Totter 1943; resite to Q.548134 April 1944; 2/C.1 Nov 1953; U/G Jan 1962; 1/F.2 Oct 1968; *In use*

Copthorne/Crawley
Opened Oct 1937 Q.330392, 19/T.3 Copthorne (Upper Common, opposite Abergavenny Arms); resite to Q.331395 (Copthorne School Tower). Granite, 1942; 2/S.4 Nov 1953; resite to Gatwick Aerodrome, renamed Crawley, Oct 1961; U/G Aug 1962; *Closed Oct 1968*

Crowborough
Opened 1925 Q.503294, 2/L.2; 2/J.1 1929; resite to Q.509298 April 1942; 2/A.2 Nov 1953; resite to Q.506296 Nov 1959; U/G Oct 1960; 1/F.3 Oct 1968; *In use*

Cuckfield
Opened 1925, 2/N.1; resite to Q.306244 1927; 2/M.1

1929; 2/S.1 May 1939; 2/O.4 April 1943; 2/L.2 Nov
1953; U/G June 1962 *Closed Oct 1968; Reopened, 2/K.1.,*
Nov 1970: In use

Cuckmere Haven
Opened April 1953; V.500981, 2/B.3; U/G April 1958;
1/G.3 Oct 1968; *In use*

East Dean/Singleton
Opened June 1929 U.898130, 2/P.2 East Dean; Totter
1942; 2/Q.4 May 1943; resite to U.882129 (date
unknown); 2/F.1, renamed Singleton, June 1959; U/G
Jan 1961; 2/H.1 Oct 1968; *In use*

Fairlight
Opened Nov 1929 O.861112, 1/H.5; 1/J.3 April 1933;
1/H.1 May 1939; 1/L.2 June 1943; 1/H.3 Nov 1953;
U/G Dec 1960; 1/H.2 Oct 1968; *In use*

Fernhurst
Opened 1925 U.898284, 2/O.2; 2/Q.2 1929; 2/M.3 Nov
1953; U/G Sept 1959; 2/G.3 Oct 1968; *In use*

Framfield
Opened 1925 Q.489206, 2/L.1; 2/J.3 1929; 2/V.2 May
1939; resite to Q.509205 May 1941; 2/A.3 Nov 1953;
U/G March 1960; *Closed Oct 1968*

Frant
Opened 1925 Q.590358, 1/J.3; 1/I.3 1929; 2/J.3 April
1939; 1/P.1 Nov 1953; U/G Oct 1961; *In use*

Hartfield
Opened June 1937 Q.478349, 19/T.1; 19/S.3 March
1938; 2/T.3 June 1939; 2/A.1 Nov 1953; U/G May 1960;
Closed Oct 1968

Henfield
Opened 1925 Q.182159, 2/M.3; resite to Q.199163
Jan 1941; Totter 1943; 2/L.3 Nov 1953; resite to
Q.222163 April 1963; U/G July 1964; *Closed 1968*

Horsham
Opened June 1929 Q.161305 (roof of, Tanners & Chart,
Drapers, Middle St), 2/M.2; resite to Q.178309 May 1934;
2/O.1 May 1939; Granite 1942; 2/P.3 Nov 1953; resite
to Q.180309 Aug 1954; resite to Q.179297 Aug 1961;
U/G Dec 1961; 2/G.2 Oct 1968; *In use*

Keymer/Ditchling
Opened 1925 Q.314154, 2/M.2 Keymer; 2/L.3 1929;
resite to Q.316149 July 1941; 2/M.4 Sept 1943; 2/D.,
renamed Ditchling, Nov 1953; resite to Q.323160
Jan 1961; U/G June 1962; 2/K.1 Oct 1968; *Closed Nov*
1970

Lewes
Opened 1925 Q.409102 (Castle Tower), 2/M.1; 2/L.2
1929; 2/C.4 Nov 1953; resite to Q.393113 (Lewes

Racecourse) Jan 1959; U/G Dec 1960; 2/K.2 Oct 1968;
In use

Mannings Heath
Opened 1925, 2/N.2; *Closed 1929*

Mayfield/Rotherfield
Opened 1925 Q.589873, 2/K.3 Mayfield; 2/J.2 1929; resite
to Q.591267 March 1942; 1/P.4, renamed Rotherfield,
Nov 1953; U/G April 1963; *Closed Oct 1968*

Midhurst
Opened 1925 U.876211, 2/0.2; 2/Q.1 1929; resite to
U.886214 (Post Office roof) Nov 1934; 2/M.1 Nov
1953; resite to U.864198 Jan 1959; U/G May 1962;
Closed Oct 1968

Newhaven
Opened 1929 Q.449001, 2/L.4; 2/L.3 July 1944; 2/C.2
Nov 1953; resite to Q.442005 Feb 1964; U/G May
1965; *Closed Oct 1968*

Newick
Opened 1925 Q.421210, 2/L.3; 2/L.1 1929; 2/S.2 May
1939; resite to Q.422199 Aug 1941; 2/V.4 Oct 1943;
2/A.4 Nov 1953; resite to Q.417227 July 1964; U/G Nov
1965; *Closed Oct 1968*

Ninfield/Catsfield
Opened 1929 Q.725134, 1/H.1 Catsfield; resite to
Q.702127, renamed J.1 Ninfield 1939; 2/H.1 1943;
1/G.4 Nov 1953; resite to Q.700128 June 1961; U/G
Jan 1962; 1/H.3 Oct 1968; *In use*

Northiam
Opened 1929 Q.824258, 1/H.1; 1/H.4 Nov 1953; U/G
Sept 1961; *In use*

Peacehaven
Opened Aug 1943, Promenade near Bolney Ave, 2/L.3;
resite to Q.414006 April 1944; 2/C.3 Nov 1953; U/G
1968; *Closed Oct 1968*

Petworth
Opened 1929 U.974213, 2/0.3; 2/Q.3 May 1939; 2/M.2
Nov 1953; resite to U.970213 Feb 1955; resite to
U.961158 Nov 1964; U/G May 1966; *Closed 1968*

Polegate
Opened 1925 Q.579073, 2/K.1; Totter 1942; 2/B.1 Nov
1953; resite to Q.618117 Oct 1961; U/G Jan 1962;
Closed Oct 1968

Pulborough
Opened 1929 Q.063187, 2/N.3; resite to Q.611189 April
1939; 2/0.2 May 1939; 2/E.1 Nov 1953; resite to
Q.065195 May 1954; U/G June 1968; 2/J.1 Oct 1968;
In use

Robertsbridge
Opened 1925, 1/H.2; 1/H.1; 1/I.3 Nov 1940; resite to Q.744260 June 1942; 1/G.1 Nov 1953; U/G Sept 1961; *Closed Oct 1968*

Rogate
Opened 1929 U.806208, 2/Q.3; 2/Q.4 April 1939; 3/B.3 June 1940; resite U.809223 Aug 1940; 2/M.4 Nov 1953; resite to U.805243 Sept 1961; U/G June 1962; *Closed Oct 1968*

Rushlake Green
Opened 1929 Q.628181, 2/K.2; 2/V.1 April 1938; Totter 1943; resite to Q.614211 Aug 1944; 1/F.3 Nov 1653; resite to Q.614208 Aug 1958; U/G Jan 1959; 1/G.1 Oct 1968; *In use*

Rye Harbour
Opened 1929 Q.941188, 1/F.1; 1/H.3 April 1938; Totter 1942; 1/H.2 Nov 1953; resite to Q.905197 Feb 1961; U/G Sept 1961; *Closed Oct 1968*

Selsey
Opened 1929; (Foreshore South of Mill House), 2/P.4; resite to Z.857923 May 1933; 2/P.3 April 1939; resite to Z.853930 (roof of "Upper Reach") June 1940; Totter 1942; resite to Z.850924 (Marine Hotel roof) Aug 1947; 2/F.3 Nov 1953; resite to Z.848947 Jan 1961; U/G Feb 1963; 2/H.2 Oct 1968; *In use*

Shoreham
Opened Aug 1939 Q.174045, 2/M.1; Totter 1942; 2/D.3 Nov 1953; resite to Q.240071 March 1962; U/G Nov 1962; *Closed Oct 1968*

Steyning
Opened 1929 Q.174112 (Steyning Grammar School), 2/N.2; 2/S.1 Oct 1943; resite to Q.174103 July 1944; 2/D.4 Nov 1953; U/G Oct 1959; 2/J.2 Oct 1968; *In use*

Ticehurst
Opened May 1925 Q.692299, 1/J.2; Totter 1943; 1/F.2 Nov 1953; resite to Q.675285 Aug 1958; U/G Oct 1959; *Closed Oct 1968*

Warbleton
Opened 1925, 2/K.1 Closed shortly afterwards

West Hoathly
Opened Oct 1937 Q.363329, 19/T.2; Granite 1942; 2/S.3 Nov 1953; resite to Q.366326 Oct 1961; U/G Sept 1962; 2/E.2 Oct 1968; *In use*

West Wickham
Opened Feb 1938 Q.381659 (Post Office roof), 19/Y.1; 2/Q.2 Nov 1953; resite to Q.396614 Sept 1958; U/G Sept 1959; *Closed Oct 1968*

West Wittering
Satellite opened Sept 1942, Z.776976, 3/M.4; *Closed July 1948*

Worthing/Lancing
Opened 1929 Q.151021, 2/N.4 Worthing (Corporation Pier); 2/N.2 May 1939; resite to Q.150024 (County Restaurant roof, Marine Parade), June 1940; 2/S.3 May 1943; 2/E.2 Nov 1953; resite to Q.182036 Oct 1961; U/G Sept 1962; renamed Lancing Oct 1962; *Closed Oct 1968*

WARWICKSHIRE

Alderminster
Opened June 1937 P.242487, 5/D.2; Granite 1942; resite to P.252443 Nov 1944 3/K.1 Nov 1953; U/G Oct 1963; *Closed Oct 1968*

Barford
Opened Dec 1937 P.288598, 5/C.2; Granite 1942; 8/E.2 Nov 1953; U/G July 1959; 3/E.2 Dec 1962; *Closed Oct 1968; Reopened, 3/A.2, May 1969; In use*

Bideford-on-Avon
Opened Dec 1937 P.113521, 5/D.1; Granite 1942; 3/E.3 Nov 1953; U/G June 1960; 3/C.2 Oct 1968; *In use*

Coleshill/Curdworth/Hurley
Opened Dec 1937 P.196901, 5/G.3 Hurley; 5/F.3 Sept 1940; 8/C.2, renamed Coleshill Nov 1953; resite to P.166932, renamed Curdworth, Oct 1964; U/G Nov 1965; *Closed Oct 1968*

Edge Hill
Opened Jan 1938 P.354450, 12/J.2; Granite 1942; 3/P.4 Nov 1953; resite to P.373468 Jan 1961; U/G March 1963; 3/D.3 Oct 1968; *In use*

Erdington
Opened Dec 1937 P.102917, 5/F.1; 8/C.1 Nov 1953; U/G Oct 1960; 8/L.1 Oct 1968; *In use*

Harbury
Opened Jan 1954 P.363598, 8/F.1; U/G Oct 160; 3/F.1 Dec 1962; 3/A.2 Oct 1968; *Closed Oct 1968*

Henley-in-Arden
Opened Dec 1939 P.155660, 5/C.3; Granite 1944; 8/E.1 Nov 1953, U/G 1960; 3/E.1 Dec, 1962; *Closed Oct 1968*

Kenilworth/Haseley Knob
Opened Dec 1937 P.304726, 5/C.1 Kenilworth; 8/R.2 Nov 1953; resite to P.259710, renamed Haseley Knob, March 1964; U/G Nov 1964; 3/A.1 Oct 1968; *In use*

Long Compton
Opened Jan 1938 P.297310, 4/Z.2; 12/Q.3 Feb 1940; 3/K.3 Nov 1953; U/G 1961; 3/F.3 Oct 1968; *In use*

Meriden
Opened Dec 1937 P.252806, 5/F.2; 8/R.1 Nov 1953; resite to P.262826 Oct 1964; U/G Nov 1965; 8/J.3 Oct 1968; *In use*

Napton-on-the-Hill/Southam
Opened Jan 1938 P.458614, 12/J.3 Southam; 5/C.4, renamed Napton 1943; Granite 1944; 8/Q.4 Nov 1953; U/G July 1959; *Closed Oct 1968*

Selly Oak/Frankley
Opened Dec 1937 P.074823, 5/E.1 Selly Oak; 5/F.4 March 1942; 8/C.2 Nov 1953; resite to P.002797, renamed Frankley, Nov 1957; U/G Aug 1960; 8/H.3 Oct 1968; *In use*

Shirley
Opened Dec 1937 P.101789, 5/F.3; 5/E.4 July 1940; resite to P.125778 April 1950; 8/R.3 Nov 1953; U/G Nov 1961; 8/H.2 Oct 1968; *In use*

Wolston
Opened 1943 P.419747, 5/B.2; 8/Q.1 Nov 1953; U/G May 1960 3/B.3 Oct 1968; *In use*

WESTMORLAND

Appleby
Opened May 1939 Y.676199, 29/V.3; 22/0.3 Nov 1953; resite to Y.674199 May 1956; U/G May 1960, 33/K.2 Oct 1968; *In use*

Bampton
Opened Nov 1938 Y.516182, 29/V.1; 22/O.2 Nov 1953; resite to Y.521175 Sept 1962; U/G March 1963; 22/K.4 Oct 1968; *In use*

Grasmere
Opened May 1940 Y.345066, 29/W.3; 21/C.1 Nov 1953; resite to Y.322108, 22/H.1, April 1963; U/G Dec 1964; 22/L.1 Oct 1968; *In use*

Kendal
Opened Nov 1938 D.526917, 29/T.2; Granite 1942; Augmented Granite 1944; 21/C.3 Nov 1953; 21/B.4 May 1962; U/G May 1965; 21/B.1 Oct 1968; *In use*

Kirby Lonsdale
Opened May 1940 D.603787, 29/P.1; Granite 1943; 21/B.3 Nov 1953; U/G June 1965; *In use*

Kirby Stephen
Opened Jan 1939 Y.779088, 29/V.2; 21/A.4 Nov 1953; U/G Nov 1962; 22/K.3 Oct 1968; *In use*

Liddlesdale
Opened June 1940 Y.476878 32/A.3; Granite 1943; 22/J.1 Nov 1953; U/G Nov 1962; *Closed Oct 1968*

Milnthorpe
Opened Nov 1938 D.484805, 29/P.4; 29/X.2 Dec 1942; Granite 1943; 21/F.1 Nov 1953; U/G June 1965; *Closed Oct 1968*

Tebay
Opened May 1940 Y.619045, 29/T.1; 21/B.1 Nov 1953; U/G Nov 1962; 22/L.2 Oct 1968; *In use*

Troutbeck/Windermere
Opened June 1940 D.413038, 29/W.2 Troutbeck; 21/C.4 Nov 1953; resite to D.427988, renamed Windermere, Nov 1963; U/G Dec 1963; *Closed Oct 1968*

WILTSHIRE

Alderbury/Bodenham
Opened Jan 1938 U.160257, 23/D.3 Bodenham; resite to U.207248, 14/B.2, Nov 1953; renamed Alderbury Aug 1954; U/G Aug 1961; 14/D.2 Oct 1968; *In use*

Amesbury
Opened Jan 1938 U.152425, 23/C.2; 14/N.3 Nov 1953; resite to U.195428 Jan 1956; resite to U.160387 Oct 1963; U/G July 1964; 14/E.3 Oct 1968; *In use*

Avebury
Opened Jan 1938 U.107695, 23/B.2; resite to U.104692 Sept 1953; 14/M.4 Nov 1953; U/G June 1961; 3/D.4 Dec 1967; 14/B.1 Oct 1968; *In use*

Blunsdon/Highworth
Opened Jan 1938 U.141904, 23/A.2 Blunsdon; 3/M.2 Nov 1953; resite to U.194924, 3/M.2, renamed Highworth, April 1959; U/G Sept 1959; *Closed 1968*

Bradford-upon-Avon
Opened Jan 1938 T.824613, 23/G.2; 9/C.4 Nov 1953; U/G Jan 1961; 9/D.1 Oct 1968; *In use*

Bratton
Opened Feb 1938 T.919528, 23/G.1; 14/A.1 Nov 1953; resite to T.921509 Feb 1961; U/G Oct 1961; 14/A.3 Oct 1968; *In use*

Chippenham
Opened Jan 1938 T.926739, 23/M.2; resite to T.922717 Sept 1940; resite to T.902718 May 1949; 14/M.3 Nov 1953; U/G May 1958; 3/D.3 Dec 1967; 14/A.1 Oct 1968; *In use*

Collingbourne Ducis
Opened Jan 1938 U.240533, 23/C.3; resite to U.227537 Aug 1953; 14/N.4 Nov 1953; U/G April 1959; *Closed Oct 1968*

Devizes
Opened Jan 1938, 23/G.3; resite to U.033601 Nov 1952; 14/M.2 Nov 1953; U/G Aug 1961; 3/D.2 Dec 1967;

14/A.2 Oct 1968; *In use*

Enford
Opened Jan 1938 U.136514, 23/C.1; 14/A.2 Nov 1953;
U/G April 1959; *Closed Oct 1968*

Great Bedwyn
Opened Jan 1938 U.278648, 23/B.3; 14/L.4 Nov 1953;
resite to U.284694 Sept 1959; U/G Aug 1961; 14/B.3
Oct 1968; *In use*

Maiden Bradley/Mere
Opened Jan 1938 T.800390, 23/E.1 Maiden Bradley;
resite to T.796377 April 1953; 9/D.4 Nov 1953; resite to
T.802353 Aug 1959; U/G July 1965, renamed Mere;
9/F.1 Oct 1968; *In use*

Malmesbury
Opened Jan 1938 T.935873 (Tower House roof), 23/M.1;
3/M.4 Nov 1953; resite to T.953855 March 1961; U/G
March 1962; *Closed April 1968*

Minety/Cricklade
Opened Jan 1938 U.026909, 23/A.1 Minety; 3/M.1 Nov
1953; resite to U.071919, renamed Cricklade, March
1960; U/G July 1962; 3/J.2 Oct 1968; *In use*

Osborne St. George
Opened Jan 1938 U.202740, 23/B.1; resite to U.216756,
14/M.1 Nov 1953; U/G June 1961; 3/D.1 Jan 1968;
Closed Oct 1968

Shrewton
Opened Feb 1940 U.052448, 23/D.4; 14/A.3 Nov 1953;
U/G March 1963; *Closed Oct 1968*

Sutton Veney
Opened Jan 1938 T.899418, 23/E.3; 14/A.4 Nov 1953;
U/G April 1959; *Closed Oct 1968*

Tisbury
Opened Jan 1938 T.941288, 23/E.2; 14/B.4 Nov 1953;
resite to T.941288 June 1954; U/G July 1960; *Closed Oct
1968*

Wootton Bassett/Swindon/Wroughton
Opened Jan 1938 U.071828, 23/A.3 Wootton Bassett;
3/M3 Nov 1953; resite to U.120835, renamed Swindon,
April 1956; U/G July 1961; site abandoned March 1967.
New site U.142795, U/G, June 1968 named Wroughton;
3/K.3 Oct 1968; *In use*

Wylye
Opened Jan 1938 U.008373, 23/O.3; resite to U.006368
1944; 14/B.1 Nov 1953; U/G June 1961; 14/D.1 Oct
1968; *In use*

WORCESTERSHIRE

Broadway
Opened Dec 1937 P.115364, 5/D.3; Granite 1943; 3/C.2
Nov 1953; U/G June 1960; *In use*

Bromsgrove
Opened Dec 1937 O.967708, 16/D.1; U/G Aug 1961;
3/K.4 Dec 1962; *Closed April 1968*

Clows Top
Opened Dec 1937 O.717718, 24/V.3; Granite 1942;
16/O.1 Nov 1953; U/G June 1959; 12/C.1 June 1965;
Closed Oct 1968

Crowle/Himbleton
Opened Nov 1937 O.945587, 24/M.2 Himbleton; resite
to O.916569 Nov 1943; 3/D.3 renamed Crowle, Nov
1953; U/G June 1960; 12/C.5 Dec 1962; *Closed Oct 1968*

Inkberrow
Opened Dec 1937 P.011569, 5/E.1; Granite, 1943; 3/E.4
Nov 1953; U/G, 3/E.3, Dec 1962; 3/C.1 Oct 1968; *In use*

Ombersley
Opened Dec 1937 O.848637, 24/M.1; 16/C.2 Nov 1953;
U/G Aug 1961; 16/L.2 Oct 1968; *In use*

Pershore
Opened Nov 1937 O.940466, 24/N.1; Granite 1942;
3/C.1 Nov 1953; U/G Nov 1961; *Closed April 1968*

Powick
Opened Nov 1937 O.827517, 24/M.3; resite to O.827521,
12/D.4, Nov 1953; resite to O.828518 April 1961; U/G
Feb 1962; 12/M.5 Jan 1963; *In use*

Redditch
Opened Dec 1937 P.038677, 5/E.2; resite to P.034690,
8/D.2, Dec 1962; U/G, 3/E.5, May 1963; *Closed April 1968*

Tenbury
Opened Dec 1937 O.596679, 24/T.3; Granite 1942;
16/O.4 Dec 1960; U/G Sept 1962; 12/C.4 June 1963;
Closed Oct 1968

Upton-upon-Severn
Opened Nov 1937 O.846402, 24/N.2, Granite 1942;
12/M.2 May 1950; resite to O.872382 Jan 1960; U/G
Aug 1961; 12/B.3 Oct 1968; *In use*

Wolverley/Arley
Opened Dec 1937 O.828801, 24/V.2 Wolverley; 16/A.3,
renamed Arley, Nov 1953; U/G April 1961; *Closed Oct
1968*

YORKSHIRE

Aldbrough
Opened Oct 1936 A.246392, 10/F.2; 18/J.2 Nov 1953;

resite to A.265385 June 1954; U/G Dec 1958; 20 /N.2
May 1964; 20/M.2 Oct 1968; *Closed 1975*

Askern
Opened Sept 1937 E.540124, 8/Y.2; resite to E.573144
Jan 1942; Granite 1943; 18/F.2 Nov 1953; U/G Jan 1961;
Closed Oct 1968

Aysgarth
Opened Sept 1938 E.006878, 9/Y.4; Granite 1943; 21/A.3
Nov 1953; U/G June 1965; 21/C.2 Oct 1968; *In use*

Barkston Ash
Opened Aug 1937 E.486362, 8/Z.2; 20/D.3 Nov 1953;
UG Dec 1957; *Closed Oct 1968*

Barningham
Opened Dec 1936 Z.078094, 30/H.3; resite to Z.083112
March 1942; Granite 1943; 23/C.3 Nov 1953; U/G Sept
1962; *Closed Oct 1968*

Barwick-in-Elmet
Opened March 1942; E.339375, 8/Z.1; Granite 1943;
20/D.4 Nov 1953; resite to E.387367 July 1958; U/G Jan
1962; 20 C.3 Oct 1968; *In use*

Bewerley
Opened Aug 1937 E.082524, 8/T.1; 21/K.4 Nov 1953;
resite to E.060522 Aug 1955; U/G June 1963; *Closed Oct
1968*

Beauchief
Opened Jan 1938 K.237813, 6/O.1; Granite 1943; 18/N.4
Nov 1953; U/G May 1959; 18/F.4 Oct 1962; 8/A.3 Oct
1968; *In use*

Bedale
Opened Dec 1936 E.260876, 9/V.2; Granite 1943; resite
to E.271887 Feb 1945; 20/H.3 Nov 1953; U/G April
1959; 23/V.3 Dec 1963; 20/B.3 Oct 1968; *In use*

Beverley/Leconfield
Opened July 1936 A.021427, 10/L.2 Leconfield; resite to
A.022388, renamed Beverley, Sept 1941; 10/N.2 March
1946; 18/S.1 Nov 1953; resite to A.009385 Nov 1963;
U/G Feb 1964; 20/L.2 Oct 1968; *In use*

Birdsall
Opened Aug 1936 E.816668, 10/J.3; 20/Q.2 Nov 1953;
resite to E.681673 Aug 1961; U/G Feb 1962; 20/D.3 Oct
1968; *In use*

Blaxton/Lindholme
Opened May 1940 E.675008, 8/R.4, Blaxton; 8/R.3 Sept
1942; 18/M.1 Nov 1953; resite to E.691075 Feb 1961;
renamed Lindholme Sept 1961; U/G May 1962; 18/H.1
May 1964; 15/A.3 Oct 1968; *In use*

Bolton-by-Bowland
Opened Nov 1938 D.775501, 29/R.3; 21/J.2 Nov 1953;

U/G June 1956; *In use*

Boston Spa
Opened Aug 1937 E.430448, 8/Z.3; 8/V.2 Nov 1942;
20/D.2 Nov 1953; resite to E.448425 April 1954; U/G
Nov 1959; *Closed Oct 1968*

Bramley
Opened July 1940 E.237351, 8/V.4; 8/Z.4 Aug 1942;
Granite 1943; 20/E.2 Nov 1953; U/G Jan 1962; 18/C.2
Oct 1964; *Closed Oct 1968*

Brandesburton
Opened Dec 1943 A.097493, 10/N.3; 18/H.3 Nov 1953;
resite to A.093501 Nov 1961; U/G June 1962; 20/M.3
Aug 1962; *Closed Oct 1968*

Brandsby
Opened Jan 1937 E.582723, 9/W.1; resite to E.589736
May 1940; 9/X.1 Oct 1944; 20/R.2 Nov 1953; resite to
E.572720 Oct 1962; U/G June 1964; 20/C.2 Oct 1968;
In use

Bridlington
Opened July 1936 A.169671 (Observation Tower,
Bridlington Grammar School), 10/G.3; 20/A.3 Nov 1953;
resite to A.167710 Sept 1957; U/G May 1959; 20/H.3
Feb 1966; 20/E.2 Oct 1968; *In use*

Bubwith
Opened July 1936 E.715365, 10/K.3; 18/G.2 Nov 1953;
U/G May 1961; *Closed Oct 1968*

Buckden
Opened Nov 1942 D.937780 8/T.4; Darky; 8/P.1 April
1947; 21/L.3 Oct 1953; resite to D.936782 May 1958;
U/G Sept 1963; 21/F.1 Oct 1968; *In use*

Burton Agnes
Opened Dec 1952 A.095656, 10/New Post; 20/B.2 June
1955; U/G, 20/J.2, Sept 1962; *Closed Oct 1968*

Burton Pidsea
Opened July 1936 A.243321 10/E.1; 18/J.3 May 1955;
resite to A.232315 Nov 1961; U/G June 1962; 20/N.3
Aug 1962; *Closed Oct 1968*

Camblesforth
Opened July 1936 E.649263, 10/A.2; 18/C.3 Nov 1953;
U/G Oct 1961; 20/P.3 Oct 1968; *In use*

Castleton
Opened Dec 1936 Z.682077, 9/R.3; 9/O.4 April 1953;
20/M.4 Nov 1953; U/G April 1959; 20/A.3 Oct 1968;
In use

Cawood
Opened March 1940 E.582389, 10/E.4; 18/G.1 Nov 1953;
U/G May 1961; 20/G.2 Oct 1968; *In use*

Attack Warning Red

Chop Gate
Opened July 1940 Z.558000, 9/Q.4; 9/S.1 July 1953; 20/L.3 Nov 1953; U/G Sept 1963; 23/M.2 Oct 1968; *In use*

Cloughton
Opened Jan 1937 A.009953, 9/S.2; 9/Q.1 Feb 1953; 20/P.1 Nov 1953; U/G Feb 1962; *Closed Oct 1968*

Cotherstone
Opened Dec 1936 Y.996177, 30/H.2; 21/A.1 Nov 1953; U/G June 1965; 23/L.4 Oct 1968; *In use*

Cowling
Opened Aug 1937 D.972426, 8/T.3; 21/K.2 Nov 1953; resite to D.985429 Feb 1960; U/G June 1963; *Closed Oct 1968*

Croft
Opened Dec 1936 Z.309070, 9/Z.3; 9/V.1 Feb 1945; 20/J.4 Nov 1953; U/G July 1961; 23/S.4 March 1967; 23/L.2 Oct 1968; *In use*

Crossland Moor/Farnley Tyas
Opened Aug 1937 E.162115, 8/W.2 Farnley Tyas; 8/Q.3 Oct 1941; resite to E.104138, renamed Crossland Moor, May 1942; Granite 1943; 18/F.4 Nov 1953; U/G Nov 1961; 18/D.3 Feb 1967; *Closed Oct 1968*

Darley
Opened Aug 1937 E.179586, 8/S.3; resite to E.208578 Sept 1941; Granite 1943; 20/F.4 Nov 1953; resite to E.218587 April 1959; U/G May 1960; 20/F.1 Oct 1968; *In use*

Danton
Opened Aug 1937 E.323118, 8/X.1; Granite 1943; 18/F.2 Nov 1953; 18/D.1 Nov 1962; resite to E.319122 Nov 1963; U/G May 1964; 20/K.3 Oct 1968; *In use*

Deepdale/Cayton
Opened Aug 1936 A.060838, 10/H.3 Cayton; resite to A.055849 July 1940; Darky 1943; 20/P.3 Nov 1953; resite to A.048851 May 1961; renamed Deepdale Oct 1963; U/G March 1964; *Closed Oct 1968*

Dent
Opened Aug 1941 D.765877, 29/T.4; 21/L.1 Nov 1953; U/G June 1965; 21/B.2 Oct 1968; *In use*

Driffield
Opened July 1936 A.025588, 10/G.2; G.L. Post 1942; 10/N.1 Dec 1943; 20/B.3 Nov 1953; U/G Sept 1957; *Closed Oct 1968*

Dunsop Bridge
Opened Nov 1938 D.657502, 29/R.1; Granite 1943; 21/H.3 Nov 1953; resite to D.661496 July 1955; U/G June 1965; 21/J.1 Oct 1968; *In use*

Easington/Out Newton
Opened Dec 1939 A.378384 10/E.4 Easington; resite to A.399205 June 1951; 18/K.2, renamed Out Newton, Nov 1953; resite to A.369242 Feb 1961; U/G, 20/T.2, Feb 1965; *Closed Oct 1968*

Ecclesfield/Hoyland
Opened Aug 1937 E.353950, 8/X.2 Hoyland; Granite 1943; 18/N.2 Nov 1953; resite to E382981 April 1965, renamed Ecclesfield; 18/F.2 April 1965; *Closed Oct 1968*

Elloughton
Opened Sept 1938 E.954284, 10/M.1; 18/S.4 Nov 1953; U/G Dec 1958; *Closed Oct 1968*

Eston
Opened Dec 1936 Z.954200, 9/P.2; resite to Z.558191 April 1937; 9/N.3 May 1945; 20/K.3 Nov 1953; resite to Z.562174 Dec 1962; U/G Sept 1963; *Closed Oct 1968*

Flambrough
Opened Dec 1939 A.252708, 10/G.4; 20/A.2 Nov 1953; resite to A.246706 May 1960; U/G Sept 1960; *Closed Oct 1968*

Fulford
Opened Sept 1936 E.612483, 10/K.1; 20/C.4 Nov 1953; U/G Oct 1961; 20/H.3 Oct 1968; *Closed, to allow road development, Dec 1973*

Gargrave
Opened Nov 1938 D.937529, 29/S.2; 8/T.4 Dec 1943; 21/K.1 Nov 1953; U/G May 1962; 21/F.3 Oct 1968; *In use*

Gilberdyke
Opened March 1939 E.836292, 10/M.3; resite to E.838275 March 1953; 18/N.2 Nov 1953; U/G Dec 1958; 20/L.3 Oct 1968; *In use*

Goathland
Opened Dec 1936 Z.832009. 9/S.4; 9/P.3 Feb 1944; 20/N.4 Nov 1953; resite to Z.839014 April 1961; 20/D.4 July 1962; U/G May 1963; 20/A.2 Oct 1968; *In use*

Goldthorpe
Opened Sept 1937 E.450040 8/R.1; resite to E.452043 Jan 1938; Granite 1943; 18/P.4 Nov 1953; U/G May 1961; *Closed Oct 1968*

Grassington
Opened Nov 1938 D.994637, 29/S.3; 8/P.2 Dec 1943; 21/J.3 Nov 1953; U/G June 1962; 21/F.2 Oct 1968; *In use*

Great Ayton
Opened Dec 1936 Z.547116, 9/Q.3; Granite 1943; 9/T.2 March 1949; 20/L.4 Nov 1953; resite to Z.543121 Sept 1963; U/G Nov 1965; 23/M.3 Oct 1968; *In use*

Greenhow Hill
Opened Sept 1943 E.111638, 8/P.4; 20/G.3 Nov 1953;
resite to E.124638 Nov 1959; U/G June 1962; 18/A.1
July 1962; *Closed Oct 1968*

Guiseley
Opened Aug 1937 E.202442, 8/V.3; Granite 1943; 20/E.2
Nov 1953; U/G July 1958; 20/F.2 Oct 1968; *In use*

Harewood
Opened Aug 1937 E.327453, 8/V.1; Granite 1943; 20/F.3
Nov 1953; U/G May 1958; *Closed Oct 1968*

Hawes
Opened Jan 1944 D.868897, 9/Z.4; 21/L.4 Nov 1953;
U/G May 1963; 21/C.3 Oct 1968; *In use*

Heckmondwike
Opened Aug 1937 E.212251, 8/W.1; 8/Q.2 Dec 1940;
Granite 1943; 20/E.3 Nov 1953; U/G Oct 1959; 18/C.3
Oct 1962; 20/J.1 Oct 1968; *In use*

Helmsley
Opened Jan 1937 E.613854, 9/V.3; Granite 1943; 9/S.3
Dec 1944; 20/S.3 Nov 1953; resite to E.578814 July
1954; U/G May 1958; *Closed Oct 1968*

Helperby/Topcliffe
Opened Jan 1937 E.463707, 9/W.3 Helperby; 9/Y.2
June 1944; resite to E.425721 March 1953; 20/R.4 Nov
1953; resite to E.414755, renamed Topcliffe, 20/E.4 Nov
1963; U/G April 1964; *Closed Oct 1968*

High Bentham
Opened Nov 1938 D.687693, 29/P.3; 21/J.1 Oct 1953;
U/G June 1965; 21/E.3 Oct 1968; *In use*

Hinderwell
Opened Dec 1936 Z.795178, 9/O.2; 20/M.2 Oct 1953;
U/G June 1960; 20/A.1 Oct 1968; *In use*

Holme-on-Spaldingmoor
Opened Sept 1938 E.822387 (Beacon Field), 18/R.4 Nov
1953; U/G May 1960; 20/L.1 Oct 1968; *In use*

Holmfirth
Opened Dec 1940 E.156043, 8/G.1; 8/Q.1 1942; Granite
1943; 18/F.3 Nov 1953; 18/D.2 Nov 1962; U/G Jan
1964; 20/J.2 Oct 1968; *In use*

Hornsea
Opened July 1936 E.207487, 10/F.3; 18/H.2 Nov 1953;
resite to E.203485 June 1954; U/G Dec 1958; *Closed
Oct 1968*

Horton-in-Ribblesdale
Opened June 1941 D.809723, 29/S.4; 29/P.4 Jan 1944;
21/L.2 Nov 1953; resite to D.810713 Nov 1964; U/G
June 1965; 21/E.1 Oct 1968; *In use*

Hovingham
Opened Jan 1937 E.668748, 9/V.2; 9/R.4 Aug 1943;
20/Q.4 Nov 1953; U/G April 1959; *Closed Oct 1968*

Howden/Goole
Opened July 1936 S.748237, 10/A.3 Goole (Post Office
roof); 18/R.3 Nov 1953; resite to E.770273, renamed
Howden, Feb 1961; U/G May 1963; 20/R.3 May 1963;
Closed Oct 1968

Keighley
Opened Aug 1937 E.046420, 8/T.2; 21/K.3 Nov 1953;
resite to E.057424 Sept 1961; U/G May 1962; 20/F.4 Oct
1968; *In use*

Keyingham
Opened March 1940 A.253244, 10/L.4; G.L.Post 1943;
18/K.4 Nov 1953; 20/T.4 March 1964; U/G Nov 1965;
20/M.3 Oct 1968; *In use*

Kirby Hill/Stavely
Opened Aug 1936 E.374696, 8/S.2 Stavely; renamed
Kirby Hill Jan 1942; 9/Y.3 May 1944; 20/F.1 Nov 1953;
U/G July 1958; 20/M.3 Oct 1968; *In use*

Kirbymoorside
Opened Feb 1937 E.666909, 9/V.1; 9/S.2 May 1953;
20/S.2 Nov 1953; U/G May 1958; 20/D.1 Oct 1968;
In use

Knaresborough
Opened July 1940 E.361597, 8/S.4; Granite 1943; 20/F.2
Nov 1953; resite to E.361594 June 1959; U/G May 1960;
Closed Oct 1968

Knottingley
Opened Sept 1937 E.506225, 8/Y.1; 18/G.4 Nov 1953;
resite to E.361594 June 1959; U/G May 1960; *Closed
Oct 1968*

Langtoft
Opened Aug 1936 A.002663, 10/H.1; 20/B.1 Nov 1953;
U/G Nov 1959; 20/E.4 Oct 1968; *In use*

Leyburn
Opened Dec 1936 E.120914, 9/Y.3; Granite 1943;
9/Z.2 Sept 1943; 20/H.4 Nov 1953; U/G, 23/V.4, June
1966; *Closed Oct 1968*

Lockton
Opened Dec 1936 E.834895, 9/Q.3; 20/N.3 Nov 1953;
U/G May 1961; *Closed Oct 1968*

Loftus
Opened Nov 1939 Z.723199, 9/R.4; 20/M.1 Nov 1953;
U/G June 1962; 20/X.1 July 1962; *Closed Oct 1968*

Malton
Opened Jan 1937 E.783722, 9/R.3; 20/Q.3 Nov 1953;
U/G May 1961; 20/F.3 Oct 1964; *Closed Oct 1968*

Market Weighton
Opened July 1936 E.873408, 10/L.1; 10/M.1 April 1940;
18/R.1 Nov 1953; resite to E.912416 June 1955; U/G
Feb 1960; 20/R.1 Oct 1962; *Closed Oct 1968*

Middlesmoor
Opened Sept 1943 E.068756, 8/P.3; 20/G.4 Nov 1953;
U/G Dec 1959; 18/A.1 Sept 1965; 20/B.2 Oct 1968; *In use*

Middleton-on-the-Wolds
Opened March 1940 E.843503, 10/J.4; 18/H.4 Nov 1953;
U/G June 1960; *Closed Oct 1968*

Northallerton
Opened Jan 1937 E.377932, 9/X.1; resite to E.384912
Dec 1939; 9/W.1 Nov 1943; 20/H.2 Nov 1953; U/G
Jan 1961; 20/B.1 Oct 1968; *In use*

North Stainley
Opened Jan 1937 E.287758, 9/Y.1; Granite 1943; 20/G.1
Nov 1953; resite to E.270764 June 1959; U/G Nov
1959; 20/C.1 Oct 1968; *In use*

Osmotherley/East Harsley
Opened Oct 1936 E.401997, 9/Z.2 East Harsley; resite to
E.455977 Aug 1942; Granite 1943; 9/S.4 May 1944;
20/S.1, renamed Osmotherley, Nov 1953; U/G April
1959; *Closed Oct 1968*

Pickering
Opened Jan 1937 E.794844 (Beacon Hill), 9/T.3; 9/R.1,
Granite, Oct 1943; 20/Q.1 Nov 1953; U/G Nov 1961;
20/D.2 Oct 1968; *In use*

Pocklington
Opened July 1936 E.811494, 10/K.3; 20/C.3 Nov 1953;
resite to E.843507 Aug 1959; U/G Oct 1960; 20/K.3 Dec
1960; 20/H.2 Oct 1968; *In use*

Redcar
Opened Dec 1936 Z.583271, 9/Q.1; resite to Z.590252
Nov 1944; 20/L.1 Nov 1953; U/G April 1959; 23/M.1
Oct 1968; *In use*

Reeth
Opened Feb 1944 E.049985, 9/Z.1; 21/A.2 Nov 1953;
U/G June 1965; 21/C.1 Oct 1968; *In use*

Richmond
Opened Dec 1936 Z.172018, 9/Y.1; 9/V.3 Oct 1939;
Granite 1943; 20/H.1 Nov 1953; U/G, 23/V.1, Sept
1962; 23/L.3 Oct 1968; *In use*

Robin Hoods Bay
Opened Jan 1937 Z.952053, 9/S.1; 9/P.2 Oct 1939;
20/N.2 Nov 1953; U/G Jan 1961; *Closed Oct 1968*

Rosedale
Opened Oct 1953 E.720944, 20/M.3; U/G Feb 1962;

20/X.3 Nov 1964; *Closed Oct 1968*

Rossington
Opened Nov 1937 K.625974, 8/R.2; 18/M.2 Nov 1953;
resite to K.626970 May 1962; U/G May 1963; 15/C.1
Oct 1968; *In use*

Rothwell
Opened Aug 1937 E.523287, 8/V.2; resite to E.343292
April 1939; 8/Z.3 Aug 1942; Granite 1943; 18/F.1 Nov
1953; resite to E.319278 Feb 1961; U/G June 1962;
Closed Oct 1968

Saltburn
Opened Dec 1936 Z.657209, 9/Q.2; 9/O.1 May 1945;
20/L.2 Nov 1953; resite to Z.653205 May 1955; U/G
June 1960; *Closed Oct 1965*

Saltend (Hull)
Opened Sept 1938 A.143293, 10/L.3; resite to A.152294
Sept 1939; 18/J.4 Nov 1953; resite to A.182248 Nov
1961; U/G June 1962; 20/N.4 Sept 1963; *Closed Oct 1968*

Sawley
Opened Aug 1937 E.239678, 8/S.1; Granite 1943; 20/G.2
Nov 1953; U/G Nov 1959; *Closed Oct 1968*

Sedbergh
Opened Nov 1938 D.662922, 29/T.3; Granite 1943;
21/B.3 Nov 1953; U/G June 1965; *Closed Oct 1968*

Settle
Opened Nov 1938 D.804436, 29/S.1; resite to D.814629
April 1943; 21/J.4 Nov 1953; U/G June 1965; 21/E.2 Oct
1968; *In use*

Sherburn
Opened June 1940 E.963767, 10/H.4; resite to E.966769
Aug 1943; 20/A.4 Nov 1953; U/G May 1959; 20/B.4
Nov 1960; 20/J.4 March 1966; *Closed Oct 1968*

Skipsea
Opened July 1936 A.169556, 10/G.1; resite to A.176548
Feb 1940; 18/H.1 Nov 1953; U/G Oct 1959; 20/E.3 Oct
1968; *In use*

Skirlaugh
Opened July 1936 A.135402, 10/F.1; 18/J.1 Nov 1953;
U/G April 1959; 20/M.1 Oct 1968; *In use*

Sowerby Bridge
Opened Aug 1937 E.066223, 8/W.3; resite to E.056211,
19/A.2 Nov 1953; U/G, 21/Q.1, May 1962; 20/J.3 Oct
1968; *In use*

Spurn Head
Opened April 1942 A.404114, 10/E.1; (The only Post
provided with barrack accommodation and staffed by a
crew of 7 Full-Time Observers); 18/A.2 Nov 1953;
Closed 1956

Stamford Bridge/Bishop Wilton
Opened Aug 1936 E.792576, 10/J.2 Bishop Wilton;
resite to E.731565, renamed Stamford Bridge, Oct 1944;
20/C.2 Nov 1953; 20/K.2 March 1963; resite to E.690561
Sept 1964; U/G Oct 1964; *Closed Oct 1968*

Stockbridge
Opened Aug 1937 K.275969, 8/X.3; Granite 1942;
Augmented Granite 1944; 18/N.1 Nov 1953; resite to
K.253971 Nov 1963; U/G Jan 1964; 18/F.1 Oct 1966;
8/A.1 Oct 1968; *In use*

Strensall
Opened Jan 1937 E.637601, 9/W.2; 9/X.2 June 1951;
20/C.1 Nov 1953; U/G Feb 1968; 20/H.1 Oct 1968; *In use*

Sunk Island/Patrington
Opened July 1936 A.313220 (Beacon Hill), 10/E.3
Patrington; resite to A.295173, renamed Sunk Island,
March 1942; 18/K.3 Nov 1953; U/G, 20/T.3, Nov 1962;
Closed Oct 1968

Thirsk
Opened Jan 1937 E.442818, 9/X.3; resite to E.422804,
9/W.3, June 1942; 20/R.1 Nov 1953; U/G April 1959;
Closed Oct 1968

Thorne
Opened July 1936 E.685129, 10/A.1; 18/Q.4 Nov 1953;
resite to E.680155 Sept 1961; U/G May 1962; 20/Q.4
March 1964; *Closed Oct 1968*

Thornton
Opened Jan 1938 E.092332, 8/W.1; 20/E.4 Nov 1953;
U/G May 1958; 18/C.4 Aug 1962; 20/F.3 Oct 1968;
In use

Tockwith
Opened Aug 1937 E.452522, 8/Z.1; 8/V.4 Oct 1942;
20/D.1 Nov 1953; U/G June 1959; 20/G.1 Oct 1968; *In
use*

Todmorden
Opened Nov 1940 E.931274, 8/W.2; 19/A.1 Nov 1953;
U/G July 1961; 21/Q.1 Jan 1962; *Closed Oct 1968*

Tollerton
Opened Dec 1939 E.517635, 9/W.3; 9/X.3 April 1944;
20/R.3 Nov 1953; U/G Oct 1959; *Closed Oct 1968*

Upsall
Opened Jan 1937 E.454873, 9/X.2; Granite 1943; 20/S.4
Nov 1953; U/G Jan 1961; *Closed Oct 1968*

Upton/Bradsworth
Opened Sept 1937 E.458147, 8/Y.3 Upton; Granite 1943;
18/P.1 Nov 1953; 18/G.1, renamed Bradsworth, U/G,
Feb 1964; 20/K.2 Oct 1968; *In use*

Wetwang
Opened Aug 1936 E.927589, 10/J.1; 20/B.4 Nov 1953;
U/G Sept 1960; *Closed Oct 1968*

Whitby
Opened April 1937 Z.905113, 9/R.2; 9/P.1 Feb 1955;
20/N.1 Nov 1953; U/G Nov 1959; 20/D.1 Nov 1964;
Closed Oct 1968

Wickersley
Opened Nov 1937 K.487920, 8/R.3; 8/X.2 Aug 1942;
resite to K.493920, 1942; Granite 1943; resite to K.417915
18/P.3, Nov 1953; resite to K.473915 Oct 1933; 8/A.2
Oct 1968; *In use*

Withernsea/Tunstall
Opened July 1936 A.368243, 10/E.2; resite to A.369238
Jan 1938; resite to A.380231 Nov 1939; resite to
A.348237 Sept 1950; 18/K.1 Nov 1953; U/G, renamed
Tunstall, Feb 1959; 20/T.1 Sept 1963; *Closed Oct 1968;*
Reopened, 20/M.2, 1975

Wykeham
Opened Jan 1937 E.965842, 9/E.1; 9/T.1 May 1937;
Granite 1943; 9/Q.2 Jan 1945; 20/P.4 Nov 1953; U/G
Nov 1959; 20/E.1 Oct 1968; *In use*

SCOTLAND

ABERDEENSHIRE

Alford
Opened July 1939 J.575164, 38/E.3; Granite 1943;
29/K.4 Nov 1953; resite to J.565143 Nov 1960; U/G
July 1962; 29/H.1 Oct 1968; *In use*

Ballater
Opened July 1939 O.266954, 38/G.3; Granite 1943;
29/A.3 Nov 1953; U/G Feb 1959; 29/G.2 Oct 1968; *In
use*

Boddam
Opened May 1940 K.127411, 38/B.4; 29/E.1 Nov 1953;
resite to K.115430 March 1960; U/G Feb 1961; *Closed
Oct 1968*

Braemar
Opened July 1940 O.146905, 38/G.4; 29/A.2 Nov 1953;
resite to O.143910 Sept 1960; U/G Jan 1962; 29/G.3 Oct
1968; *In use*

Bucksburn
Opened July 1939 J.900093, 38/D.2; 29/C.1 Nov 1953;
U/G March 1960; *Closed Oct 1968*

Cruden Bay
Opened July 1939 K.096356, 38/B.2; 29/E.4 Nov 1953;
U/G June 1959; 29/E.3 Oct 1968; *In use*

Attack Warning Red

Drumoak
Opened July 1939 J.789993 (Drum Castle Tower),
38/P.1; resite to J.790001 April 1941; Granite 1943;
resite to J.783994, 29/B.4 Feb 1960; *Closed Oct 1968*

Echt
Opened July 1939 J.741055, 38/E.2; Granite 1943;
29/B.1 Nov 1953; U/G June 1959; 29/H.2 Oct 1968;
In use

Fyvie
Opened July 1939 J.773379, 38/C.3; 29/E.3 Nov 1953;
U/G June 1959; *Closed Oct 1968*

Huntly
Opened July 1939 J.523398, 38/J.2; Granite 1943; 38/G.2
May 1946; resite to J.546385, 29/J.3, Nov 1953; U/G
March 1958; 29/D.3 Oct 1968; *In use*

Inverallochy
Opened June 1939 K.034647, 38/A.2; 29/F.1 Nov 1953;
resite to K.023644 March 1960; U/G Feb 1961; *Closed
Oct 1968*

Inverebrie Hill/Methlick
Opened July 1939 J.918340, 38/C.1 Inverebrie Hill;
resite to J.869278, 29/E.3, Nov 1953; renamed Methlick
Aug 1960; U/G Feb 1961; 29/E.4 Oct 1968; *In use*

Kennethmount
Opened July 1939 J.551285, 38/H.1; Granite 1943;
29/K.1 Nov 1953; U/G June 1959; *Closed Oct 1968*

Kildrummy
Opened July 1939 J.467179, 38/H.2; Granite 1943;
29/K.3 Nov 1953; U/G April 1960; *Closed Oct 1968*

Kintore
Opened July 1939 J.786179, 28/E.1; resite to J.796155
July 1953; 29/D.2 Nov 1953; U/G June 1961; *Closed Oct
1968*

Newburgh
Opened July 1939 K.004243, 38/D.1; resite to J.995252,
29/D.3 Nov 1953; U/G Feb 1961; *Closed Oct 1968*

New Deer
Opened July 1939 J.886463, 38/B.3; 29/F.3 Nov 1953;
U/G Jan 1958; *Closed Oct 1968*

Pitcaple
Opened July 1939 J.718261, 38/C.2; 29/D.1 Nov 1953;
U/G Dec 1961; 29/D.2 Oct 1968; *In use*

Rosehearty
Opened June 1939 J.937673, 38/A.1; 29/G.1 Nov 1953;
U/G June 1959; *Closed Oct 1968*

St. Fergus
Opened July 1939 K.102506, 38/B.1; 29/F.4 Nov 1953;

U/G May 1962; 29/E.2 Oct 1968; *In use*

Strathdon
Opened July 1939 J.354129, 38/G.1; Granite 1943; 29/A.1
Nov 1953; U/G June 1959; 29/G.1 Oct 1968; *In use*

Strichen
Opened June 1939 J.941541, 38/A.3; 29/F.2 Nov 1953;
resite to J.948559 Sept 1955; U/G Aug 1958; 29/E.1
Oct 1968; *In use*

Tarland
Opened July 1939 J.479045, 38/G.2; Granite 1943;
29/A.4 Nov 1953; U/G April 1960; 29/H.3 Oct 1968;
In use

Turriff
Opened June 1939 J.730505, 38/L.2; 38/G.3 Nov 1953;
U/G June 1959; 29/B.3 Oct 1968; *In use*

Undy Station
Opened July 1939 J.912243, 38/D.3; 38/C.4 April 1942;
29/D.4 Nov 1953; U/G June 1959; 29/J.1 Oct 1968;
In use

ANGUS

Aberlemno
Opened June 1939 O.512554, 37/G.2; Granite 1943;
29/N.3 Nov 1953; resite to O.525548 March 1959; U/G
Sept 1961; *Closed Oct 1968*

Arbroath
Opened June 1939 O.635407 (top of Water Tower),
37/C.2; 28/Y.4 Nov 1953; resite to O.647412 Dec 1955;
U/G Aug 1958; 28/E.2 Oct 1968; *In use*

Brechin
Opened June 1939 O.587610, 37/B.3; Granite 1943;
29/N.4 Nov 1953; U/G Feb 1959; *Closed Oct 1968*

Carnoustie
Opened June 1939 O.567360, 37/C.3; 28/X.3 Nov 1953;
U/G Dec 1959; *Closed Oct 1968*

Clova
Opened June 1939 O.341715, 37/F.1; 28/O.2 Nov 1953;
U/G April 1960; 28/C.1 Oct 1968; *In use*

Cortachy
Opened June 1939 O.383601, 37/G.1; Granite 1943;
28/C.3 Nov 1953; U/G Dec 1957; 28/C.2 Oct 1968; *In
use*

Downfield/Pourie
Opened Oct 1938 O.395336, 36/K.2; resite to O.391312
Sept 1953; 28/X.2 Nov 1953; U/G Dec 1957; *Closed
Oct 1968*

Edzell

Opened June 1939 O.594691, 37/H.2; Granite 1943;
29/N.1 Nov 1953; U/G Nov 1957; 28/D.3 Oct 1968;
In use

Forn

Opened June 1939 O.484622, 23/H.3; Granite 1943;
29/N.2 Nov 1953; U/G April 1960; *Closed Oct 1968*

Forfar

Opened June 1939 O.458492, 37/G.3; Granite 1943;
resite to O.459491 Oct 1952; 28/Y.2 Nov 1953; U/G
April 1963; *Closed Oct 1968*

Friockhein

Opened June 1939 O.594503, 37/C.1; Granite 1943;
28/Z.2 Nov 1953; resite to O.610495 Aug 1960; U/G
Jan 1962; *Closed Oct 1968*

Glamis

Opened June 1939 O.385454, 37/D.4; Granite 1943;
28/Y.3 Nov 1953; resite to O.371470 March 1959; U/G
April 1960; 28/C.4 Oct 1968; *In use*

Glenisla

Opened June 1939 O.221605, 37/F.3; Granite 1943;
28/P.1 Nov 1953; U/G Dec 1957; *Closed Oct 1968*

Inverkeilor

Opened June 1939 O.688508, 37/B.2; 28/X.2 Nov 1953;
resite to O.684501 March 1959; U/G April 1960; 28/E.1
Oct 1968; *In use*

Letham

Opened June O.526499, 37/D.1; Granite 1943; 28/Y.1
Nov 1953; U/G Feb 1959; 28/C.3 Oct 1968; *In use*

Lintrathen

Opened June 1939 O.292548, 37/F.2; Granite 1943;
28/O.2 Nov 1953; U/G Dec 1957; *Closed Oct 1968*

Newbiggin

Opened June 1939 O.514474, 37/D.2; resite to
O.515376 July 1939; 28/X.4 Nov 1953; U/G Jan 1961;
28/E.3 Oct 1968; *In use*

Newtyle

Opened June 1939 O.319392, 37/D.3; resite to
O.515396 Sept 1941; Granite 1943; 28/X.1 Nov 1953;
resite to O.285417 June 1962; U/G April 1963; *Closed
Oct 1968*

Tarfside

Opened June 1939 O.492801, 36/H.1; 29/P.1 Nov 1953;
U/G Dec 1957; 28/D.1 Oct 1968; *In use*

Scourie

Opened Sept 1957 C.146443, 30/P.2; resite to C.149448
Dec 1958; U/G May 1960; 30/B.5 Oct 1968; *In use*

Appin

Opened July 1940 M.923480, 35/C.4; 27/H.2 Nov 1953;
resite to M.910457 March 1959; U/G Aug 1960; 27/B.1
Oct 1968; 30/S.1 April 1973; *In use*

Arduaine

Opened Aug 1940 M.817070, 35/G.1; 27/A.4 Nov 1953;
resite to M.823064 July 1960; 27/C.2 Oct 1968; 30/R.2
April 1973; *In use*

Barr

Opened Aug 1940 S.282945, 33/H.2; Granite 1943;
25/K.4 Nov 1953; U/G Oct 1963; *Closed Oct 1968*

Bridge of Orchy

Opened Dec 1940 N.299419, 35/B.3; 27/D.2 Nov 1953;
U/G Aug 1960; 27/C.2 Oct 1968; 30/R.2 April 1973;
In use

Carradale

Opened April 1941 R.817383, 34/M.4; Granite 1943;
26/P.4 Nov 1953; resite to R.813389 June 1960; U/G,
25/P.1 Dec 1962; 25/E.2 Oct 1968; *In use*

Calchan

Opened May 1957 R.745548, 34/M.1; 26/P.1 Nov 1953;
resite to R.761568 March 1961; 27/P.1 Oct 1962; U/G
Dec 1962; *Closed Oct 1968*

Dalavich

Opened 1949; M.981114, New Post; 27/B.1 Nov 1953;
resite to M.967125 Jan 1960; U/G Oct 1960; *Closed
Oct 1968*

Dalmally

Opened July 1940 N.143277, 35/B.2; 27/C.1 Nov 1953;
resite to N.137261 Dec 1958; U/G Aug 1960; 27/C.4
Oct 1968; *Closed Jan 1969* because of local industrial
development. Scottish Home Office decided not to
resite

Glenbarr

Opened April 1941 R.672372, 34/M.2; 26/P.2 Nov
1953; U/G Dec 1960; 25/P.2 April 1962; *Closed Oct 1968*

Inveraray

Opened Oct 1943 N.121098, 35/P.3 (Town Hall roof);
resite to N.082071, 35/B.4 Nov 1952; 27/B.4 Nov 1953;
U/G Oct 1960; *Closed Oct 1968*

Isle of Oronsay/Ardvasar

Opened Aug 1955 G.696127, 30/K.3 Isle of Oronsay;
resite to G.655069 May 1958; renamed Advasar May
1961; *In use*

Kames/Tighanbruaich

Opened Oct 1941 R.978431, 34/L.4 Kames; resite to
R.994475 June 1943; 27/O.2 Nov 1953; resite to R.987712

renamed Tighanbruaich, June 1962; U/G June 1963; 25/B.4 Oct 1968; *In use*

Kildonan, Isle of Arran
Opened May 1941 S.036232, 34/N.2; Granite 1943; 26/Q.3 Nov 1953; U/G Dec 1962; 25/P.2 Oct 1968; *In use*

Lochaline/Kingairloch
Opened Sept 1940 M.858318, 35/D.2 Kingairloch; resite to M.673452 Sept 1943; 27/G.2 renamed Lochaline, Nov 1953; U/G March 1963; 30/Q.2 April 1973; *In use*

Lochgilphead/Ardrishaig
Opened June 1940 R.849860, 35/G.2 Lochgilphead; 27/A.3 Nov 1953; renamed Ardrishaig March 1960; U/G Oct 1960; renamed Lochgilphead 1962; 27/D.3 Oct 1968; 30/T.3 April 1973; *In use*

Machrihanish
Opened April 1941 R.621199, 34/M.3; resite to R.628208 July 1942 (because sea-spray splashed over Post and sound of Breakers made sound plotting difficult); 26/P.3 Nov 1953; resite to R.657216 Aug 1960; resite to R.667224, 25/P.3, Dec 1962; U/G June 1963; 25/E.3 Oct 1968; *In use*

Minard
Opened Aug 1941 R.976964, 35/F.4; 27/B.4 Nov 1953; U/G Oct 1960; 27/D.1 Oct 1968; 30/T.1 April 1973; *In use*

Oban/Connel
Opened April 1943 M.908353, 35/C.3 Oban; 27/H.3 Nov 1953; resite to M858315 May 1958; U/G Aug 1960; *Closed Oct 1968*

Salen
Opened July 1940 M.689660, 35/D.3; 27/Ç.1 Nov 1953; resite to M.688674 Jan 1964; 27/A.1 Oct 1968; 30/Q.1 April 1973; *In use*

Sacrainish, Isle of Tiree
Opened April 1972 M.994449, 27/G.5; resite to M.996447 Nov 1964; U/G Feb 1966; 27/A.4 Oct 1968; 30/Q.4 April 1973; *In use*

Seil Island
Opened July 1941 M.742176, 35/G.5; 27/A.1 Nov 1953; resite to M.769168 April 1960; U/G Aug 1960; 27/B.4 Oct 1968; 30/S.4 April 1973; *In use*

Strontian
Opened March 1952 M.810624, 35/D.1; 27/G.3 Nov 1953; U/G March 1963; *Closed Oct 1968*

Tarbert
Opened Aug 1940 R.869686, 35/G.3; resite to R.869702 Nov 1952; 27/A.2 Nov 1953; resite to R.854682 Sept

1960; U/G Dec 1962; 27/D.2 Oct 1968; 30/T.2 April 1973; *In use*

Taynuilt
Opened July 1940 N.002298, 35/C.2; 27/E.4 Nov 1953 U/G Aug 1960; 27/B.2 Oct 1968; 30/S.2 April 1973; *In use*

Tobermorey, Isle of Mull
Opened June 1962 M.533517, 27/G.4; resite to M.524529 Jan 1964; 27/A.3 Oct 1968; 30/Q.3 April 1973; *In use*

AYRSHIRE

Ballantrae
Opened Aug 1940 X.091827, 33/G.1; Granite 1943; 25/K.2 Nov 1953; resite to X.084815 Dec 1958; U/G Oct 1963; *Closed April 1968;* Reopened 25/K.2, 1974

Barrhill
Opened July 1940 X.222817, 33/H.3; Granite 1943; 25/K.3 Nov 1953; U/G Oct 1959; 25/K.2 Oct 1968; *Closed 1974*

Beith
Opened Aug 1940 S.340550, 34/G.1; 25/R.1 Nov 1953; U/G April 1960; *Closed Oct 1968*

Catrine
Opened Feb 1939 S.529261, 34/F.3; resite to S.526257, 26/T.3, Nov. 1953; U/G March 1961; *Closed April 1968*

Darvel
Opened Feb 1939 S.569377, 34/F.2; 26/T.1 Nov 1953; U/G Dec 1959; 25/G.3 Oct 1968; *In use*

Dalmellington
Opened Aug 1940 S.479055, 33/K.4; 25/J.3 Nov 1953; resite to S.461070 March 1954; resite to S.477669 April 1956; U/G July 1966; *Closed Oct 1968*

Dunlop
Opened Feb 1939 S.398497, 34/H.3; 26/R.4 Nov 1953; U/G March 1961; 25/G.2 Oct 1968; *In use*

Dunure
Opened Aug 1940 S.264162, 33/J.3; resite to S.263273 Oct 1953; 26/S.3 Nov 1953; U/G Oct 1958; *Closed Oct 1968*

Girvan
Opened March 1953, X.185991, 25/K.1; resite to X.189950 Dec 1964; U/G Sept 1965; 25/K.3 Oct 1968; *In use*

Irvine/Kilwinning
Opened July 1940 S.305386, 34/G.2. Irvine; 26/R.3 Nov 1953; resite to S.323421, renamed Kilwinning, June 1961; U/G Aug 1965; *Closed April 1968*

Joppa
Opened Aug 1940 S.419195, 33/J.2; 26/S.4 Nov 1953;
U/G March 1961; 24/J.4 Oct 1968; *In use*

Kilmarnock
Opened Feb 1939 S.443388, 34/F.4; 34/H.4 Dec 1941;
26/S.1 Nov 1953; U/G March 1961; 25/G.4 Oct 1968;
In use

Muirkirk
Opened Jan 1939 S.702281, 34/F.1; 26/T.2 Nov 1953;
U/G Dec 1959; 25/J.1 Oct 1968; *In use*

New Cumnock
Opened Feb 1939 S.614133, 33/E.1; 25/H.1 Nov 1953;
U/G, 25/T.3; March 1964; 25/J.2 Oct 1968; *In use*

Port Ellen/Isle of Islay
Opened April 1962 S.323517, 27/P.4; U/G 25/P.4,
Feb 1965; 25/E.1 Oct 1968; *In use*

Prestwick
Opened Aug 1940 S.344251, 33/J.1; 26/S.2 Nov 1953;
U/G Sept 1957; *Closed April 1968*

Skelmorlie
Opened Feb 1939 S.199671, 34/L.2; 26/O.4 Nov 1953;
resite to S.195649 May 1962; 27/O.4 Dec 1963; U/G
April 1965; 25/B.2 Oct 1968; *In use*

Straiton
Opened Aug 1940 S.381043, 33/K.3; 25/J.2 Nov 1953;
U/G Feb 1963; 25/J.3 Oct 1968; *In use*

Turnberry
Opened Aug 1940 S.211059, 33/H.1; 25/J.1 Nov 1953;
U/G May 1963; 25/K.1 Oct 1968; *In use*

West Kilbride
Opened July 1941 S.202484, 34/G.3; 26/R.2 Nov 1953;
U/G March 1961; 25/H.2 Aug 1963; 25/G.1 Oct 1968;
In use

BANFFSHIRE

Aberchirder
Opened June 1939 J.621523, 38/K.2; 29/H.2 Nov 1953;
resite to J.619563 March 1960; U/G Dec 1960; 29/D.1
Oct 1968; *In use*

Buckie
Opened June 1939 J.428650, 38/K.3; resite to J.409649
July 1951; 29/J.1 Nov 1953; U/G June 1960; 29/B.1 Oct
1968; *In use*

Cabrach
Opened Oct 1953 J.374314, 38/New Post; resite to
J.380310, 29/K.2, Aug 1958; U/G June 1960; 29/C.2
Oct 1968; *In use*

Drummuir
Opened July 1939 J.382444, 38/J.3; Darky and Granite,
1942; 29/J.2 Nov 1953; U/G June 1960; 29/C.3 Oct 1968
In use

Gardenstown
Opened June 1939 J.805644, 38/L.1; 29/G.2 Nov 1953;
U/G April 1960; *Closed Oct 1968*

Grange
Opened July 1939 J.497511, 38/J.1; Granite 1943;
resite to J.521527, 29/J.4, Nov 1953; U/G June 1960;
29/C.1 Oct 1968; *In use*

Macduff
Opened June 1939 J.708644, 38/L.3; 29/H.3 Nov 1953;
U/G June 1959; 29/B.2 Oct 1968; *In use*

Portsoy
Opened June 1939 J.582660, 38/K.1; resite to J.584663
Nov 1948; resite to J.606663, 29/H.1, Nov 1953; U/G
June 1960; *Closed Oct 1968*

BERWICKSHIRE

Berwick-Upon-Tweed
Opened Feb 1937 U.007538, (Brass Bastion on City
Wall), 30/N.1; resite to T.979548 Feb 1940; Darky
1942; 23/J.3 Nov 1953; 24/H.3 Nov 1962; U/G Feb 1964;
Closed Oct 1968

Chirnside
Opened Feb 1937 T.878572, 31/G.2; Granite 1943;
24/H.2 Nov 1953; U/G Feb 1960; *Closed Oct 1968*

Cockburnspath/Innerwick
Opened Feb 1937, 31/B.2 Innerwick; resite to T.746726
July 1942; Granite 1943; 24/J.2, renamed Cockburnspath,
Nov 1953; U/G May 1963; 24/E.2 Oct 1968; *In use*

Coldstream
Opened Dec 1937 T.841405, 31/E.1; 23/J.1 Nov 1953;
resite to T.838407 April 1954; U/G Nov 1959; 24/H.3
1963; *Closed Oct 1968*

Duns
Opened Feb 1937 T.793542, 31/D.2; Granite 1943;
resite to T.752516, 24/H.1 Nov 1953; U/G Jan 1964;
24/F.4 Oct 1963; *In use*

Eyemouth
Opened Feb 1937 T.931646, 31/G.1; 31/C.2 April 1939;
24/K.2 Nov 1953; U/G Feb 1962; *Closed Oct 1968*

Gordon/Stichill
Opened Feb 1937 T.653431, 31/F.1 Gordon; Granite
1943; resite to T.678438, 23/G.3, renamed Stichill, Nov
1953; resite to T.688437 Nov 1961; U/G, 24/G.3,
renamed Gordon, May 1963; 24/H.2 Oct 1968; *In use*

Grantshouse
Opened Feb 1937 T.814651, 31/C.1; resite to T.816649
Oct 1939; Granite 1943; 24/K.4 Nov 1953; U/G May
1961; *Closed Oct 1968*

Greenfield
Opened Dec 1953 T. 943586, 24/K.3; U/G Feb 1960;
24/F.2 Oct 1968; *In use*

Lauder
Opened Feb 1937 T.527469, 31/J.2; Granite 1943;
24/G.1 Nov 1953; resite to T.526467 June 1961; U/G
Dec 1963; 24/H.1 Oct 1968; *In use*

Longformacus
Opened Feb 1937 T.686580, 31/F.3; 31/D.1 May 1939;
Granite 1943; 24/J.3 Nov 1953; U/G May 1963;
Closed Oct 1968

Norham-on-Tweed
Opened March 1937 T.905463, 30/N.3; Granite 1943;
23/H.4 Nov 1953; resite to T.907463 May 1959; U/G
Oct 1960; 24/F.3 Oct 1968; *In use*

Oxton
Opened July 1961 T.478575, 24/New Post; U/G, 24/F.4,
Dec 1963; 24/D.2 Oct 1968; *In use*

St. Abbs Head
Opened Aug 1961 T.912691, 24/K.1; U/G May 1963;
24/F.1 Oct 1968; *In use*

Westruther
Opened Feb 1937 T.643496, 31/J.1; 31/D.3 May 1939;
24/G.2 Nov 1953; U/G May 1959; *Closed Oct 1968*

BUTESHIRE

Brodick
Opened May 1940 S.032353, 34/N.1; Granite 1943;
26/Q.1 Nov 1953; U/G, 25/Q.1 Dec 1962; 25/F.1. Oct
1968; *In use*

Rothsay/Kilchattan
Opened Dec 1940 S.105547, 34/L.3 Kilchattan; resite to
S.098644, renamed Rothsay, March 1941; 26/O.3 Nov
1953; resite to S.082562 Jan 1959; renamed Kilchattan
Bay, May 1961; U/G Sept 1961; 25/B.3 Oct 1968; *In use*

CAITHNESS

Dunbeath/Berridale
Opened June 1941 D.124238, 39/K.4 Berridale; Granite
1943; 30/R.2 Nov 1953; resite to D.123327 Jan 1958;
U/G Sept 1959; 30/F.3 Oct 1968; *In use*

Duncansby Head/John O'Groats
Opened June 1941 D.405732, 39/J.4; 30/Q.1 Nov 1953;
U/G Sept 1959; 30/C.2 Oct 1968; *In use*

Halkirk
Opened Sept 1960 D.123578, 30/New Post; U/G 30/Q.5
June 1961; *Closed Oct 1968*

Latheron
Opened May 1941 D.180315, 39/K.3; Granite 1943;
resite to D.203334, 30/R.3 Nov 1953; U/G Sept 1959;
30/F.2 Oct 1968; *In use*

Thurso/Dunnet Head/Barrock
Opened May 1941 D.204768, 39/J.3 Thurso; 30/Q.2,
renamed Dunnet Head, Nov 1953; U/G Nov 1959;
30/C.1 renamed Barrock, Oct 1968; *In use*

Watten
Opened May 1941 D.246541, 39/K.1; 30/R.1 Nov 1953;
U/G Sept 1959; 30/P.1 Oct 1968; *In use*

Wick
Opened May 1941 D.375499, 39/K.2; 30/R.4 Nov 1953;
resite to D.365530 May 1958; U/G Sept 1959; *Closed
Oct 1968*

CLACKMANNANSHIRE

Alloa/Tillicoultry
Opened Nov 1938 S.942942, 36/F.1 Tillicoultry; resite to
S.938951 June 1941; Granite 1943; 24/B.1 Nov 1953;
resite to S.886939 Oct 1961; U/G Feb 1962; 28/J.1 June
1963; 24/A.1, renamed Alloa, Oct 1968; *Closed 1971*

DUMFRIESHIRE

Auldgirth
Opened Aug 1940 X.916873, 33/A.3; Granite 1943;
Augmented Granite 1944; 25/E.2 Nov 1953; U/G Oct
1959; *Closed Oct 1968 ; Reopened, 22/B.4, 1975*

Beattock
Opened Oct 1939 T.103010, 32/K.1; resite to T.095030
April 1950; 25/G.2 Nov 1953; resite to T.085033 May
1954; U/G March 1964; 22/B.2 Oct 1968; *In use*

Bentpath
Opened Nov 1939 Y.295909, 32/L.2; Granite 1943;
22/F.3 Nov 1953; U/G June 1959; *Closed Oct 1968*

Boreland
Opened Nov 1939 Y.176919, 32/L.3; Granite 1943;
25/F.3 Nov 1953; resite to Y.178923 March 1956; resite
to Y.183917 Sept 1962; U/G April 1964; *Closed Oct 1968*

Canobie
Opened Oct 1939 Y.402779, 32/J.1; Granite 1943; 22/J.3
Nov 1953; U/G Oct 1961; *Closed Oct 1968*

Cummertrees
Opened Oct 1939 Y.141662, 32/H.2; Granite 1943;
22/K.2 Nov 1953; U/G Oct 1966; 22/E.1 Oct 1968; *In use*

Dumfries
Opened Oct 1939 X.981751, 32/H.1; 25/E.3 Nov 1953;
U/G Oct 1965 on resite to X.983752; 22/C.3 Oct 1968;
In use

Eskdalemuir
Opened Nov 1939 Y.256975, 32/L.1; 25/F.4 Nov 1953;
resite to Y.250980 June 1955; U/G Oct 1959; 22/D.1
Oct 1968; *In use*

Kirtlebridge
Opened Oct 1939 Y.224736, 32/J.3; Granite 1943;
22/K.1 Nov 1953; resite to Y.217732 May 1954; U/G
Oct 1961; 22/C.2 Oct 1968; *In use*

Langholme
Opened Dec 1950 Y.372848, 32/L.4; 22/J.4 Nov 1953;
resite to Y.366858 Nov 1959; U/G Sept 1961; 22/D.3
Oct 1968; *In use*

Lockerbie
Opened Oct 1939 Y.143820, 32/K.2; resite to Y.144816
Oct 1941; Granite 1943; 25/E.4 Nov 1953; U/G April
1964; *Closed Oct 1968*

Moniaive
Opened Aug 1940 X.769902, 33/A.4; Granite 1943;
24/H.3 Nov 1953; U/G Feb 1962; 22/B.4 Oct 1968;
Closed 1975

Parkgate
Opened Oct 1939 Y.045909, 32/E.3; Granite 1943;
25/E.1 Nov 1953; 22/E.1 Aug 1963; U/G Sept 1964;
22/C.1 Oct 1968; *In use*

Sanquhar
Opened Feb 1939 S.784105, 33/A.1; 25/G.4 Nov 1953;
U/G June 1959; 22/B.1 Oct 1968; *In use*

Thornhill
Opened Aug 1940 X.883940, 33/A.2; Granite 1943;
25/G.3 Nov 1953; U/G Oct 1958; 22/B.3 Oct 1968;
In use

DUNBARTONSHIRE

Alexandria
Opened Dec 1938 S.404798, 34/K.1; 26/N.1 Nov 1953;
U/G May 1961; 27/M.3 Oct 1962; 25/A.2 Oct 1968;
In use

Arrochar
Opened Dec 1938 N.299042, 35/F.1 (300 yds West of
Torpedo Factory on shore of Loch Long); 27/C.2 Nov
1953; resite to N.276028 Nov 1958; resite to N.297052
May 1959; U/G Aug 1960; 25/A.1 Oct 1968; *In use*

Garelochead
Opened April 1943; S.238927, 35/F.2; 27/B.3 Nov 1953;

U/G June 1959; 27/M.2 May 1963; *Closed Oct 1968*

Milngavie
Opened May 1947 S.547744, 34/K.2; resite to S.553757
Aug 1952; 26/Z.3 Nov 1953; U/G May 1961; 27/M.3
June 1962; *Closed Oct 1968*

FIFESHIRE

Cupar
Opened Feb 1937 O.385149; 28/V.4 Nov 1953; U/G
Feb 1959; 28/H.2 Oct 1968; *In use*

Crail
Opened Feb 1937 O.606077, 36/B.2; 28/C.1 Oct 1952;
24/M.1 Nov 1953; U/G Feb 1959; 28/C.1 July 1963;
Closed Oct 1968

Elie
Opened Feb 1937 O.484003, 31/B.3; 24/M.2 Nov 1953;
U/G Sept 1960; 24/B.1 Oct 1968; *In use*

Falkland
Opened Feb 1937 O.259076, 36/C.3; 28/V.3 Nov 1953;
U/G April 1963; *Closed Oct 1968*

Gaultry
Opened Dec 1941 O.364238, 36/K.4; 28/V.1 Nov 1953;
U/G Feb 1958; *Closed Oct 1968*

Inverkeithing
Opened Feb 1937 T.125833, 36/D.2; resite to T.126831
Nov 1939; resite to T:126834 Aug 1948; resite to
T.132809 May 1951; 24/C.4 Nov 1953; U/G 24/N.3
July 1959; *Closed Oct 1968*

Kelty/Thew
Opened Dec 1939 T.129937, 36/E.4 Kelty; Granite 1943;
24/C.1 Nov 1953; resite to T.148915 July 1961; U/G,
renamed Thew, April 1963; 24/B.2 Oct 1968; *In use*

Kinghorn
Opened Feb 1937 T.265867, 36/D.1; 24/A.3 Nov 1953;
U/G, 28/H.2, Jan 1959; *Closed Oct 1968*

Leslie
Opened Feb 1937 O.247043, 36/D.3; *Closed Dec 1946*
Reopened, O.250005, 24/A.1 April 1954; 28/H.1 Aug
1962; U/G April 1963; *Closed Oct 1968*

Leven
Opened Feb 1937 O.388016, 36/C.1; 24/A.4 Nov 1953;
U/G, 28/G.2 Sept 1961; *Closed Oct 1968*

Newburgh
Opened Feb 1937 O.239185, 36/A.3; resite to O.242185,
28/V.2, May 1959; U/G Sept 1961; 28/H.1 Oct 1968;
In use

Oysart/Thornton/Kirkcaldy
Opened Feb 1937 T.291969, 36/C.2, Thornton; renamed
Kirkcaldy Jan 1951; resite to T.296950, renamed 24/A.2
Thornton, Nov 1953; renamed Oysart Aug 1956; resite
to T.292954 Nov 1959; U/G Sept 1961; 24/B.3 Oct
1968; *In use*

Peat Inn
Opened March 1940 O.458099, 36/A.4; 36/C.4 April
1940; 28/W.2 Nov 1953; U/G Aug 1960; *Closed Oct
1968*

St. Andrews
Opened Feb 1937 O.523156, 36/B.1; resite to O.526159
Oct 1939; 28/W.3 Nov 1953; U/G Jan 1958; 28/H.2
Oct 1968; *In use*

Tayport
Opened Feb 1937 O.467279, 36/A.1; resite to O.454288
April 1942; 28/W.1 Nov 1953; U/G Dec 1957; *Closed
Oct 1968*

INVERNESSHIRE

Arisaig
Opened April 1942 M.649873, 35/E.2; 27/F.2 Nov 1953;
resite to M.642879 Jan 1961; U/G March 1963; *Closed
Oct 1968*

Aviemore
Opened 1968 H.895139 U/G, 29/F.3; *In use*

Beauly
Opened Aug 1940 H.519472, 39/E.3; Granite 1943;
30/Z.1 Nov 1953; U/G March 1961; 30/L.1 Oct 1968;
In use

Cannich
Opened July 1940 H.343317, 39/E.2; *Closed April 1947*
because of Hydro-Electric Development. *Reopened,*
H.327318, 30/Z.2, Nov 1953; resite to H.337313 Aug
1961; U/G Jan 1962; 30/L.4 Oct 1968; *In use*

Dalwhinnie
Opened July 1940 H.639860, 39/C.3; 30/Y.3 Nov 1953;
U/G May 1961; 30/P.3 Oct 1968; *In use*

Drumnadrochit
Opened July 1940 H.509261, 39/D.1; 30/Z.4 Nov 1953;
resite to H.505292 May 1961; U/G Aug 1961; 30/L.2
Oct 1968; *In use*

Farr
Opened July 1940 H.687340, 39/C.4; Granite 1943;
30/Y.1 Nov 1953; *Closed 1956*

Fort Augustus
Opened July 1940 H.370076, 39/D.3; 30/Z.3 Nov 1953;
resite to H.374097 July 1960; U/G Sept 1962; 30/L.3

Oct 1968; *In use*

Fort William
Opened July 1940 N.109754, 35/A.3; resite to N.111736
Jan 1950; 27/E.2 Nov 1953; resite to N.109758 Jan 1955;
U/G Sept 1960; 30/N.3 Oct 1968; *In use*

Glen Finnan
Opened April 1941 M.909807, 35/E.3; 27/F.3 Nov 1953;
resite to M.900805 Nov 1961; U/G March 1963;
30/N.4 Oct 1968; *In use*

Inverness
Opened Sept 1940 H.666451, 39/E.1; resite to H.632443
July 1952; 30/V.3 Nov 1953; resite to H.672469 April
1960; U/G May 1961; *Closed Oct 1968*

Kingussie
Opened July 1940 H.786016, 39/C.2; 30/Y.4 Nov 1953;
resite to H.772011 Nov 1958; U/G April 1961; 30/P.2
Oct 1968; *In use*

Laggan/Invergarry
Opened Aug 1940 N.299984, 35/A.1 Laggan; 27/E.1
Nov 1953; U/G Sept 1960; 30/N.1, renamed Invergarry,
Oct 1968; *In use*

Lochboisdale, South Uist
Opened June 1960 F.771203, 30/Lochboisdale; U/G,
30/A.1, Nov 1963; 30/A.2 Oct 1968; *In use*

Lochmaddy, North Uist
Opened July 1960 F.914688, 30/Lochmaddy; U/G,
30/A.3, Nov 1963; *In use*

Mallaig
Opened July 1940 M.676967, 35/E.1; 27/F.1 Nov 1953;
resite to M.675954 May 1963; 30/N.5 Oct 1968; *In use*

Onich
Opened July 1940 N.015617, 35/C.1; 27/H.1 Nov 1953;
resite to N.025614 Aug. 1960; U/G May 1963; 27/C.1
Oct 1968; 30/R.1 April 1973; *In use*

Spean Bridge
Opened April 1943 N.211824, 35/A.2; 27/E.3 Nov 1953;
U/G Sept 1960; *Closed Oct 1968*

Tomatin
Opened Jan 1953 H.802292, 30/X.2; resite to H.798299
Feb 1960; U/G July 1963; 30/M.3 Oct 1968; *In use*

Tulloch
Opened as Watcher Post, Kinlochleven Dam, Dec 1940;
resite to N.371909, 35/A.4 Observer Post, Jan 1941;
27/E.4 Nov 1953; resite to N.374812 Dec 1958; U/G
Sept 1960; 30/N.2 Oct 1968; *In use*

Whitebridge/Gorthleck
Opened July 1940 H.494157, 39/D.2 Whitebridge;

37/Y.2 Nov 1953; resite to H.490156, renamed Gorthleck,
May 1961; U/G 1963; 30/P.1 Oct 1968; *In use*

KINCARDINESHIRE

Feughside
Opened July 1939 O.641922, 38/F.4; Granite 1943;
29/B.2 Nov 1953; U/G Feb 1959; 29/K.1 Oct 1968;
In use

Greg Ness
Opened July 1940 J.752036, 38/D.4; resite to J.957037
Nov 1944; 29/C.3 Nov 1953; resite to J.952027 March
1960; U/G Sept 1960; *Closed Oct 1960*

Inverbervie
Opened June 1939 O.824727, 37/A.2; 28/M.3 Nov 1953;
U/G Sept 1961; *Closed Oct 1968*

Laurencekirk
Opened June 1939 O.716720, 37/A.3; Granite 1943;
28/M.2 Nov 1955; resite to O.713726 Jan 1957; U/G
May 1959; *Closed Oct 1968*

Port Lethan
Opened July 1939 O.938964, 38/F.2; resite to O.926961
Aug 1939; 29/C.2 Nov 1953; U/G Jan 1961; 29/J.2
Oct 1968; *In use*

St. Cyrus
Opened June 1939 O.752647, 37/B.2; 27/Z.1 Nov 1953;
29/N.1 Nov 1953; U/G April 1960; 28/D.2 Oct 1968;
In use

Stonehaven
Opened July 1939 O.878850, 38/F.3; Darky 1943;
38/B.2 May 1953; 29/B.3 Nov 1953; resite to O.688829
June 1960; U/G July 1962; 29/K.2 Oct 1968; *In use*

KINROSSHIRE

Milnathort
Opened Oct 1938 O.116059, 36/E.1; Granite 1943; 28/S.4
Nov 1953; resite to O.135045 June 1955; resite to
O.097039 March 1959; U/G Aug 1960; 28/F.4 Oct 1968;
In use

KIRKCUDBRIGHTSHIRE

Auchenblae
Opened June 1939 O.728784, 37/A.1; Granite 1943;
28/M.1 Nov 1953; U/G Oct 1962; *Closed Oct 1968*

Castle Douglas
Opened Aug 1940 X.769622, 33/C.1; Granite 1943;
resite to X.767624 Jan 1952; 25/D.2 Nov 1953; U/G
Dec 1961; 22/E.3 Oct 1968; *In use*

Carsphairn
Opened Aug 1940 X.562934, 33/K.2; 25/H.2 Nov 1953;
U/G Jan 1962; 22/A.1 Oct 1968; *In use*

Creetown
Opened Aug 1940 X.481567, 33/D.1; Granite 1943,
25/B.4 Nov 1953; U/G Oct 1959; *Closed Oct 1968*

Dalry
Opened Sept 1940 X.632821, 33/B.1; Granite 1943;
25/C.1 Nov 1953; resite to X.632814 April 1963; U/G
Jan 1964; 22/A.2 Oct 1968; *In use*

Gatehouse of Fleet
Opened Aug 1940 X.607566, 33/C.4; Granite 1943;
25/C.2 Nov 1953; U/G Aug 1959; *Closed Oct 1968*

Kirkbean
Opened Oct 1939 X.969588, 32/H.3; Granite 1943;
25/D.4 Nov 1953; resite to X.975599 Feb 1956; U/G
Oct 1959; 22/E.2 Oct 1968; *In use*

Kirkcudbright
Opened Aug 1940 X.697502, 33/C.3; Granite 1943;
25/C.3 Nov 1953; resite to X.704517 April 1963; U/G
Jan 1964; 22/A.4 Oct 1968; *In use*

Kirkgunzeon
Opened Aug 1940 X.869671, 33/B.2; Granite 1943;
25/D.1 Nov 1953; 22/D.1 Dec 1961; *Closed Oct 1968*

Parton
Opened Oct 1940 X.689704, 33/B.3; Granite 1943;
Augmented Granite 1944; 25/C.4 Nov 1953; U/G April
1960; 22/A.3 Oct 1968; *In use*

Rockliffe
Opened Aug 1940 X.857527, 33/C.2; Granite 1943;
25/D.3 Nov 1953; resite to X.858539 May 1963; U/G,
22/D.3, April 1964; *Closed Oct 1968*

LANARKSHIRE

Abington
Opened Jan 1939 S.929239, 34/E.3; 25/G.1 Nov 1953;
resite to S.921251, 25/V.4 May 1962; U/G Feb 1964;
25/H.3 Oct 1968; *In use*

Airdrie
Opened Dec 1938 S.775644, 34/B.3; 26/X.1 Nov 1953;
resite to S.777669 April 1956; U/G Nov 1959; 25/X.1
May 1963; 25/D.1 Oct 1968; *In use*

Bargrennan
Opened Aug 1940 X.355764, 35/E.1; Granite 1943;
Augmented Granite 1944; 25/L.1 Nov 1953; resite to
X.347772 Oct 1961; U/G Jan 1964; 25/M.1 Oct 1968;
In use

Attack Warning Red

Carluke
Opened Dec 1938 S.857493, 34/C.3; Granite 1943;
resite to S.866486 Jan 1960; U/G Sept 1961; 24/H.1
Oct 1968; *In use*

Douglas
Opened Jan 1939 S.847309, 34/E.1; 26/V.3 Nov 1953;
resite to S.820313 Feb 1955; resite to S.844314, 25/V.3,
Jan 1963; U/G Feb 1964; 25/H.4 Oct 1968; *In use*

Dunsyre
Opened Dec 1938 T.080485, 34/D.1; resite to T.107465
June 1952; 26/U.3 Nov 1953; resite to T.034456,
24/U.1, Oct 1963; U/G Feb 1965; *Closed Oct 1968*

Forth
Opened Jan 1939 S.937540, 34/C.2; Granite 1943; resite
to S.941543 May 1948; resite to S.939557 Sept 1951;
26/X.3 Nov 1953; U/G Oct 1959; 25/D.2 Oct 1968; *In use*

Gilbertfield/Bothwell
Opened Dec 1938 S.697589, 34/J.2 Bothwell; resite to
S.548582, renamed Gilbertfield, Nov 1951; 26/X.2 Nov
1953; resite to S.679542, 25/X.2, May 1962; U/G
March 1966; 25/D.4 Oct 1968; *In use*

Glasgow
Opened Dec 1938 S.556647 (J & P Coates Factory roof);
resite to Press Box roof, Rangers Football Ground,
Ibrox Park, Oct 1950; resite to S.554655 (Luma Co-
Operative Store roof) Sept 1951; 26/Y.3 Nov 1953;
U/G (adjacent ground), Aug 1960; 27/P.4 June 1962;
25/C.3 Oct 1968; *In use*

Lesmahagow
Opened Dec 1938 S.801384, 34/E.2; 26/V.1 Nov 1953
U/G Nov 1959; 25/Y.2 April 1963; *Closed Oct 1968*

Shotts
Opened Dec 1938 S.870606, 34/C.1; resite to S.879611
Sept 1941; Granite 1943; 26/X.4 Nov 1953; resite to
S.885612 March 1963; 25/X.4 May 1963; U/G May
1966; *Closed Oct 1968*

Stepps
Opened April 1947 S.659695, 34/J.1; 26/Y.2 Nov 1953;
U/G Feb 1960; 27/P.1 Aug 1962; *Closed Oct 1968*

Strathaven
Opened Dec 1938 S.708442, 34/H.4; 34/F.4 Dec 1941;
26W.2 Nov 1953; U/G Oct 1959; 25/D.3 Oct 1968;
In use

Tankerton
Opened Dec 1938 S.971376, 34/D.3; 26/V.2 Nov 1953;
U/G 1959; 25/H.2 Oct 1968; *In use*

EAST, MID AND WEST LOTHIAN

Aberlady (East)
Opened Feb 1937 T.464800, 31/A.3; resite to T.474828
Dec 1943; 24/L.2 Nov 1953; U/G Feb 1959; *Closed Oct 1968*

Athelstaneford (East)
Opened Feb 1937 T.532767, 31/A.2; 24/L.4 Nov 1953;
resite to T.514761 July 1961; U/G Dec 1965; *Closed
Oct 1968*

Balerno (Mid)
Opened Nov 1938 T.168660, 31/K.1; resite to T.151669
April 1939; Granite 1943; 31/D.3 April 1953; 24/D.3
Nov 1953; U/G Nov 1961; *Closed Oct 1968*

Bathgate (West)
Opened Nov 1938 S.984688, 31/L.3; resite to S.979695
June 1948; resite to S.988688 June 1950; 24/C.2 Nov
1953; U/G Oct 1959; *Closed Oct 1968*

Boness (West)
Opened Nov 1938 S.993967, 31/L.1; resite to S.998811
May 1942; resite to T.019816 Sept 1949; resite to
T.005795, 24/B.3 Nov 1953; 24/C.1 Oct 1963; 24/A.2
Oct 1968; *In use*

Braid Hills/Portobello (Mid)
Opened Dec 1954 T.251693, 24/D.4 Braid Hills; resite to
T.305705 1960; U/G, renamed Portobello, June 1962;
Closed Oct 1968

Dalkeith/Roslin (Mid)
Opened Feb 1937 T.348666, 31/L.3 Dalkeith; resite to
T.301633, 24/E.1, renamed Roslin, Nov 1953; resite to
T. 361659 July 1961; U/G, renamed Dalkeith, Dec 1963;
24/D.1 Oct 1968; *In use*

Dunbar (East)
Opened Feb 1937, T.689783, 31/E.2; 31/B.1 May 1939;
Granite 1943; resite to T.700779, 31/M.1 Oct 1953;
24/J.1 Nov 1953; resite to T.677761 May 1962; U/G
Dec 1963; *Closed Oct 1968*

Garvald (East)
Opened Feb 1937 T.587710, 31/B.3; Granite 1943;
24/J.4 Nov 1953; resite to T.579704 July 1961; U/G
May 1963; 24/E.3 Oct 1968; *In use*

Gorebridge/Heriot (Mid)
Opened Nov 1938 T.399547, 31/J.3 Heriot; 24/F.1,
renamed Gorebridge, Dec 1952; U/G Dec 1959; *Closed
Oct 1968*

Humbie (East)
Opened Feb 1937 T.459628, 31/K.2; 31/J.1 April 1939;
24/E.4 Nov 1953; U/G Jan 1961; *Closed Oct 1968*

New Mills (East)
Opened Oct 1938 T.016881, 36/E.4; Granite 1943;

24/B.4 Nov 1953; resite to T.027898 Nov 1964; U/G Oct 1965; 28/H.1 Oct 1968; *In use*

North Berwick (East)
Opened Feb 1937 T.579853, 31/A.1; 24/L.1 Nov 1953; U/G Feb 1959; 24/E.1 Oct 1968; *In use*

Penicuik (Mid)
Opened March 1938 T.238603, 31/K.2; Granite 1943; resite to T.237580, 24/E.3, Nov 1953; resite to T.235576 June 1960; U/G Feb 1961; 24/D.4 Oct 1968; *In use*

Stow (Mid)
Opened Nov 1938 T.467450, 31/H.1; 24/F.2 Nov 1953; U/G April 1961; *Closed Oct 1968*

Tranent (East)
Opened Feb 1939 T.408734, 31/M.2; Granite 1943; resite to T.413726 June 1948; resite to T.419727 May 1951; 24/L.3 Nov 1953; U/G Oct 1959; *Closed Oct 1968*

Turnhouse/Granton/Leith (Mid)
Opened Feb 1937 T.320775, 31/L.1 Leith; resite to T.286782, 31/M.1 renamed Granton 1939; resite to T.299773 (Portland House roof, 32 York Road, Edinburgh) Sept 1940; resite to T.177735, 24/D.1, renamed Turnhouse, Nov 1953; U/G April 1958; 24/C.1 Oct 1968; *In use*

West Calder (Mid)
Opened March 1939 T.025620, 31/K.4; resite to T.028623 May 1939; Granite 1943; 24/D.2 Nov 1953; U/G Oct 1959; 24/C.2 Oct 1968; *In use*

Winchburgh/Kirkliston (West)
Opened Nov 1938 T.097750, 31/L.2 Winchburgh; resite to T.099748 May 1939; 24/C.3 Nov 1953; resite to T.111743, renamed Kirkliston, Nov 1959; U/G Dec 1963; *Closed Oct 1968*

MORAYSHIRE

Carron
Opened Aug 1940 J.228438, 39/D.2; Granite 1943; 30/W.3 Nov 1953; resite to J.234441 Sept 1961; U/G Jan 1962; 29/A.3 Oct 1968; *In use*

Dallas
Opened July 1940 J.133525, 39/B.3; HSL 1942; Granite 1943; resite to J.125530, 30/W.2 Nov 1953; U/G April 1962; *Closed Oct 1968*

Elgin
Opened July 1940 J.213641, 39/B.1; resite to J.184636 Jan 1953; resite to J.196608, 30/W.4, Nov 1959; U/G Jan 1962; 30/A.2 Oct 1968; *In use*

Findhorn
Opened July 1940 J.038649, 39/A.1; 39/B.4 Oct 1941;

30/W.1 Nov 1953; U/G Feb 1959; 29/A.1 Oct 1968; *In use*

Grantown-on-Spey
Opened July 1940 J.022261, 39/C.1; Granite 1943; 30/X.2 Nov 1953; resite to J.031282 June 1961; U/G Nov 1962; 29/F.1 Oct 1968; *In use*

NAIRN

Cawdor
Opened July 1940 H.849508, 39/A.3; 30/V.4 Nov 1953; resite to H.855511 Aug 1959; U/G April 1960; 30/M.2 Oct 1968; *In use*

Glenferness
Opened Aug 1940 H.952455, 39/A.2; Granite 1943; resite to X.963444, 30/X.1 June 1961; 29/A.4 Oct 1968; *In use*

Nairn
Opened July 1940 H.898568, 39/A.1; 30/V.1 Nov 1953; U/G Dec 1961; *Closed Oct 1968*

ORKNEY

Deerness
Opened March 1960 Y.569073, 30/Deerness; 29/L.2 Oct 1968; *In use*

Kirkwall
Opened June 1960 Y.411116, 30/Kirkwall; U/G June 1962; 29/L.1 Oct 1968; *In use*

Stromness
Opened April 1960 Y.231099, 30/Stromness; U/G July 1960; 29/L.3 Oct 1968; *In use*

PEEBLESHIRE

Peebles
Opened Nov 1938 T.244413, 31/H.3; 24/F.3 Nov 1953; U/G Oct 1959; 24/C.1 Oct 1968; *In use*

Traquair
Opened April 1953 T.328343, 31/New Post; 24/U.4 Nov 1953; U/G 1962; 24/G.2 Oct 1968; *In use*

Tweedsmuir
Opened Jan 1939 T.112358, 34/D.2; 25/U.2 Nov 1953; U/G Nov 1959; 24/G.3 Oct 1968; *In use*

West Linton
Opened Nov 1938 T.147514, 31/K.3; *Closed 1948. Reopened May 1957*, T.138523, 24/E.2; U/G Oct 1959; 24/D.3 Oct 1968; *In use*

PERTHSHIRE

Aberfeldy
Opened Aug 1940 N.858489, 37/J.2; 28/Q.3 Nov 1953;
U/G April 1960; 28/A.3 Oct 1968; *In use*

Aberfoyle
Opened Dec 1938 N.520015, 34/A.1; 28/L.2 Nov 1953;
U/G May 1959; *Closed Oct 1968*

Abernyte
Opened Oct 1938 O.256326, 36/K.3; 28/T.4 Nov 1953;
U/G Sept 1961; 28/G.1 Oct 1968; *In use*

Alyth
Opened June 1939 O.234475, 37/E.2; Granite 1943;
28/P.4 Nov 1953; U/G April 1960; 28/B.2 Oct 1968;
In use

Bankfoot
Opened June 1939 O.080348, 36/K.1; Granite 1943;
28/T.2 Nov 1953; U/G April 1960; *Closed Oct 1968*

Blackford
Opened Oct 1938 N.898095, 36/H.3; Granite 1943;
Closed 1947; Reopened July 1951, N.896096, 28/R.3;
Closed Oct 1968

Blair Athol
Opened July 1940 N.868665, 37/J.1; *Closed 1945.
Reopened Dec 1955,* 28/Q.1; U/G April 1960; 28/A.1
Oct 1968; *In use*

Braco
Opened Oct 1938 N.819096, 36/G.2; resite to N.827089
April 1942; 28/F.3 Nov 1953; U/G Oct 1958; 28/J.2
Oct 1968 *In use*

Bridge of Earn
Opened Oct 1938 O.127185, 36/J.2; Granite 1943;
resite to O.145169, 28/S.1 Nov 1953; resite to
O.145178 May 1963; U/G 1964; *Closed Oct 1968*

Callander
Opened Oct 1938 N.636085, 36/G.1; 26/M.1 1953;
resite to N.635094 July 1954; resite to N.636091, 28/L1,
June 1957; U/G Sept 1963; 28/J.4 Oct 1968; *In use*

Comrie/Crieff
Opened Oct 1938 N.875222, 36/H.1 Crieff; Granite
1943; 28/R.2 Nov 1953; resite to N.768202 Jan 1959;
U/G Aug 1960; 28/F.2 Oct 1968; renamed Comrie
1969; *In use*

Crianlarich
Opened July 1940 N.386249, 35/B.1; 27/C.3 Nov 1953;
U/G Aug 1960; 27/C.3 Oct 1968; *In use*

Doune
Opened Oct 1938 N.724024, 33/G.3; 26/M.3 Nov 1953;

U/G April 1962; *Closed Oct 1968*

Dunning
Opened Oct 1938 O.018141, 36/H.2; Granite 1943;
28/S.2 Nov 1953; U/G Aug 1960; 28/F.3 Oct 1968;
In use

Dunkeld
Opened Aug 1939 O.035433, 37/E.1; Granite 1943;
Closed 1946. Reopened Dec 1955, 28/Q.3; U/G March
1961; 28/A.2 Oct 1968; *In use*

Killin
Opened July 1940 N.575331, 36/H.4; 27/D.3 Nov 1953;
U/G Aug 1960; 28/F.1 Oct 1968; *In use*

Kinloch Rannoch/Bridge of Gaur
Opened Dec 1940 N.503564, 37/J.3, Bridge of Gaur,
Watcher Post; *Closed 1945. Reopened June 1955,*
N.503564, 27/D.1, Kinloch Rannoch; resite to N.660579
Nov 1958; U/G Oct 1960; 28/Q.2; 28/A.4 Oct 1968;
In use

Kirkmichael
Opened June 1953 O.085596, 37/New Post; 28/P.4 Nov
Nov 1953; 28/P.2 April 1960; resite to O.091596 Feb
1962; U/G Oct 1962; 28/B.1 Oct 1968; *In use*

Methven
Opened Oct 1938 O.018259, 36/J.3; resite to O.025263
June 1939; Granite 1943; 28/R.1 Nov 1953; resite to
O.016265 Oct 1964; U/G March 1964; 28/G.3 Oct
1968; *In use*

Meikleour
Opened Oct 1938 O.165392, 36/K.1; 37/E.2 July 1941;
Granite 1943; 28/T.1 Nov 1953; U/G Feb 1958; *Closed
Oct 1968*

Muckhart
Opened Oct 1938 O.007015, 36/E.3; Granite 1943;
28/S.3 Nov 1953; U/G Aug 1960; *Closed Oct 1968*

Scone
Opened Oct 1938 O.144271, 36/J.1; Granite 1943;
28/T.3 Nov 1953; U/G Feb 1958; 28/G.2 Oct 1968;
In use

Strathyre
Opened May 1959 O.562199, 27/Strathyre; resite to
O.563201, 28/L.5; U/G May 1963; 28/J.1 Oct 1968;
In use

RENFREWSHIRE

Barrhead
Opened Feb 1939 S.486591, 34/H.1; 26/N.3 Nov 1953;
resite to S.493593 March 1962; 27/P.3 Nov 1963; U/G
April 1965; 25/C.4 Oct 1968; *In use*

Bridge of Weir
Opened Dec 1938 S.385650, 34/K.3; *Closed Oct 1947.*
Reopened 1953; S.393667, 26/N.2 resite to S.377654,
27/F.2, April 1962; U/G April 1965; 25/C.5 Oct 1968;
In use

Eaglesham
Opened Dec 1938 S.564511, 34/H.2; resite to S.562514
Feb 1939; resite to S.558519 Aug 1939; 26/W.3 Nov
1953; U/G May 1960; 25/W.1 May 1962; *Closed April
1968*

Gourock
Opened Dec 1939 S.237772, 34/L.1; 26/D.1 Nov 1953;
resite to S.238771 Sept 1960; 27/0.1 Nov 1963; U/G
Apri 1965; 25/B.1 Oct 1968; *In use*

Achnasheen
Opened July 1956 H.162584, 30/M.3; U/G May 1961;
30/H.3 Oct 1968; *In use*

Alness/Invergordon
Opened July 1940 H.653700, 39/F.4 Alness; Alarm Bell
system to RAF Invergordon 1941; 30/M.1 Nov 1953;
resite to H.683692 Oct 1954; U/G, renamed Invergordon,
May 1965; 30/J.3 Oct 1968; *In use*

Ardgay
Opened June 1940 H.592904, 39/G.3; Granite 1943;
30/S.2 Nov 1953; resite to H.593907 June 1959; U/G
Dec 1959; 30/E.3 Oct 1968; *In use*

Aultbea
Opened Nov 1953 J.844914, 30/N.2; resite to J.865892
Dec 1958; U/G May 1961; *Closed Oct 1968*

Balintore/Fearn
Opened Aug 1940 H.863759, 39/H.3 Balintore; 30/T.3
Nov 1953; U/G Aug 1959; 30/J.2, renamed Fearn, Oct
1968; *In use*

Cromarty
Opened June 1940 H.805664, 39/F.1; 30/T.2 Nov 1953;
U/G Oct 1961; *Closed Oct 1968*

Dingwall
Opened July 1940 H.548584, 39/F.3; Granite 1943;
39/T.3 April 1953; 30/M.4 Nov 1953; resite to H.555603
May 1961; U/G Jan 1964; 30/H.2 Oct 1968; *In use*

Fortrose
Opened July 1940 H.741563, 39/F.2; 30/V.2 Nov 1953;
resite to H.746558 June 1959; U/G May 1961; 30/M.1
Oct 1968; *In use*

Gairloch
Opened Sept 1960 H.793773, 30/Gairloch; resite to
H.800774 April 1961; U/G, 30/N.5, Dec 1964; 30/D.4
Oct 1968; *In use*

Garve
Opened Jan 1961 H.399617, 30/Garve; resite to H.39262
30/M.3, April 1964; U/G Oct 1965; 30/H.1 Oct 1968;
In use

Kinlochewe
Opened Feb 1960 H.030616, 30/M.2; U/G May 1961;
Closed Oct 1968

Kyle of Lochalsh
Opened Sept 1960 G.781314, 30/Kyle of Lochalsh
(Durinish); 30/K.4 Aug 1962; resite to G.779309
(because of shifting sands), Dec 1963; U/G March 1964;
30/K.2 Oct 1968; *In use*

Stornoway, Isle of Lewis
Opened June 1960 B.448325, 30/Stornoway; U/G,
30/A.1, Nov 1963; *In use*

Ullapool
Opened March 1956 H.134939, 30/N.3; U/G May 1960;
30/D.3 Oct 1968; *In use*

Tain
Opened July 1940 H.791816, 30/H.1; resite to H.792826
Feb 1949; 30/S.3 Nov 1953; U/G Aug 1959; 30/J.1
Oct 1968; *In use*

ROXBURGHSHIRE

Bonchester Bridge/Ashkirk
Opened Nov 1938 T.577123, 31/G.2 Bonchester Bridge;
23/E.1, renamed Ashkirk, Nov 1953; U/G Nov 1959;
24/B.1 Oct 1965; 24/J.2 Oct 1968; *In use*

Jedburgh
Opened Nov 1938 T.636196, 31/F.2; 23/E.2 Nov 1953;
U/G Sept 1961; 24/B.2. 1963; 24/J.3 Oct 1968; *In use*

Kelso
Opened Feb 1937 T.729353, 31/E.; resite to T.727349
July 1942; 23/F.2 Nov 1953; resite to T.746374 March
1954; resite to T.744347 June 1959; U/G April 1960;
24/A.2 Oct 1963; 24/H.3 Oct 1968; *In use*

Lilliesleaf
Opened Nov 1938 T.472224, 31/G.1; 23/F.4 Nov 1953;
U/G Sept 1961; 24/A.4 1965; *Closed Oct 1968*

Morebattle
Opened Feb 1937 T.775245, 31/E.2; 23/F.3 Nov 1953;
resite to T.778248 June 1959; U/G Sept 1961; 24/H.4
Oct 1968; *In use*

St. Boswells/Smailholme
Opened Nov 1938 T.569312, 31/F.3 St. Boswells;
Granite 1943; 23/F.1 renamed Smailholme, Nov 1953;
resite to T.636345 July 1959; resite to T.669359 March
1961; U/G May 1963, 24/A.1; *Closed Oct 1968*

Attack Warning Red

Steel Road
Opened Nov 1939 Y.518935, 31/A.1; 23/E.4 Nov 1953;
U/G Sept 1961; 22/F.1 Dec 1964; 22/D.2 Oct 1968; *In use*

SELKIRKSHIRE

Galashiels/Clovenfords
Opened July 1940 T.442361, 31/H.4 Clovenfords; 23/G.4
Nov 1953; renamed Galashiels Dec 1957; U/G Nov
1959; 24/G.4 1965; *Closed Oct 1968*

Yarrow
Opened Nov 1938 T.342261, 31/H2; 23/U.1 Nov 1953;
resite to T.302247 July 1959; U/G Sept 1961; 24/U.3
Jan 1964; 24/J.1 Oct 1968; *In use*

SHETLAND

Lerwick
Opened July 1960 U.447424, 30/Lerwick; U/G July
1961; 29/M.2 Oct 1968; *In use*

Sumburgh
Opened April 1960 U.392127, 30/Sumburgh; U/G 1961;
29/M.3 Oct 1968; *In use*

Voe
Opened July 1960 U.439726, 30/Voe; U/G Jan 1961;
29/M.1 Oct 1968; *In use*

Walls
Opened April 1960 U.236491, 30/Walls; U/G March
1961; 29/M.4 Oct 1968; *In use*

ISLE OF SKYE

Broadford
Opened Feb 1955 G.655235, 30/K.2; U/G Dec 1959;
30/K.4 Oct 1968; *In use*

Dunvegan
Opened April 1955 G.247483, 30/L.2; resite to
G.275480 March 1961; U/G 1962; *Closed Oct 1968*

Portree
Opened May 1958 G.473447, 30/L.3; U/G Aug 1966;
30/G.2 Oct 1968; *In use*

Uig
Opened June 1958 G.393625, 30/L.1; resite to G.400635
April 1960; U/G May 1961; 30/G.1 Oct 1968; *In use*

STIRLINGSHIRE

Bannockburn
Opened Nov 1938 S.822897, 36/P.3; Granite 1943;
24/B.2 Nov 1953; U/G May 1961; *Closed Oct 1968*;
Reopened June 1971, 24/A.1; In use

Falkirk/Bonnybridge
Opened Nov 1938 S.876786, 36/F.2 Falkirk; 26/Y.1 Nov
1953; resite to S.815808 Jan 1957; U/G, renamed
Bonnybridge, June 1961; 24/M.2 1963; 24/A.4 Oct 1968;
In use

Killearn
Opened Dec 1938 S.528863, 34/A.3; 26/Z.2 Nov 1953;
U/G March 1960; 27/N.1 Nov 1962; 25/G.1 Oct 1968;
In use

Kilsyth/Kirkintilloch
Opened Dec 1938 S.722779, 34/B.1 Kilsyth; resite to
S.741761, 26/Z.4 Nov 1953; resite to S.670756, renamed
Kirkintilloch, Dec 1961; U/G, 27/N.3, April 1963;
25/C.2 Oct 1968; *In use*

Kippen
Opened Dec 1938 S.637945, 34/A.2; resite to S.635943
July 1952; 26/Z.1 Nov 1953; U/G May 1961; 20/J.3
Oct 1968; *In use*

Slamannan
Opened Dec 1938 S.861732, 34/B.2; 26/Y.4 Nov 1953;
U/G May 1961; 24/A.3 Oct 1968; *In use*

SUTHERLAND

Altnaharra
Opened Jan 1955 C.569357, 30/P.4; U/G May 1960;
30/B.3 Oct 1968; *In use*

Bettyhill
Opened May 1941 C.702618, 39/J.1; resite to C.700627
Dec 1941; 30/P.4 Nov 1953; 30/Q.4 May 1958; U/G
Nov 1959; *Closed Oct 1968*

Brora
Opened July 1940 C.910040, 39/G.1; Granite 1943;
30/S.4 Nov 1953; U/G Dec 1959; 30/E.2 Oct 1968;
In use

Dornoch
Opened July 1940 H.803883, 39/G.2; Granite 1943;
30/S.4 Nov 1953; resite to H.816921 Dec 1956; U/G
Dec 1959; *Closed Oct 1968*

Durness
Opened Aug 1956 D.415676, 30/T.1; resite to D.394678
Nov 1956; U/G Nov 1959; 30/B.1 Oct 1968; *In use*

Elphin
Opened Sept 1960 C.218119, 30/Elphin; U/G, 30/N.4,
Aug 1962; 30/D.2 Oct 1968; *In use*

Kinbrace
Opened Dec 1954 C.865315, 30/S.1; U/G Nov 1959;
30/E.1 Oct 1968; *In use*

Lairg
Opened June 1956 C.583073, 30/P.3; U/G Dec 1959; 30/B.4 Oct 1968; *In use*

Lochinver/Stoer
Opened Jan 1956 C.042275, 30/N.1 Lochinver; U/G May 1960; 30/D.1, renamed Stoer, Oct 1968; *In use*

Melvich
Opened May 1941 C.875655, 39/J.2; 30/Q.3 Nov 1953; U/G Nov 1959; 30/C.3 Oct 1968; *In use*

Tongue
Opened Sept 1960 C.599563, 30/Tongue; U/G, 30/P.5, May 1962; 30/B.2 Oct 1968; *In use*

WIGTOWNSHIRE

Auchenmalg
Opened Aug 1940 X.228519, 33/F.2; 25/A.4 Nov 1953; U/G Nov 1959; *Closed April 1968*

Ervie of Kirkcolm
Opened Aug 1940 X.044713, 33/G.2; Granite 1943; 25/L.2 Nov 1953; resite to X.006713 Oct 1960; U/G Jan 1964; 25/L.1 Oct 1968; *In use*

Garlieston
Opened Aug 1940 X.465466, 33/D.2; 25/B.3 Nov 1953; U/G Jan 1963; 25/M.2 Oct 1968; *In use*

Kirkcowan
Opened Aug 1940 X.307610, 33/E.3; Granite 1943; *Closed 1946.* Reopened Oct 1956 X.326612, 25/A.1; U/G Nov 1959; 25/M.3 Oct 1968; *In use*

New Luce
Opened Aug 1940 X.177662, 33/F.1; Granite 1943; 25/L.3 Nov 1953; U/G Nov 1959; 25/L.2 Oct 1968; *In use*

Newton Stewart
Opened Aug 1940 X.404654, 33/E.3; Granite 1943; 25/B.1 Nov 1953; U/G Feb 1963; *Closed April 1968*

Portpatrick
Opened Dec 1952 Y.003537, 33/New Post; 25/A.2 Nov 1953; U/G Aug 1957; *Closed April 1968*

Port William
Opened Aug 1940 X.343431, 33/D.3; Granite 1943 25/B.2 Nov 1953; U/G Feb 1961; *Closed April 1968*

Sandhead
Opened Aug 1940 X.095506, 33/F.3; 25/A.3 Nov 1953; resite to X.079528 April 1963; U/G Feb 1964; 25/L.3 Oct 1968; *In use*

WALES

ANGLESEY

Amlwch
Opened Aug 1940 H.437921, 28-2/Y.1; 28-2/A.1 Oct 1941; resite to H.441933 July 1949; 17/A.1 Nov 1953; resite to H.439935 Feb 1957; U/G May 1959; *Closed Oct 1968*

Llanfaethlu
Opened Sept 1940 H.311869, 28-2/A.2; 17/A.2 Nov 1953; U/G Feb 1959; 17/A.1 Oct 1968; *In use*

Llangefni
Opened Sept 1940 H.456773, 28-2/B.3; Granite 1943; 17/A.3 Nov 1953; resite to H.456676 Oct 1959; U/G April 1960; 17/A.2 Oct 1968; *In use*

Marianglas
Opened Jan 1949 H.502838, 28-2/New Post; 17/A.4 Nov 1953; U/G Sept 1961; *Closed Oct 1968*

Newborough
Opened Sept 1940 H.416656, 28-2/B.2; Granite 1943; 17/B.2 Nov 1953; resite to H.418653 Nov 1959; U/G March 1960; 17/A.3 Oct 1968; *In use*

Rhosneigr
Opened Sept 1940 H.322733, 28-2/A.3; 17/B.1 Nov 1953; resite to H.321735 Feb 1958; U/G Aug 1960; *Closed Oct 1968*

BRECONSHIRE

Abercrave
Opened Sept 1938 N.814129, 25/M.3; 13/M.1 Nov 1953; U/G Dec 1965; 13/K.2 Oct 1968; *In use*

Abergwyessyn
Opened Sept 1938 N.80533, 25/L.1 Watcher Post; resite to N.859531, with normal Post status, Nov 1940; 13/O.2 Nov 1953; U/G Nov 1961; *Closed Oct 1968*

Brecon
Opened Sept 1938 O.040296, 25/K.3; resite to O.049269 July 1950; 13/N.4 Nov 1953; U/G Oct 1962; 12/C.3 Oct 1968; *In use*

Brynmawr
Opened Sept 1938 O.189123, 25/B.3; 12/P.3 Nov 1953; resite to O.183125 April 1961; U/G Aug 1962; 12/G.1 Oct 1968; *Closed April 1973*

Builth Wells
Opened Sept 1938 O.039508, 25/L.1; resite to O.045507 Aug 1953; 13/O.4 Nov 1953; U/G Dec 1959; *Closed Oct 1968*

Erwood
Opened Sept 1938 O.098428, 25/A.1; 12/Q.1 Nov 1953;
resite to O.095429 Sept 1961; U/G Sept 1963; 12/C.1
Oct 1968; *In use*

Hay
Opened Sept 1938; O.224433, 25/A.2; 12/Q.4 Nov 1953;
U/G April 1959; 12/C.2 Oct 1968; *In use*

Llangammarch Wells
Opened Sept 1938 N.928476, 25/L.2; 13/L.3 Nov 1953;
U/G Dec 1958; 13/E.1 Oct 1968; *In use*

Sennybridge
Opened Sept 1938 N.922288, 25/K.2; 13/N.3 Nov 1953;
U/G Oct 1959; *Closed Oct 1968*

Talgarth
Opened Sept 1938 O.159334, 25/A.3; 12/Q.2 Nov 1953;
U/G Oct 1962; *Closed Oct 1968*

Talybont-on-Usk
Opened Sept 1938 O.110230, 25/K.1; 12/P.2 Nov 1953;
U/G Aug 1962; *Closed Oct 1968*

CAERNARVONSHIRE

Abersoch
Opened Sept 1940 H.297277, 28-2/F.3; 17/D.3 Nov 1953;
resite to H.303289 Sept 1960; U/G Oct 1960; *Closed
Oct 1968*

Bangor
Opened Sept 1940 H.579712, 28-2/B.1; Granite 1943;
17/B.4 Nov 1953; U/G Feb 1959; 17/B.1 Oct 1968;
In use

Beddgelert
Opened Aug 1941 H.594481, 28-2/G.4; 17/C.4 Nov
1953; resite to H.583487 May 1963; U/G Oct 1963;
17/F.1 Oct 1968; *In use*

Capel Curig
Opened Sept 1940 H.732579, 28-2/C.1; 17/K.3 Nov
1953; resite to H.720583, U/G Nov 1963; 17/B.3 Oct
1968; *In use*

Carreg Plas/Aberdaron
Opened Sept 1939 H.163291, 28-2/F.4 Carreg Plas;
17/D.2 Nov 1953; resite to H.169265 July 1959; U/G
April 1960; 17/E.3, renamed Aberdaron, Oct 1968;
In use

Ceinant
Opened Oct 1940 H.533610, 28-2/G.1; Granite 1943;
17/B.3 Nov 1953; U/G April 1958; *Closed Oct 1968*

Chwilog
Opened Aug 1940 H.439388, 28-2/F.2; Granite 1943;

17/D.4 Nov 1953; U/G Dec 1957; 17/E.2 Oct 1968;
In use

Llandudno
Opened Aug 1939 H.776815, 26/L.1; Granire 1943;
17/L.1 Nov 1953; U/G March 1961; 17/C.1 Oct 1968;
In use

Llanfairfechan
Opened Aug 1941 H.680754, 28-2/B.4; Granite 1942;
Darky 1943; Augmented Granite 1944; resite to
H.672749 Oct 1951; 17/L.2 Nov 1953; U/G Dec 1960;
Closed Oct 1968

Nefyn
Opened Oct 1940 H.273408, 28-2/F.1; Granite 1943;
17/D.1 Nov 1953; U/G April 1960; 17/E.4 Oct 1968;
In use

Penmachno
Opened Sept 1941 H.800505, 26/V.3; 17/K.4 Nov 1953;
resite to H.793505 Jan 1961; U/G Oct 1963; *Closed Oct
1968*

Pen-Y-Groes
Opened July 1940 H.474536, 28-2/G.2; Granite 1943;
17/C.1 Nov 1953; resite to H.475534 July 1964; U/G
Nov 1964; 17/E.1 Oct 1968; *In use*

Port Madoc
Opened Aug 1940 H.561374, 28-2/G.3; Granite 1943;
Augmented Granite 1944; 17/C.3 Nov 1953; U/G 1960;
Closed Oct 1968

Trevor
Opened Aug 1940 H.366472, 28-2/F.4; Granite 1943;
17/C.2 Nov 1953; U/G Oct 1962; *Closed Oct 1968*

CARDIGANSHIRE

Aberporth
Opened Aug 1940 N.243502, 28-1/Y.2; 13/B.1 Nov
1953; resite to H.227504 Aug 1957; U/G Jan 1960;
Closed Oct 1968

Aberystwyth
Opened Oct 1942 N.593834, 28-1/O.1; 13/Q.1 Nov 1953;
resite to N. 593825 Aug 1954; resite to N.597829 Aug
1964; U/G Feb 1966; *Closed Oct 1968*

Cardigan
Opened July 1940 N.167443, 28-1/X.4; 13/C.4 Nov
1953; U/G Jan 1960; 13/C.3 Oct 1968; *In use*

Crosswood
Opened Aug 1940 N.679723, 28-1/O.3; Darky 1943;
13/Q.3 Nov 1953; U/G Dec 1959; 13/A.2 Oct 1968;
In use

Lampeter
Opened Sept 1941 N.381601, 28-1/Y.4; 13/A.1 Nov
1953; U/G Dec 1959; 13/C.1 Oct 1968; *In use*

Llandyssul/Pont Shaen
Opened Aug 1940 N.433482, 28-1/Y.1 Pont Shaen;
13/A.3 Nov 1953; resite to N.394433, renamed
Llandyssul, May 1954; U/G 1960; *Closed Oct 1968*

Llanon
Opened Sept 1940 N.521668, 28-1/O.4; 13/Q.2 Nov
1953; U/G Dec 1959; 13/A.1 Oct 1968; *In use*

New Quay
Opened Sept 1941 N.381601, 28-1/Y.4; 13/A.1 Nov
1953; U/G Dec 1959; 13/C.1 Oct 1968; *In use*

Pont-erwyd
Opened Sept 1940 N.750810, 28-1/O.2; 13/Q.4 Nov
1953; resite to N.753820 May 1961; U/G Oct 1963;
13/A.1 Oct 1968; *In use*

Tregaron
Opened Aug 1940 N.878597, 28-1/P.1; 13/A.4 Nov
1953; U/G July 1961; 13/D.1 Oct 1968; *In use*

CARMARTHENSHIRE

Carmarthen
Opened Aug 1940 N.411313, 28-1/Q.1; 13/G.1 Nov
1953; U/G June 1960; 13/H.2 Oct 1968; *In use*

Conwill
Opened July 1942 N.349277, 28-1/R.4; 13/B.3 Nov
1953; U/G June 1960; *Closed Oct 1968*

Dryslwyn
Opened Aug 1940 N.542214, 28-1/Q.3; 13/G.4 Nov
1953; resite to H.543216 May 1959; U/G Oct 1955;
13/K.1 Oct 1968; *In use*

Kidwelly
Opened Nov 1941 N.416065, 28-1/Q.4; 13/G.3 Nov
1953; U/G June 1960; 13/J.1 Oct 1968; *In use*

Laugharne
Opened 1940 N.299099, 28-1/H.1; 13/G.2 Nov 1953;
U/G 1963; 13/H.3 Oct 1968; *In use*

Llanboidy
Opened Aug 1940 N.203234, 28-1/R.3; resite to
N.206233 Nov 1942; 13/F.1 Nov 1953; U/G Jan 1960;
13/H.1 Oct 1968; *In use*

Llandovery
Opened Sept 1938 N.765354, 25/M.1; 13/H.1 Nov
1953; U/G March 1961; 13/E.2 Oct 1968; *In use*

Newcastle Emlyn
Opened Aug 1940 N.309422, 28-1/Y.3; 13/B.2 Nov

1953; resite to N.310418 May 1958; U/G Aug 1958;
13/C.2 Oct 1968; *In use*

Pencader
Opened Aug 1940 N.453371, 28-1/P.3; 13/B.4 Nov
1953; U/G March 1961; 13/D.3 Oct 1968; *In use*

Talley
Opened Aug 1940 N.636325, 28-1/Q.2; 13/N.2 Nov
1953; U/G March 1961; 13/E.3 Oct 1968; *In use*

DENBIGHSHIRE

Cerrig-Y-Druidion/Derwen
Opened Aug 1939 J.058473, 26/U.1 Derwen; resite
to H.964496, renamed Cerrig-y-Druidion, Jan 1942;
17/J.4 Nov 1953; U/G Sept 1963; *Closed Oct 1968*

Coedpoeth/Brymbo
Opened Aug 1939 J.284533, 26/N.3 Coedpoeth; Granite
1943; 16/M.2 Nov 1953; resite to J.226537 July 1955;
resite to J.284535, renamed Brymbo, May 1960; U/G
Oct 1960; 17/H.2 Oct 1968; *In use*

Llanfair Talhaiarn
Opened Sept 1939 H.931697, 26/L.2; Granite 1943;
17/K.1 Nov 1953; resite to H.929700 Nov 1959; U/G
June 1960; 17/C.3 Oct 1968; *In use*

Llangollen
Opened March 1939 J.216429, 26/O.1; resite to J.205417,
16/M.3 Nov 1953; resite to J.216429, 17/M.3; U/G,
July 1958; 17/H.3 Oct 1968; *In use*

Llanrhaiadr
Opened Aug 1939 J.133262, 26/T.2; Granite 1943;
17/Q.4 Nov 1953; U/G Sept 1965; 17/K.1 Oct 1968;
In use

Llanrwst
Opened March 1939 H.808624, 26/U.1; 26/V.1 Feb
1942; 17/K.2 Nov 1953; U/G July 1960; *Closed Oct 1968*

Llysfaen
Opened Sept 1941 H.892775, 26/L.4; Granite 1943;
17/L.4 Nov 1953; resite to H.889774 April 1961;
U/G June 1962; *Closed Oct 1968*

Nantglyn
Opened Aug 1939 J.006625, 26/M.2; Granite 1943;
19/G.2 Nov 1953; 17/N.2 1963; U/G April 1966;
Closed Oct 1968

Pentrefoelas
Opened Aug 1939 H.872512, 26/U.2; 26/V.2 March
1942; 17/J.1 Nov 1953; U/G July 1958; 17/B.2 Oct
1968; *In use*

Ruthin
Opened Sept 1939 J.111588, 26/N.2; Granite 1943;

16/M.1 Nov 1953; resite to J.112599 Sept 1959; 17/M.1
June 1961; U/G Oct 1965; 17/H.1 Oct 1968; *In use*

FLINTSHIRE

Bodfari
Opened Aug 1939 J.097719, 26/M.3; Granite 1943;
19/G.3 Nov 1953; U/G, 17/N.3, Oct 1960; *Closed Oct
1968*

Holywell/Halkyn
Opened Oct 1937 J.207706, 7/G.3 Halkyn; 19/H.1
Nov 1953; resite to J.186751, renamed Holywell, April
1964; 17/P.1 May 1964; *Closed Oct 1968*

Mold
Opened Oct 1939 J.233634, 26/N.1; Granite 1943;
Augmented Granite 1944; 19/H.2 Nov 1953; resite to
J.234619 June 1956; 17/P.2 April 1957; U/G Oct 1964;
Closed Oct 1968

Overton
Opened Sept 1938 J.374399, 26/A.2; Granite 1943;
Augmented Granite 1944; resite to J.374408 Nov 1964;
U/G May 1965; 16/C.2 Oct 1968; *In use*

Prestatyn/Mostyn
Opened Oct 1937 J.154800, 7/H.3 Mostyn; resite to
J.109832 April 1951; 19/G.4, renamed Prestatyn, Nov
1953; resite to J.079817 Jan 1961; U/G Feb 1961; 17/N.4
1966; 17/C.2 Oct 1968; *In use*

Rhyl/St. Asaph
Opened Aug 1939 J.027825, 26/M.1 Rhyl; Granite
1943; 19/G.1 Nov 1953; 17/N.1 March 1961; resite to
J.020751, renamed St. Asaph, Oct 1963; U/G Feb 1964;
Closed Oct 1968

GLAMORGANSHIRE

Amman Valley/Gwaun-Cae-Gurwen
Opened Sept 1938 N.703125, 25/M.2 Gwaun-Cae-
Gurwen, 13/M.2, renamed Amman Valley Nov 1953;
resite to N.699199 Sept 1956; U/G Oct 1959; 13/K.2
Oct 1968; *In use*

Bargoed
Opened Sept 1938 T.146299, 25/B.1; resite to T.149991
Dec 1938; resite to T.138993, 12/E.3, Nov 1953; U/G
April 1963; 12/F.2 Oct 1968; *Closed Jan 1969*

Clydach
Opened Sept 1938 N.694022, 25/H.2; 13/J.1 Nov 1953;
resite to N.699015 Nov 1954; resite to N.676006 July
1961; U/G May 1962; 13/J.2 Oct 1968; *In use*

Dowlais/Merthyr Tydfil
Opened Sept 1938 O.066080, 25/E.3 Dowlais; 13/M.4
Nov 1953; resite to O.028059, renamed Merthyr

Tydfil, April 1957; U/G Feb 1959; 12/F.1 Oct 1968; *In use*

Hirwaun
Opened Sept 1938 N.970060, 25/E.2; resite to N.951062
Sept 1950; 13/M.3 Nov 1953; U/G Oct 1959; *Closed
Oct 1968*

Llantwit Major
Opened Sept 1938 S.989691, 25/F.2; resite to S.972692
May 1940; 13/K.3 Nov 1953; U/G May 1960; *Closed
Oct 1968*

Maesteg
Opened Sept 1938 S.850907, 25/G.2; resite to S.853903
Oct 1952; 13/L.2 Nov 1953; resite to S.847908 Nov
1958; U/G Sept 1961; 13/L.1 Oct 1968; 13/L.3 Oct
1969; *In use*

Mountain Ash
Opened Sept 1938 T.479992, 25/E.1; resite to T.053974
Sept 1950; 13/L.4 Nov 1953; resite to T.056967 Nov
1958; U/G Feb 1961; 12/F.3 Oct 1968; *In use*

Penarth
Opened Sept 1938 T.253721, 25/D.3; resite to
T.193721 Nov 1938; 12/F.3 Nov 1953; resite to
T.186691 Sept 1955; U/G June 1962; 12/K.2 Oct 1968;
Closed 1975

Penclawdd
Opened June 1941 S.541975, 25/J.1; resite to S.539954,
13/H.2, Nov 1953; U/G June 1960; 13/J.3 Oct 1968;
In use

Pencoed
Opened Sept 1968 S.964826, 25/P.1; resite to S.956828,
13/K.2, Nov 1953; resite to S.963794 July 1958; U/G
Sept 1961; 13/L.2 Oct 1968; 13/L.1 Oct 1969; *In use*

Penmaen
Opened Sept 1938 S.528889, 25/J.2; 13/H.4 Nov 1953;
resite to S.534885 Sept 1962; resite to S.536883 April
1965; U/G Aug 1966; *Closed Oct 1968*

Pentyrch
Opened Sept 1938 T.100826, 25/D.2; 13/K.1 Nov 1953;
U/G Sept 1961; *Closed Oct 1968*

Pontardulais
Opened Sept 1938 N.605035, 25/H.3; resite to N.582046,
13/H.1, Nov 1953; U/G May 1962; *Closed Oct 1968*

Pontypridd
Opened Sept 1938 T.065880, 25/D.4; resite to T.068888
Aug 1939; 25/E.4 1941; 13/L.4 Nov 1953; U/G Oct
1960; *Closed Oct 1968*

Porthcawl
Opened Sept 1938 S.808775, 25/G.3; 13/J.3 Nov 1953;

U/G 1961; 13/L.3 Oct 1968; 13/L.2 Oct 1969; *In use*

Port Talbot/Britton Ferry
Opened Sept 1938 S.756892, 25/G.1 Port Talbot; resite
to S.765907 Nov 1940; resite to S.753885 Nov 1951;
13/J.4 Nov 1953; resite to S.736941 Aug 1962; renamed
Britton Ferry Jan 1964; U/G June 1964; *Closed Oct 1968*

Resolven
Opened Sept 1938 N.836027, 25/H.1; 13/L.1 Nov 1953;
resite to N.834029 Sept 1958; U/G Jan 1964; *Closed
Oct 1968*

Rhoose
Opened Sept 1938 T.061667, 25/F.3; resite to T.073666
April 1940; 13/K.4 Nov 1953; resite to T.059673 Nov
1959; U/G March 1960; *Closed Oct 1968*; Reopened
12/K.2, 1975

Rhossilli
Opened Sept 1938 S.420880, 25/J.1; 13/H.3 Nov 1953;
U/G Sept 1962; *Closed Oct 1968*

Sketty/Fforest Fach
Opened Sept 1938 S.622929, 25/J.3 Sketty; resite to
S.625939 (Cfn Coed Hospital Grounds) Aug 1939;
resite to S.618942, 13/J.2 Nov 1953; U/G, renamed
Fforest Fach, Oct 1962; *Closed Oct 1968*

MERIONETHSHIRE

Aberdovey
Opened Aug 1940 N.593969, 28-2/E.3; Granite 1943;
17/G.2 Nov 1953; resite to N.610963 Oct 1962; U/G
March 1964; *Closed Oct 1968*

Bala
Opened Aug 1939 H.916359, 26/U.2; 17/J.3 Nov 1953;
U/G Nov 1963; 17/G.3 Oct 1968; *In use*

Barmouth
Opened Oct 1940 H.603181 28-2/D.2; resite to H.681351
Sept 1943; Granite 1943; 17/E.3 Nov 1953; U/G Sept
1965; *Closed Oct 1968*

Blaenau Ffestiniog
Opened Dec 1940 H.694451 28-2/C.3; 17/E.1 Nov 1953;
resite to H.690452 March 1956; U/G May 1961; *Closed
Oct 1968*

Corwen
Opened Sept 1939 J.079444, 26/N.4; 26/U.2 July 1940;
17/M.4 Nov 1953; resite to J.051453 Feb 1958; U/G
Oct 1965; 17/G.1 Oct 1968; *In use*

Dolgellau
Opened Sept 1940 H.728186, 28-2/D.1; 17/F.1 Nov
1953; U/G Feb 1965; 17/G.2 Oct 1968; *In use*

Egylsfach
Opened April 1954, 17/G.3; U/G Sept 1965; *Closed
Oct 1968*

Llanbedr
Opened Sept 1940 H.586262, 28-2/D.3; Granite 1943;
17/E.2 Nov 1953; U/G Sept 1960; 17/F.3 Oct 1968; *In
use*

Llanegryn/Tywyn
Opened April 1942 H.593042, 28-2/E.4 Llanegryn;
Granite 1943; 17/F.2 Nov 1953; U/G July 1966; 17/J.3,
renamed Tywyn, Oct 1968; *In use*

Llanuwchllyn
Opened Aug 1941 H.879293, 28-2/D.4; 17/J.2 Nov
1953; resite to H.879393 May 1957; U/G 1960;
Closed Oct 1968

Trawsfynydd
Opened Aug 1940 H.713358, 28-2/C.4; 17/E.4 Nov
1953; U/G Oct 1968; *In use*

MONMOUTHSHIRE

Abergavenny
Opened Sept 1938 O.308154, 25/B.2; 12/P.4 Nov 1953;
resite to O.323145 Sept 1963; U/G Sept 1964; *Closed
Oct 1968. Reopened Nov 1973*, 12/G.1; *In use*

Chepstow
Opened Dec 1937, T.528937, 24/Q.3; resite to T.536917
May 1951; 12/G.3 Nov 1953; resite to T.528918 Jan
1962; U/G Dec 1962; *Closed Oct 1968*

Crosskeys/Ynysddu
Opened Sept 1939 T.223917, 25/C.2 Crosskeys; 12/F.1
Nov 1953; resite to T.197942 Sept 1962; renamed
Ynysddu, Dec 1962; U/G April 1963; *Closed Oct 1968;
Reopened, Jan 1969*, 12/F.2; *In use*

Llantilio Crossenny
Opened Dec 1937 O.395134, 24/R.3; resite to O.404141
April 1940; 12/E.1 Nov 1953; U/G Oct 1961; 12/G.2
Oct 1968; *In use*

Newport
Opened Sept 1938 T.293883, 25/C.3; 12/F.4 Nov
1953; resite to T.288902 Sept 1961; U/G June 1962;
12/H.3 Oct 1968; *In use*

Penhow
Opened Dec 1937 T.414899, 24/Q.2; resite to T.415903
April 1938; 12/C.1 Nov 1953; U/G May 1961; 12/H.2
Oct 1968; *In use*

Pontypool
Opened Sept 1938 O.295008, 25/C.1; 12/E.3 Nov
1953; U/G Oct 1961; 12/G.3 Oct *1968; Closed 1975*

St. Mellons/Llanishen
Opened Sept 1938 T.226802, 25/D.1 St Mellons; resite
to T.239832 June 1952; 12/F.3 Nov 1953; resite to
T.189851, renamed Llanishen, March 1963; U/G Jan
1966; 12/K.1 Oct 1968; *In use*

Usk
Opened Dec 1937 O.378014, 24/Q.1; 12/G.1 Nov 1953;
resite to O.392014 May 1960; U/G Dec 1962; *Closed
Oct 1968;* Reopened 12/G.3, 1975

MONTGOMERYSHIRE

Aberangell
Opened Sept 1940 H.846104, 28-2/E.1; 17/F.3 Nov
1953; resite to H.853105; U/G Feb 1966; 17/J.1 Oct
1968; *In use*

Carno
Opened Sept 1941 N.955971, 26/S.4; 17/H.3 Nov 1953;
resite to N.954670 Jan 1956; U/G May 1961; 17/L.3
Oct 1968; *In use*

Llanbrynmair
Opened Aug 1939 H.902029, 26/S.1; 17/H.2 Nov 1953;
U/G June 1961; *Closed Oct 1968*

Llanfair Caereinion
Opened Aug 1939 J.106061, 26/P.3; 26/T.1 July 1940;
Granite 1943; 16/F.4 Nov 1953; U/G May 1961;
17/R.4 July 1961; *Closed Oct 1968*

Llanfyllin
Opened Sept 1939 J.146203, 26/T.3; Granite 1943;
16/L.3 Nov 1953; U/G Sept 1965; *Closed Oct 1968*

Llangadfan
Opened Oct 1941 J.014112, 26/T.1; 26/P.4 Feb 1942;
resite to J.022118, 17/H.4, Nov 1953; U/G Feb 1962;
Closed Oct 1968

Llanidloes
Opened Aug 1939 N.945854, 26/S.2; 13/P.1 Nov 1953;
U/G Aug 1960; 13/B.1 Oct 1968; *In use*

Llanwyddyn
Opened Oct 1939 J.022196, 26/T.4 Watcher Post; Full
Post Status 1941; 17/H.1 Nov 1953; resite to J.025188
April 1961; U/G March 1962; 17/K.3 Oct 1968; *In use*

Llanymynech
Opened Aug 1939 J.263217, 26/O.4; Darky and Granite
1943; Augmented Granite 1944; 17/Q.2 Nov 1953;
resite to J.264213 Sept 1959; U/G Dec 1960; 17/K.2
Oct 1968; *In use*

Machynlleth
Opened Sept 1940 H.751013, 28-2/E.2; 17/G.1 Nov
1953; resite to H.941009 Jan 1961; U/G Nov 1961;

17/J.2 Oct 1968; *In use*

Montgomery
Opened April 1940 O.217964, 26/P.1; Granite 1943;
16/F.2 Nov 1953; U/G May 1960; 17/H.2 May 1961;
Closed Oct 1968

Newtown
Opened Aug 1939 O.116023, 26/S.3; Granite 1943;
resite to O.114923, 17/R.3 Nov 1953; U/G June 1961;
17/L.2 Oct 1968; *In use*

Pen-Y-Ffridd
Opened Sept 1941 J.311624, 7/G.4; 19/H.3 Nov 1953;
U/G Nov 1958; resite to J.308622, 17/P.3, May 1960;
Closed Oct 1968

Staylittle
Opened June 1953 N.874936, 28-1/New Post; 17/C.4
Nov 1953; U/G 1960; *Closed Oct 1968*

Welshpool
Opened March 1939 J.225081, 26/P.2; resite to J.227087
Aug 1942; Granite 1943; 16/F.1 Nov 1953; U/G Oct
1958; 17/R.1 1963; 17/L.1 Oct 1968; *In use*

PEMBROKESHIRE

Broad Haven
Opened July 1940 M.859132, 28-1/T.2; 13/E.1
Nov 1953; U/G Sept 1960; 13/F.3 Oct 1968; *In use*

Castlemartin St. Twynnells
Opened July 1940 R.915984, 28-1/S.1 Castlemartin;
13/E.3 Nov 1953; resite to R.942975 Nov 1959; U/G
July 1962; 13/C.3, renamed St. Twynnells, Oct 1968;
In use

Croes-goch
Opened Aug 1940 M.824302, 28-1/U.3; 13/D.2 Nov
1953; U/G Sept 1960; 13/F.1 Oct 1968; *In use*

Crymmych
Opened Aug 1940 N.173333, 28-1/X.2; 13/C.3 Nov
1953; resite to N.182341 Jan 1960; U/G July 1962; *Closed
Oct 1968*

Dale
Opened July 1940 M.825055, 28-1/T.1; resite to M.815047
April 1946; 13/E.2 Nov 1953; resite M.802039 Oct
1960; U/G July 1962; *Closed Oct 1968*

Fishguard
Opened July 1940 M.952368 1941, tie-line with C/G
Station; 13/D.1 Nov 1953; resite to M.954358 June
1959; U/G July 1963; *Closed Oct 1968*

Haverfordwest
Opened Aug 1940 M.929153, 28-1/T.3; 13/D.3 Nov

1953; resite to N.013155 June 1959; U/G July 1962; 13/G.1 Oct 1968; *In use*

Lamphey/Manorbier
Opened Dec 1940 N.066973, 28-1/S.3 Manorbier; resite to N.042009 Nov 1942; renamed Lamphey Feb 1953; 13/E.3 Nov 1953; U/G Sept 1960; *Closed Oct 1968*

Letterston
Opened Aug 1940 M.947294, 28-1/U.2; 13/D.4 Nov 1953; U/G Jan 1960; *Closed Oct 1968*

Maenclochog
Opened Aug 1940 N.070280, 28-1/X.3; 13/C.2 Nov 1953; U/G Jan 1960; 13/F.2 Oct 1968; *In use*

Narberth
Opened Aug 1940 N.103149, 28-1/R.2; resite to N.111124 Nov 1952; 13/F.2 Nov 1953; U/G Jan 1960; 13/G.2 Oct 1968; *In use*

Newport
Opened Aug 1940 N.064378, 28-1/X.1; 13/C.1 Nov 1953; resite to N.046391 July 1958; U/G Jan 1960; *Closed Oct 1968*

Saundersfoot/Tenby
Opened Sept 1940 N.145031, 28-1/S.2 Tenby; renamed Saundersfoot Oct 1951; 13/F.4 Nov 1953; U/G Jan 1960; *Closed Oct 1968*

RADNORSHIRE

Knighton
Opened Aug 1939 O.283718, 27/H.3; 12/B.4 Nov 1953; resite to O.300716 April 1961; U/G Oct 1962; 16/K.3 Oct 1968; *In use*

Llananno
Opened Aug 1939 O.098746, 26/O.1; 13/F.3 Nov 1953; U/G Aug 1960; 13/B.2 Oct 1968; *In use*

Llandrindod Wells
Opened March 1939 O.061605, 25/L.1; 13/O.1 Nov 1953; resite to O.065605 June 1958; U/G Dec 1958; 13/L.3 Oct 1968; *In use*

New Radnor
Opened Aug 1939 O.209612, 26/R.2; 12/A.1 Nov 1953; resite to O.217608 July 1961; U/G Oct 1962; *In use*

Rhayader
Opened Aug 1939 N.974685, 26/R.3; 13/P.2 Nov 1953; resite to N.972689 May 1954; U/G Sept 1963; *Closed Oct 1968*

ISLE OF MAN

Castletown
Opened Dec 1959 C.292692, 22/Q.4 U/G; 22/M.3

Oct 1968; *In use*

Douglas
Opened Oct 1965 C.413782, 22/Q.1, U/G; 22/M.2 Oct 1968; *In use*

Peel
Opened Oct 1965 C.258848, 22/Q.2, U/G; 22/M.4 Oct 1968; *In use*

Ramsey
Opened Oct 1965 C.451963, 22/Q.3, U/G; 22/M.1 Oct 1968; *In use*

NORTHERN IRELAND

COUNTY ANTRIM

Ballymoney
Opened June 1957 C.982236, 31/B.4 U/G; *Closed Oct 1968*

Ballycastle
Opened Aug 1957 D.076430, 31/B.3 U/G; 31/B.1 Oct 1968; *In use*

Ballymena
Opened Aug 1957 D.096056, 31/C.3 U/G; 31/D.1 Oct 1968; *In use*

Bushmills
Opened Aug 1957 C.913411, 31/B.2 U/G; *Closed Oct 1968*

Cloghmills
Opened June 1957 D.059197, 31/C.4 U/G; 31/B.3 Oct 1968; *In use*

Cushendall
Opened Aug 1957 D.244305, 31/C.1 U/G; 31/B.2 Oct 1968; *In use*

Dundrod
Opened June 1957 J.225739, 31/N.3 U/G; 31/G.2 Oct 1968; *In use*

Glenarm
Opened Jan 1961 D.333137, 31/C.4 U/G; *Closed Oct 1968*

Larne
Opened Dec 1957 D.383077, 31/D.1; resite to D.396039 Jan 1960; U/G 1961; 31/D.2 Oct 1968; *In use*

Randalstown
Opened Aug 1957 J.039938, 31/N.1 U/G; 31/D.3 Oct 1968; *In use*

Templepatrick
Opened Sept 1957 J.214879, 31/N.4 U/G; 31/G.1 Oct 1968; *In use*

Whitehead
Opened April 1946 J.479938, 31/D.2; resite to J.455918 Sept 1961; U/G Feb 1962; *Closed Oct 1968*

COUNTY ARMAGH

Armagh
Opened June 1957 H.911459, 31/H.3 U/G; 31/K.1 Oct 1968; *In use*

Lurgan
Opened Sept 1957 J.096597, 31/O.4; 31/G.3 Oct 1968; *In use*

Portadown
Opened May 1960 J.965577, 31/H.1 U/G; *Closed Oct 1968*

COUNTY DOWN

Ardglass
Opened Sept 1957 J.529349, 31/F.2 U/G; *Closed Oct 1968*

Ballynahinch
Opened Sept 1957 J.342493, 31/O.2 U/G; 31/L.1 Oct 1968; *In use*

Ballywalter
Opened June 1957 J.634659, 31/E.2 U/G; 31/H.2 Oct 1968; *In use*

Banbridge
Opened June 1957 J.150484, 31/H.2 U/G; 31/L.3 Oct 1968; *In use*

Donghadee/Groomsport
Opened June 1957 J.562826, 31/D.3 Donghadee; resite to J.528826 Jan 1961; U/G May 1961; renamed Groomsport Sept 1963; 31/H.1 Oct 1968; *In use*

Downpatrick
Opened Jan 1960 J.498448, 31/F.4 U/G; 31/L.2 Oct 1968; *In use*

Dundrum
Opened April 1959 J.385355, 31/F.3 U/G; *Closed Oct 1968*

Holywood
Opened June 1958 J.416774, 31/D.4; resite to J.515777 Sept 1960; U/G June 1961; *Closed Oct 1968*

Kilkeel
Opened Sept 1959 J.301146, 31/C.2 U/G; 31/K.2 Oct 1968; *In use*

Newry/Jerretts Pass
Opened Dec 1957 J.073322, 31/G.3 Newry; 31/K.3, renamed Jerretts Pass, Oct 1968; *In use*

Newtownards
Opened June 1958 J.478725, 31/E.1; resite to J.459748 Dec 1960; U/G Dec 1961; *Closed Oct 1968*

Portaferry
Opened Sept 1957 J.600492, 31/F.1 U/G; *Closed Oct 1968*

Rathfriland
Opened June 1957 J.184350, 31/G.1 U/G.; *Closed Oct 1968*

Saintfield/Carryduff
Opened Feb 1957 J.383626, 31/E.3 U/G; 31/H.3 Oct 1968; *In use*

COUNTY FERMANAGH

Enniskillen
Opened Sept 1957 H.264484, 31/K.3 U/G; 31/J.3 Oct 1968; *In use*

Lisnaskea
Opened Aug 1957 H.364343, 31/J.4 U/G; 31/J.2 Oct 1968; *In use*

Kesh
Opened Sept 1957 H.181672, 31/K.1 U/G; 31/J.1 Oct 1968; *In use*

COUNTY LONDONDERRY

Claudy
Opened Aug 1957 C.559097, 31/A.4 U/G; *Closed Oct 1968*

Coleraine
Opened Aug 1957 C.825338, 31/B.1 U/G; 31/A.1 Oct 1968; *In use*

Draperstown
Opened Sept 1957 H.762925, 31/M.4 U/G; 31/C.3 Oct 1968; *In use*

Dungiven
Opened June 1957 C.684071, 31/A.1 U/G; 31/C.2 Oct 1968; *In use*

Limavady
Opened June 1957 C.685217, 31/A.2 U/G; 31/A.3 Oct 1968; *In use*

Londonderry
Opened Aug 1957 C.400175, 31/A.1, U/G; 31/C.1 Oct 1968; *In use*

Maghera/Kilrea
Opened Sept 1957 C.879127, 31/M.1 Maghera; resite to C.982127 June 1961; U/G, renamed Kilrea, Feb 1962; 31/A.2 Oct 1968; *In use*

COUNTY TYRONE

Beragh
Opened Sept 1957 H.521666, 31/P.4 U/G; 31/E.2 Oct 1968; *In use*

Caledon
Opened June 1957 H.774432, 31/H.4, U/G; *Closed Oct 1968*

Clogher
Opened Dec 1957 H.547546, 31/J.2 U/G; 31/F.3 Oct 1968; *In use*

Cookstown
Opened Sept 1957 H.812796, 31/M.3, U/G; 31/F.1 Oct 1968; *In use*

Drumquin
Opened Sept 1957 H.333741, 31/L.3, U/G; 31/E.3 Oct 1968; *In use*

Dungannon
Opened Aug 1957 H.805639, 31/P.3, U/G; 31/F.2 Oct 1968; *In use*

Fivemiletown
Opened Aug 1957 H.409478, U/G; *Closed Oct 1968*

Kilskerry
Opened Aug 1957 H.296553, 31/J.1, U/G; *Closed Oct 1968*

Newtownstewart
Opened Sept 1957 H.403869, 31/L.2, U/G; 31/E.1 Oct 1968; *In use*

Index

The author would like to thank the following for providing material for the illustrations: Leonard Bridgman; K. J. Ralph; Group Captain W. Maydwell; F. J. Wheaton; G. Vincent; Ivo Peters; A. V. Cosden; John Blake; Bundesorchiv; Imperial War Museum; Associated Press; Aberdeen Journals Ltd.; Fox Photos; Central Press; Times and Post; Sport and General Press Agency.

Foreward to New Edition 1992

When the demand for a reprint of Attack Warning Red, with update pages, became apparent, I could not have foreseen that it would be a final chapter on the Royal Observer Corps in its nationwide form.

The Corps has lived through many changes but none so drastic or so unnecessarily sudden as the announcement of stand down in July 1991.

In this edition of Attack Warning Red, the 1975 text has been reproduced in its entirety and to this has been added a supplement, regrettably limited in extent due to cost considerations.

I have tried briefly to fill in the years 1975-1992 and present an overall listing of the Corps as it existed at stand down. It is hoped that this will provide a record for ex-members and for anyone in the future who is researching the remarkable history of the ROC.

Many members of the Corps have assisted with the preparation of this new edition. In particular, I would like to thank Air Commodore Mike Boddy, Observer Captain John Murphy and the staff at ROC headquarters. Derrick Ballington has drawn up the final Corps national map and collated the corrections and additions to the original edition. To all others who have helped, I extend my thanks.

Derek Wood

1992 Addendum

The Corps 1976 – 1992

The year 1976 can be described as a period of consolidation for the Royal Observer Corps, with various developments in procedures. In October Norwich, Lincoln, Edinburgh, Durham and York groups undertook an aircraft reporting trial for the RAF which proved highly successful and was continued in the following year. Six years later the Ministry of Defence decided not to proceed with the scheme.

To mark the Silver Jubilee of Her Majesty the Queen's accession in 1977, the Corps offered Her Majesty a silver model of the Elizabethan beacon lighter forming the centre-piece of the ROC badge. Members took part in numerous local celebrations and the Corps participated in the Royal Review of Reserve and Cadet Forces at Wembley Stadium.

In 1981 came the first results of a Home Defence Review which recognised the need to improve and update communications and equipment in use in UKWMO and the Emergency Control Network (ECN).

The Warning System was given first priority and by November of that year nearly all attack warning circuits, including those to carrier control points had been converted from emergency circuits to private wires. Sector and group controls had been completely re-equipped with modern push button keyboards and the installation of an improved loudspeaker telephone at posts, also operating over private wires instead of emergency circuits, had begun. This involved considerable re-clustering of posts within the groups and some transfer of posts from one group to another in order to obtain the most efficient and economical layout. New Burndept radio equipment had been installed in posts in the Maidstone group; other installations followed in groups to westward and northward until the whole of the UK was covered. Plans were also made for improving and completing radio links between groups.

With the post reclustering, a new system of designation was introduced. The post operational number was henceforth used for administrative as well as operational purposes, in the former case with the group number attached. For instance, Al Elstree became 7/60 Elstree.

New carrier receivers at posts were installed and a trial installation of a post ventilation fan was made in 1982 in No. 2 Group, soon followed by further units at two posts in each sector.

The posts themselves began to benefit from the re- equipment programme. In 1983/84 thermal linings for post floors were issued to keep out the cold which froze feet and legs, particularly during long night exercises. The term thermal lining was in itself amusing as it consisted of thick rubber belting obtained from the National Coal Board. The original task for the belting was transporting coal down the mine.

In 1981 the Scottish Home and Health Department at the request of the Director UKWMO had installed, as a trial, message switch equipment, initially at Dundee and subsequently at other groups. This equipment took the form of a micro-processor which routed messages automatically in conjunction with the existing teleprinter equipment, originally installed in the late 1960s. The Home Office realised the need to plan replacement for the ageing teleprinter system and to introduce equipment using more up-to-date technology. They, therefore, decided to introduce message switch (MSX) equipment working with visual display units and modern teleprinters capable of operating at higher speeds.

The first was installed at Maidstone and by February 1984 a further five installations had been made. Other installations proceeded apace so that by March of the following year, MSX was in use at all groups except No 31 Group Belfast (which followed in June). At this time, second private wire speech circuits were ordered for inter-group and inter-sector links. 1984 also saw a start made on the installation of a microwave radio highway for the ECN into which sector and group controls were to be linked.

In 1985/86 two new post instruments were issued, the PDRM 82 replacement for the Radiac Survey Meter No. 2 and the PDRM 82F replacement for the Fixed Survey Meter. Following these, in 1986/87, came a battery- powered electronic Fixed Survey Meter Trainer to replace the equipment which used a clockwork mechanism and celluloid pattern. The new FSMT used Electronically Programmable On-line Memory (EPROM). Up-to-date dosimeters with battery-powered transistorised charging units were also supplied.

To complete the post transformation, the ancient Villiers four–stroke engine–alternator sets, with their 12V output, were gradually to be replaced by higher capacity generators. At last post observers were really to see what they were doing! It was eventually hoped that the generator sets could be mounted above ground in a protective housing and operated from below ground. A further luxury was to have been black heat elements for warmth and cooking.

In July 1988 the first of a new generation of automated switchboards, known as SX200, was installed at Horsham and Oxford controls. These switchboards were computerised, with visual display units and typewriter keyboard. Using the national immediate dial system, the network thus had a countrywide private telephone network by March 1989 which had little or no operator intervention.

The first rumblings of possible drastic change for the Corps came with the Home Office ministerial review of UKWMO completed in December 1988, the recommendations of which were communicated to all ROC officers a year later.

In essence, the review foresaw a future warning system based on data gathering from unmanned sensors combined with automatic data processing. In the meantime, more emphasis would be placed on Regional Seats of Government and ultimately on local authorities. The final paragraph of the review presented a sober assessment of the real situation:

"The reviewers noted that consideration of change in field organisation and structure could only be taken forward if certain of the technical proposals were shown to be feasible, cost-effective and affordable; and that the development and implementation of such technical innovation would be a long process. Until then, and indeed up to the point where installation of any new equipment was completed and tested, the field organisation would continue to rely on the majority of the current arrangements - including existing instruments, communications methods and, most importantly of all, the existing structure of full- time and spare-time staff contingents which have supported warning and monitoring since its inception in its present form in the 1950s."

Over the years there had, at various times, been pressure by the Home Office for the ROC to be absorbed into UKWMO in a different form, thus losing its cherished identity, the colour of its uniform and links with the Royal Air Force. Fortunately these moves had come to nothing, as it was realised that they would result in wholesale resignations and a blight on recruiting.

As headquarters ROC was due to move from Bentley Priory owing to RAF plans for the site, it was proposed that the headquarters of UKWMO and the ROC should be co-located. In a progress report on the warning and monitoring review in June 1990 it was stated that possible co-location options had been identified at Cowley, Oxford, whence HQ UKWMO had removed, from Banbury some years earlier.

Headquarters ROC, in the meantime, had been actively searching for new roles to broaden the field of ROC operations throughout Home Defence activities. More particularly, trials were carried out with Corps volunteers assisting RAF Shortrange Air Defence (SHORAD) units equipped with Rapier missiles and in manning displays and communications cells with RAF stations' War Operations Centres and elsewhere in RAF passive defence roles.

1990 marked the fiftieth anniversary of the Battle of Britain and the Corps was involved in many events, shows and exhibitions around the UK in conjunction with the RAF. On Battle of Britain Day, September 15, 1990, there was a major parade and flypast of 168 aircraft at Buckingham Palace with representatives from all of the military and civilian organisations who were involved in the Battle. The Corps was represented by observers from the drill flights of several groups under the command of Obs Lt(W) J.C. Morris, while the banner bearer was Obs Lt D.R. Lee of 12 Group. The Corps was also represented at the service held in Westminster Abbey where the ROC provided ushers for the day.

For the RAF Benevolent Fund "Reach for the Sky" appeal in the same year, the Corps raised well in excess of £20,000 and put in some 5,000 man hours in support of RAF, RAFA and IAT charitable ventures. Throughout, this effort took priority over the Corps interests.

Another, and most important, celebration was also in the detailed planning stage, namely the Royal Review of the ROC by Her Majesty the Queen to mark the 50th anniversary of the approval of the title "Royal" in 1941 by King George VI.

Events, however, were taking place in Whitehall which would drastically affect the whole of the Corps and its future. Firm discussions on the review of warning and monitoring had been delayed, first by a further review of UK emergency planning and the all hazards approach to disaster management and then by the Gulf War.

At Bentley Priory it was anticipated that the final review outcome would be yet another reorganisation for the ROC and substantial reductions in numbers as had occurred in 1968. This would have been bad enough but the bolt from the blue which came on May 1 could not have been expected.

On May 1 the MoD and the Commandant were informed by the Home Office that the decrease in the perceived threat would allow the reshaping of the Warning and Monitoring function. Hence the UKWMO would be disbanded and the Home Office's requirement for the ROC as the field force of the UKWMO would lapse. This news could not be communicated to the Corps until the House of Commons was told - which took place on July 10, 1991. Most unfortunately, then the bulk of the Corps first learned of its fate from radio and television.

The Commandant and the Chief of Staff, Observer Captain Murphy, had fought the ROC corner through the review and countless other meetings. Now they had to fight again, as Air Commodore Boddy later put it to Area Commandants "In order that the Corps must be allowed to run down with dignity". He described the fate of the ROC as "a catastrophe which is soon to befall us".

They could and did, however, gain a respite. It was agreed with the Home Office and the Ministry of Defence that the Corps would cease active training at the end of July 1991 and would stand down in its operational role at the end of September, full-time staff continuing the run down until March 31, 1992. The ROC Royal Warrant and supporting regulations and legislation remained extant.

When the announcement was made on July 10, it came as a complete shock to the Corps as a whole. As if to add insult to injury, the Home Office public relations department told the media that both UKWMO and the ROC were being "disbanded" which was incorrect as regards the ROC which was being "stood down" - a world of difference in a word.

It was decided that, as a nationwide body, the ROC would go out with a bang and not a whimper as befitted its spirit.

On July 25, 1991, 2,000 observers from the four corners of the realm, together with distinguished guests, assembled at RAF Bentley Priory for a Royal Review and Garden Party. The Queen, accompanied by the Duke of Edinburgh, reviewed the Parade, a ceremony which was followed by the Consecration and Presentation of a new Royal Observer Corps Banner. Informal meetings with officers and observers in the gardens then took place. The close relations between the ROC and the RAF were underlined by the fly-past of a Spitfire, a Hurricane and a Lancaster of the Battle of Britain Memorial Flight.

On the penultimate day of the Corps' service, September 29, 320 officers and observers, representing every Area and Group, attended a service at St. Clement Danes in the Strand, the Central Church of the Royal Air Force. The Sovereign's Banner of the ROC, presented in 1966, was laid up and is now displayed in perpetuity, along with the Banners, Colours, Standards and Ensigns of the Royal Air Force.

While the ROC, as the field force of UKWMO, no longer exists, it is still a Corps in being. A full-time Observer Commander has been appointed as the Commanding Officer, with an Observer

Lieutenant as his deputy. They are attached to No. 11 Group RAF at Bentley Priory and will manage the 250-plus observers still in uniform and operating the Nuclear Reporting Cells (NRCs) at certain armed forces headquarters, such as Strike Command. This command element will also keep alive liaison with the Royal Observer Corps Association (referred to elsewhere in these pages), TAVRA, local authorities, etc.

It is expected that, as the Ministry of Defence completes its plans under "Options for Change", there may be further requirements for the services of ROC personnel in uniform for tasks such as outlined earlier in this chapter.

The Royal Observer Corps lives on!

Fifty years ago, my father granted you the title "Royal Observer Corps" in recognition of your contribution to victory in the Battle of Britain. It so happens that it is also fifty years since women joined the Corps. The master-mind of the Battle of Britain was Lord Dowding, and it is fitting that this anniversary should be celebrated here at Bentley Priory, which was both his and the Corps' headquarters in those critical days.

That battle was only the beginning of the Corps' invaluable services during the last War. Apart from the routine reporting of enemy aircraft, the Corps played a most important part in the rescue of many Fighter and Bomber Command crews and was instrumental in the saving of the lives of many aircrew.

Later on, the Corps had an active part in our defences against the Flying Bomb campaign and it also provided a large force of Seaborne Observers in support of the Normandy landings.

The demand for your services did not end with the War. In addition to supporting the Royal Air Force, the Corps was given the task of reporting nuclear incidents to the Home Office. That was during what became known as the Cold War. That War has now also, thankfully, come to an end and there has been a welcome reduction in international tensions.

While no one can predict what the future holds, the immediate threats which gave the Corps the reason for its existence have receded. This means an honourable Stand Down for the Corps after sixty-six years of dedicated service.

When I presented the first Banner in 1966, I said I was proud and happy to be opening a new chapter in the history of the Corps. In presenting you with this new Banner I am aware that there will now be mixed feelings, but foremost you must feel a deep sense of pride in the knowledge that all members have done their duty with selfless devotion.

It will be many years before the "old comrades" can no longer pass on the stories and traditions of the Corps, and even then the record will remain and this Banner will continue to represent the volunteer spirit which has been such a fundamental part of the philosophy of the Corps ever since it was founded.

This Banner salutes sixty-six years of dedicated voluntary service and it will ensure that that service will never be forgotten. I have had the honour to be your Air Commodore-in-Chief for the last thirty-eight years, and I want to thank each one of you most warmly for all the time and effort you have given to the Royal Observer Corps. I offer you all my very best wishes for the future.

25th July, 1991

Her Majesty the Queen's address to the Parade
at the Royal Review of the Royal Observer Corps
at RAF Bentley Priory, July 25th, 1991.

Royal Observer Corps Association

Early in 1986, the Commandant ROC sent a letter to all groups, proposing the establishment of a national association for past and serving members. The name Royal Observer Corps Association (ROCA) was adopted and a Provisional Committee held several meetings at Bentley Priory to work out a constitution, which was eventually accepted by all the group associations that had been formed.

The Provisional Committee gave itself a year in office and thereafter a Central Committee was set up with members nominated from the existing ROC Areas. Observer Captain Gerald Brown, then Assistant Commandant, became Chairman and former Observer Commander Geoffrey Paine the Honorary Secretary.

After a great deal of hard work for ROCA, both have now retired. The new Chairman is former Observer Captain Joyce Shrubbs and Honorary Secretary former Observer Captain Michael Marks.

Across the country meetings and social functions are regularly held. In 1990 and 1991 ROCA reunions were held at Pontins, Blackpool, attracting some 600 members and relatives.

With the announcement of the ROC stand down, the ROCA Constitution has had to be changed in several respects, including the position of President, previously held by the Corps Commandant. Membership of ROCA has risen sharply and now stands at over 5,500.

ROCA will have an important role to play in the future if the MoD, or some other Authority, requires volunteers and needs to recruit people with certain types of expertise which only former ROC members possess. ROCA would be the focus for contacts.

The Association will also have a key part to play in the activities of the ROC Benevolent Fund and each group association will have an Honorary Benevolent Fund Officer.

Royal Observer Corps Seaborne Association

The late Obs. Lt. A.J.T. Court of No 12 Group launched the idea of the Seaborne Association in 1986 to improve communication between those of the ROC who served on the D-Day invasion fleet and to maintain the friendship and camaraderie of these days. In addition, it was intended to preserve and extend the records of the Seaborne unit. During the six years since the Association was formed, 45 members have joined, plus a handful of honorary members, but sadly 12 have since died. One Seaborne member, Observer Wally Shonfield of 2 Group, was still serving at stand down and attended the Royal Review.

Annual reunions are held and a quarterly newsletter published. The President is ex-ROC Commandant Air Vice Marshal George Black and the Committee consists of Peter Jay and Derek James, the latter being Honorary Secretary.

ROC/LMK

Over the years very close links have been forged between the Royal Observer Corps and the Luftmeldekorpset (LMK), the Danish Ground Observer Corps. The connection began in July 1971 with a visit of Danish officers to Lincoln Group. In the following year, a 23-strong party, representing HQ ROC and the five ROC areas, flew to Denmark in an RAF Andover on a fact finding mission.

It was fitting that the party was led by the then Commandant, Air Commodore E.B. Sismore, who had been awarded the Danish Order of Dannebrog for his part in the raid on the Gestapo headquarters in Copenhagen in March 1945.

In 1974 the ROC was invited to send a team to Denmark to compete in an aircraft recognition contest. A return match was arranged for the following year when the LMK crossed the Channel to visit the ROC. In 1976, the LMK presented a Challenge Shield which was competed for annually in alternate countries, except in 1980. When the ROC team for the 1991 contest took off from Northolt in May, on board a 32 Squadron Andover, they little imagined that it would be the last such event.

At stand down, the Shield had been competed for on sixteen occasions and the score stood at ROC 9, LMK 7.

Informal visits between members of the LMK, and now ex- members of the ROC, continue and the link will be maintained, albeit on an individual basis.

The ROC Museums

Opened in 1980, the Royal Observer Corps Museum at Winchester is an important element in keeping the history and traditions of the Corps alive.

As with most things connected with the ROC, the effort has been entirely voluntary and has resulted in a unique collection of display items and records which is continuously being extended.

Located at what was the HQ of Winchester Group, in a wartime ROC Centre, the Museum is being considered by the Hampshire County Council for support at a permanent location. The Museum curator is Mr. Neville Cullingford.

Other homes for ROC memorabilia, equipment and records will be the RAF Museums at Duxford and Hendon and the Museum of Flight at East Fortune Airfield near Edinburgh.

ROC Training Camp Venues 1976 – 1991

1976 Little Rissington, 1977 Cosford, 1978 Cosford, 1979 Cosford, 1980 West Raynham, 1981 West Raynham, 1982 West Raynham, 1983 Scampton, 1984 Scampton, 1985 Leeming, 1986 University of Newcastle-upon-Tyne, 1987 Waddington, 1988 Waddington, 1989 Watton, 1990 Watton, 1991 (Royal Review).

Location of ROC Posts at Stand Down, September 1991, with National Grid References

No 1 Group MAIDSTONE

10 Borough Green TQ 613573. 11 Knockholt TQ 472615. 15 Hoo TQ 779735. 16 Eastchurch TQ 993708. 17 Rodmersham Green TQ 898613. 20 Minster TR 316656. 21 Kingsdown TR 376491. 22 Barham TR 217509. 23 Herne Bay TR 171649. 25 Linton TQ 764510. 26 Cranbrook TQ 763355. 27 Penshurst TQ 526470. 30 Pluckley TQ 921459. 31 Wye TR 055460. 32 Ham Street TR 007332. 35 Frant TQ 591357. 36 Chiddingly TQ 548134. 37 Crowborough TQ 506295. 40 Ticehurst TQ 676285. 41 Pevensey TQ 646027. 42 Cuckmere Haven TV 495979. 45 Northiam TQ 824253. 46 Fairlight TQ 861112. 50 Folkestone TR 205382. 51 Dungeness TR 025198. 52 Dymchurch TR 105316.

No 2 Group HORSHAM

10 Weybridge TQ 081661. 11 Clandon TQ 051507. 12 Camberley SU 911592. 13 Windsor SU 972771. 15 Dulwich TQ 341726. 16 Wallington TQ 288622. 20 Herriard SU 673446. 21 Farnham SU 837495. 22 Bordon SU 794339. 25 Cranleigh TQ 018357. 26 Horsham TQ 179297. 27 Fernhurst SU 898284. 30 Redhill TQ 295479. 31 West Hoathly TQ 366326. 32 Holmwood TQ 172456. 35 Froxfield Green SU 727258. 36 Hambledon SU 649146. 37 Cheriton SU 582281. 40 Havant SU 685065. 41 Singleton SU 882129. 42 Selsey SZ 848947. 45 Pulborough TQ 065195. 46 Steyning TQ 175103. 47 Littlehampton SU 996033. 50 Cuckfield TQ 306244. 51 Lewes TQ 393113. 53 Brighton TQ 329045.

No 3 Group OXFORD

10 Broadway SP 115364. 11 Inkberrow SP 011569. 12 Bidford on Avon SP 111521. 15 Edge Hill SP 373468. 16 Brackley SP 584374. 17 Bloxham SP 451345. 20 Stow on the Wold SP 192266. 21 Andoversford SP 049219. 25 Long Compton SP 297310. 26 Enstone SP 372239. 27 Hailey SP 347129. 28 Carterton SP 251072. 30 Boars Hill SP 486029. 31 Middleton Stoney SP 543238. 32 Wantage SU 404870. 35 Whitchurch SP 795209. 36 Cheddington SP 916170. 37 Thame SP 721059. 38 Buckingham SP 703323. 40 North Cerney SP 029081. 41 Cricklade SU 071919. 42 Kemble ST 967963. 45 Ashbury SU 271847. 46 Wroughton SU 142795. 50 Watlington SU 711936. 51 Great Missenden SP 924022. 52 Beaconsfield SU 924893.

No 4 Group COLCHESTER

10 Cherry Hinton TL 493546. 11 Bottisham TL 562623. 12 Kentford TL 714653. 15 Bacton TM 062668. 16 Beyton TL 943626. 17 Bury St Edmunds TL 829647. 20 Stradbroke TM 237743. 21 Westleton TM 445692. 22 Wickham Market TM 305551. 25 Wickhambrook TL 752540. 26 Great

Dunmow TL 646246. 27 Henham TL 548282. 28 Linton TL 554465. 30 Sudbury TL 885434. 31 Earls Colne TL 857282. 32 Clare TL 771439. 35 Langham TM 009305. 36 Hadleigh TM 035425. 37 Tendring TM 144247. 40 Crowfield TM 159562. 41 Alderton TM 347408. 42 Woolverstone TM 195373. 45 Good Easter TL 629117. 46 Billericay TQ 670916. 47 Chipping Ongar TL 559057. 50 Woodham Ferrers TQ 798988. 51 Wickham Bishop TL 855127. 52 Bradwell on Sea TM 011074. 55 Rainham TQ 549829. 57 Chigwell TQ 434947. 60 Leigh TQ 835873. 61 Foulness TR 004929.

No 6 Group NORWICH

10 Middleton TF 672159. 11 Brancaster TF 772428. 12 Dersingham TF 695319. 15 Gressenhall TF 955188. 16 South Creake TF 851351. 17 Melton Constable TG 041378. 20 West Beckham TG 140388. 21 Mundesley TG 301367. 22 Aylsham TG 187253. 25 Upwell TF 504022. 26 March TL 404949. 27 Parson Drove TF 379098. 30 Narborough TF 741072. 31 Watton TF 929040. 32 Downham Market TF 601035. 35 Brundall TG 343082. 36 Honingham TG 094102. 37 Hellesdon TG 201113. 38 Stalham TG 392251. 40 Sutton TL 441801. 41 Southery TL 616947. 42 Soham TL 601773. 45 Garboldisham TM 015816. 46 Lakenheath TL 727826. 47 Mundford TL 807952. 48 Thetford TL 864854. 50 Diss TM 115810. 51 Wymondham TM 126988. 52 Bungay TM 322865. 55 Fleggburgh TG 460114. 56 Lowestoft TM 546959. 57 Barnby TM 462878.

No 7 Group BEDFORD

10 Cold Overton SK 806097. 11 Sutton Bassett SP 777907. 12 Clipston SP 703826. 15 Duddington SK 991007. 16 Market Deeping TF 142082. 17 Whittlesey TL 285981. 20 Sawtry TL 157841. 21 Kettering SP 861752. 22 Benefield SP 960899. 25 St Ives TL 278688. 26 Ramsey TL 275849. 27 Willingham TL 412651. 30 Brixworth SP 757709. 31 Earls Barton SP 870648. 32 Duston SP 713604. 35 Olney SP 892457. 36 Pavenham SP 973557. 37 Riseley TL 047626. 40 Sandy TL 152495. 41 Arrington TL 321502. 42 Ampthill TL 027378. 45 Great Offley TL 136271. 46 Ashwell TL 268385. 47 Markyate TL 058155. 50 Brent Pelham TL 425315. 51 Much Hadham. TL 436198. 52 Hertford TL 293146. 55 Kings Langley TL 067019. 56 Welwyn TL 207111. 60 Elstree TQ 181948. 61 Bowes Park TQ 301904. 62 Northolt TQ 093851.

No 8 Group COVENTRY

10 Stocksbridge SK 253971. 11 Wickersley SK 472915. 12 Beauchief SK 327813. 15 Buxton SK 089756. 16 Hartington SK 129600. 20 Ashover SK 358637. 21 Whitwell SK 529771. 22 Farnsfield SK 635585. 25 Uttoxeter SK 112361. 26 Rugeley SK 061188. 27 Ipstones SK 017501. 30 Ambergate SK 354512. 31 Melbourne SK 365249. 32 Brassington SK 227553. 35 Burton Joyce SK 643448. 36 Clifton SK 540336. 37 Hucknall SK 515491. 40 Harlaston SK 196097. 41 Shenstone SK 116053. 42 Church Gresley SK 279179. 45 Rearsby SK 663137. 46 Birstall SK 590107. 47 Hathern SK 495218. 50 Shirley SP 129765. 51 Frankley SP 002792. 52 Erdington SP 102917. 55 Stoke Golding SP 398955. 56 Fleckney SP 638932. 57 Lutterworth SP 520855. 60 Meriden SP 262825. 61 Barford SP 288598. 62 Hasely Knob SP 259710. 65 Wolston SP 419747. 66 Daventry SP 587626. 67 Chipping Warden SP 505519.

No 9 Group YEOVIL

10 Shirwell SS 565403. 11 Torrington SS 530240. 12 Croyde SS 437383. 15 Lynton SS 726482. 16 South Molton SS 713246. 20 Exford SS 839379. 21 Dunster ST 005444. 22 Holford ST 162429. 25

Shepton Mallet ST 605428. 26 Bradford on Avon ST 812615. 27 Frome ST 765485. 30 Kingston St Mary ST 233304. 31 Wellington ST 152234. 32 Bampton SS 973187. 35 Chard ST 309091. 36 Chilton Polden ST 386382. 37 Langport ST 418285. 40 Yetminister ST 599102. 41 Crewkerne ST 429072. 42 Marston Magna ST 590255. 43 Templecombe ST 701216. 45 Mere ST 803350. 46 Fontmell Magna ST 865181. 50 Kentisbeare ST 053070. 51 Seaton ST 234911. 52 Sidmouth SY 110868. 55 Buckland Newton ST 680050. 56 Dorchester SY 681911. 57 Portland Bill SY 681712. 58 Burton Bradstock SY 480907. 60 Worth Matravers SY 984784. 61 West Lulworth SY 819799. 62 Bere Regis SY 857947.

No 10 Group EXETER

10 Holsworthy SS 350038. 11 Kilkhampton SS 257134. 15 Winkleigh SS 619094. 16 Lydford SX 527856. 20 Stockleigh Pomeroy SS 885032. 21 Witheridge SS 767114. 25 Callington SX 368692. 26 Otterham SX 148885. 27 Launceston SX 334842. 30 Drewsteignton SX 712909. 31 Pinhoe SX 996933. 32 Christow SX 829829. 35 St Columb Major SW 923622. 36 Mitchell SW 841537. 37 St Agnes SW 727486. 40 St Breward SX 098775. 41 Par SX 104556. 42 Bodmin SX 068664. 45 Millbrook SX 433515. 46 Downderry SX 314547. 47 Liskeard SX 257648. 50 Modbury SX 677547. 51 Plymstock SX 498518. 52 Bere Alston SX 455652. 53 Sharpitor SX 557699. 55 Ashburton SX 754683. 56 Torquay SX 926698. 57 Brixham SX 945566. 58 Strete SX 837469. 60 Madron SW 438334. 61 Helston SW 649273. 62 The Lizard SW 712121. 65 Penryn SW 759354. 66 Mevagissey SX 006423. 67 Veryan SW 920374.

No 12 Group BRISTOL

10 Erwood SO 094429. 11 Brecon SO 047270. 15 Peterchurch SO 362394. 16 Pontrilas SO 387268. 17 Hay SO 224433. 18 New Radnor SO 217608. 20 Leominster SO 514577. 21 Pencombe SO 618531. 22 Burghill SO 483451. 23 Lyonshall SO 325563. 25 Upper Sapey SO 709626. 26 Ombersley SO 848637. 27 Upton on Severn SO 873382. 28 Powick SO 828518. 30 Trumpet SO 681372. 31 Lea SO 672220. 32 Harewood End SO 528274. 35 Ynysddu ST 197944. 36 Mountain Ash ST 055967. 37 Merthyr Tydfil SO 028069. 40 St Biravels SO 560039. 41 Abergavenny SO 323145. 42 Llantilio Crossenny SO 404141. 45 Dursley ST 733996. 46 Stroud SO 831086. 47 Leighterton ST 830893. 51 Llanishen ST 189851. 55 Usk ST 412991. 56 Penhow ST 414903. 57 Newport ST 288902. 60 Little Sodbury ST 767838. 61 Marshfield ST 773729. 62 Clevedon ST 408720. 63 Hallen ST 552800. 65 Clutton ST 642600. 66 West Harptree ST 546561. 67 Bleadon ST 345578.

No 13 Group SOUTH WALES

10 Crosswood SN 679723. 11 Tregaron SN 677598. 12 Llanon SN 518668. 13 Ponterwyd SN 753820. 15 Llananno SO 097745. 16 Llandrindod Wells SO 061602. 17 Llangammarch Wells SN 928476. 20 Newcastle Emlyn SN 310418. 21 Cardigan SN 165443. 25 Lampeter SN 581481. 26 Pencader SN 451371. 27 Newquay SN 383601. 30 Maenclochog SN 070280. 31 Broadhaven SM 859132. 32 Croesgoch SM 822301. 35 Narbeth SN 111124. 36 St Twynnells SR 942975. 37 Haverfordwest SN 013155. 40 Kidwelly SN 416065. 41 Laugharne SN 299099. 42 Llanboidy SN 206233. 43 Carmarthen SN 411213. 45 Dryslwyn SN 543214. 46 Talley SN 636325. 47 Llandovery SN 765354. 48 Amman Valley (Gwaun-cae-Gurwen) SN 699119. 50 Penclawdd SS 539954. 51 Abercrave SN 814129. 52 Clydach SN 676005. 55 Pencoed SS 963791. 56 Porthcawl SS 808775. 57 Maesteg SS 847908.

No 14 Group WINCHESTER

10 Devizes SU 033601. 11 Bratton ST 921509. 12 Chippenham ST 903718. 15 Great Bedwyn SU 283653. 16 Avebury SU 104692. 20 Streatley SU 574801. 21 Shiplake SU 759778. 22 Bradfield SU 602713. 25 Broadchalke SU 028254. 26 Wylye SU 006369. 27 Amesbury SU 160387. 28 Alderbury SU 207248. 30 Newbury SU 451651. 31 Hurstbourne Tarrant SU 376527. 32 Grateley SU 268409. 35 Stratfield Turgis SU 702590. 36 Kingsworthy SU 495337. 37 Overton SU 521497. 40 Fordingbridge SU 168142. 41 Christchurch SZ 143954. 42 Witchampton SU 005056. 45 Botley SU 498117. 46 Stone Point SZ 457986. 47 Lyndhurst SU 289089. 48 Stockbridge SU 381353. 50 Freshwater SZ 353858. 51 Newport SZ 518891. 52 Niton SZ 508761.

No 15 Group LINCOLN

10 Scotter SE 896009. 11 Eastoft SE 805155. 12 Winterton SE 933189. 15 North Kelsey TA 053014. 16 Wootton TA 077152. 17 Roxton TA 183117. 20 Burgh on Bain TF 214841. 21 Fulstow TF 340971. 25 Louth TF 337848. 26 Mablethorpe TF 502863. 27 Alford TF 410741. 30 Blyth SK 635861. 31 Rossington SK 626970. 32 Lindholme SE 691075. 35 East Markham SK 729737. 36 Wiseton SK 756917. 37 Dunham on Trent SK 822738. 40 Market Rasen TF 090876. 41 Navenby SK 983547. 42 Hackthorn SK 997790. 45 Baumber TF 229734. 46 Coningsby TF 259564. 47 Billinghay TF 133562. 48 Bardney TF 125689. 50 Little Steeping TF 426617. 51 Skegness TF 556656. 52 Boston TF 331486. 55 Newark SK 756572. 56 Claypole SK 850487. 57 Harby SK 745306. 60 Grantham SK 902330. 61 Billingborough TF 106336. 62 Buckminster SK 873224. 65 Quadring Eaudyke TF 237335. 66 Holbeach TF 364263. 67 Bourne TF 096227.

No 16 Group SHREWSBURY

10 Helsby SJ 493754. 11 Altringham SJ 715889. 15 Knutsford SJ 748794. 16 Poynton SJ 932827. 17 Rushton Spencer SJ 940632. 20 Overton SJ 375410. 21 Malpas SJ 495480. 25 Silverdale SJ 815477. 26 Audlem SJ 661448. 27 Middlewich SJ 708663. 30 Bomere Heath SJ 485201. 31 Minsterley SJ 371053. 32 Nesscliff SJ 387187. 35 Market Drayton SJ 660346. 36 Oakengates SJ 693101. 37 Great Bolas SJ 630210. 40 Standon SJ 818344. 41 Weston on Trent SJ 981279. 42 Gnosall SJ 842211. 45 Upton Magna SJ 549125. 46 Much Wenlock SO 614986. 47 Church Stretton SO 465929. 50 Cheslyn Hay SJ 969081. 51 Brierley Hill SO 916896. 52 Stottesdon SO 683826. 53 Pattingham SO 817971. 55 Ludlow SO 504744. 56 Knighton SO 300716. 57 Lydbury North SO 359859.

No 17 Group NORTH WALES

10 Amlwch SH 439935. 11 Marianglas SH 502838. 12 Bangor SH 579712. 13 Newborough SH 418653. 15 Llandudno SH 776815. 16 Pentrefoelas SH 872512. 17 Capel Curig SH 720583. 20 Prestatyn SJ 079817. 21 Llanfair Talhaiarn SH 929700. 25 Neston SJ 316796. 26 Aldford SJ 417586. 27 Holywell SJ 186751. 30 Chwilog SH 439388. 31 Aberdaron SH 169265. 32 Nevin SH 275408. 33 Pen-y-Groes SH 475534. 35 Llanbedr SH 586262. 36 Beddgelert SH 583487. 37 Trawsfynydd SH 713358. 40 Corwen SJ 051453. 41 Llanuwchllyn SH 879293. 45 Llangollen SJ 216429. 46 Ruthin SJ 112599. 47 Brymbo SJ 284533. 50 Tywyn SH 593042. 51 Dolgellau SH 728186. 52 Aberangell SH 853105. 53 Machynlleth SH 741009. 55 Llanymynech SJ 264213. 56 Llanwyddyn SJ 025188. 57 Llanrhaiadar SJ 131261. 60 Newtown SO 114923. 61 Llanidloes SN 947847. 62 Carno SN 956970. 63 Welshpool SJ 227087.

No 20 Group YORK

10 Northallerton SE 384912. 11 Bedale SE 271887. 15 Birdsall SE 861673. 16 Kirby Moorside SE 666909. 17 Pickering SE 794844. 20 Bridlington TA 167710. 21 Skipsea TA 176548. 22 Langtoft TA 002663. 23 Wykeham SE 965842. 25 Buckden SD 936782. 26 Grassington SD 994637. 27 Settle SD 814629. 28 Horton in Ribblesdale SD 810713. 30 North Stainley SE 270764. 31 Kirby Hill SE 374696. 32 Darley SE 218587. 33 Middlesmoor SE 086756. 35 Pocklington SE 843507. 36 Tockwith SE 452522. 37 Brandsby SE 572720. 38 Strensall SE 637601. 40 Guiseley SE 202442. 41 Thornton SE 092333. 42 Keighley SE 037424. 43 Gargrave SD 937529. 45 Camblesforth SE 649263. 47 Fulford SE 619499. 50 Holme on Spalding Moor SE 822387. 51 Beverley TA 009385. 52 Gilberdyke SE 838275. 55 Tunstall TA 311319. 56 Keyingham TA 253244. 57 Skirlaugh TA 135402. 60 Holmfirth SE 156043. 61 Sowerby Bridge SE 056209. 62 Heckmondwike SE 212251. 65 Barwick in Elmet SE 388366. 66 Upton SE 458147. 67 Darton SE 319122.

No 21 Group PRESTON

10 Ramsey SC 451963. 11 Douglas SC 405781. 12 Castletown SC 292692. 13 Peel SC 256848. 15 Flookburgh SD 368752. 16 Barrow in Furness SD 172690. 17 Broughton in Furness SD 218889. 20 Kendal SD 525917. 21 Dent SD 765877. 25 Kirkby Lonsdale SD 603787. 26 High Bentham SD 687693. 27 Forton SD 496504. 28 Heysham SD 409601. 30 Fleetwood SD 325482. 31 Lytham SD 335274. 35 Longridge SD 621389. 36 Catforth SD 455368. 40 Padiham SD 797347. 41 Dunsop Bridge SD 661496. 42 Bolton by Bowland SD 775501. 45 Burscough SD 427105. 46 St Helens SJ 487945. 47 Woodvale SD 304095. 50 Brinscall SD 593230. 51 Turton SD 724143. 52 Atherton SD 692044. 55 Bacup SD 865228. 56 Glossop SK 046947. 57 Prestwich SD 832048.

No 22 Group CARLISLE

10 Parkgate NY 045909. 11 Dumfries NX 983752. 12 Auldgirth NX 916873. 15 Steele Road NY 518935. 16 Langholm NY 366858. 17 Eskdalemuir NY 240981. 20 Bellingham NY 847838. 21 Great Whittington NZ 008714. 22 Kielder NY 631919. 25 Cummertrees NY 144661. 26 Kirkbean NX 975599. 27 Kirtlebridge NY 217732. 30 Dalston NY 380484. 31 Caldbeck NY 338391. 32 Wigton NY 252493. 33 Carlisle NY 384592. 35 Roadhead NY 519748. 36 Gilsland NY 641660. 37 Brampton NY 529604. 40 Alston NY 724462. 41 Whitfield NY 779576. 42 Haydon Bridge NY 838658. 43 Slaley NY 973579. 45 Allonby NX 087431. 46 Eskdale NY 134002. 47 Whitehaven NX 986189. 48 Workington NY 009295. 50 Penrith NY 504291. 51 Threlkeld NY 307244. 52 Bassenthwaite NY 229328. 55 Culgaith NY 614295. 56 Appleby NY 674200. 57 Kirby Stephen NY 779088. 58 Bampton NY 521175. 60 Tebay NY 619046. 61 Hawkshead SD 351978. 62 Grasmere NY 332108.

No 23 Group DURHAM

10 Bamburgh NU 165350. 11 Embleton NU 226224. 12 Hart Heugh NT 986253. 13 Millfield NT 931346. 15 Otterburn NY 909951. 16 Byrness NT 782031. 20 Shilbottle NU 191081. 21 Harbottle NT 936057. 22 Whittingham NU 073114. 25 Stannington NZ 212802. 26 Hartburn NZ 099856. 27 Longhorsley NZ 142944. 28 Ellington NZ 285925. 30 Castleside NZ 086483. 31 Prudhoe NZ 092623. 32 Ponteland NZ 156695. 33 Whitley Bay NZ 351713. 35 Tow Lane NZ 134384. 36 Westerton NZ 245312. 37 Wearhead NY 854388. 38 Stanhope NY 992407. 40 Sacriston NZ 223480. 41 Easington NZ 430468. 45 Woodland NZ 050244. 46 Croft NZ 309070. 47 Cotherstone NY 996177. 50 Sedgefield NZ 364302. 51 Hartlepool NZ 485337. 52 Sadberge NZ 338166. 55 Great

Ayton NZ 544121. 56 Redcar NZ 590252. 57 Chop Gate NE 557999. 60 Castleton NZ 681075. 61 Hinderwell NZ 794178. 62 Goathland NZ 839014. 65 Richmond NZ 172018. 66 Aysgarth SE 006878. 67 Hawes SD 868897. 68 Reeth SE 049985.

No 24 Group EDINBURGH

10 Kelty NT 148915. 11 Dysart NT 292954. 12 Eile NO 484003. 15 West Calder NT 028625. 16 Slamannan NS 860732. 17 Bonnybridge NS 815807. 18 Bannockburn NS 819898. 19 Bo'ness NT 004794. 20 Dalkeith NT 361659. 21 Penicuik NT 235576. 22 West Linton NT 138523. 23 Turnhouse NT 177735. 25 North Berwick NT 561844. 26 Cockburnspath NT 746726. 27 Garvald NT 579704. 30 Carluke NS 866487. 31 Abington NS 921251. 32 Douglas NS 844314. 35 Forth NS 933553. 36 Tweedsmuir NT 095247. 37 Beattock NT 085035. 38 Thankerton NS 971376. 40 Lauder NT 526467. 41 Traquair NT 328343. 42 Peebles NT 244413. 43 Oxton NT 478575. 45 St Abbs Head NT 873683. 46 Greenfield NT 947585. 47 Norham NT 905463. 48 Duns NT 752516. 50 Ashkirk NT 502197. 51 Jedburgh NT 636196. 52 Teviotdale NT 395042. 53 Yarrow NT 302247. 55 Gordon NT 688437. 56 Kelso NT 744374. 57 Morebattle NT 778248.

No 25 Group AYR

10 Lochgilphead NR 850859. 11 Minard NR 976964. 21 Tarbert NR 855682. 15 Alexandria NS 404798. 16 Arrochar NN 296053. 20 Kilchattan Bay NS 082561. 22 Gourock NS 238771. 23 Skelmorlie NS 195649. 25 Bridge of Weir NS 377654. 26 Killearn NS 529866. 27 Kirkintilloch NS 670756. 28 Glasgow NS 531654. 30 Machrihanish NR 667224. 31 Port Ellen NR 323517. 32 Carradale NR 813389. 35 Kildonan NS 038218. 36 Brodick NS 032352. 40 Kilmarnock NS 451396. 41 West Kilbride NS 207488. 42 Dunlop NS 401495. 43 Darvel NS 572379. 45 Barhead NS 493593. 46 Airdrie NS 777669. 47 Strathaven NS 708442. 48 Gilbertfield NS 644581. 50 Turnberry NS 211059. 51 Girvan NX 189950. 52 Ballantrae NX 084815. 55 Joppa NS 419195. 56 Muirkirk NS 693280. 57 New Cumnock NS 614133. 58 Straiton NS 381043. 60 Ervie NX 006713. 61 New Luce NX 177662. 62 Sandhead NX 079528. 65 Kirkcowan NX 322612. 66 Bargrennan NX 347772. 67 Port William NX 343431. 70 Carsphairn NX 562934. 71 Dalry NX 632814. 72 Parton NX 689705. 73 Castle Douglas NX 768624. 74 Kirkcudbright NX 704517. 75 Sanquhar NS 784105. 76 Thornhill NX 883940.

No 28 Group DUNDEE

10 Methven NO 014264. 11 Kinloch Rannoch NN 660579. 12 Aberfeldy NN 858489. 13 Dunkeld NO 035433. 15 Alyth NO 234475. 16 Blair Atholl NN 868665. 17 Kirkmichael NO 091596. 20 Cortachy NO 383601. 21 Letham NO 526499. 22 Glamis NO 371470. 23 Clova NO 341717. 25 Edzell NO 594691. 26 Tarfside NO 492801. 27 St Cyrus NO 752647. 30 Dunning NO 018141. 31 Comrie NN 768204. 32 Killin NN 575332. 35 Newbigging NO 513377. 36 Abernytc NO 257324. 37 Inverkeilor NO 684501. 38 Arbroath NO 622399. 40 Braco NN 828088. 41 Kippen NS 634942. 42 Callander NN 638088. 43 Strathyre NN 563201. 45 Scone NO 143272. 46 Milnathort NO 097038. 50 St Andrews NO 526155. 51 Cupar NO 385149. 52 Newburgh NO 242185.

No 29 Group ABERDEEN

10 Sumburgh HU 392127. 11 Walls HU 236491. 12 Voe HU 439726. 13 Lerwick HU 447424. 15 Kirkwall HY 411116. 16 Deerness HY 569073. 17 Stromness HY 231099. 20 Carron NJ 235441. 21 Glenferness NH 963447. 22 Findhorn NJ 038649. 23 Elgin NJ 195608. 25 Drummuir NJ 382444. 26

Tomintoul NJ 164182. 27 Buckie NJ 409649. 28 Grange NJ 521527. 30 Turriff NJ 730505. 31 Huntly NJ 546385. 32 Cabrach NJ 380310. 33 Aberchirder NJ 619563. 34 Macduff NJ 708644. 35 Cruden Bay NK 098356. 36 Strichen NJ 948561. 37 St Fergus NK 102506. 40 Grantown-on-Spey NJ 038282. 41 Dalwhinnie NN 637860. 42 Kingussie NH 772011. 43 Aviemore NH 898136. 45 Methlick NJ 870378. 46 Pitcaple NJ 718261. 47 Alford NJ 565163. 48 Strathdon NJ 350132. 50 Udny Station NJ 912243. 51 Portlethen NO 923961. 52 Echt NJ 740052. 53 Kintore NJ 796155. 55 Tarland NJ 487035. 56 Ballater NO 366954. 57 Braemar NO 143910. 60 Stonehaven NO 868829. 61 Auchenblae NO 728784. 62 Feughside NO 641922.

No 30 Group INVERNESS

10 Stornoway NB 448325. 11 Lochboisdale NF 771203. 12 Lochmaddy NF 914688. 13 Harris NB 154002. 15 Melvich NC 875655. 16 Kinbrace NC 856312. 17 Altnaharra NC 569358. 18 Durness NC 394678. 19 Tongue NC 599564. 20 Barrock ND 205765. 21 John O'Groats ND 405732. 22 Latheron ND 203334. 23 Watten ND 246541. 25 Stoer NC 042275. 26 Scourie NC 149448. 27 Elphin NC 218119. 28 Ullapool NH 124939. 29 Gairloch NG 797778. 30 Dunbeath ND 124237. 31 Brora NC 886022. 32 Lairg NC 583060. 35 Fearn NH 864760. 36 Tain NH 795816. 37 Ardgay NH 593907. 40 Portree NG 472452. 41 Uig NG 406635. 45 Dingwall NH 555603. 46 Achnasheen NH 176589. 47 Garve NH 392628. 48 Invergordon NH 683692. 50 Broadford NG 646233. 51 Lochcarron NG 946444. 52 Kyle of Lochalsh NG 779309. 53 Ardvasar NG 655065. 55 Beauly NH 519472. 56 Drumnadrochit NH 505292. 57 Gorthleck NH 489155. 58 Fort Augustus NH 374079. 59 Cannich NH 337313. 60 Fortrose NH 747558. 61 Cawdor NH 855511. 62 Tomatin NH 798299. 65 Fort William NN 110758. 66 Glenfinnan NM 900805. 67 Mallaig NM 675954. 68 Invergarry NN 298984. 69 Tulloch NN 374812. 70 Lochaline NM 673452. 71 Tobermory NM 524529. 72 Scarinish NL 996447. 73 Salen NM 688674. 75 Appin NM 910457. 76 Taynuilt NN 001302. 77 Arduaine NM 822065. 78 Seil Island NM 769168. 80 Onich NN 025614. 81 Bridge of Orchy NN 301419. 82 Crianlarich NN 382246.

No 31 Group BELFAST

10 Limavady IC 685217. 11 Dungiven IC 684071. 12 Londonderry IC 400174. 15 Cloghmills ID 059197. 16 Coleraine IC 825338. 17 Ballycastle ID 076428. 20 Ballymena ID 097056. 21 Kilrea IC 892127. 22 Cushendall ID 244305. 25 Clogher IH 547546. 26 Drumquin IH 333741. 27 Newtownstewart IH 403871. 28 Beragh IH 521666. 30 Castle Dawson IH 902930. 31 Cookstown IH 813796. 35 Temple Patrick IJ 210884. 36 Randalstown IJ 039938. 37 Larne ID 396039. 40 Enniskillen IH 264484. 41 Kesh IH 181672. 42 Lisnaskea IH 365343. 45 Portadown IH 965577. 46 Banbridge IJ 150484. 47 Armagh IH 911460. 48 Dungannon IH 805639. 50 Hillsborough IJ 236557. 51 Carryduff IJ 382627. 52 Ballynahinch IJ 342493. 55 Groomsport IJ 527836. 56 Ballywater IJ 634659. 57 Ardglas IJ 529349. 60 Jerretts Pass IJ 037322.

Posts closed prior to stand-down, with national grid reference. Date of closure in brackets.

1/12 Greenhithe, TQ 608734 (1989). 1/47 Ninfield, TQ 700128 (1990). 4/56 Stratford, TQ 416824 (1989). 12/50 Rhoose, ST 065679 (1990). 20/46 Barkston Ash (1989). 25/21 Tighnabruaich, NR 967712 (1989). 31/61 Kilkeel, IJ 325148 (1989).

Location of ROC Area and Group Headquarters at Stand Down September 1991

METROPOLITAN AREA

1 Group, 57 London Road, MAIDSTONE, Kent. Semi-sunk. Admin: adapted residence.

2 Group, Denne Road, HORSHAM, W Sussex. Surface. Admin: purpose built co-located with Metropolitan area.

3 Group, Rowan House Annex, James Wolfe Road, Cowley, OXFORD. Semi-sunk. Admin: purpose built. Co-located with HQ UKWMO.

4 Group, Errington Lodge, 22 Lexden Road, COLCHESTER, Essex. Surface. Admin: adapted residence.

14 Group, Abbots Road, WINCHESTER, Hants. Surface. Admin: Standard Secco Type ROC Centre.

MIDLAND AREA

6 Group, Chartwell Road, NORWICH. Semi-sunk. Admin: hutting

7 Group, Days Lane, Biddenham, BEDFORD, Beds. Semi-sunk. Admin: Standard Secco type ROC Centre.

8 Group, Lawford Heath, RUGBY, Warwickshire. Semi-sunk. Admin: purpose built.

15 Group, Fiskerton, LINCOLN. Semi-sunk. Admin: purpose built, co-located with HQ Midland Area.

20 Group, Shelly House, Acomb Road, YORK. Semi-sunk. Admin: brick built hutting.

SCOTTISH AREA

24 Group, RAF Turnhouse, EDINBURGH. Semi-sunk. Admin: brick built.

25 Group, Monkswell House, 17 Waterloo Road, PRESTWICK, Ayrshire. Surface. Admin: adapted residence.

28 Group, Craigiebarns, DUNDEE, Angus. Semi-sunk. Admin: adapted residence, co-located HQ Scottish Area.

29 Group, Quarry Road, Northfield, ABERDEEN. Surface. Admin: brick built hutting.

30 Group, King Duncan's Road, INVERNESS. Adapted. Admin: purpose built.

SOUTHERN AREA

9 Group, 53 Southwoods, Hendford Hill, YEOVIL, Somerset. Semi-sunk. Admin: Standard Secco type ROC Centre less Ops Room.

10 Group, Poltimore Park, EXETER, Devon. Surface. Admin: in part of converted SOC.

12 Group, Lansdown, BATH, Avon. Adapted building. Admin: purpose built.

13 Group, Picton Terrace, CARMARTHEN, Dyfed. Surface. Admin: purpose built.
16 Group, Holywell Street, SHREWSBURY, Salop. Surface. Admin: purpose built.

WESTERN AREA

17 Group, Borros Park Road, WREXHAM, Clwyd. Surface. Admin: purpose built.
21 Group, Longley Lane, Goosnargh, PRESTON, Lancs. Adapted building (SOC). Admin: prefabricated building, co-located with HQ Western Area.
22 Group, Grindledyke, Kingstown, CARLISLE, Cumbria. Surface. Admin: hutting.
23 Group, The Sands, DURHAM CITY. Surface. Admin: on roof of protected building.
31 Group, Knox Road, LISBURN, Co Antrim, N Irerland. Adapted building (AAOR). Admin: prefabricated building.

ROC Senior Officers
Deputy Commandants/Chiefs of Staff

Obs Capt W Rusby OBE	1953 – 1969
Obs Capt R A R Falconer OBE DFM	1969 – 1972
Obs Capt C J Rowlands MBE	1972 – 1977
Obs Capt H M Williamson	1977 – 1983 (Dec)
Obs Capt S L Coffey ISO	1984 – 1988 (Jan 84 Chief of Staff/Deputy CDt)
Obs Capt J Murphy BA	1988 – 1992 (Stand Down)

Assistant Commandants

Observer Captain W R Wilkinson OBE JP	1961 – 1981
Observer Captain J W Foster OBE DFC	1981 – 1983
Observer Captain K Terry FCII	1983 – 1986
Observer Captain D J Bridle	1986 – 1987
Observer Captain K G Brown	1988 to date
Observer Captain (W) J Shrubbs MBE AIAgs	1989 to date

Southern Area

Area Commandants

Observer Captain ID Sims OBE	1946 – 1978
Observer Captain J Bridle	1978 – 1981
Observer Captain S Deedman	1981 – 1985
Observer Captain C Topliss	1986 – 1988
Observer Captain A G Price-Talbot	1988 – 1991

Group Commandants

No 9 Group:

Observer Commander J Bridle	1975 – 1976
Observer Commander P Robshaw	1976 – 1979
Observer Commander H Daniel	1979 – 1988
Observer Commander S Sedwell	1988 – 1991

No 10 Group:

Observer Commander K Tyres BSc	1971 – 1981
Observer Commander J Shrimpton BSc MSc(Eng), C ENG DIC MBE ACSM FIMM FGS	1981 – 1986
Observer Commander M Richards	1986 – 1988
Observer Commander A J Child	1988 – 1991
Observer Commander M Davies	1991 – 1991

No 12 Group:

Observer Commander R Pitt	1970 – 1978
Observer Commander P Robshaw	1979 – 1982
Observer Commander C Topliss	1982 – 1986
Observer Commander A Price-Talbot	1986 – 1988
Observer Commander H Daniel	1989 – 1991
Observer Commander J Morris	1991 – 1991

No 13 Group:

Observer Commander L Watkins	1969 – 1976
Observer Commander J Neville	1976 – 1981
Observer Commander J Evans	1981 – 1991

No 16 Group:

Observer Commander P Barber	1955 – 1981
Observer Commander J Adams	1981 – 1986
Observer Commander D Jones	1986 – 1991

Scottish Area

Area Commandants

Observer Captain J Stewart OBE DFC MA	1969 – 1979
Observer Captain W M Holmes	1979 – 1990
Observer Captain J E G Martin BEd	1990 – 1991

Group Commandants

No 24 Group:

Observer Commander W M Holmes	1973 – 1979
Observer Commander V Campden MBE	1979 – 1987
Observer Commander M Duncan	1987 – 1991

No 25 Group:

Observer Commander R Pate	1975 – 1983
Observer Commander A Williams	1984 – 1988
Observer Commander J Sharpe	1988 – 1991

No 28 Group:

Observer Commander A Douglas	1969 – 1980
Observer Commander D Woods	1980 – 1986
Observer Commander J Carr	1987 – 1991

No 29 Group:

Observer Commander C F Campbell	1975 – 1979
Observer Commander D W Inkster MA	1979 – 1984
Observer Commander J E G Martin BEd	1984 – 1990
Observer Commander M J Mann	1990 – 1991

No 30 Group:

Observer Commander D Bell	1970 – 1976
Observer Commander J G Walford MBE BSc F/nst DL	1976 – 1985
Observer Commander G Boyd BSc Dip MRTPI MICD	1986 – 1991

Midland Area

Area Commandants

Observer Captain J W Chilton	1970 – 1981
Observer Captain B K Cooper BA Dip ED	1982 – 1984
Observer Captain (W) Shrubbs MBE AIAGS	1984 – 1989
Observer Captain M J Marks	1989 – 1991

Group Commandants

No 6 Group:

Observer Commander H J Teague MBE	1971 – 1989
Observer Commander B H Watson	1989 – 1991

No 7 Group:

Observer Commander W J Gooden MBE FRSH	1967 – 1978
Observer Commander B K Cooper BA Dip ED	1979 – 1982
Observer Commander (W) J Shrubbs MBE AIAGS	1982 – 1984
Observer Commander M J Marks	1984 – 1989
Observer Commander (W) P D Austin MBIM	1989 – 1991

No 8 Group:

Observer Commander L M J Mitton	1976 – 1986
Observer Commander J S Adams	1986 – 1989
Observer Commander M H Bosworth	1989 – 1991

No 15 Group:

Observer Commander R H Johnson DL	1966 – 1982
Observer Commander P Jex	1982 – 1991

No 20 Group:

Observer Commander C Burton	1963 – 1979
Observer Commander R S Perkins	1979 – 1983
Observer Commander J Millington	1983 – 1991

Metropolitan Area

Area Commandants

Observer Captain J W Foster OBE DFC	1964 – 1981
Observer Captain D J Bridle	1981 – 1985
Observer Captain S G Deedman	1985 – 1987
Observer Captain B W L McCarthy MCIOB MICD	1987 – 1991

Group Commandants

HQ No 1 Group:

Observer Commander B W L McCarthy MCIOB MICD	1976 – 1987
Observer Commander R C Saunders ASW MBASW	1987 – 1991

HQ No 2 Group:

Observer Commander J D Ballington	1974 – 1983
Observer Commander R Bent LRSC AITO	1983 – 1991

HQ No 3 Group:

Observer Commander D N James	1959 – 1984
Observer Commander T N Austin FCA	1984 – 1991

HQ No 4 Group:

Observer Commander E G J W Kent FCA	1961 – 1980
Observer Commander L W Strover BSc MCIT	1980 – 1986
Observer Commander G C Webb	1986 – 1991

HQ No 14 Group:

Observer Commander S G Deedman	1972 – 1981
Observer Commander P W Robshaw	1982 – 1985
Observer Commander A B Maasz MBIM MIME MReS	1985 – 1991

Western Area

Area Commandants

Observer Captain K Terry FCII	1968 – 1983
Observer Captain J G Brown	1984 – 1987
Observer Captain H Archer	1988 – 1991

Group Commandants

No 17 Group:

Observer Commander R E Wilcox-Jones	1964 – 1980
Observer Commander N Etchells BEd	1980 – 1987
Observer Commander J B Jones	1987 – 1991

No 21 Group:

Observer Commander J G Brown	1972 – 1984
Observer Commander G Scurrah	1984 – 1986
Observer Commander R Burnett	1986 – 1991

No 22 Group:

Observer Commander D H Edgar	1975 – 1983
Observer Commander H Archer	1983 – 1988
Observer Commander K W Dodd BSc	1988 – 1991

No 23 Group:

Observer Commander K Whitfield	1973 – 1991

No 31 Group:

Observer Commander J J Barnes	1965 – 1979
Observer Commander W S Sullivan Boomer	1979 – 1987
Observer Commander J R McDonald	1987 – 1991

THE ALLOCATION OF GROUP NUMBERS AND AREA ADMINISTRATIVE RESPONSIBILITIES FROM 1940 – 1992

(To be used in conjunction with the allocation of ROC service numbers record)

Groups 1940-92	1940 – 1953		1953 – 1968		1968 – 1992	
	Group	Area	Group	Area	Group	Area
1 Gp	Maidstone	Southern	Beckenham	Metropolitan	Maidstone	Metropolitan
2 Gp	Horsham	Southern	Horsham	Metropolitan	Horsham	Metropolitan
3 Gp	Winchester	Western	Oxford	Southern	Oxford	Metropolitan
4 Gp	Oxford	Western	Colchester	Metropolitan	Colchester	Metropolitan
5 Gp	Coventry	Midland	Watford	Metropolitan		
6 Gp	Derby	Midland	Norwich	Eastern	Norwich	Midland
7 Gp	Manchester	North West	Bedford	Eastern	Bedford	Midland
8 Gp	Leeds	Northern	Coventry	Western	Coventry	Midland
9 Gp	North York	Northern	Yeovil	Southern	Yeovil	Southern
10 Gp	East York	Northern	Exeter	Southern	Exeter	Southern
11 Gp	Lincoln	Midland	Truro	Southern	Truro (1968-73)	Southern
12 Gp	Bedford	Midland	Bristol	Southern	Bristol	Southern
13 Gp			Carmarthen	Southern	South Wales	Southern
14 Gp	Bury St Edmunds	Midland	Winchester	Southern	Winchester	Metropolitan
15 Gp	Cambridge	Midland	Derby	Eastern	Lincoln	Midland
16 Gp	Norwich	Midland	Shrewsbury	Western	Shrewsbury	Southern
17 Gp	Watford	Southern	Caernarvon	Western	North Wales	Western
18 Gp	Colchester	Southern	Leeds	Northern		
19 Gp	Beckenham	Southern	Manchester	Northern		
20 Gp	Truro	Western	York	Northern	York	Midland
21 Gp	Exeter	Western	Lancaster	Western	Preston	Western
22 Gp	Yeovil	Western	Carlisle	Western	Carlisle	Western
23 Gp	Bristol	Western	Durham	Northern	Durham	Western
24 Gp	Gloucester	Western	Edinburgh	Scottish	Edinburgh	Scottish
25 Gp	Cardiff	Western	Ayr	Western	Ayr	Scottish
26 Gp	Wrexham	North West	Glasgow	Scottish		
27 Gp	Shrewsbury	North West	Oban	Scottish		
28 Gp	Carmarthen	Western	Dundee	Scottish	Dundee	Scottish
28/2 Gp	Caernarvon	North West				
29 Gp	Lancaster	North West	Aberdeen	Scottish	Aberdeen	Scottish
30 Gp	Durham	Northern	Inverness	Scottish	Inverness	Scottish
31 Gp	Galashiels	Scottish	Belfast	Western	Belfast	Western
32 Gp	Carlisle	North West				
33 Gp	Ayr	North West				
34 Gp	Glasgow	Scottish				
35 Gp	Oban	Scottish				
36 Gp	Dumfermline	Scottish				
37 Gp	Dundee	Scottish				
38 Gp	Aberdeen	Scottish				
39 Gp	Inverness	Scottish				
40 Gp	Portree (Skye)	Scottish				

ROC AREA HQ LOCATIONS 1940 – 1992

Southern	1935 – 1953 RAF Uxbridge		1953 – 1990 RAF Rudloe Manor		1990 – 1992 Lansdown, Bath
Western	1937 – 1953 RAF Rudloe Manor		1953 – 1965 RAF Barton Hall		1965 – 1992 Goosnargh, Preston
Scottish	1937 – 1943 Edinburgh	1943 – 1947 Inverness	1947 – 1973 Carleton Tce Edinburgh		1973 – 1992 Craigiebarns, Dundee
Midland	1938 – 1942 RAF Grantham	1942 – 1953 RAF Whatnall	1953 – 1968 Disbanded	1968 – 1976 RAF Spitalgate	1976 – 1992 Fiskerton, Lincoln
Metropolitan			1953 – 1972 RAF Uxbridge	1972 – 1992 TA Centre, Horsham	
North Western	1940 – 1953 RAF Barton Hall		1953 Disbanded		
Northern	1938 – 1943 RAF Hucknall	1943 – 1953 RAF Catterick	1953 – 1968 Acomb, York		1968 Disbanded
Eastern			1953 – 1963 RAF Horsham St Faith	1963 – 1968 RAF Old Catton	1968 Disbanded

SECONDARY TRAINING CENTRES (STCs)

These were previous Group Headquarters that were stripped of their group status and clerical support staff but were retained as stand-by operational buildings and as additional training facilities:

STC	Dates	Parent Admin Unit
(+) Beckenham	1959 – 1968	Maidstone
Bury St Edmunds	1953 – 1968	Norwich
Caernarvon	1962 – 1968	Wrexham
Cambridge	1953 – 1965	Bedford
Cardiff	1953 – 1968	Bristol
($) Derby	1961 – 1974	Lincoln
Dumfermline	1953 – 1968	Dundee
Gloucester	1953 – 1976	Bristol
Lancaster	1961 – 1967	Preston
($) Lincoln	1953 – 1961	Derby
(+) Maidstone	1953 – 1959	Beckenham
Manchester	1961 – 1970	Preston
(*) Oban	1968 – 1973	*Inverness
Watford	1968 – 1973	Metropolitan Area

(+) Beckenham and Maidstone Groups swopped responsibilities in 1959.

($) Derby and Lincoln Groups swopped responsibilities in 1961

(*) Oban control remains in existance. From 1973-1992 it was a stand-by communications centre for Inverness Group HQ manned by an NRC team.

Additionally, Truro Group HQ (previously 11 Gp) was retained from 1973 to 1992 manned by an Exeter NRC team

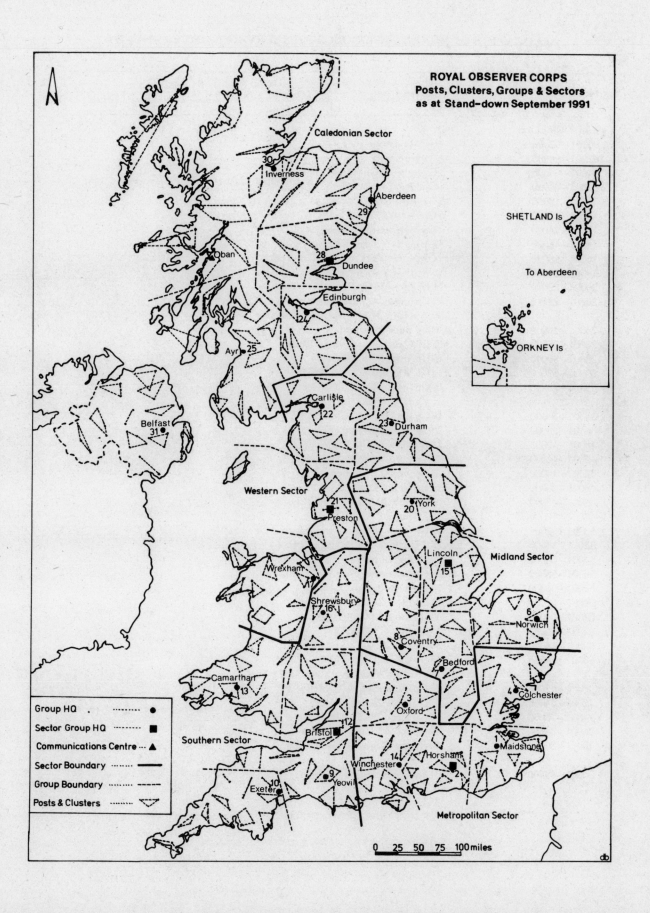

ROYAL OBSERVER CORPS
Posts, Clusters, Groups & Sectors
as at Stand-down September 1991

Caledonian Sector

30
Inverness

Aberdeen
29

Oban

28
Dundee

Edinburgh

24

Ayr 25

Carlisle
22

23 Durham

Western Sector

York
20

21
Preston

Lincoln
15

Midland Sector

Wrexham

Shrewsbury
16

6
Norwich

8 Coventry

Bedford

Camarthan

13

4 Colchester

3
Oxford

12
Bristol

1 Maidstone

Southern Sector

14
Winchester

Horsham
2

9
Yeovil

10
Exeter

Metropolitan Sector

Belfast
31

SHETLAND Is

To Aberdeen

ORKNEY Is

Group HQ	●
Sector Group HQ	■
Communications Centre	▲
Sector Boundary	
Group Boundary	
Posts & Clusters	

0   25   50   75   100 miles

ALLOCATION OF ROYAL OBSERVER CORPS SERVICE NUMBERS 1947–1991

Numbers	Issued to
Initial Allocation	Jan 47
00001 – 02000	1 GP Maidstone
02001 – 04000	2 GP Horsham
04001 – 06000	3 Gp (now 14 Gp) Winchester
06001 – 08000	4 Gp (now 3 Gp) Oxford
08001 – 10000	5 GP (now 8 Gp) Coventry
10001 – 12000	6 Gp Derby (Closed 1968)
12001 – 14000	7 Gp Manchester (Closed 1968)
14001 – 16000	8 Gp Leeds (Closed 1968)
16001 – 18000	9 GP North York (now 20 Gp) York
18001 – 20000	10 Gp East York (now 20 Gp) York
20001 – 22000	11 Gp (now 15 Gp) Lincoln
22001 – 23215	12 Gp (now 7 Gp) Bedford
	23216-24001 Not Issued (786 Nos)
24001 – 26000	14 Gp Bury St Edmunds (Closed 1953)
26001 – 28000	15 Gp Cambridge (Closed 1953)
28001 – 30000	16 Gp (now 6 Gp) Norwich
30001 – 32000	17 Gp Watford (Closed 1968)
32001 – 33840	18 Gp (now 4 Gp) Colchester
	33841-34000 Not Issued (160 Nos)
34001 – 36000	19 Gp Beckenham (Closed 1959)
36001 – 38000	20 Gp Truro (Closed 1973)
38001 – 40000	21 Gp (now 10 Gp) Exeter
40001 – 42000	22 Gp (now 9 Gp) Yeovil
42001 – 44000	23 Gp (now 12 Gp) Bristol
44001 – 46000	24 Gp Gloucester (Closed 1953)
46001 – 48000	25 Gp Cardiff (Closed 1953)
48001 – 50000	26 Gp (now 17 Gp) Wrexham
50001 – 52000	27 Gp (now 16 Gp) Shrewsbury
52001 – 54000	28/1 Gp (now 13 Gp) Carmarthen
54001 – 56000	28/2 Gp Caernarvon (Closed 1962)
56001 – 58000	29 Gp Lancaster (now 21 Gp) Preston
58001 – 60000	30 Gp (now 23 Gp) Durham
60001 – 62000	31 Gp (now 24 Gp) Edinburgh
62001 – 64000	32 Gp (now 22 Gp) Carlisle
64001 – 66000	33 Gp (now 25 Gp) Ayr
66001 – 68000	34 Gp Glasgow (Closed 1968)
68001 – 68886	35 Gp Oban (Closed 1968)
	68887-70000 Not Issued (1114 Nos)
70001 – 72000	36 Gp Dunfermline (Closed 1953)
72001 – 74000	37 Gp (now 28 Gp) Dundee
74001 – 76000	38 Gp (now 29 Gp) Aberdeen
76001 – 78000	39 Gp (now 30 Gp) Inverness
78001 – 80000	40 Gp Isle of Skye (Closed 1953)
80001 – 82000	31 Gp Belfast Feb 54

Numbers	Issued to	Date	Numbers	Issued to	Date
82001 – 92000	Northern Area	Dec 58			
			82001 – 83000	19 Gp (Manchester)	Dec 58
			83001 – 84000	20 Gp	Dec 58
			84001 – 85000	18 Gp (Leeds)	Dec 58
			85001 – 87000	23 Gp	Dec 58
			87001 – 92000	*Not Issued (5000 Nos)*	
92001 – 102000	Met Area	Sept 60			
			92001 – 93341	1 Gp (Beckenham)	Sep 60
			93342 – 94000	*Not Issued (658 Nos)*	
			94001 – 96000	2 Gp	Sep 60
			96001 – 98000	5 Gp (Watford)	Sep 60
			98001 – 99085	4 Gp	Sep 60
			99086 – 102000	*Not Issued (12915 Nos)*	
102001 – 112000	Eastern Area	Mar 62			
			102001 – 103276	6 Gp	Mar 62
			103277 – 106000	*Not Issued (2724 Nos)*	
			106001 – 107200	7 Gp	Mar 62
			107201 – 109000	*Not Issued (1800 Nos)*	
			109001 – 110885	15 Gp (Derby)	Mar 62
			110886 – 112000	*Not Issued (1115 Nos)*	
112001 – 122000	Sou Area	Mar 62			
			112001 – 113000	14 Gp	1962
			113001 – 114000	13 Gp	1962
			114001 – 115000	11 Gp (Truro)	1962
			115001 – 116000	10 Gp	1971
			116001 – 117000	13 Gp	1972
			117001 – 117681	9 Gp	1976
			117682 – 118000	*Not Issued (318 Nos)*	
			118001 – 118696	12 Gp	1978
			118697 – 122000	*Not Issued (3304 Nos)*	
122001 – 132000	Wes Area	Dec 62			
			122001 – 123884	31 Gp	Dec 62
			123885 – 124000	*Not Issued (116 Nos)*	
			124001 – 126000	17 Gp (Caernarvon)	Dec 62
			126001 – 127447	16 Gp	Dec 62
			127448 – 128000	*Not Issued (553 Nos)*	
			128001 – 129603	22 Gp	Dec 62
			129604 – 130000	*Not Issued (397 Nos)*	
			130001 – 131247	21 Gp (Lancaster)	Dec 62
			131248 – 132000	*Not Issued (753 Nos)*	

Numbers	Issued to	Date	Numbers	Issued to	Date
132001 – 142000	Sco Area	Apr 65			
			132001 – 133554	24 Gp	1965
			133555 – 134000	*Not Issued (445 Nos)*	
			134001 – 135261	25 Gp	1965
			135262 – 137000	*Not Issued (1739 Nos)*	
			137001 – 137974	28 Gp	1965
			137975 – 139000	*Not Issued (1026 Nos)*	
			139001 – 140000	29 Gp	1965
			140001 – 141789	30 Gp	1965
			141790 – 142000	*Not Issued (211 Nos)*	
142001 – 152000	Wes Area	Mar 67			
			142001 – 143734	23 Gp	Jan 63
			143735 – 152000	*Not Issued (8266 Nos)*	
152001 – 162000	Met Area	Oct 67			
			152001 – 152500	2 Gp	Oct 62
			152501 – 153000	3 Gp	Oct 67
			153001 – 153467	14 Gp	Apr 80
			153468 – 153500	*Not Issued (33 Nos)*	
			153501 – 153901	3 Gp	Jan 81
			153902 – 154000	*Not Issued (99 Nos)*	
			154001 – 154320	2 Gp	Dec 81
			154321 – 162000	*Not Issued (7680 Nos)*	
162001 – 172000	Mid Area	Jan 68			
			162001 – 162958	8 Gp	Mar 62
			162959 – 168000	*Not Issued (5042 Nos)*	
			168001 – 168866	20 Gp	Jan 68
			168867 – 172000	*Not Issued (3134 Nos)*	
172001 – 182000	Sou Area	Jun 87	*172001 – 174000*	*Not Issued (2000 Nos)*	
			174001 – 174229	10 Gp	1971
			174230 – 178000	*Not Issued (3771 Nos)*	
			178001 – 178108	13 Gp	1989
			178109 – 182000	*Not Issued (3892 Nos)*	
182001 – 192000	Wes Area	Nov 88	182001 – 182079	31 Gp	1989
			182710 – 192000	*Not Issued (9291 Nos)*	
192001 – 202000	Sco Area	Jun 89	192001 – 192090	29 Gp	1989

192091 Onwards not issued.   192090 Service Numbers   78342 Not Issued
(113749 Observers have served in the Corps since January 1947)

Lists prepared by former Observer Lieutenant Commander A.P. Angrove FITD MBIM

Observer Kelway's death

Reference was made in the original edition (see page 178) to Observer Kelway, the only observer to have been killed in action in World War 2 – apart from those who died in the Seaborne venture. New information has become available on this incident, much of it collated by former Corps member Charles Parker.

In March 1945 the Luftwaffe planned a "last ditch" series of intruder attacks against Bomber Command under the code name Operation Gisella. These were unexpected, as no German piloted aircraft had been officially reported over the United Kingdom since August 1944 (in fact there had been several flights unnoticed, by jet-propelled Arado 234s).

On the night of March 3/4, 541 RAF bombers had been operating on raids, which included the main targets of Kamen and the Dortmund Ems Canal. On returning they were met by some 140 German night fighters.

Shortly after one o'clock in the morning, Lancaster I NG502 of 460 squadron RAAF Binbrook was attacked. The pilot, F/O Warren managed to force-land safely near the railway line at Barfield House Farm, Langworth, with his flight engineer and wireless operator dead and three other crew injured. As they scrambled out of the aircraft, the intruder returned making several attacks on the burning wreckage. In Langworth village, Observer P. Taylor was just getting ready to go to Fox Two, Greetwell Post for the 02.00 – 06.00 shift. Hearing the gunfire he went outside and saw the intruder diving off towards Scothern at about 300 ft. and as it approached Scampton, the pilot could apparently see the partially blacked out lights of a car on the Welton- Spridlington road. He immediately attacked with cannon fire. Coming in too low, the pilot hit a telephone pole and wires at the side of the road, causing him to crash on to his target. The driver was Observer Jack Perotti Kelway who was going on duty at Love One, Hackthorn post. An extremely keen Observer, he was normally in the habit of sleeping at the post before going on watch but on this occasion had driven from his home in Lincoln. The force of the impact pushed his car across two fields killing him and the crew of the intruder.

An extract from Hackthorn post's diary reads as follows:

00.45 Hostile fighter activity – glow in sky at 33 (bearing) and A/c at 50 (bearing).

01.35 Fire at 26 (bearing) - gunning from low altitude, direction of Hemswell, Faldingworth and Wickenby and also at (bearing) 26.

03.05 Re fire in direction 26 timed at 01.35. This was caused by machine crashing, which most unfortunately swept across the Welton to Spridlington road at Cold Hanworth Lane end, hitting Observer J. Kelway's car and killing him instantly.

The body of Obs. Kelway was taken to Scampton and he was buried at Newport Cemetery on 7th March, 1945, guards of honour being provided by both the ROC and the Air Cadets. The grave bears the inscription "To the memory of Jack Perotti Kelway, killed by enemy aircraft near Hackthorn on 4th March 1945. Father of Tony, Pat and Christine." It is not in the military section of the cemetery and his Corps' service is not mentioned.

The nightfighter involved in the incident was Junkers Ju 88G-6c C9-RR of the 7th Staffel of NJG5 and the four crew are buried in Scampton village churchyard. The Luftwaffe shot down 20 RAF aircraft that night and three German fighters which hit the ground due to low flying - including C9-RR – were the last to crash on English soil during the war.

Corrections and Additions to 1975 Edition

Page	Column	Alteration
99		line 8 'Inchrie' should read 'Inchrye'
151		line 18 'Ockill hills' should read 'Ochil Hills'
203		line 23 'eight years' service should read 'nine years' service
253	2nd	line 3 'White–Boycott' should read 'Wight–Boycott'
254	1st	line 17/18 under '1945-1960' add 'Mr Wills (HEO)'
267	1st	line 25 'Aberdeen' should read 'Ayr'
268	1st	'Bromley/Beckenham': line 6 '1945' should read '1941 (destroyed by E/A)' between line 6–7 insert: 'Masonic Hall, Mason Hill, Bromley 1941–45'
275	2nd	'Winchester': line 5 '1929' should read '1937' line 6 '1929' should read '1937'
276	1st	'Wrexham' between lines 21–22 insert; 'Observer Commander Kirby'
277		line 16 'RAC' should read 'RAF'
279	2nd	'Parson Grove' should read 'Parson Drove'
284	1st	'Devonshire' should read 'Devon'
285	2nd	Between 'Seaton' and 'Shirwell' insert: 'Seven Rocks' Satellite (C/G Station); Disposed Mar 1946'
286	1st	'Dorsetshire' should read 'Dorset'
286	2nd	Between 'Canford Cliffs' and 'Fontwell Magna' insert: 'Charmouth' Satellite (C/G Station); Disposed Mar 1946 'Dancing Ledge' Satellite (C/G Station), 22/N.3; Disposed Oct 1944
286	2nd	Between 'Gillingham' and Maiden Newton' insert: 'Grove Point' Satellite (C/G Station), 22/J.2; Disposed Mar 1946 'Kimmeridge' Satellite (C/G Station), 22/E.2; Disposed Mar 1946 'Langton Herring' Satellite (C/G Station), 22/Q.3; Disposed Mar 1946
287	1st	After 'Preston' add: 'St Albans Head' Satellite (C/G Station); Disposed Oct 1944 'Seven Rocks' Satellite (C/G Station); Disposed Mar 1946
287	1st	After 'Wareham' add: 'West Bay' Satellite (C/G Station); Disposed Nov 1945 'West Boxington' Satellite, 22/S.2; Disposed Mar 1946
287	1st	After 'Worth Matravers' add: 'Wyke Regis' Satellite (C/G Station); Disposed Mar 1946

287	1st	'West Lulworth' line 1 'Lampton' should read 'Langton'
287	2nd	'Sedgefield' line 1 'Z.364302' should read 'NZ.364302'
287	2nd	'Hastings Hill/Washington' line 3 '23/H.I' should read '23/N.I'
288	2nd	'Castle Headingham' should read 'Castle Hedingham'
289	2nd	'New Malden' and all post details to P.291 between 'Newcross/ Dulwich' and 'Stratford'
289	2nd	Between 'Orsett' and 'Rochford' insert: 'Rainham' Opened Oct 1937, Q.523820, 19/P.2 (roof of telephone exchange) U/G, 1960, 4/K.2; Oct 1968; Q.549829
291	1st	'Harrow/Colindale' line 5 after '1961' add '5/A.1, 1963'
291	1st	'Newcross/Dulwich' line 7 '2/B.1' should read '2/B.2'
291	1st	'Uxbridge/Northolt' line 3 after 'Station' add '5/M.1, 1963'
292	1st	'Hardley' should read 'Handley'
292	1st	'Hambledon' line 1 '3/D.2.1' should read '3/D.2'
292	1st	'Havant' line 3 '2/G.1' should read '2/H.3'
292	1st	'Hayling Island' line 3 '2/G.1' should read '2/G.2'
292	1st	'Headley/Borden': line 1 after '1926' and '3/B.1, 1926-40' line 2 after '3/L.1' add '1940-66'
292	2nd	After 'Hill Head/Lee-on-Solent' add: 'Hurstbourne Tarrant' In use 1991
294	2nd	'Walkington' should read 'Wallington' all post details to P.291 between 'Uxbridge/Northolt' and 'Winchmore Hill'
295	1st	'Bearsted' line 2 'Q.694560' should read 'Q.794560'
295	2nd	'Cranbrook' line 3 '1930' should read '1929'
301	2nd	'Aldeby' and all post details to P.303 under 'Northamptonshire'
303	2nd	'Corby' and all post details including 'Earls Barton' to P.304 under 'Northamptonshire'
303	2nd	'Clipston' should read 'Clipstone'
303	2nd	'Daventry' line 1 delete 'Closed Oct 1968' add '1st Oct 1968, 3/B.2 and returned COV/66 1st Sep 1982; In use'
306	2nd	'Rutlandshire' should read 'Rutland'
309	1st	'Armitage' should read 'Armitage/Rugeley'
309	2nd	'Glascote/Polesworth' line 3 delete 'In use' add 'Closed (no date)'
309	2nd	'Shenstone' line 3 after '1968' add 'Re-opened March 1983'
311	2nd	'Stratford' and all post details to P.291 between 'Newcross/ Dulwich and Uxbridge/Northolt'
312	1st	'Farnham' all grid refs should read 'U' not 'Q'
312	1st	'Knaphill/Camberley/Deepcut': line 1 '4/L.3' should read '3/L.3' line 2 '1954' should read '1944' line 4 '2/D.3' should read '2/D.2'
312	1st	'Arundel/Littlehampton' line 2 'Q.189065' should read 'Q.018056'
312	2nd	'Bognor/Middleton': line 2 'Z.89200' should read 'Z.989200' line 3 'A.933989' should read 'Z.933989'
312	2nd	After 'Catsfield' add 'See Ninfield'
312	2nd	Between 'Catsfield' and 'Chiddlingly' insert: 'Chichester/Dell Quay' 2/P.1 1953 redesignated 2/F.4; Closed 1968
313	1st	'Fairlight' line 1 '0.861112' should read 'Q.861112'